D0722733

Evaluation
to Improve
Learning

Evaluation to Improve Learning

Benjamin S. Bloom
University of Chicago

George F. Madaus
Boston College

J. Thomas Hastings
University of Illinois

McGraw-Hill Book Company
New York St. Louis San Francisco Auckland Bogotá Hamburg Johannesburg
London Madrid Mexico Montreal New Delhi Panama Paris São Paulo
Singapore Sydney Tokyo Toronto

EVALUATION TO IMPROVE LEARNING

567890 DODO 898765

This book was set in Primer by Black Dot, Inc. The editors were Phillip A. Butcher and Susan Gamer; the design was done by Caliber Design Planning; the production supervisor was Leroy A. Young. The drawings were done by J & R Services, Inc.
R. R. Donnelley & Sons Company was printer and binder.

Library of Congress Cataloging in Publication Data

Bloom, Benjamin Samuel, date
    Evaluation to improve learning.

    A major revision of the authors' Handbook on formative and summative evaluation of student learning, pt. I.
    Includes index.
    1.   Educational tests and measurements.
I. Madaus, George F., joint author. II. Hastings,
John Thomas, date   joint author. III. Title.
LB3051.B532   371.2'6   80-25580
ISBN 0-07-006109-2   AACR1

Contents

Preface

This is a book about the "state of the art" of evaluating students' learning, intended primarily for present and future classroom teachers. Properly used, evaluation should enable teachers to make marked improvements in their students' learning. It is the improvement of students' learning which is the central concern of this book.

This book is *not* addressed to the selection and use of intelligence, aptitude, and standardized achievement tests—the typical student in school is likely to take only one or two standardized tests each year. Rather, it is addressed to the improvement and proper use of the fifty to sixty *teacher-made* quizzes, progress tests, and other examinations that the typical student takes each year.

Busy teachers, responsible for large classes with a great variety of students, have been so concerned with the instructional processes that they have often given little time or attention to the evaluation processes. Furthermore, it is likely that they have not been able to keep abreast of the growing literature on the art and science of evaluation. This book, by bringing together the best of evaluation techniques, is intended to help the teacher use evaluation to improve both the teaching process and the learning process.

A very important development in instruction during the past decade has been the widespread use of mastery learning, which enables most students to reach high levels of learning in school and college courses. The effect of the mastery-learning approach is to improve students' learning, increase their interest in the subject, and give them increased confidence in their ability to learn. Most teachers who use mastery learning develop a new view of students' learning potential. Teachers also find themselves spending more time on managing the learning of their students and less time on managing and disciplining their students.

Chapters 1 to 3 present a point of view about education and educational objectives and describe in detail how evaluation may be used to help bring students up to mastery levels of learning.

Chapters 4 to 6 are intended to help teachers become aware of the different purposes of evaluation and the ways in which different types of evaluation instruments can be developed for use in the classroom. The teacher will find ways of improving the summative evaluation he or she now uses; and the discussions of diagnostic and formative evaluation are likely to present new and very different ways in which evaluation can be used to improve teaching and learning.

Chapter 7 describes the general techniques for writing test items and for selecting items for particular testing purposes. Chapters 8 to 11 are organized around the taxonomies of educational objectives. These chapters present models and techniques for constructing valid evaluation instruments for the different types of objectives found at all levels of education and in most subject fields. For easy reference, the taxonomy of cognitive and affective objectives is summarized in the Appendix.

While the book is intended primarily for teachers in schools, it is also designed for students in teacher-training programs and graduate programs in departments of education. The reader should not regard it as a book to be read from cover to cover. It is, rather, a handbook to be used as the teacher (or student) encounters various evaluation problems at the beginning of the teaching cycle for an academic year and at each stage in this cycle, including the final summative stage.

The reader should become familiar with the ideas contained in the book so that he or she may return for a more careful reading to particular chapters that relate to specific curriculum, instructional, and evaluation problems he or she is attempting to solve at different times during the school year.

The book should also prove useful to students in courses on test construction. Since the entire book is related to the taxonomies of educational objectives, test makers will be able to find a large number of evaluation techniques relevant to the objectives and behaviors they want to evaluate. The detailed tables of contents or chapter highlights and the index will enable test constructors to find models and illustrations they need.

But the entire book is a handbook, to be used in a variety of teaching contexts and learning contexts. It is our hope that students in teacher-training institutions will secure the book early in their student careers, that they will refer to it in the curriculum courses they take, that they will use it to provide illustrations and models for evaluation courses, that they will find it useful in their methods courses as they attempt to relate instructional and learning approaches to the feasible objectives of courses in their field, and that the evaluation procedures will help them become clearer about the meaning and significance of the objectives. As they do their practice teaching, they should find the book helpful in improving their evaluation practices. Finally, we hope they find this book so useful that they continue to use it during their teaching careers as they face choices having to do with curriculum and instructional approaches, improvement of evaluation procedures, and the maintenance and development of a point of view about education, mastery learning, and evaluation.

We believe that the skilled teacher may eventually go beyond the limits provided by this book—when this occurs, let us hope that it will no longer be needed or that new books will be available. In the meantime, it is our hope that the full significance of what education can be is not lost in details of translating tables of specifications into learning experiences and evaluation procedures. These are operations intended to enable more teachers to realize the seductive dream which drew them into education—the fullest educational development of their students.

Benjamin S. Bloom
George F. Madaus
J. Thomas Hastings

Evaluation
to Improve
Learning

1 A View of Education

THE FUNCTION OF EDUCATION

Selection versus Development

Education throughout the world has for many centuries emphasized a selective function. Much of the energy of teachers and administrators was devoted to determining the students to be dropped at each major stage of the education program. The culmination of the public education system has been conceived of as entrance into or completion of a university program. Thus, of 100 students entering into formal education, some 10 percent were regarded as fitted by nature or nurture for the rigors of higher education. Little interest was felt by educators in the 90 percent to be dropped at the different stages of the education system.

Back of this very wasteful procedure was the notion that it is the rare individual who is really equipped to complete secondary school or to enter and complete a college program. The basic task of education was assumed to be the identification of the few who were to be permitted to enter and complete the secondary school academic program and then be admitted to higher education. The effect of this selection process, especially when the major decisions were made early—before age 12—was to weed out most of the children from the working-class group and to give special advantages to children of professional parents. While one may wish to argue about genetic differences between these children, it is becoming more and more evident that the observable differences between children of different social classes lie in the development of standard language, motivation to secure as much education as possible, willingness to work for teachers' approval or long-term goals, and acceptance of the learning tasks set by the schools with a minimum of rebellion.

There is little doubt that appropriate home and school conditions can significantly modify these characteristics. And there is a rapidly growing body of evidence showing the effects of early modifications of these characteristics on later school learning (Bloom, Davis & Hess, 1965; Bronfenbrenner, 1974; Kennedy, 1978; Weikart, Bond, & McNeil, 1978).

Quite in contrast to the notion of using schools for selection purposes is the view that education has as its primary function the development of the individual. Under this view, the central task of the schools is to develop those characteristics in students

2

which will enable them to live effectively in a complex society. The underlying assumptions are that talent can be developed by educational means and that the major resources of the schools should be devoted to increasing the effectiveness of individuals rather than to predicting and selecting talent.

Many of the highly developed countries are rapidly moving into a situation where a greater proportion of the labor force than 10 percent will need some form of higher education. This movement is largely dictated by changes in the economic system and the need for more highly trained workers. It is in part a consequence of greater affluence and the desire of a broader segment of the population for upward social and economic mobility. In almost every country in the world, the demand for education at every level exceeds the facilities and opportunities presently available. One symptom of this demand is that, with few exceptions, the largest single expenditure of public moneys in almost every nation is devoted to education—and the demand is rising very rapidly for increased expenditures.

Two countries of the world are especially distinctive in the proportion of the age group that at present completes secondary education—the United States, with about 75 percent of the 18-year-olds finishing high school; and Japan, with approximately 90 percent of the 18-year-olds completing secondary education. It is likely that in the next decade, a sizable number of countries will have at least four-fifths of the age group completing secondary education.

In short, education, at least through secondary school, will be provided for the large majority of young people. Selection procedures, prediction, and other judgments to determine who is to be given educational opportunities are quite irrelevant when most young people complete secondary schooling (or, in the more distant future, 2 or 4 years of college). Education must be increasingly concerned about the fullest development of all children and youth, and it will be the responsibility of the schools to seek learning conditions which will enable each individual to reach the highest level of learning possible for him or her.

But education does not end with the completion of secondary or higher education. The nature of change in modern society requires that formal as well as informal education continue throughout life. Most workers at the skilled level or above must relearn their jobs many times throughout their career. The worker who desires to advance to another level of work (in terms of complexity of task or responsibility) must learn the new skills and duties required. One no longer plans a curriculum for any profession or occupation on the assumption that this will be the last time the learner will have to learn. Most occupational fields now recognize the need for continuing learning and are finding ways of providing educational opportunities at different stages in the career of the worker.

However, continuing learning is not restricted to increased vocational competence. One must learn how to be an effective parent, citizen, and consumer (or producer) of the arts, and how to understand the changes in the world and their effects on each of us. Education, whether by the schools or other means, must be regarded as a process that never fully ceases (Faure et al., 1972).

If education is to serve youth and society under these new and very fluid conditions, it is evident that the schools and the teachers must learn to work in new ways. While this is a book about evaluation rather than curriculum and instruction, it is clear that both evaluation and teaching must undergo marked transformations if they are to be adequate to the new demands placed on them. It is the task of this chapter to delineate some of the new views of education (and evaluation) that appear to us to be in harmony with the new educational tasks.

The Changing Place of Evaluation

Education throughout the world has been conceived of as a set of learning tasks which presumably are more difficult as one proceeds from the first to the last year of formal schooling. It has also been assumed that as students move up this education ladder, fewer and fewer will have the necessary native endowments or acquired skills and attitudes to negotiate the higher rungs successfully. Education has for centuries been thought of as a pyramid, with all or most of the younger age groups attending school at the bottom and very few ever reaching the apex.

Examinations of some kind have been used to make the decision about who is to be permitted to go to the next level. As part of the process, the results of examinations and teachers' judgments have been turned into a grading system in which all students are classified annually or more frequently.

Thus, education has been viewed as having a fixed curriculum, a graded set of learning tasks, and a mixed group of learners to be classified at each major time unit in the system. Examinations or other evaluation procedures are used to make critical and often irreversible decisions about each student's worth and future in the education system. These decisions and classifications frequently affect a student's entire career.

The consequences of this system for learning or for the welfare of the individual student have not been a major concern of the people running it—teachers and administrators. While there are rumblings from time to time in each society about the education system, rarely is there concerted action to do more than alter some small piece of the overall framework. The system does produce a small proportion of individuals who have successfully negotiated the hurdles provided—and some of these do make very significant contributions to society.

The effect of this system on the unsuccessful students—and the largest fraction of those who begin education are unsuccessful at some stage in the system—is not of central concern to teachers and administrators. The system of categorizing students is generally designed to approximate a normal distribution of marks (such as A, B, C, D, and F) at each grade or level. Since the system is highly consistent from one grade or level to the next, our research finds that some students are rewarded with an A or B at each grade,

whereas others are reminded over and over again that they are D or F students (Bloom, 1964; Hicklin, 1962; Payne, 1963). The result of this method of categorizing individuals is to convince some that they are able, good, and desirable from the viewpoint of the system and others that they are deficient, bad, and undesirable. It is not likely that this continual labeling has beneficial consequences for the individual's educational development, and it is likely that it has an unfavorable influence on many a student's self-concept. To be physically (and legally) imprisoned in a school system for 10 or 12 years and to receive negative classifications repeatedly for this period of time must have a major detrimental effect on personality and character development (Bloom, 1976; Kifer, 1977; Stringer & Glidewell, 1967).

The purpose of evaluation, as it is most frequently used in the existing systems of education, is primarily the grading and classifying of students. It is designed to find those who have failed (D or F), those who have succeeded (A or B), and those who have gotten by (C). As testing and other forms of evaluation are commonly used in the schools, they contribute little to the improvement of teaching and learning, and they rarely serve to ensure that all (or almost all) learn what the school system regards as the important tasks and goals of the educational process.

The intent of this book is to present a broader view of evaluation and its place in education. We are primarily concerned with its use to improve teaching and learning. Briefly, our view encompasses

1. Evaluation as a method of acquiring and processing the evidence needed to determine the student's level of learning and the effectiveness of the teaching
2. Evaluation as including a great variety of evidence beyond the usual final paper-and-pencil examination
3. Evaluation as an aid in clarifying the significant goals and objectives of education and as a process for determining the extent to which students are developing in these desired ways
4. Evaluation as a system of feedback-corrective to determine at each step in the

teaching-learning process whether the process is effective or not, and if not, what changes must be made to ensure its effectiveness before it is too late

5. Finally, evaluation as a tool in educational research and practice for ascertaining whether or not alternative procedures are equally effective in achieving a set of educational ends

Education as a Process of Change

Education for us is a process which changes the learners. Given this view we expect each program, course, and unit of education to bring about some significant change or changes in the students. Students should be different at the end of a unit from what they were before it. Students who have completed a unit of education should be different from those who have not had it. Although it is true that some of the differences in a learner between the beginning and end of secondary school are to be attributed to maturation, growth, and the influences of varied experiences, we are here concerned with the changes produced by education and in the last analysis determined by the school, curriculum, and instruction.

It is here that we become concerned with means and ends. No doubt an individual student can be markedly affected by specific teachers; by the process of interaction among students, teachers, and subject matter; and by particular combinations of experiences. For research purposes, it may be important to disentangle this great variety of processes and experiences in order to determine what has influenced each student. We are interested in evaluation, however, as an attempt to describe, appraise, and in part influence the changes which take place rather than to analyze all the processes which bring them about. Thus, we wish to distinguish the role of evaluation, whose primary purpose is to describe and influence change, from that of research methodology, which may seek an understanding of cause and effect or undertake a detailed analysis of the variables regarded as significant in producing change in

learners. *Evaluation, as we see it, is the systematic collection of evidence to determine whether in fact certain changes are taking place in the learners as well as to determine the amount or degree of change in individual students.*

In proposing these views of the educational process, we are registering our faith (and there is much evidence to support it) that education can produce significant changes in learners. This is not to say that all learners will change in exactly the same way and to the same degree. Nor is it to say that all teachers, curricula, and schools will be equally effective in changing their students or will do so in the same way and to the same degree.

If the role of education is to produce changes in learners, then someone must decide what changes are *possible* and what are *desirable*. Every teacher-student interaction is based on some implicit conviction on the part of both the teacher and the student about the possibility and desirability of certain changes. It is not really possible to ignore these basic questions. Each teaching act and each learning act come out of answers to them. The teacher who does not want to state his or her educational objectives is merely avoiding an explicit verbal answer to these questions: the teacher's actions and interactions with students are implicit answers.

However, making verbal formulations of goals does not ensure that the implicit goals are congruent with the explicit. Nor does it ensure that the explicit goals will be realized. This is one of the uses of evaluation—to relate the actualities of changes in students to the stated formulation of changes sought.

Establishing Objectives

Having argued that the questions of possible and desirable changes cannot really be avoided, we still face the problem of who should answer these questions. There is no doubt that the students must be involved in the process of decision about educational goals and objectives. They must accept and to some degree understand the goals if they are to exert the appropriate learning effort. We recognize that this is difficult for very young learners, who are less able to grasp or be moved by long-term goals than older learners, who may more readily accept distant aims and deferred rewards. We also recognize that many students are not in the best position to participate actively in setting goals which they find hard to comprehend fully before they have achieved them. At the very least, it is to be desired that the learners accept the goals. At the other extreme, it is to be desired that the learners have some sense of participation in setting them. However, we would argue that the full responsibility for setting goals cannot be placed on the students, who in most cases will not be able to foresee the alternatives available and in many cases cannot fully appreciate the implications of particular choices.

There is no doubt that the task of determining the objectives of instruction must rest largely with the teacher. It is on this assumption that much of our book is written. We believe that at the beginning of the year the teacher should make explicit—to himself or herself as well as to the students—the changes that are expected to take place in the students as a result of the course. With these goals in mind, the teacher will consciously select materials, teaching procedures, and instruction strategies; will use appropriate evaluation techniques; and will find ways of working with individual students and groups of students in order to accomplish the given aims. And in working with particular groups of students, the teacher will modify goals as necessary to adjust the plan to the actualities in the classroom.

The teacher is not alone in setting the goals for a particular course or subject. Whether we like it or not, textbooks and syllabi have always had a major effect on the aims of instruction. During the past three decades, a great deal of work has been done by teachers, curriculum teams, professional associations, and other expert groups in thinking through the goals of each subject in the school curriculum. Bloom, Hastings, and Madaus (1971) have attempted to bring together some of the best work in selected subject fields. The teacher of a course in science, social studies, or literature, for example, will be guided in part by the work of others in thinking through both the content and the objectives of instruction. However, it is not likely that the teacher can simply borrow specifications created by others. In dealing with particular groups of learners, teachers must find ways of modifying the curriculum specifications of others to suit the local conditions they face. One may hope also that the individual teacher will find ways of going beyond such curriculum specifications to include objectives and procedures which are in some sense an advancement over what others have been able to do.

Teaching is a cycle which is repeated across groups of students. The cycle is repeated in subsequent years on new students or, if the teacher has several sections of the same course, concurrently with several groups. It is thus possible for the dedicated teacher to strive for more effective teaching and learning as the cycle is repeated. Evaluation, if used properly, gives some of the information necessary to determine where improvement is needed. Although it may give clues as to where to make the improvement, the teacher will usually have to find additional bases for determining how to remedy the situation. Teachers may discover correctives by observing variations in the students and by referring to experience accumulated in dealing with individual differences. They may also find possible answers by consulting with other teachers or experts. The literature on learning and psychology, on cultural differences in students, and on instruction in particular subjects may furnish additional ideas for remedies. Supported by these resources, evaluation should provide teachers with evidence on the effectiveness of the procedures they use.

Thus, the professional growth of teachers is dependent on their ability to secure the evaluation evidence and other information and material they need to constantly improve their teaching and their students' learning. Repetition provides a possibility of learning from one cycle for improvement in another.

Also, evaluation can serve as a means of quality control to ensure that each new cycle secures results as good as or better than those in previous cycles.

However, the teacher working alone must have a very limited set of objectives. Especially at the junior and senior high school levels, any one teacher usually has the students for only a fraction of their school time. Certain objectives can be realized in relation to a given subject matter, but others will undoubtedly transcend its boundaries. Here it is possible for a number of courses (and teachers) either to oppose each other or to reinforce and support each other. The cumulative effect of several courses with related objectives may be far more powerful than the mere sum of these courses taken one at a time. Especially in the so-called "higher mental processes" and the more deeply rooted attitudes and values, there is a necessity for educational goals to be determined by groups of teachers who work with the same group of students. This is necessary not only for subjects being taken simultaneously by the same students but also for those which will be taken over a period of years. There are complex problems of integration and sequence in learning which have a bearing on the selection of objectives; and here it is important to recognize that groups of teachers (and in fact the entire school) must be involved at one stage or another in decisions about the changes to be produced in students by the cumulative effect of learning experiences over a number of years.

At a more remote point from the classroom is the curriculum maker. A curriculum—whether it is a textbook, a complete set of materials and activities, or a whole school program—must have some ends in view. It must be constructed in relation to some purposes. Ideally, these should be formulated in terms of the changes the curriculum is intended to bring about in students. Without an explicit set of goals and specifications, the curriculum is primarily an artistic expression of its maker. We do believe that every curriculum and set of instructional materials must reflect the insights, special skills, and uniqueness of the designers. That is, it represents to some degree the artistry of those who create it. But it must also be designed to produce particular types of learning in selected groups of students. Explicit specifications of content and objectives define in part what the curriculum includes and what it is intended to accomplish. Unless the teachers or staff involved in selecting and using curriculum material are fully aware of the specifications it incorporates (and the evidence of its effectiveness in accomplishing given goals), they must accept or reject it on the basis of their views about the curriculum maker, their beliefs about what it may accomplish, or the salesmanship of its promoters. We are convinced that the users of curriculum programs and materials will increasingly demand to be provided with explicit sets of specifications and with evaluative evidence of their effectiveness under prescribed conditions (see Tyler, Klein, & Michael, 1971).

Sources of Objectives

As we have said, there are two types of decisions about curriculum objectives which must be made by teachers and curriculum makers—what is *possible* and what is *desirable*. The first of these is somewhat easier to determine than the second.

What is *possible* is essentially a problem of what has already been accomplished elsewhere. It is here that the research literature in education can be very valuable. Objectives that are possible in particular subject areas have been summarized in the writings on each subject field. The two handbooks of the *Taxonomy of Educational Objectives—Cognitive Domain* and *Affective Domain*—do indicate some of the broad classifications of educational objectives which are possible of attainment by students (Bloom, 1956; Krathwohl, Bloom, & Masia, 1964).

Bloom, Hastings, and Madaus (1971) indicate the types of objectives which careful teachers and expert groups believe are possible in each field. But we must hasten to emphasize that this is what such experts believe (or have found to be the case) under present conditions. As new research is pursued and new curriculum procedures are devised, it is highly likely that present limits on objectives will have to be altered. Thus, educators are finding that when culturally deprived children are provided with appropriate learning conditions, they can learn more rapidly and achieve a greater range of educational objectives·than seemed possible a few years ago. Also, in Chapters 3 and 6 we describe how the careful use of formative (or diagnostic progress) evaluation devices, accompanied by a variety of instructional resources, makes it possible for the majority of students to achieve objectives which previously had been attained by only a small proportion of students in the same class or course.

That an educational objective may be possible for some students to attain does not mean that it is possible for all. Clearly age and level and type of previous learning are important factors here. The teacher confronted with a particular group of students, who have varying levels of ability and varying interests and attitudes toward learning tasks, must determine what is possible for them. Teachers may seek some evidence in the literature which bears on students of the type they are teaching, but this is difficult to locate. In general, it is the teachers who, in the last analysis, must decide which objectives their students are likely to attain. They will implement their decisions in their methods of instruction and interaction with students. A teacher may err by expecting too much or too little, but it is the teacher's expectations and procedures that determine the objectives toward which the students will work and the extent to which they attain them.

Many teachers believe that the decision about what is possible should be based not on the students' characteristics but on the teacher's teaching style, ability, experience, and personality. We recognize that teachers do differ in their capabilities and especially in their self-confidence in relation to particular objectives. However, it is our considered judgment that most teachers can learn new ways of teaching students and that, if they will make the appropriate effort, most can help their students attain a great variety of educational objectives. The *teacher* does not, in our thinking, represent the major factor in determining the objectives which are possible. It is the *teaching* which determines the objectives which are possible. If teachers are convinced of the need and are provided with the necessary training and experience, they can become effective in teaching for most of the important objectives in their field.

A more difficult problem in determining objectives is what is *desirable*. This is a question of values; the use of evidence can help, but the question cannot be answered by evidence alone (Bloom, 1966; Tyler, 1950). What is desirable for particular students and groups of students is in part dependent on their present characteristics and their goals and aspirations for the future. If we were able to know in advance a person's entire life pattern, there would be little doubt about the desirable educational objectives. This lacking, objectives must be selected which are likely to give our students maximum flexibility in making a great variety of possible life decisions. Thus, what is desirable for the individual student may coincide with the greatest range of possibilities available in the light of the student's ability, previous achievement, and personality. If education is really to be development, objectives must be selected which maximize the range of possible developments.

Some help in determining the appropriate range of objectives for groups of students may be found in the study of the existing society. Social scientists have been attempting to determine the forces behind changes currently occurring and to foresee the likely changes in many aspects of the society. Not all of these have a direct impact on the work of the schools, but many of them have considerable relevance to the question of desirable objectives in education. It is clear that the nature of careers will be much affected by changes in the society; what implications do these have for desirable educational objectives? It is quite evident that increased leisure will be available to a large segment of the society in the near future; what implications does this have? Changes in social structure, government, communication and transportation, and other areas all bear on the desirability of some educational objectives as contrasted with others.

While we do not believe that each teacher must function as a social scientist in order to determine desirable objectives, we do believe that teachers should become increasingly aware of the consequences of social trends for decisions about educational objectives. It will be more and more necessary for teachers to have concise statements available about social changes and their implications for the work of the schools. Perhaps national and regional commissions could assume the central task of helping schools and teachers to these ends.

Another source of decisions on the desirability of particular objectives is the educational philosophy of the teachers and the school. While everyone involved in education, including parents, does have an implicit philosophy of education, it is difficult for people to spell it out explicitly. All too frequently such a statement seems so trivial and banal that the author hesitates to dignify it as a philosophical statement. However, an educational philosophy that makes clear the author's conception of the good person and the good life can be a powerful tool in determining what educational objectives are desirable. An educational philosophy that makes explicit the role of particular subjects and the role of personality and character in a society may be extremely useful in selecting objectives. Moreover, especially for a schoolwide committee, a statement of philosophic position can help determine the relations among courses and teachers with regard to the educational objectives (and instruction) which are desirable.

In Bloom, Hastings, and Madaus, 1971, where major objectives are described for each subject field as seen by experts, there are brief attempts to suggest the rationale for these—some from the viewpoint of the nature of the subject matter, some from societal conditions and trends, and some from a set of philosophic propositions about the school and the good life. The reader may find these useful as suggesting some of the bases for determining the desirability of particular objectives.

Structure of a Subject versus Structure of the Learning Process

A great deal has been written about the structure of a subject field. Many writers appear to believe that the structure of a field is synonymous with the proper structure of instruction in the subject field (Elam, 1964; Ford & Pugno, 1964). We take issue with this view of structure.

At a certain stage of sophistication in a subject, the scholar and the research worker are able to see relations among ideas and phenomena that form powerful conceptual tools for further study. Thus, Einstein's theory of relativity puts a great range of physical phenomena in a new perspective. Role theory in sociology and psychology is a very useful model for organizing a plethora of behavioral data, and constitutes a highly important set of ideas for new research. Set theory does much the same for mathematics. There is no doubt that the structuring of a subject field around a few theoretical formulations or conceptual models is extremely useful for the scholar and researcher. Whether in fact such ideas are useful for instruction is not to be decided upon by their usefulness for specialized scholarship.

There is no argument with the view that the learning in a subject field should have a structure which helps relate various aspects of the learning and gives increasingly deeper meaning to what otherwise might be a large number of unconnected specifics. There is much evidence in the research on learning to demonstrate that parts are more easily grasped and remembered in relationship to each other than in isolation.

The usefulness of a structure for learning has to do with the ability of students to comprehend it and to use it as an organizing factor in their learning. There is no clear relation between the usefulness of a structure for scholars and its usefulness (and meaningfulness) for students. Furthermore, when alternative structures are available in a subject field, it may well be that overlearning one structure will incapacitate the student to learn other structures later.

In contrast to the structure of a subject field is the structure of the learning process. The structure of the learning process should be one in which students can successfully move from one phase of learning to another. They should continually be offered clues and stimuli which are meaningful at each stage. Students should be able to participate actively in the learning process and be repeatedly rewarded by successful mastery as they advance to increasingly more complex learning tasks. It is possible that the end result of the learning will be a structure of the subject that resembles one scholars find useful. As we said, however, the structure of teaching and learning must be based on pedagogical considerations and need not mirror the scholar's view of a field.

Components of the Learning Process

In both curriculum making and teaching, there is the act of breaking a subject and a set of behavioral objectives into a series of tasks and activities. If this is done properly, it will result in the student's developing the cognitive and affective characteristics which are the intended outcomes of the educational process.

The art of teaching is the analysis of a complex final product into the components which must be attained separately and in some sequence. To teach anything is to have in view the final model to be attained while concentrating on one step at a time in the movement toward the goal. One gets a glimpse of the great power of pedagogy when it is applied to very complex new ideas in mathematics, the sciences, philosophy, the social sciences, and other fields. Einstein's theory of relativity, DNA genetic coding, and set theory are all examples of significant new

ideas which when first developed could be understood by only a small number of scholars in the respective fields. Such ideas may now be understood by millions of students at the secondary level because curriculum workers and teachers have found ways of explaining them to a great variety of learners. Evidence of this is the fact that many parents have difficulty comprehending some concepts which their children can use with great facility.

The analysis and organization of the learning process are difficult to describe when one is dealing with such complex ideas as the above. It is easier to convey something of this work by describing a simple and readily observed learning procedure. One begins to teach a child how to ride a two-wheel bicycle with a mental picture of the child's operating the bicycle smoothly at the end of the learning process. Then the good teacher breaks the learning task into the steps of adjusting the bicycle to the child's size, the child's balancing, getting started and building sufficient momentum, braking the bicycle, steering it, and so forth. In addition, the teacher is likely to be concerned with special problems such as safety and signals to other vehicles. Given this breakdown, the teacher then determines the appropriate sequence of learning steps. In teaching the child, the teacher is aware of the special problems the rider is having and the corrections needed. The teacher also attempts to reward and encourage the learner whenever possible.

This learning task exemplifies the analysis of the parts to be mastered and the arrangement of those parts in the most appropriate sequence of learning steps. The teacher has subdivided the whole unit of learning into the equivalent of a breakdown chart or a blowup diagram with the conception of a naive learner at the beginning and a competent cyclist at the end. Each of the parts has its own special learning characteristics (Figure 1-1).

Other, more complex learning tasks may be viewed in much the same fashion, although the time required for learning may be years instead of hours.

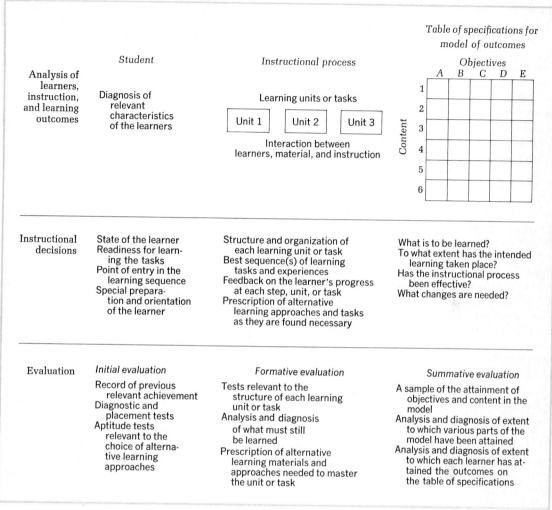

Figure 1-1 The relation among evaluation, instructional decisions, and the analysis of learners, instruction, and learning outcomes.

Essentially, the structure of a learning process may be broken into several major parts: a model of outcomes, the diagnosis of the learner at the beginning of the learning unit, and the instructional process.

Model of Outcomes and Table of Specifications

The teacher has in mind a model of the outcomes of instruction. While it may be rather general, the careful teacher is fully aware of many of the specifics in the model and may even have worked it out to the point where an inventory of the characteristics of the end product can be listed and checked off. The teacher also tries to help the student become aware of the final model and strive to attain it as the goal of learning.

The model of outcomes or objectives of instruction can be expressed in many ways. Some teachers (and courses of study) specify in great detail the subject matter or content the student should have learned by the end of the year, term, course, or other unit. This is very useful, but it does not specify in what sense the student should have "learned" the subject. In most contemporary developments of instruction and curriculum, there is some attempt to define the objectives or behaviors which the student should attain. These are statements of the ways in which students should be able to think, act, or feel about the subject matter. They may also be statements on how the students should be able to think, act, or feel about themselves, about others, about social institutions, and so forth—that is, the objectives need not always be confined to a course or subject. We have found it useful to represent the relation of content and behaviors or objectives in the form of a two-dimensional table with the objectives on one axis, the content on the other. The cells in the table then represent the specific content in relation to a particular objective or behavior. The development and use of objectives is spelled out in greater detail in Chapter 2. Bloom, Hastings, and Madaus (1971) have attempted to describe in some detail possible models of outcomes for selected subjects and programs of instruction. Various users may refer to the tabular form of the model as the "master chart," "table of specifications," or "matrix of content and behaviors," among other titles; we will call it the "table of specifications."

We believe that one of the most difficult problems in stating the specifications in the model is to make them precise enough to convey clear ideas of what is intended not only to the person making the model but also to other teachers, education workers, and related professional people. All too frequently language fails us as we try to describe the characteristics we intend to develop in our students. The statements become bland and relatively meaningless, even to their author.

One way of making the objectives more detailed is to specify the behaviors that a student who has attained the objectives should possess or exhibit. The use of behavioral statements is developed further in Chapters 2 and 4, and in Chapters 8 through 11 for each type of objective.

Another way of giving further clarity to the specifications of outcomes is to represent them in the form of the problems, questions, tasks, and the like which students should be able to do or the kinds of reactions they should give to specific questions or situations. What is being suggested here is that the summative evaluation instruments, when finally constructed, offer an operational definition of the model of specifications. To construct or select an appropriate evaluation instrument is to define something about what the students should learn and to give a detailed operational definition of a sample of the problems, questions, tasks, and situations to which they should be able to respond in an appropriate manner. This idea will be further developed throughout the entire book and is treated in a very detailed way in Chapter 4.

Diagnosis of the Learner at the Beginning of the Learning Unit

A teacher does attempt to determine what the learner has brought to the learning task that is relevant and what special problems the student may have in relation to previous related learning. In our bicycle illustration, a very young learner will be seen as different from a much older learner. A child who can ride a tricycle will begin a bit differently from one who has never ridden any type of cycle.

When teachers or curriculum makers are specifying the outcomes of instruction, they must have in mind the kinds of students or learners who are likely to be able to attain these outcomes in a reasonable period of time under the given learning conditions. The teacher may assume that students possess certain characteristics when they enter the course or program. However, these assumptions may not be entirely accurate, and the teacher may gradually learn that the students lack particular important characteristics. If this is the case, the expectations or the nature of the learning tasks, or both, must be revised.

The teacher must be able to diagnose the relevant characteristics of his or her students at the time they enter the course or program:

that is, the teacher must know the students' readiness for the learning tasks, must know the point of entry into a learning sequence that is appropriate for individual learners or the group, and must be able to determine what special preparation and orientation will be necessary before the students begin the sequence of learning tasks.

Evaluation can play a vital role in providing the teacher with the information needed to make decisions about individual learners or the entire group. Part of this initial evaluation will be provided by records of previous evaluations made of the students. Other aspects may require special diagnostic and placement tests or even the use of particular aptitude tests and other instruments, which may suggest alternative learning approaches. The use of initial evaluation procedures is discussed more fully in Chapter 5.

The Instructional Process

During each step of the learning there is interaction among the learner or learners, the material or problems, and the teacher. It is this interaction which is the heart of the instructional process.

The teacher, having selected a model of the outcomes of instruction, has to make decisions about what *materials* to use, what *methods* of teaching are appropriate, and what *activities* on the part of the learner are likely to be helpful in attaining the objectives desired. Although these topics are more properly a part of teaching and curriculum than of evaluation, we would be remiss if we did not communicate something about the nature of these decisions. We discuss this further in Chapters 3 and 6.

Materials

Never before have teachers had the wealth of instructional materials now available. A quarter of a century ago, the primary (and usually the only) instructional materials were textbooks. Now the teacher may make use of readings, workbooks, programmed materials, games, films and other audiovisual media, concrete materials (including laboratory materials), problem materials (including pamphlets and readings giving the necessary background to a complex problem), carefully designed drill materials, and other types. Although these materials may be used by entire groups of students, the teacher is likely to find that a "learning laboratory" with a great range of alternative materials to fit the special needs of individual learners at particular stages in the learning will yield far greater results than those obtained under a single set of required materials for all.

The decisions on materials to be used will in part be determined by the experience the teacher has had in the past in working toward particular objectives. In general, materials which are purely descriptive are likely to be most useful for objectives of the knowledge and comprehension types, whereas problem materials are likely to be most useful for the higher cognitive objectives such as application and analysis (see Chapters 8, 9, and 10).

Methods of instruction

Each teacher tends to use a single general method of instruction—lecture, recitation, or discussion, for example. However, as teachers clarify the range of objectives they are seeking, they will find it necessary to use a greater variety of instructional methods. For some purposes they may see all instruction as ranging from didactic to dialectical (Ginther, 1964; Rippey, 1969). Didactic instruction is largely a one-way form of communication from teacher to learners, and dialectical instruction is predominantly interactive processes between learners and teachers around problems and questions. In other connections teachers may view instruction as including tutorial methods; problem sessions of the discovery type; small-group work sessions (with or without the aid of the teacher); larger-group methods such as having students read, listen, or work in some way; recitation to determine whether they have learned what was intended, with corrections as needed; and lectures to very large groups of students. While many other possibilities are available, these are likely to be combinations of the few methods already listed.

Again, the choice of method must be dependent on the objectives of the instruction. Didactic teaching is likely to be very effective for the lower mental processes, although dialectical teaching will probably be necessary for the higher mental processes. Methods which maximize the reinforcement of the learning and the students' success are likely to lead to greater interest in and more favorable attitudes toward the subject and learning in general.

When one considers the variety of students involved in a course and the size of the class which must be taught as a group, it is likely that the methods to be used will be dictated by the practical considerations confronting the teacher. It is, however, quite probable that the attainment of a range of objectives will require a variety of instructional methods. It is also likely that alternative methods must be provided for those students who are not showing the desired development under the instructional approaches being used for the group (see Chapters 3 and 6).

Learning units or tasks

Learning takes place over time, and the instructional material and process must be organized into smaller units than an entire course, grade, or program.

The instructor or curriculum maker must determine the learning steps by which students can be helped over a period of time to attain the outcomes regarded as important and desirable. This requires that there be an overview of the structure of the subject or ideas to be learned, a breakdown of this structure into a series of steps or units to be learned in some sequence, and a further analysis of what is included in each learning unit or task.

Each unit or task may be conceived of as comprising the learning to take place in a relatively short period of time—a day, a week, or a month, perhaps. Each learning unit may also be conceived of as a series of subtasks which can best be learned as a series of short steps, each related to the others, building from relatively simple and concrete elements (terms, facts, procedures) to more complex and abstract ideas (concepts, rules, principles, processes) to even more abstruse ideas (theories, models, applications, and analyses). The art of instruction, as we have pointed out, consists in large part of breaking down a relatively complex idea or process into a series of smaller elements or steps and then finding a way of helping individual students learn these elements.

The breakdown of the learning task provides the specifications for formative evaluation tests or procedures (see Chapter 6). If such instruments are well used, they can furnish information to the teacher and the students about how adequately each unit is being learned as well as provide feedback on what is still necessary if the unit is to be mastered by individual students and the entire group. Formative evaluation may be utilized as one basis for decisions on alternative learning tasks and procedures (see Chapters 3 and 6). Thus, we are suggesting that the proper use of formative evaluation—evaluation during the formation of learning—can do much to ensure that the outcomes of instruction are attained by the largest proportion of the learners.

SUMMARY

In this chapter we have attempted to spell out in some detail the point of view about teaching and learning which is central in this book. We take the position that the main task of the education process is to change the learners in desirable ways, and that it is the primary task of teachers and curriculum makers to specify in precise terms the ways in which students will be altered by the learning process.

There is a series of decisions which teachers must make if they are to be effective in helping learners change in the desired ways, and it is the role of evaluation to provide appropriate evidence to help both teachers and learners attain the goals of instruction. The remainder of the book attempts to delineate the specific evaluation procedures and techniques which may be utilized or constructed to provide the information needed at each step in the education process.

REFERENCES

Bloom, B. S. (Ed.). *Taxonomy of educational objectives: The classification of educational goals.* Handbook 1. *Cognitive domain.* New York: McKay, 1956.

Bloom, B. S. *Stability and change in human characteristics.* New York: Wiley, 1964.

Bloom, B. S. The role of the educational sciences in curriculum development. *International journal of educational sciences,* 1966, *1,* 5–16.

Bloom, B. S. *Human characteristics and school learning.* New York: McGraw-Hill, 1976.

Bloom, B. S., Davis, A., & Hess, R. *Compensatory education for cultural deprivation.* New York: Holt, 1965.

Bloom, B. S., Hastings, J. T., & Madaus, G. F. *Handbook on formative and summative evaluation of student learning.* New York: McGraw-Hill, 1971.

Bronfenbrenner, U. *Is early intervention effective?* Washington, D.C.: U. S. Department of Health, Education, and Welfare, Office of Child Development, 1974.

Elam, S. (Ed.). *Education and the structure of knowledge.* Chicago: Rand McNally, 1964.

Faure, E., et al. *Learning to be.* Paris: UNESCO; London: Harrap, 1972.

Ford, G. W., & Pugno, L. (Eds.). *The structure of knowledge and the curriculum.* Chicago: Rand McNally, 1964.

Ginther, J. R. Conceptual model for analyzing instruction. In J. P. Lysaught (Ed.), *Programmed instruction in medical education.* Rochester, N.Y.: University of Rochester Clearing House, 1964.

Hicklin, W. J. *A study of long-range techniques for predicting patterns of scholastic behavior.* Unpublished doctoral dissertation, University of Chicago, 1962.

Kennedy, M. M. Findings from the Follow-Through Planned Variation study. *Educational Researcher,* 1978, 7, 3–11.

Kifer, E. The impact of success and failure on the learner. (Monograph.) In B. H. Choppin and T. N. Postlethwaite (Eds.), *Evaluation in education.* Oxford: Pergamon Press, 1977.

Krathwohl, D. R., Bloom, B. S., & Masia, B. B. *Taxonomy of educational objectives: The classification of educational goals.* Handbook 2. *Affective domain.* New York: McKay, 1964.

Payne, A. *The selection and treatment of data for certain curriculum decision problems: A methodological study.* Unpublished doctoral dissertation, University of Chicago, 1963.

Rippey, R. M. The Ginther model: Four dimensions of research on instruction. *Elementary School Journal,* 1969, 69, 215–223.

Stringer, L. A., & Glidewell, J. C. *Early detection of emotional illnesses in school children.* (Final Rep.) St. Louis, Mo.: St. Louis County Health Department, 1967.

Tyler, L. L., Klein, M. F., & Michael, W. B. *Recommendations for curriculum and instructional materials.* Los Angeles: Tyl Press, 1971.

Tyler, R. W. *Basic principles of curriculum and instruction.* Chicago: University of Chicago Press, 1950.

Weikart, D. P., Bond, J. T., & McNeil, J. T. *The Ypsilanti Perry preschool project: Preschool years and longitudinal results through fourth grade.* Ypsilanti, Mich.: High Scope Educational Research Foundation, 1978.

2 Formulating and Selecting Educational Objectives

Chapter Contents

In Chapter 1 we saw that a premise central to this book is that education is a process which helps the learner to change in intended ways. Given this premise, one of the principal tasks of teachers and administrators is to decide how they want the student to change and how they can assist in the process. The changes in students that teachers intend are the educational objectives or ends of instruction.

DEFINING EDUCATIONAL OBJECTIVES

In stating an objective the teacher seeks to clarify in his or her own mind and to communicate to others the sought-for change in thoughts, actions, or feelings that a particular unit or educational program should help a student realize. Statements of educational objectives describe in a relatively specific manner what a student should be able to do or produce, or what the characteristics are that the student should possess, after completing the unit or course. To formulate useful statements of educational objectives the educator must choose words that, as far as possible, are interpreted in the same sense by intended readers. This chapter deals with the problem of writing and selecting meaningful, unambiguous statements of intended educational outcomes which can serve as guides for instruction and for formative and summative evaluation.

In Chapter 1 we also saw that in planning the ends of instruction, two decisions must be made: first, is a potential objective possible; second, is it desirable? We saw that characteristics of students and teachers must be considered when one is deciding whether an objective is possible and that studying the existing society and philosophies of education is useful in judging whether an objective is desirable. It is quite possible to write or select an objective that is specific and unambiguous but is nonetheless either impossible of attainment or undesirable for an individual or group. However, the very process of formulating or selecting unambiguous educational objectives can often reveal previously hidden ideas about what is desirable, as well as presuppositions about what is possible. The

process of writing or selecting statements of educational objectives should inform, and be informed by, the process of making decisions about their feasibility and desirability. Such decisions and judgments should not be neglected or hurried through, and the reader is referred to the discussion in Chapter 1 of the various screens that may be used in this process. (On feasibility the reader might also wish to see Case, 1975; on desirability, MacDonald and Clark, 1973.)

Though objectives are by definition the *intended* outcomes of instruction, they in no way comprise all outcomes. Given the complexity of most subject fields and the dynamic social system of the classroom, it is quite impossible to anticipate the full range of outcomes that will result from instruction. Nor would teaching be an art without unanticipated outcomes. As the course progresses, unanticipated outcomes—some positive, others unfortunately negative—often develop. Some of these are quickly identified; others may go unrecognized. Attempts to specify *all* the outcomes in advance can stultify teaching and evaluation. A teacher may mistakenly feel that only outcomes planned in advance are important, and may thus neglect situations where other outcomes become possible or evaluate only those outcomes explicitly detailed in advance. The formulation or selection of objectives needs to be viewed as an ongoing, cyclical process. Planned outcomes often will need to be reconsidered in the light of experience. Further, many of the unanticipated outcomes will become objectives the next time the course or unit is taught. In short, the interactive classroom situation is both a source of objectives and the crucible in which the feasibility and desirability of planned objectives are evaluated.

This is not to imply that careful consideration should not be given before instruction to what outcomes are possible, desirable, and thus systematically to be sought. Such planning is an essential step in instruction and evaluation, and this chapter deals with how to formulate and select maximally useful statements of educational objectives. However, it is important to emphasize that other significant outcomes will usually become evident as instruction proceeds, and the teacher should be alert to them. We shall deal more directly in this book with the evaluation of anticipated outcomes.

IMPORTANCE OF EDUCATIONAL OBJECTIVES

Much attention in American education has been given to the process of stating objectives. There is probably no aspect of instruction about which more has been written. Books on methods of teaching all stress the importance of defining objectives. Those in charge of teacher-training courses routinely require them as part of the lesson plans prepared by student teachers. National commissions, state and local curriculum groups, and individual classroom teachers have worked long and hard to delineate educational goals and instructional objectives. Seldom, however, have these efforts had any impact on classroom instruction or evaluation. This lack of impact has led to confusion about the importance and debate over the worth of statements of objectives. Do they really help improve the educational process, or is their formulation merely a rite of passage for the novice and a ritualistic exercise for the more experienced educator? Why *bother* studying about educational objectives?

Specific behavioral objectives have been at the heart of recent major developments that are bound to affect teachers: competency-based graduation programs, programmed learning, computer-assisted instruction, mastery-learning projects, performance-based teacher education, criterion-referenced testing, performance contracting, needs-assessment programs, and the accountability movement—all require specific, unambiguous statements of objectives. Public Law 94-142 and state counterparts like Chapter 766 in Massachusetts further exemplify major developments which directly involve the teacher. These laws mandate individualized educational programs for handicapped students and other students with special needs. They require that the students' regular classroom teacher cooperate closely with special teachers and other professional staff members in the formulation of a specific educational program for each student with special needs. Each individualized program must include the student's initial level of performance (techniques for determining this are described in Chapter 5; the short- and long-term objectives stated in specific, behavioral fashion (the concern of this chapter); and a description of how these long-term objectives will be assessed (the concern of Chapters 4 and 6).

If the listed developments are indeed of major importance, then the educational objectives movement—an essential component of all of them—itself is a development of enormous importance. To evaluate the implications, strengths, limitations, uses and abuses of such programs, or to participate actively in one or more of them, today's teacher must know about behavioral objectives.

It is not enough to "know about" educational objectives. Today's teachers must also know how to formulate and select them—a process which carries with it a variety of benefits. The first of the benefits is that *the process of writing or selecting clear, specific, behavioral statements of objectives requires a teacher to think quite seriously about the changes he or she wants to help the student realize.* The activity itself is beneficial. Broad, general statements of objectives no longer suffice; ends that were vague and implicit are sharpened and made explicit. The process of sharpening and making explicit the ends of instruction *can reveal hidden judgments* about the desirability and feasibility of certain objectives (MacDonald-Ross, 1973).

In addition to requiring teachers to think explicitly about changes in students' behavior, *the process helps teachers recognize trivial objectives and identify those that are missing.* Implicit objectives or general statements of ends can easily mask trivial or rote objectives by vague language.

It is interesting to note that critics of the process of defining behavioral objectives argue that it tends to produce a list of outcomes that place a heavy emphasis on rote learning and the recall and recognition of information, definitions, rules, etc. This is so because these so-called "lower-level" outcomes more easily translate into specific actions or products than "higher-level" outcomes do (Broudy, 1970). The latter should not be neglected, of course. On the other hand, lower-level outcomes should not necessarily be denigrated or considered trivial. The important point is that precisely because the writing and selecting process demands specific statements, it becomes easier for a teacher to recognize whether there is a preponderance of certain kinds of outcomes, whether certain outcomes are missing entirely or others underrepresented. In short, objectives can be added or deleted from the list on a rational basis (Popham, 1969).

A third benefit associated with the process of formulating or selecting objectives is that *clearly stated goals help the teacher in making decisions about the proper placement of students.* We shall discuss diagnostic and placement evaluation in Chapter 5. Suffice it to say at this point that once a list of specific objectives has been determined, it is possible through the use of a pretest to discover which objectives have already been mastered. This in turn may permit the formulation of different groupings and the selection of different materials and experiences for various pupils. Further, once one has the list of objectives, one is in a better position to identify the behaviors prerequisite to the pursuit of new objectives. Assessment of prerequisite skills is a key feature of legislation like Public Law 94-142 and Chapter 766, mentioned above.

The benefits associated with proper placement having been realized, *a list of the ends of instruction is itself an aid in selecting methods, materials, and experiences for their attainment.* The teacher who has a clear statement of the ends desired is in a better position to consider the appropriateness and possible efficacy of various means. Clearly stated objectives neither prescribe nor proscribe means but do suggest them.

Two different teachers considering the same behavioral objective might very well follow quite different ways of teaching for it. Differences in methods, materials, experiences, etc., are the result of differences in teaching style, classroom composition, and even educational philosophy. For example, Cazden (1971) describes an objective shared by three different types of preschool programs: "the ability to speak in complete sentences." The means employed to achieve the common goal differ substantially. One program, which emphasizes sequence and structure, includes "recitation lessons in which children are expected to respond in carefully specified ways, even repeat sentences after the teacher"; the other two programs, which have much less structure imposed by the teacher, "rely on more natural conversational contexts" (p. 355).

There is considerable evidence that successful programs begin with clearly stated ends, structure instruction to meet these ends, give feedback and correctives to students on their progress toward these ends, and use evaluation techniques that reflect these ends (see Block, 1971, 1974; Bloom, 1976; Iwanicki, 1972; Madaus, Airasian, & Kellaghan, 1980; Stodolsky, 1972). Thus planning helps a teacher, and the keystone in planning is clearly stated instructional objectives.

While clearly stated ends suggest rather than prescribe possible means that may be used to obtain them, they do provide a starting point and a frame of reference for planning how one will teach. Trying beforehand to intelligently relate means to ends will not of course tell a teacher exactly what to do or say at any particular moment in the classroom; the classroom is too complex a situation for one to predict the nature of the interaction. The situation is analogous to planning an automobile trip. A map affords an excellent plan. However, it does not tell the driver how to adjust to the flow and volume of traffic or to road and weather conditions. These variables have to be experienced, and one's driving rhythm has to be guided by them. Further, it is often true that in classroom interaction a teacher may have to abandon planned methods or discard prepared material in the light of puzzled expressions, incorrect answers, looks of boredom, or unexpected questions. In addition, opportunities to pursue unanticipated outcomes might dictate the abandonment of planned activities in favor of the "teachable moment."

Given the fact that new objectives can emerge, nevertheless a substantial number of important ends are known in advance and can be clearly and specifically stated. The existence of such clearly stated instructional objectives is the starting point in planning methods, selecting materials, and structuring assignments and experiences to help the student attain the intended goals.

From our point of view, one of the prime benefits is that *clearly stated instructional objectives suggest the most direct methods for evaluating students' achievement.* If, for example, one has the objective "students can correctly use a microscope," then a paper-and-pencil test on the parts of a microscope is of questionable validity. The relationship of objectives to the development of formative and summative evaluation techniques is discussed later in this chapter and runs throughout the remainder of this book; it will not be pursued at this point, except to emphasize that the first step in developing valid evaluation techniques is to write or select specific behavioral objectives.

An often overlooked benefit associated with formulating and stating objectives is that *clearly stated instructional objectives help ensure communication between teachers.* The list of specific instructional objectives can improve a dialog between teachers of the same course or sequential courses (Geis, 1972). Often in talking about the ends of instruction, teachers use words like "understanding," "application," "motivation," and "comprehension." These words are nominal or descriptive terms, constructs invented to describe certain observable behavior patterns. MacDonald-Ross (1973) has called such verbs "verbs of state" rather than "verbs of action." No one has ever seen "understanding." Instead, certain observable behavior

patterns or products are given the nominal or descriptive label "understanding" by an observer. For example, different teachers may describe, as occurrences of "understanding," applying previously learned principles to solve a novel problem, or listing a series of dates, or translating graphic information into one's own words. The problem is that broad constructs like "understanding" are open to various interpretations by different teachers.

If the word "understands" were used alone, without further specification, two teachers in adjoining classrooms could think they were attempting to achieve the same instructional objective when in fact the two classes could differ entirely in both the desired and the actual outcomes. Thus, in discussing a supposedly common objective, "understanding," two teachers might very well engage in conversation without communication. Clearly specific instructional objectives, on the other hand, are stated in terms of observable actions or products of students. These behavior patterns or products become indicators of the general construct "understanding." (Pages 30 to 34 of this chapter discuss how a teacher can describe nominal constructs such as "understanding," "appreciation," and "comprehension" in terms of observable actions or products of students.)

It is never possible to eliminate ambiguity completely from instructional objectives. Even when instructional objectives are stated in terms of observable actions or products, there can still be various interpretations of intention on the part of different teachers (see Gardner, 1977; Geis, 1972; MacDonald-Ross, 1973). However, ambiguity and misunderstandings are enormously reduced by using observed actions or products in discussing instructional objectives. Teachers are in a better position to discuss whether their intents are limited to recall and recognition. They are in a position to discuss the worth and feasibility of their instructional objectives. Finally, they are in a better position to identify and explore the presuppositions about ends and means held by their colleagues and explain their own presuppositions (MacDonald-Ross, 1973).

In much the same way that stated objectives improve communication between teachers, they *can improve communication between the teacher and the students.* If students know at the outset of instruction what it is that they are expected to achieve, then they are in a better position to structure their study than if they are forced to infer objectives from teachers' examining or grading practices. A list of objectives can provide the students with an "advanced organizer" of the subject and an opportunity to compare their performance with the criteria in the objectives (Duchastel & Merrill, 1973; Faw & Waller, 1976).

Some students are too young to benefit fully from a list of clearly specified instructional objectives. Older students will need to be convinced that the stated objectives are the teacher's *real* objectives. That is, students must have confidence that there is a congruence between the stated and the evaluated objectives. Such confidence can be built by firsthand experience with the teacher or by accepting a tradition handed down from past classes. When older students are convinced that the stated objectives are in fact the actual objectives of a course, or unit, they will begin to structure their studying in a more intelligent manner.

A final but nevertheless important benefit associated with clearly stated objectives is that *they can improve communication between the teacher and parents.* A list of skills, products, or observable actions provides a more precise means for reporting to parents what a student has mastered than the more traditional reporting form. Examples of report forms stated in terms of observable actions or products are described in more detail in Chapter 4. Reporting students' progress in terms of clear instructional objectives gives both parents and students a clearer picture of strengths and weaknesses. Further, such reports serve as a basis for a clearer dialog between teachers, parents, and students on what steps might be taken to remedy weaknesses.

The next section explores alternative approaches to defining educational objectives in order to arrive at the two elements that characterize appropriately stated objectives.

INSTRUCTIONAL OBJECTIVES AND TWO OUTCOME MODELS

Before describing in more detail how to write and select maximally useful statements of objectives, we return to the discussion of outcome models begun in Chapter 1. Outcome models in the instructional objective movement can follow one of two approaches: task analysis or the Tyler approach. MacDonald-Ross (1973) has labeled the former a "feed-forward" model of planning, the latter a "cyclical" or "feedback" model. A comparison of the two approaches is useful in that it reveals different ways of planning the ends and means of instruction and evaluation.

Task Analysis

The task analysis approach grew out of the applications of industrial psychology to military and industrial training. During World War II and the Korean conflict the military turned to industrial psychologists for help in training personnel. The psychologists were asked to develop efficient programs to equip trainees with identical, well-defined competencies. Often the competencies required were for interactions between human beings and machines. It was clear what the desired skill was and how it was to be used. Barring changes in technology, the skill was meant to be fairly permanent. Thus, when the Army wished to train soldiers to assemble and disassemble an M-1 rifle, the psychologists began by specifying the training objectives through a technique that became known as "task analysis." The skill or performance desired of the trainee at the end of the unit of instruction was described and then analyzed into a "repertoire of behavior structures" that were built up sequentially to arrive at the terminal performance. The analysis was sometimes based on the characteristics of the particular human-machine system (e.g., the operation of a radar set) and sometimes on observing the actions of an experienced or "master" performer (MacDonald-Ross, 1973).

In training, unlike general education, learning a sequence of steps by rote will ensure that the trainee acquires the desired skill. Prescribing the most efficient set of hierarchical steps to be learned then becomes essential. The task description details the competence the trainee should have at the end of the course; the task analysis goes beyond this to specify the conditions thought to be directly related to learning. Thus task analysis takes the "macro" performance and breaks it down into "micro" behavior components, which are the building blocks of instruction.

Gardner (1977) describes the process as one of decomposition where there is "(1) an essentially unmanageable complex whole which can be dealt with by (2) a process of decomposition to a level of manageable parts which are then (3) added up to reconstitute a now manageable whole" (p. 387).

The techniques of the military psychologists were adopted, with modifications, by experimental psychologists investigating classroom learning, by those interested in programmed or computer-assisted instruction, and, more recently, by those working in the area of individualized instruction. The first step in developing material in all these applications is a detailed description of the target behavior.

One of the purposes of the detailed task analysis is to bring principles derived from learning theory to bear on the sequencing of instruction. What school of learning theory the psychologist adheres to will of course determine the character of the resulting analysis and the methods used in the instruction sequence.

The work of Glaser and Reynolds (1964) offers an example of a task analysis done in terms of stimulus-response (Figure 2-1). The top box in Figure 2-1, "Telling time to the nearest minute," can be considered as one objective in a large first-grade arithmetic specifications table, and hence a summative objective. It is divided into three subobjectives: writing the hour and minute in sequence, saying the minutes and hours in sequence, and saying "o'clock" on the hour. In turn, each of these is broken down into component behaviors, which are arranged hierarchically (designated by the symbols $A1$, $A2$, $A3$, etc.). These separate components are also related to the task horizontally (indicated by the lateral lines in the flowchart). The analysis works backward from the overall objective until the curriculum builder is willing to accept certain behaviors as assumed at this particular age or grade. Subobjectives are defined in very specific terms that will be described in more detail presently.

The technique of task analysis is not equally applicable to all areas of the curriculum. It is most useful in dealing with objectives that involve skills:

> Skills are usually useful and are performed to give standards. They become refined, reportable, routinised, predictable and eventually may come to be performed subconsciously. In any event, it is easy to find types of educational experiences which have nothing to do with skills—learning for learning's sake for instance. The distinction between knowledge and skills is deeply embedded in our ordinary language for the excellent reason that it is meaningful and functionally necessary. To have a skill is to have the ability to execute useful tasks to publicly agreed standards of performance. This clearly implies that a task analysis procedure might be effective for skills but inadequate for general education. (MacDonald-Ross, 1973, p. 23)

Skills form a basic component of the educative process. There are numerous cognitive and psychomotor skills in most areas of the curriculum that we want all students to acquire. Much of the criticism of schools is directed at the belief that many young people graduate without basic skills in mathematics, reading, and writing. Task analysis is most useful in teaching and evaluating those skills we want all students to acquire, either because they are ends in themselves (e.g., telling time, driving safely) or because they are prerequisites for later instruction and

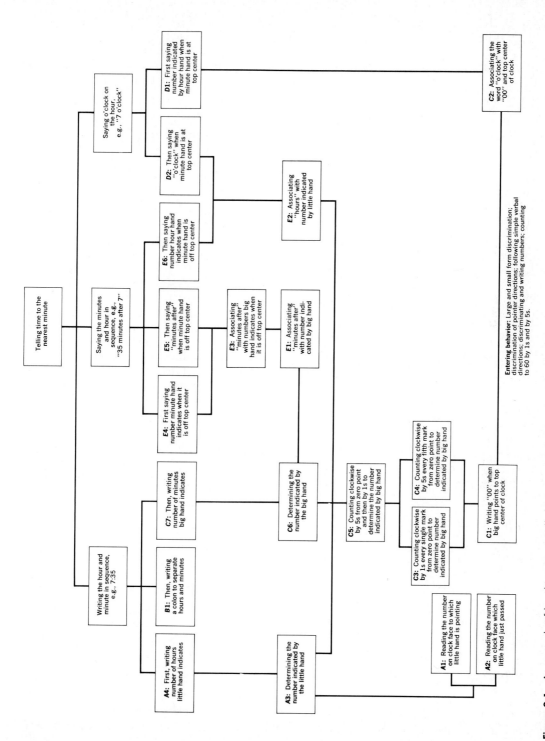

Figure 2-1 An example of breaking an overall objective into component behaviors. (Glaser & Reynolds, 1964, p. 64. © 1964 by University of Pittsburgh Press; reproduced by permission of University of Pittsburgh Press.)

The boxes contain the following:

Telling time to the nearest minute

Writing the hour and minute in sequence, e.g., 7:35

Saying the minutes and hour in sequence, e.g., "35 minutes after 7"

Saying o'clock on the hour, e.g., "7 o'clock"

A4: First, writing number of hours little hand indicates

B1: Then, writing a colon to separate hours and minutes

C7: Then, writing number of minutes big hand indicates

E4: First saying number minute hand indicates when it is off top center

E5: Then saying "minutes after" when minute hand is off top center

E6: Then saying number hour hand indicates when minute hand is off top center

D2: Then saying "o'clock" when minute hand is at top center

D1: First saying number indicated by hour hand when minute hand is at top center

A3: Determining the number indicated by the little hand

C6: Determining the number indicated by the big hand

E3: Associating "minutes after" with numbers big hand indicates when it is off top center

E1: Associating "minutes after" with number indicated by big hand

E2: Associating number "hours" with number indicated by little hand

A1: Reading the number on clock face to which little hand is pointing

A2: Reading the number on clock face which little hand just passed

C3: Counting clockwise by 1s every single mark from zero point to determine number indicated by big hand

C5: Counting clockwise by 5s from zero point and then by 1s to determine the number indicated by big hand

C4: Counting clockwise by 5s every fifth mark from zero point to determine number indicated by big hand

C1: Writing "00" when big hand points to top center of clock

C2: Associating the word "o'clock" with "00" and top center of clock

Entering behavior: Large and small form discrimination; discrimination of pointer directions; following simple verbal directions; discriminating and writing numbers; counting to 60 by 1s and by 5s.

23

learning (e.g., basic reading, writing, and mathematics skills).

In education, unlike training, we do not expect all students to use acquired skills in exactly the same way. The higher one proceeds on the educational ladder, the more apparent this becomes. For example, two students might learn certain skills as a result of an introductory physics course in high school. One may use this ability only in the role of an intelligent citizen who reads with interest about progress being made in the space program, whereas the other may build on these same behaviors as a major in college physics. At the elementary school level, on the other hand, certain skills, such as reading, spelling, grammar, and the acquisition of the number facts, are prerequisites for later instruction. Here training techniques may be more appropriate, although even at this level mere rote learning will not be adequate.

From the point of view of evaluation, the work of the task analysis group is most helpful for illuminating the concept of formative evaluation. Once the overall objective has been broken down into its component objectives, the student's progress can be evaluated at each step in the sequence. The results can then be used to determine whether students should go on to the next step or should receive further instruction at the present step.

Figure 2-1, from Glaser and Reynolds, is an exemplar, formidable in scope and detail. Because of constraints of time and training, classroom teachers may not be able to produce such detailed plans. Furthermore, the average teacher is generally not called upon to develop a programmed text, a computer-aided instruction program, or curriculum material. Instead, an existing curriculum is a given, generally in the form of a textbook and accompanying teacher's guide. It is also becoming common for publishers to provide subobjectives for each unit. Chapter 6 describes how the teacher can use analyses provided by the publisher or infer the objective and subobjectives for a unit from the materials. Teachers should acquaint themselves with the technique of task analysis, for it may prove helpful in thinking about and

analyzing skills. The ability to analyze a task is becoming increasingly important in performance-based graduation programs where students must display mastery of certain basic skills before certification is granted.

The Tyler Approach

Since the 1930s Ralph Tyler's work in curriculum, instruction, and evaluation has been built on the premise that education is a systematic process designed to help produce behavioral changes in the learner. The function of evaluation, as Tyler sees it, is primarily to determine the extent to which students have or have not changed in relation to the set of desired behaviors.

The importance of carefully defining educational objectives for the improvement of curricula and instruction is central to all of Tyler's work. In his rationale for curriculum development (1950), statements of objectives serve as the first step in the development of improved curriculum materials and instruction techniques. Further, these same statements serve as guides to teachers in building evaluation instruments to appraise the effectiveness of newly developed materials or techniques.

The cyclical nature of the approach is shown in Figure 2-2. The shaded area of the rectangle represents preactive teaching—that is, decisions made before the teacher enters the classroom (Jackson, 1966). The remaining area represents interactive teaching—decisions made, often subconsciously, in the classroom itself. Figure 2-2 shows that some objectives are planned while others emerge spontaneously in the interactive situation. Similarly with the means used to obtain the ends: some are planned; others emerge as the teacher "plays it by ear" in the classroom. Evaluation is also a part of both preactive and interactive teaching. The teacher is continually making on-the-spot evaluations during teaching, based on subtle cues from pupils. These evaluations can influence how the teacher interprets the results of formal evaluation (e.g., quizzes). The arrows indicate that the path proceeds from objective through

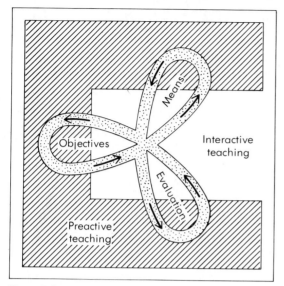

Figure 2-2

means, and through evaluation to a return to a reconsideration of objective. Though this is not depicted in Figure 2-2, when the path returns to reconsidering objectives, it returns on a slightly higher plane, a change made possible by the initial circuit. This approach requires that instructional objectives be stated in terms of students' behavior and of the subject matter to be conveyed. However it does not require the specificity found in the task analysis approach. Though Tyler's approach does include evaluation of instruction in progress, historically his main emphasis was on summative evaluation. Evaluation data were used mainly to make judgments at the conclusion of the course; evaluation became largely summative in nature; it stressed grading, selecting, and certifying students and determining the effectiveness of the curriculum compared with alternative curricula. Unfortunately, it was this aspect of Tyler's thinking rather than the improvement of instruction and curriculum that received the greatest emphasis by those who subsequently used his work.

However, as we shall see, this approach can be followed equally well if one wishes to develop formative units and evaluation techniques. Basic to the Tyler approach is the

specification of an outcome model analogous to that shown in Table 2-1. The model consists of a table of specifications, which presents the course objectives in the form of a two-dimensional matrix. There are three steps involved in arriving at a table of specifications.

First, general objectives, stated temporarily in rather broad terms, must be decided upon by the teacher or curriculum builder. The next step is to break each of these objectives down into a content component and a behavior component. As we saw previously, "content" refers to the specific subject matter to be conveyed, and "behavior" refers to what we want the student to do with the material.

Once the first two steps have been accomplished, a table of specifications can be drawn up. Each behavior is listed along one axis, and the different content areas are specified along the other. The interaction of each behavior (B) with each content area (C) results in a chart composed of $B \times C = n$ behavior-content cells. Table 2-1 is a master table of specifications for objectives in preschool early language development (Cazden, 1971, p. 348). (Actually Table 2-1 incorporates the language objectives of several preschool programs.)

Many cells in such a table may well remain empty—that is, no such intersection of content and behavior is among the objectives of the course. Thus in Table 2-1, the x's in the various cells mean that a behavior applies to that content in at least one of the language programs reviewed by Cazden; the remaining cells are "empty."

Each of the general objectives contained in the table can then be further specified by describing the objective in more detail. Thus the objectives of the Bereiter-Engelmann program contained in Table 2-1 are described in more detail in Table 2-2 (Cazden, 1971, p. 357).

The way in which the table of specifications is used points up the distinction between formative and summative evaluation and between formative and summative uses for objectives. Each target cell of the specifications matrix is evaluated at the end of the

TABLE 2-1 TABLE OF SPECIFICATIONS FOR PRESCHOOL EDUCATION: OBJECTIVES IN EARLY LANGUAGE DEVELOPMENT

	BEHAVIORS									
	Cognitive									Affective
CONTENT	Understand and produce simple language forms	Understand and produce elaborated language: describe	Understand and produce elaborated language: narrate	Understand and produce elaborated language: generalize, explain, and predict	Use language effectively for specific purposes to others: communication	Use language effectively for specific purposes to oneself: cognition	Operate on language: analyze	Operate on language: transform and translate	Operate on language: evaluate	Demonstrate the use of language frequently and with enjoyment
	A	B	C	D	E	F	G	H	I	J
1. Sounds	X							X	X	X
2. Words	X						X	X	X	X
3. Grammar	X						X	X	X	X
4. Objects		X		X						X
5. Events			X	X						X
6. Ideas				X						X
7. Reality: discussion					X					X
8. Fantasy: dramatic play					X					X
9. Thought						X				X

Source: Cazden, 1971, p. 348.

course or sequence (i.e., summatively). In few subjects is it possible to evaluate the student on the total matrix in one summative test; therefore, summative evaluation is usually directed at a sample of the cells, with the view of making inferences about the students' competency on the full range of objectives. The matrix serves as a blueprint in designing a summative test. A weight or value can be assigned to each of the instructional objectives contained in each target cell. Chapter 4 discusses in detail various ways of assigning values to each cell. However, no matter how these values are assigned, the relative value afforded each cell in the matrix helps to ensure that any test instru-

TABLE 2-2 TABLE OF SPECIFICATIONS SHOWING OBJECTIVES OF THE BEREITER-ENGELMANN PROGRAM

Cognitive domain				Affective domain
Use language				
A. Understand and produce simple language forms	*B–D. Understand and produce elaborated language*	*E, F. Use language effectively for specific purposes*	*G–I. Operate on language*	*J*
Speak in sentences made up of clearly pronounced, distinct words (*A*-1–*A*-3). Repeat sentences (*A*-3).	Master the use of structural words and inflections which are necessary for the expression and manipulation of logical relationships (*D*-4–*D*-6). Use language to acquire, process, and transmit information; perform operations on concepts: e.g., explain, describe, inquire, hypothesize, compare and deduce (*D*-4–*D*-6).	Carry on sustained dialogue with self or others, to accumulate and use information (*E*-7). Talk to oneself for planning and controlling behavior (*F*-9).	Recombine words, e.g., *green and red* to *red and green* (*G*-3, *H*-2). Transform sentences, e.g., imperatives to declaratives (*H*-3). Make and evaluate rhymes (*H*-1, *I*-1).	

Source: Cazden 1971, p. 357. (From Bereiter & Engelmann, 1966, 1968, undated; and Osborn, 1968.)

ment will have content validity. This may be accomplished by having the number of test items that are written to measure each objective in the matrix approximate the value assigned to each cell.

Formative evaluation, on the other hand, deals with only a segment rather than the total specifications matrix, but does so in a more detailed and exhaustive fashion. Parts of the table can be learned in relative isolation from other parts. Thus, it is conceivable that one cell may be treated as an independent learning unit, but it is also possible that a group of cells may naturally go together in the learning process.

Cazden (1971, p. 383) describes a formative unit comprising various cells from Table 2-1. The arrows in Table 2-3 indicate the

27

TABLE 2-3 TABLE OF SPECIFICATIONS FOR A UNIT ON RELATIONAL WORDS

	Cognitive domain				Affective domain
	Use language				
	A. Understand and produce simple language forms	B–D. Understand and produce elaborated language	E, F. Use language effectively for specific purposes	G–I. Operate on language	J
	Understand and produce words of relative position or location (A-2) "on" "in" "out" "under" "over" "between" "next to" "behind" "in front of"	Understand and produce sentences expressing a coordination of two or more spatial relationships (B-4): "The ball is in the box under the chair."	Describe or give directions taking into account differences in visual perspective between speaker and listener (E-7, E-8).	Demonstrate understanding that some pairs of relational words are polar opposites (H-2) by answering the question: "What is the opposite of over?" or by naming a pair of opposites.	
	Answer question "Where is X?" in complete sentence (A-3).				

Source: Cazden 1971, p. 383.

28

structure of the unit and the temporal sequence of instruction, that is, objective A-2 must be taught before objective B-4 because it is a component of B-4, etc. Other ways of identifying formative units with an overall table of specifications are described in Chapter 6.

The approaches of the task analysis school and the Tyler school complement and supplement one another despite their differences in emphasis. For example, Tyler stops at a description of the desired behavior, whereas task analysis goes on to prescribe a very detailed behavior repertoire. That is, as we shall see presently, the two viewpoints differ on the degree of specificity required in the statement of the objective. Tyler's approach does not require the specificity which task analysis entails. The Tyler approach can be used to define objectives in a general education whereas the task analysis approach works best in the area of training for specific skills.

The two points of view agree, however, on at least three points: (1) Instruction has as its goal helping students to change their behavior—the students must be able to do something after instruction that they could not do before. (2) The degree of success of a program must be evaluated. (3) General objectives must be described in terms of observable actions or products. Both approaches consider formative and summative evaluation important; the principal difference lies in emphasis.

CHARACTERISTICS OF APPROPRIATELY STATED INSTRUCTIONAL OBJECTIVES

We now consider in more detail the two characteristics of an instructional objective—content and behavior—and discuss the issue of the level of specificity needed in stating objectives. We shall next describe strategies a teacher can employ in developing educational objectives either by writing them or by selecting them. Finally, we shall describe sources from which a teacher can select statements of educational objectives. A statement of an instructional objective should have two characteristics: it must specify the content area, and it should describe in specific terms what a student should be able to do or produce after the instruction that he or she could not do beforehand. This section explains in more detail how to describe educational objectives in terms of these two characteristics. As a result the reader should be able to write instructional objectives that include both characteristics or, if selecting objectives, be able to distinguish between statements that contain or lack one or both of the characteristics.

A well-written instructional objective should succeed in communicating the teacher's intent. Communication is successful when a knowledgeable person can look at a student's actions or products and decide whether or not the objective has been reached. In fact, the degree to which different people can agree on whether a performance reflects a desired objective is an index of the reliability or clarity of the statement.

It must be firmly kept in mind, however, that success in communicating an instructional objective does not mean that the objective is necessarily desirable or possible. These attributes must be determined using the criteria suggested in Chapter 1. Proper formulation of an objective makes accurate observation possible but does not necessarily ensure its educational worth or guarantee that students can attain it.

Specification of Content

The first half of a properly stated instructional objective consists of a description of the *content*. This element is usually neglected in standard treatments of "behavioral" objectives. In standard treatments the reader is advised that content needs to be specified, and thereafter the focus is on specifying behavior. We think that considerably more attention should be given to the specifying and sequencing of content.

The content of an objective can sometimes flow from the behaviors sought. For example, Kamii (1971) points out that for socioemotional, perceptual-motor, and cognitive objectives at the preschool level the content can be literally anything found in a child's environment. Kamii narrows this down by conceptualizing the content as consisting of "the self, people in the immediate and distant environment, objects in the immediate and distant environment, and properties of things, for example, colors and sizes." Each of these categories can be further specified. Thus objects in the environment might include "glasses, spoons, pebbles, paint, and so forth" (p. 293).

In areas like mathematics and science, the subject field dictates topics. For example, Table 2-4 presents a synopsis of the grade placement of topics in mathematics (Wilson, 1971). However, vocabulary and readings in second-language learning can be dictated by the choice of text (Valette, 1971). The content description of an objective can be more easily specified for topics not likely to change much in the future (e.g., history, classical languages). If, on the other hand, knowledge in a discipline is expanding rapidly, then specifying content is more difficult.

Specification of content should not be hurried over. The teacher of a particular subject should become familiar with discussions of the content and topics by national curriculum groups. Part II of *Handbook on Formative and Summative Evaluation of Student Learning* (Bloom, Hastings, & Madaus, 1971) contains a discussion of content and topics in eleven areas of learning, written by experts in each area.

Other sources of content for teachers to consider are banks of objectives developed to permit teachers to select instructional objectives. For example, the New York State Education Department has developed a bank of instructional objectives for reading called the *System for Pupil and Program Evaluation and Development (SPPED)* (O'Reilly, Cohen, & Algozzine, 1973). In this bank, the content section of each reading objective is delimited; the topics covered by the objectives are defined as shown in Figure 2-3. *SPPED* resource material then lists specific elements of content under each of the topics shown in Figure 2-3. (Banks, or pools, of objectives are discussed further on page 44.)

Teachers should also be aware of specialized reference works that can be used in defining content. For example, Carroll, Davies, and Richman's *American Heritage Word Frequency Book* (1971) is an excellent resource for teachers of English and language arts.

Finally, the very important concept of sequencing content receives excellent treatment in the work of Posner and Strike (1976). Their sequencing principles are analogous to the more familiar *Taxonomy of Educational Objectives* (Bloom, 1956), which concentrates on the behavioral component of objectives. Posner and Strike describe five major types of content sequence and important subcategories under each. The use of the categories is illustrated with examples of the sequence within which specific content could be taught.

Perhaps because the content component of an objective is so important there is sometimes a temptation to focus exclusively on content. Content by itself is often meaningless. What is the student supposed to be able to do with or to the content? Bruner (1966) has put it in this way:

> One must begin by setting forth the intellectual substance of what is to be taught, else there can be no sense of what challenges and shapes the curiosity of the student. Yet the moment one succumbs to the temptation to "get across" the subject, at that moment the ingredient of pedagogy is in jeopardy. For it is only in a trivial sense that one gives a course to "get something across," merely to impart information. There are better means to that end than teaching. Unless the learner also masters himself, disciplines his taste, deepens his view of the world, the "something" that is got across is hardly worth the effort of transmission. (p. 73)

Specification of Students' Actions or Products

We saw earlier that to describe students' actions teachers often use terms which are open to various interpretations. The following are examples:

TABLE 2-4 APPROXIMATE GRADE PLACEMENT OF MATHEMATICS TOPICS

Topic	K–3	4–6	7–8	9	10	11–12	
Number systems	Concept of zero and whole numbers. Place value. Counting. Addition and subtraction up to 3 place numbers.	Numeration systems. Nature, properties, and techniques of the operations on integers. Factors, primes, and exponents.	Nature, properties, and techniques of the operations on rationals. Introduction to negative integers. Decimal system. Factors, primes, and exponents.	Operations on negative numbers.		Irrational numbers. Real number system. Complex numbers.	
Algebra			Solutions of open sentences. Introduction to algebra.	Solutions of equations. Polynomials and factoring. Algebraic expressions.		Polynomials and factoring. Equations, systems of equations. Polynomial functions. Transcendental functions.	Transcendental functions. Algebra of trigonometry. Theory of equations.
Geometry	Awareness and definitions of common shapes.	Sets of points. Sides and relationships of triangle.	Informal plane geometry (coordinates, similarity and congruence).		Characteristics of lines, triangles, solid figures, other polygons, etc. Congruence and similarity. Loci and constructions.	Analytical geometry of quadratics. Graphs of functions.	Analytical geometry.
Measurement	Awareness of common systems.	Linear and angular measurement. Area.	Linear and angular measurement. Area. Volume. Metric systems.		Measurement as a system. Proofs involving measurements. Area, perimeter, etc.		
Application	Application of measurement. Simple arithmetic operations.	Application of measurement. Application of area. Problems involving more than one operation.	Application of measurement. Application of rational numbers. Area. Volume.	Application of algebra to solution of problems.	Application of loci.	Application of logarithms and trigonometry.	Introduction to calculus. (Tangent to a curve.) Probability and statistics. Functions.
Analysis, Logic, Statistics, etc.		Introduction to sets.	Sets. Graphs and measures of central tendency.		Proof (deductive).	Mathematical induction.	

Source: Adapted from Romberg and Kilpatrick, 1969, p. 285.

1. The student has knowledge of . . .
2. The student comprehends a . . .
3. The student thinks critically about . . .
4. The student understands a . . .
5. The student has an appreciation of . . .
6. The student has an interest in . . .
7. The student fully appreciates . . .
8. The student grasps the significance of . . .
9. The student can memorize . . .
10. The student learns . . .
11. The student respects . . .
12. The student expands his or her horizons.
13. The student works effectively.
14. The student speaks effectively.
15. The student speaks correctly.
16. The student reads with ease.
17. The student uses basic skills.

Adjectives	Initial consonants
Antonyms	Logical relationships
Classification	Main ideas
Compound grammatical elements	Medial consonant diagraphs
Compound words	Medial consonants
Consonants	Opinion
Contractions	Possessives
Diction	Prefixes
Emotions	Prepositions
Etymology	Propaganda and persuasion
Fables and morals	Rhyming words
Fact and fantasy	Roots
Figurative language	Sequence
Final consonant digraphs	Singular and plural
Final consonants	Skimming and outlining
Heteronyms	Suffixes
Homonyms	Syllables
Initial consonant digraphs	Synonyms
	Symbols and objects
	Verbs
	Vowels

Figure 2-3 Topics covered by lists of elements for generic objectives for the evaluation of pupils and programs. (O'Reilly, Cohen, & Algozzine, 1973, p. 13.)

The difficulty with terms like those in the first 12 items is that the constructs involved cannot be directly observed. One cannot see "understanding" or "memorization" or observe "critical thinking" or hear or feel "appreciation." While it is perfectly correct initially to state an instructional objective using these general constructs, one must then elaborate further the observable actions or product that will be accepted as indicative of the more general construct. It must be kept clearly in mind that it is the general construct (e.g., understanding, knowledge, appreciation) which is really the objective, *not* actions or products per se. It should be kept in mind also that the observed actions or products which a teacher uses to describe these more general constructs do *not* define the construct but instead are *indicative* of it, since many other actions or products may also be apropos (Cronbach, 1971; MacDonald-Ross, 1973). The teacher is testing understanding, appreciation, comprehension, knowledge, etc., through the student's behavior or product (Sockett, 1973; White, 1971). Thus, the problem in correctly specifying objectives that involve nonobservable constructs is to describe the actions or products that are *indicative* of the construct.

As White points out, items 13 through 17 are of a different nature. Here, the behavior is observable: one can directly witness reading, speaking, and working. What is sought is the behavior itself, not a construct, as was the case in items 1 through 12 (White, 1971). However these kinds of objectives can be misinterpreted because of the modifier or object of the verb. The criteria for correctness, effectiveness, and ease differ from person to person, as does the meaning of "basic skills." These modifiers or objects of the verb need to be further clarified.

To define objectives so that they are not open to multiple interpretations involves translating verbs open to inference into action verbs that entail direct observation of a student's actions and, when appropriate, specifying the criteria to be used in interpreting modifiers and adjectives. The overt behavior, or the procedure for observing it, is described in such a way that all who read the description can agree whether or not a student's performance or product testifies to the presence of the objective in question.

Let us first consider objectives that involve constructs like the first twelve listed above, where the construct is not directly observable but can be inferred through behavior. These objectives need to be clarified by using active operational verbs that are not open to misinterpretation. The following are examples of correctly stated objectives (additional action verbs for affective objectives are given in Chapter 11):

1. To state the relationship between . . .
2. To distinguish between . . .
3. To match . . .
4. To put into one's own words . . .
5. To translate a passage . . .
6. To predict . . .
7. To evaluate . . .
8. To volunteer answers . . .
9. To use conventional grammatical form . . .
10. To compute in base two . . .
11. To charge out library books . . .
12. To name . . .
13. To list the consequences of . . .
14. To diagram the flow of . . .
15. To classify . . .
16. To apply principles to new situations . . .
17. To construct a proof . . .
18. To solve . . .
19. To read . . .
20. To identify . . .
21. To graph . . .
22. To complete . . .
23. To construct . . .
24. To paint . . .
25. To arrange in order . . .
26. To explain . . .
27. To ask . . .
28. To join . . .

29. To cut . . .
30. To point to . . .
31. To eliminate the cause of . . .
32. To interpolate . . .
33. To adjust the . . .
34. To pronounce correctly . . .
35. To speak on a topic in . . .

Action verbs like those listed can help determine the instruction sequence and the evaluation procedures to be used. Suppose this objective is stated: "The student has knowledge of the decimal system." Until "has knowledge" is further defined by an action verb, this objective is subject to various interpretations. One teacher might decide to accept as evidence of knowledge the student's ability to write numerals in expanded notation. This teacher might want the instruction sequence to emphasize practice in breaking numerals into units, tens, hundreds, and onward, using exponential notation for each position. The evaluation procedure might simply present a set of numerals to be written by the student using expanded notation. The fact that a place system will work with any base need not be taught, and other bases need not be introduced.

Another teacher may expect the student to be able to perform additional operations involving carrying in bases other than ten. The behaviors indicative of knowledge for this teacher would call for practice in a system of notation with a different base—say, base two or seven—as well as practice with addition in that base. The evaluation procedure might require the student to perform addition which involves carrying, using a base system not specifically studied—say, base three. The point is that, since the behaviors accepted as evidence of knowledge differ, the instruction sequences will probably differ, as will the evaluations.

We shall now consider situations like those listed in items 13 through 17 on page 31, where the behavior itself (i.e., reading, writing, speaking, pronouncing, spelling, etc.) is the objective sought. We commented above that, while one can directly observe these behaviors or the resulting products (e.g., an essay, a business letter), ambiguity can be caused by the modifier or object of the verb in question. Terms like "effectively," "correctly," "with ease," "accurately" need further specification. A standard can often be set that further defines these terms. For example, "speaks effectively" might be further clarified by the following: "Speaks in sentences made up of clearly pronounced, distinct words" (Cazden, 1971, p. 357). In the objective "Uses language effectively for specific purposes," "effectively" may be further clarified by the following description: "Plan, talk over, and explain experiences; ask increasingly penetrating questions, engage in dramatic play" (Cazden, p. 355). The objective "The student can spell correctly" might be further clarified by the following:

The student can recognize eighteen of twenty misspelled words.
The student spells correctly eighteen of twenty words dictated to him or her.
The student's essay is free of spelling errors.

In short, ambiguous words that modify the behavior can be further clarified by giving examples of acceptable performance.

The task analysis school would go even further in specifying an instructional objective. For example, in addition to describing the action of students or the product that results from an action, Mager (1962) would require two additional characteristics. The first of these is a description of the important conditions under which the behavior is expected to occur. Consider this objective: "Given a map of the world, the learner must be able to correctly mark the ocean currents with arrows on the map." Here the details of the evaluation situation and what is expected of the student in it are contained in the statement of the objective.

The second characteristic Mager requires is a designation of how accurate the performance must be. Thus the previous objective could be further clarified by stating it this way: "Given a sketch and map of the world, the student must be able to correctly mark six ocean currents with arrows on the map in a 15-minute time period." Here the number of correct responses is indicated along with the

time in which the student must finish. A minimal acceptable performance is described, giving further specificity to the statement of the objectives. Objectives stated in this fashion are sometimes called "performance objectives."

Gagné (1965, p. 34), summarizing the high degree of specificity described in the work of Mager (1962) and Miller (1961), breaks the statement of an objective into four basic components. The four are illustrated in this sentence taken from Gagné: "Given two numerals connected by the sign +, the student states orally the name of the number which is the sum of the two." First, the statement contains words denoting the *stimulus situation* which initiates the performance ("Given two numerals connected by the sign +"). Second, there is an action word or verb which denotes *observable behavior*. Third, there is a term denoting the *object acted upon* (which sometimes is simply implied). Finally, there is a phrase indicating the *characteristics of the performance* that determine its correctness ("the name of the number which is the sum of the two"). Performance objectives then are described in very specific and detailed terms. How specific and detailed should a statement of an instructional objective be? The next section attempts an answer.

Level of Specificity

One of the thorniest problems associated with describing instructional objectives is the question of how specific the descriptions need to be. If a general objective like "understanding" is broken down into statements of very specific performance objectives, the writing task can become burdensome. The level of specificity then is partly a function of whether the classroom teacher is writing objectives or is choosing them from available sources. (These sources will be described presently.) If the teachers are writing them, then the detail required in the Mager-Gagné approach would probably be too time-consuming for some. If, on the other hand, the teacher is selecting objectives from available sources or is supplementing those he or she has written, then time is less of a problem and the specificity of the Gagné-Mager type of objective can be more helpful than a less specific description in suggesting evaluation techniques.

The level of precision necessary in stating an objective is also a function of the learning experiences planned, and the generalizability of the behavior sought. If the student is expected to interact almost exclusively with learning materials contained in a programmed text or computer, then the objectives must be stated very specifically. This is true if for no other reason than that such materials cannot be built without a detailed task description. However, as the variables in the learning situation increase (teacher, number of students, and type of materials, among others), it becomes more difficult to arrive at highly specific formulations. Statements of the objectives hoped for at the end of the course or year would transcend the particular content used during instruction and instead describe more generalizable and transferable skills.

Occasionally the content description of a long-term objective can be relatively detailed. This is particularly true of courses that are sequential, requiring knowledge or comprehension of specifics to build on in hopes of subsequently developing more generalizable skills. Further, if the subject matter is viewed as more or less closed and not likely to change much in the future, the objective may stress knowledge or comprehension. If, on the other hand, the content of the discipline is expanding rapidly, then the aims may stress transferable competencies.

Statements of educational objectives formulated by national curriculum groups or commissions are often very broad in scope— for example, "to use leisure time productively," "to develop good citizenship," "to build an appreciation of the value and power of mathematics in our technological society." Often such broad statements are criticized on the grounds that they give no indication of the kinds of changes to look for in students who have purportedly reached the stipulated goal. While such attempts by blue-ribbon committees often result in excellent philosophical declarations of purpose that can give overall

direction to a school system, they are too Delphic in nature to help the classroom teacher in the daily management of instruction. In other words, because of their vagueness, they cannot serve as a model for instruction or evaluation of the kind described in Chapter 4.

If the purpose of such broadly worded statements were to guide instruction and evaluation, then of course this criticism would be valid. However, they are not intended for that use. They are designed rather to give direction to policymakers at the national, state, and local levels. Though lofty, they are still explicit enough to suggest certain types of action to school boards and administrators.

Perhaps these general statements of purpose would be better labeled "goals" than "objectives." A goal is something broader, longer-range, and more visionary than an objective. It is "something presently out of reach; it is something to strive for, to move toward, or to become. It is an aim or purpose so stated that it excites the imagination and gives people something they want to work for, something they don't yet know how to do, something they can be proud of when they achieve it (Kappel, 1960, p. 38)."

Goals must of course be translated into school programs and activities. In turn, the explicit behaviors that a program will help the student develop are its immediate objectives and should be related to the statement of long-range purpose that initiated it. It is these more immediate aims that must be made precise enough to guide instruction and evaluation. (See Figure 2-4, page 37, for an illustration of the translation of goals into specific objectives at various levels.)

Educators can easily lose sight of the relationship between short-term objectives and long-range purposes. Thus, some teachers and administrators assert that their *real* objectives are intangible or unidentifiable and hence impossible to state in terms of the change in students. The claim is made that the student develops certain attitudes, values, or skills that are not immediately apparent and may not reveal themselves until much later in life, long after school has been completed. Teachers often argue that these intangibles are the only important objectives and that one cannot anticipate what form or direction these outcomes will take. This attitude is sometimes summed up by the cliché "More is caught than taught."

Now, no one will deny that there are many enigmatic, intangible, and unidentifiable long-term outcomes, good and bad, that result from instruction. Often more is "caught than taught" in the dynamic of the classroom. But to claim that these intangibles are the only important objectives for the classroom teacher is to adopt the untenable position that one cannot prove that anything has ever been taught. Further, it neglects the almost universally agreed-upon assumption that pupils must acquire at the very least the basic skills of reading, writing, and mathematics. For purposes of meaningful evaluation at least, objectives must be stated in terms of more readily observable outcomes or changes on the student's part, so that a teacher can determine whether the student is making progress.

The relationships between long-range purposes, short-term objectives, and "success in life" are extremely complex. This chapter concerns itself with the more immediate objectives of instruction. The hope is that the outcomes sought in day-to-day instruction will contribute to the realization of long-range goals. However, sophisticated longitudinal data are needed to determine the ultimate success of a school's programs in fulfilling its broad declarations of purpose. For a more complete discussion of the place of goals in education the reader is referred to Peters (1973).

Ultimately, then, the generalized behavior described in statements of long-term objectives must be specified in more detail for evaluation purposes. Figure 2-4 shows how two broadly stated system goals—one in physical education and another in music—are made progressively more specific as one proceeds from planning through teaching to evaluation. For the evaluation stage the statement of objectives possesses the four characteristics of a Gagné-Mager type of statement (Ferry & Scofield, 1974a, 1974b).

Thus there are various levels of precision with which one can specify an objective and still communicate the intention of instruction. The teacher should bear in mind that there is no one "correct" way to state instructional objectives; other approaches will be illustrated in this and subsequent chapters. In determining the level of specificity of an objective the teacher will take into consideration the amount of time available for either writing or selecting objectives, the number of lessons for which objectives are needed, and the nature of the learning situation and materials.

STRATEGIES AND SOURCES FOR DEVELOPING EDUCATIONAL OBJECTIVES

What strategies can teachers pursue in writing or selecting objectives to ease the workload associated with this essential task? The strategies which follow are arranged more or less in the most efficient order. In addition to knowing efficient strategies for writing and selecting objectives, teachers today need also to know the way through the proliferation of sources of behavioral objectives. And finally, in using these sources, teachers need to observe certain cautions. First, we consider strategies for developing educational objectives.

Strategies for Developing Educational Objectives

Cooperation between colleagues

The first strategy that can ease the burden of writing and selecting instructional objectives is cooperation between colleagues. We have already noted that the writing of educational objectives useful in the planning and evaluation of instruction is not a particularly easy job. It takes a great deal of careful thought and analysis, which in turn require large amounts of time. The job can be made easier if teachers in the same department or grade level develop the objectives in common. A collective effort will minimize the time and work required of each teacher in specifying the objectives.

		Music	Physical education
P L A N N I N G	System goal:	The student will acquire knowledge, skills, and values in esthetic and creative fields that will help to enrich personal and social life.	The student acquires good health habits and understands the conditions necessary for the maintenance of physical and emotional well-being.
	Program goal:	The student is able to sing and use musical instruments to satisfy personal needs and standards; to explore, experiment, and discover.	The student knows rules and is able to apply strategies in a variety of physical education activities and sports.
	Course goal:	The student is able to arrange pulse and duration into a variety of rhythmic patterns.	The student knows the body mechanics, form, and skills for passes in basketball including one-hand, two-hand, chest, bounce, underhand, and "baseball."
	Instructional goal:	The student is able to use a steady pulse beat as a cue for improvising a rhythmic pattern.	The student knows that the following characteristics contribute to the appropriate form for passing in basketball: (1) fingers grip ball, (2) arm and wrist impart force, (3) arms extend for follow-through, (4) step is taken in direction of pass.
M E A S U R E M E N T	Behavior objective:	Given an introductory and continuing pulse beat played on another instrument, the student is able to play an accompanying rhythmic pattern on a classroom drum.	Given a list of four characteristics which contribute to the appropriate form for passing in basketball and four characteristics which do not contribute, the student is able to identify the contributing characteristics.
	Performance objective:	Given a primary classroom drum, drumsticks, and an introductory and continuing pulse beat played in $\frac{4}{4}$ time on another instrument, the student is able to play without additional prompts a rhythmic pattern which varies from the pulse but retains the tempo.	Given a list of four characteristics which contribute to the appropriate form for passing in basketball and four characteristics which do not contribute, the student is able to identify the contributing characteristics with 100 percent accuracy.

Figure 2-4 An example of further specifying a generally defined educational objective in music and physical education. (Adapted from Ferry and Scofield, 1974a and 1974b, p. iii.)

Group participation also helps ensure that students taking the same course of study from different teachers are working toward the attainment of an identical core of objectives. Too often classes taking the "same" course from different teachers achieve entirely different outcomes. Not that there is no longer room for individual teachers to have unique educational objectives; however, the determination of *all* objectives for a common course cannot be left entirely to the discretion of each instructor. Within the framework of a common set of objectives, there is still sufficient freedom for the teacher to work toward unique goals. Further, in realizing the unified aims, the teacher can follow many paths. Common objectives do not imply common methods or the need to stifle a teacher's creativity. Admittedly, capable and conscientious educators may dispute the value of an identical core of objectives, placing instead a premium on diversity and differences between their own objectives and those of others. But to the extent that common skills and knowledge are seen as valuable, cooperative development of objectives is highly recommended.

A further benefit of group participation in the developing of objectives is the formation of a pool of test items. An item pool consists of a large number of test questions, each coded by behavior, content, and approximate grade level, useful for building tests. A full discussion of the formation and use of item pools is given in Chapter 7. Suffice it to say at this point that cooperation in developing objectives is a necessary first step in the development of an item pool.

Analysis of the curriculum materials

Teachers formulating common instructional objectives should begin with an analysis of the text and materials adopted. It should be noted that one should proceed from developing objectives to the choice of test and materials—*not*, as is more frequently the case, from an adopted text to objectives. However, the developing of useful objectives cannot begin in a vacuum, and the process may in turn uncover deficiencies in the books and materials already in use.

One indication of the influence of the behavioral objectives movement is the fact that the major textbook publishers now provide teachers' editions of their textbooks which contain instructional objectives for each unit or lesson. Thus the strategy of analyzing the adopted or proposed curriculum material can lead to discovery of a rich source of already formulated objectives. For example, the *Macmillan Mathematics, Teacher's Edition* (Thoburn, Forbes, Bechtel, & Nelson, 1976) provides a description of the learning base needed to begin a unit and states the purpose of the unit in terms of the tasks children should be able to perform at the end of the unit, as illustrated in Figure 2-5 for the unit on subtraction.

A large number of publishers today incorporate statements of objectives as an integral

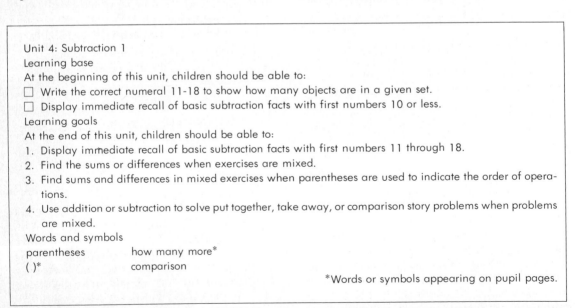

Unit 4: Subtraction 1
Learning base
At the beginning of this unit, children should be able to:
☐ Write the correct numeral 11-18 to show how many objects are in a given set.
☐ Display immediate recall of basic subtraction facts with first numbers 10 or less.
Learning goals
At the end of this unit, children should be able to:
1. Display immediate recall of basic subtraction facts with first numbers 11 through 18.
2. Find the sums or differences when exercises are mixed.
3. Find sums and differences in mixed exercises when parentheses are used to indicate the order of operations.
4. Use addition or subtraction to solve put together, take away, or comparison story problems when problems are mixed.
Words and symbols
parentheses   how many more*
( )*   comparison

*Words or symbols appearing on pupil pages.

Figure 2-5 Description of learning base and learning goals for a unit on subtraction. (Thoburn et al., 1976, p. 69a.)

part of their material. Further, most publishers also provide diagnostic and placement tests (described further in Chapter 5), formative units and tests (described in Chapter 6), and summative tests (described in Chapter 4).

The cooperating teachers should begin the process of developing their course objectives by examining statements of instructional objectives that may accompany the adopted or proposed text. However, there is no need for teachers to limit themselves to the stated objectives of an adopted or proposed text. Objectives accompanying similar textbooks by other publishers should also be examined for additional objectives. This strategy will also reveal both the commonality and the uniqueness of various instructional objectives in different texts in the same subject at the same grade level. Such information is useful in deciding on the feasibility and desirability of different objectives. A discussion by cooperating teachers of publishers' statements of objectives can be beneficial in bringing out differences in approach, emphasis, and sequencing.

It must be kept in mind that although an instructional objective is described by a publisher of a text in terms of some observable action, teachers need not adopt it as their own. They must carefully study the objectives of the given curriculum in relation to the particular situation. Knowledge of previous instruction, available time for teaching, the specific needs of a group of students, and the interest or qualifications of the teacher may individually or collectively militate against the adoption of certain objectives examined.

Analysis of objectives by national curriculum groups

During the past decade regional laboratories and various groups, composed mainly of university scholars and skilled teachers interested in curriculum reforms, have produced new sets of objectives for almost all the subjects taught in the elementary and secondary schools. Hence another strategy to follow in deciding on objectives is to study the new sets of objectives produced by these national curriculum groups. In the case of a few projects—the Cambridge Conference on School Mathematics (1963), for example—the goals have been visionary and long-range so that educators may have some informed notion of the direction in which they should be moving. However, in most cases these groups have translated their objectives into curriculum materials for classroom use, and many are now commercially available, as mentioned above.

Sets of objectives from national curriculum groups serve as a frame of reference indicating what a selected body of experts regard as important in the discipline. Teachers can then compare what they themselves think important, and what authors and text publishers think important, with what a national curriculum group thinks important.

Analysis of teacher-made tests

A different strategy to employ is an analysis of the examinations used in past years. By analyzing test questions one can draw inferences about the kinds of behaviors required of students in answering each. It needs always to be kept in mind that for students the objectives that really matter are those implicitly embedded in the tests on which their grades are based. This is precisely the reason it is important to ensure congruence between objectives and evaluation procedures.

It must be emphasized that the validity of such inferences depends on an accurate knowledge of the background—at least the in-school experience—that the student brings to the item. The same item may elicit entirely different behaviors from different students: a test question may involve simple recall of memorized facts for students who have discussed the specific material in class, while it may require high-level analysis and application by those who have never seen the material but have covered relevant principles during instruction.

Despite differences in students' backgrounds, however, this strategy can give insights into the actual behaviors intended by the teachers, thereby providing some guidelines for specifying objectives. The *Taxonomy of Educational Objectives* (Bloom, 1956), to be discussed in more detail below, is a useful frame of reference for classifying test questions (Madaus & Macnamara, 1970).

Classroom observations

The formulation of objectives can also be facilitated by observing classes to identify the changes in students that are *actually* taking place. Students' performance reveals the actual outcomes of instruction, which often are quite different from the objectives stated at the outset (Brickell, 1976; Scriven, 1974).

In this strategy, the observer looks not only for expected outcomes but also for unanticipated outcomes. The procedure is based on the assumption that while the text or course materials have content validity, it is difficult to envision *all* the resulting behaviors beforehand. Too often unexpected negative and positive outcomes of the course are overlooked because evaluation concentrates exclusively on previously formulated objectives. The Illinois Elementary School Science Project utilized such an approach in assessing its strengths and weaknesses. As J. Myron Atkin (1963), then project director, put it:

> Project personnel are beginning a series of classroom observations in an attempt to identify unexpected behavioral changes in students. In the customary methods of course development and evaluation, such a procedure seems backwards. The standard practice is to identify the changes desired in the students, then see if the course is effective in producing the changes. Instead we are observing classes for the purpose of identifying changes that are not predicted or recognized at the start. (p. 132)

Classroom observation, then, helps identify unanticipated outcomes, results in more comprehensive and reliable evaluation, and identifies which objectives should be added, preserved, or deleted.

Classroom experience

The insights of observers need to be supplemented by the insights of the teacher; reflections on daily teaching, if made regularly and recorded, can be one of the most valuable sources of objectives. In Chapter 1 we saw that a principal source of objectives was the

needs of students, particularly the interests of students. What better place than the classroom to discover these interests? Gardner (1977), in his analysis of Kohl's book *36 Children* (1968), showed how Kohl, a first-year teacher in a sixth-grade ghetto school, was initially unsure about what his objective ought to be:

> The ends which emerge in Kohl's work both emerge and are substantively determined by the essentially *experiential* character of the method. Kohl discovers what to teach from his study of the children—their needs, feelings, thoughts, language, their life experience—and *how* he teaches is determined by what he wishes to teach. (p. 391)

In the cyclical view of developing objectives (see Figure 2-2), a beginning teacher should, by the second year, have a clearer, expanded picture of the instructional objectives. The list of planned objectives and means of achieving them can grow as a result of each year's experience. It must be emphasized that many skills and behaviors that a teacher wants students to master can be specified in advance, even by beginning teachers. Nonetheless, *new* objectives and methods will emerge, and planned objectives will be modified, as the result of teaching. New ends that emerge can be added to the planned list, perhaps crowding out previous objectives.

Taxonomy of Educational Objectives

In developing objectives the two-volume *Taxonomy of Educational Objectives* (Bloom, 1956; Krathwohl, Bloom & Masia, 1964) is invaluable. Each *Taxonomy* is summarized in the Appendix, and each will be treated more fully in Chapters 8–11. However, a brief description of the two volumes is in order here.

Handbook 1, *Cognitive Domain*, was published in 1956; it classifies objectives which involve intellectual tasks. For some of these objectives the student has to do little more than remember; for others the student must determine the essential problem and then reorder given material or combine it with ideas, methods, or procedures previously learned. (See Chapters 8–10 for a more detailed discussion of the categories in the *Cognitive Domain*.) Handbook 2, *Affective Domain*, completed in 1964, categorizes objectives which emphasize feeling, emotion, or degree of acceptance or rejection (see Chapter 11 for a more detailed discussion of the *Affective Domain*).

The *Taxonomy* is the work of a group of college examiners who developed this classification system for educational objectives to facilitate communication among themselves and their colleagues about objectives, test items, and test procedures. They were aware that the lack of precision in classification was responsible for much of the ambiguity, misinterpretation, and conversation-without-communication which greeted educators' attempts to share ideas about objectives and testing. A third taxonomy for the psychomotor domain was developed by Harrow (1972). (For a discussion of other taxonomies of educational objectives, see DeLandsheere, 1977.)

The three taxonomies place the behavioral aspect of the objective within a hierarchical framework: each category is assumed to include behavior more complex, abstract, or internalized than the previous category. In the *Cognitive Domain* these categories are arranged along a continuum from simple to complex. In the *Affective Domain* the continuum is one of internalization; that is, the ordering describes the process by which a given phenomenon or value progresses from a level of bare awareness to a position of some power to guide or control a person's action. Harrow has arranged psychomotor behaviors along a continuum from the lowest level of observable behavior—reflex movements—to the highest nondiscursive movement.

In each volume each category is illustrated by examples of educational objectives taken from the literature, a description of the behaviors involved at the particular level, and sample test items designed to measure the described behaviors.

Teachers may use the *Taxonomy* in various ways. First, if a group of teachers have a set of objectives stated in broad terms, the *Taxonomy* can help specify them more precisely. Thus, if one of the objectives is "The student understands economic information presented in graphic form," the teacher can make the objective more precise by choosing various behaviors from the *Cognitive Domain* and by using the illustrative test items. For teachers struggling with the problems of stating objectives, the *Taxonomy* provides a common point of reference and a common terminology on which to center their discussions.

Second, one of the principal values of the *Cognitive Domain* has been that it has called teachers' attention to the possibility of measuring objectives more complex than the recall of facts. The test items in the *Taxonomy* can be used by teachers as models in building similar items peculiar to their content-area needs. The *Taxonomy* abounds in model items designed to measure all types of behavior from simple to very complex. Teachers generally have little difficulty testing straightforward recall of facts but are not so adept at building items to measure higher-order mental processes or affective outcomes of instruction. One of the main criticisms teachers level at objective tests is that they examine only very simple skills. The model items in the *Taxonomy* should disabuse teachers of this notion and give them direction in constructing items measuring more complex behavior.

Third, the *Taxonomy* can suggest classes of objectives not previously considered. Used in this manner, it becomes a guide for a more comprehensive screening of course outcomes.

Fourth, as mentioned above, the *Taxonomy* can be used to help teachers analyze objectives implicit in tests (Madaus and Macnamara, 1970). As Krathwohl (1964) has said, teachers have the feeling that standardized tests are:

> . . . put together by experts who know more than they do, and though they may feel a vague discontent with the test, too often they do not analyze the content of these tests against their objectives to determine how well

they match. Here again, by using the taxonomy as a translating framework one can compare the test with the teachers' goals. In its simplest form this may be a determination of the proportion of items in each of the major taxonomy categories. This alone is often enough information to help a teacher determine a test's relevance. (p. 34)

Finally, the *Taxonomy* has been used as a classificatory system by various groups that have built large pools, or banks, of objectives and test items (which will be discussed below). Some textbook publishers also use the cognitive taxonomy in describing the goals or objectives for their textbooks. Thus, a working knowledge of the various taxonomies will aid teachers in their consideration of objectives banks and statements of objectives published by textbook houses.

Sources for Selecting Objectives

As we have mentioned, the task of developing and writing instructional objectives can be time-consuming. Further, because teachers generally teach more than one subject—elementary teachers are usually responsible for a number of curricular areas—they would have to write a large number of instructional objectives. For example, if a teacher has two objectives for each lesson, and five different lessons a day, there would be a need to write 50 instructional objectives per week—quite a time-consuming task, particularly for a beginning teacher.

However, in recognition of this burden, and also of the value of clearly stated objectives, a number of sources have been developed that permit busy teachers to *select* for their use educational objectives stated in terms of content and actions desired. We have already discussed three such sources in the preceding sections: teachers' editions of textbooks, statements of national curriculum groups, and the three taxonomies of educational objectives. In this section we shall discuss several additional sources from which teachers can select well-formulated statements of instructional objectives. These sources obviate the need of planning a course

from scratch. Using these sources avoids duplication of effort by taking advantage of the thought and effort of curriculum experts and countless classroom teachers. Further, these sources serve as a bench mark against which a teacher or group of teachers can compare their ideas about the ends of a curriculum with those developed either by specialists in the field or by other school systems or districts. Before proceeding with a description of these sources, however, we need to emphasize the following precautions governing their use.

1. *Is the objective desirable?* Just because an objective appears in print and is clearly stated in terms of behavior and content, it is not necessarily a worthwhile objective. Desirability needs to be determined in each case in relation to the school's or teacher's philosophy, the learning process, and the needs of the students (see Chapter 1).

2. *Is the objective feasible?* An objective may not be feasible in a particular situation. The content may be inappropriate in terms of the texts and resource material available, or the outcomes may not be possible because of certain characteristics of the student population (e.g., bilingualism, maturational differences, handicaps). A decision of feasibility needs to be made for each objective under consideration.

3. *Is the content of the objective within a teacher's competence?* Some teachers without in-service training may not be prepared to teach certain content and concepts that might appear as part of an objective, for example in a *new* mathematics or social studies course.

4. *Does the content component of the objective fall within the appropriate stage of the content sequence?* The important but often neglected matter of content sequencing is discussed above.

5. *Can colleagues agree on the meaning of a particular statement of an objective?* Statements of objectives should be clear enough, in terms of both content and observable action or products, so that

teachers can agree on the outcome in question. If not, and if the objective is still considered important, the teachers should be able to further clarify it.

6. *Does the source include only objectives that can be measured by a paper-and-pencil test?* If the source has this restriction—and many do—a variety of important goals may be excluded. For example, this restriction would suppress objectives measurable only by "hands-on" methods—dissection, manipulation, modeling, repairing a carburetor, playing an instrument, using a microscope, preparing food, sewing, making a speech, etc.

The Eight-Year Study

One of the first extensive lists of behavioral objectives was produced as part of the famous Eight-Year Study of secondary education for the Progressive Education Association. A group of high schools labeled "progressive" were attempting to develop new curricula and approaches to instruction and learning. Those in charge of the programs anticipated that their graduates might find it difficult to gain admission to college: since these students would not have followed "traditional" high school curricula, some colleges might feel that they lacked sufficient prerequisite credits. The Eight-Year Study enlisted the cooperation of colleges to admit students of progressive high schools so that the development of the new programs could continue to be carefully evaluated longitudinally through the four years of higher education. For comparison purposes, students from traditional schools were also followed longitudinally. It became critical to the success of this study that the objectives of the new curricula be stated in clear, unambiguous terms, so that appropriate evaluation instruments and techniques could be developed to appraise the effectiveness of the curricula. Smith and Tyler's book *Appraising and Recording Student Progress* (1942), one of five volumes describing the Eight-Year Study, contains example after example of educational objectives described in terms of content area and observable actions (see Chapter 11 for an example). While some of these objectives are dated, a large number are still applicable, particularly affective objectives.

National Assessment project and state needs-assessment projects

The National Assessment is a project that systematically takes a censuslike survey of knowledge, skills, understanding, and attitudes at four age levels—9 years, 13 years, 17 years, and adult,—in the following ten areas: art, career and occupational development, citizenship, literature, mathematics, music, reading, science, social studies, and writing (Womer, 1970).

In order to carry out these periodic surveys, a specific set of objectives had to be developed for each of these ten areas. These objectives were written by subject matter specialists and then reviewed for final selection by lay panels in each of the areas. Each objective selected is further clarified by an exercise, that is, a description of the test question or task used in the survey to gather information about mastery of that objective. Booklets are available from National Assessment describing each of the objectives in each of the ten areas. The following is an example of an objective taken from the booklet (Norris & Bowes, 1970) describing music objectives:

III. Listen to music with understanding.
A. *Perceive the various elements of music, such as timbre, rhythm, melody and harmony, and texture.*
  1. Identify timbres.
    Age 9: Identify by categories the manner in which the instrument is played (e.g., struck, bowed).
    Identify individual instrumental timbres—unaccompanied.
    Identify individual instrumental timbres—with accompaniment.
    Age 13 (in addition to Age 9): Identify individual vocal timbres—with accompaniment.
    Identify ensemble timbres, instrumental and vocal.
    Age 17 and adult: Identify by categories families of related timbres (e.g., woodwinds, plucked strings).

Identify individual instrumental timbres
—unaccompanied.

Identify individual instrumental and vocal timbres—with accompaniment.

Identify ensemble timbres, instrumental and vocal. (pp. 11–12)

The lists of objectives in each of the ten areas, while not extensive, are valuable in that they describe for teachers those objectives in each field that both subject matter experts and panels of laypeople agree are important.

Many state education departments have conducted needs assessments in various subject areas. Often as part of these assessments, panels of teachers and laypeople develop educational objectives, and these are often described in terms of content areas and student performance. Teachers selecting objectives in states that have carried out these assessments would do well to obtain from their state department of education a description of the needs-assessment objectives for their area of the curriculum.

Competency-based graduation and certification programs

A number of states and local school districts have begun to develop competency-based graduation or certification programs. In such programs certain outcomes thought to be important in life, sometimes called "minimal competencies," are required of a student in order to graduate. These outcomes are described in terms of content and actions or products. Teachers in the process of selecting objectives from available sources in states or districts that are moving toward such programs should try to obtain lists of these minimal graduation competencies. Such a list can be used to select certain objectives or check the representativeness of objectives selected from other sources.

Commercially available criterion-referenced tests

Many test publishers have recently developed criterion-referenced tests (see Chapter 5) in reading and mathematics or offer services whereby school districts can receive customized criterion-referenced tests. Items on such tests are geared to statements of objectives for reading or mathematics. These statements of objectives are available to teachers in accompanying materials (e.g., manuals, technical reports). These lists, often classified by grade level, are an excellent source of objectives.

Objective pools

As we noted previously, for many areas of the curriculum there now exist large pools, or banks, of statements of educational objectives. Pools of test items accompany many of these objective pools (item banks will be discussed in Chapter 7). Generally a pool has a description of broad content topics that are further subdivided into specific elements. Each objective can then be coded by subject, by topic within the subject (see Figure 2-3), and by specific element within a topic. Generally objectives are stated in terms of outcomes and then in more detail by a series of subobjectives or test items or exercises. A coding scheme is generally employed to classify each objective in terms of outcomes—often the categories of the *Taxonomy of Educational Objectives* are used for the coding. See Figure 2-6 for a representative example of an objective from one such pool. Each pool is generally accompanied by a description of how it was built, the assumptions underlying it, and the directions on how to use it for selecting objectives. A variety of examples of such pools may help illustrate their scope and use and in part their coding system. The following is a list of the major objective pools that a teacher might want to consult:

1. *Westinghouse Learning Press* (1975a, 1975b, 1975c, 1975d); Flanagan & Shanner (1971a, 1971b, 1971c, 1971d) has objective pools for science, mathematics, social studies, and language arts.
2. *The Alaska Statewide Instructional Support System* prepared by the Northwest Regional Educational Laboratory (1976)

CONSONANTS
Initial single

Code number: WPC 1.1.   .B   Item type: Oral word–word recognition

Objective

The student will be given an oral word containing a single initial consonant sound *(b, hard c, soft c, etc.)*. Then, from among four words listed in a row, the student will select the word that begins with that sound and circle it.

The student will be required to distinguish the correct word from the following three incorrect options:

1. A word with an intial consonant and sound similar to the initial sound of the given word
2. A word with a final consonant sound identical to the initial consonant sound of the given word (to identify a consonant reversal)
3. A word which rhymes with the given word.

Coding scheme

WPC   1.1.____.B

Word identification skills   Oral word–Word recognition
Phonetic analysis   item type
Consonants   Specific content tested
    Single consonant
    Initial single consonant

Figure 2-6   Objective taken from the Alaska Objectives and Item Bank with an explanation of the coding scheme. (Adapted from Northwest Regional Education Laboratory, 1976.)

contains objective pools for reading and arithmetic.

3. *The New York State System for Pupil and Program Evaluation and Development* (O'Reilly, Cohen, & Algozzine, 1973) contains three resource packages that permit teachers working at the local level to construct their own objective pool. The first, *Resource 5000*, contains a large pool of statements of objectives that teachers may select from. These objectives are described in terms of the stimulus materials and the student behaviors but leave the choice of objective to the second and third resources. The second, *Resource 5001*, permits the teacher to further elaborate selected objectives in terms of criterion performance expected: the third, *Resource 5002*, permits the teacher to fur-

ther elaborate the content of selected objectives. A manual describes how the teachers use the three resources to prepare individualized lists of instructional objectives.

4. One of the largest collections of objective pools has been assembled by the *Instructional Objective Exchange* (IOX, 1972). This collection contains pools of cognitive and affective objectives and measurement items for a large number of curriculum areas.

In addition to these sources a number of school districts have produced excellent objective pools through the cooperative effort of teachers in the system, often working in conjunction with curriculum or evaluation specialists. For example, Holliston, Massachusetts, has developed a large pool of objectives for various areas in the middle school curriculum; West Hartford, Connecticut, has a pool for the elementary curriculum; Downers Grove, Illinois School District 97, has extensive pools in language arts, mathematics, social studies, and science at the primary, intermediate, and junior and senior high school levels; the Sequoia Union High School District in Redwood City, California, has developed large pools of objectives for fourteen subjects; the Tri-County Goal Development Project of the Multnomah County Intermediate Education District in Oregon has developed a twelve-volume set of 15,000 objectives in twelve basic subjects for kindergarten through grade 12.

Teachers wishing to select objectives would be advised to inquire into these various projects. The curriculum library of a school district or curriculum department might be able to acquire such pools, permitting teachers to develop, through selection, their own list of objectives.

Handbook on Formative and Summative Evaluation of Student Learning (Part II)

As we noted earlier, Part II of the *Handbook on Formative and Summative Evaluation of Student Learning* (Bloom, Hastings, & Madaus, 1971) consists of eleven chapters written by specialists in preschool education, language arts, social studies, art education, science, mathematics, literature, writing, second-language learning, and industrial education. Each chapter is organized around an instructional-evaluation model in the form of a content-behavior matrix. [Our Table 2-1 (page 26) is the matrix taken from the chapter by Courtney Cazden, "Evaluation of Learning in Preschool Education: Early Language Development."] Each chapter then proceeds to discuss each nonempty cell of the matrix further in terms of both content and observable outcomes. Next, specific techniques for evaluating each objective are illustrated. Formative and summative evaluation are discussed, and finally each chapter presents an example of a formative unit (see Table 2-3). Teachers working in the eleven curriculum areas covered in the *Handbook*

should consult the appropriate chapter for objectives for their own courses.

EXERCISES

1. Select one major skill from your subject field of interest. Perform a task analysis for this skill.
   a. Begin with a statement of the target behavior.
   b. Decompose this target behavior into its component parts. For each component state the desired behavior.
   c. Arrange your results in a form similar to Glaser and Reynolds's chart (Figure 2-1 of this chapter). Indicate the interrelationships of the component parts.
   d. What entry behaviors would you assume of your students? How would you establish whether or not this assumption was warranted?
   e. Review the chart you have produced. Does each statement include an observable, identifiable behavior?

2. Select a unit of instruction from your subject field of interest. This time use the Tyler approach to develop a set of instructional objectives for the unit.
   a. Use whatever sources you consider appropriate to select the content to be covered; texts, curriculum materials, your own lesson plans, tests, workbooks, etc.
   b. Begin by stating some broad general unit objectives. They should encompass in general terms everything to be covered in the unit.
   c. Break the objectives down into content and behavior components and display them in a table of specifications. Indicate which of the cells are empty and which are target cells.
   d. For each target cell write detailed objectives at the level of specificity you feel appropriate.

3. For each of the detailed objectives in 2(d) above:
   a. Underline the content component.
   b. Underline the behavior component

twice. Is the verb an observable behavior?

   c. Classify the desired behavior as indicative of a construct (e.g., "understanding") or a behavior sought for its own sake (e.g., "to read").

4. Select five or six of your objectives and rewrite them in the form of performance objectives.

5. Select another subset of five or six objectives. For each of these suggest several alternative learning activities.

REFERENCES

Aho, W., Alberti, D., Perkes, V., Sheldon, R., Thomas, T., & Ward, R. *The McGraw-Hill evaluation program for ESS.* New York: McGraw-Hill, 1974.

Atkin, J. M. Some evaluation problems in a course content improvement project. *Journal of Research in Science Teaching*, 1963, *1*, 129–132.

Block, J. H. (Ed.). *Mastery learning: Theory and practice.* New York: Holt, 1971.

Block, J. H. (Ed.). *Schools, society, and mastery learning.* New York: Holt, 1974.

Bloom, B. S. (Ed.). *Taxonomy of educational objectives: The classification of educational goals.* Handbook 1. *Cognitive domain.* New York: McKay, 1956.

Bloom, B. S. *Human characteristics and school learning.* New York: McGraw-Hill, 1976.

Bloom, B. S., Hastings, J. T., & Madaus, G. F. *Handbook on formative and summative evaluation of student learning.* New York: McGraw-Hill, 1971.

Brickell, H. M. Needed: Instruments as good as our eyes. *Evaluation Center Occasional Paper Series #7.* Kalamazoo: Western Michigan University, 1976.

Broudy, H. S. Can research escape the dogma of behavioral objectives? *School Review*, 1970, *79*, 43–56.

Bruner, J. S. *Toward a theory of instruction.* Cambridge, Mass.: The Belknap Press of Harvard University, 1966.

Cambridge Conference on School Mathematics. *Goals for school mathematics: The report of the Cambridge Conference on School Mathematics.* Boston: Houghton Mifflin, 1963.

Carroll, J. B., Davies, P., & Richman, B. *The American Heritage word frequency book.* New York: American Heritage; Boston: Houghton Mifflin, 1971.

Case, R. Gearing the demands of instruction to the developmental capacities of the learner. *Review of Educational Research*, 1975, *45*(1), 59–87.

Cazden, C. B. Evaluation of learning in preschool education: Early language development. In B. S. Bloom, J. T. Hastings, & G. F. Madaus (Eds.), *Handbook on formative and summative evaluation of student learning.* New York: McGraw-Hill, 1971.

Cronbach, L. J. Test validation. In R. L. Thorndike (Ed.), *Educational measurement* (2nd ed.). Washington, D.C.: American Council on Education, 1971.

California Test Bureau (CTB)/McGraw-Hill. *Prescriptive reading inventory interpretive handbook.* Monterey, Calif.: Author, 1972.

DeLandsheere, V. On refining educational objectives. In B. H. Choppin & T. N. Postlethwaite (Eds.), *Evaluation in education: International progress* (An International Review Series), 1977, *1*(2), 73–90.

Duchastel, P. C., & Merrill, P. F. The effects of behavioral objectives on learning: A review of empirical studies. *Review of Educational Research*, 1973, *43*(1), 53–69.

Faw, H. W., & Waller, T. G. Mathemagenic behaviors and efficiency in learning. *Review of Educational Research*, 1976, *46*(4), 691–720.

Ferry, C., & Scofield, S. *Course goals in physical education, K-12.* Portland, Oregon: Tri-County Goal Development Project, Multnomah County Intermediate Education District, 1974. (a)

Ferry, C., & Scofield, S. *Course goals in music, K-12.* Portland, Oregon: Tri-County Goal Development Project, Multnomah County Intermediate Education District, 1974. (b)

Flanagan, J. C., Shanner, W. H., & Mager, R. F. *Science behavioral objectives.*

Palo Alto, Calif.: Westinghouse Learning Press, 1971. (a)

Flanagan, J. C., Shanner, W. H., & Mager, R. F. *Mathematics behavioral objectives.* Palo Alto, Calif.: Westinghouse Learning Press, 1971. (b)

Flanagan, J. C., Shanner, W. H., & Mager, R. F. *Language arts behavioral objectives.* Palo Alto, Calif.: Westinghouse Learning Press, 1971. (c)

Flanagan, J. C., Shanner, W. H., & Mager, R. F. *Social studies behavioral objectives.* Palo Alto, Calif.: Westinghouse Learning Press, 1971. (d)

Gagné, R. M. The analysis of instructional objectives for the design of instruction. In R. Glaser (Ed.), *Teaching machines and programmed learning.* Vol. 2. *Data and directions.* Washington, D.C.: National Education Association, 1965.

Gardner, L. Humanistic education and behavioral objectives: Opposing theories of educational science. *School Review,* May 1977, pp. 376–394.

Geis, G. L. *Behavioral objectives: A selected bibliography and brief review.* ERIC Clearinghouse on Media and Technology. Stanford, Calif.: Stanford University Press, April, 1972.

Glaser, R., & Reynolds, J. Instructional objectives and programmed instruction: A case study. In C. M. Lindvall (Ed.), *Defining educational objectives.* Pittsburgh: University of Pittsburgh Press, 1964.

Harrow, A. J. *A taxonomy of the psychomotor domain: A guide for developing behavioral objectives.* New York: McKay, 1972.

Instructional Objectives Exchange (IOX). *Attitudes toward school.* Los Angeles: Author, 1972.

Iwanicki, E. F. *An empirical study of the contributions of the cognitive objectives of an instructional system to the instructional process.* Unpublished doctoral dissertation, Boston College, 1972.

Jackson, P. W. *The way teaching is.* Washington, D.C.: Association for Supervision and Curriculum Development, 1966.

Kamii, C. K. Evaluation of learning in preschool education: Socio-emotional, perceptual-motor, cognitive development. In B. S. Bloom, J. T. Hastings, and G. F. Madaus (Eds.), *Handbook on formative and summative evaluation of student learning.* New York: McGraw-Hill, 1971.

Kappel, F. R. *Vitality in a business enterprise.* New York: McGraw-Hill, 1960.

Kohl, H. *36 children.* New York: Signet Books, 1968.

Krathwohl, D. R., Bloom, B. S., & Masia, B. B. *Taxonomy of educational objectives: The classification of educational goals.* Handbook 2. *Affective domain.* New York: McKay, 1964.

MacDonald, J. B., & Clark, D. Critical value questions and the analysis of objectives and curriculum. In R. M. W. Travers (Ed.), *Second handbook on research on teaching.* Chicago: Rand McNally, 1973.

MacDonald-Ross, M. Behavioral objectives: A critical review. *Instructional Science,* 1973, 2, 1–52.

Madaus, G. F., Airasian, P. W., & Kellaghan, T. *School effectiveness: A reassessment of the evidence.* New York: McGraw-Hill, 1980.

Madaus, G. F., & Macnamara, J. *Public examinations: A study of the Irish Leaving Certificate.* Dublin, Ireland: Educational Research Centre, St. Patrick's College, 1970.

Mager, R. F. *Preparing objectives for programmed instruction.* San Francisco: Fearon, 1962.

Miller, R. B. The newer roles of the industrial psychologist. In B. Gilner (Ed.), *Industrial psychology.* New York: McGraw-Hill, 1961.

Norris, E. L., & Bowes, J. E. *Music objectives.* Ann Arbor, Mich.: National Assessment of Education Progress, 1970.

Northwest Regional Educational Laboratory. *Alaska statewide instructional support system. Objective and item directory reading: Word identification skills.* Juneau: Alaska Department of Education, 1976.

Ontario Department of Education. *Living and learning: The report of the Provincial Committee on aims and objectives in education.* Ontario, Can.: Author, 1968.

O'Reilly, R. P., Cohen, A. S., & Algozzine,

J. *Training manual for the use of objectives in the bank of objectives, items and resources in reading. System for pupil and program evaluation and development.* Albany: University of the State of New York, The State Education Department, Bureau of School and Culture Research, 1973.

Peters, R. S. (Ed.). Aims of education: An interdisciplinary inquiry. *London Educational Review,* 1973, 2(3).

Popham, W. J. Objectives and instruction. In W. J. Popham, E. Eisner, H. J. Sullivan, & L. L. Tyler (Eds.), *Instructional objectives* (American Educational Research Association Monograph Series on Curriculum Evaluation, No. 3). Chicago: Rand McNally, 1969.

Posner, G. J., & Strike, K. A. A categorization scheme for principles of sequencing content. *Review of Educational Research,* 1976, 46(4), 665–690.

Romberg, T. A., & Kilpatrick, J. Preliminary study on evaluation in mathematics education. In T. A. Romberg & J. W. Wilson (Eds.), *The development of tests* (NLSMA, Report No. 7). Stanford, Calif.: School of Mathematics Study Group, 1969.

Scriven, M. Evaluation perspectives and procedures. In W. J. Popham (Ed.), *Evaluation in education.* Berkeley: McCutchan Publishing Corp., 1974.

Smith, E. R., & Tyler, R. W. *Appraising and recording student progress* (Adventure in American Education Series, Vol. 3). New York: Harper, 1942.

Sockett, H. Behavioral objectives. *London Educational Review,* 1973, 2(3) 38–45.

Stake, R. E. *Priorities planning judges the importance of individual objectives.* Los Angeles: Instructional Objectives Exchange, 1972.

Stodolsky, S. S. Defining treatment and outcome in early childhood education. In H. T. Walberg & A. T. Kopan (Eds.), *Rethinking urban education.* San Francisco: Jossey Bass, 1972.

Thoburn, T., Forbes, J. E., Bechtel, R., & Nelson, L. *Macmillan mathematics, teachers edition.* New York: Macmillan, 1976.

Tyler, R. W. *Basic principles of curriculum and instruction.* Chicago: University of Chicago Press, 1950.

Valette, R. M. Evaluation of learning in a second language. In B. S. Bloom, J. T. Hastings, & G. F. Madaus (Eds.), *Handbook on formative and summative evaluation of student learning.* New York: McGraw-Hill, 1971.

Westinghouse Learning Press. *Learning objectives for individualized instruction: Science.* Sunnyvale, Calif.: Author, 1975. (a)

Westinghouse Learning Press. *Learning objectives for individualized instruction: Language arts.* Sunnyvale, Calif.: Author, 1975. (b)

Westinghouse Learning Press. *Learning objectives for individualized instruction: Mathematics.* Sunnyvale, Calif.: Author, 1975. (c)

Westinghouse Learning Press. *Learning objectives for individualized instruction: Social studies.* Sunnyvale, Calif.: Author, 1975. (d)

White, J. P. The concept of curriculum evaluation. *Journal of Curriculum Studies,* 1971, 2(2), 102–112.

Wilson, J. W. Evaluation of learning in secondary school mathematics. In B. S. Bloom, J. T. Hastings, & G. F. Madaus (Eds.), *Handbook on formative and summative evaluation of student learning.* New York: McGraw-Hill, 1971.

Womer, F. B. *What is National Assessment?* Ann Arbor, Mich.: National Assessment of Educational Progress, 1970.

3 Learning for Mastery

Chapter Highlights

INTRODUCTION

Let us begin with a statement of ours that has been widely quoted:

> Each teacher begins a new term or course with the expectation that about a third of his students will adequately learn what he has to teach. He expects about a third to fail or to just "get by." Finally, he expects another third to learn a good deal of what he has to teach, but not enough to be regarded as "good students." This set of expectations, supported by school policies and practices in grading, is transmitted to the students through the grading procedures and through the methods and materials of instruction. This system creates a self-fulfilling prophecy such that the final sorting of students through the grading process becomes approximately equivalent to the original expectations. (Bloom, Hastings, and Madaus, 1971, p. 43)

This set of expectations, which fixes the academic goals of teachers and students, is the most wasteful and destructive aspect of the present educational system. It reduces the aspirations of both teachers and students, it reduces motivation for learning in students, and it systematically destroys the ego and self-concept of a sizable group of the students, who are legally required to attend school for 10 to 12 years under conditions which are frustrating and humiliating year after year. The cost of this system in reducing opportunities for further learning and in alienating youth from both school and the community at large is so great that no society can tolerate it for long.

Most students (perhaps more than 90 percent) can master what we have to teach them, and it is the task of instruction to find the means which will enable them to master the subject under consideration. A basic task is to determine what we mean by "mastery of the subject" and to search for the methods and materials which will enable the largest proportion of our students to attain such mastery.

In this chapter we will consider one approach to learning for mastery and the underlying theoretical concepts, research findings, and techniques required. Basically, the problem of developing a strategy for mastery learning is one of determining how individual differences in learners can be related to the learning and teaching processes.

Background

Some societies can utilize only a small number of highly educated people in the economy and can provide the economic support for only a small proportion of the students to complete secondary or higher education. Under such conditions, much of the effort of the schools and the external examining system is devoted to finding ways of rejecting the majority of students at various points in the education system and to discovering the talented few who are to be given advanced educational opportunities. Such societies invest a great deal more in predicting and selecting talent than in developing it.

The complexities of the skills required by the work force in the United States and in other highly developed nations mean that we can no longer operate on the assumption that completion of secondary and advanced education is for the few. The increasing evidence (Bowman, 1966; Schultz 1963) that investment in the education of humans pays off at a greater rate than does capital investment suggests that we cannot return to an economy of scarcity of educational opportunity.

Whatever might have been the case previously, highly developed nations must seek to find ways to increase the proportion of the age group that can successfully complete both secondary and higher education. The question is no longer one of finding the few who can succeed. The basic problem is to determine how the largest proportion of the age group can learn effectively the skills and subject matter regarded as essential for their own development in a complex society.

However, given another set of philosophic and psychological presuppositions, we may express our concern over the consequences for intellect and personality of a lack of clear success in the learning tasks of the school. Learning throughout life (continuing learning) will become necessary for an increasingly larger segment of the work force. If school learning is regarded as frustrating and even impossible by a sizable proportion of students, then little can be done at later levels to kindle a genuine interest in further learning. School learning must be successful and rewarding as one basis for ensuring that learning can continue throughout life as needed.

Even more important in modern society is the malaise about values. As the secular society becomes more and more central, the values remaining for the individual have to do with hedonism, interpersonal relations, self-development, and ideas. If the schools frustrate the students in the latter two areas, only the first two are available to them. Whatever the case may be for each of these values, the schools must strive to assure all students of successful learning experiences in the realms of ideas and self-development.

There is little question that the schools now do provide successful learning experiences for some students—perhaps as many as one-third. If the schools are to provide successful and satisfying learning experiences for at least 90 percent of the students, major changes must take place in the attitudes of students, teachers, and administrators as well as in teaching strategies and the role of evaluation.

The Normal Curve

As educators we have used the normal curve in grading students for so long that we have come to believe in it. Achievement measures are designed to detect differences among our learners—even if the differences are trivial in terms of the subject matter. We then distribute our grades in a normal fashion. In any group of students we expect to have some small percentage receive a grade of A. We are surprised when the figure differs greatly from about 10 percent. We are also prepared to fail an equal proportion of students. Quite frequently this failure is determined by the rank order of the students in the group rather than by their failure to grasp the essential ideas of the course. Thus, we have become accustomed to classifying students in about five levels of performance and assigning grades in some relative fashion. It matters not that the failures of one year performed at about the same level as the C students of another year. Nor does it matter that the A students of one school do about as well as the F students of another.

Having become conditioned to the normal distribution, we set grade policies in these terms and are horrified when some teacher attempts to recommend a very different distribution of marks. Administrators are constantly on the alert to control teachers who are "too easy" or "too hard" in their grading. A teacher whose grade distribution is normal will avoid difficulties with administrators. But even more important, by our grading system, and even by our system of quizzes and progress testing, we effectively convince students that they can do only C or D work. Finally, we proceed in our teaching as though only the minority of our students should be able to learn what we have to teach.

There is nothing sacred about the normal curve. It is the distribution most appropriate to chance and random activity. Education is a purposeful activity, and we seek to have the students learn what we have to teach. If we are effective in our instruction, the distribution of achievement should be very different from the normal curve. In fact, we may even insist that our educational efforts have been *unsuccessful* to the extent that the distribution of achievement approximates the normal distribution.

"Individual differences" in learners are facts that can be demonstrated in many ways. That students vary in many ways can never be forgotten. The notion that these variations must shape learning standards and achievement criteria is a reflection more of our policies and practices than of the necessities of the case. The basic task in education is to find strategies which will take individual differences into consideration but which will do so in such a way as to promote the fullest development of the individual.

THE VARIABLES FOR MASTERY-LEARNING STRATEGIES

A learning strategy for mastery may be derived from the work of Carroll (1963), supported by the ideas of Bruner (1966), Glaser (1968), Goodlad and Anderson (1959), Morrison (1926), Skinner (1954), and Suppes (1966). In presenting these ideas, we will refer to some of the research findings which bear on them. However, our main concern here is with the major variables in a model of school learning and the ways in which these variables may be utilized in a strategy for mastery learning.

Put in its briefest form, the model proposed by Carroll (1963) makes it clear that if the students are normally distributed with respect to *aptitude* for some subject (mathematics, science, literature, or history, for example) and all the students are provided with exactly the *same instruction* (same in terms of amount and quality of instruction and time available for learning), the end result will be a normal distribution on an appropriate measure of achievement. Fur-

thermore, the relation between aptitude and achievement will be fairly high (a correlation of +.70 or higher is to be expected if the aptitude and achievement measures are valid and reliable). Conversely, if the students are normally distributed with respect to aptitude but the kind and quality of instruction and the amount of time available for learning are made appropriate to the characteristics and needs of *each* student, the majority of students may be expected to achieve mastery of the subject. And the relationship between aptitude and achievement should approach zero. It is this basic set of ideas we wish to develop in the following discussion.

Aptitude for Particular Kinds of Learning

Teachers have come to recognize that individuals do differ in their aptitudes for particular kinds of learning, and over the years test makers have developed a large number of instruments to measure these differences. In study after study, it has been found that aptitude tests are relatively good predictors of achievement criteria (achievement tests or teacher's judgments). Thus, for example, a good set of mathematics aptitude tests given at the beginning of a course in algebra will have a correlation of as high as +.70 with the achievement tests given at the end of the year.

The use of aptitude tests for predictive purposes and the high correlations between such tests and achievement criteria have led many of us to the view that high levels of achievement are possible only for the most able students. From this it is an easy step to some notion of a causal connection between aptitude and achievement. The simplest notion of causality is that the students with high levels of aptitude can learn the complex ideas of the subject while the students with low levels of aptitude can learn only the simplest ideas of the subject.

Quite in contrast to this is Carroll's view that *aptitude is the amount of time required by the learner to attain mastery of a learning task.* Implicit in this formulation is the assumption that, given enough time, all students can conceivably attain mastery of a learning task. If Carroll is right, then learning to mastery is theoretically available to all, if we can find the means for helping each student. This formulation of Carroll's has the most fundamental implications for education.

One type of support for this view is to be found in the grade norms for many standardized achievement tests. These norms demonstrate that selected criterion scores achieved by the top students at one grade level are achieved by the majority of students at a later grade level. Further support is provided by studies of students who are allowed to learn at their own rate. These show that, although most students eventually reach mastery of each learning task, some achieve it much sooner than others (Atkinson, 1967; Glaser, 1968).

Can all students learn a subject equally well? That is, can all master a learning task at a high level of complexity? From a study of aptitude distributions in relation to students' performance, we have become convinced that there are differences between the learners at the extremes and the remainder of the population. At the top of the aptitude distribution (the upper 1 to 5 percent), there are likely to be some students who have an unusual talent for the subject. These are able to learn and use the subject with greater fluency than others. The student with special aptitudes for music or foreign languages can learn these subjects in ways not available to most other people. Whether this is a matter of native endowment or the effect of previous training is not clear, although this must vary from subject to subject. It is likely that some people are born with sensory organs better attuned to sounds (music, language, and so forth) than are others, and that these constitutional characteristics give them special advantages in learning the related subjects. For other areas of study, such factors as special training and particular interests may develop these high-level aptitudes.

At the other extreme of the aptitude distribution, there are students with special disabilities for particular kinds of learning. The tone-deaf will have great difficulty learning music; the color-blind will have special problems in learning art; and the individual who thinks in concrete forms will be at a disadvantage in learning highly abstract conceptual systems, as in philosophy. Again, it is believed that these students may constitute less than 5 percent of the distribution, but this will vary with the subject and the aptitudes.

In between are approximately 90 percent of the learners, about whom the writers believe (as does Carroll) that aptitudes are predictive of rate of learning rather than the level or complexity of learning that is possible. Thus, we are expressing the view that, given sufficient time and appropriate types of help, 95 percent of students (the top 5 percent plus the next 90 percent) can learn a subject with a high degree of mastery. To say it another way, we are convinced that the grade of A as an index of mastery of a subject can, under appropriate conditions, be achieved by up to 95 percent of the students in a class.

It is assumed that it will take some students more effort, time, and help to achieve this level than it will others. There will be those for whom the effort and help required may make it prohibitive. Thus, to learn high school algebra to a point of mastery may require more than a year for some students but only a fraction of a year for others. Whether mastery learning is worth the great effort the first group must invest is highly problematic. A basic problem for a mastery-learning strategy is to find ways of reducing the amount of time the slower students require to a point where it is not prohibitively long.

It is not assumed that aptitude for particular learning tasks is completely stable. There is evidence (Bloom, 1964; Hunt, 1961) that aptitudes may be modified by environmental conditions or learning experiences in the school and the home. The major task of education programs concerned with learning to learn and general education should be to produce positive changes in the students' basic aptitudes. It is likely that these aptitudes can be most markedly affected during the early years in the home and during the elementary school period. Undoubtedly, however, some changes can take place at later points in a learner's career.

However, even if marked changes do not occur in the individual's aptitudes, it is highly probable that more effective learning conditions can reduce the amount of time which all students and especially those with lower aptitudes require to master a subject. It is this problem which must be directly attacked by strategies for mastery learning.

Quality of Instruction

The schools have usually proceeded on the assumption that there is a standard classroom situation for all students. Typically, this has been expressed in the teacher-student ratio of 1 to 30, with group instruction as the central means of teaching. There is the expectation that each teacher will present the subject in much the same way as other teachers. The standardization is further emphasized by the adoption of a textbook which specifies the instructional material to be provided each class. Closely related to this is the extensive research during the past 50 years which has sought to find the one instructional method, material, or curriculum program that is best for all students.

Thus, over the years, researchers have fallen into the "educational trap" of specifying quality of instruction in terms of good and poor teachers, teaching, instructional materials, curriculum—all as related to *group* results. They persist in asking such questions as, What is the best teacher for the group? What is the best method of instruction for the group? What is the best instructional material for the group?

One may start with the very different assumption that individual students may need very different types and qualities of instruction to achieve mastery. That is, the same content and objectives of instruction may be learned by different students as the result of very different types of instruction. Carroll (1963) defines the *quality of instruction in terms of the degree to which the presentation, explanation, and ordering of elements of the task to be learned approach the optimum for a given learner.*

Much research is needed to determine how individual differences in learners can be related to variations in the quality of instruction. There is evidence that some students learn quite well through independent study while others need highly structured teaching-learning situations (Congreve, 1965). It seems reasonable to expect that some students will need more concrete illustrations and explanations than others will, some will need more examples to get an idea than others, some will need more approval and reinforcement than others, and some may need to have several repetitions of the explanation while others may be able to get it the first time.

We believe that if every student had a very good tutor, most students would be able to learn a particular subject to a high degree. The good tutor attempts to find the qualities of instruction (and motivation) best suited to a given learner. And there is some evidence (Dave, 1963) that middle-class parents do make an effort to tutor their children when they believe that the quality of instruction in school does not enable their children to learn a particular subject. In an unpublished study, one of the writers found that one-third of the students in an algebra course in a middle-class school were receiving as much tutorial instruction at home in the subject as group instruction at school. Their grades for the course were comparatively high, and the relationship between their mathematics aptitude scores at the beginning of the year and their achievement in algebra at the end was almost zero. In contrast, for the students who received no instruction other than the regular classroom instruction, the relationship between their mathematics aptitude scores and their algebra achievement scores was very high (+.90). While this type of research needs to be replicated, this small study makes it evident that the home-tutoring help was providing the quality of instruction needed by the recipients to learn the algebra—that is, the instruction was adapted to the needs of the individual learners.

The point to be stressed is that the quality of instruction should be assessed in terms of its effects on individual learners rather than on random groups of learners. We may hope that the research of the future will lead to the definition of the qualities and kinds of instruction needed by various types of learners. Such research may suggest more effective group instruction, since it is unlikely that the schools will be able to provide instruction for each learner separately.

Ability to Understand Instruction

In most courses at the high school and college levels, there is a single teacher and a single set of instructional materials. A student who finds it easy to understand the teacher's communications about the learning and the instructional material (usually a textbook) will have little difficulty learning the subject. A student who finds it hard to understand the instruction, the material, or both, will be likely to have great difficulty learning the subject. *The ability to understand instruction may be defined as the ability of the learner to understand the nature of the task to be learned and the procedures to be followed in learning it.*

Here is a point at which the students' abilities interact with the instructional materials and the instructor's skill in teaching. For the student in our highly verbal schools, it is likely that the ability to understand instruction is determined primarily by verbal ability and reading comprehension. These two measures of language proficiency are significantly related to achievement in the majority of subjects, and they are highly correlated (+.50 to +.60) with grade-point averages at the high school or college level. What this suggests is that verbal ability (independent of specific aptitudes for each subject) determines some general ability to learn from teachers and instructional materials.

While it is possible to alter an individual's verbal ability by appropriate training, there are limits to the amount of change that can be produced. Most change in verbal ability can be produced at the preschool and elementary school levels, with less and less change being likely as the student gets older (Bloom, 1964). However, vocabulary and reading skill may be improved to some extent at all age levels, even though the utility of this approach diminishes with increasing age. Improvements in verbal proficiency should result in improvements in the learner's ability to understand instruction.

The greatest immediate payoff in dealing with this ability is likely to come from modifications in instruction to meet the needs of individual students. There is no doubt that some teachers do attempt to tailor their instruction to a given group of students. Many focus on the middle group of their students, others on the top or bottom group. However, these are reflections of teachers' habits and attitudes, and are by no means determinants of what is *possible* for them to do. Given help and various types of aids, individual teachers can find ways of modifying their instruction to fit the differing needs of their students.

Group study

Group study should be available to students as they need it. In our own experience we have found that small groups (two or three students) meeting regularly to go over points of difficulty in the learning process were most effective, especially when the students could help each other without any danger of giving each other special advantages in a competitive situation. Where learning can be turned into a cooperative process with everyone likely to gain from it, small-group learning procedures can be very effective. Much depends on the composition of the group and the opportunities it affords each person to expose his or her difficulties and have them corrected without demeaning one member and elevating another. The group process provides occasions for the more able students to strengthen their own learning as they help others grasp an idea through alternative explanations and applications (S. Bloom, 1976).

Tutorial help

The one-to-one relationship between teacher and learner represents the most costly type of help and should be used only where alternative procedures are not effective. However, tutoring should be available to students as they need it. Ideally, the tutor should be someone other than the teacher, since a tutor should provide a fresh way of viewing an idea or process. The tutor must be skillful in detecting the points of difficulty in the student's learning and should help in such a way as to free the student from continued dependence on him or her.

Another approach to differences in students' ability to understand instruction is to vary the instructional material.

Textbooks

Textbooks vary in the clarity with which they explain a particular idea or process. The fact that one text has been adopted by the school or the teacher does not necessarily mean that others cannot be used at particular points in the instruction when they would be helpful to a student who can't grasp the idea from the adopted book. The task here is to determine where a learner is having difficulty understanding the instruction and to then provide alternative textbook explanations if they are more effective.

Workbooks and
programmed instruction units

These may be especially helpful for some students who can't grasp the ideas or the procedures in the textbook form. Some students need the drill and specific tasks which workbooks can provide. Others need the small steps and frequent reinforcement built into programmed units. Such materials may be used in the initial instruction or as students encounter specific difficulties in learning a given unit or section of the course.

Audiovisual methods and academic games

Some students may learn a particular idea best through concrete illustrations and vivid graphic explanations. For these learners,

filmstrips and short motion pictures which can be used by individual students as needed may be very effective. Others may need concrete experiences, as with laboratory experiments, simple demonstrations, and blocks and other relevant apparatus, in order to comprehend an idea or task. Academic games, puzzles, and other interesting but not threatening devices may be useful. Here again, the point is that some ways of communicating and comprehending an idea, problem, or task may be especially effective for some students although others may not use or need such materials and methods. We need not place the highest priority for all on abstract and verbal ways of instructing.

With regard to instructional materials, the suggestion is not that particular materials be used by particular students throughout the course. It is that each type of material may serve as a means of helping individual students at selected points in the learning process—and that individual students may use whatever variety of materials they find useful as they encounter difficulties in their learning.

In all use of alternative methods and materials of instruction, the essential point to be borne in mind is that these are attempts to improve the *quality of instruction* in relation to the ability of each student to *understand the instruction*. As feedback methods inform teachers of particular errors and difficulties the majority of students are having, it is to be expected that the regular group instruction will be modified so as to correct these problems. As particular students are helped, the goal should be not only to help the student over specific learning difficulties but also to help the student become more independent in learning and to help the student identify the alternative ways by which he or she can comprehend the new ideas. But most important, the presence of a great variety of instructional materials and procedures should help both teachers and students to overcome feelings of defeatism and passivity about learning. If the student can't learn in one way, he or she should be reassured that alternatives are available. The teacher should come to recognize that it is the learning which is important and that alternatives exist to enable all or almost all the students to learn the subject to a high level.

Perseverance

Carroll defines "perseverance" as *the time the learner is willing to spend in learning.* Obviously, if a student needs a certain amount of time to master a particular task and spends less than this amount in active learning, it is not likely that he or she will learn the task to the level of mastery. Carroll attempts to differentiate between spending time at learning and the amount of time a student is actively engaged in the learning.

Perseverance does appear to be related to attitudes toward and interest in learning. In the *International Study of Educational Achievement in Mathematics* (Husén, 1967), the relationship between number of hours of homework per week reported by students (a crude index of perseverance) and the number of years of further education desired by them is +.25.

There is no doubt that students vary in the amount of perseverance they bring to a specific learning task. However, they appear to approach different learning tasks with different degrees of persistence. The student who quickly gives up efforts to learn an academic subject may persevere an unusually long time in learning to repair an automobile or play a musical instrument. It would appear to us that as students find their efforts rewarding, they are likely to spend more time on a particular learning task. If, on the other hand, they are frustrated in learning, they must, in self-defense, reduce the amount of time devoted to it. Though the frustration level of students may vary, we believe that all must sooner or later give up a task if it is too painful for them.

While efforts may be made to increase the amount of perseverance in students, it is likely that manipulation of the instruction and learning materials will be more effective in helping them master a given learning task, regardless of their present level of perseverance. Frequency of reward and evidence of success in learning can increase the student's perseverance in a learning situation. As mastery of a given task is attained, the student's perseverance in a related learning task is likely to increase.

In research at the University of Chicago, it has been found that the demand for perseverance may be sharply reduced if students are provided with the instructional resources most appropriate for them. Frequent feedback accompanied by specific help in instruction and material as needed can decrease the time (and perseverance) required. Improvement in the quality of instruction (explanations and illustrations) may lessen the amount of persistence neccessary for a given learning task (B. S. Bloom, 1976).

There seems to be little reason to make learning so difficult that only a small proportion of the students can persevere to mastery. Endurance and unusual perseverance may be appropriate for long-distance running; they are not great virtues in their own right. The emphasis should be on learning, not on vague ideas of discipline.

Time Allowed for Learning

Throughout the world, schools are organized to give group instruction with definite periods of time allocated for particular learning tasks. A course in history at the secondary level may be planned for an academic year, another course may be planned for a semester, and the amount of instruction time allocated for a subject like arithmetic at the fifth grade may be fixed. Whatever the amount of time allowed by the school and the curriculum for particular subjects or learning tasks, it is likely to be too much for some students and not enough for others.

For Carroll, the time spent on learning is the key to mastery. His basic assumption is that aptitude determines the rate of learning, and that most if not all students can achieve mastery if they devote the amount of time needed to the learning. This implies that the student must be *allowed* enough time for the learning to take place.

There seems to be little doubt that students with high levels of aptitude are likely to be more efficient in their learning and to require less time for it than those with lower levels of aptitude. Whether most students can be helped to become highly efficient learners in general is a problem for future research.

The amount of time students need for a particular kind of learning has not been studied directly. One indication comes from studies of the amount of time they spend on homework. In reviewing the data from the *International Study of Educational Achievement in Mathematics* (Husén, 1967) on how long 13-year-old students worked on mathematics homework, we find that if we omit the extreme 5 percent of the subjects, the ratio is roughly 6 to 1. That is, some students spend six times as much time on mathematics homework as do others. Other studies of students' use of time suggest that this is roughly the order of magnitude to be expected.

If instruction and students' use of time become more effective, it is likely that most students will need less time to master a subject, and the ratio of time required by the slower learners to that needed by the faster learners may be reduced from about 6 to 1 to less than 2 to 1 (Bloom, 1974).

In general, we find a "zero relationship" or a slightly negative relationship between final grades and amount of time spent on homework. In the *International Study* just mentioned, the average correlation for twelve countries at the 13-year-old level is approximately $-.05$ between achievement test scores in mathematics and number of hours per week of homework in mathematics as reported by students. Thus, the amount of time spent on homework does not seem to be a very good predictor of achievement in the subject.

We are convinced that it is not the sheer amount of time spent in learning (either in or out of school) that accounts for the level of learning. Each student should be allowed the time he or she needs to learn a subject. And this time is likely to be affected by the student's aptitudes and verbal ability, the quality of instruction he or she receives in class, and the quality of the help he or she receives out of class. The task of a strategy for mastery learning is to find ways of altering the time individual students need for learning as well as to find ways of providing whatever time is needed by each one. Thus, a strategy for mastery learning must find some way of solving the problems of instruction as well as of school organization (including the question of time).

ONE STRATEGY FOR MASTERY LEARNING

There are many feasible strategies for mastery learning. Each must incorporate some way of dealing with individual differences in learners by relating the instruction to their needs and characteristics. Each strategy must find some way of dealing with the five variables discussed in the foregoing section.

Were it not so costly in human resources, the provision of a good tutor for each student might be an ideal strategy. In any case, the tutor-student relationship is a useful model to consider when one attempts to work out the details of a less costly strategy. Also, the tutor strategy is not so far-fetched as it may seem at first glance. In the preschool period, most of the child's instruction is tutorial—usually provided by the parents. In many middle-class homes, the parents or older siblings continue to give tutorial help as needed by the child during much of his or her school career.

Other strategies include permitting students to go at their own pace (Keller, 1968), guiding students with respect to courses they should or should not take, and establishing different tracks or streams for different groups of learners. The nongraded school (Goodlad & Anderson, 1959) represents one attempt to provide a structure that permits and encourages mastery learning.

The Carroll model (Carroll, 1963) postulated that learners differ in their rate of learning and that this rate may be predicted from an aptitude or intelligence test. While there was some ambiguity about the permanence or stability of the rate of learning, this model was the basis for the idea that most learners can achieve high levels of learning in a school subject—if each student is provided with the time and help needed.

This construct, as Carroll presented it, suggested that if all learners are given the same instruction in a subject and the same amount of time to learn it, the resulting scores on an achievement test over the subject will be normally distributed. If, however, the instruction and time are adapted to each student's needs, the achievement distribution will be highly skewed: most of the scores would pile up on the high end of the achievement measure. Under these conditions, the achievement scores at the end of the term cannot be predicted from an aptitude or intelligence test given at the beginning of the term.

Using the concept of mastery learning, Bloom and his students at the University of Chicago sought to find ways by which slower learners could be given the extra time and help they needed. From this research, in both educational laboratories and classrooms, it has become evident that a large portion of slower learners can learn to the same achievement level as the faster learners. When the slower learners do succeed in attaining the same criterion of achievement as the faster learners, they appear to be able to learn equally complex and abstract ideas, they can apply these ideas to new problems, and they can retain the ideas equally well, in spite of the fact that they learned with more time and help than was given to others. Furthermore, their interest in and attitudes toward the subject in which they attain the achievement criterion are as positive as those of the faster learners (Yildiran, 1977).

Research on mastery learning has been done in many countries and at all levels of education, including primary schools, secondary schools, junior colleges, four-year colleges, and advanced professional schools such as schools of medicine, nursing, and engineering. Most of the different subject courses at each level have been shown to yield excellent results under mastery methods (Block, 1974; Block & Anderson, 1975; Block & Burns, 1976; B. S. Bloom, 1976; Jones, Gordon, & Schechtman, 1975).

The mastery-learning approach developed by the Chicago group has been to supplement regular group instruction by using diagnostic procedures and alternative instructional methods and materials in such a way as to bring a large proportion of the students to a predetermined standard of achievement. In this approach, the goal is for most of the students to reach mastery levels of achievement within the regular term, semester, or calendar period in which the course is usually taught. Undoubtedly, some students will spend more time than others in learning the subject. But if the majority reach mastery levels at the end of the time allocated for the subject, this will have affective as well as cognitive consequences.

In working on this strategy over the past 15 years, the group has attempted to spell out some of the preconditions necessary, develop the operating procedures required, and evaluate some of the outcomes of the strategy for both students and teachers.

Preconditions

Achievement criteria

In order to develop mastery learning in students, one must be able to recognize when they have achieved it. Teachers must be able to define what they mean by mastery, and they must be able to collect the necessary evidence to establish whether or not a student has attained it.

The specification of the objectives and content of instruction is one necessary means of informing both teachers and students of the learning that is expected. The translation of the specifications into evaluation procedures helps define further what it is that the student should be able to do when he or she has completed the course. The evaluation procedures used to appraise the outcomes of instruction (summative evaluation) help the teacher and student know when the instruction has been effective.

Implicit in this way of defining the outcomes and preparing evaluation instruments is a distinction between the teaching-learning process and the evaluation process. At some points in time, the results of teaching and learning can be reflected in the evaluation of the students. But these are separate processes. That is, teaching and learning are intended to prepare the student in an area of learning, while summative evaluation is intended to appraise the extent to which the student has developed in the desired ways. Both the teacher and the learner must have some understanding of what the achievement criteria are, and both must be able to secure evidence of progress toward these criteria.

If the achievement criteria are primarily competitive—that is, if the student is to be judged in terms of his or her relative position in the group—then the student is likely to seek evidence on his or her rank order in the group while progressing through the learning tasks. It is recognized that competition may be a spur to students who view others in competitive terms, but much of learning and development may be destroyed by a primary emphasis on competition.

Much more preferable in terms of intrinsic motivation for learning is the setting of standards of mastery and excellence apart from competition among students, followed by appropriate efforts to bring as many students up to these standards as possible. This suggests some notion of absolute criteria and the use of grades or marks which will reflect them. Thus, it is conceivable that all students will achieve mastery and the grade of A. It is also possible in a particular year in a specific course that few or none of the students will attain mastery or a grade of A.

While it would be desirable to use absolute standards carefully worked out for each subject, we recognize the enormous difficulty of arriving at them. In some of the mastery-learning work, we have made use of standards derived from previous experience with students in a selected course. For example, in

one course in 1977 the students were informed that the grades for that year would be based on standards set in that course in 1976. The grades of A, B, C, D, and F would be given on an examination parallel to that used in 1976 and would be set at the same performance levels as those established in 1976. The class was informed that the proportion of students receiving each grade was to be determined by performance level rather than by rank order in the group. Thus, the students were not competing with each other for grades; they were to be judged on the basis of standards of achievement set in an earlier year.

In other situations, teachers have set their grading standards on their control classes and then used the same achievement standards with the same (or parallel) summative tests for the mastery classes. There are various ways of arriving at achievement standards; the point is that students must feel they are being judged in terms of level of performance rather than on a normal curve or some other arbitrary and relative set of standards. What is being recommended is that realistic performance criteria be developed for each school or group and be followed by instructional procedures which enable the majority of students to attain them.

One effect of this method of setting achievement standards is that it enables the students to work with and help each other without being concerned about giving special advantages (or disadvantages) to others. Cooperation in learning, rather than competition, is a clear result of this method of setting achievement criteria.

Orientation for students

At the beginning of the term, the teacher should explain to students how the mastery-learning course will differ from the typical course. The teacher should convey to the students his or her confidence that most of the students should be able to learn each unit of the course or chapter of the textbook to a high level and that, if they do their part in the learning of each unit to the mastery level, they should do very well on the tests and examinations used for grading purposes. They should understand that the grading procedure will be based on set standards and not on rank in the class. That is, it is possible for all of them to earn the highest grade, if their performance warrants it. The teacher should explain that the students who need it will be given extra time and help to learn the ideas they have difficulty with on each of the formative tests. The teacher should also stress that the students who make the extra effort needed will find that gradually they need less and less extra effort to achieve mastery on each new unit or chapter. Finally, the students should be reassured that they are likely to find greater interest and enjoyment in the learning process and that these procedures should eventually help them to learn other subjects to a higher level than they usually do.

The teacher should also explain that under mastery learning the group instruction and the learning materials will be much the same as those used in the regular, or control, class in this subject. The additional component of mastery learning will be the inclusion of a formative test (formative test A) at the end of each learning unit to give both the teacher and the student feedback on what has been learned well and what still needs to be learned before each student has mastered the unit. The student, with the aid of corrective suggestions and with the help of other students, is to review and correct the ideas he or she has missed on the first formative test. Then within 2 to 3 days, he or she will take a second parallel form of the formative test (formative test B) and answer only those problems or questions that were missed on the first form of the test (formative test A).

Operating Procedures

In most mastery-learning work, the instructor teaches a mastery-learning class and a control class in much the same way. That is, the materials, the methods of instruction, and the time schedules and plans of the courses are as similar as possible. The major difference between the two classes is the use of systematic feedback-corrective procedures in the mastery-learning class, while quizzes and other testing procedures for marking purposes are more central in the control class. Incidentally, the control class may be a class being taught by the instructor during the same term as the mastery class; it may be a class that was taught in a previous term by the instructor; or it may even be a comparable class taught by another instructor with the same materials and summative examinations as the mastery class.

Group instruction produces errors in learning at each stage of a course or school term, no matter how effective the teacher is. These errors in learning are compounded with later learning errors. The errors resulting from this system of group instruction determine each student's final achievement, and only rarely is the individual able to recover fully from them.

A major thesis in the mastery-learning strategy is that a system of feedback to teachers and students can reveal the errors in learning shortly after they occur. And if appropriate correctives are introduced as needed, the instruction can be self-correcting so that the learning errors made at one time can be corrected before they are compounded with later learning errors.

The essence of mastery-learning strategies is *group instruction* supplemented by frequent *feedback and individualized corrective help* as each student needs it. The *group instruction* is the same as the regular instruction presently provided by the teacher. The *feedback* is usually in the form of brief diagnostic formative tests, which indicate what each student has learned and what he or she still needs to learn before the learning task has been mastered. These tests are used at the end of each unit of instruction.

The *individualized corrective help* is provided to enable each student to learn the important points he or she has missed. This help may be provided by an aide, by other students, by the home, or by referring the student to the appropriate places in the instructional material. When this is done well, most students can be brought to mastery of each learning task.

The major change for mastery-learning

teachers is that they do less judging and grading of students on what they have learned by a particular date and do more to see to it that each student learns what he or she needs as preparation for the next learning task or tasks. When this process of group instruction, supplemented by feedback and individualized correctives, is used for each learning task, we find that almost all students gradually become similar in their learning effectiveness and in their interest and motivation for further learning. For most students, the extra time and help (in the classroom or outside) needed at the end of each 2 week period is typically only an hour or so.

Formative Evaluation

Formative tests

The formative tests are intended to provide feedback to both teachers and students. Each formative test covers a unit or part of the course. The unit may correspond to a chapter in a textbook, a well-defined content portion of the course, or a particular time unit within the course. We tend to think of learning units for formative testing as involving about 2 weeks of learning activity or approximately 8 to 10 hours of instruction in the class. In the early primary grades the unit may be only about a week of instruction, while at more advanced levels of learning (college and graduate or professional school level) the unit may be as long as 3 or 4 weeks of instruction. The major point in formative testing is to maximize the learning time and minimize the testing and corrective time. Typically, a formative test should take about 20 to 30 minutes of testing time.

We have found it useful to construct formative tests on the basis of a set of specifications of the content and objectives of each learning unit. The *Taxonomy of Educational Objectives* (Bloom, 1956) has been useful in analyzing a learning unit into specific terms and facts, complex ideas such as concepts and principles, and complex processes such as application of principles or analyses of the underlying assumptions, ideas, and methods in the learning unit. We have also made use of

the ideas of Gagné (1965) in determining the hierarchical relationships among the elements in a learning unit.

Once the specifications have been developed by two or more expert teachers or testers, it is then possible to construct valid test items or other evaluative procedures for each of the important elements in the unit. Typically, two parallel forms of the test are constructed with some attempt to get at the underlying ideas or elements in each form with different test items. These steps in setting specifications and constructing appropriate formative test items are described in detail in Chapter 6, Formative Evaluation.

At the end of the instruction over a particular learning unit, one form of the formative test is administered to all the students in the class. This test is then marked (usually by the students themselves) to determine which items were answered correctly and which ones were wrong. The teacher reads the key or the right answers as the students mark their own test. The mastery score (usually 80 to 85 percent of the number of test items) is announced, and students who achieved the mastery level are identified by a show of hands or other means and encouraged by the teacher and other students.

For the students who have mastered the unit, the formative tests should reinforce the learning and assure them that their present modes of learning and approaches to study are adequate. Students who consistently demonstrate mastery on the recurring tests should become less anxious about their achievement, since it is highly likely that they will do well on the summative achievement tests.

Corrective process

The teacher identifies the test items which were answered *incorrectly* by the majority of the students (perhaps two-thirds of the students or more). This may be done by having the students hold up their hands for the correct responses on each item as the teacher reads the key or by inspecting a sample of the test papers after they have been marked. These items indicate special difficulties in the instructional materials or the instructional process (or they may indicate faulty test items). The ideas underlying these test items should be reviewed by the teacher and, if possible, explained differently from the way they were explained in the original instruction. This review of selected ideas should be done shortly after the test has been taken or at the next meeting of the class.

The students who have not mastered the unit are expected to learn the ideas they missed and to demonstrate this learning by answering the parallel questions on the second form of the formative test given several days after the first form of the test. Usually, the students are expected to answer only the questions parallel to those that they missed on the first form of the test.

The test questions in the formative test are related to particular pages of the textbook or other instructional material used in the course, to particular pages in alternative textbooks which explain the idea in a different way, to specific pages of workbooks or programmed materials, to other material such as lecture notes and special sound cassettes which explain each idea, or to relevant audiovisual material. We suspect that no specific learning material or process is indispensable. The presence of some variety of instructional materials and procedures, and specific suggestions regarding which ones to use, help students recognize that if they can't learn in one way, alternatives are available.

The most effective procedure for the corrective learning process found thus far is to have small groups of students—two or three— meet for about 30 minutes or so to review the results of their formative test and to help each other overcome the difficulties identified on the tests. Ideally, each student in the group may *learn* from the others as well as *help* the others on some of the items missed by one or more of the students in the group. At the beginning of the term, this group corrective process may be done during a classroom period. But it is to be hoped that this mutual help may take place outside of class after the students have learned how to help each other most effectively. It should be remembered that the students in the class have received

instruction over the material and ideas included in the corrective process. They are not teaching each other—they are sharing ideas about how they have understood the materials and the problems posed in the formative tests.

Tutorial help may be of value in this corrective process, especially at the primary school level. This help may be provided through the use of aides, tutors, or parents and siblings in the home. However, we have found that, from the third grade on, the most effective corrective process involves brief periods of help by peers in the class (S. Bloom, 1976).

About 2 or 3 days after the first form of the formative test (formative test A) has been administered, the students who did not reach mastery on that test should be given the parallel test (formative test B). They should answer only the test items (parallel questions) they missed on the first form of the formative test. Mastery is now determined by the number of correct answers they had on form A of the test, plus the number of correct answers on form B of the formative tests. (Again 80 to 85 percent is mastery.) Here, the students who reached mastery by the second test should be encouraged and praised for their extra work. Rarely are students held for a third formative test if they did not get mastery on form A or B.

The entire group of students should move on to the next unit of instruction after completion of the *first form* of the formative test and the teacher's review of the ideas that the majority of the students got wrong. Other than the classroom time for giving formative tests, the use of some time for the review of common errors, and the initial orientation of the students to the group corrective work, the classroom schedule for the mastery class should be much the same as that of the control classes in the same subject.

OUTCOMES OF THE MASTERY LEARNING STRATEGIES

Favorable learning conditions such as mastery learning have profound effects on students' cognitive achievement and on the effectiveness of their learning. Such conditions also have major effects on students' attitudes, interests, and self-concepts. Perhaps of equal significance are the effects on teachers' views of students and on their instructional procedures.

Cognitive Outcomes of a Mastery Strategy

Achievement
The typical finding of the mastery-learning studies in the schools is that about 80 percent of students in a mastery class reach the same final criterion of achievement (usually at the A or B+ level) as approximately the top 20 percent of the class under conventional group instruction. Much of this research contrasts a mastery group of students with a control group of students taught the same subject by the same teacher with as nearly as possible the same instructional methods and instructional material. The two groups of students are initially equivalent in terms of previous levels of learning, aptitude, or intelligence measures (Block, 1974; Block & Burns, 1976; B. S. Bloom, 1976).

As would follow from the Carroll model (1963), mentioned above, the achievement of the upper 20 percent of the control students is predictable from the aptitude tests, intelligence tests, or previous achievement tests, while the achievement of the upper 80 percent of the mastery students is not predictable from these earlier measures.

In general, the students in the mastery classes need about 10 to 15 percent more time than the students in the control classes—however, the extra time and help are used only by those students who need them. It should be pointed out that the control and mastery classes have about the same schedule of instruction and that the corrective work of the students who need it in the mastery class is usually done outside of the classroom.

Students in a mastery class who need but do not make use of the formative test feedback and who do not make the corrections indicated *do not* attain mastery on the formative tests or attain high levels of achievement on the summative tests. A student's presence in the mastery class is no guarantee of improved learning unless the student can be motivated to make the extra effort needed to correct learning difficulties at the end of each learning unit.

Increased learning effectiveness
The majority of students under mastery-learning conditions reach high levels of cognitive achievement on the summative tests used for grading purposes. They also do very well on measures of retention and higher mental processes when compared with the top fifth of the control group of students. Furthermore, almost all the mastery-learning students who make use of the corrective procedures achieve above the average of the control students (Block & Burns, 1976; B. S. Bloom, 1976).

If mastery-learning procedures are utilized in the introductory courses in a subject field (arithmetic, science, reading, mathematics, social studies, second language, etc.), the students tend to maintain these new learning approaches in subsequent courses in the same field with less and less need for further special help or extra time.

If mastery learning is used on a wide scale (that is, in the major academic courses or subjects), students appear to show major gains in that elusive quality termed "learning to learn." The students devote more of their classroom time to active learning, and they appear to be enjoying the learning. They develop skill in providing feedback to themselves about what they have learned well and what they need to do to improve their learning where they have learned less well. They become skillful in seeking answers and securing help from books, friends, and teachers where they need to overcome special and detailed learning difficulties in a subject.

To summarize, if favorable learning conditions are provided at the beginning of new subjects or new school situations, less and less need will be found for these procedures in subsequent courses in a subject—although the new learning abilities may need to be supported to some extent in these later subjects or terms until they are strong enough to be self-maintaining.

Affective Outcomes for Students

As we have pointed out, educators for the past century have conceived of mastery of a subject as being possible for only a minority of students. With this assumption, they have adjusted the grading system so as to certify that only a small percentage of the students, no matter how carefully selected, are awarded a grade of A. If a group of students learns a subject better than a previous group, teachers persist in awarding the A to only the top 10 or 15 percent. They grudgingly award grades of D and C to the majority of the students, whom they see as having merely "gotten by." Mastery and recognition of mastery under the present relative grading system are unattainable for the majority—but this is the result of the way the education system has been "rigged."

Mastery must be both a subjective recognition by the student of his or her competence and a public recognition by the school or society. The public recognition must be in the form of appropriate certification by the teacher or the school. If students are denied such recognition, then no matter how much they have learned, they must come to believe that *they* are inadequate, rather than the system of grading or the instruction. Subjectively, the student needs to gain feelings of control over ideas and skills and must come to recognize that he or she "knows" and can do what the subject requires.

If the system of formative evaluation (diagnostic-progress tests) and summative evaluation (achievement examinations) informs the student of mastery of the subject, the student will come to believe in his or her own competence. A student may be informed by the grading system as well as by the discovery that he or she can adequately cope with the variety of tasks and problems in the evaluation instruments.

When the student has mastered a subject and receives both objective and subjective indications of this, there are profound changes in the student's self-concept and view of the outer world.

Perhaps the clearest evidence of affective change is the interest the student develops for the subject he or she has mastered: the student begins to "like" it and to want more of it. To do well in a subject opens up further avenues for exploring it. Conversely, to do poorly in a subject closes an area to further voluntary study. Students desire some control over their environment, and mastery of a subject gives them some feeling of control over a part of their environment. Interest in a subject is both a cause of mastery of the subject and a result of mastery. Motivation for further learning is one of the more important consequences of mastery.

At a deeper level is the student's self-concept. Each person searches for positive recognition of his or her worth and one comes to view oneself as adequate in those areas where one has received assurance of competence or success. A student who is to see himself or herself in a positive light must be given many opportunities to be rewarded. Mastery and its public recognition provide the necessary reassurance and reinforcement to help students look upon themselves as adequate. One of the more positive aids to mental health is frequent and objective indications of self-development. Mastery learning can be one of the more powerful sources of mental health. We are convinced that many of the neurotic symptoms displayed by students are exacerbated by painful and frustrating experiences in school learning. If 90 percent of the students are given positive indications of adequacy in learning, one might expect them to need less and less in the way of emotional therapy and psychological help. Centrarily, frequent indications of failure and learning inadequacy are bound to be accompanied by increased self-doubt in the student and a search for reassurance and adequacy outside the school (B. S. Bloom, 1976; Kifer, 1973).

Finally, modern society requires continual learning throughout life. If the schools do not promote adequate learning and reassurance of progress, the student must come to reject learning—both in the school and in later life. Mastery learning can give zest to school learning and can develop a lifelong interest in learning. It is this continual learning which should be a major goal of the educational system.

Teachers' Beliefs about Students' Learning Capabilities

As we said earlier, teachers begin a new term or course with the view that some of the students will learn well, some will learn very poorly, and some will learn only moderately well. Usually by the end of the first month of the term the teachers have sorted their students into some such categories as these, and it is likely that this sorting process will remain much the same throughout the course. The teacher is very effective in conveying these categories to students through subtle techniques in the interaction that takes place during the class. Teachers rarely expect most of the students to learn well—and the students come to accept the teacher's view of them and their learning capabilities.

Research findings, lectures, and injunctions to teachers to have greater faith in the learning potential of their students are not very effective. Teachers can and will change their beliefs in the learning capabilities of each student *only* by discovering this in the classroom (Guskey, 1979).

In our work on mastery learning in the schools, we have insisted that teachers compare learning under the mastery condition with learning under conventional procedures in a control class. The teachers using the mastery-learning procedures find that the majority of students become very successful in their learning. Most teachers note the differences in students' learning between the mastery and control class within the first 4 or 6 weeks, although some may take longer to discover this. As one teacher put it, "My classroom suddenly became overpopulated with good students."

It is of interest to note that teachers who have found these teaching-learning procedures effective continue to use such procedures thereafter on their own without administrative urging. Also, such teachers refuse to use control classes (their conventional procedures) thereafter, even if they are suggested as a basis for further study about the process. They view the request to continue using control procedures as immoral or indecent: Would you deny the use of a health-giving drug like penicillin to those who need it, just for research purposes?

EXERCISES

Objective: Compare a mastery learning strategy and traditional instruction in terms of the assumptions about human learning, the learning process, and the results of instruction.

Preparation: Refer to a text in educational measurement or elementary statistics and briefly review the characteristics of the normal curve.

1. *Graphic comparisons.* Sketch graphs to illustrate the following situations. Label the horizontal axis with characteristics involved (aptitude or achievement) and the vertical axis with number or percentage of people.
   a. Aptitude of a random group of people as traditionally defined.
   b. End-of-year grades for a heterogeneous group of students accepting a traditional definition of aptitude and the consequent view of instruction and learning.
   c. Aptitude as defined by Carroll.
   d. End-of-year grades accepting Carroll's definition of aptitude and the consequent view of instruction and learning.
2. *Comparing models of instruction and learning.* Construct a chart which compares and contrasts Bloom's mastery learning strategy with a traditional model of group instruction. Suggested categories for comparison are listed below. Add others as you see fit.
   a. Definition of aptitude.
   b. Relationship of aptitude to learning in school.

    c. Variables considered by a teacher in planning instruction.

    d. Role of group instruction.

    e. Role of the child's peers in instruction.

    f. Influence of individual differences on instruction and learning.

    g. Role of evaluation in instruction.

    h. Role of corrective help.

    i. Anticipated results in terms of achievement.

3. *Obstacles to implementation.* Assume that you want to implement a mastery learning model in your classes or your school. Consider what would be the difficulties of and obstacles to such implementation. Divide a piece of paper into two columns. In the first column list the difficulties and obstacles. In the second column list possible rebuttals and solutions.

REFERENCES

Atkinson, R. C. *Computerized instruction and the learning process.* (Tech. Rep. 122.) Stanford, Calif.: Institute for Mathematical Studies in the Social Sciences, 1967.

Block, J. H. (Ed.). *Schools, society, and mastery learning.* New York: Holt, 1974.

Block, J. H., & Anderson, L. W. *Mastery learning in classroom instruction.* New York: Macmillan, 1975.

Block, J. H., & Burns, R. B. Mastery learning. In L. S. Shulman (Ed.), *Review of research in education 4.* Itasca, Ill: F. E. Peacock, 1976.

Bloom, B. S. (Ed.). *Taxonomy of educational objectives: The classification of educational goals.* Handbook 1. *Cognitive domain,* New York: McKay, 1956.

Bloom, B. S. *Stability and change in human characteristics.* New York: Wiley, 1964.

Bloom, B. S. Time and learning. *American Psychologist,* 1974, 29, 682–688.

Bloom, B. S. *Human characteristics and school learning.* New York: McGraw-Hill, 1976.

Bloom, B. S., Hastings, J. T., & Madaus, G. F. *Handbook on formative and summative evaluation of student learning.* New York: McGraw-Hill, 1971.

Bloom, S. *Peer and cross-age tutoring in the schools.* Washington, D. C.: National Institute of Education, 1976.

Bowman, M. J. The new economics of education. *International Journal of Educational Sciences,* 1966, 1, 29–46

Bruner, J. S. *Toward a theory of instruction.* Cambridge, Mass.: Harvard University Press, 1966.

Carroll, J. A model of school learning. *Teachers College Record,* 1963, 64, 723–733.

Congreve, W. J. Independent learning. *North Central Association Quarterly,* 1965, 40, 222–228.

Dave, R. H. *The identification and measurement of environmental process variables that are related to educational achievement.* Unpublished doctoral dissertation, University of Chicago, 1963.

Gagné. R. M. *The conditions of learning.* New York: Holt, 1965.

Glaser, R. Adapting the elementary school curriculum to individual performance. In *Proceedings of the 1967 Invitational Conference on Testing Problems.* Princeton, N. J.: Educational Testing Service, 1968.

Goodlad, J. I., & Anderson, R. H. *The nongraded elementary school.* New York: Harcourt, Brace, 1959.

Guskey, T. R. *Inservice education and teacher change.* Unpublished doctoral dissertation, University of Chicago, 1979.

Hunt, J. McV. *Intelligence and experience.* New York: Ronald Press, 1961.

Husén, T. (Ed.). *International Study of Educational Achievement in Mathematics: A comparison of twelve countries* (2 vols). New York: Wiley, 1967.

Jones, E. L., Gordon, H. A., & Schechtman, G. L. *Mastery learning: A strategy for academic success in a community college.* Los Angeles: ERIC Clearinghouse for Junior Colleges, 1975.

Keller, F. S. "Goodbye Teacher . . . ." *Journal of Applied Behavior Analysis,* 1968, 1, 79–89.

Kifer, E. *The effects of school achievement on the affective traits of the learner.* Unpublished doctoral dissertation, University of Chicago, 1973.

Morrison, H. C. *The practice of teaching in the secondary school.* Chicago: University of Chicago Press, 1926.

Schultz, T. W. *The economic value of education.* New York: Columbia University Press, 1963.

Skinner, B. F. The science of learning and the art of teaching. *Harvard Educational Review*, 1954, 24(2), 86–97.

Suppes, P. The uses of computers in education. *Scientific American*, 1966, 215(51), 206–221.

Yildiran, G. *The effects of level of cognitive achievement on selected learning criteria under mastery learning and normal classroom instruction.* Unpublished doctoral dissertation, University of Chicago, 1977.

4 Summative Evaluation

Chapter Contents

The purpose of this chapter is to describe the steps one follows in carrying out a summative evaluation of students' learning. As we have seen, a summative evaluation has as its primary goals grading or certifying students or judging the effectiveness of a program of instruction. In this chapter we shall discuss the way in which summative data can be used to grade and certify students or to judge the effectiveness of a program or curriculum. We will pay particular attention to the grading of students, the single most important function that distinguishes summative evaluation from all other measurement.

DISTINCTIONS BETWEEN SUMMATIVE AND FORMATIVE EVALUATION

In Chapters 1 and 2 distinctions were made between formative and summative evaluations of learning: the three distinguishing characteristics have to do with *purpose* (expected uses), *portion of course covered* (time), and *level of generalization* sought by the items in the examination used to collect data for the evaluation. Since these characteristics are not absolute, it seems useful to give some examples of how formative and summative evaluation differ in regard to each.

The main purpose of *formative observations* (there are other ways besides paper-and-pencil tests to make inferences about student progress) is to determine the degree of mastery of a given learning task and to pinpoint the part of the task not mastered. Perhaps a negative description will make it even clearer: the purpose is *not* to grade or certify the learner; it is to help both the learner and the teacher focus upon the particular learning necessary for movement toward mastery. On the other hand, *summative evaluation* is directed toward a much more general assessment of the degree to which the larger outcomes have been attained over the entire course, or some substantial part of it. For example, in fifth-grade arithmetic, summative evaluation would have as its major purpose to determine the degree to which a student can translate word problems into quantitative expressions in order to solve them, or the extent of the student's accuracy and rapidity in handling division. Further purposes would be to grade students and to report the grades to parents or administrators. However, evaluation is definitely *not* synonomous with grading. Performance or product can be evaluated without ever being assigned a grade. Formative evaluation does *not* involve grading. Formative evaluation seeks to discover whether a deficiency in solving word problems is due to vocabulary inadequacies or to inability to demonstrate arithmetic formulations; and in evaluating accuracy in division, the type of error made is of interest.

A teacher might wish to try deriving both kinds of evaluation from one examination, but there is a danger that such a combination will give the learner a different message from that of a formative test alone. A formative test needs to be free of any overtones of grading so that the student does not come to fear it but instead sees formative tests as an aid to learning. Also, the attempt to combine them would very likely require a test much longer and more complex than advisable.

The second of the three characteristics mentioned above also helps differentiate summative from formative evaluations. Tests for formative purposes tend to be given at much more frequent intervals than summative tests. It follows from the purpose described above that formative tests should be utilized whenever the initial instruction on a new skill or concept is completed. Summative evaluation looks at mastery of several such new skills or concepts. Summative tests are *not* reserved solely for final examinations, although certainly the final examinations given in most colleges and some secondary schools for grading and certification are summative. More frequently, tests of a summative nature are used two or three times within a course to contribute grades toward an overall grade reported to students and parents. In the elementary situation it is more common to see teacher-made tests given for grading purposes every 4 to 6 weeks. Clearly, minimal-competency tests used to award a high school diploma are also summative.

Perhaps *level of generalization,* the third characteristic, differentiates summative from formative evaluation more sharply. Chapter 2 discussed, among other things, the work of Tyler and Gagné on behavioral objectives. It was suggested that Tyler's approach tends to produce descriptions of desired behaviors, while Gagné's task analysis approach produces very detailed "prerequisite capabilities" for each large aim. The difference is one of generalizability or transferability. For example, in algebra one might have as an objective "the ability to construct and interpret graphs dealing with linear data." This implies possession of a number of skills and facts—for example, the ability to locate points in a coordinate system and the ability to use signed numbers correctly." In formative evaluation an attempt would be made to observe the underlying prerequisite behaviors; summative evaluation would focus much more on the broad ability represented by the phrase "construct and interpret."

ESSENTIAL CHARACTERISTICS OF SUMMATIVE TESTS

A teacher who wishes to use a test to make important decisions about an individual or group must be sure that the test possesses two absolutely essential chacteristics— *validity* and *reliability.* Before we discuss the steps a teacher might follow in constructing and then revising a summative test, it is essential that the reader consider each of these characteristics in some detail. The steps one follows in building a test are designed to produce ultimately a valid and reliable instrument. Therefore in this section we shall discuss validity and reliability in general terms. Specific suggestions for assuring validity and formulae for computing reliability will be found in subsequent sections dealing with test construction and revision.

Validity

On the basis of a person's (or group's) performance on a test, the test user can make three inferences about that person or group: inferences about the person's or group's achievement relative to a domain of skill or knowledge the test represents; inferences about the degree to which the person or group possesses a certain trait such as creativity, intelligence, or school readiness; inferences about the person's or group's performance on some variable other than that measured by the test itself, e.g., inferences about success in college on the basis of an SAT score given in high school (APA, 1974). Test validity then is a question of the correctness or appropriateness of inferences made on the basis of the test score or scores. One cannot talk about the validity of a test in general, only about whether the test is valid for particular uses or inferences. Test validity is divided into three categories on the basis of the type of inferences one might wish to make from performance on a test: content, construct, and criterion validity (APA, 1974). These categories are not mutually exclusive, and one category of validity can often be used to demonstrate another. Let us consider each category briefly in terms of summative achievement tests. For a more detailed treatment of validity the reader is referred to Campbell and Fiske (1959), Cronbach (1971), and Messick (1975).

Content validity

When one wishes to infer the extent of an examinee's mastery of a domain of skills or a universe of objectives on the basis of performance on a test, then it is necessary to consider the content validity of the test: Do the items of the test in fact represent the objectives or skills about which one wishes to make inferences?

Content validity of a summative test refers to the correspondence between achievement test items and instruction. For example, an item in a mathematics test which samples recall of trigonometric functions would not have content validity in an achievement test used for a course in which those functions were not meant to be taught. This book insists throughout that both instruction and examinations to evaluate learning should be tied to the same table of behavior-content specifications: this is really an insistence on content validity. In a summative test we wish to make inferences about the degree to which the larger outcomes outlined in the table of specifications have been mastered. If our test item or items properly represent and sample the content and behavior of the target cells of the table of specifications, then the test can be said to be content-valid.

An appropriate technique for checking the content validity of items involves the use of judges competent in the subject area. Perhaps they will be fellow teachers, or they may be specialists from a nearby college or university. The judges must also be provided with explanations of the meaning of the content rows and behavior columns in the table of specifications. Given this information, they should be asked to match the items to cells in the table. There is bound to be some disagreement over designations among the judges or between the judges and the teachers. However, if we get 75 percent agreement or better, we can feel comfortable about the content validity of the test. If the agreement is less than 50 percent, we should reexamine our items or discuss the actual teaching with the judges. It may be, for example, that items which we expect to measure application to new situations will impress the judges as measuring knowledge—simply because they think the instruction specifically includes these particular applications.

Recent attempts to use so-called "minimal-competency tests" as prerequisites for graduation have often failed to adequately consider the content validity of the tests. In particular, attempts to measure "life" or "survival" skills overlook whether such skills were ever specifically taught in the curriculum. To deny a diploma on the basis of deficiencies in skills which were never addressed in school is both morally and legally questionable (Madaus & Airasian, 1977; Airasian, Madaus, & Pedulla, 1979; McClung, 1977; Madaus & McDonagh, 1979).

Construct validity

When one wishes to infer to what degree an examinee possesses a certain construct or trait, one must examine construct validity. A construct is a "theoretical idea developed to explain and to organize some aspect of existing knowledge" (APA, 1974, p. 29); examples are anxiety, motivation, intelligence, musical aptitude, reading comprehension, creativity, interest in mathematics, and mathematics problem solving. Construct validity is most frequently associated with ability tests (for instance, intelligence tests) or personality tests. Very generally it means that hypotheses about the relatedness of behaviors prove correct. Suppose that we develop test X (say, on interest in mathematics) and hypothesize that those who score high on it will also score high on a test known to measure problem solving in mathematics. Empirical evidence that this occurs is used as support for construct validity—meaning that the two sets of test scores are related as we believe that interest and problem solving are related. Notice that in this process we are simultaneously validating the test and our hypothesis about the construct "interest in mathematics." If the hypothesized relationship was not present—that is, if interest in mathematics was not related to problem solving—it could be either because our test was not measuring the construct "interest" or because the hypothesis about the relationship between interest and achievement was incorrect.

Very often discussion about the validity of an achievement test is limited to a consideration of content validity. This is a mistake. For instance, if on the basis of an achievement test a teacher wishes to make inferences about reading comprehension, which has been a central concern of instruction, then he or she must ask whether the test is a valid measure of the construct "reading comprehension." If, for example, many of the pupils can answer questions based on a passage to be read without bothering to read that passage, then inferences about reading comprehension would not be warranted (Madaus, Airasian, & Kellaghan, 1980).

In designing items to measure the behav-ior axis of the table of specifications a teacher needs to consider whether or not the items actually measure such constructs as knowledge, comprehension, application, analysis, and evaluation. (Chapters 8 to 10 consider the techniques and problems in designing items to measure various taxonomic constructs.)

Criterion validity

When one wishes to infer from a previous test score an individual's performance or standing on some other measure (the criterion), then one must ask about the criterion validity of the test. Criterion validity can be *predictive* in nature; that is, we wish to predict future performance on the criterion from a present test score. For example, on the basis of a score on a ninth-grade French test, one might wish to predict a person's grade-point average in tenth-grade French. Criterion validity can also be *concurrent* in nature; that is, the test may be used to estimate the person's present, rather than future, standing on the criterion. For example, performance on a teacher-made French test might be used to estimate performance on a standardized French test.

It is sometimes useful to view performance on formative tests (see Chapter 6) as predicting performance on a summative test or tests. The purpose of formative examinations is to determine whether the students have attained mastery and, if not, to discover what is missing in their knowledge, skills, and abilities. Since summative examinations are intended to test the larger behaviors which rest upon these kinds of learning, we would expect overall performance on the series of formative instruments to predict the results of the summative measures. Obviously, if the instruction is so successful that all students do very well on all of the mastery tests, the correlation between these and the summative examination scores will tend toward zero, since dispersion of scores is a necessary condition for a positive or negative relationship. On the other hand, if all do well on the formative tests but there are a sizable number of poor scores on the summative test, this should lead to a reexamination of the assumptions underlying both sets of examinations and their logical relationships. The reader should note here the close relationship between predictive validity and construct validity.

In our discussion of content validity we argued that if life or survival skills were not taught specially, a test for such skills would not be content-valid. Assuming, however, that the skills in the tests were taught, the question of how well they predict future life performance (an interesting construct itself) must be addressed. In other words, if the test purports to measure survival skills, then it should predict some construct of adult performance. Only a longitudinal study could determine if such tests really measure survival skills.

Concurrent validity is demonstrated by evidence that students maintain the same rank order on one test (for example, an arithmetic examination) as they have on another which purportedly measures the same capabilities. This sort of validity has been relied on widely by test developers who want to show that a new test measures the same powers as a respected intelligence test, such as the Binet. Notice again that this also relates to construct validity. This approach is seldom helpful with achievement tests, since it is difficult to decide which test one is validating if both tests consist of samples of items from a table of specifications.

The notion of concurrent validity can be of use if we wish to inquire into the relation between an indirect and a more direct measure of some behavior. Here again, construct validity is also at issue. A straightforward example of this occurs in composition skills. Most teachers will say that a direct measure of writing ability can be had only when the student actually prepares a composition. On the other hand, a widely used device is a composition with known errors which the student is asked to proofread and correct. There are advantages in this approach in that it saves time and allows all students to be given the same task. However, the proofreading instrument is useful only if it correlates substantially with carefully developed scores on compositions written by the students. This, in effect, is the application of the idea of concurrent validity to two tests developed for the same purpose, one of which offers a less direct measure than the other does. If the two measures are highly related, then one also has evidence about the construct validity of the indirect measure of writing. If the two methods are not highly related, one must question whether the proofreading and correcting can be used to make inferences about how well a student writes.

In summary, the heart of the validity question is: Validity *for what?* What uses will be made of the test? What inferences will be made on the basis of test performance? If a final examination in a particular course is used to determine at what point in a subsequent course each student should begin, then it is valid if and only if it works. The expression "it works" means that if on the basis of the test we start student X on instruction A and student Y on instruction B, both will learn more than they would have learned had both started at the same point and received the same instruction. In terms of predictive validity, discussed a few paragraphs earlier, we are judging the validity of the test by its usefulness in predicting an appropriate starting point. What we are talking about here is discussed at some length in Chapter 5, on diagnosis. The reason for mentioning it here is that this use is discussed fairly frequently in connection with subject areas which are seen as sequential.

As another example, it is obvious that if the final examination is given simply for the purpose of assigning grades to the students' work, then the test is valid only if the grade assigned corresponds to the real category of worth. The test must consist of items representing the actual behaviors which are the objectives of the course.

Reliability

A characteristic which may be considered separately from validity, but upon which validity in part depends, is reliability. The reliability of a set of test scores refers to the consistency with which the results place students in the same relative position if the test is given repeatedly. If the same test were administered to a group in the morning and again in the afternoon, we would ordinarily expect the examinees to be ranked much the same each time. If this were not so, we would say that the results were not stable. Similarly, if two samples of items representing the same content-behavior cells were given one after the other and the students were not ranked in approximately the same way, we would say the results were not consistent. As a third example, if the same students take a given test again—or a different one sampling the same ability—after a lapse of 6 months, and do not come out in about the same order, we would say that the results lack consistency. However, in this last example, we might claim that we did not expect a high degree of consistency because the students had received instruction during the 6 months. The three examples suggest at least three types of reliability.

The first example—the same test given twice within a very short time—reflects consistency in the testing procedure or instrument. Such things as ambiguities in items may cause examinees to interpret the questions or the instructions differently at different times. The scoring procedure—an important part of the testing procedure—may be such that the same responses are scored differently on the two occasions. This is more likely to be true of supply items, for which students supply their own answers and the scorer must judge correctness, than of multiple-choice items, for which one scoring key can be used identically by a number of scorers or by the same scorer on a number of occasions. Methods of improving reliability are described later in this chapter under steps for constructing and revising a test. Suffice it to say at this point that ambiguities in either questions or directions can be reduced. As for scoring inconsistencies, greater care can be taken in scoring with a key and greater agreement can be sought between scorers or

between scores assigned by the same person at different times.

The second example described above—two samples of items representing the same content-behavior cells which are given with a very short time lag or none at all—also reflects consistency in the testing procedure or instruments. However, a new factor enters here: the equivalence of the samples of items, that is, how well they represent all possible items testing that cell. Generally one can increase reliability—that is, decrease inconsistency in results—by adding more items to a test. Very simply, if we wanted to test the ability to divide a three-digit numeral by a two-digit numeral, we would expect to get more reliable results from 6 items than from 2. Obviously, we would have to be concerned also with ambiguities and with consistency as in the earlier example.

The third example—in which a relatively long time elapsed before second testing with the same or a different sample of items—reflects a third type of reliability: stability of the trait. If we are dealing with students' interests for purposes of predicting vocational success, we expect some stability over time. However, if we are dealing with writing ability during a period when instruction is being given, we do not expect high stability. In summative evaluation, this sort of reliability seldom has major importance, although in the use of tests for certification or prediction of success, stability should be of real concern. (For a fuller treatment of stability and methods of estimating it, the reader should see Stanley, 1971.) The earlier problems with ambiguity and scoring consistency apply here also.

The opening sentence of this discussion on reliability stated that validity depends in part upon reliability. The converse is not true. One could construct a test which was quite invalid (such as one for measuring the ability to interpret data which consisted solely of questions of knowledge of terminology) but highly reliable in terms of both testing procedure and item sampling. However, even if we found general agreement among appropriate judges that a certain set of items measured ability to interpret data, thus establishing content validity, we could not think of our test as valid if we discovered that its reliability was low. Reliability limits validity. A measure which gives inconsistent results cannot give valid results.

For each type of reliability there are a number of quantitative estimates (Stanley, 1971). Later in this chapter we shall discuss two such formulae, fairly easy to apply, which estimate consistency of the testing procedure and the consistency across a sample of items, matters of prime concern to those who deal with examinations for summative evaluation of students' learning.

GENERAL STEPS IN CONSTRUCTING SUMMATIVE TESTS

Whatever one's point of view on education and appropriate instruction procedures, there are six general steps which can be of help in the construction of a summative test. They are listed here for convenience. Each is then discussed separately in the pages which follow:

1. Develop (or borrow and adapt) a table of specifications for the subject and grade.
2. Write or select test items for the cells of the matrix.
3. Choose items which test the various cells by sampling in some rational way.
4. Arrange the chosen items systematically.
5. Design an objective scoring scheme to furnish the kind of information desired.
6. Develop unambiguous directions for the examinees.
7. Inspect the final product.

Formative tests are discussed in Chapter 6. In this chapter we are ignoring the uses of formative instruments. The word "test" or "examination" occurs frequently in this chapter without the adjective "summative," but unless it explicitly states otherwise, the discussion at all times concerns tests intended as a basis for summative evaluation.

1. Develop (or Borrow and Adapt) a Table of Specifications for the Subject and Grade

Steps in developing or selecting a specifications matrix are treated in detail in Chapter 2, and the reader should review the points made in that chapter about the content and behavior dimensions of the grid. Table 4-1 presents a table of specifications for a high school course in biology. We shall refer to Table 4-1 throughout this chapter to illustrate points associated with constructing a content-valid summative test. Though it deals with specific contents and behaviors, illustrations from it are readily applicable to other subjects and grades.

2. Write or Select Test Items for the Cells of the Matrix

Suggestions for writing test items are covered in Chapter 7; Chapters 8 to 10 cover ways of framing items for various levels of the cognitive and affective taxonomy.

3. Choose Items Which Test the Various Cells by Sampling in Some Rational Way

If you believe that each outcome is as important as the next, then your selection will follow the rules of random sampling of all possible items. You can obtain a sampling of items across the entire table of specifications by assigning numbers to each item and using the numbers for a sampling across content or themes or both.

If, on the other hand, you see the purpose of your summative evaluation as that of testing a few generalized objectives, then you should decide which cells you should sample. For example, working from Table 4-1, you might want to use only items representing behavior category D, *Demonstration of relationships between bodies of knowledge.* You would put together a random sample of items which test behaviors D.1, D.2, and D.3, and so on for the particular contents or themes you choose.

TABLE 4-1 TABLE OF SPECIFICATIONS FOR SECONDARY-LEVEL BIOLOGICAL SCIENCES

	BEHAVIORS													
CONTENT	Recall and recognition of materials learned A.0	Terminology A.1	Specific facts A.2	Conventions A.3	Trends and sequences A.4	Classifications and categories A.5	Criteria A.6	Methodolgy A.7	Principles and generalizations A.8	Theories and structures A.9	Application of knowledge to new concrete situations B.0	Nonquantitative B.1	Quantitative B.2	Use of skills involved in understanding science problems C.0
1.0 Evolution														
1.1 Data of Change														
1.2 Theories of Change														
2.0 Diversity of Types and Unity of Pattern														
3.0 Genetic Continuity														
4.0 Complementarity of Organisms and Environment														
5.0 Biological Roots of Behavior														
6.0 Complementarity of Structure and Function														
7.0 Homeostasis and Regulation														
8.0 Intellectual History of Biological Function														
9.0 Science as Inquiry														

Source: Adapted from Klinckmann, 1963, p. 20.

As we will discuss more fully after step 5, for grading purposes you might wish to sample both content and behavior; for certification purposes a more appropriate sampling might cover only those cells which are desirable for the job or the next course in question.

Since our emphasis has been that a table of specifications affords the main support for content validity, it seems appropriate in this section to discuss ways of selecting items for a summative test. It seems obvious that in a broad subject area—the concern of final examinations—the number of recall, recognition, or application items will be exceedingly

BEHAVIORS

Interpretation of qualitative data	Interpretation of quantitative data	Understanding of the relevance of data to problems	Screening and judging of the design of experiments	Screening of hypotheses	Identification of problems	Identification of assumptions and unanswered questions	Analysis of scientific reports	Demonstration of relationships between bodies of knowledge	Comparison	Extrapolation	Application to another biological area	Application to other fields	Analysis of relationships	Interrelating of facts, principles, and phenomena in a new way	Development of a new set of interrelated concepts
C.1	C.2	C.3	C.4	C.5	C.6	C.7	C.8	D.0	D.1	D.2	D.3	D.4	D.5	D.6	D.7

large. Certainly there will be far too many to include in any one examination. This forces a decision on which items to use. As we will see, an important preliminary question is how one expects to score the test and use the results. In the meantime, let us look at two general criteria for sampling items.

As always in testing, there is first the issue of values. Using our familiar Table 4-1, an instructor might consider that the materials on *Diversity of types and unity of pattern* (2.0) and *Intellectual history of biological function* (8.0) are together more important than the materials indicated by the other content rows of the matrix. Given this value judgment, more items for these content rows should be sampled. Moreover, it should be understood that even if a teacher does not make explicit value judgments, he or she nonetheless de facto values the content rows equally if the items are chosen at random.

A good question at this point is how value weights are assigned to content areas. Some teachers make quick and strong decisions about how the weights should be assigned. They *know* which categories of a subject are most valuable; their conviction is based on such things as what seemed to be good for them as they went through their own training or what the texbooks emphasize in terms of pages devoted to the topics.

Other teachers find it useful, even necessary, to adopt a value order which stems from the department or school curriculum guide. They prefer, and possibly should prefer, to rely on the judgments of certain local authorities, such as the department head or the supervisor or the committee on curriculum organization.

Some teachers attack the problem of valuing the content areas from the standpoint of *logical connections* with later courses or with the total subject. As an example, the concepts involved in a number line probably will have more connections with other mathematics than the operations of multiplication do. Additionally, a teacher may investigate the literature in the field to see which concepts and topics are most frequently encountered.

A second criterion used in sampling across the learning areas in a subject is that of *equivalence among the tasks involved.* For example, a biology teacher who knows that the terminology and symbols used in the study of circulation are used also in another area, such as respiration, might well avoid sampling both. A third-grade teacher concerned with arithmetic may be sampling from a specifications table which has a behavior column called *Speed and accuracy in computation* and content rows which include addition, subtraction, multiplication, and division. For the purpose of sampling, this

teacher may decide that division problems provide evidence concerning subtraction and multiplication, and may therefore sample more heavily from division items.

Table 4-2 is a table of specifications for a course in auto mechanics, in which the distribution of items by cell has been entered. The weighting of items was achieved by having the instructor make an independent judgment of the relative emphasis to be placed on each cell. The instructor could distribute 100 points among the cells in accordance with the value emphasis he or she considered appropriate. Accordingly the first three columns in Table 4-2 account for most of the items and explain why Baldwin (1971) points out that "little emphasis is placed on the highest level of cognitive functioning. Problems with which the auto mechanic is expected to deal in this subject-matter area involve primarily knowledge, understanding, and the application of knowledge to routine problems (p. 869)." Such tables of item weights help ensure proper coverage of important content and behaviors. They help avoid the tendency to write too many items that tap only knowledge of facts.

Part of the task of weighting items in a test is necessarily empirical. To take a simple case, let us suppose that an arithmetic teacher includes 10 items each on the four fundamental operations. The equal number of items does not necessarily mean that each part contributes the same weight to the total score. Let us imagine that the class has learned addition and multiplication well, whereas subtraction and division were learned in varying degrees of mastery. If these two outcomes are reflected in the test results, it may be that all the students will make the same score on multiplication and addition but will vary considerably in their scores on subtraction and division.

Here is an illustration of the effect of weighting. In the example just given, each student might answer correctly 9 or 10 of the multiplication and addition items. Total scores on these two skills therefore will range from 18 to 20. On subtraction and division items, however, the scores might range from

TABLE 4-2 SUMMATIVE TEST SPECIFICATIONS FOR A COURSE IN CHASSIS, SUSPENSION, AND BRAKING SYSTEMS (SHOWING NUMBER OF ITEMS BY CONTENT AND LEVEL)

	Knowledge	Understanding	Application of knowledge	Application of understanding	Row Totals	
	A	B	C	D		
I. Chassis and suspension						
A. Fundamentals						
1. Springs and shocks	5	3			8	
2. Alignment	5	5	1		12	
B. Operating principles						
1. Steering mechanisms	2	1			3	
2. Stabilizer principles	3	4		1	8	
C. Service and repair						
1. Diagnosis of troubles		5	4		9	
2. Tool usage	5	1			6	
3. Alignment techniques	1	1	2	1	5	
4. Steering and balancing	1		1		2	
II. Braking systems						
A. Fundamental types						
1. Drums and shoes	2	2			4	
2. Disc	1	2			3	
3. Hydraulic	2	1			3	
B. Operating principles						
1. Pressures, mechanical-hydraulic	2	3	7	1	13	
2. Friction coefficients	2	3			5	
C. Diagnosis and service						
1. Indications of trouble and adjustments	4	3	7		14	
2. Drum, line, and cylinder repair	2	1	1		4	
3. Tool and equipment usage	1				1	
Totals	38	35	24	3	100	

Source: Adapted from Baldwin, 1971, p. 870.

4 to 10. Total scores of these two parts will therefore range from 8 to 20. Looking at total scores for all four parts, we see that they range from 26 to 40, a spread of 14 points. However, the main differences among the students across this range are explained by the wider variations in scores on the division and subtraction items. The addition and multiplication items can separate the students only by 2 points, whereas the other parts of the test can separate them by many more.

An extreme case of this same sort would be one in which all students make exactly the same score on one part of the test but vary considerably on the other. Then the total score will differ from student to student only as much as the students differ on the second part. The first part, on which they all performed alike, adds nothing to discriminating among individuals. It only adds a constant factor to scores on the second part. The discovery that *all* have mastered the first part is nevertheless an important piece of information.

What the foregoing says to us is that even though teachers do think through the weighting of items, they can be sure of the relative impact only after administering a test and discovering which responses contributed in which ways to the total score. The relative number of items in the various parts will not govern summative contributions to the total score per se. The spread in scores will.

Another empirical idea enters into weighting. Let us assume this time that in the sample of items representing the themes in Table 4–1, it is decided that C.4, C.5, and C.8 have equal value. Let us assume further that *Screening and judging of the design of experiments* (C.4) and *Screening of hypotheses* (C.5) are highly correlated. That is, students who do well with one also do well with the other, and similarly, students who do poorly with one do poorly with the other. Moreover, let us say that the items testing C.8, *Analysis of scientific reports,* are not correlated so strongly with the items from the other two behaviors. That is, students do not always score comparably on C.8 and on C.4 and C.5 items. In such a case, then, the items

most highly correlated will add more weight to the total score than the number of those items would suggest.

From the examples given above, it becomes apparent that the weight or value given to the components of any test—that is, to the number of items for a cell—reflects the weighting of these components in the total score if, and only if, (1) the examinees vary equally in their responses to the components, and (2) the relationships among the components are the same. These two conditions are rarely met in any test. The maker of a summative examination should still consider carefully the weightings which he or she wishes to give to various parts of a test if it has been decided to sample from the whole specifications matrix.

4. Arrange the Chosen Items Systematically

In certain cases it may be desirable to arrange test items by subgroups representing types of behavior. In other cases the items may be grouped by content. When the choice of items is such that they are relatively homogeneous with respect to content and behavior, it may be well to assemble them along a scale ranging from relatively easy (many students passing) to relatively difficult (few students passing). With different types of items—multiple-choice, matching, true-false—it is generally useful to group by types simply because directions are easier for the teacher to give and the students to remember. Another consideration in arranging items physically is ease of scoring. The student can be directed to put the letter of the correct option in a column to the right of the items. Alternatively, commercially available answer sheets that can be machine-scored may be used. If you do not have access to such answer sheets, another possibility is to design a separate answer sheet. An example of a portion of a simple 50-item answer sheet which could be mimeographed for use in the classroom is shown in Figure 4-1.

Hambleton, Eignor, and Swaminathan

Number right _____

Student's name _____ Class _____
Name of test _____ Date _____

Mark through the answer you think is correct in this way:

EXAMPLE   A   B̸   C   D

Mark only one answer to each question.

1	A	B	C	D		26	A	B	C	D
2	A	B	C	D		27	A	B	C	D
3	A	B	C	D		28	A	B	C	D
4	A	B	C	D		29	A	B	C	D
5	A	B	C	D		30	A	B	C	D
6	A	B	C	D		31	A	B	C	D
7	A	B	C	D		32	A	B	C	D
8	A	B	C	D		33	A	B	C	D
9	A	B	C	D		34	A	B	C	D
10	A	B	C	D		35	A	B	C	D

Figure 4-1 Separate answer sheet for four-item multiple-choice test. (Educational Testing Service, n.d.)

(1978, p. 42) offer the following guidelines in assembling items on the test:

1. Make sure that test items are spaced so that they can be read, answered, and scored with the least amount of difficulty. Double-space between items.
2. Make sure all items have generous borders.
3. Multiple-choice items should have alternatives listed vertically beneath the stem.
4. Do not split an item onto two separate pages.
5. With interpretation exercises, place the introduction on a single page with all related items on a single facing page.
6. If no answer sheet is used, the space for answering should be down the right side of the page.
7. The most convenient method of response is circling the correct answer.
8. Items should be numbered consecutively throughout the test.
9. Tests reproduced by processes available to school systems should be duplicated on one side of the sheet only.
10. If a separate answer sheet is used, test booklets can be reused. They should be numbered so that a check can be made for complete sets of materials after test administration.

5. Design an Objective Scoring Scheme to Furnish the Kind of Information Desired

The phrase "objective scoring" describes procedures which yield uniform results, regardless of the scorer, when used to mark (correct) a test. Objective scoring of examinations is not a topic which pertains solely to summative evaluation. However, there are reasons for special concern with objectivity in the scoring of the final test for a given course. When one is doing diagnostic examining or the kind of formative evaluation which takes place during the course, there are always opportunities for correcting the conclusions derived from the data. With a final examination—at the end of a course or a large unit—the general expectation is that we will have no further data for correcting the inferences we have drawn.

Objectivity in scoring has to do not only with fairness but with validity and reliability. No matter how well the items of a test match the table of specifications of intended outcomes, if any element of the scoring brings about inaccuracies in its application, then content validity is lowered. If any bias in the scoring causes the same behavior to be scored differently for different examinees, then both the validity and the reliability of the results are lowered. By way of example let us first take a reasonably simple case in which we have a choice test.

If the teacher keying the test has somewhat different notions from his or her colleagues on which alternatives are right and wrong for each item, then there is question whether the test is being scored objectively even though the same scores will be given to all students choosing the same alternatives. There are many cases in the biological sciences, for example, in which competent biology teachers will key different alternatives for the same item as the "best response." When the key for a final examination lacks uniformity, the validity of the results is affected. The implication of these statements is that, even when items correspond closely with a specifications matrix, the results of the test will not necessarily have content validity unless there is agreement on the keying of responses. This is another case in which it is important to have the agreement of competent judges (other teachers, experts on the subject matter, or people with training and experience in testing). This means not a mere "nose count" of options but a discussion of the reasons for choosing the alternative keyed as correct. If this agreement cannot be reached on a given test item, it is doubtful whether the item

should be used. It may be possible, however, to alter the wording of the item, without departing from the intent of the content-behavior cell, in a way that meets with the judges' approval.

In a choice test, once the key is made, the only reason for different scoring of examinees who have given the same responses is pure error in using the scoring key. If this happens, we do have lowered reliability and validity. About the only corrective for this kind of error is independent scoring, either by different scorers or by the same scorer at different times, using the same key.

With supply items the case is different, whether the student is called on to give a one-word answer, as in a simple completion or blank-filling test, or to write a page or two, an operation frequently referred to as an "essay answer." Unfortunately, the terminology which designates choice tests as "objective" and supply tests as "essay" was developed quite a number of years ago and obtains to this day. Readers know that essay tests are quite frequently not essays in the literary meaning of the term. In the sense used here, objective tests are merely tests without bias in scoring once the key is set, be they choice or supply tests. It should be noted that with proper safeguards, the responses on a supply test can be as objectively scored as those on a choice test. It should also be noted that in a choice test, some person or group must judge which responses afford the best answer.

In the scoring of a supply test which calls for one-word or one-phrase completions, there are those who will accept a rather liberal range of terms as long as it seems that the meaning is "within the ball park." For example, the following item was culled from a ninth-grade algebra final examination:

What name do we attach to the following set of equations?

$$3x + 2y = 18$$
$$x - 4y = 6$$

The keyed response for this item was "a set of simultaneous linear equations." Some students filled the blank with exactly that phrase. Many supplied statements which were clearly incorrect. A number of students answered "a set of equations in two unknowns." In this particular example, some teachers scoring the test accepted only the expression "a set of simultaneous linear equations" as correct. Anything else was marked wrong. Other teachers also accepted the response "a set of equations in two unknowns" as correct, but only for some students. As a hypothetical example, if Mary, a student who had repeatedly been unable to understand various concepts in algebra, gave this response, the answer was marked incorrect. If, on the other hand, Alice gave exactly the same response, it was marked correct simply because her teacher knew that she was highly familiar with the concept. This is an example of bias on the part of the marker.

There are two points about the foregoing example which need to be made. First, even when a group of teachers agree that a particular response is the only acceptable one, there is still a danger that the item will be rendered invalid by a student's thinking of another way to state the idea accurately. Second, in the latter part of the example, identical responses by different students were marked differently because of additional knowledge which the scorer had concerning the students. Even if this additional knowledge is perfectly accurate, it remains true that such differential scoring (nonobjectivity) lowers the reliability and the validity of the test.

Other causes of bias are poor handwriting by the student and fatigue on the part of the scorer. Bias, once insinuated into the scoring, can considerably affect the validity and reliability of the test. Bias is much more likely to occur when several sentences or paragraphs are to be written in response to a given item. The scorers, even when they agree closely on the aspects of the response to look for in marking, are apt to be diverted by extraneous information. This can happen in two ways.

First, the scorer may be influenced by irrelevant errors in the responses. If a paper contains some paragraphs with sentences which are carelessly constructed, the marker may give the response a lower score than a paper which contains the same points stated without grammatical errors. An effective way to correct this kind of bias is to mark the item independently for grammar or spelling or handwriting. By scoring independently facets of each response that do not pertain to the purpose of the item, the scorer should be able to concentrate more fully upon those facets relevant to the table of specifications.

The other source of bias most common in scoring supply items is the knowledge the scorer has of how a particular student did on earlier items in a test. For example, let's say that there is an item on which a number of different responses are correct, some less obviously so than others. Some teachers, in looking at the less correct answers will tend to score according to how well the student has done on preceding items. One who has missed many items "probably does not know what he (or she) is writing about." One who has been quite successful on previous items "possibly grasped the correct idea but doesn't express himself (herself) very well." This kind of bias is perhaps best overcome by the use of the following procedure:

1. Remove the identifying name or set of initials from each response sheet, perhaps by cutting it off, after numbering the two sections of the sheet with the same number. (This need will be anticipated in well-designed tests).

2. Shuffle the response sheets for the entire group before starting to mark any of them. Since they now carry no names, it is very difficult to identify who wrote a given sheet unless the number of students is exceedingly small. Teachers who correct the papers of the same students over the course of the year will get to know most students' handwriting—particularly at the elementary level. The point is nevertheless to make every effort to overcome the bias associated with "knowing what a student meant to say."

3. If there are several items, score all papers on one item only. Then reshuffle the sheets so that they are not in the same order and

proceed to score the next item on all papers.

4. Enter the score for each item either on a separate sheet or on the response sheet in such a fashion that it cannot be seen when you are scoring the next item.

The foregoing suggestions may seem to entail an excessive amount of work. However, insofar as they prevent irrelevant judgments from biasing the scoring, they will also prevent lack of objectivity from decreasing both the validity and the reliability of the test results.

A final consideration under point 5 is whether to plan for a single score or for multiple scores. In assignments of *grades*, a single score—even though it is the sum of several others—is most useful. In *certification* a score may be obtained on each special skill or on particular abilities across specific subject areas. (In Table 4-1 the subject areas are themes.) For *prediction* purposes a single score is most useful for statistical analysis, although multiple forecasts (see any good statistics book) allow the teacher to assess whether the various behavior-content cells should be weighted differently for the best possible prediction. To place students in future courses, the scoring system should afford a range of scores applicable to the objective of the next course. For *feedback* to students, the scheme should tell them which objectives

they have mastered and which they need more work on, and therefore separate scores should be given for different objectives.

6. Develop Unambiguous Directions for the Examinees

Each type of item needs a clear set of directions on how to proceed. If the type changes, new directions should be provided. The directions should tell the students how to proceed in answering items; whether they are to choose the one best answer or look for a correct response; how much time they have for the test and each of its subparts. Figure 4-2 shows a set of general directions that can be used with the multiple-choice format.

The directions shown in Figure 4-2 can easily be modified for true-false items. For matching items the basis for matching, and directions for placing the correct answer, should be clearly described. For short-answer supply-type items the degree of precision required should be made clear, particularly if the questions involve arithmetic computations.

If the essay question is used, the examinee needs directions for each question on the form and length of the answer desired, on any points that should be covered in the question, and on the suggested time one should spend on the question. The criteria for scoring the questions need to be described; will they be

---

This is a 40-minute test. It contains 50 questions. Mark only one answer to each question. Make all your marks on the separate answer sheet.

If a question seems to be too difficult, make the most careful guess you can rather than waste time puzzling over it. If you finish early, go back and look over your answers. Your score is the number of correct answers you mark.

EXAMPLE

Test Booklet		Answer Sheet
Columbus discovered America in		A B C D
A 1066		
B 1492		
C 1008		
D 1776		

Figure 4-2 General directions for multiple-choice test. (Educational Testing Service, n.d.)

marked for substance only, or also for spelling, grammar, and style? As we discussed above, structured essay questions where expectations are clearly spelled out in the directions can be more objectively scored than unstructured essay questions where the scope, length, and nature of the answers are left entirely to the interpretation of the examinee.

One problem that needs to be handled in the general test directions is guessing. Should the examinees try to answer all items or only those they feel they know? A venerable criticism of the multiple-choice test is that it encourages guessing. Formulae have been suggested that purportedly correct for guessing. However such formulae are based on the assumption that examinees make blind guesses, and when this does not happen, these formulae either overcorrect or undercorrect. In fact, blind guessing can happen; it is rare, however, if items are carefully constructed and students have sufficient time to try all items (Wood, 1977). Most examinees act either on partial information—they can confidently eliminate one or two distractors—or on incorrect information when answering a multiple-choice item. Unless otherwise directed, students who are cautious may omit items about which they are not absolutely sure. When this happens, the cautious student is put at a disadvantage relative to the more assertive ones who will have a go at any item or play a hunch when not sure. In order to overcome these two response sets, test directions should encourage students to try all items, as in Figure 4-2.

7. Inspect the Final Product

Following the six steps listed above, the test maker eventually arrives at a finished product. The following checklist, adapted from Neill, 1978 (pp. 80–81), and used by permission of the American Association of School Administrators (1801 N. Moore St., Arlington, Va. 22209), can be profitably used to give the summative test a final inspection before use. (The checklist can be used equally well with formative tests).

Item format
____ 1. Are the items in the test numbered?
____ 2. Is each item complete on a page?
____ 3. Does the reference material for an item appear on the same page as the item or on a facing page?
____ 4. Are the item responses arranged to achieve both legibility and economy of space?

Scoring arrangement
____ 1. Has consideration been given to the practicability of a separate answer sheet?
____ 2. Are answers to be indicated by symbols rather than underlining or copying?
____ 3. Are answer spaces placed in a vertical column for easy scoring?
____ 4. If answer spaces are placed at the right of the page, is each answer space clearly associated with its corresponding item?
____ 5. Are the answer symbols to be used by the students free from possible ambiguity due to careless handwriting or deliberate hedging?
____ 6. Are the answer symbols to be used by the students free from confusion with the substance or content of the responses?

Distribution of correct responses
____ 1. Are correct answers distributed so that the same answer does not appear for a long series of consecutive questions?
____ 2. Are correct answers distributed to avoid an excessive proportion of items in the test with the same answer?
____ 3. Is patterning of answers in a fixed, repeating sequence avoided?

Grouping and arrangement of items
____ 1. Are items of the same type requiring the same directions grouped together in the test?
____ 2. When juxtaposition of items of markedly dissimilar content is likely to cause confusion, are items grouped by content within each item-type grouping?

_____ 3. Are items generally arranged from easy to more difficult within the test as a whole and within each major subdivision of the test?

Directions for answering questions

_____ 1. Are simple, clear, and specific directions given for each different item type in the test?

_____ 2. Are directions clearly set off from the rest of the test by appropriate spacing or type style?

_____ 3. Is effective use made of sample questions and answers to help clarify directions for unusual item types?

Correction for chance

_____ 1. If deductions are to be made for wrong answers, are students so informed?

_____ 2. If no deductions are to be made for wrong answers, are students advised to answer every question according to their best judgment?

Printing and duplicating

_____ 1. Is the test free from annoying and confusing typographical errors?

_____ 2. Is the legibility of the test satisfactory from the viewpoint of type size, adequacy of spacing, and clarity of printing?

_____ 3. Is the length of line neither too long nor too short for easy comprehension?

TEST DEVELOPMENT FOR SPECIFIC PURPOSES

The summative examination may serve a variety of functions. There are steps in the construction and scoring of tests which help optimize each of these uses. It is quite true that the results of a given test may be employed in several different ways. If the intended aim or aims are established clearly before the test is constructed, the results can be utilized more satisfactorily.

Test outcomes are not equally applicable to all uses at all levels of schooling or in all subject areas. Among the most commonly mentioned uses of test results are the following:

Assignment of grades
Prediction of success in subsequent courses
Initiation point for instruction in a
subsequent course
Feedback to students
Certification of skills and abilities

Each of these is discussed in the following pages *with reference to test development* and to cautions to be observed in carrying out the intended uses.

Assignment of Grades

From elementary school through college and graduate work, summative tests are used more often for assigning grades than for any other purpose. Various technical and other considerations in actually assigning grades are discussed later in this chapter. However, the eventual grading must also be considered in constructing the test. In the discussion of mastery learning we saw that almost all students can attain a grade of A. That is, a level of performance equal to that assigned a grade of A for mastery learning is achieved. When mastery learning is not pursued, grading, as the root of the word implies, usually attempts to categorize each student's learning in relation to that of other students. This purpose most often reflects the view that usually there are a few in the top achievement category, more in the second group, a large number who are "average," and fewer in the lower categories. If this is the intent of the grading process, then there is a way of optimizing the spread of students in the process of constructing the test. A new criterion must be added in the selection of items which represent particular cells from the table of specifications. This criterion concerns item difficulty and item discrimination.

Item difficulty is the percentage of examinees who pass the item. A good separation among individuals can be obtained if the average difficulty of the items is around 50 or 60 percent and if the items vary in difficulty from about 20 to 80 percent. Obviously, test questions which are passed by all or nearly all students do nothing to differentiate the examinees—that is, spread them out. The same can be said for items which few or none pass.

Item discrimination is an index comparing the percentage of top students with the percentage of poorer students who pass the same item. The words "top" and "poorer," or "more capable" and "less capable," usually refer to the total score on the test. However, other measures of quality (for example, the teacher's estimate from classroom observations) can be used. Given a separation of the students into two such sets, the measure works as follows: If 50 percent of each group pass the item, it is said that the item does not discriminate. The same is true with any other close pair of percentages. If, on the other hand, 50 percent of the better group pass the item while only 30 percent of the poorer group do, the item is said to discriminate positively. If the total test score has been used to divide the examinees, this merely means that the item is spreading students in the same direction as the whole test. If on another item, 60 percent of the top students but 80 percent of the poorer students pass, the item is working in the opposite direction from the total test. To spread the student's scores for the purpose of grading, the discrimination index of all items should be positive (that is, more of the better students should pass the item); and the difficulty index (proportion passing) should vary from 20 to 80 percent, with the average around 50 or 60 as noted above.

The foregoing discussion implies that every test must be tried out with the same or similar students before it is used for grading. Obviously this is impractical for most classroom teachers. However, indices of item difficulty and discrimination can be calculated after the test has been given, and these indices can be noted and used as *estimates* for future tests with similar students. In the section on test revision, simple methods of calculating item difficulty and discrimination are illustrated and discussed.

The teacher who does not have indices of difficulty or discrimination for items before the test is assembled has two alternatives. The difficulty index can be approximated by experienced teachers. This is by no means a perfect substitute for trying out the items, but

it is better than having no estimate. When estimating item difficulty, teachers must be careful not to confuse item difficulty with the taxonomic level of the item. The fact that an item is designed to measure application, for example, does not necessarily imply that it is more difficult than one which has been designed to measure comprehension or knowledge. To memorize *Paradise Lost* would be a Herculean feat; to ask the students to write it out would be to measure recall, the lowest level of the taxonomy. By contrast, judging the adequacy of an experiment (evaluation) may not be nearly so difficult as writing out *Paradise Lost,* particularly when difficulty is thought of as the percentage of students who can successfully answer both questions. There is a definite distinction then between the difficulty level of an item and its level in the taxonomy (Madaus & Macnamara, 1970).

The second alternative requires four steps. First, develop the test according to the best estimates of difficulty and discrimination available (experienced judgments of teachers, past experience with the items, or both). Second, give the test to the students. Third, compute the indices of difficulty and discrimination. Fourth, base the final score for each student upon only the items which meet the criteria of difficulty and discrimination above. This solution to the problem can be costly in terms of the items dropped because they fail to meet the criteria. However, if what is wanted is a spread of scores with most students falling in the center category, the expense in lost items must be accepted; ordinarily less than 10 percent of the items will be lost.

For those who view education as being directed at mastery, at whatever level or in whatever subject, and who will undertake changes in instruction time and procedures to accomplish this, the two criteria just discussed are of little importance. They may select behaviors and contents from a specifications table or task analysis chart in accordance with the value they attach to them. All or almost all students may pass the items constructed to test these outcomes, in which case the examinees are assigned the highest category of grades. It may happen that a large number do not pass some of the items, in which case the teacher may conclude that the instruction procedures are at fault. Of course another inference is possible in this situation: it might be that the instruction was fine but the items were poorly written. As the instruction improves, more students should get more of the items correct. This is the view which formative evaluation espouses (see Chapter 3 and 6).

The foregoing discussion does not purport to cover all aspects of the use of test results for assigning grades and does not treat the process of actually awarding a grade to a test performance. It is intended to alert the teacher to some of the considerations in item selection related to this particular application.

If the purpose of testing is assignment of grades, then some attention should be given to the various suggestions in test construction steps 3, 4, and 5, discussed above. Referring to Table 4-1, the Table of Specifications for Secondary-Level Biological Sciences (see page 78), the teacher might wish the test at the end of the course to include items which sample each of the behavioral categories, A.0 to D.7, across all the content themes (step 3). If so, the procedure should probably be to arrange the items according to type or format (step 4) and to assign one score (step 5) to the whole test. The reason for a single score is that a sampling of the entire table (unless the test is extremely long) would not furnish enough items for each of the content areas to allow a reliable score on a given behavior or theme. Within the format groups, a teacher might wish to arrange items from easy to difficult. The score from such a test would have to be interpreted as a general index of attainment in the course as a whole—and as a consequence, the grade assigned to the score would be interpreted in the same way. It is important to point out that a grade, while based on a test score, can be quite distinct from the score itself, especially where the test score is not based on 100 percent. The fact that two students obtaining the same score might not have been successful on many of the same items (sometimes called the "compensatory principle" in scoring) would make the score useless for feedback or diagnosis. It follows of course that a summative grade (whatever symbol is used) based on identical test scores also masks differences between individual performances on the test items.

To make the point clearer, let us take a different example. Suppose another teacher decides that a summative examination at the end of a course should focus upon behavior categories C.0 and D.0, *Use of skills involved in understanding science problems* and *Demonstration of relationships between bodies of knowledge* (step 3). Let us say the teacher also decides that the themes of *Evolution* (1.0) and *Complementarity of organisms and environment* (4.0) are crucial. Sampling from these restricted areas of the table of specifications, the teacher could score four subgroups of items, one set for each of the categories of behavior with each of the two content aspects. In this approach the teacher should plan on having at least 12 or 15 items in each subgroup—48 to 60 items in the test—in order to feel somewhat secure about the reliability of the subscores. In general, the more items per score, the more reliable—or stable—it is.

It should be noted in this connection that when the design of the test (step 4) and the plan for scoring (step 5) afford more than one overall score, the chances are improved for using the test results for purposes of feedback, initiation of later instruction, and certification. The multiple score will carry more meaning than a single score representing biology accomplishment generally across the entire specifications table or some part of it.

An average summative grade is often based on several summative tests or assignments. Ways of combining and weighting separate summative tests or assignments to arrive at a grade are discussed under techniques for grading. It should be noted here that a common overall grade of, say, B+, based on four separate summative tests, masks differences in performance on these four tests that may exist between students. Again, like the compensatory principle mentioned above in assigning a grade to a test score, an overall grade based on the average of several grades also can hide more than it shows.

Prediction of Success
in Subsequent Courses

For purposes of academic guidance, it is sometimes claimed, a summative test predicts success in a subsequent course. In other words, the test has predictive validity. For example, it is suggested that an eighth-grade arithmetic examination may be quite helpful in predicting success in ninth-grade algebra or general mathematics. The first caveat to be observed regarding this use for a summative test is that it assumes two things: (1) There is, in fact, empirical evidence of predictive validity; and (2) once predictive validity is established, the subsequent course does not involve changes in method, content, or students' learning characteristics. These are broad assumptions, but they may indeed hold in a setting in which the teachers see the subject (in the example, algebra) as relatively stable.

Ideally, the teacher or group of teachers constructing a test that has predictive validity should try various plans reflecting combinations of behavior and content in a series of tests. The reason for this may be illustrated from Table 4–1; knowledge of terminology (A.1) and knowledge of conventions (A.3) may be good predictors for a more advanced biology course, but the use of skills involved in understanding science problems (C.0) may be a better predictor than the knowledge outcomes for subsequent work in physics or chemistry. In the example of arithmetic and algebra, skill with computation may be a good predictor for *some* algebra courses, whereas ability to translate verbal problems into conventional formulae may provide a better forecast for others—depending on the contents, methods, and purposes the two courses embody.

In very general terms, students who score high on summative examinations in any academic field tend to score high in other fields. In this connection, however, many questions are still unanswered; it is not yet known whether this pattern is due to a general factor (such as intelligence), a special ability (as in test taking), or some relationship in learning between the subject areas involved. It is our view that great care must be taken in using summative examination results for predictions regarding subsequent courses and that technical help should be sought for the task, as recommended in the discussion of certification.

Initiation of Point of Instruction
in a Subsequent Course

Especially in elementary school an important use of summative examinations—usually given at the end of the year—is for deciding at what point instruction should begin in the next grade. From one perspective this is much like formative evaluation; from another, it represents some of the suggested strategies in Chapter 5, Diagnostic Evaluation.

In constructing summative tests a single score may not be very helpful; for example, a score in third-grade arithmetic is of little use to the fourth-grade teacher in establishing a behavior-content point at which to begin instruction. A table of specifications should be agreed upon, in general at least, by the third- and fourth-grade teachers. Steps 3, 4, and 5 of the general procedures for constructing a test must be so handled that there will be several scores representing the important behavior-content cells. The fourth-grade teacher who will use the results for locating the point at which to begin instruction in arithmetic—to stay with the example—must fully understand the score categories.

Feedback to Students

The very essence of formative evaluation is to tell students as soon as possible what progress they are making. Summative evaluation can be used in this fashion also. As stated before, summative tests may be given at various points within a course and cover relatively large units, or they may be "finals" at the end of a course. It if is truly the end of a unit or course ("Well, we'll never touch that again!"), the feedback of score or grade information may have little effect in terms of changing the student's behavior.

If the examination is intended for feedback to students, then it should be so constructed that the interpretations of scores will direct the student's attention to useful things to do to make up for deficiencies. The feedback should tell the students which specific objective samples they have mastered and which remain to be mastered. A simple communication of a single grade—C, let us say— merely tells the student that in some fashion or other he or she did better than others or did not do as well as others. A similar statement can be made about numerical scores: a mark of 76, whether it refers to percentage of items, a percentile score, or an actual count of right or wrong answers, gives the student as little guidance as the frequently used admonition, "Try harder." Such scores do not tell the students what they can do in any absolute sense.

Even if a summative test is a general end-of-term test, if it is built and scored astutely, we may infer from the results that the student did reasonably well in aspects which involve, for example, vocabulary but rather poorly in those which demand recognition of relationships between concepts. It is possible that the student will find the information of some use for future learning. Even this is difficult to establish for an end-of-course examination unless one can point out that subsequent courses require some of the same processes. The first statement implies that the test items are so built that they can reveal various processes which are reasonably generalizable, and the second presupposes some sort of agreement between teachers across several courses or curricula regarding desirable behavior.

Providing feedback to students is a legitimate purpose of summative evaluation, even though formative evaluation focuses on this intent. However, the results of summative tests are more likely to be used for feedback if careful attention is paid to the decisions and alternatives described in steps 3, 4, and 5 of the general test-construction procedures. Multiple scores, particulary on behavior categories related to the cells tested, can be helpful to the student if they are based on a sufficient number of items for reliability.

Certification of Skills and Abilities

There are occasions on which the main purpose of a summative examination is to certify that a given student possesses, at least at that time, certain skills, kinds of knowledge, and abilities. These situations are perhaps most likely to occur in technical training in the secondary school or junior college. In a growing number of states, partly in response to the belief that many students are leaving high school without basic competencies in reading, writing, and computation, graduation from secondary school may depend in part on passing a minimal-competency test. Any student who cannot demonstrate mastery of processes, knowledge, or skills which the state (or local community) considers essential for functioning in the world is not certified (Madaus & Airasian, 1977). The general idea of certification is also present in other school settings: the student is able, from the standpoint of reading skills, to handle social studies reading material; the student has mathematical skills and concepts which are needed for a beginning course in statistics; the applicant has skills in the science laboratory and the ability to attack science problems which qualify him or her to handle an assistantship.

In each of these settings, the focus is mainly upon the level of behavior with a given content. The implication is that the items on the certification test must be so selected that specific behavior-content cells of a known table of specifications may be scored (steps 1, 2, and 3). There is the further assumption that a known level of performance exists, above which most students can do the specified job and below which most cannot (Cronbach, 1960). This becomes a question of predictive validity and is highly desirable if not necessary for confidence. It is true that careful subjective judgments by those who have experience with performers may substitute as estimates until empirical evidence is collected.

Certification, as described in the foregoing paragraphs, is a legitimate use of summative evaluation. The development of tests for this purpose may require consultation with specialists for the technical aspects. Building tests to measure minimal competencies involves several technical issues of test validity, test length, and cutoff scores which are beyond the scope of this book. They are highly technical matters, and the issues are not completely resolved even among experts (Glass, 1977).

In Summary: Purposes

In summary, the intent of this section has been to raise questions about the purpose of giving summative examinations. It is possible for one examination to serve two or three different uses, though in general not efficiently. It must be remembered that the rules concerning objectives set forth in Chapter 2 apply to every instrument, whatever purpose it serves. These rules stipulate that objectives should be stated in terms of observable and replicable acts. Summative examinations do not differ from formative or diagnostic examinations in the requirement that they be based on clearly stated objectives. Nor do they differ in the fact that the items used to measure the objectives must be carefully written, as outlined in Chapter 7.

GENERAL STEPS IN REVISING TESTS

We have listed six steps in test construction and have discussed the application of these steps to various purposes for administering summative examinations. Such concepts as item difficulty and discrimination were explained in connection with using tests to assign grades. The idea of reliable multiple scores was discussed, especially with regard

to feedback to students. Now is the time to draw some of these elements together by describing a few revision steps which if followed will improve a test's validity and reliability. Some of these steps can be followed before the test is given; others are based on having administered the test once and using data from that administration to improve the test's reliability and validity for subsequent use.

Any test can be improved if the following steps are taken.

1. Tryout

Give the test individually to a small number of students and ask each one to do his or her reading, thinking, and answering out loud. This step in revising a test is discussed fully in Chapter 7, Item Writing and Item Selection. It is an excellent procedure to follow to identify weaknesses and ambiguities in items and directions, as well as problems with format and layout.

2. Assessment of Content Validity

Show the items of the test and the specifications table to a competent judge or judges (preferably several)—a teacher or teachers in the same area—and ask which cell or cells of the table would be identified with each item. If the judges are *not* familiar with the actual instruction, they may misclassify some items, assuming, for example, that something which you are calling "application" was specifically taught in class and is therefore "knowledge," or that something which you classify as "knowledge" is "comprehension." Nevertheless, if points of disagreement between the judges and the test maker are discussed, the finished test will generally be improved. Both the test maker and the judges will find it helpful to have each item set forth on a separate card (3 by 5, or 4 by 6 inches), with full directions for each type of item written on another card (see Chapter 7, Item Writing and Item Selection). The card system is also helpful in the development of an item pool and useful in constructing new tests.

3. Computation of Mean and Median Scores

Compute the median and mean of the test scores obtained from the tryout group. Both of these measures of average can be used in later steps of test revision. The median can be used in figuring the discrimination index, which was discussed under the heading "Assignment of Grades." The mean is necessary for the procedures described in steps 4 and 7, which concern standard deviation and reliability and, as will be discussed below, is necessary if one wishes to use standard scores in the grading process. These measures of "central tendency," or average, are useful also in comparing the performance of different groups on the same test. Their computation is described in Figure 4-3.

4. Computation of Standard Deviation of Scores

Compute the standard deviation of the test scores. This group measure is useful, along with the mean, in estimating reliability (see step 7). It is useful too in comparisons between groups and comparisons of tests. The standard deviation, which we denote by the letter s, is a measure of dispersion of scores. Two groups might take the same test and have approximately equal means or medians, and at the same time the sets of scores for the two groups might spread out above and below

the mean or median quite differently. For example, suppose two groups take an arithmetic test of 50 items. Suppose further that group A's scores vary from 10 to 48 and group B's from 25 to 40. Group A would have the larger dispersion as measured by the standard deviation. The standard deviation is a distance from the mean in terms of score units. It tells how widely the scores vary around the mean. The larger the standard deviation, the more the scores vary. (For a detailed discussion of the concept of standard deviation it is suggested that you consult an introductory statistics book.)

The computation of s is not difficult, especially if one has access to a hand calculator (Figure 4-4). Many hand calculators now have functions which allow the user to easily calculate both the mean and the standard deviation. The test scores are entered in sequence, and the teacher needs only to press one key to obtain the mean and another to obtain the standard deviation. Even less sophisticated hand calculators make it easy to calculate the standard deviation by following the formula in Figure 4-5.

5. Formulation of Item Statistics

Obtain item statistics for all items. The difficulty index of an item was discussed in general terms in the section "Assignment of Grades." The index represents the proportion of students answering an item correctly. To obtain it one merely divides the number of students passing the item by the total number of students who attempted it. For test revision

---

Very simply, the median (Md) is the score which divides the examinees into two parts, the score above and below which one-half of the cases fall. To obtain this measure, arrange the scores in order from highest to lowest and count from the bottom up (or the top down) to the middle score. If there is an even number of scores, choose a point between the two middle scores.

The *mean* (M) is found by adding all scores and dividing them by the number of scores. The mean is that score which would be assigned to every pupil in the class if all the scores were pooled and distributed equally among the members of the class. If a test is administered to 50 students and their scores add up to 1,500, the mean is 20: that is, 1,500 divided by 50.

Figure 4-3 Computation of median and mean.

The availability and relatively low cost of hand-held electronic calculators make the task of calculating item and test statistics for a teacher-made classroom test quick and easy. The data used in this figure to illustrate the computation of mean, standard deviation, item difficulty, and item discrimination are taken from Table 4-3 (page 100). Table 4-3 shows the distribution of item answers and total test scores for 20 pupils on a 10-item test.

Before any calculations are attempted, the total scores on the 10 items are arranged from highest to lowest as in Table 4-3. For each of the 10 items record a "1" for a correct answers and an "0" for an incorrect answer.

If we use the steps for calculating the mean described in Figure 4-2, then the mean for our hypothetical class shown in Table 4-3 is 6.35—that is, the sum of the 20 scores, 127, divided by the number of samples (20).

The median for the distribution is 6.5; there are 10 scores above and 10 below this point.

Using the formula for computing the standard deviation described in Figure 4-5 we find that the

$$\text{standard deviation} = s = \sqrt{\frac{909}{20} - (6.35)^2} = \sqrt{45.45 - 40.32} = \sqrt{5.13} = 2.26$$

Figure 4-4 Calculating descriptive statistics with an electronic hand-held calculator.

The steps for computing standard deviation, s, are as follows. First, square every score. Second, add the squares to obtain a total. Third, divide this total by the number of scores in the group. Fourth, subtract from this total the square of the mean (see Figure 4-3). Fifth, take the square root of the difference you obtain in the fourth computation. That square root is the standard deviation, s, for the sample of test scores. The formula for the five computations, if you prefer an equation to prose, is

$$s = \sqrt{\frac{\Sigma X^2}{N} - M^2}$$

where Σ = "the sum of"
X = a score
X^2 = the score squared
N = the number of scores
M = the mean
$\sqrt{}$ = "the square root of"

Figure 4-5 Computation of standard deviation.

it is very helpful to know the difficulty of each item. If you are using a test to spread students out (rather than to assess mastery), you will want to reject items which everyone or almost everyone either passes or fails. Remember that a good spread of results can be obtained if the average difficulty of the items is around 50 or 60 percent and items vary in difficulty from 20 to 80 percent. The difficulty index is also needed in computing the dis-

crimination index (see step 6). Figure 4-6 describes the computation of item difficulty.

Rejecting an item which is very high or very low in difficulty is not always necessary. You can alter its difficulty by changing some of the alternatives in a multiple-choice question or by altering the language of the item. When you make such changes, however, it is very important to make sure that the item is still measuring the same behavior (see the

The difficulty index for an item is the proportion of students answering the item correctly, as shown by the column totals in Table 4-3 (page 100). To obtain the difficulty index for an item, simply divide the column total by the total number of students (in this example 20). A check on the row and column sums is obtained by making sure the total of the row totals equals the total of the column totals (in this example 127). The difficulty indices for each item are shown in Table 4-3. Since every student answered item 1 correctly, its difficulty is 1.00. Note that, paradoxically, the easier the item—that is, the more people answering it correctly—the higher the difficulty index. (It is often suggested that the term "index of difficulty" be replaced by the term "index of facility").

Figure 4-6 Calculating difficulty of items.

discussion of validity and see also steps 1 and 2 in this section).

The discrimination index was discussed in general terms in the section "Assignment of Grades." The index of discrimination at its simplest level involves obtaining the difficulty index for those who do well on the test and those who do poorly. A common method calls for calculating the difficulty index separately for those above and for those below the median. If the index for the better students is larger than that for the poorer students—that is, if more of the better ones pass the item—the item discriminates positively and hence properly. This merely reflects in numbers the fact that we expect good students to do better on the average with each item than poor students. A way of approximating item discrimination is shown in Figure 4-7. Remember that to spread students' scores for norm-referenced grading, the discrimination should be positive and as high as possible.

If an item does not discriminate properly, it can be discarded. However, because time and energy have gone into every item, discarding the item is expensive. Therefore, it is wiser to attempt to revise the item. A common reason for negative discrimination is that the item contains subtle language which misleads the better students but is ignored by the poorer. For revision, using step 1 can help locate the trouble; again, however, as stated in step 5, care must be taken in revising an item so that its intent is not altered. Another reason for negative discrimination is that the item has been keyed incorrectly.

Carver (1974) suggests that, ideally, for a criterion-referenced test the difficulty index

is close to 0 before instruction and approaches 1.00 after instruction. That is, most students get the item wrong before the instructional sequence while most students answer it correctly after instruction has taken place. The following formula can be used to calculate item statistics for a criterion-referenced test:

$$\frac{\left(\begin{array}{l}\text{Proportion of students} \\ \text{answering the item} \\ \text{correctly on the} \\ \text{posttest}\end{array}\right) - \left(\begin{array}{l}\text{Proportion of students} \\ \text{answering the item} \\ \text{correctly on the} \\ \text{pretest}\end{array}\right)}{(1) - \left(\begin{array}{l}\text{Proportion answering item} \\ \text{correctly on pretest}\end{array}\right)}$$

The larger the value, the more instructionally sensitive the item. For example, if only 10 percent of the students answered the item correctly in the pretest and 90 percent answered it correctly in the posttest, the result would be:

$$\frac{.90 - .10}{1.00 - .10} = \frac{.80}{.90} = .89$$

This figure of course depends on the feasibility of administering a pretest. Giving items to students before they have had instruction can be demoralizing (Wood, 1977). Until better psychometric techniques are developed for criterion-referenced tests, teachers who do not have pretest data will have to rely on their own judgment in selecting items for criterion-referenced tests. Once again, it needs to be emphasized that content validity and not item statistics should be the prime consideration in selecting items, regardless of whether one wishes to make norm- or criterion-referenced inferences about performance.

The discrimination index provides a measure of how well an individual item discriminates between students who do well on the test and students who do poorly on the test. The exact value of this discrimination index is obtained by correlating the 0, 1 values for an item with the total test score (shown in Table 4-3). Many calculators have a correlation-function key, making the procedure relatively easy. An alternative approach to calculating the discrimination index is to identify the top and bottom 27 percent of the students, in terms of total test score. The figure 27 percent is approximate. In our example we include the first six pupils in our "high" group and the lowest six in our "low" group (see Table 4-3). One can then obtain an approximate measure of the discrimination index for each item by using this formula:

$$\text{Discrimination index} = \frac{\begin{array}{c}\text{number of students getting item}\\\text{right in high-scorer group}\end{array} - \begin{array}{c}\text{number of students getting item right}\\\text{in low-scorer group}\end{array}}{\text{number of students in either group}}$$

For example, all six students in the high group got item 3 right while none of the students in the low group got item 3 right. Applying our approximation formula, we obtain:

$$\text{Discrimination index} = \frac{6-0}{6} = 1.0$$

The value 1.0 is highest discrimination index that can be obtained; it indicates that the item discriminates perfectly between the high and low groups.

Let's look at item 10. Two students in the high group and four students in the low group answered it correctly:

$$\text{Discrimination index} = \frac{2-4}{6} = \frac{-2}{6} = .333$$

The negative sign indicates that more students in the low group answered the item correctly. One might first check to see that the item has been keyed correctly; if the key is correct, then the item should be examined for ambiguities.

Table 4-3 shows the approximate discrimination indices for each of the 10 items and the exact discrimination indices calculated using the correlational technique. The reader will note that while the difference between exact and approximate item discrimination indices varies from 0.02 to 0.18, the interpretation of the item discrimination power is the same for both techniques.

Figure 4-7 Calculating discrimination of items.

A case can be made for computing traditional item statistics for items written for a criterion-referenced test. The indices would be used for identifying weaknesses in items so that they can be revised or excluded. As we note in Chapter 7, Item Writing and Item Selection, item writers are fallible, and item statistics can be a starting point in identifying ambiguous items, such as items with more than one correct answer or items that have been keyed incorrectly.

As noted in Chapter 7, item statistics computed on another group of examinees or on small samples must not be taken too literally. When an item is used again with students of different ability or in a different test configuration, difficulty and discrimination indices can shift. For classroom tests, therefore, the parameters for item selection suggested above are just that—suggestions. There are no hard and fast cutoff points, and considerations of content validity are as important as these statistical indices.

6. Assessment of Reliability

Compute and examine the reliability of the test results. The meaning and importance of reliability were discussed earlier in this chapter. At this point let us see how to obtain a reliability measure when the test has been given and is being revised. The higher the reliability of the test, the better. Achievement tests should have reliability of .80 or higher.

There are a number of different types of reliability and a number of different formulae for obtaining a reliability coefficient. We will present just one type of reliability—internal consistency of items on a test—and two formulae for computing it. The reader who wishes to go more deeply into reliability (and we would urge it) should refer to Stanley (1971).

Our choice of these two procedures out of the many available was made because for achievement tests in the classroom the main concern is whether the items selected from the many possible constitute a good sample. Also, they are relatively easy to use if one is already collecting information about item difficulty.

In 1937 G. Frederic Kuder and Marion W. Richardson, in their article "The Theory of the Estimation of Test Reliability," presented a number of formulae for the reliability coefficient. We have chosen to demonstrate two of these, K-R formulae 20 and 21. Figures 4-8

and 4-9 show the computations of K-R 20 and K-R 21 respectively. Figure 4-10 takes the reader through the calculation of K-R 21 for the class of twenty students shown in Table 4-3 (page 100). Both 20 and 21 overestimate the consistency if speed is a large factor in the test; these formulae probably should not be used unless 90 to 95 percent of the students are able to complete the examination.

A reliability coefficient applies to the test as a whole, while the standard error of measurement, which can be estimated from the reliability coefficient, gives an estimate of the error associated with each person's score. An individual's test score (observed score) can be viewed as an estimate of his or her "true" score—the person's score on the test if there were no such thing as measurement error. There is another way of thinking about a person's true score: if a person could take the test over and over again without any change in the conditions of the test or the examinee (tiring, learning, daydreaming, etc.), the person's true score would be the average (mean) of the repeated testing. The standard error of measurement would be the standard deviation of the distribution of scores from the

---

Kuder-Richardson formula 20 is: $r = \dfrac{k}{k-1}\left(1 - \dfrac{\Sigma pq}{s^2}\right)$

In this formula r is the reliability coefficient. The letter k represents the number of items in the test. Σ, as in Figure 4-5, means "the sum of." The letter p stands for the proportion of students passing (giving the correct answer on) a given item, and q represents the proportion not passing (giving the wrong answer). The figures for p and q must add up to 1.00; or, stated another way, q is obtained by subtracting p from 1.00. The symbol s^2 stands for for square of the standard deviation, s, for which a formula was given in Figure 4-5. To calculate K-R formula 20:

1. Obtain the item difficulty (p) for each item.
2. Multiply p by q (which is 1.00 -p) for each item.
3. Add the product of $(p \times q)$ for all items in the test (Σpq).
4. Divide this figure by s^2
5. Subtract the quotient from 1.00.
6. Multiply the remainder from step (5) by the quotient of the number of items (k) divided by one less than the number of items

The resulting figure is r, the index of reliability.

Figure 4-8 Computation of reliability (K-R formula 20).

Kuder and Richardson present another formula, number 21, which somewhat simplifies the calculation of reliability. This formula uses the number of items in the test, k; the mean of the set of scores (see Figure 4-3); and the square of the deviation, s^2 (see Figure 4-5). It is:

$$r = \frac{k}{k-1}\left(1 - \frac{M(k-M)}{ks^2}\right)$$

In this formula it is assumed that the difficulty index is approximately the same for all items, varying from only about 0.3 to 0.7. If the values of p vary much more than this, the r will be a serious underestimate of the "true" index of consistency. To calculate K-R formula 21:

1. Subtract the mean (M) from the number of items on the test $(k\text{-}M)$
2. Multiple the remainder from step (1) by the mean (M).
3. Multiply the number of items (k) by the square of the standard deviation (s^2).
4. Divide the figure obtained in step 2 by that obtained in step 3.
5. Subtract the quotient obtained in step 4 from 1.
6. Multiple the remainder obtained in step 5 by the quotient of the number of items (k) divided by one less than the number of items $k - 1$.

The resulting figure is r, the index of reliability.

Figure 4-9   Computation of reliability (K-R formula 21).

The formula for internal consistency of reliability coefficient (r) according to the Kuder-Richardson formula 20 was given in Figure 4-8. If a calculator is available which has a summation function key, the calculation of the reliability coefficient is straightforward. Take the difficulty index (p) from Table 4-3 (page 100), and calculate q: i.e., $(1 - p)$. The product $p \times q$ is obtained for each item, then summed. The standard deviation was found to be 2.26; squared, it is 5.13. The number of items is 10. These values are substituted in the reliability formula in Figure 4-8 to obtain $r = 0.6773$, or 0.68.

Item	Difficulty (p)	$q = 1 - p$	$p \times q$
1	1.00	0.00	0.00
2	0.85	0.15	0.1275
3	0.50	0.50	0.25
4	0.80	0.20	0.16
5	0.65	0.35	0.2275
6	0.45	0.35	0.2475
7	0.50	0.50	0.25
8	0.60	0.40	0.24
9	0.50 '	0.50	0.25
10	0.50	0.50	0.25

$\Sigma pq = 2.0025$

$$r = \frac{k}{k-1}\left(1 - \frac{\Sigma pq}{s^2}\right) = \frac{10}{9}\left(1 - \frac{2.0025}{5.13}\right) =$$

$1.1111(1 - 0.39035) = 1.1111(0.60965) = 0.6773$

Figure 4-10   Calculating K-R formula 20 for the class of 20 pupils shown in Table 4-3.

PUPIL/ITEM	1	2	3	4	5	6	7	8	9	10	Total	x^2
High group												
Joe	1	1	1	1	1	1	1	1	1	1	10	100
John	1	1	1	1	1	1	1	1	1	1	10	100
Mary	1	1	1	1	1	1	1	1	1	0	9	81
Sarah	1	1	1	1	1	1	1	1	1	0	9	81
Eileen	1	1	1	1	1	1	1	1	1	0	8	64
Matthew	1	1	1	1	1	1	0	1	1	0	8	64
Christopher	1	1	1	0	1	0	1	1	1	0	7	49
Sean	1	1	1	1	1	0	0	1	1	0	7	49
Elizabeth	1	1	1	1	1	0	1	0	1	0	7	49
George	1	1	1	1	1	0	1	0	0	.	7	49
Martha	1	1	0	0	1	1	0	1	0	1	6	36
Brendan	1	1	0	1	0	0	1	1	1	0	6	36
Tom	1	1	0	1	1	0	0	1	0	1	6	36
Pat	1	0	0	1	0	1	1	0	1	1	6	36
Low group												
Glen	1	1	0	1	0	1	0	1	0	0	5	25
Anne	1	1	0	1	0	0	0	0	0	1	4	16
Catherine	1	1	0	1	0	0	0	0	0	1	4	16
Bill	1	1	0	0	0	0	0	0	0	1	3	9
Edward	1	0	0	0	1	0	0	0	0	1	3	9
Marion	1	0	0	1	0	0	0	0	0	0	2	4
Total (Σ)	20	17	10	16	13	9	10	12	10	.0	Σ 127	Σ 909
Difficulty index	1.00	.85	.50	.80	.65	.45	.50	.60	.50	.50		
Discrimination index (approximate)	.00	.33	1.00	.33	.83	.83	.83	.83	.83	−.33		
Discrimination index (exact)	.00	.50	.82	.35	.67	.62	.69	.67	.69	−.20		

TABLE 4-3 EXAMPLE OF RESULTS FROM A 10-ITEM TEST FOR A CLASS OF TWENTY PUPILS

Note: "I" indicates that the student answered the item correctly; "0" indicates that the student answered incorrectly. All indices rounded to nearest 100th.

repeated testing. Obviously we cannot repeatedly test students. However, the standard error of measurement can be estimated from the reliability and standard deviation of the test. Figure 4-11 shows how to calculate the standard error for test data on the twenty students shown in Table 4-3. Once obtained, it can be used to set up a confidence band around a person's observed score. Sixty-eight times out of one hundred the person's true score would fall in a band plus and minus 1 standard error from the observed score. Ninety-five times out of one hundred it would

fall between plus and minus 2 standard errors. For example, in Table 4-3 Brendan obtained a score of 6. The standard error of measurement is 1.28 (see Figure 4-11). The score of 6 plus or minus 2.6 (2 times 1.28) yields a range of scores from 3.6 to 8.6. We can be reasonably confident that if Brendan repeatedly took the test, ninety-five times out of a hundred his score would be between 3.4 and 8.6. The reader should note that the higher the reliability of tests with the same standard deviation, the smaller the standard error of measurement.

The standard error of measurement can be obtained directly from the reliability coefficient and the standard deviation of the test by use of the following formula:

$$\text{Standard error of measurement} = s \sqrt{1 - r}$$

where s is the standard deviation of the test (see Figure 4-5) and r is the reliability of test (cf Fig. 4-8). The standard error of measurement for our class of 20 pupils shown in Table 4-3 is:

$$2.26 \sqrt{1 - 0.6773}$$
$$= 2.26 \sqrt{0.3227}$$
$$= 2.26 \, (0.568)$$
$$= 1.28$$

Figure 4-11 Calculating the standard error of measurement.

The standard error of measurement should be taken into account when assigning a grade to a test. For example, Mary has 32 items correct on a test and Joe has 28. If a teacher decides to give a grade of B to all scores over 30 and a C to scores between 20 and 29, Mary would receive a B, Joe a C. If the standard error of the test is 4 points, however, sixty-eight times out of a hundred we could be reasonably sure Mary's score would fall between 36 and 28, and Joe's between 32 and 24. Notice that when the standard error is considered, Mary's "true" score could be as low as 28, a C, and Joe's as high as a B. Grading involves a value judgment about the worth of a test score. When assigning grades to test scores, therefore, the teacher needs to keep in mind that the test is subject to error. The standard error of measurement gives the teacher an estimate of this error in terms and score points. Whenever possible the teacher should consider the standard error when making value judgments about the range of scores that will be assigned a particular grade.

There are several suggestions that can help improve test reliability.

1. Clarifying ambiguities in items and directions (revision step 1, page 93) will generally improve both reliability and validity.
2. Increasing the agreement of scores, or among scores by a single scorer on different occasions (see construction step 5, page 83), will improve reliability; but unless this is done in a very rational and careful manner—certainly not by mere "voting counts"—it can decrease validity.
3. Adding more items of similar content validity to the test or subtest will increase reliability of the resultant scores, as long as attention is paid to quality of items and scoring (1 and 2 above).
4. Improving the discrimination power of items (revision step 5, page 94), other things being equal, will increase reliability. In increasing discrimination, however, one must be careful not to make alterations which affect content validity.

THE USE OF DATA-PROCESSING EQUIPMENT IN REVISING TESTS

The use of basic data-processing equipment can reduce the burdensome clerical scoring and statistical work necessarily associated with systematic evaluation. Most school systems have on hand basic unit-record equipment, such as a keypunch, card sorter, card reproducer, printer, and collator, as part of their business, commercial, or vocational education programs. Some systems also have optical scanning machines, as well as small computers. Lacking these, a school system can often make use of such equipment found in nearby banks, factories, business offices, or colleges. Some school systems, especially those located in metropolitan areas, may also have a formal arrangement with a nearby university computer center.

Correcting Multiple-Choice Examinations

Correcting multiple-choice examinations by hand is a slow, tedious, and boring task. While in some systems paraprofessionals can relieve teachers of this clerical function, the time lag between the administration of the test and the reporting of results is directly proportional to the number of questions and examinations. Further, hand-scoring does not provide the item- and test-analysis data so necessary in test revision.

If a school system has mark-sensing equipment on its reproducing punches, students can record their answers to test items on mark-sensing cards. These cards can be processed through the reproducer to punch the students' responses and then through a card printer to obtain a rapid printout of the responses. If the cards are run through the sorter first, the answers can be ordered in various ways before the printing. This technique is particularly useful for formative tests since patterns of item responses, the basis for formative decisions, can be inspected from the printout. Easily learned routines can be set up for the use of these machines to expedite scoring.

If a school owns or has access to any optical scanning machine, the burdensome clerical work associated with test scoring can be all but eliminated and the reporting of test results greatly speeded up. Judgment must be exercised as to when it is desirable and more efficient to machine-score tests instead of correcting them manually. In the case of formative tests, it may be best to have students correct the tests themselves immediately, and later to process them by machine for a more detailed analysis of response patterns. Quizzes given to small classes may be more efficiently and quickly scored by hand according to a simple answer key. Essay examinations will have to be hand-scored, at least for the immediate future. However, there is little doubt that machines can score longer multiple-choice examinations administered to regular-sized classes more cheaply, quickly, and accurately than is possible manually.

The student records responses with an ordinary number 2 pencil on a specially calibrated answer sheet. All that the teacher need do is bring the answer sheet along with the scoring key to the machine operator. The sheets can be scored rapidly, at the rate of twenty to thirty per minute, by the optical scanner. The machine will print a raw score for subtests and the total test on the side of each answer sheet. Perhaps the most important benefit associated with using such equipment is that it will also produce a computer card for each student containing an identification number and responses to each question on the exam. These cards can be processed in various ways by the sorter, but—more important—they can be used as input to a computer for test and item analysis.

Test and Item Analysis

Small computers, which are available in many school systems, can handle test analyses. Moreover, prepackaged programs for test scoring and statistical analyses are available, which teachers can very quickly learn how to operate.

The punched output from a test-scoring machine and another card describing the test (number of questions, options, examinations, and keyed answers) become the basic input to the computer.

The computer, depending on the program used, can produce various kinds of output (Figure 4–12 depicts the actual output produced by a small computer using a program that accepts punched cards from the optical scanner as basic input):

1. A card for each student with an 0 or 1 for each question depending on whether it was answered incorrectly (0) or correctly (1). This card yields very valuable formative data.
2. A card containing each student's raw score for each subtest and the total test. Both this and the previous card can become part

1. Pass-fail for each item; raw scores on two subtests and total raw score; percent each raw score is of the possible total. This is produced on IBM cards.

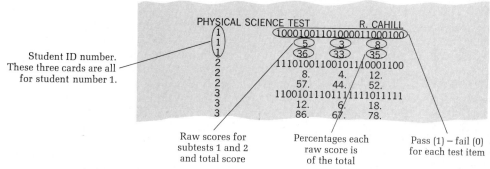

Student ID number. These three cards are all for student number 1.

PHYSICAL SCIENCE TEST   R. CAHILL

Raw scores for subtests 1 and 2 and total score

Percentages each raw score is of the total

Pass (1) − fail (0) for each test item

2. Printout of each student's performance.

Student identification

IDENT	NO. RIGHT	NO. WRONG	NO. OMITTED	RIGHTS AS PERCENT OF POSSIBLE	RIGHTS CORRECTED GUESSING
1	8	15	0	34	5
2	12	11	0	52	10
3	18	5	0	78	17
4	9	14	0	39	6
5	10	13	0	43	7
6	5	18	0	21	1
7	9	14	0	39	6
8	8	15	0	34	5
9	6	17	0	26	2
10	9	14	0	39	6
11	17	6	0		16
12	15				13
13	6				
14	8				

Class listing by ID number for total test

3. Item discrimination and difficulty indices.

ITEM NUMBERS	DISCRIMINATION INDEX	DIFFICULTY INDEX
1	.4343	.8965
2	.3382	.6896
3	.5480	.1379
4	.2433	.2758
5	.2090	.3793
6	.0781	.3448
7	.5063	.3793
8	.4632	

4. Reliability and standard error of measurement for the total test.

RELIABILITY	.67184
ST. ERROR MEAS.	2.05454

Figure 4-12 Sample computer output from a test-analysis program.

of an information system maintained on each student for later evaluation.

3. An index of item difficulty and discrimination (see Figures 4-6 and 4-7). These indices for each question are useful in updating each item in an item pool.

4. The Kuder-Richardson reliability index, formula 20, for each subtest and the total test (see Figure 4-8).

5. The standard error of measurement, an absolute index of test reliability (see Figure 4-11).

In Summary: Computers

In sum, then, the computer can quickly and accurately provide teachers working on the development of an item pool with the necessary evidence for item and test refinement (see Chapter 7, Item Writing and Item Selection). Its use eliminates the uneasiness many teachers experience when asked to compute test statistics, as well as the actual time-consuming computations. Further, it radically reduces the need to train teachers in statistical techniques, computations, and the use of statistical formulas. The machine alters the teacher's role from that of producer to that of consumer of test- and item-analysis data. It should be noted here that the new hand calculators are so versatile and easy to operate that they also reduce time-consuming hand calculations and make it easy for the teacher to calculate test statistics.

While many teachers might feel apprehensive over the thought of using a computer, the actual mechanics are very easily mastered, given proper guidance by the operator in charge of the equipment. Teachers do not learn actually to operate the computer but merely how to set up the input in the form of a data deck, which is then left for the operator to process.

Not all school systems have an optical scanner or a computer. Also, systems which have a small computer might find that their machine does not have enough memory capacity to perform the test scoring and analysis described above. This need not be a reason to forgo the time- and labor-saving assistance the computer can contribute to the development of an evaluation system. A school system without the necessary equipment should be able to affiliate with an outside computer center. Even school systems with adequate machinery for the requisite analyses find that an affiliation with a computer center can give their evaluation system additional flexibility. For example, the larger and more versatile machines, as well as the skills of programmers and systems experts generally found in universities, can result in an increased capability to improve tests used for summative and formative evaluation.

GRADING

A teacher continually evaluates students' performance, without necessarily grading that performance. The teacher praises correct responses, calls attention to errors, points out strengths and weaknesses, and in short judges the quality of a student's performance or product without assigning a grade of A, B, or C, etc. This of course is what we mean by formative evaluation. Most schools, however, require that teachers periodically grade their students. In elementary and secondary schools this requirement usually falls due every 6 or 8 weeks; in colleges it generally occurs only at the end of a semester. These grades are generally entered on a report card and recorded on a student's cumulative record card. In addition to these required grades, teachers often assign a grade to summative tests or other assignments and use these grades to arrive at the report card grade.

Traditionally grades have been used to provide information to parents and students about achievement; to serve as incentives for studying; to certify the successful completion of a grade or level of education; to select students for a particular curriculum, track, or program; to satisfy administrative record-keeping requirements; and to assist students in educational and occupational planning (Warren, 1975). (For a detailed history of grading practices the reader is referred to Cureton, 1971.) Educators, students, and parents have often attacked each of these functions and the very process of grading itself (see Ebel, 1974; Terwilliger, 1977; Warren, 1975, 1977 for a detailed discussion of the pros and cons of grading). Despite critics, assigning grades to students is still very much a part of education and undoubtedly will continue to be for the foreseeable future.

Any discussion of grading techniques must begin with the clear understanding that assigning a grade to a student's performance or product is a judgmental, value-laden process. It is one thing for a teacher to praise a student's essay or point out incorrect spelling, poor grammar, errors of fact, or mistakes in computations or reasoning; it is quite another to give a composition a grade of A, a term paper a grade of B, or a summative test a grade of C. There is no statistical or completely objective method that can be used to assign grades to a student's test score or a student's product; ultimately a judgment of the worth or value of that score or product must be made by the teacher.

Fairness in Grading

Since the consequences of a grade can be serious, whatever factors ultimately influence the assignment of grades, the process of grading not only must be fair, but must be so perceived by those whom it affects. In order to help ensure fairness in grading, the bases on which grades are assigned should be made as explicit as possible. Unfortunately, extraneous factors, such as the student's home background, speech, sex, sociability, appearance, and personality, can unconsciously influence a teacher when a grade is being assigned. Teachers must continually be on guard against the subtle influence of these extraneous factors when assigning a grade to a student's test score or product.

The student should be told whether or not the overall grade on the report card reflects effort, growth, or a determination of the degree to which the student is successful in attaining the course objectives. It is our position that the grade should reflect achievement of the course objectives. If necessary, effort, conduct, and other social or classroom factors should receive a separate grade but—as far as is humanly possible—should not influence the assignment of the course grade. Obviously this is a value judgment on our part—a judgment some will disagree with. However, we make the assumption that the course grade should reflect a level of achievement, not motivational or personal factors.

The student should also know how performance on a test or some other assignment will be converted into a grade; how various test scores or grades assigned to these will be weighted in arriving at an overall grade; how other assignments or class performance will be weighted in the overall grading process. The teacher needs to be clear about what the overall grade reflects; does it indicate how the student performs relative to his or her peers (norm-referencing), or does it reflect some standard of performance that is independent of how others in the class perform (criterion-referencing)? These questions need to be carefully considered by a teacher when grades are being determined. Let us examine several methods that have been used to convert the score on a summative test into a grade. (For more detailed discussion of these and other grading practices the reader is referred to Ebel, 1974; Gronlund, 1974; Terwilliger, 1971, 1977.)

Methods of Grading

Grading on the basis of percent correct

Perhaps the most common method teachers use to grade their classroom tests is a scale of 0 to 100. Points can be assigned to each item on the test so that the total number of points adds up to 100; alternatively, the number of raw score points attained is converted to a percentage by dividing the number correct by the total number of points possible. (If the student gets 37 items correct out of 50, the percentage correct is 74). Percentages are translated into A's, B's, C's, D's, and F's (sometimes with a plus or minus gradation added) according to a widely accepted popular convention: 100–90=A, 89–80=B, 79–70=C, 69–60=D; and anything below 60=F. Using this system, a grade for a marking period is attained either by averaging the grades on each test or by averaging the percentage mark on each test and converting the average percentages to an overall letter grade.

This system is *presumably* based on absolute judgments about students' performance. That is, for any student the percent correct, the grade assigned, or both, are independent of how his or her classmates do on the test (Airasian & Madaus, 1972; Terwilliger, 1971). While this system is widely used and seemingly unambiguous, there are several problems associated with it that the teacher should be aware of.

First, this system, while not linked directly to norm-referenced performance, is not necessarily criterion-referenced. That is, unless the test consists of items directly keyed to a well-defined domain of behaviors or tasks, the percentage score or equivalent grade tells nothing about what a student can or cannot do in an absolute sense. Further, when more than one objective is sampled in a summative test, which is most often the case, identical scores are not directly comparable. For example, suppose that two students have scored 85 percent. One student could do well on items measuring cell A.1 in Table 4-1 and poorly on those measuring cell B.2 and obtain a percent score of 85 and a grade of B; another student could do well on items keyed to objective B.2 and poorly on those related to objective A.1 and also receive a percent score of 85, or a grade of B. Neither grade tells us anything about the particular strengths and weaknesses of the two students—the identical percentages are not comparable in any performance-based sense (Airasian & Madaus, 1972). This lack of a performance referent and lack of comparability between students is not a problem if the summative test is designed to sample across a specification matrix and provide an overall index of general achievement in relation to the course specifications.

Another common difficulty associated with grades based on percentage marking is that neither the grades nor the percentages are comparable across tests. The percent correct is a direct reflection of the general ease or difficulty of the test as a whole (Terwilliger, 1971). That is, 80 percent on a summative test which was composed of relatively easy knowledge items may not be comparable to 80 percent on a test measuring more difficult, higher-level behaviors. If one simply averages the two percents together to arrive at an overall grade, then the 80 percent on the easy test would count equally with the 80 percent obtained on the more difficult test.

There is still another problem associated with combining percent scores or grades based on percentages in arriving at an overall summative grade. Suppose a teacher has given two summative tests, X and Y. On test X the percents ranged from 50 to 100, while on test Y they ranged from 75 to 100. For whatever reason, test Y was easier than test X, and there was less variability in scores. If the teacher were simply to average the two percentages, the average percentage—and consequently the grade—would be determined largely by performance on test X. This can be seen if we compare the performance of two students, Martha and Sarah, on the two tests. Martha received the highest percent (100 percent) on test X and the lowest on test Y (75 percent), while for Sarah the reverse was true: she received the lowest percentage on test X (50 percent) and the highest on test Y (100 percent). Martha's average score was 87.5, which was assigned a grade of B. Sarah's average score was 75, assigned a grade of C. However test X and test Y did not contribute equally to the overall percentage score and hence to the grade. This is because the contribution that a test makes to a composite score is a function of the variability of the scores on the test. If the teacher does not care about the relative contribution of each test, then obviously there is no problem. However, the teacher should be aware that the two tests are not contributing equally to

106

the overall grade. If, on the other hand, the teacher wishes both tests to contribute equally to the final grade, then the scores need to be adjusted to take into account the variability of the two measures. A method of adjusting scores according to the standard deviation will be described below when we discuss z scores or standard scores in grading. An alternative suggested by Gronlund (1974) is to use the range (the highest score minus the lowest score) to adjust for variability. In our example, the range for test X is 50 (100–50); for test Y, 25 (100–75). If the teacher multiplies each score on test Y by two, thus weighting the ranges equally, then each test will contribute equally to the average percentage score. Figure 4-13 illustrates this procedure. Notice that if the teacher makes the value judgment that tests X and Y should contribute equally to the final grade, the variability of the two tests must be made equal. Notice also that when the variability of the test Y is adjusted, Martha and Sarah receive identical weighting averages and now, presumably, identical overall grades of B.

Very often teachers make the value judgment that a particular test, say the final exam, should contribute more to the overall grade than, let us say, a unit test. Using the same data as in Figure 4-13, let us assume that test Y with a range of 25 points is the final exam and test X with a range of 50 points is the unit exam. One could expect less variability in the final in a mastery-learning situation. The teacher wants the final (test Y) to count twice as heavily as the unit test (test X) in determining the overall grade. Since the range on the final is half that of the unit exam, each final score must be multiplied by a factor of 4 before the final can count twice as much; this would give the final a range of 100, twice that of the unit exam. (Alternatively, one could divide the scores of the unit test by a factor of 4. Figure 4-14 illustrates this procedure. It is clear from Figure 4-14 that Sarah's overall grade changes dramatically when the test scores are weighted to actually reflect the value of the teacher's judgment on the relative importance of the two evalua-

Range on test X = 100 − 50 = 50
Range on test Y = 100 − 75 = 25
Range on test X is twice that of test Y. Therefore, to have the score on test Y contribute equally with that on test X, multiple each Y score by two.

	Martha's actual score	Martha's weighted score	Sarah's actual score	Sarah's weighted score
Test X	100	100	50	50
Test Y	75	150	100	200
Total	175	250	150	250
Average	÷2	÷3	÷2	÷3*
	87.5	83.3	75.0	83.3

*To find the weighted average the teacher divides by 3, because test Y in effect is counted twice and test X once.

Figure 4-13 Adjusting scores on two tests to equate their contribution to a final grade.

tions. The concept of the variability of the two tests is crucial. A teacher who thinks that merely doubling the final grade weights it twice as much as the unit test is mistaken. Doubling the final score will result in averages identical to those obtained in Figure 4-13, and in fact Martha and Sarah will receive the same overall average, 83.3, and hence the same grade.

To generalize the example, the unit test range is divided by the range on the final exam, and this value is multiplied by the desired weight that the final has relative to the unit test. Thus in figure 4-13, where we wish both tests to be weighted equally, we see that $50/25 = 2$, multiplied by the relative weight of 1. Therefore each score on test Y is multiplied by 2. The weighted scores are added, and the average is found by dividing by the factor we multiplied by plus 1.

In Figure 4-14, where we wanted the final to count twice as much as the unit test, we see that $50/25 = 2$, multiplied by the weight of 2, which is 4. Each student's final grade is multiplied by 4, and the average is found by

Range on unit exam = (100 − 50) = 50
Range on final exam = (100 − 75) = 25
Range on unit exam is twice that of final.

Therefore, to have the final score contribute twice as much as the unit score, multiply each final score by four or divide each unit score by two.

	Martha's actual score	Martha's weighted score	Sarah's actual score	Sarah's weighted score
Test X unit exam	100	100	50	50
Test Y final exam	75	300	100	400
Total	175	400	150	450
Average	÷2	÷5*	÷2	÷5*
	87.5	80.0	75.0	90

*To find the weighted average the teacher divides by 5 because test Y in effect is counted four times and test X once.

Figure 4-14 Adjusting scores on two tests so that one contributes twice as much as the other to the final grade.

dividing the weighted sum by 4 plus 1. This can be further generalized to any number of test scores for any number of weights.

Assigning grades according to a predefined cutoff point

In this system the teacher makes a judgment about the level of performance on a test that will be accepted as indicative of mastery; that is, the teacher decides on a cutoff point or score. Scores above the cutoff point are assigned a grade of "pass," "satisfactory," or "mastery," while those below it are assigned a grade of "fail," "unsatisfactory," or "lack of mastery." There are several ways to determine the cutoff point. The first is simply to say that the student must answer a fixed percentage (usually 70–85 percent) of the items correctly; the problem with this approach is that the percentage set is arbitrary, depending on how strict or lenient the teacher is. Adjusting downward the percentage of

items answered correctly will generally mean that more students are classified as mastering or passing, but Glass (1977) points out that such judgments are subject to whim and idiosyncrasy and questions the meaning of classifications based on such judgments. Very complex statistical formulae are sometimes offered as a way of setting cutoff points, but the pros and cons of these methods are still debated; in any event these formulae are too technical to be useful to most teachers.

Another approach is to use the past performance of other students as the criterion. This technique takes norm-referenced judgments and uses them to form the basis for future criterion-referenced judgments. For example, the average score of past classes on a given test could become the cutoff score for mastery for succeeding classes. Under mastery we feel that all students can obtain a grade of A. Therefore we suggest that the score assigned an A on a summative test given in the past becomes the cutoff score in determining whether or not students now are certified as having mastered the material. It needs to be clearly understood that the establishing of a criterion score in this way is in fact based on the performance of former classes.

There is another method of determining grades by making judgments about cutoff scores. This method uses estimated norms as the standards. The teacher looks at the test items and—on the basis of knowledge of these items and of performance of past classes—makes two judgments. First, the teacher, after considering the test, asks what score (number of items right) a student must get so that it can be said that this student is doing outstanding work and deserves a grade of A. Next, the teacher asks what minimum number of items the student must get correct in order to pass—that is, to be given a D. These two judgments, rooted in experience, reflect the teacher's standards for outstanding work and for the minimal acceptable performance. These two points can be plotted on a graph on which one axis represents raw scores and the other represents percentages or grades. On

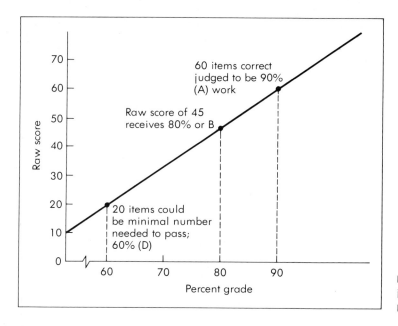

Figure 4-15 Determining grades by judgmentally establishing two score points.

the 70-item test illustrated in Figure 4-15 the teacher has decided that the student must answer 60 items correctly to get an A (90 percent) and 20 items correctly in order to get a D (60 percent). Since two points determine a straight line, the percentage grade associated with the remaining raw scores can be read from the graph. Thus a raw score of 45 receives a grade of 80 percent (B). With this technique there is no fixed percentage of A's, B's, C's, etc., that the teacher will assign. Theoretically all students could be given an A. It needs to be pointed out that a grade or classification ("pass," "fail," "mastery," etc.) using this system tells us nothing about a student's specific strengths and weaknesses but rather reflects the teacher's judgment, based on experience, about the overall summative achievement of the student—still to a degree of subjective judgment. One problem with this technique is that of combining grades on several tests or assignments derived in this manner to arrive at an overall grade. The problem of variability affecting the contribution of each test or assignment to the overall grade, as discussed in the preceding section, still remains.

Grading on the curve

In grading on a curve the raw scores on a test are arranged in rank order, and grades are distributed according to a fixed percent which approximates a normal distribution. The percentage allocations generally are A's, 10 percent; B's, 20 percent; C's, 40 percent; D's, 20 percent; F's, 10 percent. As with other techniques of grading there are weaknesses associated with grading on a curve. However, we feel that the drawbacks associated with this system of grading are especially serious. There are four problems with grading on a curve (Terwilliger, 1977):

1. Teacher-made tests—especially in a mastery-learning situation—are not designed to yield a normal score distribution. In fact, teacher-made tests generally are negatively skewed; that is, scores tend to pile up at the high end of the score range.
2. The typical class size is too small to expect a normal distribution.
3. An extremely competitive environment is created by assuming in advance a particular portion of A's, B's, C's, etc. for a given class.

4. Assigning a grade on the curve avoids explicit consideration about the quality or worth of the achievement or work.

In addition to these four weaknesses the problem of combining or weighting grades on several measures to arrive at an overall summative grade still remains.

Standard scores as a basis for arriving at an overall grade

One approach to grading is to convert each raw score on the test into a z score or standard score. A major advantage is that a student's z scores across several tests can be directly compared. Further, since z scores and standard scores are expressed in terms of standard deviation units, weighting can be directly applied to them. As long as they are based on the same class, z and standard scores on different tests can be directly compared across individuals and averaged to arrive at a weighted overall z or standard score on several summative tests or assignments. The use of z or standard scores is a more refined way of taking into account differences in the variability of performance on two or more tests, when weighting them to arrive at an overall grade. We saw previously how the range could be used to adjust for differences in variability. Before discussing how grades can be assigned to z scores and standard scores, let us consider in more detail how they can be computed and used.

Consider three students in a class with raw scores on two quizzes and one test as shown in Table 4-4. Also assume that the test is weighted twice as heavily as either quiz in obtaining the student's final average. The appropriate weighting is indicated in the column labeled "Weighted total."

As can be seen from Table 4–4, Joe scores highest of the three students on both quizzes but lowest on the test. Mary scores highest on the test, lowest on quiz 2, and in the middle on quiz 1. John scores in the middle on quiz 2 and the test and lowest on quiz 1. The problem is one that every teacher must face—how to compare the performance of these students across several tests. One possible approach would be to take the total number of raw score points obtained by each student on all three measures. These figures are given in Table 4-4 in the column labeled "Total." On the basis of these totals, Mary appears to have performed best and Joe worst. In Table 4-4 the weighted totals that result when the test score is multiplied by 2 preserve this same relationship.

The question is whether either of the two sets of totals in Table 4-4 is appropriate for assigning grades to students. The answer is no. One reason is that more information than is captured by either of the two totals is necessary. The scores need to be equated somehow. One way of doing this is to convert the raw scores to a percent of the total possible number of correct answers. In our example, each quiz had a maximum raw score of 20 points, and the test had 100 possible points. Use of the percent of total as a test mark is, as we saw, a fairly common procedure followed by teachers. Table 4-5 converts the raw scores in Table 4-4 to percents and shows the weighted mean of these percents, i.e., the test score weighted twice as heavily as either quiz.

Table 4-5 results in inferences different from those to be drawn from Table 4-4. In Table 4-5, Joe and John have switched posi-

TABLE 4-4 RAW SCORES FOR THREE STUDENTS

STUDENT	Quiz 1	Quiz 2	Test	Total	Weighted total
Joe	12	16	75	103	178
Mary	10	12	95	117	222
John	9	13	83	105	188

TABLE 4-5 PERCENTS OF TOTAL POSSIBLE SCORES

STUDENT	Quiz 1	Quiz 2	Test	Weighted mean
Joe	60	80	75	72.5
Mary	50	60	95	75.0
John	45	65	83	69.0

tions, with John now having the lowest rank. How defensible is this approach? The approach used in Table 4-5 is an improvement on the total points method but is still not right. In averaging the percents, one is assuming that Joe's score of 60 on quiz 1 is the same as Mary's score of 60 on quiz 2. The assumption is made that the same scores on the different measures are equal. This assumption, as we saw earlier, does not generally hold.

There is a way to make the scores on different measures comparable and thus to average across measures. More information about how the total class did on the measures is necessary, however. The two essential pieces of information for each measure are the mean—a measure of average or central tendency (see Figure 4-3)—and standard deviation (see Figure 4-5), a measure of variability. These values are shown in Table 4-6.

Using the values in Table 4-6, one can calculate scores for each student that reflect how his or her performance compares with that of the total class. These new scores, called "z scores," express each student's raw score in terms of standard deviation units above or below the class mean. The formula for calculating the z score is

$$z \text{ score} = \frac{(\text{raw student's score}) - (\text{class mean})}{(\text{class standard deviation})}$$

Applying this formula to the raw scores in Table 4-4 in conjunction with the means and standard deviations in Table 4-6, one obtains the z score values shown in Table 4-7. Since these z values are comparable across tests, a weighted mean can easily be calculated by applying the desired weight directly to the scores in question. These weighted means are shown in Table 4-7. The formula transforms

each quiz or test distribution into a new distribution with a mean of 0 and a standard deviation of 1.

Some interpretation of the z values in Table 4-7 may be helpful. Joe's score for quiz 1 is +2.0, indicating that he scored 2 full standard deviations higher than the class mean (now set at 0) on this measure. Recall (see Tables 4-4 and 4-6) that in the original distribution Joe's score was 12, the class mean was 11, and the standard deviation was .5. Similarly, on quiz 2 Mary's raw score (12) was 2 standard deviations (standard deviation = 1 lower than the class mean, 14). Thus, Mary's z score for quiz 2 is −2.0, that is, 2 standard deviation units below the new mean of 0. The weighted means may now be interpreted as indicating the relative performance of these three students. Recall that our teacher valued the test twice as heavily as either quiz. Thus Joe has clearly performed best, with a weighted average z score of +.75; Mary was a second best, with a weighted average z score of −.75; and John was worst, with a weighted average z score of −1.3.

The reader should note the dramatic difference in interpretation of results when the methods in Tables 4-4, 4-5, and 4-6 are used to judge students' performance. Joe, who was judged lowest in Table 4-4, moved to the middle rank in Table 4-5; but when the variability of the test was taken into account in Table 4-7, he was judged as the best student.

The method of z scores is different from what most students and teachers are accustomed to use in determining averages for grading purposes (generally the method used in Table 4-5). The method of z scores for

TABLE 4-6 CLASS MEAN AND STANDARD DEVIATION

	Quiz 1	Quiz 2	Test
Class mean	11.0	14.0	85.0
Class standard deviation	.5	1.0	20.0

TABLE 4-7 z SCORES FOR EACH STUDENT

STUDENT	Quiz 1	Quiz 2	Test	Weighted total	Weighted average z*
Joe	+2.0	+2.0	−.5	3.0	+0.75
Mary	−2.0	−2.0	+.5	−3.0	−0.75
John	−4.0	−1.0	−.1	−5.2	−1.3

*Divide weighted total by 4 since the test counts twice.

determining averages must therefore be adequately explained to students before it is used to assign grades. However, when it is presented as a way of equating scores from various tests, and of rewarding students for exceptional performance on a particularly difficult test, or of protecting them from penalties for poorer performances on a test on which the whole class did poorly, the method should be acceptable to most students. It should also be made clear to students, however, that poor performance on a test in which the majority of the class does well is weighted more negatively when the z score approach is used.

Some teachers do not like z scores, because they are expressed in terms of decimals and negative numbers. This drawback can easily be overcome by transforming the z scores to standard scores, where the mean is set at 500 and the standard deviation at 100, by multiplying the obtained z score by 100 and adding 500. Thus z scores are transformed to standard scores by using the following formula: standard score = $100z + 500$. The weighted mean z scores in Table 4–7 become 575, 425, and 370 respectively. The standard score of 575 shows that Joe is ¾ of a standard deviation (75 points) above the new mean (500). Notice that this transformation is the same used by the College Entrance Examination Board, which reports SAT and achievement scores in terms of a mean of 500 and a standard deviation of 100. The advantage of using the overall z scores is that the scores can be weighted in any way the teacher wants, and an overall weighted z score can be calculated and grades can be based on this z-weighted score. This approach overcomes the problem discussed above of different tests' not contributing to the overall grade in the way in which the teacher would like. Once the teacher has z scores for each test or assignment, weights can be applied to each to arrive at an overall weighted z score.

The problem remains: How does one assign an overall grade to the weighted z score shown in Table 4–7 above? Once again, judgment enters. Remember that z scores are norm-referenced units; that is, they describe the student's performance in terms of distance from the average performance of the class. Given this norm-referencing orientation, one approach is for the teacher to decide in advance how many A's, B's, C's, D's, etc., to award. These percentages need *not* to be fixed in reference to a normal distribution. The teacher could decide that 40 percent of the scores will receive A's. Once a distribution for each grade is determined, the overall z scores can be arranged in rank order and grades assigned to the scores according to the predetermined formula. However, when the percentage of grades is fixed in advance, competition among students is increased, and this for many teachers is a drawback.

Another method is to arrange the weighted overall z score in rank order from high to low and to inspect the distribution for naturally occurring gaps. Letter grades can then be assigned where these gaps occur. One weakness in this approach is that when the class is used as a sole referent, differences between classes are not taken into account. However, we feel that if a teacher wishes to make norm-referenced grades and to differentially weight tests and assignments, then converting to standard or z scores is a good approach. When adopting a mastery approach to instruction, the z score to which an A was assigned in previous years can be used as the standard of mastery. Under mastery conditions most students should be able to obtain the z score equivalent of an A of previous years.

In the final analysis the assigning of a grade of A, B, C, D, or "pass-fail" depends on a subjective judgment by the teacher about the value of the raw score, percentage, or z score on a given summative test or on the value of some combination of tests, assignments, or both. Problems of weighting and comparing performance on several tests and assignments must be addressed when assigning an overall summative grade. Extraneous factors that might influence judgments about worth or value should be kept clearly in mind. The judgment should be based as far as is humanly possible on considerations of what constitutes an acceptable level of performance or achievement.

SUMMARY

This chapter has suggested that summative examinations may have a variety of purposes, one being simply to give grades and another being to certify competence in a given area. A test may serve to provide feedback for students or predictions of later success, among other uses. We have suggested that as the purposes vary, so will some of the procedures for developing and scoring the test. We have strongly emphasized that content validity will come only after the appropriate valuing of the behavior-content cells in a table of specifications. After all, content validity is the *sine qua non* of a final examination. The chapter was intended to give some help with ways in which one might set about weighting the parts of a test. In that section of the discussion, it was pointed out that the actual weight of elements of a test in the total score does depend upon the empirical characteristics of variance and correlation. We also discussed the problem of weighting several tests and assignments in arriving at an overall grade. Finally, different procedures for assigning grades and the judgmental nature of these processes were discussed.

EXERCISES

Objective: Construct, administer, score, and grade a summative evaluation instrument.
Preparation:

A. Gather the table of specifications prepared at the end of Chapter 2 and the test items prepared for Chapters 8 through 10.
B. If these materials are not available, you may want to review Chapter 2 and prepare a set of objectives and table of specifications. Alternatively, select or borrow such a table. Bloom, Hastings, and Madaus (1971) has several good examples.

1. *Constructing the test:* Construct a summative test following the six general steps outlined in the chapter.
   a. For step 3 explain your sampling rationale.
   b. Which criteria did you use in step 4 for ordering the items? Why?
   c. If you have essay items, ensure that your scoring scheme spells out the criteria to be used in scoring.
   d. For which of the five specific purposes is your test being constructed? How did this influence the construction process?
   e. Use Neill's checklist (1978) to review your test.
2. *Revising the test:* Revise your test using, where possible, the general steps suggested in the chapter.
   a. Note that content validity should be ensured prior to administration by having a judge other than you match the items to your specifications.
   b. After a trial (or the only) administration, compute and interpret the item statistics. How can these results be used to improve your test?
3. *Grading the test:* Select, defend, and apply a grading scheme for the test.

REFERENCES

Airasian, P. W., & Madaus, G. F. Criterion-referenced testing in the classroom. *Measurement in Education*, 1972, 3, 1–8.

Airasian, P. W., & Madaus, G. F. & Pedulla, J. J. *Minimal Competency testing.* Englewood Cliffs, N.J.: Educational Technology Publications, 1979.

American Psychological Assocation. *Guidelines and standards for education evaluation: Report of the Joint Committee of APA, AERA, NCME.* Washington, D.C.: Author, 1974.

Baldwin, T. S. Evaluation of learning in industrial education. In B. S. Bloom, J. T.

Hastings, & G. F. Madaus (Eds.), *Handbook of formative and summative evaluation of student learning.* New York: McGraw-Hill, 1971.

Bloom, B. S., Hastings, J. T., & Madaus, G. F. *Handbook of formative and summative evaluation of student learning.* New York: McGraw-Hill, 1971.

Campbell, D. T., & Fiske, D. W. Convergent and discriminant validation by the multitrait-multimethod matrix. *Psychological Bulletin*, 1959, 56, 81–105.

Carver, R. P. Two dimensions of tests: Psychometric and edumetric. *American Psychologists*, 1974, 29, 512–518.

Cronbach, L. J. *Essentials of psychological testing* (2nd ed.). New York: Harper, 1960.

Cronbach, L. J. Test validation. In R. L. Thorndike (Ed.), *Educational measurement* (2nd ed.). Washington, D.C.: American Council on Education, 1971.

Cureton, L. W. The history of grading practices. *Measurement in Education*, 1971, 1–8.

Ebel, R. L. Shall we get rid of grades? *Measurement in Education*, 1974, 1–5.

Educational Testing Service (ETS). *Making your own test* (sound filmstrip). Princeton, N.J.: Cooperative Test Division, Educational Testing Service, n.d.

Glass, G. V. *Standards and criteria* (Paper No. 10, Occasional Paper Series). Kalamazoo, Mich.: Western Michigan University, Evaluation Center, 1977.

Gronlund, N. E. *Improving marking and reporting in classroom instruction.* New York: Macmillan, 1974.

Hambleton, R. K., Eignor, D., & Swaminathan, H. *Criterion referenced test development and validation methods.* Amherst, University of Massachusetts, AERA Precision Materials Laboratory of Psychometric and Evaluation Research, 1978.

Klinckmann, E. The BSCS grid for test analysis. *BSCS Newsletter*, 1963, No. 19. pp. 17–21. (Biological Sciences Curriculum Study, University of Colorado.)

Madaus, G. F., & Airasian, P. W. Issues in evaluating student outcomes in competency based graduation programs. *Journal of Research and Development in Education*, 1977, 10(3), 79–91.

Madaus, G. F., Airasian, P. W., & Kellaghan, T. *School effectiveness: A reassessment of the evidence.* New York: McGraw-Hill, 1980.

Madaus, G. F. & McDonagh, J. T. Minimum competency testing: Unexamined assumptions and unexplored negative outcomes. In Lennon, R. T. (Ed.), Impactive changes on measurement, *New Directions for testing and measurement*, 3, 1979, pp. 1–14.

Madaus, G. F. & Macnamara, J. *Public examinations: A study of the Irish Leaving Certificate.* Dublin, Ireland: Educational Research Centre, St. Patrick's College, 1970.

McClung, M. S. Competency testing: Potential for discrimination. *Clearing-house Review*, August 1977, pp. 439–443.

Messick, S. The standards problem: meaning and values in measurement and evaluation. *American Psychologist*, 1975, 30, 955–966.

Neill, S. B. *The competency movement*, (AASA Critical Issues Report). Sacramento, Calif.: Education News Service, 1978.

Stanley, J. C. Reliability. In R. L. Thorndike (Ed.), *Educational Measurement* (2nd ed.). Washington, D.C.: American Council on Education, 1971.

Terwilliger, J. S. *Assigning grades to students.* Glenview, Ill.: Scott, Foresman, 1971.

Terwilliger, J. S. Assigning grades: Philosophical issues and practical recommendations. *Journal of Research and Development in Education*, 1977, 10(3), 21–39.

Warren, J. R. *The continuing controversy over grades* (TM Report 51). ERIC Clearinghouse on Tests, Measurement and Evaluation. Princeton, N.J.: Educational Testing Service, 1975.

Warren, J. R. Evaluation motivation and grading. In *Evaluation and Student Motivation, UCLA Educator*, 1977, 19(2), 22–25.

Wood, R. Multiple choice: A state of the art report. *Evaluation in Education: International Progress*, 1977, 1(3), 191–280.

5 Diagnostic Evaluation

Chapter Contents

We saw in Chapters 1 and 2 that learners bring to a new task a unique history which differentially influences how well, how fast, or whether they eventually master the task. We also saw that much of the variation in the learning of any task may be accounted for by variation in the achievement, motivational, and attitudinal history of the students. Further, we argued that *if* all learners possess the necessary cognitive and affective prerequisites, and *if* the quality of instruction is appropriate to the students' backgrounds and characteristics, then all or most students should be able to master the new task.

INTRODUCTION: THE ROLE OF DIAGNOSTIC EVALUATION

Diagnostic evaluation is an essential ingredient of good teaching, undertaken to adapt instruction to the needs and backgrounds of learners. "Diagnosis" in education is not limited to the identification of deficiencies or problems. It is a broader concept that includes the identification of strengths and special talents. A teacher diagnoses in order to facilitate learning, not to label a student. The results should not be used to shunt students who lack prerequisites into some watered-down course where they languish indefinitely; the purpose is to plan a program that will remove blocks to learning. Further, by identifying students who have already mastered some or all of the material, experiences can be planned that build on strengths and forestall boredom and complacency.

At the beginning of a course or new unit the traditional practice is to start all students at an imaginary "zero point." That is, the implicit assumption is made that no student has mastered any of the planned objectives but that all have the cognitive, affective, and psychomotor prerequisites necessary to begin the course or unit. This assumption of homogeneity of educational background is dubious (Balow, 1962; Goodlad & Anderson, 1959; Yates, 1966). A crucial function of diagnostic evaluation is the identification of students who fall above or below the zero point, so that they may be placed in the most beneficial instructional sequence.

Diagnostic evaluation performed prior to instruction, then, has placement as its primary function and may take several forms. It may seek to determine the "readiness" of a student to begin school. Subsequently, diagnostic evaluation may focus on entry behaviors or skills judged to be prerequisite for the course or unit. It may attempt to establish whether the student has mastered some or all of the objectives, which finding would permit the student to begin at a more advanced level. Finally, diagnostic evaluation may aim to classify students according to certain characteristics—interest, personality, background, aptitude, skill, or instructional history—hypothesized to be related to a particular teaching strategy or instructional method.

One of the problems of students who have not been successful, and in particular of disadvantaged students, is that they often have been required to begin a course or unit without the basic prerequisites and they fall below our imaginary zero point. Therefore it may be necessary to first help some students, and particularly those who are disadvantaged, to acquire the prerequisite skills. (This, of course, is the objective of many of the compensatory educational programs developed under Title I of the Elementary and Secondary Education Act.)

Some students, on the other hand, may be well beyond the zero point, having mastered all or many of the competencies the course or unit has been designed to develop. Another form of diagnosis involves the determination of the degree to which a student already has mastery over the objectives planned for a course. Students who have already achieved all or a number of planned objectives should either elect another course or have instruction start at the most appropriate place. Proper placement can help avoid boredom and lack of interest for those who have already mastered objectives and can avoid discouragement and frustration for those lacking prerequisites.

Diagnostic evaluation for this type of placement can begin by pretesting the students with an alternative form of the summative examination designed for the course. A student who reaches some previously determined level of mastery on the test could be given credit for the course and be placed in a more advanced one or, in the case of nonsequential courses, be allowed to elect another course. Such a system works particularly well at higher levels of education, where scheduling and elective courses allow for more individualization of a student's program. In self-contained classrooms or in systems that do not permit flexible scheduling, the teacher can at least make provisions for an enrichment program of more advanced work for students who have displayed an adequate level of mastery on the summative pretest. Techniques for constructing summative examinations are discussed in Chapters 4, 7, 8, 9, and 10 and will therefore not be taken up here.

Some students might not display the required level of mastery on the summative pretest but still possess some of the competencies the course seeks to develop. If this is the case, it may be possible to tailor the course more intelligently by locating the optimum starting point for instruction somewhere beyond the imaginary zero point. If a teacher has broken the course down into formative units and has built formative tests for each unit as described in Chapter 6, then these tests may be used to diagnose not only the appropriate unit at which instruction should begin but also the proper starting point within the structure of that unit. When formative tests are not yet available, a teacher can gain valuable diagnostic information through a careful analysis of errors on more traditional types of teacher-made tests used as pretests for placement purposes.

Diagnostic evaluation performed while instruction is under way has as its primary function determining the underlying causes of repeated learning deficiencies that have not responded to remedial instruction. As we saw in Chapter 2, the diagnostic evaluation of children with learning disabilities is a key feature of Public Law 94–142 and its state counterparts, such as Chapter 766 in Massachusetts. Under these laws the teacher plays a central role: initially identifying a child with learning disabilities, referring the student for further evaluation, and also assisting in the collection and interpretation of data about the child. After evaluation the teacher, working with others, helps to design an appropriate individual educational plan (IEP) for the child and is then responsible for implementing it.

The causes for a student's difficulty may be related to inappropriate goals, to instruction methods, or to materials. If these can be ruled out as causes of repeated difficulty, the teacher will then need to consider whether the learning difficulty may involve causes which are physical, emotional, cultural, or environmental in nature. If these kinds of learning blocks are suspected, the teacher will refer students to a guidance counselor, school psychologist, or outside agency. Such referrals give both the teacher and the student the benefit of special training and expertise.

In this chapter we shall first discuss steps that a teacher can follow in determining a child's readiness to begin school. We shall then turn to steps a teacher can follow to determine the proper placement in the instructional sequence. Next we shall look at the part commercially available tests can play in the process of placement and diagnosis. Finally, we shall consider steps the teacher can follow when a student gives evidence of repeated inability to profit from instruction.

EVALUATION OF SCHOOL READINESS

Many school systems admit children to kindergarten or first grade solely on the basis of chronological age. However, a child who enters formal schooling lacking the prerequisites can be trapped in a vicious cycle of failure, frustration, anxiety, and further failure. If, on the other hand, deficiencies in socioemotional, perceptual-motor, cognitive, and language behaviors can be identified, then remedial instruction or emotional and other support can be provided. In assembling a readiness battery to screen incoming kindergarten or first-grade pupils, teachers must first decide what variables should be assessed. The literature indicates that the following are important dimensions for readiness: health, gross and fine motor coordination, general cognition and language skills, and socioemotional skills (Cazden, 1971; Kamii, 1971; D. K. Walker & Bryk, 1976).

Having decided which dimensions of readiness to assess, teachers can then either develop screening techniques themselves or select from available instruments and techniques. Many aspects of readiness can be assessed by observing the child in a controlled situation. Teachers can devise or select techniques and—more important—relevant criteria for acceptable performance. An example of specifying the relevant criteria used to judge a student's eye-hand coordination, an important component of readiness, is offered in Figure 5-1, where lines *a* through *f* are used to clarify the criteria listed.

For other dimensions of readiness, teachers may wish to select from available instruments. There are many standardized cognitive readiness measures available commercially, and checklists to assess socioemotional readiness are to be found in the research literature. There are a number of excellent sources teachers can use to locate such readiness measures (Kamii, 1971; Cazden, 1971; Gislason, 1975; Guthrie & Horne, 1971; Simon & Boyer, 1970; Rosen, 1971; Johnson & Bonmarito, 1971; Hoepfner, Strickland, Stangel, Jansen, & Patalino, 1970; Collier, 1971; Buros, 1972; Boyer, Simon, & Karafin, 1973). Gislason (1975) has developed a bibliography on school readiness testing to assist school systems that wish to develop procedures to evaluate readiness. Another source for the identification of readiness measures—as well as other types of educational and psychological tests—is *Directory of Information on Tests,* published by ERIC Clearinghouse on Tests, Measurement and Evaluation at Educational Testing Service (Backer, 1977). This monograph provides a directory of books, other printed materials, and information systems that one could consult for test-related information. It also offers strategies that might be employed in mounting an information search about potential techniques.

In selecting readiness measures, teachers should pay close attention to:

1. Special problems associated with testing young children: e.g., short attention span; distractability, novel situations; strange people administering the instrument (see Bradley & Caldwell, 1974).

2. Mode of administration (individual or group).
3. Validity. (Do the dimensions assessed by the test actually predict success in kindergarten or first grade?)
4. Reliability. (How stable are the estimates of the dimensions being assessed?)
5. The extent to which the test and test manual meet the standards set forth in APA-AERA-NCME *Standards for Educational and Psychological Tests* (APA, 1974).
6. Problems of assessing minority group children (see Oakland & Phillips, 1975).
7. Cost effectiveness of the test relative to other possible instruments.

Once the instruments and techniques have been selected and administered, the information on each incoming child may be made available to the teacher in the form of a class list. Such a list enters the children's names along a horizontal axis and the various readiness components along the vertical. A simple check ($\sqrt{}$) in one of the cells indicates a variable that the screening process identified as a possible problem for a particular child. The pattern of checks across all cells along a particular readiness dimension provides a profile of the group's readiness on that dimension.

Once deficiencies in essential characteristics of readiness have been diagnosed, then the teacher must prescribe learning experiences that will aid the child in realizing the necessary skills. Prescription is the key. Too often the evaluation of readiness has been used to *delay* instruction for some students rather than to move them more quickly into the normal instructional sequence.

DETERMINING THE PROPER PLACEMENT OF STUDENTS

Each September as students move from one grade to the next, teachers need to determine whether they have the prerequisite skills for the new academic year and, if so, the extent to which some students have already mas-

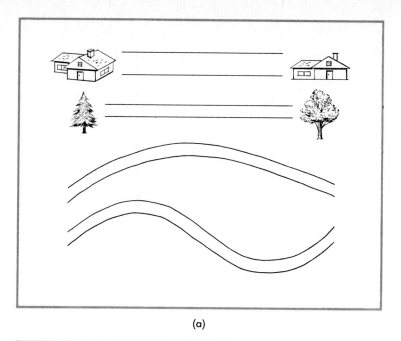

(a)

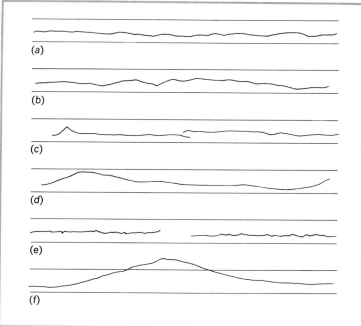

(a)

(b)

(c)

(d)

(e)

(f)

(b)

Criteria

a. Draws an unbroken line between the lines from one end to the other as shown.

b. Lifts pencil from paper but continues the line without a break as shown.

c. Lifts pencil from paper and makes a break, fork, or sharp angle as shown.

d. Touches the edge of the road as shown.

e. Makes a sketched, corrected, or broken line as shown.

f. Goes outside the edge of the road as shown.

Comments:

_____

_____

(c)

Figure 5-1 Technique and criteria for evaluating eye-hand coordination. (a) Illustrative procedures for evaluating eye-hand coordination. (Frostig. 1963, pp. 1a, 1b; items 2, 3, 6, 7. By permission of Consulting Psychologists Press, Inc. Cited by Kamaii, 1971, p. 308.) (b, c) Scoring criteria for eye-hand coordination tasks. (Frostig, 1966, pp. 18–19. By permission of Consulting Psychologists Press, Inc. Cited by Kamii, 1971, pp. 308–309.) See Kamii and Frostig for how these criteria might be used.

tered some of the planned objectives. The determination of what prerequisites are appropriate is not an easy task, and the teacher's judgment comes into play to a large extent. It is easier to detail necessary entry behaviors for sequential courses, such as reading, arithmetic, mathematics, science, and foreign languages, than for courses more self-contained, such as history or English literature. Even in the latter courses, however, such general cognitive ability as reading comprehension can be considered a prerequisite; subject-related interest and a positive attitude toward self and school might also be considered prerequisites. In the following sections we shall describe techniques for determining where in the instructional sequence the student should be placed. We shall not discuss instrument construction per se but instead focus on how information from various sources can be used in the placement process.

Records of Performance in the Previous Year

In sequential subjects, material presented in one unit often becomes the foundation of the next, and the foundation laid in one year is built upon in the next. In sequential courses failures can quickly become cumulative. This is perhaps clearest in one of the most sequential of all school subjects—the study of a foreign language. One study found that 60 percent of students who received C in first-year French or Spanish received a D or failed in the second year, while one-third who received D in the first year failed the second. It was very rare for a student to improve his or her grade from the first to the second year (Pimsleur, Sundland, & McIntyre, 1966). Because of the sequential nature of many basic elementary and secondary school subjects, diagnostic evaluation for placement purposes performed at the beginning of the year often depends heavily on the results of summative evaluations of the previous year's work.

Typically in education, summative evaluation has resulted in the student's being assigned a single score (75 percent) or grade

(C+) for the course or subject. The summative grades are sometimes used diagnostically to group, or "track," students. Thus in September a fifth-grade teacher, on the basis of summative grades in fourth-grade arithmetic, might divide the class into three groups—advanced, average, and slow—for differential instruction. The practice of using summative results in this fashion, if not planned and judiciously monitored, has dubious validity at best and can cause irreparable harm by trapping some students in a self-fulfilling prophecy of failure. Repeated failure or even continued grouping in a track for which there is a low expectation of success can destroy students' faith in their ability to perform. Even second-graders quickly learn the level of expectation the teacher has for such innocuously named reading groups as the "Robins," the "Blue Jays," and the "Cardinals." Chapter 3, Learning for Mastery, discussed how the use of gross summative measures for placement has had adverse results on self-concept.

Moreover, whatever its administrative convenience, a single grade precludes an adequate description of the student's performance on the various objectives of the course. It is unlikely that a student will have performed consistently, at the same level of competence, on all objectives. In other words, the single grade hides more than it shows. It does not reveal the variation in learning from objective to objective and therefore does not provide adequate diagnostic information for intelligent placement. An overall grade of A or B *may* indicate that the student is ready for work at the next level. However, grades of C or D give no clue as to the kind of remediation necessary before the student should begin the next year's work.

It is possible to design summative report forms that *do* indicate levels of mastery on various objectives and subskills within a course and give more diagnostic information than a single grade. The Mathematics Goal Record Card of the Winnetka, Illinois, Public Schools shown in Figure 5-2 is an example. A check in a box on the side of the goal card indicates an arithmetic ability, skill, or con-

Winnetka Public Schools

MATHEMATICS GOAL RECORD CARD 1

Pupil __________ *Teacher* __________ *Year* ____

	Check
Recognizes number groups up to 5	
Recognizes patterns of objects to 10	
Can count objects to 100	
Recognizes numbers to 100	
Can read and write numerals to 50	
Recognizes addition and subtraction symbols	
Understands meaning of the equality sign	
Understands meaning of the inequality signs	
Can count objects:	
By 2s to 20	
By 5s to 100	
By 10s to 100	
Recognizes geometric figures:	
Triangle	
Circle	
Quadrilateral	
Recognizes coins (1¢, 5¢, 10¢, 25¢)	
Knows addition combinations 10 and under using objects	
Knows subtraction combinations 10 and under using objects	
Recognizes addition and subtraction vertically and horizontally	
Shows understanding of numbers and number combinations (check one)	
1. Using concrete objects	
2. Beginning to visualize and abstract	
3. Making automatic responses without concrete objects	
Can tell time	
1. Hour	
2. Half hour	
3. Quarter hour	

	Check
Addition combinations 10 and under (automatic response)	
Subtraction combinations 10 and under (automatic response)	
Can count to 200	
Can understand zero as a number	
Can understand place value to tens	
Can read and write numerals to 200	
Can read and write number words to 20	
Uses facts in 2-digit column addition (no carrying)	
Roman numerals to XII	

CARD 2

Pupil __________ *Teacher* __________ *Year* ____

	Check
Calendar (months, days of week, dates)	
Coins and their equivalent value to 25¢	
Recognizes 50¢ coin and $1.00	
Recognizes and uses 1/2, 1/4, 1/3 of a whole	
Addition facts to 18 (aim for mastery)	
Subtraction facts to 18 (aim for mastery)	
Word problems: (check one)	
1. Can set the problem up	
2. Can understand the process involved	
3. Can notate word problems	

Comments:

Figure 5-2 Adaption of Winnetka Public Schools Mathematics Goal Record Card. (Winnetka Public Schools, undated, sides 1 and 2.)

tent which the student has mastered. Lack of a check indicates that the student has yet to master the objective in question.

Similarly, it is possible to design a cumulative record card for a given subject indicating levels of mastery of various skills and objectives across several years of schooling. Figure 5–3 shows a portion of the Brockton Public Schools Cumulative Reading Record for grades K–6. The blacked-out areas of the card indicate that the particular skill is *not* an objective in that grade. For example, under "II. Word Identification, B. Phonetic Analysis," objective 1c ("Blends and diagraphs") is not pursued in kindergarten; it is an objective in grades 1 and 2 but not thereafter. The explanation to the teacher shows that one diagonal in a cell indicates weakness while a cross diagonal indicates mastery of the skill. Not shown are those parts of the Cumulative Reading Record that report on skills related to comprehension, study skills, and literary analysis or to results of standardized diagnostic and achievement tests.

Report forms like those used in Winnetka and Brockton have both immediate and long-range benefits. Immediately, they give a clear picture of the student's strengths and weaknesses in the particular subject. Such reports convey with greater clarity than a single overall grade where the teacher or parent can work to help the student to improve. Perhaps even more important, since such reports follow students to the next grade, the new teacher is provided with information about what they still need to master. Learners' behavioral needs are identified. Individual and group remedial needs are pinpointed in terms of observed skills and objectives. Such criterion-referenced data are of more value for placement than the single summative grade or percentage.

However, even the criterion-referenced report forms, although they are an enormous improvement over a single letter grade, can mislead a teacher. Students may well have "mastered" the indicated objective at the time of reporting but may have lost this mastery over the summer months; hence the prerequisite skills and knowledge are not available in September. Thus the new teach-

er should supplement criterion-referenced competency-based report forms like the ones illustrated in Figures 5-2 and 5-3 by administering a review test on the past year's objectives and competencies. This task is greatly simplified by the fact that target objectives have already been specified. Such a review test can be teacher-made (techniques for building summative tests are detailed in Chapter 4), or it may be commercially available, supplied by the textbook publisher, or some combination of these types. Information from such a review test or tests can identify students who are in need of a refresher before beginning new material.

Diagnosis of Prerequisite Study Skills

One reason for various levels of performance in the previous year is the presence or absence of proper study skills and habits. A student who does not know how to budget time and energy, how to keep track of assignments, how to take notes, how to use a library—in a word, how to study—is at an immediate disadvantage across all areas of the curriculum. Therefore teachers at the beginning of the year should try to determine the degree to which these prerequisite study skills have been attained so that, where needed, steps can be taken to develop or improve them. One approach is to have students at the beginning of the year anonymously complete a checklist of study habits. Figure 5-4 presents a portion of such a checklist developed by one school. The complete list also contains questions in the following areas: classroom activities, examinations, study habits related to reading. After filling out the checklist the student is asked to notice those items for which "rarely" or "sometimes" was checked, and is then provided with a booklet that contains the following chapters (Bidaud, 1974):

1. A five-step method to study
2. Note-taking
3. Behavior leading to work-study skills
4. Learning to listen
5. Effective skills in taking tests, quizzes, and examinations

Brockton Public Schools ———— CUMULATIVE READING RECORD   K-6

Name _____   School _____   Birthdate _____

LAST   FIRST   MIDDLE   Mo.   Day   Year

Date Entered Brockton _____   Date Left Brockton _____

Mo.   Day   Year   Mo.   Day   Year

Instructional Level

Year	K	1	2	3	4	5	6
September							
June							

Explanation To The Teacher

A blank space indicates the child has not mastered the skill.

The headings (K, 1, 2, 3, 4, 5, 6) indicate the approximate difficulty levels of the skills making up the reading program.

Mark the column according to these directions:

1. ☐ which indicates a **Weakness** and/or need to complete.

2. ☒ which indicates **Mastery** of the skill.

Any skill marked ☐ (indicating **Weakness**) must be worked on until **Mastery** may be indicated according to the code ☒

I. Pre-Reading

A. Language Development
  1. Listening
    a. Vocabulary
    b. Thinking Skills
      (1) Classification
      (2) Sequence
        (a) Special relationship
        (b) Time relationship
        (c) Following directions
      (3) Causation
      (4) Comparison
  2. Speaking
    a. Vocabulary
    b. Talking in complete sentences
    c. Thinking Skills
      (1) Classification
      (2) Sequence
      (3) Causation
      (4) Comparison

B. Motor Skills
  1. Gross motor
  2. Fine motor
  3. Fine visual-motor
  4. Left to right progression

C. Visual Skills
  1. Body awareness
  2. Figure-ground perception
  3. Perception of spatial relationships
  4. Perception & discrimination size & shape
  5. Visual memory

D. Auditory Skills
  1. Perception of audio stimuli
  2. Recognizing rhymes & rhyming sounds
  3. Auditory memory

E. Interest Development

II. Word Identification

A. Vocabulary
  1. Configuration
  2. Sight
  3. Context clues

B. Phonetic Analysis
  1. Consonants
    a. Initial and final
    b. Medial
    c. Blends and diagraphs
    d. Silent letters
    e. Variability of consonants
  2. Vowels
    a. Long and Short
    b. Diagraphs and dipthongs
    c. Vowel principles
    d. Variability of vowels
  3. Phonograms

C. Structural Analysis
  1. Inflectional endings
  2. Identification of root words
    a. Prefixes
    b. Suffixes
  3. Compound words
  4. Contractions
  5. Syllables
    a. Meaning
    b. Auditory and visual recognition
    c. Application of vowel principles
  D. Abbreviations

III. Word Meaning

A. Sight Vocabulary
  1. Associates pictures to words
  2. Uses context clues

B. Vocabulary Development
  1. Multiple meanings
  2. Synonyms, antonyms, homonyms, etc.
  3. Classification
  4. Meaning of prefixes, suffixes, root words
  5. Selecting of dictionary meaning
  6. Figurative speech and idioms
  7. Development of vocabulary in content area
  8. Analogies

Figure 5-3 Portion of the Brockton Public Schools Cumulative Reading Record. (Brockton Public Schools, n.d., side 1.)

	Rarely	Sometimes	Usually

1. Health habits which affect studying
   a. Get at least 8 hours sleep a night.
   b. Have a regular program of physical exercise.
   c. Eat well-balanced meals.
   d. Read and study in a good light.
   e. Have regular periods for relaxation.
2. Time scheduling
   a. Maintain a daily study schedule with hours planned in advance.
   b. Have a regular place to study.
   c. Schedule study periods so that they precede or follow directly the given subject being studied.
   d. Study hard during free hours of the day to avoid doing all study at night.
   e. Make ample allowances in daily, weekly, and semester schedules for term reports and special proejcts.
   f. Have regular daily and weekly review periods.
   g. Make allowances for short, daily periods of recreation.
   h. Schedule social life so that it does not seriously interfere with studying.
3. Note taking
   a. Have a large notebook with plenty of paper.
   b. Listen to the professor for cues on what is important.
   c. Avoid trying to write each word the lecturer says.
   d. Take down only the main ideas and key facts in a lecture.
   e. Concentrate and think critically during the entire lecture or class discussion.
   f. Write down formulas, equations, and diagrams quickly and accurately.
   g. Space notes so that they are not too crowded.
   h. Go over each set of lecture notes as soon after class as possible.
   i. Organize notes so that major headings stand out from minor headings.
   j. Segregate notes in sections by courses.
4. Studying an assignment
   a. Be certain that the purpose and nature of the assignment are clear.
   b. Start to work without delay.
   c. Skim through textbook chapters to get a general picture before reading carefully.
   d. Practice self-recitation at regular intervals during reading.
   e. Keep notes of main ideas and key facts in reading assignments.
   f. Recheck written problems to be sure they are right.
   g. Build a list of unfamiliar terms.
   h. Stay with an assignment until it is completed, even though it may be difficult.
   i. Avoid distractions, noises, and useless conversation.
   j. Stop and relax briefly about once each hour.
   k. Have occasional conferences with instructor.

Figure 5-4 Study habits checklist. (Bibaud, 1974, p. 2–3.)

Each section concludes with a personal-inventory for the student to complete on the skill in question.

This type of *self*-evaluation and diagnosis reflects the importance of good study habits and recognizes the need for specific suggestions for improving these habits. An alternative to a self-evaluation would be for the teacher to administer such an inventory anonymously. On the basis of the group data a period or two could be planned for specific suggestions and guidance to improve study and work habits.

Diagnostic Assistance from the Curriculum Designer or Textbook Publisher

Teachers need to be aware that the designers of some of the newer curriculum packages suggest prerequisite skills. For example, the teachers' manual for *Study Guides for PSSC Physics* (Friedman & Stickland, 1975) suggests that only students who are facile with second-year high school algebra take the PSSC course. A diagnostic algebra test is provided to determine whether the students have sufficient skills in algebra to undertake the PSSC course. Students who need more than a short three-class review should be counseled to pursue mathematics for the year and then try PSSC the next year. In giving the diagnostic algebra test the teacher is advised to emphasize that the test is diagnostic *only* and will not be graded, in the hope of eliminating unwarranted preparations or anxiety. Another prerequisite that should be tested before starting PSSC is conversion of physical units. Recognizing that many students are weak in conversion, PSSC provides a sample lesson for the teacher to use for remediation.

Increasingly, textbook publishers are providing, as part of their supplementary materials, pretests and placement tests for use with their books. Generally there is a test for each unit or chapter in the book with each test item corresponding to a performance objective. Some publishers suggest that success on pretest items allows the student to skip those pages in the text related to the objective measured by the items.

These pretests and placement tests can aid a teacher interested in proper diagnosis and placement, but they need to be used with caution. Unlike tests built by test publishers, pretest or placement tests provided by *some* textbook publishers contain no psychometric or technical data. Information about validity and reliability is lacking. Further, when only one or two items are used to measure an objective, the student can very easily be misclassified as having mastered or not mastered an objective.

Teachers need to examine technical information about these tests when it is provided (e.g., how many items for each objective, where the items were tried out). If this type of information is not provided, teachers should use these tests with caution. Instead of placing students on the basis of these tests, they may wish to use such tests to screen them for making a more detailed diagnosis. Alternatively, the publisher's tests could be supplemented by teacher-made placement tests and the teacher's observations.

One of the outgrowths of the major curriculum projects has been the recognition that there is no single best way to organize or approach the development of a new course. These groups have perceived the need to offer diversity and variation in their approaches and materials, so that alternative routes to the same goal are open to both teachers and students. A statement by F. James Rutherford describes the rationale underlying one large project's decision to design alternative approaches and is equally applicable to other areas of the curriculum.

> Practical considerations, as well as educational and psychological theory, suggested the direction taken by Project physics. As you look out at the real world of students, teachers, and schools in this country you see that great diversity exists; and there appear to be no imminent educational or social developments likely to change that situation in the foreseeable future. It seems a matter of practical good sense, therefore, to accept diversity as a fact of life, and to build enough flexibility into our physics course to accommodate and even to take advantage of that diversity. This acceptance was neither reluctant nor despairing. Far

from being disturbed by the existence of diversity, we applaud and foster it. Thus the Project set out to design a course that permitted and indeed encouraged variation. We have been trying to develop a flexible physics course that allows a teacher to complement his strengths and supplement his weaknesses, that make it possible for him to take into account student differences, and that is workable within a wide variety of school situations. (Rutherford 1967, p. 216)

Many new curriculum projects have designed alternative curriculum packages to be used as different approaches to the achievement of the same goal. Other projects working more or less independently of each other have produced a wealth of packages in the same subject area but each with a different approach or emphasis.

The fact that alternative curricula containing diverse and varied materials are now available to schools raises the possibility of placing students according to some characteristic in the curriculum that would be maximally beneficial. This type of placement goes beyond the usual homogeneous ability grouping in fast, average, and slow—or college preparatory, commercial, and vocational— tracks. As we pointed out earlier, the heterogeneity of aptitudes, interests, educational backgrounds, aspirations, and countless other characteristics within these "homogeneous" groups argues against using the single criterion of track or level to determine the types of instruction a student receives. Instead, the more sophisticated approach asks which students, regardless of track or level, can best profit from the various approaches available in the same subject field.

Unfortunately, there are few empirically based attempts to adapt the method of instruction to students' characteristics. Tobias (1976) describes the situation as follows:

Existing adaptions generally consist of varying instructional *rate* to student needs rather than instructional method. When instructional method has been suited to student, such adaptions are typically based on the artistry of the practitioner, rather than on a systematically formulated set of precepts that have been verified by empirical research. (p. 61)

As Tobias indicates, differential placement in alternative programs or treatments still involves a large measure of artistry. Teachers can take into consideration a student's existing academic background or ability level in making decisions about the appropriateness of a particular curriculum or version of a multiversion curriculum. Published evaluations, studies, and reviews of a new curriculum often offer suggestions as to the types of students who benefit most from alternative offerings. For example, on the basis of their research, the makers of the BSCS Biology Project offered the following placement information regarding their Special Materials track:

The class mean for SM classes should not exceed the 40th percentile on a general ability test or a test of reading comprehension; and, for any individual in the class with an ability test score of over the 50th percentile, . . . there should be a written explanation of his/her presence in the class. (Grobman, 1965a, p. 764)

Thus various kinds of differential placement are often possible. Teachers must keep abreast of instructional research in their subject as one guide to the kinds of diagnosis necessary. They also should carefully study any placement recommendations made by the publisher or curriculum group that designed alternative versions of a course. If no information or direction for improved placement of students is available from these two sources, interested teachers within a department can pool their own observations and experiences. They might also analyze alternative curricula (see B. Wilson & Van Etten, 1977) to try to determine whether different approaches designed to reach the same goal presume different educational backgrounds or skills on the part of the student. Teachers might themselves develop alternative methods geared to different learning styles: primarily visual for some students, auditory for others, manipulative for others, or a combination of these three modalities for still others. They can experiment with small and large groups, one-to-one tutoring, individual study, and tutoring by peers. All these methods can supplement a mastery-learning approach which emphasizes feedback and correctives well before a summative grade has to be given.

Teacher-Made Diagnostic Placement Charts

When teacher-made tests are used for diagnosis, the way in which performance is portrayed often governs their usefulness in prescribing remediation. One technique that helps teachers in the use of diagnostic test results is the construction of a diagnostic placement chart.

The Gary, Indiana, Program in Compensatory Education—Intensive Language Arts, under the direction of Sophie Bloom (see S. Bloom, 1975), affords an example of an easy-to-interpret teacher-made diagnostic placement chart. This program has developed oral and written diagnostic instruments for both the receptive and the expressive language skills. The language skills in question are broken down into a hierarchy of sequential subskills. The results are then placed on the diagnostic chart shown in Figure 5-5.

Only three colors are required to give teachers the necessary detailed information concerning the children's specific needs. Blue indicates mastery; yellow, near mastery; and red, a skill which has not been learned. (These colors have been replaced by three different shadings in Figure 5-5.)

Coded charts like this one show at a glance the strong and weak subskills of the children. When the chart is read vertically, the coding indicates groups in the class which have mastered various subskills. When the pattern is inspected horizontally, it conveys to the teacher the status of an individual child. The teacher can see specific weaknesses more clearly and where instruction might most effectively begin.

Each child receives his or her portion of the outcome map and keeps track of progress toward mastery of subskills during the ensuing formative units by removing red tags and replacing them with yellow and then blue. The concepts "pass" and "fail" are avoided by

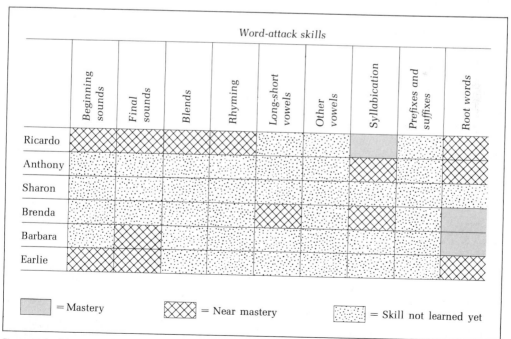

Figure 5-5 Diagnostic chart for word-attack skills. (Adapted from S. Bloom, 1975, p. 29.)

the use of terms like "has learned" and "still to be learned" in connection with the tags. The students are told that they can master each skill and are allowed to arrive at mastery according to their own schedule. The issue is not passing or failing but only when the last "still to be learned" tag can be replaced by a blue tag signifying mastery.

Here is an example of how the schools, while unable to remove the environmental and cultural causes of underdeveloped language skills, can intervene with necessary remedial instruction to help ensure that the students will acquire the verbal skills prerequisite to profiting from later verbally dependent learning experiences.

The diagnostic report form of the Gary public schools is of course adaptable to other areas of the curriculum, such as arithmetic. Whether such reports are modeled after the Gary form or on some other visual scheme, their strength lies in the fact that they are easy to interpret and that they indicate levels of mastery for each subskill or objective.

Diagnosis of Affective Prerequisites

There is little doubt that affect has an important influence on what is learned and how it is learned. In fact, affective entry characteristics can account for up to one-fourth of the variation on cognitive achievement measures (B. S. Bloom, 1976). There is a great deal of variation in students' affective entry characteristics. Some students eagerly approach the beginning of a new year or a new course; their interest in learning is high, and they have been successful throughout their school careers. Others expect to learn and get good grades but have little interest, enthusiasm, or delight in the subject; their motives instead are more pragmatic, such as getting into college or pleasing their parents. Still other students approach the new tasks with anxiety and defensiveness; in the past they have had negative experiences while pursuing the subject. In short, they may have a negative attitude either toward school in general or toward certain subjects in particular, and they hold negative perceptions of their own academic abilities. One way to treat negative

affect toward a subject is by helping the student to achieve. Very often affect toward a subject improves when cognitive competencies are developed. Because cognitive and affective outcomes are so closely intertwined, the teacher should determine a student's entry-level affect so that appropriate experiences geared to improve affect can be planned.

At the beginning of each course or year teachers should assess the student's affect. Chapter 11, Evaluation Techniques for Affective Objectives, describes in detail how to construct or select measures of subject-specific affect and of general school-related affect. Therefore, as mentioned earlier, we shall not discuss instrument design or selection per se but instead will focus on how affective information can be used for diagnostic purposes. Such information might take the form of the class list shown in Figure 5-6. The information in Figure 5-6 is specific to a particular commercially available instrument, *Survey of School Attitudes* (Hogan, 1975); teachers can, of course, select from a number of specific interest inventories that give similar information (see Chapter 11).

Figure 5–6 contains many different kinds of valuable individual and group information. First there is information on individual item responses—like (L), dislike (D), neutral (N)—for four subject areas: reading and language, mathematics, science, and social studies. Further, there is a section labeled "Local" where students' responses to items designed by the local district are reported. In this case the items dealt with the students' perceptions of the textbooks used in various subjects. Thus, in mathematics, Mary Carter indicated that she liked the mathematics activity described in item 5, and was neutral to the one described in item 33, and disliked the one described in item 45. This item information provides the teacher with the student's specific likes and dislikes in a subject. The raw scores shown at the right are derived by giving each "like" response a weight of 2, each "neutral" response a weight of 1, and each "dislike" response a weight of 0. The raw score, however, gives us little information until it is converted into one or

Teacher Mrs. Leicy

School Jefferson Elementary

System Pleasantville   Date 10/19/75

Grade 4   Form A

Level Primary

Norms Used Grade 4

Class List Report

SSA | HBJ Scoring Service

Summary of School Attitudes

Student	Level Scores R/L	LM	S	SS	Percentile Ranks R/L	M	S	SS	Raw Scores R/L	M	S	SS
Carter, Mary	5	5	4	3	87	85	42	27	28	27	22	17
DeWolfe, Cheryl	5	3	4	4	97	27	55	41	30	23	24	20
Goodes, Laurie	4	3	3	3	66	32	22	23	25	17	18	16
Graham, Lorie	5	3	4	3	73	32	48	23	26	17	23	16
Haymaker, Susan	4	2	3	2	52	4	12	6	23	7	15	10
Keister, Jeff	4	2	5	5	45	9	91	75	22	10	29	26
Rallston, Kristy	4	3	5	4	52	36	77	57	23	18	27	23
Sanger, Randy	3	3	4		17	7	51		16	13	22	
Weyman, Daniel	5	2	5	4	87	9	84	69	28	10	28	25

Individual Item Responses

	READING / LANGUAGE	MATHEMATICS	SCIENCE	SOCIAL STUDIES	LOCAL
Carter, Mary	LLLLLDLLLLLLL	LLLLLLLnLLDLL	nLLnLDLLLLnLnDL	nLDLLLnnLLDDLD	LnLnLn
DeWolfe, Cheryl	LLLLLLLLLLLLL	nDLnDLDDD-LDDLL	nnLLLLLDLLLn-L	nLDDLDnLLLnLLn	nDLLnD
Goodes, Laurie	nLLLLLnLLLLDn	nDnLDnLnLLnDDLL	LnLnLnnLnnnLDnLD	nDnnLDnLLnnnLD	nDLnLL
Graham, Lorie	nLLLLLLnLnLLn	LnLnnLnDnnnDnLn	LLLLLLLnnLLDn	nLDLLnLDLLDLDnnD	LnLnDD
Haymaker, Susan	nLLLnDLLLLLLLn	nDnnDnDnDDDnDn	nnLDDLnLDnnnnn	DnDnnLnDnnDnDD	LDnnnD
Keister, Jeff	LLLnLnnnLDLnLn	DDDDDnDDnLLLL	LLLLLnLLLLLLL	LLDLLLnLnLLLLL	LnLnmL
Rallston, Kristy	DLLLLnLLnnDLLL	LnnnDnLnnDnLnL	LLnDLLLLLLLLL	DLLLLnnLnLLnnLL	LDLLnn
Sanger, Randy	LnLLLDnnLD-DDLD	Ln--nn-DD-nnn-n	DDDnDnnD-LLLLD	Ln-LDLLLnnLLLnn	nnnLLn
Weyman, Daniel	LLLLLLLLLLnLLn	DDDnDDDnnLLDLnD	LLLLnLLLLnLLLL	LnnLLLLLLnLnLn	LDLLDD

		READING / LANGUAGE	MATHEMATICS	SCIENCE	SOCIAL STUDIES
Median Raw Scores		24.1	13.2	25.4	22.0
Percentile Rank of Median Raw Scores		59	17	63	51
Distribution of Level Scores		freq.	freq.	freq.	freq.
	5	9	2	12	8
	4	10	3	9	9
	3	7	10	5	8
	2	0	7	0	1
	1	0	3	0	0
Data based on following number of students		26	25	26	26

Legend: L = Like, n = neutral, D = Dislike, - = omit

Figure 5-6 Sample class list report. (Hogan, 1975, p. 23. Copyright © 1975 by Harcourt Brace Jovanovich, Inc.; all rights reserved; reproduced by permission.)

TABLE 5-1 CONVERSION OF RAW SCORES TO LEVEL SCORES AND DESCRIPTIONS OF LEVEL SCORES

Raw score	Level score	Verbal description
26-30	5	Expresses a liking for all or nearly all aspects of the curricular area.
19-25	4	Expresses a liking for most aspects of the area, but may dislike or be indifferent to some aspects of the curricular area.
12-18	3	Is indifferent to most aspects of the curricular area or expresses about an equal number of likes and dislikes.
5-11	2	Expresses a dislike for most aspects of the area, but may like or be indifferent to some aspects of the curricular area.
0-4	1	Expresses a dislike for all or nearly all aspects of the curricular area.

Source: Hogan, 1975, p. 23. Reproduced from the Survey of School Attitudes by permission. Copyright © 1975 by Harcourt Brace Jovanovich, Inc. All rights reserved.

more derived scores—in this case, level scores or percentile ranks. Table 5-1 describes the level score associated with various raw scores. The reader will note that the level score describes the individual's raw score in terms of a continuum ranging from liking all or nearly all aspects of the subject to disliking all or nearly all aspects.

The more common derived score, used by almost all standardized test publishers, is the percentile rank reported in column 3, Figure 5-6. For this reason it is important that teachers understand the concept and interpretation of percentiles. Percentile ranks are discussed in Figure 5-7 in terms of the performance of one of the students from the sample class list report; however, the treatment of percentiles in Figure 5-7 is applicable to any use of this derived score.

In Figure 5-6, the median raw score for the class is reported at the bottom of the column for each scale. The median is a measure of central tendency, or average, and corresponds to the midpoint, or 50th percentile, of the score distribution. That is, the

median score is the score above and below which 50 percent of the scores fall. Thus in Figure 5-6 the median raw score for the class of twenty-six students in the reading and language scale was 24.1. The median of the class (24.1) is also converted to the percentile rank that score would correspond to in the norming population—in this case, the 59th percentile. The median raw score for this class was above the median raw score for the norm group.

A class list similar to that shown in Figure 5-6 has the potential for the following kinds of diagnostic information (Hogan, 1975, pp. 28–29). (Only nine of the twenty-six pupils in the class are shown in detail in Figure 5-6.)

1. Twenty of the twenty-five students are indifferent to, or express a dislike for, most or nearly all aspects of the mathematics curriculum. This could be seen from an inspection of the item responses and the distribution of level scores reported at the bottom of the mathematics column, i.e., ten pupils with a level score of 3 (indifferent), seven with a level score of 2, and three with a level score of 1 (dislike for all or nearly all).

2. Item responses can be visually examined to detect *patterns* of positive or negative reactions to aspects of the curriculum.

3. Cheryl, Jeff, Kristy, and Daniel all revealed little interest in mathematics, as shown by their level scores and their percentile ranks. These pupils need special attention to increase their interest in, and curiosity about, mathematics.

4. Susan's negative attitude toward social studies—a level of 2—might be remediated by capitalizing on her interest in reading activities—a level score of 4.

As Hogan points out, the comments above are far from exhaustive. There is considerably more individual and group information contained in the printout. However, the comments illustrate how teachers can use affective information in a diagnostic way to plan learning experiences for groups or for an individual.

A percentile rank is a norm-referenced, derived score that shows as a percent the proportion of the norm group which received the same score or a lower score. In Figure 5-6 Mary Carter received a raw score of 28 on the reading/language scale. The percentile rank corresponding to the raw score is 87. Mary's percentile rank (87th percentile) indicates that she received a raw score that was as high as, or higher than, 87 percent of the norm group; 13 percent of the norm group scored higher than Mary on the reading/language scale. In science Mary's raw score is 22, which converts to a percentile rank of 42, meaning that Mary scored as high as or higher than 42 percent of the norm group, while 58 percent of the norm group scored higher than Mary. Notice that Mary's raw scores have no meaning until converted to a percentile rank. It is meaningless, and potentially misleading, to directly compare her raw score of 28 in reading/language with the score of 22 in science. Mary's scores take on meaning only in comparison with the performance of the norm population. Clearly the relative closeness of the raw scores 28 and 22 is not reflected in their respective percentiles, 87 and 42.

The percentile rank is the derived score least open to misinterpretation (other derived scores will be discussed presently). Two cautions are in order, however. First, a percentile rank should *not* be misread as the percentage of "correct" answers; it is, rather, the relative position of a person in the distribution of the norm group.

Second, when the scores are distributed normally (i.e., there is a bell-shaped distribution), percentile ranks become elastic. That is, the difference between two adjacent percentile ranks is not the same at all points across the score distribution. A percentile cuts off 1 percent of the area under curve of a distribution of scores. In the normal curve shown the distance along the horizontal axis between score points needed to cut off 1 percent of the area increases as one moves away from the center of the distribution. Thus the difference in raw score points between percentiles in the center of the distribution—i.e., between the 50th and 55th percentiles, or 5 percent of the area under the curve—is nowhere near as large as the difference in raw score points between percentiles at the tail, i.e., between the 94 and 99 percentiles—also 5 percent of the area under the curve.

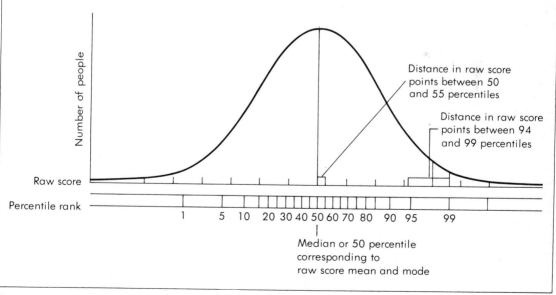

Figure 5-7 Explanation of percentile ranks. (The illustration of the normal curve is adapted from Psychological Corporation, 1955, p. 2.)

It is possible for the artful teacher to plan experiences that capitalize on interests or are aimed at developing interests. Hogan (p. 327) offers the following suggestions:

1. Spend 5 minutes within each lesson on activities designed to foster interest: brain teasers, games, crossword puzzles, etc.
2. Design class or individual projects, running concurrently with a lesson, that will stimulate interest.
3. Supplement the traditional curriculum with a movie, slides, field trips, and speakers.
4. Coordinate activities with instruction: for example, some students might be encouraged to compute batting or earned-run averages, others to read about a local team and its players.
5. Identify the outside interests of students, and through these try to build interest in a given curriculum area.

There are at least two instruments that are designed to elicit information about students' leisure time, interests, and activities—the *Background and Experience Questionnaire* (Maier & Anderson, 1964b) and the *Independent Activities Questionnaire* (Evaluation Testing Service, 1965).

General attitudes toward school or self are more resistant to change than subject-specific attitudes; hence it is important that general attitudes be assessed as early as possible. When children have a negative attitude toward school or a poor concept of their academic abilities, it is important that they begin to experience successes in school. The teacher can try to plan materials and assignments that will give students with negative attitudes toward school a needed sense of accomplishment. Perhaps the best way of developing positive affect is by improving the student's skills and competencies. Success in a subject generates positive affect which in turn increases the likelihood of continued success. Reversing negative affect is not an easy task. However, the early diagnosis of negative affect permits the teacher to begin working toward the reversal of such negative affect.

Identifying Gifted and Talented Students

Among the children who need to be identified so that they may be placed in proper educational programs are the academically gifted or extremely talented students. The teacher is a key person in identifying the exceptionally gifted student. Stanley, George, and Solano (1977, p. 9) suggest that teachers use the following fifteen criteria to identify the academically gifted child:

1. Uses large vocabulary easily and accurately.
2. Is effective in spoken and written communication.
3. Has a rich reading background, and shows evidence that he thinks about his reading and likes to discuss it.
4. Shows a wide range of interests, or in exceptional cases a heavy concentration on one.
5. Spends time beyond usual assignments or schedules on things that interest him.
6. Spends much time on special projects of his own.
7. Performs significantly above grade level in school projects.
8. *Usually* scores high on standardized tests.
9. *Usually* receives good marks in school classes.
10. Tends to figure out what is wrong with an activity and show how it could be done better.
11. Gives refreshing twist to even old ideas.
12. Shows little patience with routine procedures and skills.
13. Asks penetrating questions, particularly about causes and reasons.
14. Likes to seek answers to problems and puzzles.
15. Is quick to recognize relationships.

A gifted child does not of course have to meet all the criteria but will usually meet some combination of them. There is, however, a risk that nonconforming students or gifted students who are not working up to their potential may be overlooked (Stanley, George, & Solano, 1977). Teachers need to be constantly on the lookout for gifted children; and once such students have been identified, care should be taken to provide them with a challenging educational program (see Stanley, George, and Solano for a description of programs to develop intellectual talent).

THE USE OF COMMERCIALLY AVAILABLE TESTS IN DIAGNOSTIC EVALUATION

Commercially produced tests are a major source of diagnostic information. Such tests can give valuable information about prerequisite skills, as well as skills and objectives already mastered. However, it is important that teachers know the strengths and weaknesses of such tests in diagnosis. Further, a teacher needs to know how to interpret scores that accompany such tests. This section describes the uses of norm-referenced achievement tests, diagnostic achievement tests, and criterion-referenced achievement tests. Scores associated with these tests are described (percentile ranks have already been treated). Once again it must be emphasized that a teacher needs to know how to interpret correctly various scores provided by test publishers. Most school systems have a testing program, and if the results are to be used correctly and not abused, teachers must know how to interpret them.

Norm-Referenced Achievement Tests

Commercially available norm-referenced achievement batteries are routinely given by school systems early in the school year or in the spring. Such a battery can help a teacher identify general levels of a student's performance in such important skills as reading, computation, spelling, and mechanics of writing. (Katz, 1973, offers guidelines that teachers can use when selecting norm-referenced achievement tests.)

Norm-referenced tests by definition allow the teacher to *compare the performance of a student of a given grade level or age with that of a normative group,* in basic curricu-

lar areas. Norm-referenced tests, as we saw in Chapter 4, are not designed to tell what specific objectives a student has mastered, but instead how the student's performance compares with the performance of the norm group. As we noted previously, in order to make inferences about performance the person's raw score—the number of items answered correctly—must be converted to a score that reflects the performance of the norm group. The most common derived scores reported to teachers are percentile ranks (explained in Figure 5-7), standard scores (Figure 5-8), stanine scores (Figure 5-9), and grade-equivalent scores (Figure 5-10). Figure 5-11 shows the relationship of various derived scores to one another and to the normal score distribution. Teachers need to understand these concepts in order to properly interpret performance and explain results to parents—and often students.

In interpreting derived scores it is very important that the user know the characteristics of the norm group on which the derived scores are based. Most publishers provide the user with national norms and in addition have regional and state norms as well as norms based on school characteristics (e.g., public, private, or parochial; urban, suburban, or rural; size of school district). Further, when publishers score the tests for the user, district, school, and even class norms can be computed. Local norms can differ quite significantly from national norms. It is entirely possible for a raw score of 25 on a test to correspond to percentile ranks of 85 nationally and 55 locally. Before making inferences based on derived scores, the users must be sure that they understand the characteristics of the norm group on which the scores are based. Further, users should determine whether the norm group was drawn in such a way that it in fact represents what it purports to represent. Users should read the publisher's technical manual carefully in order to make a judgment about the representativeness of the norm group. In using norms with minority group students the teacher needs to check that the publisher has adequately represented minority groups in the norm sample.

Standard scores permit the user to directly compare a pupil's performance across various subtests. Basically, a standard score is one expressed in terms of a fixed mean and standard deviation. The mean for the norm group of each test is set to common mean which for most test publishers is 50, although, as shown in Figure 5-11, the mean could be set to 0, 50, or 500. The standard deviation of the norm group for each test is set to a common value; for a mean of 50, the standard deviation is set to 10.

The standard deviation of a distribution of scores is an index of the variability of the scores from the mean of the distribution and represents a *distance* in score units along the score axis. If two groups took the same test, and the mean (average) score for each was 43 and the standard deviation for group 1 was 9 and for group 2 was 3, this would indicate that group 2 was more homogeneous in its performance than group 1. There are fewer extreme scores in group 2 than in group 1, and students tend to cluster closer to the mean in group 2. (See Chapter 4 for a further discussion and a method of computing the standard deviation).

Standard scores are expressed in terms of the *new* standard deviation units (1, 10, 100, etc.), above and below the *new* mean (0, 50, 500). Standard scores based on the same norm group permit a user to compare the performance of a student across tests. For example, if the standard score is based on a mean of 50 and a standard deviation of 10, then a standard score of 60 on an arithmetic computation means that the student's performance is one standard deviation above the mean (60–50) of the norm group; a standard score of 35 in arithmetic problem solving means that the student's performance on the test is 1½ standard deviations (35–50) below the mean performance of the norm group. Thus it is clear that the student's performance relative to the norm group on computation is quite a bit higher than the performance in the area of problem solving. Similarly, the standard score used to report CEEB results is based on a mean of 500 and a standard deviation of 100. Thus a student who has a verbal SAT score of 650 and a mathematics score of 400 is 1½ standard deviations above the mean of the norm on the verbal test but 1 standard deviation below the mean on the mathematics test.

Figure 5-8 Explanation of standard scores.

Further, the user should check the manual to see that consideration has been given to selecting items that are as far as possible free of cultural bias (see Fitzgibbon, 1975, and Oakland and Phillips, 1975, for a further discussion of problems in using standardized tests with minority group students).

Derived scores from one publisher on a subtest like arithmetic computation are not directly comparable with those from other publishers. In other words, a percentile rank of 84 on the test produced by one publisher does not necessarily represent the same level of performance or the same percentile rank for another publisher's test. In order to compare a student's or group's performance on one major commercial test of arithmetic computation with performance on another pub-

lisher's test, a teacher would have to convert both scores to a third derived score using a table provided by the National Anchor Study (Bianchini & Loret, 1974). This study permits a test user to equate performance in certain grades across a series of tests which are commercially available, standardized, and norm-referenced in nature.

Most major test makers provide the teacher with an individual student profile chart—a graphic picture of the student's overall level of achievement. Figure 5-12 (see page 138) presents a sample of an individual profile chart prepared by one major test maker. Basically the chart allows the teacher to compare visually a student's performance on various sub-tests with the performance of a norm group. The student's raw score is

Stanine, another norm-referenced score, derives its name from the fact that it is a standard score of nine units. The scale ranges from 1 to 9, with the mean (or average) stanine at 5 and a standard deviation of 2. Stanines are normally distributed, and each represents approximately the same range of raw score (except for the extreme scores of 1 and 9 (see the diagram). The advantage of the stanine is that the person's score is expressed as a single digit; however, this simplicity is gained at the expense of precision, particularly for scores 1 and 9. The normal curve shown describes the relationships of stanine scores to the "normal" curve and to percentile ranks. When stanines are used the following verbal descriptions are appropriate; 9, highest level; 8, high level; 7, well above average; 6, slightly above average; 5, average; 4, slightly below average; 3, well below average; 2, low level; 1, lowest level.

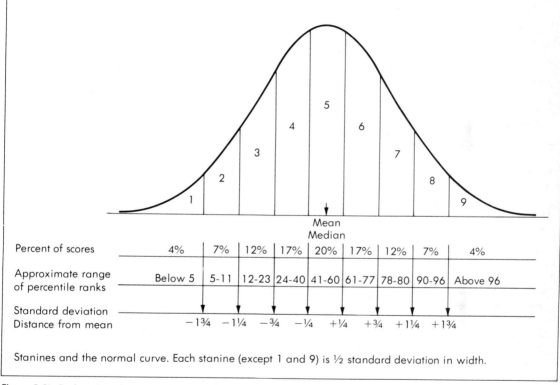

Percent of scores	4%	7%	12%	17%	20%	17%	12%	7%	4%
Approximate range of percentile ranks	Below 5	5-11	12-23	24-40	41-60	61-77	78-80	90-96	Above 96
Standard deviation Distance from mean		$-1\frac{3}{4}$	$-1\frac{1}{4}$	$-\frac{3}{4}$	$-\frac{1}{4}$	$+\frac{1}{4}$	$+\frac{3}{4}$	$+1\frac{1}{4}$	$+1\frac{3}{4}$

Stanines and the normal curve. Each stanine (except 1 and 9) is ½ standard deviation in width.

Figure 5-9 Explanation of stanine scores. (Mitchell, undated.)

reported in terms of one or more derived scores. The Stanford individual profile pictured in Figure 5-12 uses grade equivalents, percentile ranks, and stanines. It also provides a space for the teacher to enter the student's scale score. (Scale scores have equal-interval properties and are used primarily for longitudinal growth studies because they permit school officials to measure growth from grade to grade and from one level of the Stanford to another; Madden, Gardner, Rudman, Karlsen & Merwin, 1973.)

The grade equivalent (GE) score is one of the most widely used derived scores, but unfortunately the most widely misinterpreted. Because the GE is widely abused, *Standards for Educational and Psychological Tests* (APA, 1974) recommended that such scores be abandoned or their use discouraged (Standard 05.2.3, p. 23). However, since the GE is still very popular, it is important that this score be examined to point out its proper uses, its limitations, and its pitfalls. (See Vollbrecht, 1977, for an annotated bibliography on grade equivalent scores; see also Echternacht, 1977, and Plas, 1977, for a further discussion of the limits of grade equivalents).

The grade equivalent is derived in the following manner. Suppose a test maker is setting norms for an arithmetic test, designed for third-graders in the month of September. In addition to administering the third-grade test to the third-grade sample, the test maker would also administer it to samples of second-, fourth- and, fifth-graders. On the basis of these administrations it is now possible to compute the average raw score (most often the median is used) on the third-grade test for the second-, third-, fourth-, and fifth-grade samples. These average raw scores for each of the four grades can be plotted on a graph—raw scores along one axis, grade placement along the second axis. Since there are ten months in the school year, there would be ten units between any two adjacent grades along the grade-placement axis, i.e., ten units between grades 2 and 3. The average scores (median scores) for the September administration for each grade can now be plotted. Thus the average score the fifth grade would be assigned would be a grade-placement score of 5.0. The average raw score for grades 2.0, 3.0, 4.0, and 5.0 can then be connected. Raw scores corresponding to grade placement in months between grade levels (i.e., 3.4-third grade, fourth month) can be interpolated. Grade equivalent scores below 2.0 and above 5.0 can be extrapolated from the graph. The fact that grade equivalent scores are largely interpolated or extrapolated is one of the weaknesses associated with this type of score, since it is based on an assumption of uniform growth throughout the school year.

However, it is in the interpretation of the GE that the principal danger lies. Suppose a third-grader receives a grade equivalent of 4.6. This means that performance *on third-grade material* is equal to the performance of a student in the sixth month of the fourth grade *on third-grade material*. It does *not* mean that the third-grader can do fourth-grade arithmetic. Simiarily, if the third-grader were to receive a grade equivalent of 2.0 this would mean that performance was equivalent to that of a student in the first month of the second grade *on third-grade material*. Beyond elementary school, grade equivalents have little meaning. Clearly, a grade equivalent of 10.6 on a sixth-grade arithmetic test does not mean that the student can do algebra or geometry.

A further difficulty with grade equivalents is that they can mislead teachers who wish to compare the performance of a student across subtests. Not uncommonly a student's raw scores on two subtests are assigned the *same* grade equivalent but *different* percentile ranks within the pupil's own norm group. Conversely, raw scores for two subtests could receive the *same* percentile rank and quite *different* grade equivalent scores. This is because GE scores cut across grade samples and therefore can differ from one subject to another, while percentile ranks are based only on the performance of student in the same grade. Thus it could happen that a third-grade pupil received a GE score of 5.0 for both reading and mathematics; this should not be interpreted to mean that the level of performance is the same in both subjects, because when compared with the third-grade norm group the reading score may fall at the 90th percentile and mathematics at the 75th percentile. Teachers should use grade equivalents with extreme caution—percentile ranks, standard scores, or stainines being preferable norm-referenced scores.

Figure 5-10   Explanation of grade equivalent (GE) scores.

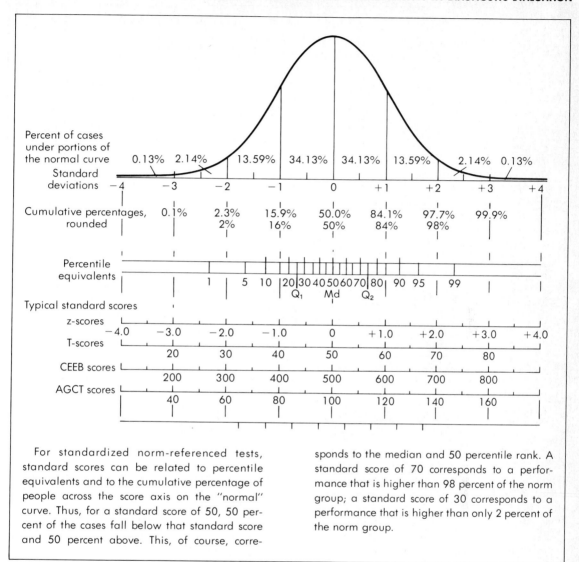

For standardized norm-referenced tests, standard scores can be related to percentile equivalents and to the cumulative percentage of people across the score axis on the "normal" curve. Thus, for a standard score of 50, 50 percent of the cases fall below that standard score and 50 percent above. This, of course, corresponds to the median and 50 percentile rank. A standard score of 70 corresponds to a performance that is higher than 98 percent of the norm group; a standard score of 30 corresponds to a performance that is higher than only 2 percent of the norm group.

Figure 5-11 Relationship of various types of derived scores to the normal curve. (Illustration adapted from Psychological Corporation, 1955, p. 2.)

Name: GR **Age:** 10.0
Grade: 4.2 **OLMAT Raw Score:** 54
School: Hillview **OLMAT IQ:** 95

	Number Right	Scaled Score	Grade Equiv.	%ile Rank*	STANINE* (circled)
TEST 1: Vocabulary	30	149	4.4	56	5
TEST 2: Reading Comp.	47	141	3.8	46	5
TEST 3: Word Study Skills	32	136	3.6	44	5
TEST 4: Math, Concepts	14	137	3.5	32	4
TEST 5: Math, Computation	10	127	2.2	8	2
TEST 6: Math, Applications	13	135	3.2	28	4
TEST 7: Spelling	22	138	3.3	26	4
TEST 8: Language	22	124	2.4	20	3
TEST 9: Social Science	29	145	4.4	56	5
TEST 10: Science	15	122	2.7	22	3
TEST 11: Listening Comp.	29	134	3.4	38	4
Total Battery (Test 1 through Test 11)	263	136	3.6	32	4
Total Auditory (Test 1 + Test 11)	59	139	4.0	46	5
Total Reading (Test 2 + Test 3)	79	140	3.7	44	5
Total Mathematics (Test 4 + Test 5 + Test 6)	37	133	3.1	20	4

*Percentile Ranks and Stanines based on tables for Beginning ⊠ End ☐ of Grade

---

Name: JK **Age:** 8.8
Grade: 4.2 **OLMAT Raw Score:** 48
School: Hillview **OLMAT IQ:** 95

	Number Right	Scaled Score	Grade Equiv.	%ile Rank*	STANINE* (circled)
TEST 1: Vocabulary	24	137	3.4	32	4
TEST 2: Reading Comp.	53	148	4.4	58	5
TEST 3: Word Study Skills	39	147	4.6	58	5
TEST 4: Math, Concepts	25	163	5.8	86	7
TEST 5: Math, Computation	33	166	5.9	96	9
TEST 6: Math, Applications	27	174	6.8	94	8
TEST 7: Spelling	37	152	4.6	64	6
TEST 8: Language	36	147	4.3	58	5
TEST 9: Social Science	32	150	4.7	64	6
TEST 10: Science	32	153	5.2	76	6
TEST 11: Listening Comp.	24	127	2.8	22	3
Total Battery (Test 1 through Test 11)	362	148	4.3	66	6
Total Auditory (Test 1 + Test 11)	48	130	3.0	24	4
Total Reading (Test 2 + Test 3)	92	148	4.5	60	6
Total Mathematics (Test 4 + Test 5 + Test 6)	85	166	6.0	96	9

*Percentile Ranks and Stanines based on tables for Beginning ⊠ End ☐ of Grade

Figure 5-12 Pupil profile chart of the Stanford Achievement Test, Primary Level III, Battery Form A. (Madden et al., 1973, p. 15. Copyright © 1973 by Harcourt Brace Jovanovich, Inc.; all rights reserved; reproduced by permission.)

The authors of the Stanford profile present a typical diagnosis of a general deficiency revealed in the Individual Profile Chart for the students JK and GR in Figure 5-12:

> Comparing the potential of these two pupils we find that each has an Otis-Lennon Mental Ability Test (OLMAT) IQ of 95 which is in the upper limit of the stanine of 4. On the Total Auditory score we find a stanine of 5 for GR and a stanine of 4 for JK.
>
> The profiles of JK and GR are, however, very different. JK has only 3 stanines which are below 5. These three are in Vocabulary, Listening Comprehension, and Total Auditory, the only areas in which JK probably has had no direct instruction or has made no studied effort to achieve. JK has no percentile rank in studied subjects below 58, but his achievement on the Total Auditory indicates superiority to only one-fourth of the normal sample. On the other hand GR has no stanine above 5. He also is at a low percentile rank of the stanine 5 band in Reading Comprehension and Word Study Skills and has percentile ranks ranging from 8 to 28 in five tests. With the same measured potential in terms of IQ and with less measured potential as shown by Total Auditory, JK outpaces GR in achievement by a long way. The most challenging comparison of the two pupils is in Mathematics. JK has a grade equivalent of 6.8 in Mathematics Applications while GR has only a grade equivalent of 3.2.
>
> After a review of the test results, how does the teacher proceed with these two pupils? JK needs special instruction in listening. GR needs special instruction in mathematics, with immediate priority given to computation, and in spelling. (Madden et al., 1973, p. 15)

An important caution in using norm-referenced achievement data for diagnosis is in order: The standardized achievement test can alert the teacher to the fact that a student is weak in a certain general area like reading or arithmetic computation when compared with some normative group, but it does not reveal the exact nature and cause of the difficulty. More sensitive diagnostic instruments are needed for this task.

In order to achieve a somewhat finer diagnosis of weaknesses on a particular subtest, some test publishers suggest using item data. This technique involves examining the response pattern of a student. If a student misses several items all dealing with the principle of carrying in addition, then a workable hypothesis might be that the student needs remedial instruction in this skill. Most test makers provide some type of item-analysis chart. However, it is a simple matter for a teacher to construct one that gives an individual or group item-analysis profile based on how each item was answered. Figure 5-13 is an example of such a chart.

The teacher simply lists the name of each student in the class (the patterns for only six students are shown in Figure 5-13). Along the top of the chart are listed the item numbers, arranged according to subtest, objective, content, or behavior; vertical lines enclose each group or related items. In this case the items were grouped according to computational skills. A plus sign indicates that the item was answered correctly, and a zero that it was answered incorrectly. If the chart is read across, the individual's pattern of re-

	Addition							Subtraction							Multiplication				Division					
	1	2	7	9	10	12	14	3	4	5	6	11	13	15	16	18	19	20	21	22	23	24	25	26
Mary Ryan	+	+	+	+	+	+	+	+	+	+	0	0	+	0	0	0	0	0	+	+	+	+	0	+
Martha Smith	+	0	+	0	0	0	0	0	0	0	+	0	+	0	0	0	0	0	+	0	+	+	0	+
Joseph O'Brien	0	+	+	0	+	+	+	0	+	+	0	0	+	+	0	+	+	0	+	0	+	+	0	+
George Carlson	+	+	+	+	0	0	+	0	0	0	+	0	+	0	0	0	0	0	+	0	+	+	+	+
Eileen Jones	0	0	0	+	0	+	+	0	+	0	0	0	+	+	0	0	0	0	+	0	+	+	0	+
Sarah Allen	+	+	0	+	+	+	+	0	0	0	0	+	0	0	0	+	+	0	0	0	+	+	0	+

Figure 5-13 An example of part of an item analysis chart that could be constructed by a classroom teacher.

sponses on the related items is revealed; if the chart is read down, the pattern of the class response is shown. These patterns can then be examined to determine whether it appears that an individual or the class as a whole is consistently missing a certain type of item and therefore might be in need of remedial instruction.

While the practice of examining response patterns on standardized tests can be helpful, it often lacks the refinement needed for an accurate diagnosis of specific learning disabilities in a given content area. The reason is that often there are not enough items of a specific type to make a reliable judgment on mastery. Further, some skills within a subject field may not be measured at all. This, of course, is not the fault of the test; no standardized test can hope to have a sufficient number of items for all the local objectives contained in a unit of instruction. The practice of analyzing responses on standard tests, if used with caution, can at least provide the teacher with testable hypotheses about the instructional needs of students. However, more sensitive diagnostic instruments are required to pinpoint the exact nature and cause of the difficulty.

Standardized Diagnostic Tests

Standardized diagnostic tests evaluate a particular subskill in much greater detail than is possible for an achievement test, which must cover many general areas rather broadly. Diagnostic tests are not limited to identifying weakness in *prerequisite* skills and abilities: they can also be used for diagnosis well into the school year to try to determine the cause of repeated learning difficulties. Since a diagnostic test is designed to categorize weaknesses among students who are below average on a subskill, these instruments have a greater proportion of easy items than do achievement tests, which are designed to measure the entire range of attainment. Beatty, Madden, and Gardner (1966) point out that this relative ease of diagnostic items means that:

. . . pupils who may be frustrated by even a well-developed achievement test should experience a good deal of success on the diagnostic test. Futhermore, more accurate, reliable measurement of below average performance is afforded by the less difficult nature of a diagnostic test. In order to increase the reliability of measurement in identifying weaknesses of pupils and still keep the test administration time within reasonable limits, precision in measurement for the upper levels of performance is sacrificed in a substantial number of subtests. A high level of performance on a diagnostic subtest indicates that a certain area is *not* a weakness for a pupil or group, although it may not indicate exactly how strong the pupil or group is in that area. (p. 3)

The Stanford Diagnostic Mathematics Test (SDMT) is an example of this type of standardized norm-referenced instrument. The SDMT measures key arithmetic subskills across the elementary grades (Figure 5–14). Such tests can be individually administered or given to groups of students. The interpretation of a diagnostic test like the SDMT involves looking for patterns of responses; once scored, the student's raw score is converted to one or more derived scores and plotted on a profile chart. If a student receives a low stanine or percentile rank on a subskill (a norm-referenced interpretation), the teacher should go back to specific responses to begin the diagnosis. This latter kind of interpretation comes closer to being content- or criterion-referenced.

Figure 5-14 presents a student profile prepared by the publisher of the SDMT. A teacher can begin to use this profile by placing a check against any score below the suggested cutoff. In Kathy's case all scores in the "Concept/skill domain" but one (geometry and measurement) are below the suggested cutoff. Notice that a raw score of 5 in two skills falls below the cutoff, while in a third it falls above. In helping to interpret the profile the authors offer the following observations and advice:

On the Number System and Numeration subtest, Kathy obtained a Progress Indicator of "−" on the highest priority Concept/Skill Do-

Stanford Diagnostic Mathematics Test

Teacher ROBERT BOCCI

School COURTHOUSE ELEMENTARY

System GOTHAM CITY   Grade 5

INDIVIDUAL DIAGNOSTIC REPORT

for   COLLINS   KATHY M

Group 1

CONCEPT/SKILL DOMAIN ANALYSIS

DOMAIN CODE	NUMBER OF ITEMS TOTAL	PI	CONCEPT/SKILL DOMAIN	RAW SCORE +	RAW SCORE −
1.0			NUMBER SYSTEM AND NUMERATION		
1.1	21	15	WHOLE NOS & DEC PL VALUE		9
1.2	3	2	RATIONAL NOS & NUMERATION		1
1.3	12	7	OPERATIONS & PROPERTIES		5
2.0			COMPUTATION		
2.1	6	5	ADDITION OF WHOLE NOS		4
2.2	12	8	SUBTRACTION OF WHOLE NOS		5
2.3	12	8	MULTIPLICATN OF WHOLE NOS		3
2.4	9	5	DIVISION OF WHOLE NOS		0
2.8	9	5	NUMBER SENTENCES		2
3.0			APPLICATIONS		
3.1	12	7	PROBLEM SOLVING		3
3.2	9	4	RDG & INTERP TBLS & GRAPHS		3
3.3	9	5	GEOMETRY & MEASUREMENT	5	

PI = Progress Indicator cutoff score; + means score at or above PI cutoff
                  − means score below PI cutoff

NOTES

Kathy was absent
38 days last year.

OTHER PUPIL DATA:

Age (Yrs/Mos) 9 / 11

Other Information

TEST INFORMATION:

Level GREEN   Form A   Date of Testing 10/04/76

Norms Used GRADE   4.6–5.5

RAW SCORES	NUMBER OF ITEMS	GRADE EQUIV-ALENTS	SCALED SCORES	PERCENTILE RANK & STANINE SCORES LOCAL PR	S	NAT'L PR	S	SUBTEST AND TOTAL SCORES	STANINE PROFILE 1 2 3 BELOW AVERAGE	4 5 6 AVERAGE	7 8 9 ABOVE AVERAGE
15	36	3.4	303			15	3	1.0 NUMBER SYSTEM AND NUMERATION	−3−		
14	48	2.9	283			6	2	2.0 COMPUTATION	−2−		
11	30	3.3	315			19	3	3.0 APPLICATIONS	−3−		
40	114	3.1	283			8	2	TOTAL	−2−		

Please see notes on back.

Process No.   000-0000-000

Data Services

Figure 5-14   Individual diagnostic report. (From Stanford Diagnostic Mathematics Test. Copyright © 1976 by Harcourt Brace Jovanovich, Inc.; all rights reserved; reproduced by permission.)

main, "Whole Numbers and Decimal Place Value" (1.1). This indicates that she probably does not understand how to count by multiples, read and interpret numerals in the thousands, and rename numbers well enough to progress to higher level concepts. Lack of understanding in this area will undoubtedly hinder her progress in computation when renaming is involved. The fact that she also obtained "–" Progress Indicators for the "Addition of Whole Numbers" and "Subtraction of Whole Numbers" domains, both of which involve renaming, supports this conclusion. Working with tangible sets of objects and the number line, reading numerals aloud, and analyzing computation examples that involve renaming should help Kathy to understand the concepts of decimal place value. Instruction should progress slowly and by small steps when pupils like Kathy are having only limited success in working with numbers. (Beatty, Madden, Gardner, & Karlsen, 1976, p. 55)

As the reader can see, the interpretation involves both norm- and criterion-referenced inferences about Kathy's weaknesses in arithmetic.

Most standardized diagnostic tests have been developed to assess basic skills in arithmetic, reading, and language. The SDMT described above is an example in arithmetic. The Illinois Test of Psycholinguistic Abilities (McCarthy & Kirk, 1961), is a diagnostic test which helps identify nine specific psycholinguistic abilities and disabilities in children between 2⅓ and 9 years of age. The basic skill of reading has been the target of many fine standardized individual and group diagnostic tests. The interested reader is referred to the books by Bond and Tinker (1974) and R. M. Wilson (1967), each of which contains an excellent treatment of these tests, as well as a description of some informal methods that can be employed to diagnose reading difficulties.

In response to the need for diagnostic tests in compensatory programs and to screen children with potential learning disability, several diagnostic tests have been designed for individual administration by a teacher, teacher aide, or trained volunteer. Further, these tests generally provide the teacher with

both norm- and criterion-referenced interpretations. The following are a few examples of this type of diagnostic instrument: the *Key-Math Diagnostic Arithmetic Test* (Connolly, Nachtman, & Pritchett, 1976); *Woodcock Reading Mastery Tests* (Woodcock, 1973); the *Peabody Individual Achievement Test* (Dunn & Markwardt, 1970); the *Brigance Diagnostic Inventory of Basic Skills* (Brigance, 1976); and the *Bilingual Syntax Measure* (Burt, Dulay, & Hernandez, 1976a). A potential user of any one of these tests—or any diagnostic test, for that matter—should screen the test according to the suggestions outlined earlier in this chapter.

Some of the new tests are criterion-referenced in nature. For example, the *Bilingual Syntax Measure* (Burt, Dulay, & Hernandez, 1976a) is a criterion-referenced test designed to diagnose weakness in a very important prerequisite entry behavior—the student's oral proficiency in English. The number of school children whose first language is not English is increasing, and the largest group of such children have Spanish as their native tongue. It is important that students whose native tongue is not English be assessed for proficiency in English and in their native tongue as well. Failure to remedy faulty English can result in frustration for the student. The degree to which language or verbal skills can be altered is inversely related to the age at which remediation begins. It is more difficult to produce significant changes in later grades. Therefore it behooves school systems to identify non-English speakers early and to provide remedial programs as soon as possible.

The *Bilingual Syntax Measure* (Burt et al., 1976a) provides the teacher with a criterion-referenced statement of the child's Spanish-English syntactic proficiency, language dominance, level of second-language acquisition, and degree of maintenance or loss of the first language.

Teachers or other school personnel who speak and work with Spanish and English can administer the *Bilingual Syntax Measure*. The test is first administered in what the teacher feels is the child's native tongue,

SPANISH PROFICIENCY LEVEL	ENGLISH PROFICIENCY LEVEL				
	LEVEL 1 No English	LEVEL 2 English comprehension only	LEVEL3 Survival English	LEVEL 4 Intermediate English	LEVEL5 Proficient English
LEVEL 1 No Spanish	Children whose scores would appear in these boxes did poorly in both languages and need special diagnosis by a speech therapist or school psychologist. If these children do not have a speech problem, a learning disability, or emotional disturbance, they may have been uncooperative when tested and should be retested.			English monolingual	English monolingual
LEVEL 2 Spanish comprehension only				English monolingual	English monolingual
LEVEL 3 Survival Spanish				English dominant	English dominant
LEVEL 4 Intermediate Spanish	Spanish monolingual	Spanish monolingual	Spanish dominant	Balanced bilingual (intermediate in both)	English dominant
LEVEL 5 Proficient Spanish	Spanish monolingual	Spanish monolingual	Spanish dominant	Spanish dominant	Balanced bilingual (proficient in both)

Figure 5-15 Definition of language dominance categories. (Burt, Dulay, & Hernandez, 1966, p. 40. Copyright © 1975 by Harcourt Bruce Jovanovich, Inc.; all rights reserved; reproduced by permission.)

either English or Spanish. Then a few days later the student is tested again in the other language. From the two administrations the teacher obtains one of five score levels of proficiency in both English and Spanish. When English-level proficiency and Spanish-level proficiency are taken together, the student can be classified into one of the language-dominance categories shown in

Figure 5-15. Each proficiency level is criterion-referenced in terms of the status of the child with respect to specific points along a developmental psycholinguistic continuum. Further, each level itself is described further in the manual in criterion-referenced terms. The teacher is also provided with brief instructional suggestions for each proficiency level. The following is an example of a

143

criterion-referenced description of the English proficiency of students whose native tongue is Spanish:

> *Level 2:* Children in Level 2 are able to understand varying amounts of everyday English. These children are able to produce some English verbal routines, and they are also able to repeat short sentences or questions in English. However, they cannot yet use the language to communicate their thoughts and opinions. When children who are in Level 2 know that the person speaking to them understands their dominant language, they will sometimes respond in that language. This often happens when children are eager to communicate but cannot do so in English. (Burt, et al., 1976, p. 12)

The caution expressed in Figure 5-15 is an important one; it directs the teacher to refer a student to some specialist equipped to make a finer diagnosis. It is important that teachers realize that they are not equipped to make a complete diagnosis in many instances and know when to refer a student.

Many publishers provide graphic representations of test performances of single individuals. This pictorial representation of test scores is helpful in diagnosing a person's strengths and weaknesses across various skills. However, as always in interpreting test scores—norm- or criterion-referenced—a user must proceed with proper caution. Gardner (1970, pp. 3–9) has described the following eight cautions a user should observe in interpreting achievement profiles similar to those shown in the above figures.

1. *Be sure the scores plotted are in comparable units.* As we saw earlier, raw scores on different tests are not comparable. Check to be sure that when you plot or use a profile, it is based on one of the following scores: standard scores; stanines; percentile ranks; grade equivalents.
2. *Be sure the score scales on the profile are based on the same or strictly comparable populations which have been tested at the same time.* This caution reminds the test user of our earlier admonition to know the norm group and be sure that all the derived scores plotted on the profile are based on the same norm group. Do not mix norm groups in plotting a profile.
3. *Do not depend upon observed differences alone.* It is not enough to "eyeball" the profile. What might appear to be differences in performance between two tests could simply be a result of the scale used. To avoid this pitfall the user should heed the next caution carefully.
4. *Check on the reliability and the standard error of measurement of each test and each difference score.* Two test scores that appear to be different from each other may in fact overlap when the standard error of measurement of both is taken into consideration. Many publishers build into their profiles methods that permit the user to determine if an apparent difference in test scores is a significant difference.
5. *Be concerned about the independence or lack of independence of the variables shown on the profile.* Since differences in score patterns are of interest, the reliability of differences between scores is a function not only of the reliability of the two tests but also of the degree to which the two tests are related to each other. When two measures are highly correlated, the reliability of differences between them is less than between the two measures that are not highly related.
6. *Be sure that all necessary supporting information is included as part of the labeling on a profile.* Gardner here reminds the user plotting a profile to immediately write down all pertinent information: norm group, type of score plotted, date of testing, etc. These data can be quickly forgotten and a month later can be very hard to reconstruct.
7. *Remember that profiles using lines joining points are not graphs in the usual sense.* Graphs generally picture continuous functions, but in this case lines have meaning and represent values associated with values between the plotted points.
8. *Base your interpretation on test scores aided by the profile.* Depending on the order in which tests are plotted, one can

achieve quite different visual effects. Therefore, interpretation is based primarily on the scores and is aided by the profile rather than the other way around.

This caution can take another form. Merwin and Joselyn (1971) point out that a student could have an identical percentile rank across all the tests, but if the grade-equivalent score is plotted, this flat, even profile will not necessarily be reflected, and it could appear that the student performed better in one subject than others (see Figure 5-10, which discusses grade equivalents).

Before going on to the next section, we should point out that once a profile is interpreted, remedial actions based on this interpretation need to be planned and implemented. Remember that diagnosis without prescription is a charade.

Criterion-Referenced Achievement Tests

In increasing numbers publishers are marketing criterion-referenced achievement tests (CRTs) or batteries in reading and in arithmetic. (C. B. Walker, 1977; Kosecoff, Fink, and Klein, 1976; and Hambleton and Eignor, 1978, offer procedures and standards that teachers can use to evaluate and select criterion-referenced tests.) Unlike norm-referenced achievement tests, the criterion-referenced tests can readily serve a dual diagnostic function: determination of the performance level of prerequisite entry behaviors and placement within a course or unit. The criterion-referenced tests are geared to a set of behavioral objectives like those described in Chapter 2. Each objective is measured by 3, 4, 5, or more items. The mastery criterion for an objective is set at a fixed number of items answered correctly, (e.g., 3 out of 3; 4 out of 5). Table 5-2 shows the probability of attaining a mastery level on the basis of chance alone. Table 5-2 shows that if there are 5 multiple-choice items, each with four options measuring an objective, and the mastery level is set at 3 items correct, then the probability of answering 3 out of 5 items correctly on the basis of chance is .104.

TABLE 5-2 PROBABILITY OF ATTAINING MASTERY BY CHANCE ALONE

MASTERY CRITERION	Total Number of items per objective (Each item has four choices)				
	1	2	3	4	5
1 or more correct	0.250	.438	.578	.684	.764
2 or more correct	—	.063	.156	.262	.368
3 or more correct	—	—	.016	.051	.104
4 or more correct	—	—	—	.004	.016
5 correct	—	—	—	—	.001

Source: SRA, 1975, p. 5. © 1975, 1974, The Regents of the University of California. Reprinted by permission of the publisher, Science Research Associates, Inc.

To accompany these criterion-referenced tests, test publishers provide report forms that provide the teacher with diagnostic information. For example, Figure 5-16 shows a portion of the teacher's management record for Houghton Mifflin's *Individual Pupil Monitoring System*. The chart shows the number of items a student answered correctly out of a total of 5 for each skill or objective. Such a chart can be interpreted in terms of the class; e.g., skill 633, homonyms, needs review since the average number of items answered correctly out of a possible 5 is 2.6. It can also be interpreted in terms of an individual student; e.g., Paula C. appears deficient on all the objectives shown. The teacher can use this information to plan individual or group remediation.

Most publishers also cross-reference each objective measured by their criterion-referenced tests to the reading or mathematics programs of major publishers. This guide identifies pages in the reading materials that give the best instruction on those behaviors not yet mastered by each individual student. The teacher is provided with a program reference guide that cross-references each objective to major reading programs. The cross-referencing permits the teacher to prescribe review and practice from the adopted text for students who are weak on one objective or any combination of objectives measured by the test. It also identifies extra review and practice materials from other reading series.

VOCABULARY AND COMPREHENSION Level 6 Skills	Names of students	Paula C.	Susan C.	Robert K.	Karen H.	Bill S.	Class average
631. Unknown words (meaning of non-sense word from context)		2	5	4	4	5	4
632. Synonyms/antonyms: Choose word from context		2	5	4	3	2	3.2
633. Homonyms: Choose from phonetic spelling in context		1	4	2	3	3	2.6
634. Multi-meaning words: Identify meaning from context		2	4	4	3	4	3.4

Figure 5-16 Portion of teacher's management record for the *Individual Pupil Monitoring System.* (Houghton Mifflin, 1974. Copyright ©1974 by Houghton Mifflin Co., reprinted by permission.)

Publishers also provide teachers with guides for forming instructional groups on the basis of their criterion-referenced test performance. For example, Harcourt Brace Jovanovich provides the following guide for grouping according to students' mastery level on various reading skills measured by its *Skills Monitoring System: Reading* (1975, pp. 30–31):

Skill Cluster Groups
Group 1—Word Meaning in Context
(Skills 1, 2*, 3, 4, 5, 6, 7)
These learners have difficulty in using context clues to discover the meaning of a word.

Group 2—Sentence Meaning
(Skills 8*, 9, 10*, 11, 12, 13)
These learners have difficulty in understanding the meaning of a sentence.

Group 3—Stated Concepts
(Skills 14, 15*, 16, 17*, 18)
These learners have difficulty in understanding the meaning of directly stated material, such as following a sequence, identifying a stated detail, or identifying a directly stated main idea.

Group 4—Interpretation
(Skills 19*, 20, 21, 22*, 23, 24, 25, 26, 27, 28, 29)
These learners have difficulty in identifying the main idea when it is not directly stated as well as difficulty with various inferential skills.

Group 5—Critical Reading and Characterization
(Skills 30, 31, 32*, 33, 34, 35)
These learners have difficulty in analyzing what they read, such as differentiating between fact and opinion, and in recognizing different types of content. They also have difficulty in recognizing character traits and in interpreting a character's behavior. (Reproduced by permission. Copyright © 1975 by Harcourt Brace Jovanovich, Inc. All rights reserved.)

The publisher recognizes that having multiple groups in class results in management problems for the teacher and suggests the management pattern which is shown in Figure 5–17.

TIME (minutes)	Group I	Group II	Group III	Group IV
15	Teacher instruction	Supplementary reading Games, puzzles, etc.	Independent application of skill previously taught Supplementary reading	Independent application of skill previously taught
15	Independent application of skill previously taught	Teacher instruction	Supplementary reading Games, puzzles, etc.	Independent application of skill previously taught Supplementary reading
15	Independent application of skiil previously taught Supplementary reading	Independent application of skill previously taught	Teacher instruction	Supplementary reading Games, puzzles, etc.
15	Supplementary reading Games, puzzles, etc.	Independent application of skill previously taught Supplementary reading	Independent application of skill previously taught	Teacher instruction

Figure 5-17 Classroom management pattern for skill instruction. (Harcourt Brace Jovanovich, 1975, p. 32. Copyright © 1975 by Harcourt Brace Jovanovich, Inc.; all rights reserved; reproduced by permission.)

The commercially available criterion-referenced tests offer the teacher a wealth of diagnostic information both in terms of proper placement and in terms of prerequisite skills. In the latter case the performance on the objectives appropriate to the year below the grade of interest can provide excellent information concerning prerequisite skills; information on the mastery of objectives appropriate to the present grade can provide excellent placement information. Teachers who are unable to avail themselves of commercial criterion-referenced test information should nonetheless study the publisher's interpretative handbook for tips on diagnosis.

DIAGNOSIS OF THE CAUSES OF REPEATED INABILITY TO PROFIT FROM INSTRUCTION

Up to this point we have discussed diagnosis primarily in terms of prerequisite entry behaviors and placement within a course or unit. Every teacher recognizes that despite such diagnosis, some students who are properly placed initially are still unsuccessful learners. When this occurs, a teacher must try to diagnose the probable cause of the student's inability to profit from instruction. The cause of repeated failure for an individual or group of pupils may be related to the instruction, materials, or test questions asked. If these causes can be ruled out, then the difficulty very likely is nonacademic. If this is true, then several cautions are in order. First, although teachers are not expected to be experts on deep-seated noneducational causes of learning disabilities, they should recognize the symptoms associated with such causes. Second, teachers should be aware of the special agencies available if these symptoms are observed. Third, teachers should realize that they are an integral part of a team that together can diagnose causes of learning disability and plan a program to bring the student back on the learning track. Fourth, teachers should realize that while there may still be failures despite such diagnosis, many students can be—and are being—helped by diagnostic teams.

Causes Related to Instruction, Materials, or Test Questions

Case (1975) makes the excellent point that logical analysis of the components of a learning unit can fail to uncover psychological blocks to learning. These undetected blocks are a function of the interaction between the material and the developmental level of the student. He recommends that teachers examine students' errors for consistency by asking, "Is there a different question for which these answers would actually be correct?" Case argues that students answer the wrong question because of an inability to overcome their natural way of responding to a situation or an inability to coordinate all the relevant information. If the teacher considers that students are answering questions different from the ones intended, then the teacher needs to plan more effective instruction to help learners obtain the objective sought.

Case suggests that a teacher might be able to facilitate learning in these situations by following these four steps:

> The first is to enable the subject to discriminate between the question he was asked and the question he answered.
>
> The second is to enable him to discriminate

between the salient cues on which he focused and the relevant (embedded) cues on which he *should* have focused.

> The third is to enable him to understand the rationale underlying the correct response.
>
> The fourth is to enable him to understand the *relationship* between the correct response and the one which he gave. (p. 81)

Orasanu (1976) points out that "the likelihood that a person will demonstrate a particular skill may depend on the materials used to test the skill, rather than in proficiency at the skill itself. Yet inferences are drawn about the skill, not about familiarity with the materials" (p. 8). Thus repeated failures may be the result of one or both of two factors—a mismatch between the material and the capacities of the learner or a mismatch between the methods used to test the skills in question and the capacities of the learner.

Orasanu reviews studies which show clearly that constraints of text, directions, or the setting used to measure certain cognitive skills can result in an *incorrect* inference that a student has not attained a skill. This is a question of test validity: Does the test measure what it purports to? Directions that are fine for adults may not "make sense" for children; unfamiliar material or a new setting for testing can also adversely affect the student's ability to demonstrate skills that he or she in fact possesses. Orasanu points out, "If it can be shown that, outside of the testing situation, children possess and use abilities which they are assumed to lack on the basis of their test performance, our diagnosis and prescriptions for their future school experiences ought to be modified appropriately" (p. 28).

Noneducational Causes

A teacher who suspects a noneducational factor to be the cause of learning disabilities should look for behavior symptomatic of physical, psychological, or environmental problems. If several such symptoms are observed, the teacher may use available screening devices to check this hypothesis further. When these devices support such conjectures, the teacher should then refer the student to the proper authorities or agency for additional diagnosis and prescription. When the screening devices do not sustain the hypothesis, the teacher should search for alternative explanations for the symptoms. Some other rather simple factor may account for the observed behavior. For example, perhaps the student is experiencing difficulty in another class and it is affecting his or her work in all classes; perhaps the student's parent has been laid off or is experiencing legal or medical problems; perhaps a close relative has died. Failing to find an alternative explanation, the teacher should refer the student to the proper authorities or agencies for further diagnosis.

In programs such as those required by Public Law 94–142, the teacher is the person who provides the psychologist with an analysis of the student's specific behavioral abilities and with a comparison of those abilities to the tasks contained in the regular classroom program. The teacher also provides a statement of school readiness or achievement and a description of behavioral, perceptual, social, or emotional problems noted in class. The teacher plays an integral part in interpreting all the data and designing a reasonable academic program. Thus it is most important for teachers to be alert for symptoms of physical, psychological, or environmental problems if the student is to be helped.

In the category of physical problems, visual, auditory, motor, speech, dietary, general health, glandular, or neurological conditions may cause or contribute to a student's learning disability.

Under the classification of psychological problems are a host of emotional factors which can impair a student's ability to profit from instruction. A poor self-concept, the negative emotional effects of a broken home, neurosis or more debilitating mental disorders, or simply the tensions concomitant with adolescence can all make it impossible for a student to profit from the usual type of learning experience.

Similarly, the category of environmental problems includes many factors which can contribute to a student's learning difficulties. As we saw previously, some of these, especially those caused by cultural deprivation, such as poor language and reading skills, can be detected, and the student can be placed in the proper compensatory class. Other environmental factors, ranging from the marital difficulties of a student's parents to a bilingual problem, will not necessarily be picked up by ordinary placement diagnosis.

We shall not go into a detailed treatment of each of the noneducational causes of learning problems since there are several excellent sources available. The reader is referred to Gardner (1977), Kessler (1966), and R. M. Wilson (1967) for a detailed discussion of the classroom symptoms of physical, psychological, and environmental causes of learning disabilities. These books contain descriptions of symptoms, screening devices, and referral agencies for the various causes.

SUMMARY

Good diagnosis helps the teacher to place students properly in the instructional sequence and to identify causes of repeated failure to learn. Teachers should make the implicit assumption that all students bring similar cognitive and affective experiences, prerequisites, and skills to their class or subject at the beginning of each year. A teacher must take the time and effort to identify the presence or absence of prerequisite skills, attitudes, and habits; those students who have already mastered some or all of the objectives; and those gifted or talented individuals who need special attention. The success of the instruction and learning during the year will depend in good part on the accuracy and depth of the diagnosis performed at the outset.

EXERCISES

Objective: Design, implement, and interpret a variety of diagnostic procedures in a classroom setting.

Preparation: In doing the exercises below you will need access to test battery profiles on your students and a source for diagnostic test instruments. If you are not currently engaged in teaching, perhaps you could enlist the cooperation of a teacher in gaining access to these materials.

1. Interpreting test scores for diagnostic purposes.
   a. Examine standardized test battery scores for several students.
   b. Write up a diagnostic narrative for each student. Consider the following:
      (1) What kinds of tests were used?
      (2) What kinds of scores were reported?
      (3) Examine the individual profile (if it has been provided) for each pupil. Are there any ways such a profile could be misleading?
      (4) What are the limitations of the information you are examining for diagnostic purposes?
      (5) What other kinds of information would be useful?
      (6) Prescribe remediation where warranted by your narrative.
2. Group-administered diagnostic evaluation.
   a. Either prepare or select a diagnostic instrument to assess one of the following:
      (1) School readiness
      (2) Study skills
      (3) Cognitive prerequisites
      (4) Affective prerequisites
   b. Administer the instrument.
   c. Interpret the results with an emphasis on prescription of placement, materials, and methods to provide the best learning experience for each child or group of children.
3. Individually administered diagnostic evaluation.
   a. If possible, administer—with trained assistance if necessary—one of the individually administered diagnostic instruments mentioned in the chapter.
   b. Interpret the results, again with emphasis on prescription.

REFERENCES

American Psychological Association. *Standards for educational and psychological tests.* Washington, D.C.: Author, 1974.

Backer, T. E. *A directory of information on tests* (TM Report 62). Princeton, N.J.: Educational Testing Service, ERIC Clearinghouse on Tests, Measurement and Evaluation. 1977.

Balow, I. H. Does homogeneous grouping give homogeneous groups? *Elementary School Journal*, 1962, 62(1), 28–32.

Beatty, L. S., Madden, R., & Gardner, E. F. *Manual for administering and interpreting Stanford Diagnostic Arithmetic Test.* New York: Harcourt, Brace and World, 1966.

Beatty, L. S., Madden, R., Gardner, E. F., & Karlsen, B. *Manual for administering and interpreting Stanford Diagnostic Mathematics Test.* New York: Harcourt Brace Jovanovich, 1976.

Bianchini, J., & Loret, P. *Anchor Test Study: Final report.* (34 vols.) Berkeley, Calif.: Educational Testing Service, 1974.

Bibaud, C. R. *Learning to learn.* Shrewsbury, Mass.: St. John's High School, 1974.

Bloom, B. S. *Stability and change in human characteristics.* New York: Wiley, 1964.

Bloom, B. S. *Human characteristics and school learning.* New York: McGraw-Hill, 1976.

Bloom, B. S., Hastings, J. T., & Madaus, G. F. *Handbook of formative and summative evaluation of student learning.* New York: McGraw-Hill, 1971.

Bloom, S. *Peer and cross-age tutoring in the schools: An individualized supplement to group instruction.* Gary, Ind.: Gary Public Schools Program in Compensatory Education, 1975.

Bond, G., & Tinker, M. A. *Reading difficulties: Their diagnosis and correction* (2nd ed.). New York: Appleton Century Crofts, 1974.

Boyer, E. G., Simon, A., & Karafin, G. (Eds.). *Measures of maturation: An anthology of early children observation instru-*

ments (3 vols.). Philadelphia: Research for Better Schools, 1973.

Bradley, R. H., & Caldwell, B. M. *Issues and procedures in testing young children* (TM Report 37). ERIC Clearinghouse on Tests, Measurement and Evaluation. Princeton, N.J.: Educational Testing Service, 1974.

Brigance, A. H. *Brigance Diagnostic Inventory of Basic Skills.* Newton, Mass.: Curriculum Association, Inc., 1976.

Brockton Public Schools. *Brockton Public Schools Cumulative Reading Report.* Brockton, Mass.: Brockton Public Schools, undated.

Buros, O. K. (Ed.). *The seventh mental measurement yearbook.* Highland Park, N.J.: Gryphon Press, 1972.

Burt, M. K., Dulay, H. C., & Hernandez, C. E. *Bilingual Syntax Measure.* New York: Harcourt Brace Jovanovich, 1976. (a)

Burt, M. K., Dulay, H. C., & Hernandez, C. E. *Manual for Bilingual Syntax Measure.* New York: Harcourt Brace Jovanovich, 1976. (b)

Burt, M. K., Dulay, H. C., & Hernandez, C. E. *Technical handbook.* New York: Harcourt Brace Jovanovich, 1976. (c)

California Test Bureau (CTB)/McGraw-Hill. *Prescriptive Reading Inventory Interpretive Handbook.* Monterey, Calif.: Author, 1972.

Case, R. Gearing the demands of instruction to the developmental capacities of the learner. *Review of Educational Research,* 1975, 45(1), 58–87.

Cazden, C. B. Evaluation of learning in preschool education: Early language development. In B. S. Bloom, J. T. Hastings, & G. F. Madaus (Eds.), *Handbook on formative and summative evaluation of student learning.* New York: McGraw-Hill, 1971.

Collier, A. R. *The assessment of "self concept" in early childhood education.* (ERIC Clearinghouse, ED 050–822) Princeton, N.J.: Educational Testing Service, 1971.

Connolly, A., Nachtman, W., & Pritchett, E. *Key Math Diagnostic Arithmetic Test.* Circle Pine, Minn.: American Guidance Services, 1976.

Dunn, L. M., & Markwardt, F. C., Jr.

Peabody Individual Achievement Test. Circle Pine, Minn.: American Guidance Services, 1970.

Echternacht, G. Grade equivalent scores. *NCME Measurement in Education,* 1977, 8(2).

Educational Testing Service. *Independent Activities Questionnaire.* Princeton, N.J.: Author, 1965.

Fagan, W. T., Cooper, C. R., & Jensen, J. M. *Measures for research evaluation in the English language arts.* ERIC Clearinghouse on Reading and Communication Skills & National Council of Teachers of English. Urbana, Ill.: National Institute of Evaluation, 1975.

Fitzgibbon, T. J. *The use of standardized instruments with urban and minority group pupils.* New York: Harcourt Brace Jovanovich, 1975.

Friedman, C. P., & Strickland, J. S. *Study guides for PSSC physics: Teacher's manual.* Washington, D.C.: Georgetown University Center for Personalized Instruction, 1975.

Frostig, M. Developmental test of visual perception. Palo Alto, Calif.: Consulting Psychologists Press, 1963.

Frostig, M. *Developmental test of visual perception: Administration and scoring manual.* Palo Alto, Calif.: Consulting Psychologists Press, 1966.

Gardner, E. F. Interpreting achievement profiles—Uses and warnings. *NCME Measurement in Evaluation,* January, 1970, 1(2), 1–11.

Gardner, W. I. *Learning and behavior characteristics of exceptional children and youth.* Boston: Allyn & Bacon, 1977.

Gislason, B. J. *School readiness testing: A bibliography* (TM Report 54). ERIC Clearinghouse on Tests, Measurement and Evaluation. Princeton, N.J.: Educational Testing Service, 1975.

Goodlad, J. I., & Anderson, R. H. *The nongraded elementary school.* New York: Harcourt Brace, 1959.

Grobman, H. Assignment of students to tracks in biology. *American Biology Teacher,* 1965, 27, 762–764.(a)

Grobman, H. Background of the 1963–64 evaluation. *BSCS Newsletter*, 1965, No. 24, 16–24. (Biological Services Curriculum Study, University of Colorado.) (b)

Guthrie, P. D. *Measures of social skills: An annotated bibliography* (Head Start Test Collection). Princeton, N.J.: Educational Testing Service, 1971.

Guthrie, P. D., & Horne, E. V. *School readiness measures: An annotated bibliography* (Head Start Test Collection). Princeton, N.J.: Educational Testing Service, 1971.

Hambleton, R. K., & Eignor, D. R. Guidelines for evaluating criterion-referenced tests and test manuals. *Journal of Educational Measurement*, Winter 1978, *15*(4), 321–328.

Harcourt Brace Jovanovich. *Skills Monitoring System: Reading. Teacher Handbook, Comprehension.* New York: Author, 1975.

Hoepfner, R., Strickland, G., Stangel, G., Jansen, P., & Patalino, M. *CSE Elementary School Test Evaluations.* Los Angeles: UCLA Graduate School Center for the Study of Evaluation, 1970.

Hogan, T. P. *Survey of school attitudes: Manual for administering and interpreting.* New York: Harcourt Brace Jovanovich, 1975.

Houghton Mifflin. *Individual Pupil Monitoring System: Level 6, Teacher's Management Record.* Boston: Author, 1974.

Johnson, O. G., & Bonmarito, J. W. *Tests and measurement in child development: A handbook.* San Francisco: Jossey Bass, 1971.

Josselyn, E. G., & Merwin, J. C. Using your achievement test score reports. *NCME Measurement in Education,* 1971, 3(1).

Kamii, C. K. Evaluation of learning in preschool education: Socio-emotional, perceptual-motor, cognitive development. In B. S. Bloom, J. T. Hastings, & G. F. Madaus (Eds.), *Handbook on formative and summative evaluation of student learning.* New York: McGraw-Hill, 1971.

Katz, M. *Selecting an achievement test: Principles and procedures.* Princeton, N.J.: Educational Testing Service, 1973.

Kessler, J. W. *Psychopathology of childhood.* Englewood Cliffs, N.J.: Prentice-Hall, 1966.

Kosecoff, J., Fink, A., & Klein, S.P. *A system for describing and evaluating criterion-referenced tests.* ERIC Clearinghouse on Tests, Measurement & Evaluation. Princeton, N.J.: Educational Testing Service, 1976.

Levin, J. *Learner differences: Diagnosis and prescription.* New York: Holt, 1977.

McCarthy, J. J., & Kirk, S. C. *Examiner's Manual, ITPA.* Urbana, Ill.: University of Illinois, 1961.

Madden, R., Gardner, E. F., Rudman, H. C., Karlsen, B., & Merwin, J. C. *Stanford Achievement Test, Primary Level III Battery. Teachers Guide for Interpreting.* New York: Harcourt Brace Jovanovich, 1973.

Maier, M. H., & Anderson, S. B. Growth Study: 1. Adolescent behavior and interests. *Research Bulletin RDR–64–5, No. 6.* Princeton, N.J.: Educational Testing Service, 1964. (a)

Maier, M. H., & Anderson, S. B. *Background and experience questionnaire.* Princeton, N.J.: Educational Testing Service, 1964. (b)

Mitchell, B. *A glossary of measurement terms* (Test Service Notebook 13). New York: Harcourt Brace Jovanovich, undated.

Northwest Regional Education Laboratory. *Alaskan Statewide Instructional Support System: Objective and Item Directory Reading: Word Identification Skills.* Juneau: Alaska Department of Education, 1976.

Oakland, T., & Phillips, B. N. *Assessing minority group children.* New York: Behavioral Publications, 1973.

Orasanu, J. Constraints of text and setting of measurement of mental ability (Working Paper 3). New York: Rockefeller University Laboratory of Comparative Human Cognition and Institute for Comparative Human Development, 1976.

Otis-Lennon Mental Ability Test (OLMAT) IQ. New York: Harcourt Brace Jovanovich, 1974.

Pimsleur, P., Sundlan, D. M., & McIntyre, R. D. *Underachievement in foreign language learning.* New York: Modern Language Association, 1966.

Plas, J. M. If not grade equivalent scores—then what? *NCME Measurement in Education,* 1977, 8(2), 4–7.

Psychological Corporation. *Methods of expressing test scores* (Test Service Bulletin 48). New York: Author, 1955.

Purves, A. C. Evaluation of learning in literature. In B. S. Bloom, J. T. Hastings, & G. F. Madaus (Eds.), *Handbook on formative and summative evaluation of student learning.* New York: McGraw-Hill, 1971.

Resnick, L., & Glasser, R. Problem solving and intelligence. In L. Resnick (Ed.), *The nature of intelligence.* New York: Wiley, 1976.

Rosen, P. *Language development tests: Annotated bibliography* (Head Start Collection). Princeton, N.J.: Educational Testing Service, 1971.

Rutherford, F. J. Flexibility and variety in physics. *Physics Teacher,* 1967, 5, 215–221.

Rutherford, F. J., et al. *Harvard Project Physics Unit Tests.* Cambridge, Mass.: Harvard Project Physics, 1966. (a)

Rutherford, F. J., et al. *Pupil Activity Inventory.* Cambridge, Mass.: Harvard Project Physics, 1966. (b)

Rutherford, F. J., et al. *Semantic Differential Test.* Cambridge, Mass.: Harvard Project Physics, 1966. (c)

SRA. *Criterion-referenced measurement program: An evaluation tool. MASTERY: The guide to mastery.* Chicago: Science Research Associates, 1975.

Simon, A., & Boyer, E. G. (Eds.), *Mirrors for behavior: An anthology of classroom observation instruments.* Philadelphia: Research for Better Schools, 1970.

Suydom, M. Unpublished instruments for evaluation in mathematics education: An annotated bibliography. ERIC Information Analysis Center for Science, Mathematics and Environment Education. Columbus: Ohio State University, 1974.

Stanley, J. C., George, W. C., & Solano, C. H. *Educational programs and intellectual prodigies.* Baltimore: Johns Hopkins, 1977.

Tobias, S. Achievement test information. *Review of Educational Research,* 1976, 46(1), 61–74.

Vollbrecht, M. T. *Grade equivalent scores: An annotated bibliography.* ERIC Clearinghouse on Tests, Measurement and Evaluation. Princeton, N.J.: Educational Testing Service, 1977.

Walker, C. B. Standards for evaluating criterion-referenced tests. Los Angeles: Center for the Study of Evaluation, 1977. (Mimeo)

Walker, D. K., & Bryk, A. S. The development of a kindergarten assessment battery for the evaluation of the Brookline Early Education Project: Report of spring 1974 and spring 1975 kindergarten pilot studies. Brookline, Mass.: Brookline Early Education Project, 1976.

Wilson, R. M. *Diagnostic and remedial reading for classroom and clinic.* Columbus: Merrill, 1967.

Wilson, B., & Van Etten, C. Materials analysis. *Journal of Learning Disabilities,* 1977, 9(7), 408–416.

Winnetka Public Schools. *Mathematics Goal Record Card.* Winnetka, Ill.: Winnetka Public Schools, undated.

Woodcock, R. W. *Woodcock Reading Mastery Tests.* Circle Pines, Minn.: American Guidance Services, 1973.

Yates, A. (Ed.). *Grouping in education.* New York: Wiley, 1966.

6 Formative Evaluation

Chapter Highlights

INTRODUCTION: TYPES OF SYSTEMATIC EVALUATION

We have chosen the term "summative evaluation" to indicate the type of evaluation used at the end of a term, course, or program for purposes of grading, certification, evaluation of progress, or research on the effectiveness of a curriculum, course of study, or educational plan. In Chapter 4 we considered in some detail the special problems of constructing tests and using test data for this type of evaluation. Perhaps the essential characteristic of summative evaluation is that a judgment is made about the student, teacher, or curriculum with regard to the effectiveness of learning or instruction, *after* the learning or instruction has taken place. It is this act of judgment which produces so much anxiety and defensiveness in students, teachers, and curriculum makers. We do not believe it is possible to avoid using summative evaluation, nor would we wish to do so. However, there is another type of evaluation which all who are involved—student, teacher, curriculum maker—would welcome because they find it so useful in helping them improve what they wish to do.

In searching for a term to describe this other type of evaluation, we found "formative evaluation," first used by Scriven (1967) in connection with curriculum improvement. Scriven points out that once a curriculum has been put in final form, everyone connected with it resists evidence which would make for major alterations. It is his view that formative evaluation involves the collection of appropriate evidence *during* the construction and trying out of a new curriculum in such a way that revisions of the curriculum can be based on this evidence.

We regard formative evaluation as useful not only for curriculum construction but also for instruction and students' learning. Formative evaluation is for us the use of systematic evaluation in the process of curriculum construction, teaching, and learning for the purpose of improving any of these three processes. Since formative evaluation takes place during the formation stage, every effort should be made to use it to improve the process. This means that in formative evaluation one must strive to develop the kinds of evidence that will be most useful in the process, seek the most useful method of reporting the evidence, and search for ways of reducing the negative affect associated with evaluation—perhaps by reducing the judgmental aspects of evaluation or, at the least, by having the users of the formative evaluation (teachers, students, curriculum makers) make the judgments. The hope is that the users of the formative evaluation will find ways of relating the results of the evaluation to the learning and instructional goals they regard as important and worthwhile.

NEED FOR FEEDBACK AND CORRECTIVES

In Chapter 3, Learning for Mastery, we pointed out that group instruction does not provide equality of learning opportunity for all the students in a classroom. Observations of teachers and students in classrooms (Brophy & Good, 1970) demonstrate that teachers quite unconsciously direct their teaching and explanations to some students and ignore others, give positive reinforcement and encouragement to some students but not to others, and encourage active participation from some students and discourage it from others. Typically, the students in the top fourth or third of the class are given the greatest attention and encouragement by teachers, while the students in the bottom half of the class are given the least attention and support.

As we noted in Chapter 3, group instruction produces errors in learning at each stage of a course or school term, which are then compounded with later learning errors. The errors produced by this system of group instruction determine the final achievement of each student, and only rarely is the individual student able to fully recover from them.

We also explained in Chapter 3 a major thesis of the mastery-learning stragegy which bears repeating here: A system of feedback to the teachers and students can reveal the errors or difficulties in learning for each student shortly after they occur. If appropriate correctives are introduced as they are needed, the educational system can be a self-correcting system so that learning errors can be corrected before they are compounded with later learning errors.

This self-correcting system is the essential process in most mastery-learning strategies. *Group instruction* is supplemented by frequent *feedback* and *individualized corrective help* as each student needs it. The *group instruction* is the same as the regular instruction at present provided by the teacher. The *feedback* is usually in the form of brief *formative* progress tests which indicate what each student has learned and what he or she still needs to learn in order to master the learning task. The *individualized corrective help* is provided to help each student learn the important points he or she has missed. This help may be provided by referring the student to particular instructional materials, by having students help each other over their specific difficulties, or by the use of an aide or tutor.

Feedback and correction is a concept only rarely used in regular group instruction. This concept is, we believe, most important if all students are to learn well. While the usual quiz or progress test used by teachers can furnish feedback, it is used primarily for grading or judging the students on what they have learned by a given point in time. The important point to be stressed is that the feedback (to both the student and the teacher) must be accompanied by corrective procedures if the students are to be adequately prepared for the subsequent learning tasks. To use a crude analogy, the usual test or quiz given during the course is like a thermometer which measures the temperature of a room. It may be very accurate, but nothing is done about the temperature of the room, other than to record or measure it. In contrast, a *thermostat* registers the temperature of the room in relation to a set criterion temperature and then institutes corrective procedures (the furnace or air conditioner is turned on or off) until the room temperature is equal to the criterion temperature. The thermometer provides information, while the thermostat provides *feedback and correctives* until the desired temperature of the room is attained.

ANALYSIS OF LEARNING UNITS

The Unit of Learning

Most fundamental to the use of formative evaluation is the selection of a unit of learning. Within a course or education program there are parts or divisions which have a separable existence such that they can, at least for analytic purposes, be considered in relative isolation from other parts. While these parts may be interrelated in various ways so that the learning (or level of learning) of one part has consequences for the learning of others, it is still possible to consider the parts separately.

The nature of the unit may vary for different purposes. In curriculum construction it may be desirable to regard the unit as a single lesson or learning session. However, for the practical purposes of instruction and learning, it appears to us that a useful unit would be something larger than the single session. In some of our work we have found that a unit of learning could be the content covered in a chapter of a textbook or the material covered in 1 to 2 weeks of instruction. The delineation of the unit may be arbitrary; ideally it should be determined by natural breaks in the subject matter or by the content that makes a meaningful whole.

Specifications for the Unit

A unit of learning, however conceived, consists of subject matter to be learned over a given period of time. For the purposes of formative evaluation, it is necessary to analyze the components of this unit. The task of determining the specifications for formative evaluation is much the same as that of creating specifications for summative evaluation.

It is possible for curriculum makers to construct a unit by beginning with a set of specifications in which they outline in some detail the content to be included as well as the behaviors or objectives to be achieved in relation to this content. Ideally the curriculum makers may also determine the standard they desire to be met in the attainment of the specifications. Given the set of specifications, *instructional materials personnel* attempt to create the material and set the learning experiences which will enable students to develop in the ways specified. The same types of specifications can be used by *evaluation specialists* or *teachers* to construct formative evaluation instruments which can be used to determine when students have attained the competence defined by the specifications as well as to indicate in which aspects of the specifications the students' development is satisfactory or unsatisfactory.

Content

In our own work at the University of Chicago on formative evaluation, we have begun with existing instructional material and have at-tempted to analyze a learning unit into its components. The first step, which in some ways is the simplest, is to determine what *new* content or subject matter has been introduced in the new unit. What are the new terms, facts, relations, procedures which have been explained, defined, illustrated, or otherwise presented in the learning material?

We find that the usual textbook is relatively clear in signaling the new content that has been developed in a particular chapter. In either the textbook or the teacher's guide the new material is indicated by changes in print or color, comments in the margin, the summary at the end of the chapter, and the index.

Two or more independent judges who know the subject field rarely have difficulty agreeing on the new elements of content or subject matter that are included in a particular learning unit. In our work with teachers and graduate students, we find agreement between judges to be on the order of 90 percent or higher when they independently list the details of content that have been introduced in a particular textbook chapter or set of instructional materials.

Behaviors

A second type of analysis is undertaken to determine the behaviors or learning outcomes related to each new element of content. That is, given a new idea, relation, statement of truth, or other information, what is the student expected to learn? What is the student expected to remember? What is the student expected to be able to do with the specific subject matter introduced in the learning unit?

We have found it useful to classify the new elements of subject matter or content according to some of the categories in the *Taxonomy of Educational Objectives*, Handbook 1, *Cognitive Domain* (Bloom, 1956). These classifications attempt to define a hierarchy of levels of behavior that relate to the difficulty and complexity levels of the learning process. We have used the following levels:

Knowledge of terms

The "terms" are the specific vocabulary of a subject that the students are to learn. They may be expected to define the term, recognize illustrations of it, determine when the term is used correctly or incorrectly, or recognize synonyms. This category represents the lowest or simplest behavior level in the *Taxonomy*. (*Knowledge of terms* is defined in more detail in Chapter 8.)

Knowledge of facts

"Facts" are the specific types of information which the students are expected to remember. Facts may include dates, names of persons or events, and descriptions; in general they are the particular details which are to be known simply because someone regards or as essential for other kinds of learning. Students are expected to recall or remember these as discrete and separable content elements. They may be expected to recall the specific bit of information, to distinguish between accurate and inaccurate statements of it, and to remember the correct fact when asked about it in a relatively direct manner. (This category is also defined in more detail in Chapter 8.)

Knowledge of rules and principles

This classification entails recall of the major ideas, schemes, and patterns by which the phenomena and ideas in a subject area are organized. Rules and principles bring together a large number of facts or describe the interrelationships among many specifics in such a way that a large body of information can be organized in a parsimonious manner. Students are expected to know the rule or principle, to remember the illustrations of it used in the instruction, to recall situations in which it is applicable, and to remember the conditions under which it is or is not applicable. Rules and principles are likely to be more abstract and more difficult to learn than specific terms and facts. However, it is important to recognize that this category deals only with the recollection of the rules and principles and not with their application. (See

Chapter 8 for a fuller definition and illustrations of this category.)

Skill in using processes and procedures

This category is not included in the *Taxonomy*. We found, after inspecting a number of courses and especially some of the newer curriculum materials, that students are frequently expected to be able to use certain procedures and operations accurately and rapidly. Quite frequently these are particular steps in a process which the students learn in the appropriate sequence. It is sometimes possible for students to learn a process before they have a name or rule to identify it—for example, they may be able to speak correctly before they have grammatical rules, or to take the square root of a number by following correct steps before they have a rule or principle which "explains" the operation. In this category the emphasis is on the students' being able to use the process or procedure accurately. That is, the students can do the steps in the procedure in the correct order, can perform the operation in an appropriate manner, and can get the correct result with a minimum of awkward or extraneous activity.

Ability to make translations

This category involves the transformation of a term, fact, rule or principle, or process or procedure from one form to another. In translation the students can put the idea in their own words; they can take a phenomenon or event presented in one mode or form and represent it by an equivalent form or mode. For example, the representation may move from a verbal to a symbolic form, from a concrete to a more abstract form, or from a general to a more specific illustration, and vice versa. The students will be able to use new illustrations of a term, fact, rule, or other matter, and determine when a new illustration is an appropriate or inappropriate one for it. In general, translation is being employed when the students put an idea in their own words or use relatively new examples of what they have already learned. (This category is further defined and illustrated in Chapter 8.)

Ability to make applications

"Application" is the use of rules and principles to solve problems presented in situations which are new or unfamiliar to the students. The primary behavior required at the application level is the use of a rule or principle learned in one context to solve a problem presented in a new context. If a problem is one the students have encountered many times previously, except that new data are substituted, the behavior to be performed can be classified as translation rather than application. It is difficult to identify examples which represent true application without some knowledge of the learning materials or context within which the students originally encountered the relevant rules and principles. In application the students must recognize the essentials of the problem; determine the rules, principles, generalizations, and so forth which are relevant; and then use these ideas to solve a problem which is different from those previously encountered in the instruction or instructional materials. This is the most complex of the categories in that it depends on some of the previous classifications but requires the students to apply the ideas in new situations or problems. (This category is further defined and illustrated in Chapter 9.)

The classification of the detailed content according to these categories of behavior is more difficult than the identification of the content. However, we find that after a little explanation and some practice in applying the behaviors to given material, judges (teachers, psychologists, researchers) can agree on 85 percent or more of the classifications, with most of the errors having to do with distinctions between facts and rules or principles and between translations and applications (Airasian, 1971). It is evident that teachers of a subject have less difficulty making these distinctions than psychologists and research workers who have never taught the subject. The teachers are familiar with the content, they are more clearly aware of what the instructional material is intended to

do, and they have a clearer model of what students should be able to do after they have completed the learning unit. In general, teachers are able to apply these categories to a specific learning unit with a few hours of practice.

Table of Specifications

We have found it useful to organize the specifications for a unit of learning and for formative evaluation in tabular form. On one axis of this table we place the major behavior categories. Under each of these we list the appropriate subject matter elements or details. Then, by using connecting lines, we attempt to show the interrelations among the elements. That is, if an element at one level is necessary for an element at a more complex level, this is shown by a line connecting the two elements. In Tables 6-1, 6-2, 6-3 and 6-4 we illustrate the use of tables of specifications in analyzing units of learning in chemistry, biology, algebra, and arithmetic. On each chart we have indicated in circles the numbers of relevant formative test items, some of which will be given in the following section, "Formative Test Construction."

The process of developing specifications in this manner is highly revealing to teachers since it enables them to see in a very compact form the elements in a unit of learning as well as the relations among these elements as developed in the unit. Teachers and curriculum workers are especially sensitive to gaps revealed by the specifications table—it immediately shows terms, facts, or rules which are to be learned without being used in translations or applications. Quite frequently a unit of learning will consist simply of a large number of terms or facts to be learned with a minimum of interrelation. The specifications describe the elements, behaviors, and interrelationships as they are developed in the instructional material. If most of the elements fall under a particular category of behavior, this becomes apparent. If the elements are introduced in isolation from each other, this becomes apparent also. Teachers

TABLE 6-1 TABLE OF SPECIFICATIONS FOR A CHEMISTRY UNIT

A. Knowledge of terms	B. Knowledge of facts	C. Knowledge of rules and principles	D. Skill in using processes and procedures	E. Ability to make translations	F. Ability to make applications
Atom ①		Boyle's law ⑫			
Molecule ②		Properties of a gas ⑬			
Element ③		Atomic theory ⑯		Substance into diagram ㉒	
Compound ④		Chemical formula ⑲		Compound into formula ㉑ ②	Writing and solving equations to fit experimental situations ㉘
Diatomic ⑤	Diatomic gases ⑪	Avogadro's hypothesis ⑭			㉓
Chemical formula ⑥		Gay-Lussac's law ⑮			㉔
Avogadro's number ⑦		Grams to moles ⑱			㉕
Mole ⑧					㉖
		Molecular weight ⑰	Molecular weight ⑳		㉗
Atomic weight ⑨					㉙
Molecular weight ⑩					

TABLE 6-2 TABLE OF SPECIFICATIONS FOR A BIOLOGY UNIT

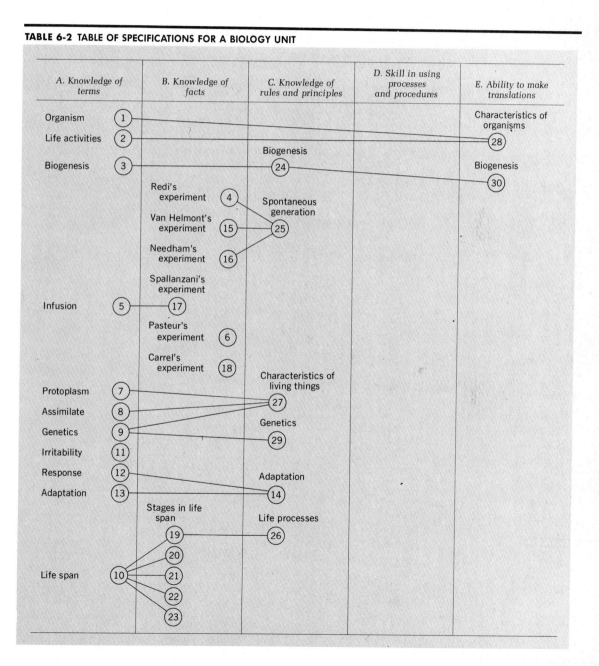

A. Knowledge of terms	B. Knowledge of facts	C. Knowledge of rules and principles	D. Skill in using processes and procedures	E. Ability to make translations
Organism ①				Characteristics of organisms
Life activities ②				㉘
Biogenesis ③		Biogenesis ㉔		Biogenesis ㉚
	Redi's experiment ④	Spontaneous generation ㉕		
	Van Helmont's experiment ⑮			
	Needham's experiment ⑯			
Infusion ⑤	Spallanzani's experiment ⑰			
	Pasteur's experiment ⑥			
	Carrel's experiment ⑱			
Protoplasm ⑦		Characteristics of living things ㉗		
Assimilate ⑧				
Genetics ⑨		Genetics ㉙		
Irritability ⑪				
Response ⑫		Adaptation ⑭		
Adaptation ⑬				
	Stages in life span ⑲	Life processes ㉖		
	⑳			
Life span ⑩	㉑			
	㉒			
	㉓			

TABLE 6-3 TABLE OF SPECIFICATIONS FOR AN ALGEBRA UNIT

	A. Knowledge of terms	B. Knowledge of facts	C. Knowledge of rules and principles	D. Skill in using processes and procedures	E. Ability to make translations	F. Ability to make applications
Variable	①					
Replacement set	②					
Variable expression	③					
Term	④					
Factor	⑤					
Coefficient	⑥				Identifying coefficients ⑯	
Exponent	⑦			Evaluating an expression ⑮ ⑱		
Base	⑧					
Power	⑨					
Open sentence	⑩			Solving open sentences ⑭		
Root	⑪					
Solution set	⑫			⑰ ⑲ ⑳	Problem statements into algebraic sentences ㉑ ㉒ ㉓	Solving problems with open sentences ㉔ ㉕
Inequality	⑬					

162

TABLE 6-4 TABLE OF SPECIFICATIONS FOR A THIRD-GRADE ARITHMETIC UNIT

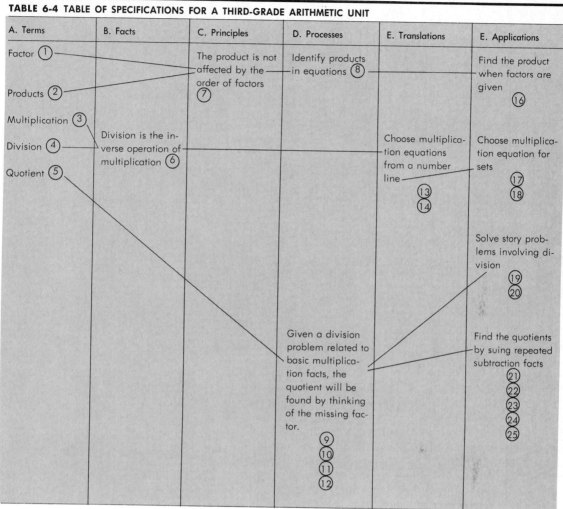

A. Terms	B. Facts	C. Principles	D. Processes	E. Translations	E. Applications
Factor ①		The product is not affected by the order of factors ⑦	Identify products in equations ⑧		Find the product when factors are given ⑯
Products ②					
Multiplication ③					
Division ④	Division is the inverse operation of multiplication ⑥			Choose multiplication equations from a number line ⑬ ⑭	Choose multiplication equation for sets ⑰ ⑱
Quotient ⑤					Solve story problems involving division ⑲ ⑳
			Given a division problem related to basic multiplication facts, the quotient will be found by thinking of the missing factor. ⑨ ⑩ ⑪ ⑫		Find the quotients by suing repeated subtraction facts ㉑ ㉒ ㉓ ㉔ ㉕

Note: This unit and the formative test items for this unit were developed by Betty L. Thomas under the guidance of Michael Katims; both are employed by the Chicago Board of Education.

or curriculum workers may have some views about what can or should be done with a particular unit of learning, and they can compare their model of what might be with the material as it is organized in the learning unit. Teachers especially can see what they must do with the instructional materials if they are to achieve the outcomes they desire.

The specifications table is useful in the construction of formative evaluation instruments because one can determine what should be included in the formative test and something about the hypothesized relations among the test items.

FORMATIVE TEST CONSTRUCTION

Essential versus Nonessential Elements

After the unit is appropriately analyzed into content and behavior, the constructor of a formative evaluation instrument (teacher, evaluation expert, curriculum maker, or other professional) must determine which elements in the unit are important or essential and which are unimportant or useful only as background for the essential material. For example, in a chemistry unit, the names of originators of ideas, the dates when they lived, or the countries where they were born may be useful as interesting background for presenting the idea but may be of little cognitive importance in the unit. Such specific facts may be included in the specifications but dropped at the time of testing. The point is that not everything included in the specifications is of equal importance, and the curriculum maker, the teacher, or the formative evaluator must apply some judgment and draw on experience to determine what is essential in the unit and what is trivial— that is, what may be omitted from the test without impairing the student's mastery of the unit.

General Principles of Formative Evaluation Test Construction

Formative evaluation should include all the important elements in a unit as detailed by the table of specifications. Thus, if there are twenty-five important elements in the table, each of these should be represented by one or more test items. This is in contrast with summative evaluation, where it is feasible, in the testing time available, only to sample the range of contents and behaviors outlined in a table of specifications.

The formative evaluation should include items at each of the behavior levels specified. Virtually the same subject matter may be included as a term, specific fact, rule, process, translation, and application, if all are included in the specifications. This means that the tester must clearly distinguish an item that appraises the student's knowledge of a term or fact from the item that determines whether or not the student can translate an idea into a new form or apply a rule or principle to a new problem.

In Tables 6-1 to 6-4 we have presented the structural diagrams for four units of learning.

We have also indicated the item numbers of the formative tests for each unit. It will be noted that the items are generally arranged in the test with the simpler behaviors first, followed by increasingly more complex behaviors. This is especially useful in the corrective process, when the students correct their knowledge errors before attempting to correct the more complex ideas and behaviors which they had missed on the formative tests.

Although Chapters 8 to 11 of this book go into more detail on appropriate classifications of behavior and testing techniques, we have illustrated those used at each level of the specifications in formative tests constructed for learning units in chemistry, biology, algebra, and arithmetic. So that the reader may relate the test items to their place in the structure of these units (see Tables 6-1, 6-2, 6-3, and 6-4), we have used the same numbers in the charts and in the cell codes of the following illustrative questions. Although all these items are in the multiple-choice form for rapid administration and ease of scoring, it is of course possible to use other testing forms appropriate to the content and behaviors being examined.

Knowledge of terms (A)

Chemistry: A.5
1. A molecule that contains only two atoms, both of the same element, is called a(n)
   a. monatomic molecule
   b. noble gas
   c. diatomic molecule
   d. ionic compound

Biology: A.1
2. Complete and entire living things composed of living substances and performing life activities are
   a. organisms
   b. frogs and grasses
   c. rock and water
   d. nonliving things
   e. protoplasm

Algebra: A.10
3. Which of the following is an open sentence?
   a. 3x
   b. 3x + 1
   c. 3x + 1 = 8
   d. 7 + 1 = 4 + 4
   e. none of these

Algebra: A.12

4. The set whose members make an open sentence true is called the_____of the open sentence.
   a. replacement set   d. erector set
   b. solution set   e. none of these
   c. variable set

Arithmetic: A.1

5. Factors are the numbers we_____.
   a. add b. multiply c. subtract d. none of these

Arithmetic: A.3

6. Multiplication is the product of two_____.
   a. answers b. factors c. divisors d. none of these

Knowledge of facts (B)

Chemistry: B.11

7. Hydrogen, oxygen, and nitrogen are
   a. noble gases   c. diatomic gases
   b. compounds   d. monatomic gases

Biology: B.15

8. The outline of a method of producing mice from grains of wheat and human sweat was given by
   a. Jan van Helmont
   b. Francesco Redi
   c. John Needham
   d. Lazzaro Spallanzani
   e. Louis Pasteur

Knowledge of rules and principles (C)

Chemistry: C.19

9. In order to write a chemical formula, you have to know
   a. only the symbols of the elements that are in the compound
   b. only the proportions in which the atoms of elements combine
   c. both the symbols of the elements that are in the compound and the proportions in which the atoms of elements combine
   d. the atomic weight of the elements that form the compound

Biology: C.24

10. The principle of biogenesis states that
    a. living things have a cellular organization
    b. life arises from nonliving materials
    c. living things are capable of response
    d. organisms are capable of growth
    e. life arises from life

Arithmetic: C.7

11. Complete this problem:
    $9 \times 8 = 72$ so $8 \times 9 =$ _____
    a. 9   b. 8   c. 72   d. none of these

Skill in using processes and procedures (D)

Chemistry: D.20

12. The molecular weight of a gas can be determined experimentally by
    a. weighing 22.4 liters of the gas
    b. comparing the weight of a known volume of the gas with the weight of a different volume of another gas of known molecular weight
    c. comparing the weight of a known volume of the gas with the weight of 22.4 liters of the same gas
    d. comparing the weight of a known volume of the gas with the weight of the same volume of another gas of known molecular weight

Algebra: D.19

13. Find the roots of $3x + 5 = 8$ and $y - 2 = 11$. The *sum* of their roots is
    a. 10
    b. 14
    c. 40/3
    d. 52/3

Arithmetic: D.10

14. $6 \div 2 = N$ Think ? $\times 2 = 6$
    a. 6
    b. 2
    c. 3
    d. 2

Ability to make translations (E)

Chemistry: E.21

15. The correct formula for the compound dinitrogen tetroxide is
    a. N_1O_2
    b. NO_1
    c. NO_2
    d. N_2O_1

Biology: E.30

16. Select an example of the principle of biogenesis:
    a. puppy growing into a dog
    b. bud blooming into a flower
    c. moth hatching from a cocoon
    d. flies coming from meat
    e. salmon laying eggs

Arithmetic: E.13

17. Choose the multiplication equation for these pictures:

    0   5   10   15   20   25   30   35   40   45   50

    a. $9 \times 5 = 45$
    b. $5 \times 5 = 25$
    c. $9 \times 1 = 9$
    d. none of these

Algebra: E.23

18. A notebook costs 28 cents more than a pencil. The pencil costs x cents. Five pencils and two notebooks cost 91 cents. Which of the following describes the situation?

a. $x + (x + 28) = 91$
b. $2x + 5(x + 28) = 91$
c. $5x + 2(x + 28) = 91$
d. $5x + 2x + 28 = 91$
e. $2x + 5x + 140 = 91$

Ability to make applications (F)

Questions 19 and 20 are based on the following new situation.

An evacuated container was weighed, then filled with oxygen and weighed again. The container was evacuated, filled with an unknown gas, and weighed again. Both gases were weighed at the same temperature and pressure. The following data were obtained:

Container empty	150.10/g
Container + oxygen gas	151.41/g
Container + unknown gas	151.82/g

Chemistry: F.26

19. What is the weight of one molecule of the unknown gas as compared with one molecule of oxygen?

a. .761
b. 1.01
c. 1.30
d. 1.00

Chemistry: F.28

20. It is determined experimentally that the unknown gas contains carbon and hydrogen atoms in the ratio of 1 to 2. What is the simplest formula?

a. CH
b. C_2H
c. C_2H_2
d. CH_2

Algebra: F.24

21. A team won three times as many games as it lost. It played 172 games. The *difference* between the number won and the number lost is

a. 28   c. 48
b. 38   d. 86

Arithmetic: F.19

22. Mark is putting candy in bags for a Halloween party. He has 18 pieces. He puts 3 pieces in each bag. How many bags can he fill?

a. $18 \div 3 =$
b. $3 \times 6 =$
c. $3 + 12 =$
d. none of these

If there is a hierarchy in learning difficulty (see Gagné, 1965, 1968), then the responses of students to the test should reveal this hierarchy. That is, the test items for knowledge of specific facts or terms should be passed by more students than those for knowledge of rules and principles or skill in the use of processes. Also, the test items involving translation and application are likely to be more difficult, and thus to be passed by fewer students.

The items in the test may also form a hierarchy in that passing the lower-level item is necessary for the mastery of the higher-level item (if this is indicated by the specifications). The item analysis might then conform with a pattern such as this:

		Higher-level item	
		Fail	Pass
Lower-level	Pass	35%	35%
item	Fail	30%	0%

That is, if the lower-level item is necessary for success on the higher-level item, then those students who fail the lower item should also fail the higher item—none who fail the first should be able to pass the second (except by chance or guessing). On the other hand, it is possible for some of the students who pass the lower item to fail the higher one, if the lower item is *necessary but not sufficient* for mastery of the higher item. Appropriate item analysis procedures can be used to determine whether the hierarchy of items established by the table of specifications is in fact borne out by students' performance. Airasian (1971) found that three-fourths or more of the students' responses showed the pattern of correct and incorrect responses indicated in the specifications for a chemistry and an algebra unit.

One analysis of the formative evaluation test should be made in terms of mastery or nonmastery. We have used accuracy levels of

80 to 85 percent on each formative test as an indication of mastery. This is arbitrary, however, and individual teachers may want to set the score for mastery higher or lower. If the accuracy level is too high (95 to 100 percent), it is likely to be obtained by only a few students, and there will be little positive reinforcement for mastery for very many students. On the other hand, if the mastery level is too low (50 to 60 percent), then a large number of students may have the illusion that they have mastered the unit of learning when in fact they have made many errors.

Block (1972) did a study in which he set the mastery level at different percents of the possible score. He found that the final achievement scores increased as the mastery levels were set higher on the formative tests. However, he found that if the mastery level was set above 85 percent, the students' interests and their attitudes toward the subject became more negative. The 85 percent level was approximately the level at which both cognitive and affective outcomes were maximal. One hopes that this type of research will be explored further to determine what is the ideal level of mastery for each formative test.

Another type of analysis of formative evaluation tests should reveal to the students the errors they have made. We have found it useful to provide students with an answer sheet on which they can mark their errors.

Where possible, the record of errors should be accompanied by a detailed prescription of the alternative instructional materials (textbooks, workbooks, programmed instruction, films, and so forth) the students should consult to correct the errors and strengthen their mastery of the unit under consideration.

These remedial suggestions might appear on the test booklet or on the answer sheet, as shown in Figure 6-1. It is desirable to make the prescriptions very specific with regard to pages to be read, films to be seen, and the like.

THE USE OF FORMATIVE EVALUATION BY STUDENTS

The most important value of formative evaluation, in our view, is the aid it can give students in learning the subject matter and behaviors for each unit of learning. As has been indicated in Chapter 3, Learning for Mastery, it is possible to have the large majority of students attain mastery of the subject if instruction is appropriately individualized. One step in individualizing instruction can be formative evaluation accompanied by a variety of materials and instructional procedures for students to use in remedying the particular gaps in their learning of a specific unit. We discuss this in more detail in the next section.

The Scoring and Corrective Process

In our work with mastery-learning classes we have usually constructed two parallel formative tests for each learning unit. The two tests have parallel numbered questions, but the questions in the second test are asked in a somewhat different way. That is, the same idea or process is tested but with different examples, different choices (if multiple-choice questions are used), and different applications or problems. The procedure for scoring and correcting was described in Chapter 3; we repeat it here for our readers' convenience.

Immediately after the instruction over a particular learning unit has been completed, the students are given the first form of the formative test for that unit. They record their answers to the questions on an answer sheet such as the one indicated on Figure 6-1. After they have completed this test, they put the same answers on a second answer sheet. The first answer sheet is kept by the student, while the second answer sheet is collected by the teacher. Then the answers to the questions are read by the teacher, and students mark their answer sheets to indicate which questions they got right and which ones wrong. (In some cases, students may ex-

CHEMISTRY TEST

Answer sheet

Name_____

Date _____ Test number ____2____

CIRCLE your answer for each question. When you score this test, put an R beside each correct answer. Leave your incorrect answers blank.

Alternative learning resources: This test is designed to inform you of your learning difficulties. This test will not count as part of your final grade. Below is a list of learning materials which will explain the ideas you still need to learn. For each item you did not get right, read across to find where the correct answer or idea is explained.

						Right (R)	Textbook: Chemistry: An Experimental Science	Chemistry: A Science of Matter, Energy, & Change by Choppin and Jaffe	
1.	A	B	C	D	E		Page 21	Page 19	
2.	A	B	C	D	E		Page 21	Page 18	
3.	A	B	C	D	E		Page 28	Page 14	
4.	A	B	C	D	E		Page 28	Page 15	
5.	A	B	C	D	E		Page 31	Page 76	
6.	A	B	C	D	E		Page 31	Page 16	
7.	A	B	C	D	E		Page 33	Page 86	
8.	A	B	C	D	E		Page 32	Page 84	
9.	A	B	C	D	E		Page 33	Page 84	
10.	A	B	C	D	E		Page 33	Page 84	
11.	A	B	C	D	E		Page 31	Page 77	
12.	A	B	C	D	E		Page 17	Page 53	
13.	A	B	C	D	E		Page 21	Page 19	
14.	A	B	C	D	E		Page 25	Page 71	
15.	A	B	C	D	E		Pages 25-26	Pages 69-70	
16.	A	B	C	D	E		Page 28	Page 50	
17.	A	B	C	D	E		Page 33	Page 98	
18.	A	B	C	D	E		Page 34	Page 105	
19.	A	B	C	D	E		Page 31	Page 16	
20.	A	B	C	D	E		Lab manual Pages 14-18	Page 81	
21.	A	B	C	D	E		Page 32	Page 136	
22.	A	B	C	D	E		Page 28	Page 50	
23.	A	B	C	D	E		Page 27	Pages 69-71	
24.	A	B	C	D	E		Page 34	Page 106	
25.	A	B	C	D	E		Page 34	Page 106	
26.	A	B	C	D	E		Pages 25-26	Pages 81-82	
27.	A	B	C	D	E		Page 34	Pages 86-87	
28.	A	B	C	D	E		Page 37	Pages 88-91	
29.	A	B	C	D	E		Page 33	Page 98	
30.	A	B	C	D	E		Page 38	Pages 104-105	

Figure 6-1 Remedial instructional materials keyed to items on a formative chemistry test.

change answer sheets and then mark them, or the teacher may believe it is important that the answer sheets be marked by the teacher or an aide. However, since the teacher has a second copy of the answer sheet for each student, there is little incentive for individual students to claim more right answers than they have earned.)

After the answer sheets are marked, the number of right answers is put on the top of the answer sheet. Students who have obtained 80 percent correct (or 85 percent, depending on the criterion set by the teacher) are deemed to have mastered the learning unit. The teacher may have these students hold up their hands or stand up while the teacher and other students applaud, or there may be other methods of showing approval for students who have reached mastery. Students with less than this percent correct are deemed not to have mastered the unit; they are expected to correct their learning difficulties, and they will be tested again on this unit in a few days.

The teacher then identifies the test items which were answered incorrectly by most of the students (usually two-thirds of the students or more). These are regarded as indicating faulty test items or the presence of special difficulties in the instructional materials or instructional process. The ideas underlying these test items should then be reviewed for the entire class by the teacher. If possible, they should be explained in a different way from in the original instruction. This should be done shortly after the test has been taken or at the next meeting of the class.

For the students who lack mastery of the unit, the formative test should reveal the particular points of difficulty—that is, the specific questions they answered incorrectly and the ideas, skills, and processes they still need to work on. It has been observed that the students respond best to the formative test results when they are referred to particular instructional materials or processes intended to help them clear up their difficulties.

As was pointed out earlier (Chapter 3), the test questions in the formative test are related to particular pages of the original textbook or other instructional material, to particular pages in alternative textbooks which explain the idea in a different way, to specific pages of workbooks or programmed material, or to specific other material such as lecture notes, special sound cassettes which explain each idea, or other relevant audiovisual material. We suspect that no specific learning material or process is indispensable in this corrective process. The presence of some variety of instructional materials and procedures—and specific suggestions regarding which ones to use—help students to recognize that if they can't learn in one way, alternatives are available to them.

The most effective procedure found thus far is to have small groups of students (two or three students in each group) meet for about half an hour (or longer) to review the results of their formative tests and to help each other overcome the difficulties identified on the tests. This works best where each student is helped on some items by the other students and in turn each student provides help to the others on one or more items. This group process may initially be done in class, but later on the corrective process may be done outside of the class, especially after the students have learned how to help each other most effectively.

Tutorial help may be of value in this corrective process, especially at the primary school level through the use of aides, tutors, or the parents and siblings in the home. However, we have found that from the third grade on, brief periods of help by peers in the same class is the most effective corrective process.

The teacher sets a date for the second form of the formative test—usually 2 or 3 days after the first form of the formative test was taken. The students who did not attain mastery are encouraged to study and review the questions they answered incorrectly. When the second form of the formative test (a parallel test) is taken, the students answer *only* the parallel items or questions they got wrong on the first form of this test. (In some cases, the teachers may have the students answer all the questions in the second form of the formative test. However, we have obtained our best results when the students answer only the ones they got wrong on the first form.) Again, the students answer the questions on two answer sheets and submit one answer sheet to the teacher before the tests are marked. The answers to all the questions are read, and the student (or another student) marks the answer sheet and counts the number of correct answers.

Typically, mastery is regarded as answering 80 percent (or 85 percent) of the answers correctly. This is now the number of questions answered correctly on the first form of the test *plus* the number of correct answers on the second form of the test (these were the student's errors on the first form). Students who obtained mastery through the corrective process are again identified and encouraged in some way for their progress.

If students do the necessary corrective work on each formative test, gradually more and more of the students should reach mastery on the first forms of the formative tests on the subsequent learning units.

The Pacing of Students' Learning

Another effective use of formative evaluation is in pacing students' learning. When subject matter is sequential in a course, that is, when learning units 1 and 2 are prerequisites to subsequent units, it is of importance that the student master units 1 and 2 before 3 and 4, 3 and 4 before 5 and 6, and so forth. This is most evident in subjects like algebra, where the first three or four units of the subject are basic to everything that follows. In such a subject, poor learning of the early units is likely to result in poor learning of all ensuing ones.

In sequential subjects, formative evaluation can set goals for learning as well as a time schedule for each unit. There is some educational literature, summarized by Anthony (1967), Merkhofer (1954), and Stephens (1951), indicating that the frequency of quizzes and other testing, when accompanied by detailed feedback to the examinee, is related to the final performance level of the students. One way in which this operates is by pressing students to put the appropriate effort into studying the subject for each of the periods covered by the quizzes. Students are always faced with conflicting demands on their time, and they are likely to postpone work and study where the demands are less urgent. If they anticipate a quiz or a progress test, they are likely to make the appropriate preparation before the test.

Thus formative evaluation helps students by breaking the entire learning sequence into smaller units and by pressing them to make more adequate preparation while they are learning a particular unit. Although pacing the students is of the utmost importance when the learning units form a hierarchical sequence, it is still of some importance for the students to learn in a scheduled way even if the units are not arranged hierarchically. Especially is this true when there is a great deal to be learned, so that students who postpone their study too long will be faced with an overwhelming amount of material, usually too great to be learned well just before the final summative evaluation.

Reinforcement of Mastery

It is difficult for students to determine whether their learning is satisfactory, particularly with an instructor and a subject new to them. For students who have achieved mastery or near mastery of a unit of learning, the results of the formative evaluation can be an effective reward or reinforcement. This is especially useful for providing the student with positive reinforcement over small units of learning. The repeated evidence of mastery is a powerful reinforcement which will help ensure that the student will continue to invest the appropriate effort and interest in the subject.

It is less certain that grading students on quizzes or formative evaluation is a useful reinforcement. A student who is given a C repeatedly on a series of tests comes to believe that C is the mark he or she will finally receive in the course; and this is highly probable if the quiz grades are averaged and counted as part of the final grade. C students must defend their self-concept by investing an amount of time and effort commensurate with getting a C. Thus it is highly likely that students who receive frequent Cs or lower grades on quizzes will adjust their investment in the subject so as to protect their ego when they finally get C for the course. They must convince themselves that it is impossible for them to get a higher grade, they could never learn this subject, they didn't really try, and so on.*

For this reason, we believe formative evaluation should simply inform the students whether they have or have not mastered the unit, and if not, indicate that there are certain steps they should take before leaving the unit.

In sequential units we have found that many students become progressively more able as they master the essential earlier units. That is, if students do the necessary learning or relearning over the first few units, the attainment of mastery levels on later units becomes more probable. This progressive development of mastery as well as the repeated evidence of mastery serves as a very powerful reinforcement, and the students come to look forward to this reassurance and to the tests which provide it. Furthermore, the students are likely to anticipate the tests and make the necessary preparation for them in advance.

Even students who haven't achieved mastery on a particular formative test may be assured of what they have learned and what they still need to work on. If the results can be put in positive terms, they can be reinforced for what they have learned. A parallel form of

the formative test is given to students who did not attain mastery on the first form of the test but who did attempt to relearn those parts of the content and behaviors they missed the first time. The repeated administration of the formative evaluation test can then further reinforce those who attained mastery or near mastery on the second administration. We have rarely made use of a third or fourth formative test. Two such tests are usually all that is needed for about 90 percent of students to reach the standard for mastery.

Prescription of Alternative Remedial Measures

While the formative evaluation test can only locate the problems students are having, it is possible to relate these diagnostic aspects of the test results to alternative ways in which they may overcome their difficulties.

It will be noticed that the illustrative answer sheet in Figure 6-1 refers the student in each case to the appropriate page or pages in the textbook and laboratory manual assigned to the class and an alternative textbook. Other types of material might be suggested as well, such as a programmed unit and a workbook.

These represent relatively simple alternative instructional materials. Ideally each alternative should have some qualities not possessed by the others, such as clearer or simpler explanations, concrete illustrations, and drill and practice work on specific problems. It would be desirable to create special remedial materials—for example, short motion pictures explaining specific ideas, sound recordings, and even games or other devices—to help the student over a particular difficulty. We can even imagine the possibility of developing a set of cards each of which contains a test problem with a brief discussion of why certain answers are wrong, an explanation of why a particular answer is correct, and a short exposition of the idea being tested.

Two alternatives that are not included on the answer sheet are tutorial assistance and

---

*It is to be noted that some students may reduce their learning effort when their test results are not graded. One possibility for such students is to grade them on both formative and summative tests but to give them the alternative of having the final grade in the course be the average of both formative and summative tests or of only the summative tests, whichever is higher.

special group cooperation. In our own work, as we pointed out on page 169, we have found that small groups of two or three students, meeting on a scheduled basis (a special study period, a regular meeting time, or the like) after each formative test, are most effective in helping each other overcome specific learning difficulties as pointed up by the test results. (See also Chapter 3.) While not all groupings of students work equally effectively (and some groups may need reorganization from time to time), we are convinced that all students can profit from reviewing particular ideas together and that this is of greatest value when the review is focused by the results of formative tests. When able students help less able ones, they gain increased understanding of the ideas as well as increased social sensitivity and cooperativeness. The less able students frequently get a new way of comprehending an idea, since it must be explained in a form they can understand. We believe the time is well spent for all who participate in these helping relations.

It is likely that there will be individual differences in students which will make given alternatives more effective for some than for others. At this stage in our work, we are not able to indicate which of various remedial measures is likely to be of greatest value for a particular student. Perhaps in the future it will be possible to accumulate data on each student as to the effectiveness of each alternative and to prescribe the one or two remedial measures that are likely to work best for him or her. However, it is possible that the greatest value in providing alternative procedures is that students will come to believe that even if they can't learn the ideas from one instructional method or set of materials, they can learn them from another. This would enable them, we hope, to come to see that it is the learning which is central rather than a particular textbook, teacher, or instructional method. We may hope also that each student will come to recognize the particular approach to learning which is most effective for him or her.

THE USE OF FORMATIVE EVALUATION BY TEACHERS

Scriven (1967) has proposed the use of formative evaluation by curriculum makers. He recommends that they try out their materials and methods with selected samples of students and teachers and that they secure evidence on the effectiveness of these materials as well as on the specific aspects of the curriculum that are in need of revision. The type of formative testing we have suggested in this chapter is likely to be of great value in this tryout process since it can be used to locate specific difficulties that students are having with a particular portion of a curriculum. However, it is clear from Scriven's article that he would not confine his formative evaluation for curriculum development purposes to testing procedures; nor would we. Teachers' comments, subject specialists' criticisms, interest and attitudinal reactions of students are all relevant for formative evaluation. The advantages of the type of cognitive formative test we have stressed in this chapter are that it can accurately represent the structure of a curriculum unit, it can show the difficulties students are having, and it can represent the behavioral hierarchies and patterns of students' responses. The appropriate use of such tests enables the curriculum maker to test hypotheses and hunches about specific aspects of a curriculum and the relations among the elements in a particular unit of learning. We will not dwell on the use of formative evaluation for curriculum development, since we are primarily concerned in this book with learning and instruction.

Feedback to Teachers

Teachers have usually made use of quizzes, progress tests, and other evaluation techniques over brief periods of learning. However, though these are to some degree formative instruments, they are primarily used to motivate students and to mark their work at frequent intervals. For the most part these teacher-made tests are summarized to show the scores or marks of individual students. Only rarely does a teacher use them as a basis for modifying instruction. The primary change in the teacher's use of formative testing proposed here is that it be directed to yielding information which can be used to alter instruction or to review those ideas on which students are having great difficulty.

It is suggested that at the end of each learning unit, the teacher prepare an analysis of the errors that students in a particular class have made on each item in the formative test. This can be done in a few minutes if the teacher places the students' answer sheets side by side and counts the number of correct or incorrect answers made on each item by the group. For items answered incorrectly by a sizable portion of the students, the teacher may want to count the number of times students made a specific wrong answer on a particular item, since this can reveal some of the confusions or types of difficulties the students are having.*

The results of this item analysis can be used to identify terms, facts, rules, and so forth, with which the students are having difficulty. If the majority of students answer a particular item incorrectly, this would appear to represent an element of the learning unit which has not been adequately mastered by the class. It is suggested that the teacher regard errors made by a substantial proportion of the students (we suggest 65 percent or more, but each teacher may have his or her own criterion of what constitutes a "substantial proportion") as stemming from difficulties in the instructional material or the instructional process. Such items chould be reviewed for the entire class, and efforts

should be made to find a different approach in explaining these ideas. One might expect the teacher to use different illustrations, to attempt to discover what the stumbling block was and remove it, or to relate the idea to other ideas which the majority have adequately learned, among other techniques. The teacher may get clues to the cause of the difficulty by noting the kinds of errors made by the students as well as the place of these items in the entire structure of the unit (see Tables 6-1 to 6-4).

In sum, then, errors on a formative test made by less than the majority of a class are errors to be corrected by individual students. In contrast, errors made by the majority of students are regarded as difficulties in the instructional material or process and should be corrected by group instructional procedures. In the section on the corrective process, we suggested that these group errors should be resolved in the same session as that in which the test was taken. In any case, they should be corrected as soon as possible after the time the formative test is taken.

Quality Control

Each new cycle of a course is in some respects related to previous cycles. That is, each time the course is given to a new group of students, the teacher may make use of previous experience with it.

If the course is similar in content and objectives and includes some of the same units as before, the teacher may use the formative tests of an earlier term or year, with or without modification. Since the tests are to be used to help the students in the learning process (rather than for grading purposes), there is little danger that a student will be given any great advantage by consulting previous students in order to get help on the tests in advance of their distribution to the class.

The teacher may compare the results from the new group of students with those obtained previously, for quality control purposes. Thus the proportion of students attain-

---

*If the class is relatively large, the teacher may wish to make the item analysis of a sample of twenty to twenty-five answer sheets. If the sample is selected at random, or if the answer sheets are arranged in order of total score and every second, third, or fourth answer sheet is taken (depending on the number of examinees and the size of the sample to be analyzed), the sample should be quite representative of the entire group.

ing mastery on each test in the formative series may be compared from one year to another. When the results are lower for the current term, the teacher may wish to study the item analysis of test outcomes in the two terms to note where the difficulties lie. If the results are equal, or if the current performance shows an improvement over that of the previous class, the teacher may expect that, if succeeding test results are equally favorable, the final results on the summative tests will be at least as good as those in the previous term.

Especially in sequential units, the formative tests used as quality-control indices can be used to determine whether the current class is doing as well as previous classes or better. Also, the teacher can use the results of formative tests to seek ways of improving the current class's achievement over that of previous classes who took the same course.

Where an earlier group of students had special difficulties with particular ideas or units, the teacher may wish to try a different instructional approach to these and to note whether the formative test results are indicative of the desired improvement in the learning process.

All this is to suggest that teachers should maintain a record of the formative test results of a particular year and use them as a set of norms or expectancies for new classes taking the same course. It is to be hoped that each new cycle of the course can be improved through an analysis of the results from a previous cycle and that the improvement can be discerned through a comparison of the formative test results on each unit with the previous results as well as with the results on parallel summative examinations over several years.

Charting the Progress of the Mastery-Learning Class

Formative tests are achievement tests over particular units of learning. Summative tests are achievement tests over a number of units of learning. Since there is usually some overlap between the two tests with regard to subject matter, behaviors, and even evaluation procedures, it is likely that the two types of test results will be related. In our own work we have found a relatively high correlation between the performance of students on two or more formative tests and their performance on summative tests given several months later.

From these relationships, which appear to hold for individual students as well as groups of students, it is possible to predict results on summative tests several months in advance. That is, it is possible to anticipate results on summative tests while the instruction and learning process is still going on. And if the teachers and learners so desire, it is possible to change the forecast.

In Figure 6-2 we show an idealized graph of results of mastery learning. When the mastery-learning process is working well, the proportion of students achieving mastery on each new formative test (A) should increase. Such results will be found in most mastery-learning classes if the corrective process is used well.

Thus, in Figure 6-2, approximately 20 percent of the students attained the mastery criterion on formative test 1-A. If most of the remainder of the students make use of the corrective process to correct their errors, about 75 percent of students (or more) should attain mastery after the corrective process. (That is, about 55 percent more students attain mastery on formative test 1-B). If this results, then the proportion of students attaining mastery on formative test 2-A should now be greater than the proportion originally attaining mastery on formative test 1-A, and so on to each new learning unit.

It will be noted in this chart that smaller and smaller proportions of students need to use the corrective process as the course proceeds from learning unit to learning unit.

Such results are to be expected if the majority of students enter each new learning unit with an adequate grasp of the prerequisite learning (cognitive entry) for that unit. Also, such results are to be expected if the majority of students enter each new learning unit with confidence that they can learn the

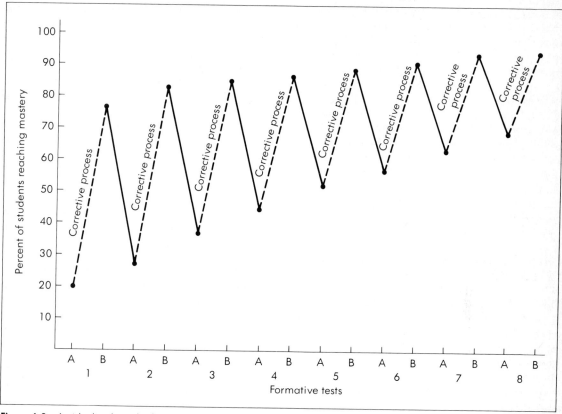

Figure 6-2 An idealized graph of mastery learning results. *Note:* Form A of the formative test is given at the end of a unit of instruction. Form B of the formative test is given after the corrective work.

new unit well because they have learned the previous units to a high level. Such results also indicate that the students are likely to be more purposive, interested, and involved in the classroom learning processes for each new learning unit.

Charts such as Figure 6-2 make it clear that mastery learning depends on the effectiveness of the corrective process. If more and more students attain mastery either initially or through the corrective process, the summative test results for the mastery-learning class will be much superior to the summative results for the control class taught the same material by the same instructor. If the corrective process does not work at all, then the proportion of students attaining mastery on the B formative tests will be no greater than

the percentages attaining mastery on the A formative tests. Under such conditions, the summative results of the mastery and control classes should be about the same.

In many mastery-learning classes, the major record kept of the class progress is a chart such as the one shown in Figure 6-2. It is frequently placed on the bulletin board of the classroom, so that all members of the mastery class are aware of the results for the entire group. This appears to be effective in getting a large proportion of the students to strive for mastery before as well as after the corrective process.

We believe that formative tests can be of vital importance in helping the teacher and students determine the quality of learning that is taking place and can allow them to forecast the results of summative tests some time in advance of the summative testing. Such results may be used as a basis for altering the teaching-learning situation early enough to change the immediate learning as well as to alter the forecast.

Learning is a process which can be observed and evaluated as it is taking place. Formative evaluation can be used to make the process more effective long before the summative evaluation. Recognition of the interactions among formative evaluation, teaching and learning, and summative evaluation can do much to improve teaching and learning before it is too late.

COOPERATIVE CONSTRUCTION OF FORMATIVE TESTS

The typical one-semester course includes about ten learning units or textbook chapters, while the typical academic-year course may include as many as twenty learning units. The development of mastery-learning material for each learning task or learning unit includes a set of specifications and at least two parallel formative tests with corrective suggestions. If this is multiplied by 10 or 20, it may be seen that it would be a formidable task for a single teacher to prepare all the material for a semester or a full year. Where this has been done by a single teacher in some programs we have encountered, it took a single teacher about 10 weeks of full-time work.

In a number of school systems that have tried to develop mastery-learning procedures it has been found possible to have as many as ten teachers work together in pairs to produce the mastery-learning materials they needed. Under these conditions, each teacher selected one chapter or learning unit. In such instances one teacher developed a set of specifications for the chapter while a second teacher produced an independent set of specifications for the same chapter. The two teachers then discussed the differences in the two sets of specifications and agreed on a single common set of specifications for that chapter or unit.

Then, the first teacher produced two sets of test items for the specifications while the second teacher reviewed the items in relation to the specifications, criticized the items, and suggested changes or new items. The first teacher made changes until both teachers were in agreement that the specifications and formative tests were both valid and satisfactory. Then the first teacher produced the corrective suggestions for the chapter, and the second teacher criticized them and made additional suggestions.

In turn, the second teacher produced the materials for a second chapter or unit, with the first teacher serving as critic and validator for this material.

In this way, each teacher served as the responsible person or author for the mastery-learning materials for one chapter and as the critic or reviewer for another chapter. This care devoted to the preparations of the materials usually resulted in an excellent set of mastery-learning materials with considerable validity for each chapter or unit. Each teacher assumed responsibility for developing approximately 10 percent of the material and served as critic or reviewer for another 10 percent of the material. Once the teachers had some brief training in the necessary procedures, the actual effort required of each teacher for a one-semester course was approximately 1 week of work.

While such cooperative work can produce a satisfactory set of mastery materials for use by other teachers using the same instructional materials or textbook, it is clear that each teacher using the materials should be able to adapt or revise the materials to fit his or her own instructional needs. Each teacher using mastery materials prepared by others may wish to have the students answer only the questions stressed in the instruction and delete those questions which are less important or which the students have had little opportunity to learn. The teacher may also wish to add a few questions which he or she regards as very important or believes the students should have learned. Such revisions and additions may be made toward the end of the instruction over the particular chapter or learning unit. When the formative tests are used and adapted in this way, teachers can be confident that they are not "teaching for the test" and that the emphasis they want to give in their instruction is determined by their own views of what is important.

SELECTION OF FORMATIVE TESTS

In recent years a number of textbook publishers have published sets of mastery-learning material, while others have produced sets of formative tests with or without corrective suggestions. Some of these materials have been excellent; others have been little more than quickly built sets of specific knowledge questions for each chapter in a textbook.

It is suggested that teachers (ideally, working cooperatively) review these formative tests and corrective materials with the following criteria in mind:

1. Are the formative tests valid instruments in relation to the specifications (or objectives) for each chapter or learning unit? Can they be improved on, and with what extra effort and cost?
2. Are there two or more parallel tests for each learning unit?
3. Are the corrective suggestions for each formative test likely to be useful to the students? Are there several different corrective suggestions for each item in the test?
4. Is there any evidence that teachers who have used these formative tests and corrective suggestions have found significant improvements in the summative examination results for their students under mastery-learning conditions?

If a group of teachers working cooperatively review existing material, they can determine whether they could improve the existing material or make their own better-suited to the special conditions in their classrooms. The teachers considering this should review the suggestions made above for the cooperative construction of formative tests.

EXERCISES

Objective: Apply the techniques of formative evaluation by constructing and administering a formative test and applying feedback and corrective procedures based on the test results.

Preparation: If you have a table of specifications available from the exercises at the end of Chapter 2, that table can serve as the basis for the table needed below.

1. *Building a table of specifications.* Build a table of specifications appropriate to formative evaluation instrument construction. In order to ensure content validity, have a colleague independently build a table of specifications for the same unit.
    a. Define a managable unit.
    b. Include material new to this unit on the content dimension.
    c. Use the *Taxonomy* for the cognitive domain as the basis for the behavior dimension.
    d. Indicate on your table the interrelationships among the content elements.
    e. Check for content validity. Compare your own table with the table built by your colleague.

2. *Test construction.* Construct a formative evaluation instrument based on the above table. If time permits, write enough items to construct two forms of the test.
    a. Ensure that all essential elements are included.
    b. You may use items written as exercises for Chapters 8, 9, and 10 in the building of the test.
    c. Screen the items on the basis of Hambleton and Eignor's checklist, presented at the end of Chapter 7.
    d. Check for content validity of the test items. Have an independent judge classify the test items by behavioral levels of the *Taxonomy*. Have the items checked against your table of specifications.
    e. Compile the items into a test. What

criteria do you use in determining the order of the items?

f. Construct an answer sheet suitable for the test. What kinds of information will the answer sheet provide for?

3. *Using the test.*

a. Prior to using the test, determine the level of performance which will represent mastery.

b. If possible, teach this unit and administer the formative test.

c. Score the tests. Determine common errors; i.e., those items missed by two-thirds of the students. How will this determination influence the feedback and corrective process?

d. Provide feedback and corrective suggestions to the students who did not achieve mastery.

(1) Describe the feedback and corrective techniques.

(2) Explain the rationale behind these techniques.

e. After corrective measures have been applied, administer to each "nonmaster" items parallel to those he or she had missed.

(1) Repeat (c) and (d) above.

(2) Analyze the results of the retest. How many students have now achieved mastery? Are there particularly difficult areas which are holding up the other students? How are feedback and corrective processes for the retest different from those for the original test?

REFERENCES

Airasian, P. W. The use of hierarchies in curriculum analysis and instructional planning. *California Journal of Educational Reseach*, 1971, 22, 34–41.

Anthony, B. C. *The identification and measurement of classroom environmental process variables related to academic achievement.* Unpublished doctoral dissertation. University of Chicago, 1967.

Block, J. H. Student learning and the setting of mastery performance standards. *Educational Horizons,* 1972, 50, 183–191.

Bloom, B. S. (Ed.) *Taxonomy of educational objectives: The classification of educational goals.* Handbook 1. *Cognitive domain.* New York: McKay, 1956.

Brophy, J. E., & Good, T. L. Teachers' communication of differential expectations for children's classroom performance: Some behavioral data. *Journal of Educational Psychology,* 1970, *61,* 365–374.

Gagné, R. M. *The conditions of learning.* New York: Holt, 1965.

Gagné, R. M. Learning hierarchies. *Educational Psychologist,* 1968, 6, 1–9.

Merkhofer, B. E. *College students' study behavior.* Unpublished doctoral dissertation, University of Chicago, 1954.

Scriven, M. The methodology of evaluation. *AERA Monograph Series on Curriculum Evaluation,* 1967, No. 1, pp. 39–83.

Stephens, J. M. *Educational psychology: The study of educational growth.* New York: Holt, 1951.

Item Writing and Item Selection

Chapter Contents

In Chapter 2 we saw that the starting point in planning instruction and evaluation is the formulation of instructional objectives in terms of a specific content and observable actions or productions of students. Further, we saw how a task analysis or a table of specifications can serve as a blueprint for both instruction and evaluation. The component behaviors resulting from a task analysis or the objectives associated with the target cells of the specification matrix become the focal point in evaluating the outcomes of instruction.

INTRODUCTION: SPONTANEOUS VERSUS SYSTEMATIC EVALUATION

Much instruction, of course, is spontaneous and unplanned; this is also true of evaluation. Teachers constantly evaluate their students in every class, during every lesson. They do this spontaneously without the intrusion of anything that would normally be called a test. Often the teacher's cue is a momentary facial expression, a tone of voice, a shift in posture; at other times, of course, the teacher takes account of students' oral answers to questions. These cues, which Jackson (1968) has aptly called the "language of classroom behavior," continually tell the teacher how well he or she is communicating with the students. These spontaneous judgments fit neatly our definition of formative evaluation; they are assessments made while teaching is in progress for the purpose of guiding that teaching. Without them teaching could hardly be called teaching.

However, because this type of evaulation is unplanned, it is different from the *systematic* and *quantitative* types of evaluation—placement, formative, diagnostic, and summative—proposed in this book. This is not to suggest that spontaneous, informal evaluation is of little worth or that there is any basic contradiction between informal and formal evaluation. Quite the contrary. However, throughout this book we emphasize that informal evaluation should be supple-mented by more systematic sorts of evidence gathering.

One such systematic technique is the widely used common or garden variety of paper-and-pencil test in which the student responds by writing or marking an answer to a series of oral or written questions or problems—commonly referred to as "items" —set by the teacher. The purpose of this chapter is to give the reader suggestions that should help in both writing and selecting good items. The primary focus of the chapter is on the mechanics of good writing—things to do and things to avoid if one wishes to produce a well-written, clear, and concise question for the student to respond to. Compared with the informal, spontaneous evaluations made during instruction, formal paper-and-pencil evaluations are relatively more difficult to carry out, if for no other reason than that, compared with speech, writing is relatively clumsy, lengthy, and slow. Questions posed by the teacher during instruction almost always benefit from the greater expression made possible through the ability to stress certain words orally by speed, pitch, and articulation and through such bodily cues as a wink, nod of the head, shrug, frown, and smile (Cherry, 1966). Teachers intuitively use such cues to clarify for students the problem being posed. The ability of the teacher to employ these contextual cues is intimately related to the teacher's reading of verbal and bodily cues given off by students—hesitancy, whispered speech, a blush, a smile, a puzzled expression, the hand shooting up, etc. However, when writing an item for a test, the teacher can easily lose sight of the fact that these contextual, verbal, and bodily cues are no longer available to either the teacher or the student.

FOCI OF THIS CHAPTER

In this chapter we shall outline problems of a general nature associated with the mechanics of writing most kinds of test items, and specific problems associated with writing particular types of items. The final section of this chapter describes how teachers can develop or use item pools to select items for inclusion on their tests.

For most of us communication through the written word is seldom easy. Item writing is a particularly difficult form of writing. Test items stand alone. Unlike most other forms of writing, they cannot benefit from context. Test items are relatively short statements, and it seems it is always more difficult to write effectively when limited to one or two sentences than when less constrained by length. Each test item is read very carefully by most examinees: each word becomes important, and the examinee is constantly asking what the item or word *really* means. If the item is not framed precisely, the examinee may read things into the item that the writer had not allowed for. It does little good, after the test, to argue with the student, "But you should have known that is not what I intended." Teachers can expect to make mistakes when writing items; even professional item writers make mistakes. Much of the criticism of standardized testing has been directed at poorly worded multiple-choice items (Hoffman, 1962; Houts, 1977). The wording of essay questions also has been the target of criticism (Coffman, 1971; Madaus & Macnamara, 1970; Stalnaker, 1951).

The point is that item writing, like the formulation of objectives, is a cyclical process. Teachers should not underestimate the difficulty of framing a good item, whether an objective item or an essay question. Nor should the teacher be paralyzed or traumatized by the task of item writing. The teacher needs to make every attempt initially to write items that are technically sound. Items once written can be improved by careful review, the critiques of colleagues, and the reactions of students before the test is given. Further help in improving an item can be gleaned from item analyses once the test is over. (Techniques for item analysis are discussed in Chapter 4.) Informal evaluations also complement and supplement data about the appropriateness of an item or group of items.

That is, if a student or a number of students can demonstrate the behavior associated with a given objective in spontaneous evaluations in the class but fail on a paper-and-pencil test, then the teacher should begin to examine the written questions to see if the difficulty lies with the items, rather than with the student or the instruction.

Many items will be discarded along the way; many others can be improved with hindsight. A teacher should not at once be discouraged by the fact that many items are poorly written; they can be criticized and improved. Like all good writing, writing a test item involves working it over, editing it, polishing it, and sometimes abandoning it to start again. If the teacher keeps in mind the fact that item writing is not a one-shot, night-before-the-test exercise, but an ongoing cyclical process, eventually there will develop a pool of well-written, tried-and-true items that can be used to evaluate instruction.

The emphasis, then, in this chapter is on improving the basic mechanics of writing test items. Techniques for designing items that measure various levels of the cognitive and affective taxonomies are dealt with specifically in Chapters 8 to 11. The reader should be aware, however, that the very first requirement in constructing an item to measure any level of either taxonomy is that the item be well written. Time spent, for example, designing an item to measure application can be wasted if the item is misunderstood because it is awkwardly worded or if it can be answered correctly solely on the basis of some grammatical clue.

Similarly, the suggestions we shall make for writing unambiguous, concise, mechanically correct items apply equally to items written for norm-referenced tests and to those written for criterion-referenced tests. For either type of test, clarity and grammatical and mechanical considerations are equally important.

Finally, in using item pools the general and specific suggestions for writing items become important criteria in screening items for inclusion on a test. The presence of an item in an item pool does not necessarily mean that the item is well written. The item writer, like all of us, is susceptible to making the kinds of errors that will be outlined in this chapter. In selecting items from a pool, a teacher needs to take the time to carefully review each in terms of the general and specific suggestions to be outlined below.

PRELIMINARY CONSIDERATIONS

Instructional Objectives and Table of Specifications

The starting point in item writing is a careful consideration of the instructional objective (see Chapter 2). The list of objectives summarized in a table of specifications becomes a blueprint to follow in planning a paper-and-pencil test (see Tables 2-1 and 4-1 for examples of a table of specifications). In Chapter 2 we saw that each target cell of the specification matrix can be assigned a value weight in terms of the teacher's judgment of the overall relative importance of that cell. This judgment might be based on the amount of instructional time or emphasis devoted to the particular cell; or it may be based on the perceived importance of the objective in terms for future instruction; or all cells may be judged to be equally important. Regardless of the criteria used to weight each cell, a rough percentage figure can be assigned to each cell and these percentages can then be used to estimate the number of items one should write for each cell. This helps ensure content validity (see Chapter 4); that is, the test reflects the relative importance of the instructional objectives.

If a cell were assigned a relative weight of 20 percent and a 50-item test were planned, one would want approximately 10 items for this cell. Considerations of test length in terms of test reliability are discussed further in Chapter 4. A general rule of thumb in writing objective items is that the writer should write about three times the number of items needed, because roughly 2 out of 3 items will be discovered to be flawed

in some way (although this number will decrease with practice). In our example, then, a teacher should plan to write about 30 items to come up with the 10 or so needed. Once the cells have been assigned a value weight, and the approximate number of items needed for each cell has been determined, then items need to be written to elicit the behavior associated with the cell.

Choice of Types of Items

What type of item should be written to measure the objective in question? As we shall see in the next section, there are two basic types of items: *supply*, where the student writes an answer to a question; and *selection*, where the student chooses the correct answer from among competing alternatives. As we shall see, under these two categories there are alternative item types. The choice of item type must be governed by the nature of the objective or objectives to be measured. The method that permits the student most directly to exhibit the desired behavior should be preferred at the outset. It may be that more indirect item types can be used eventually, but their validity should be established; in other words, the performance of individuals on the indirect items must rank them in the same way as their performance on the direct method of assessment. For a large number of objectives, the paper-and-pencil, supply, and selection types are direct measures of the target objectives. However, the teacher needs to keep in mind that many objectives cannot be measured *directly* by paper-and-pencil tests—for example, speaking skills, pronunciation in a foreign language, the correct use of laboratory techniques, the use of a microscope, or the repair of a carburetor.

In addition to categorizing test questions on the basis of whether they require students to supply or to select an answer, items are also categorized as either essay or objective in nature on the basis of how they are scored.

As we will see, each essay needs to be read by someone knowledgeable in the field being examined. No single answer can be categorically listed as correct, and therefore clerks cannot score students' answers. A subjective judgment on the quality of the answer enters into the scoring. In fact, one of the principal weaknesses of the essay question is that different readers can fail to agree on the correctness of the answer, and even the same reader at different times can score the answers differently.

Objective items, on the other hand, are those in which correct answers can be scored by clerks or by machine. All selection-type items are thus objective in nature. The short-answer supply type generally is also objective, but the item writer must take care in constructing the short-answer item so that in fact a single answer is clearly correct. Classroom teachers often ask whether they should use the essay or some form of objective question. This question ultimately should be answered in terms of what the teacher wishes to measure. In some cases—for example, measuring writing skills—only the essay question permits the student to exhibit the desired behavior. In other cases, such as measurement of a student's knowledge of facts, the objective format is superior. In still other cases, such as the application of principles, both types may serve equally well. The teacher should ask what format permits the student to most directly exhibit the desired behavior. After that, a comparison of the characteristics of essay and objective items should be kept in mind when deciding between the two forms. Table 7-1, a summary prepared by Educational Testing Service, compares the essay and objective items on the basis of several important characteristics.

Too often, items written to measure a particular skill bear little relationship to the way that skill was taught. When this happens, students need an additional set of skills, not directly related to the content, to respond. For example, when writing and spelling skills are measured by the indirect means of having students recognize examples of poor writing and incorrect spelling, the behaviors measured are quite different from those of producing a well-written business letter or short story, or spelling correctly while writing (Madaus, Airasian, & Kellaghan, 1980). Rice

(1897) was one of the first persons to recognize that one's choice of item format can influence the inferences made about students' achievement. Rice found that the way in which words were pronounced by teachers on a dictated spelling test affected students' performance. He subsequently devised two additional tests of spelling; in the first, words to be spelled were in a sentence, and care was taken to avoid words where pronunciation would give clues to the spelling. The second was to correct for spelling in an essay. Test validity is primarily a question of the correctness of the inference made from the test. The teacher should always keep in mind that the choice of item format can influence the inferences one makes about students' achievement.

Of course a teacher can—and often should—use different item formats to measure the same objective. Inferences about students' progress based on many sources of evidence are always preferable to those based on a single type of evidence. The point to keep firmly in mind is that the choice of item type should be made on the basis of the objective to be measured.

The Item-Writing Process

Once the number of items and the type of items to be written have been determined, the teacher is ready to begin the item-writing process. The teacher now might well begin by identifying resource material, textbooks, workbooks, newspapers, magazines, etc., that might be used to generate ideas for items. The larger the variety of resources consulted, the more likely it will be that a sufficient number of items can be written so that the required number of items can be realized. Further, once the teacher moves beyond writing simple recall or recognition items, extra class material is needed to provide the basis for items that measure higher-level skills.

Each item should be written on a separate index card. Various changes made in the item can be added to the card, along with item-analysis data when it becomes available

TABLE 7-1 A COMPARISON OF ESSAY ITEMS AND OBJECTIVE ITEMS

Essay	Objective
Abilities measured	
Requires the student to express himself in his own words, using information from his own background and knowledge.	Requires the student to select correct answers from given options, or to supply answer limited to one word or phrase.
Can tap high levels of reasoning such as required in inference, organization of ideas, comparison and contrast.	Can *also* tap high levels of reasoning such as required in inference, organization of ideas, comparison and contrast.
Does *not* measure purely factual information efficiently.	Measures knowledge of facts efficiently.
Scope	
Covers only a limited field of knowledge in any one test. Essay questions take so long to answer that relatively few can be answered in a given period of time. Also, the student who is especially fluent can often avoid discussing points of which he is unsure.	Covers a broad field of knowledge in one test. Since objective questions may be answered quickly, one test may contain many questions. A broad coverage helps provide reliable measurement.
Incentive to pupils	
Encourages pupils to learn how to organize their own ideas and express them effectively.	Encourages pupils to build up a broad background of knowledge and abilities.
Ease of preparation	
Requires writing only a few questions for a test. Tasks must be clearly defined, general enough to offer some leeway, specific enough to set limits.	Requires writing many questions for a test. Wording must avoid ambiguities and "give-aways." Distractors should embody most likely misconceptions.
Scoring	
Usually very time-consuming to score.	Can be scored quickly.
Permits teachers to comment directly on the reasoning processes of individual pupils. However, an answer may be scored differently by different teachers or by the same teacher at different times.	Answer generally scored only right or wrong, but scoring is very accurate and consistent.

Source: Educational Testing Service, 1973, p. 5.

(see Chapter 4). A scheme for coding each item according to taxonomic level and content area can also be added to the card, as will be discussed later. The first advantage in using a separate index card for each item is that it is easier to review separate items. Secondly, the item cards can be arranged in various orders—according to the estimated difficulty of the item, by the content area, or by the behavior—until the teacher is satisfied with a particular sequence; the test can then be typed from the final arrangement of the cards. Finally, placing each item on a separate card is one step in building an item pool which will be discussed in more detail later.

TYPES OF ITEMS AND SPECIFIC RULES FOR WRITING THEM

As we saw in the previous section, an item can be of either the supply type or the selection type. In this section we shall illustrate various item formats associated with different types of supply and selection items. The illustrations will not be exhaustive, since additional item types are illustrated in Chapters 8, 9, and 10. Rules for writing each type will then be outlined. General rules that apply to *all* types of items will be discussed in a subsequent section.

Supply-Type Items

Supply items require the pupil to write an answer in response to the question or problem set by the teacher. The pupil must *supply* the answer rather than selecting the answer from among alternatives. There are two principal forms the supply item can take: the essay question and the short-answer item.

Essay questions

The essay question is the item type perhaps most frequently used by teachers. Stalnaker (1951) describes the essay question as a test item

> . . . which requires a response composed by the examinee, usually in the form of one or more sentences, of a nature that no single response or pattern of responses can be listed as correct, and the accuracy and quality of which can be judged objectively only by one skilled or informed in the subject. (p. 495)

However, Coffman (1971) points out that it is possible to construct an essay question in which the answers are relatively short and where the acceptable answer can be outlined in advance.

The following is an example of a college-level essay question which requires an extended response, one for which no single response could be listed as correct and which must be subjectively judged:

> Write an essay in which you show how two authors have treated one of the following legends. In your essay compare the authors as to the use of specific incidents from the legend they have selected, their point of view in telling the legend, their attitude toward the characters in the legend, and their interpretation of the significance of the legend. You should select one of the following: Electra, the fall of Troy, Job, the wanderings of Ulysses, Antigone, or Samson and Delilah. (Purves, 1971, p. 726)

The student is asked to compare literary treatments of a legend as the basis of several listed criteria. Obviously the responses to this question will vary in length, content, and quality, and each answer will have to be judged subjectively by the teacher. (Techniques for scoring this type of question are discussed in Chapter 4, Summative Evaluation.)

An essay question which imposes somewhat more structure for the response is the following:

Directions: Describe the organization of The Adoration of the Magi in terms of balance, proportion, and representation—discussing the use of each of the elements: line, plane, volume, mass, texture, light and dark, and color. (20 minutes).

(University of Chicago, Examiners' Office)

The following are essay questions for which the answers will be relatively short and for which the acceptable answer can be outlined in advance.

Directions: Explain how you would analyze a building according to these four points. (10 minutes)
Site (3 lines for writing)
Materials (3 lines for writing)
Construction (3 lines for writing)
Functions or purpose (7 lines for writing)

(University of Chicago Examiners' Office)

Directions: Choose five of the following words. For each write two sentences, one illustrating the literal use of the word, the other its nonliteral use:

astronomical	Cassandra	foggy
antidote	collosus	Rubicon
ballast	doldrums	oasis

(College Entrance Examination Board, Commission on English, 1963, p. 3)

Suggestions for writing essay questions

*1. **Be sure that the question is focused.*** The amount of freedom allowed should be restricted and clearly made known to examinees. The reason for this suggestion is twofold. First, if the question is too broad or vague, many students under the initial pressure of an exam and then of working against the clock will produce poorly written, rambling discourses. Second, the less-structured the question, the more likelihood that subjective judgments will influence the scoring.

The following essay question is too broad and open to too many interpretations:

Choose two novels and compare them in terms of their being representative of the age in which they were written.

(Purves, 1971, p. 727)

Because of its ambiguity the item places a premium on the compositional aspects of the answer rather than on literary knowledge. This in turn increases the subjective element in scoring the consensus. If more than one scorer is involved, one may end up with a measure of the graders' preference of literary style rather than a rating of literary knowledge. A more structured form of the same question would be:

No matter how timeless, a work of literature is first of all representative of the age in which it was written. It reflects the ideas, attitudes, and customs that prevailed during the author's lifetime.

Choose two novels written in different countries or at different times and show how they are or are not representative of the age in which they were written, with respect to one of the following: women, war, marriage, education, the good life, success. In your essay, show first what the belief or attitude of the time was and then how the work you have chosen reflects, attacks, or criticizes that belief.

(Purves, 1971, p. 727)

While more focused than the first attempt, this formulation of the question still leaves it to the examinee to choose the topic, the novels, and the relationships between the two novels. Purves suggests that it would be better for the item writer to make these choices for the examinee in a still more focused question such as:

Choose two novels written in different periods of literary history and compare the attitudes expressed by their authors toward marriage. In your essay show what each author appears to think a good marriage is: how it is related to love, duty, honor, or money; and how he makes

his attitude apparent to the reader. Finally, compare the two works as to both the author's attitude and the techniques by which that attitude is made apparent.

(Purves, 1971, p. 728)

These three versions of an essay question designed to measure literary knowledge illustrate the need for the item writer to narrow and focus the topic—to direct the student toward the content and behavior the item is intended to measure so that all examinees understand the problem to be addressed.

2. *Do not permit examinees to choose from among several essay questions those that they will answer.* Allowing optional questions undermines the major function of a summative exam, i.e., comparing the performance of students on a common task (Madaus & Macnamara, 1970).

3. *Decide in advance how the essay question will be scored.* One of the principal weaknesses associated with the essay question is that there can be considerable inter- and intra-scorer disagreement when reading the question. When the rules for marking are neither very explicit nor very complete, the person marking the question becomes inconsistent from one reading to the next, and if more than one person marks the question, there is apt to be substantial disagreement (Madaus & Macnamara, 1970). If the essay question is used to make a summative judgment, then it is extremely important that the scoring be reliable. (Techniques for increasing marker reliability in reading essay questions are discussed in Chapter 4, Summative Evaluation.)

Short-answer items

The short-answer item requires the student to supply a word or phrase, number, or one or two sentences. The simplest short-answer form is the completion item, which lends itself to a variety of applications.

The name of the third president of the United States is_____.

The Crimean War took place in the years _____to_____ .

The completion type is often used in arithmetic and mathematics.

The set with no elements is called the

_____ .

$6 - (-3) =$ _____

$a/b + c/d =$ _____

The completion type also lends itself to measuring rules, patterns and words, morphology, or usage in foreign languages.

Répondez aux questions suivantes. Employez le même verbe.
1. Allez-vous au cinéma? Oui, nous
_____*au cinéma.*
   (Response: *allons*)
*2. Allez-vous au théâtre? Oui, je*_____*au théâtre.*
   (Response: *vais*)
[Answer the following questions. Use the same verb. (1) Are you going to the movies? Yes, we_____to the movies. (Response: are going) (2) Are you going to the theater? Yes, I_____to the theater. (Response: (am going)]

(Valette, 1971, p. 828)

Knowledge of morphology
Completion
1. Elle_____couche. [She is going to bed.]
2. Vous_____lavez. [You are washing up.]
3. Je_____lève. [I am getting up.]
4. Nous_____amusons. [We are having fun.]
5. Ils_____habillent. [They are getting dressed.]
(Responses: (1) se, (2) vous, (3) me, (4) nous, (5) s')
(Valette, 1971, p. 849)

The short-answer item also lends itself to the direct request for a proof, definition, construction, or short translation.

Prove by induction that

$$\sum_{k1}^{n} k^3 = \frac{n^2(n+1)^2}{4}$$

(J. W. Wilson, 1971, p. 682)

Construct a triangle *ABC* on segment *AB* such that △ *ABC* is similar to △ *PQR*.

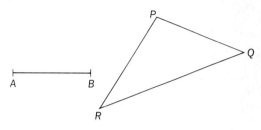

(J. W. Wilson, 1971, p. 669)

There is one other type of supply item which bears mentioning. This is one in which the stimulus for recall is visual or auditory. Following are two examples.

For each of the following figures, write the name below the figure.

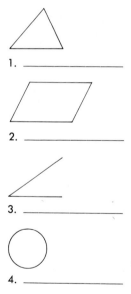

1. _____

2. _____

3. _____

4. _____

Directions: Study the reproduction of Fra Filippo Lippi's "Madonna and Child" [Figure 7-1; see page 188] and then in the box to the right make a line diagram showing the *two* major circular forms and the *two* major triangular forms of the painting's composition.

(Davis, 1968, item 4.
Quoted in B. G. Wilson, 1971, p. 534)

187

(a)

(b)

Figure 7-1 (a) Fra Filippo Lippi's *Madonna and Child* (National Gallery of Art, Washington, D.C., Samuel H. Kress Collection); (b) scoring guide for Lippi's composition. (B. G. Wilson, 1971, p. 534.)

Suggestions for writing short-answer and completion items

*1. **Make sure that the questions can be answered with a simple or unique phrase or word and that there is only one correct answer.*** "What country did the Pilgrims come from?" is a bad item because an examinee could answer either "England" or "Holland." "The Crimean War took place in _____" has several appropriate answers. If the fact being tested is the years in which the war took place, then the following wording avoids the possibility of the student's supplying remote but appropriate answers: "The Crimean War took place in the years_____to_____."

*2. **Use an appropriate format.*** For ease in scoring, the space provided for the examinee's response should be in a column to the right of each question.

*3. **Do not mutilate completion-type items.*** An example of a mutilated completion item from a geometry test is the following:

Two_____are_____if they have _____ and _____ of one equal respectively to _____ and_____of the other.

Items like this reduce the examinee to "reading tea leaves."

4. *Avoid giving clues.* Do not give clues to the correct answer in a completion item by having the length of the blanks vary according to the length of the expected word or phrase; also, avoid giving the first letter of the correct word or phrase.

If the indefinite article "a" or "an" is needed before a blank, write the article in the form "a(n)" to avoid giving the examinee a clue as to whether the required word begins with a vowel or a consonant:

A mathematical rule taken to be true without formal proof is called a(n)_____.

5. *Indicate how precise answers must be.* If the problem involves computation of decimals or fractions, specify clearly the degree of precision expected.

Selection-Type Items

Selection-type items require the student to select the correct answer from information supplied by the examiner. Like the supply type, these items assume several forms.

True-false items

The true-false items require that the students judge a declarative statement as either true or false. For example:

For each of the following staements, put a T or an F in the blank in front of the statement, according to whether you believe it is true (T) or false (F).

   a. _____ The opposite sides of a parallelogram are equal.
   b. _____ A quadrilateral has four equal angles.
   c. _____ An isosceles triangle has three equal sides.

The true-false format readily lends itself to measurement of the knowledge outcomes and permits the teacher to obtain a large sample of a student's command of facts in a relatively short testing period. It can also measure higher-level taxonomic skills:

The next term in the series 3, 4, 7, 11, 18 is 29   (T)
(Ebel, 1971, p.421)

One variation of the true-false format asks the student to indicate whether an equation, sentence, or phrase is right or wrong:

Has the boy choosed his prize yet?   (W)

$a (b+c) = ab+ac$ (R)

Another variation asks the student to respond "yes" or "no" to a direct question:

Are "run" and "water" both verbs?   (Yes)

Suggestions for writing true-false items

1. *Make absolutely sure that the item is unambiguously true or false.* The following two items are examples of ambiguity:

Christopher Columbus discovered America.   T   F

The greatest painter of the twentieth century was Pablo Picasso.   T   F

2. *Do not lift items verbatim from the text.* Sentences or phrases lifted out of context seldom are universally true or false.

3. *Do not write trick items.* Such items are those which attempt to trip up the examinee on the basis of such things as misspelling, a name using an incorrect middle initial, etc.

4. *Avoid negative statements.*

5. *Avoid double-barreled statements.* For example, the following item has two parts to it:

Vitamins play a role in the regulation of metabolism, but do not provide energy.   T   F

6. *Use an appropriate format.* For ease of scoring, answers should be indicated in a column to the left of each question or marked on a separate answer sheet.

7. *Avoid "specific determiners."* There are a number of words called "specific determiners" which qualify the problem or statement posed by a test question. For example, words such as "usually," "as a rule," "generally," "often," "rarely," are generally used in true-false items that are true. Another type of specific determiner is a word like "all," "always," "each," "every," "none." When such words are used in a true-false question, the questions are generally false. A wise examinee follows the rule that "all statements containing 'all' are false, including this one" (Payne, 1951). As is implied in the previous statement, the clever item writer can sometimes construct true-false items in which words like "all," "always," "never," etc., make the item true. The novice item writer, however, must be on guard against inadvertently using specific determiners, since many respondents will be able to answer the item correctly on the basis of the word clue rather than on the basis of mastery of the objective in question.

8. Avoid having the correct answers fall into patterns. Item writers need to be on guard against having the correct answers fall into some recognizable routine pattern (e.g., T, F, T, F, T, F). Having the correct answers fall into a recognizable pattern can be avoided by assigning the correct answer to a position at random by simply flipping a coin.

Matching items

This format consists of a list of premises and a corresponding list of responses. The student is directed to match one of the responses to each premise. As a rule, a response may be used once, more than once, or not at all:

Identify the author of each title in the left-hand column by putting the letter which appears before the name in the right-hand column in the blank before the title. An author may have written several of the works named or none of them.

____1. The Taming of the Shrew   a. Benét
____2. Ode on a Grecian Urn   b. Byron
____3. Talifer   c. Keats
____4. Moby Dick   d. Longfellow
____5. John Brown's Body   e. Melville
____6. Tristram   f. Robinson
   g. Shakespeare

Like the true-false item format, the matching format lends itself most readily to the measurement of a student's knowledge of facts and provides efficiency in terms of coverage per unit of testing time. For example, eleven separate identifications are asked for in the following item.

Directions: Each group of questions below consists of five lettered headings followed by a list of numbered questions. For each numbered question select the one heading which is most closely related to it. Each heading may be used once, more than once, or not at all.

Questions 1-5 concern the following particles:
A Protons
B Neutrons
C Electrons
D Cations
E Anions

Which particles have the characteristics described in each of the following questions?
1. These have no electrical charge.
2. These are charged particles contained in the nucleus of every atom.
3. These are constituents of all atoms and are negatively charged.
4. These have a much smaller mass than any atom.
5. These carry the positive charge in electrolysis.

Questions 6-11 are concerned with aqueous solutions of the following compounds:
A Iron (III) chloride
B Copper(II) chloride
C Magnesium nitrate
D Silver nitrate
E Sodium carbonate

Select the salt which in aqueous solution most closely fits the description given in each question below.
6. Gives a blue precipitate with sodium hydroxide solution
7. Gives a white precipitate with dilute hydrochloric acid
8. Bubbles vigorously with dilute hydrochloric acid
9. Gives a white precipitate with sodium chloride solution
10. Gives a white precipitate with sodium hydroxide solution but no precipitate with sodium chloride solution
11. Gives a white precipitate with barium chloride solution but no precipitate with sodium chloride solution

(University of London General Certificate of Education Examination: Chemistry 2, June 1974)

Again, like the true-false item, the matching variety can be used to measure higher taxonomic levels, particularly when the student is asked to classify statements on the basis of a set of rules, principles, or propositions:

Directions: In the following items you are to judge the effects of a particular policy on the distribution of income. In each case assume that there are no other changes in policy which would counteract the effects of the policy described in the item. For each item, blacken the appropriate space on the answer sheet.

A—if the policy described would tend to reduce the existing degree of inequality in the distribution of income.

B—if the policy described would tend to increase the existing degree of inequality in the distribution of income.

C—if the policy described would have no effect, or an indeterminate effect, on the distribution of income.

1. Increasingly progressive income taxes.
2. Introduction of a national sales tax.
3. Provision of educational and medical services and low-cost public housing.
4. Reduction in the degree of business monopoly.
5. Increasing taxes in periods of prosperity and decreasing them in periods when depressions threaten.

Suggestions for writing matching items

1. Make sure that both the premises and the options to be matched are homogeneous. In the following item, neither the premises (below) nor the options (top of opposite column) are homogeneous; notice that an examinee can quickly and superficially limit the two premises that call for dates (6 and 12) to two options (1791; 1789). (Although the item is broken across columns on this page, that would not of course be done on a test.)

[Premises:]

___ 1. Fourth president of the United States
___ 2. Member of the first cabinet
___ 3. Presiding officer at the Constitutional Convention
___ 4. Refused to attend the Constitutional Convention
___ 5. Proposed Articles of Confederation
___ 6. Bill of Rights ratified
___ 7. Author of the Declaration of Independence
___ 8. Principal author of *The Federalist*
___ 9. First Vice-president
___10. Proposed the "Connecticut Compromise"
___11. Absent from the Constitutional Convention for diplomatic reasons
___12. The first Congress elected under the new Constitution

[Options:]

a. George Washington
b. Benjamin Franklin
c. 1791
d. Alexander Hamilton
e. Thomas Jefferson
f. John Adams
g. Patrick Henry
h. Oliver Ellsworth
i. 1789

2. Use an appropriate format. List the homogeneous premises on the left, the options to be matched on the right. For ease of scoring, leave a blank space beside each numbered premise for the letter of the match.

3. The basis for matching each premise and option should be made clear. For example, in the following item (which we cited earlier) the basis for the matching is title with author.

Identify the author of each title in the left-hand column by putting the letter which appears before the name in the right-hand column in the blank before the title. An author may have written several or none of the works named.

___1. The Taming of the Shrew
___2. Ode on a Grecian Urn
___3. Talifer
___4. Moby Dick
___5. John Brown's Body
___6. Tristram

a. Benét
b. Byron
c. Keats
d. Longfellow
e. Melville
f. Robinson
g. Shakespeare

Notice that the directions explicitly point out that there is no one-to-one correspondence between titles (premises) and authors (options). Lack of one-to-one correspondence is good procedure in writing matching items.

Multiple-choice items

The multiple-choice format consists of two main components: the stem, which presents the student with a direct question or an incomplete statement, and two or more options, one or more of which can be correct and the remainder incorrect (distractors, decoys, or foils). The multiple-choice item is the most versatile of all selection items. Subsequent chapters on measuring various levels of the cognitive taxonomy illustrate its applicability across all taxonomic levels (see Chapters 8 to 10). The multiple-choice format lends itself to a number of variations. The principal variations will be presented here. Other varieties are given in Chapters 8 through 10.

1. The direct-question variety. The stem consists of a direct question followed by alternative answers. Sometimes only one of the alternatives is correct.

For example:

Which of the following Supreme Court cases set the precedent for the Supreme Court's assumption of judicial review?
  a. Marbury *v.* Madison
  b. Baker *v.* Carr
  c. McCulloch *v.* Maryland
  d. Plessy *v.* Ferguson

(Orlandi, 1971, p. 490)

In other instances two or more of the alternative answers are correct or appropriate in some sense, and the student is asked to pick the best (most correct) answer. The following two items are examples.

Which of the following asserted the most clear influence on the writing of James Joyce?
  a. Charles Darwin   d. Sigmund Freud
  b. Karl Marx   e. Benedetto Croce
  c. Sir James Jeans

(Purves, 1971, p. 729)

The steps leading to the swimming pool appear bent where they enter the water. Which one of the following gives the best explanation of this phenomenon?
  a. Diffraction of light by the surface of the water
  b. Dispersion of light on entering water
  c. Refraction of light due to difference in speed of light in air and water
  d. Light not traveling in straight lines in water
  e. Suspended particles in the water

The alternative responses need not be verbal. For example:

Which of these groups of trademarks [in Figure 7-2] most effectively conveys a feeling of strength and dependability?

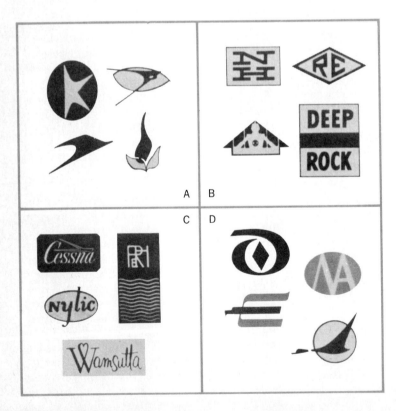

Figure 7-2 Groups of trademarks used with the Education through Vision Text. (Trismen, 1968; from B. G. Wilson, 1971, p. 531.)

The stem can be a combination of a verbal question and a figure, drawing, map, or diagram. For example:

The arrows show the direction of the velocity and acceleration vectors for a car at five separate instants of time. The car travels chiefly toward the east, but changes direction at times.

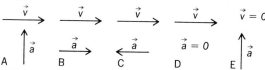

Which diagram represents the car at an instant while turning a corner?

a. Diagram A   c. Diagram C   e. Diagram E
b. Diagram B   d. Diagram D

(Adapted from Rutherford et al., 1966a.
Cited in Klopfer, 1971, p. 592)

[On the basis of the maps shown in Figure 7-3,] which of the following factors seem to be most related?

a. Major types of food and population
b. Major types of food and rainfall
c. Population and rainfall
d. Population and religion

(Association of American Geographers, 1967, p. 6, item 20.
Cited in Orlandi, 1971, p. 479)

It is of course possible and usually very desirable to ask additional questions based on a map, diagram, or illustration such as is shown in the above question. If you have students spend time digesting such maps or illustrations, then the time should be compensated for by asking as many questions as possible consistent with your objectives. Further, to recover the cost of reproducing complex material you should be pre-

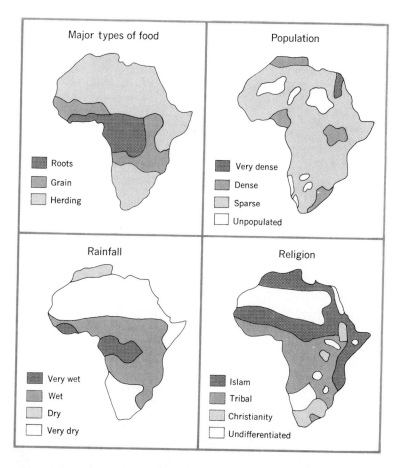

Figure 7-3 Maps of distribution of human and natural resources in Africa. (Association of American Geographers, 1967, p. 6. Cited in Orlandi, 1971, p. 479.)

pared to elicit as much evaluative information as possible.

2.   *The incomplete-statement variety.*   Here the stem consists of an incomplete statement followed by a list of responses, one (or more) of which completes the stem. As was the case with the direct question variety, the alternative answers can be constructed so that an option is the single correct choice or one that is clearly the best among choices that are all correct in varying degrees. The following is an example of the single-correct-answer approach:

Suppose that an operation $\triangle$ on any numbers a and b is defined by $a \ \triangle \ b = a + (a \times b)$. Then $5 \ \triangle \ 2$ equals
 a. 10
 b. 12
 c. 15
 d. 20
 e. 35

(J. W. Wilson, 1971, p. 674)

The following item is an example of the best-answer approach (in this item the student has an excerpt from *King Lear* in which the lines of the excerpt are numbered).

The statement which best explains the diction of lines 7-11 [from *King Lear*] is
 a. Only the language used in these lines is really appropriate to a king.
 b. The language reveals Lear's innate tendency to exaggeration in circumstances that excite his anger.
 c. The language, chosen by the playwright primarily with a view to the effect on the spectator or reader achieves a skillful contrast by the creation of emotional stress after the emotional relations in lines 1-6.
 d. The imaginative quality of the language vividly show Lear's awareness, as a result of his own painful experience, of the suffering of the poor in general.

Like the direct-question variety, the incomplete variety can be made up of a combination of verbal and figural elements in the stem, in the responses, or in both.

Here is an example:

A dual trace oscilloscope is connected to points *P* and *Q* in the grounded base amplifier circuit shown below. Select the pattern you would see on the oscilloscope.

(Klopfer, 1971, p. 876)

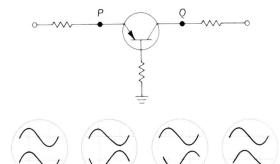

(a)*   (b)   (c)   (d)

The incomplete stem can consist of a mathematical problem:

$24 + 76 = 76 + \square$
 a. 24
 b. 34
 c. 52
 d. 100
 e. None of these

(J. W. Wilson, 1971, p. 672)

3.   *The completion variety.*   Here the stem consists of a statement from which a word or phrase has been deleted. One of the suggested alternatives completes the statement. Notice that this selection item resembles the supply type completion item, differing in that the student selects from alternatives provided.
   For example:

Judicial review is best described as an example of_____in the American Constitution.
 a. federalism
 b. checks and balances
 c. states' rights
 d. democracy

(Orlandi, 1971, p. 490)

The number 30 is a _____number
  a. fraction
  b. decimal
  c. whole
  d. negative

Le brouillard était si épais qu'on _____*plus rien.*
  a. *ne voyait*
  b. *n'entendait*
  c. *ne sentait*
[The fog was so thick that we could no longer _____anything. (a) see, (b) hear, (c) smell]
(Valette, 1971, p. 837)

4. The negative variety.
When certain questions have several equally appropriate or correct answers, it is possible to frame a question which asks the student to pick the alternative that is inappropriate or incorrect.

Which of the following CANNOT be a plane figure?
  a. circle
  b. quadrilateral
  c. tetrahedron
  d. trapezoid
  e. pentagon
(J. W. Wilson, 1971, p. 670)

Which of the following is the LEAST adequate criterion for making aesthetic judgments?
  a. The manner in which the parts are related.
  b. The sensitivity with which the artist has used his materials.
  c. The pleasure one derives from viewing the work.
  d. The absence of a center of interest.
(B.G. Wilson, 1971, p. 538)

5. The ordering variety.
Here the stem presents a basis for arranging objects, numbers, events, stages, etc., in a sequence or order. The alternatives present various possible orders or sequences from which the student is required to pick the correct one. For example:

If the following rational numbers are arranged in order of their closeness to 1, then the order would be

a. $\frac{3}{4}, \frac{3}{2}, \frac{1}{3}, \frac{7}{8}, \frac{4}{3}$

b. $\frac{1}{3}, \frac{3}{4}, \frac{7}{8}, \frac{4}{3}, \frac{3}{2}$

c. $\frac{3}{2}, \frac{4}{3}, \frac{7}{8}, \frac{3}{4}, \frac{1}{3}$

d. $\frac{7}{8}, \frac{3}{4}, \frac{4}{3}, \frac{3}{2}, \frac{1}{3}$

e. $\frac{3}{2}, \frac{1}{3}, \frac{3}{4}, \frac{7}{8}, \frac{4}{3}$

(Wilson et al., 1968f, p. 206.
Cited in J. W. Wilson, 1971, p. 669)

Which of the following lists gives the stages in the life history of the housefly in their correct order?
  a. pupa, larva, egg, adult
  b. egg, larva, pupa, adult
  c. larva, egg, pupa, adult
  d. egg, larva, adult, pupa
  e. pupa, egg, larva, adult
(Adapted from Hedges, 1966, p. 36.
Cited in Klopfer, 1971, p. 592)

6. The multiple-response variety.
Here the student is required to mark *all* the correct alternatives.

For example:

Which of the following numbers, expressed in base 7 numeration, are both prime and odd?
  (a) 10
  (b) 11
  (c) 12
  (d) 13
  (e) 14
Key: a, c, e.

7. The combined-response variety.
Closely related to the multiple-response variety is the combined-response variety. Here the item writer includes combinations of separate distractors as additional alternative answers.

For example:

Movement of materials through the cell membrane is dependent upon
  a. the size of the materials, the composition of the membrane, and the concentration of the materials.
  b. the temperature and the pressure of the surrounding environment.
  c. the degree of solubility of the material in water and the electrical charge of the membrane.
  d. a and b.
  e. a, b, and c.
(Klopfer, 1971, p. 629)

Alternatively, the item writer may present two or more separate answers and a separate set of coded responses which indicate various combinations of the alternatives. The student is required to select from the coded list the set which describes the combination of correct alternatives.

The illustrative question refers to the following experiment:

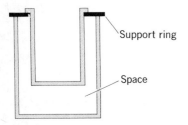

A student, desiring to do some experiments to determine the specific heat of various substances, constructed his own calorimeter. He used two tin cans, nested one inside the other, as shown in the diagram above. The hot sample will be dropped into water held in the inner can.

Which of the following would have to be known to obtain accurate results with this apparatus?
   I. The specific heat of the inner can
   II. The specific gravity of the inner can
   III. The mass of the inner can
      a. I only
      b. II only
      c. III only
      d. I and II
      e. I and III

(Adapted from Educational Testing Service, 1963b, p. 16, Item 25. Copyright 1963 by Educational Testing Service. All rights reserved. Cited in Klopfer, 1971, pp. 599-600)

Suggestions for writing multiple-choice items

1. Make sure that the stem clearly sets the problem. For most multiple choice items the examinee should be able to answer the question or complete the sentence without having to read each option.

2. Words that would otherwise have to be repeated in each option should be placed in the stem. Any word that can go in the stem should. Consider the following item:

If the philosophy in the Allgeyer v. Louisiana case had been applied to the Slaughter House case, the decision in the latter
   a. would have been sustained.
   b. would have been reversed.
   c. would have been undecided.
   d. would have been based on the police power.

Here the phrase "would have been" in front of each option should be dropped and instead placed in the stem immediately after the word "latter."

3. If possible, avoid negatively stated items. Negatively stated items tend to be more difficult for examinees since they are used to selecting the correct, rather than the incorrect, answer. This source of difficulty is generally extraneous to the concept being examined, and therefore whenever possible, negative items should be avoided. Further, item phrasing has a better chance of being understood when expressed positively (Payne, 1951). However when an item can only be tested through the negative approach, then emphasize the negative word by capitalizing each letter and underlining it.

Political alienation is expressed by United States citizens in all of the following ways EXCEPT their
   a. failure to vote in local elections.
   b. attempts to impose their views on others.
   c. expression of views that differ from those of their political leaders.
   d. attempts to organize armed resistance to government policies.

(Adapted from Schultz, 1967, p. 13, item 2. Quoted in Orlandi, 1971, p. 472)

Also remember that when using a negative stem, all but *one* option must be a *correct* answer to the problem posed.

4. If the best-answer variety is used, be sure that the keyed option is clearly the best.

5. If the item is testing the definition or meaning of a word, the word to be defined or explained should be in the stem, while the distractors consist of alternative definitions or meanings. For example, after reading a passage the examinee was asked a series of questions about words in the passage including the following:

The word exact as underlined and used in this passage means about the same as
   a. precise. b. difficult. c. incorrect. d. exaggerated.

(Moore & Kennedy, 1971, p. 435)

6. Four- or five-option items are more desirable than those with fewer options. When the number of options drops below four, the item can be weakened (Wood, 1977).

Inexperienced item writers might find it easier to construct four- rather than five-option questions. In many cases the writer is hard put to come up with four good distractors to go with the correct option. There obviously is no hard and fast rule as to four or five options; the nature of the content or problem being measured and the skill and art of the writer will ultimately be the deciding factors.

7. Each distractor should be plausible and attractive to students who have not mastered the material being examined. Plausible and attractive distractors are those which incorporate common errors, misunderstandings, and misinformation. Constructing good distractors involves the experience of the teacher in dealing with the common types of errors students make in homework and class recitation and the types of misunderstandings revealed through their questions. Another recommended technique for generating plausible distractors is to initially frame a supply question and use the pool of incorrect answers as a source of distractors. However, some incorrect answers to a supply-type question are too obviously incorrect when they are included among distractors in a multiple-choice item (Wood, 1977).

In general, the more homogeneous the distractors in terms of content, form, and structure, the more difficult the item. Thus one way to attempt to control an item's difficulty is by varying the degree of homogeneity among its distractors. Once an item has been used, the percentage of students choosing each distractor can be determined; when and if the item is revised, distractors which attract very few examinees become prime candidates for replacement. When distractors are relatively homogeneous, there is less likelihood that students who have not mastered the material will be able to eliminate one or more distractors as obviously incorrect and then answer by guessing.

8. When possible, arrange distractors in a logical or sequential order. For example:

The sum of the angles of a triangle
  a. is between 90° and 180°.
  b. is 180°.
  c. is between 180° and 360°.
  d. depends on the sizes of the angles.

(J. W. Wilson, 1971, p. 671)

When variables, dates, etc., are arranged in sequence, the correct answer should occasionally be the first or last in the sequence. This helps to overcome the tendency of both item writers and examinees to disregard the extremes of a sequence as not being likely candidates for the correct answer. Item writers sometimes unconsciously set up a sequence or list centering on the correct figure or date.

Where there is no logical or sequential order to the distractors, they should be arranged randomly using one of the two techniques described below. This will ensure that the correct option will not appear noticeably more often in one particular position.

9. Use the option "none of the above" or "none of these" sparingly The option "none of the above" should only be used with care. It should *not* be used with the best-answer multiple-choice item, only with the correct-answer type. Wood (1977) suggests it be used only with items that must be solved first before referring to the distractors; however, even with this type of item, it probably should not be the correct choice, since an examinee could be given credit for a wrong answer. For example, consider an item measuring a computational skill like division where "none of these" is the keyed, or "correct," answer. An examinee could do the division, come up with the wrong answer, and not finding this mistake among the distractors, therefore pick "none of these," the correct answer, for quite the wrong reason. Wesman (1971) suggests that one way around this problem is to use "none of these" as an obviously correct answer very early in the test but sparingly thereafter.

10. Distractors should be independent of one another. In the following example, options a and d are synonymous:

Which is longest?
  a. 36 inches
  b. 3½ feet
  c. 1 meter
  d. 1 yard

In the following example, the options overlap and if d is correct, a, b, and c are also correct.

In the Northeast, the median income for a family of four to live comfortably is more than
  a. $15,000.
  b. $16,000.
  c. $16,500.
  d. $17,000.

11. Avoid giving clues to the correct response. Apart from violating conventions of good writing, grammatical inconsistencies can give students a clue to the correct answer. For example, consider the following item:

Frank Lloyd Wright was an
  a. potter.
  b. architect.
  c. sculptor.
  d. watercolorist.

Only one of the options, "architect"—the correct choice—is properly modified by "an." The item can easily be improved by dropping "an" from the stem and placing the correct article in front of each distractor:

Frank Lloyd Wright was
  a. a potter.
  b. an architect.
  c. a sculptor.
  d. a watercolorist.

The point is that grammatical construction can permit students who may not have the knowledge to answer the item correctly. Similarly, the following item provides a grammatical clue.

Which of the following scientists are famous for their work with DNA?
  a. Einstein
  b. Morgan
  c. Muller
  d. Crick and Watson

Only one distractor, d, fits the plural construction found in the stem.

In addition to grammatical clues, Millman and Pauk (1969, p. 66) describe the following ten characteristics of poorly written multiple-choice items which generally allow students to recognize the correct option:

  a. Length: It will be longer than the incorrect one.
  b. Qualification: It will be qualified to give it precision.
  c. Generalization: It will be generalized to give it wider application than the incorrect options.
  d. Physical position: It will *not* be the first or last option.
  e. Logical position: It will *not* be one of the extremes of a set of options which can be put in some natural order (e.g., options which are all numbers).
  f. Similarity or oppositeness: It will be one of two similar statements, or it will be one of two options which state the idea or fact in diametrically opposite fashion.
  g. Phraseology: It will be in a sentence bearing familiar or stereotyped phraseology.
  h. Language: It will not contain language or technical terms which the student is not expected to know.
  i. Emotive words: It will not contain such extreme words as "nonsense," "foolhardy," "harebrained," etc.
  j. Silly ideas: It will *not* be a flippant remark or a completely unreasonable statement.

12. Avoid having correct options fall into a pattern. The item writer must be on guard against discernible patterns of correct response (e.g., abcd, abcd, abcd). Two randomized techniques are possible (ETS, 1963).

First, when there is no logical order to the options for each question (e.g., numerical order, dates), they can be positioned by alphabetizing the options. For example, consider the following item:

Perspective refers to
   a. lightness-darkness.
   b. the color of objects.
   c. line drawings.
   d. two dimensions.
   e. the illusion of depth.

(B. G. Wilson, 1971, p. 536)

The options would be alphabetized as follows:

   a. lightness-darkness.
   b. line drawings.
   c. the color of objects.
   d. the illusion of depth.
   e. two dimensions.

A second way to accomplish the same randomization of the options across the items of the test is to use a table of random permutations of the letters of the alphabet like the one shown in Table 7-2.

To use Table 7-2, an item writer, without looking, places a pencil on the figure on one of the permutations and rearranges the options according to the letters of the permutation. For example, let us say that the writer's pencil hit the circled permutation CDAB and that the item was originally written thus:

Michelangelo did numerous works in
   a. lithography.   c. mobiles.
   b. woodcut.   d. marble.

(Adapted from B. G. Wilson, 1971, p. 536)

TABLE 7-2 RANDOM PERMUTATIONS TO BE USED IN ARRANGING THE CHOICES IN FOUR-CHOICE ITEMS

DABC	ADCB	DACB	DBCA	BDCA	ACDB
ABDC	BACD	BCDA	CDAB	CABD	ACBD
CBAD	BDAC	ABCD	DBAC	ADBC	CDBA
DCAB	BADC	CADB	BCAD	CBDA	DCBA

Source: Educational Testing Service, 1963.

This item would be retyped with the options arranged as follows:

   a. mobiles.
   b. marble.
   c. lithography.
   d. woodcut.

For the next item one would move to the permutation to the right or left or above or below the circled one and rearrange the original options as indicated. This procedure would continue until all of the items had had their options recorded.

GENERAL SUGGESTIONS FOR WRITING OR SELECTING ITEMS

There are a number of very basic suggestions that should be followed in writing both supply and selection items. These same basic suggestions can also be used as criteria for selecting items from an item pool or item bank.

The suggestions to be discussed below will at first blush appear obvious. Since these suggestions deal with aspects of the mechanics of writing, the reader's immediate reaction may be, "But of course." This reaction would be a serious mistake. However obvious and mundane these suggestions may appear, they are consistently overlooked by persons writing test items. There is a tendency for someone who has written an item to accept uncritically what has been written. The question is perfectly clear to the writer—after all he or she wrote it; consequently there is a tendency to assume that the question must also be clear to the examinee. However, each examinee brings a slightly different perspective to an item. Furthermore, item writers are adults, and examinees are often children or adolescents; words that are clear to the writer may be interpreted differently or simply not understood at all. A sentence or phrase that is clear to the writer may be awkward or complex to an examinee. Writers must constantly guard against taking too much for granted, and must be aware of their shortcomings as writers; item writers, no matter how experienced, *will* make mistakes. The suggestions which follow will assist item writers to be more critical of their products and to check against the subtle fault of taking too much for granted.

1. The item should clearly pose a single definite problem. On reading the item stem the student should fully understand what he or she is being asked to do. It is one thing to be unable to answer a question but quite another not to understand what is being asked. The item stem needs to be clear in and of itself; since it stands alone, it cannot take on additional meaning or clarity from context, as verbal questioning in the classroom can. If the item can be interpreted differently from the way intended by the writer, then it probably will be. As we noted earlier, it is of no help to the student for the teacher to argue, after the fact, "But you should have known what I meant."

Consider the following items from the point of view of posing a single definite problem:

Slave codes
   a. gave slaves their rights.
   b. showed that Southerners were afraid of slave revolt.
   c. were uniform throughout the country.
   d. helped runaway slaves escape.

In this case the stem poses no problem and the examinee must read all the alternative answers in order to infer what is being asked.

Now consider the following example of ambiguity:

The Crimean War took place in
_____.

This short-answer question, as we noted earlier in this chapter, is ambiguous; an examinee would be justified in answering—among other possible responses—any date between 1853 and 1856, "the Crimea," "the nineteenth century," "southern Russia." The writer no doubt was after one fact, perhaps the year in which the war was fought. However, the item can take on numerous interpretations as it stands, and it would be wrong for a teacher to try to justify a single interpretation as correct.

Here is an item that asks for too much interpretation:

Choose two novels and compare them in terms of their being representative of the age in which they were written.

Purves (1971), in criticizing this previously discussed essay question, points out that the word "representative" can be interpreted in terms of subject matter, attitude, theme, style, or all four. He asks, further, Should the student choose works from the same or different literary periods? Purves concludes that "the student has so many questions that he may spend half the examination period settling on his topic and not write enough to allow one to judge the quality of his work" (p. 727).

The point to observe in each of the items discussed above is that the problem was poorly posed. The objective being measured in each case might be important, but a poorly written item caused some students to exhibit behaviors other than those the item was intended to tap. The likelihood that a student will demonstrate a particular skill or action or produce a particular product can depend in large measure on the way in which an item is posed rather than on the student's mastery of the objective itself. *However, generally when a students fails an item, inferences are made about the student's lack of mastery, not about the item.* If the item is clearly and unambiguously written and the student fails, the inference about lack of mastery may be valid; if, on the other hand, the item is poorly written, the inference may well be invalid. The suggestions that follow are in fact corollaries of the need to clearly pose a simple definite problem for the examinee.

2. The reading and linguistic difficulty of the item should be appropriate for the examinees. The weakest student in the class should be able to read and understand the item. The understanding of the problem posed by an item, or of the directions preceding a group of items, should not depend primarily on the examinee's vocabulary or reading comprehension level. When this happens, some students who have in fact mastered the skill or objective may fail the item because of a problem associated with reading comprehension.

When adults write items for children, instructions or questions which are adequate for adolescents and seem reasonable to the adult may not provide a child with an equivalent understanding of the problem (Orasanu, 1977). Klein (1971) reviewed two studies of the instructions accompanying standardized tests and concluded:

> The findings (Jones, 1970; Kennedy, 1970) are rather impressive but upsetting. They noted among other things that the short term memory load and linguistic requirements of the instructions used in measures for early elementary pupils demand far more than one could reasonably expect from such statements. In other words, the student's score on a measure may largely be a function of his ability to understand unusual and difficult syntax and to follow complex directions rather than of his ability to answer the questions themselves. (p. 3)

The problem is not limited to writing items for young children: reading comprehension and vocabulary levels vary for students at all grade levels and vary even in college and graduate school. One way to check on the linguistic appropriateness of individual items on a test is to administer the test individually to a small number of students known to represent a rather broad band of ability, and to ask each to do the reading, thinking, and answering out loud. Taking rather full notes (or using a recorder) so that there is a record of the process that went into answering the item, one can use these data to make inferences concerning the clarity of the vocabu-

lary and graphic materials (if any) in both the directions and questions. As few as five to eight students can give considerable help in picking out points to revise. One can do this with individual items, but it helps to try out the complete test since there are frequently interrelationships among items.

Students' responses in this type of tryout are likely to give the teacher clues for revision which would not emerge during the original test construction. The classroom teacher may not be able to try out items in this way beforehand but after the test could ask five or eight students chosen to represent the various ability levels in the class to go over the test; having the examinee read the question out loud and say what it means will greatly aid the teacher in the cyclical process of item development. Further, as a result of this *post hoc* procedure the teacher could discount certain items and rescore the test.

3. Each item should avoid repetition and be as brief as possible, consistent with clarity. The item writer should take pains to avoid the inclusion of phrases, sentences, or words that are not necessary to an understanding of the problem posed. For example,

The name of the bee that lays eggs and does no other work is the
    a. worker.
    b. drone.
    c. queen.
    d. scout.

The phrase "and does no other work" could be eliminated from the item without damaging the intent of the question.

Irrelevant sentences, phrases, or words increase the time students spend reading items, thus in turn decreasing the number of items that can be asked and giving fast readers an unfair advantage. Further, irrelevant sentences, phrases, or words generally increase reading difficulty. Schmeiser and Whitney (1973) found that stems which include window dressing—that is, material not necessary to answer the item—were appreciably more difficult than those without such irrelevancies.

As a general rule of thumb, Payne (1951) suggests that a question should contain no more than twenty words, while Storey (1970) would have no item stem and single alternatives exceed twenty to twenty-five words or one average-length sentence.

4. Simple words should be used whenever possible—words which have a precise and unambiguous meaning. While the previous suggestion spoke to the desirability for brevity of expression, this suggestion speaks to the issue of clarity. It seems only obvious to state that the item writer's precision in choosing words is crucial in conveying the exact problem or issue which the writer had in mind. Nevertheless, imprecise items abound. Cherry (1966) describes the importance of correct wording this way:

> If words of a language do not name things, actions, events, relationships, and so on, with precision, then language itself must be a source of imprecision in communication? Indeed it is. And the degree of this imprecision depends to a great extent upon the choice of words by the writer or speaker, upon his skill in selecting words, and upon his artistic sense in using them to set his audience into the right frame of mind. (p. 71; by permission of M.I.T. Press)

The choice of a particular word over a near synonym can subtly change the meaning or emotional tone of a sentence. Often the full effect of a word is felt only in context.

Simple, familiar words should be used, since they contribute to brevity, readability, and clarity. Orasanu (1977), in her review of constraints of text and setting in the measurement of mental ability, found that the frequency with which a word is encountered dramatically controls the nature of an adult's response to word-classification questions. She then asks, rhetorically, if this would not also be the same for children.

There are a number of excellent lists of frequently used words (Carroll, 1971; Thorndike & Lorge, 1944) that teachers could refer to with benefit. However even such lists contain words which can pose problems for the item writer. Many common words have two or more meanings. Payne (1951) lists 1,000 frequent or familiar words, and one out of every twelve words in the list is designated as a "problem word." (Examples of problem words are "give," "always," "anything," "bad," "every," "only," "people," "poor," etc.) "Poor," for example, is designated as a problem word because some people can confuse the "rich-poor" idea with the "good-poor" idea (Payne, 1951). A third of the words on Payne's list of 1,000 have ten or more meanings: among common multimeaning words are "after," "act," "fit," "fire," "fly," "hand," "open," "repeat," "where." For example, the examinee's frame of reference in answer to a question with "where" in it can vary:

Where would you go to find out who is the Chief Justice?

Students can interpret "where" in terms of a place (library), a section in a book, a person (civics teacher), etc. The reader is referred to Payne's list and his excellent discussion of problem words and words with multiple meanings. When writing items it is a good practice to keep a dictionary and thesaurus handy to check the intended meanings and at the same time to check other meanings the word might have that might lead to misinterpretation.

Certain types of words should be avoided when possible, such as "government," "country," "America," "art," etc. These words take on meaning in terms of the respondent's conceptualization, and this conceptualization can be quite different from that intended by the item writer. Payne (1951) suggests that when we use such general concept-type words we can easily end up with a "blab-blab question" such as:

Should our country (blab) be more active (blab) in world affairs (blab)?

(p. 150)

The words "country," "active" and "affairs" clearly can take on numerous meanings across respondents.

Another set of words that need to be used with precision are "should," "could," and "might." For example, consider the following questions:

Outline what should be done to improve the United States' balance of payments.

Outline what could be done to improve the United States' balance of payments.

Outline what might be done to improve the United States' balance of payments.

Each version carries a distinct connotation that changes the way in which a respondent answers the question. "Should" wordings connote a moral issue of needs; "could" connotes the issue of possibility; "might" conveys the issue of probability (Payne, 1951).

Idioms, slang, or colloquialisms can result in ambiguity and should be avoided. Similarly, when a passage is lifted verbatim from the textbook and stands alone as a test item, the passage can lose its original context and meaning and can become trivial or meaningless.

5. The grammar and punctuation of the item should be faultless. Like all good writing, item writing is subject to rules of grammar, punctuation, and sentence structure.

All items should be punctuated properly. If the item is a direct question, it should end with a question mark. If the direct question is a multiple-choice item and the distractors are complete sentences, then the first word of each distractor should begin with a capital letter and end with a period or question mark.

In the past, glaciers covered the Great Lakes region. Which of the following offers the most direct experimental support for this statement?
   a. The region is relatively cool in the summer.
   b. Unsorted deposits are found in the region.
   c. Igneous rocks are found in the region.
   d. Ice sheets are still present in Greenland.
   e. Tropical vegetation is absent in the region.

If the direct question in the stem is not followed by complete sentences, then each distractor begins with a capital letter but does not have any terminal punctuation. If the stem of the item is an incomplete sentence, then the first word in each distractor should begin with a lower-case letter and the distractor should end with a period. If the distractors for the incomplete stem are proper names, then of course they should be capitalized and followed by a period.

Sometimes a student encounters a confusing pronoun, such as "it," "its," "this," "that," "these," "those." Such words should not be used unless their antecedents are absolutely clear. If there is any question about the antecedent, then restate it (Payne, 1951). Confusing antecedents can be a particular problem with essay questions or indirect-interview questions, which are discussed in Chapter 11.

6. Clues to the correct response should be avoided. In writing items the writer must always be on guard against giving clues that permit students who have not actually mastered the material to answer the item correctly. We have already illustrated how specific determiners such as "always," "never," "sometimes," etc., can give unwarranted clues on true-false items. We have also illustrated how faulty grammar in a multiple-choice item can signal the correct response.

7. Each item should be edited. After writing each item on a separate card, the item writer should put the cards away for a few days, then go back and proofread each item carefully, starting with the stem and checking it against the various suggestions described above. Without looking at the options, the writer should answer the questions and then check to see that the answer *is* one of the options. Next, each option should be checked against the rules of writing, vocabulary, and grammar described above. The writer should make sure that none of the distractors are in fact correct and that none are simplistic or outrageous. One must check to be sure that there are no inadvertent clues to the correct answer in the stem or in the options. As one proofreads, some items will have to be changed, others discarded, and new ones written.

Because many writers have difficulty proofreading, if at all possible the items should *also* be submitted to colleagues or friends for their reactions. As we pointed out previously, students themselves are another excellent source for criticizing items. Item analysis (see Chapter 4) after the test has been given is no substitute for careful editing and proofreading before the test is typed in final form.

ITEM POOLS

Introduction: General Considerations

We saw in Chapter 2 that for educational objectives there are large pools or banks of statements. These objective pools give teachers the flexibility of selecting objectives in addition to, or in lieu of, writing their own. Accompanying most of these objective pools are large item pools from which teachers can select items designed to measure the objectives in the pool. An item bank or item pool is simply a large number of items—each coded by behavioral aim, content, and approximate grade level—that can be used to assemble instruments to evaluate outcomes.

Teachers should be aware of these pools, since these collections can reduce substantially—although they can never eliminate completely—the time teachers spend on writing items.

In using pools developed commercially or by state or local agencies, a teacher should make sure that the selected item or items do in fact measure the desired objective. The teacher must be satisfied that the item actually gives the examinee the opportunity to exhibit the outcome desired. The fact that the objective code agrees with the item code does not necessarily mean the item is valid. Many item pools, unfortunately, are limited to selection-type items, and some objectives simply cannot be directly measured using this item type. It should be kept in mind, however,

that there is no reason why an item pool cannot include all types of items—supply or selection.

Further, the user needs to keep in mind that simply because an item appears in an item pool, it does not follow that it is well written. No item writer is immune from making mechanical, stylistic, or grammatical errors. Each item should be carefully proofread and checked against the general and specific suggestions for item writing described earlier in this chapter and checked against the criteria for good items summarized on pages 208–209.

It is increasingly common for groups of teachers to cooperatively develop item pools for their own needs. Before describing the steps in developing an item bank, we should point out that there needs to be a cooperative effort between teachers, administrators, and—where needed and available—outside consultants in evaluation and testing. Because the item bank is to serve the needs of teachers, they should have the central role in its development. This role, however, assumes at least four prerequisites: first, an in-service training program which enhances the relevant skills of teachers; second, cooperation so that no one individual will have to carry too heavy a load; third, released time to work on the project; and finally, leadership to direct and coordinate the work. The function of the leader is to convene the group; make provision for necessary in-service training; organize subgroups which will carry out specific tasks; arrange with the administration for proper released time, facilities, and budget; and generally guide the group.

A few school systems may be fortunate enough to have the services of an evaluation specialist, just as they have specialists in music, art, and guidance. Such a person would be an ideal leader to direct teachers in the development of an item pool. Other school systems may be able to release a teacher who already has acquired, or who can acquire, the needed expertise. Most likely the task of leadership will simply fall on a department head or an interested teacher. In this case the leader's job would include—in addition to coordinating the activities—procuring consultant help from a local college or university when technical assistance is needed. Whoever the leader is, it should be emphasized that the task is to coordinate the work of teachers, to work with them, and to make it possible for them to develop and to screen items for inclusion in the pool.

Developing an Item Pool

Specifications
It is important to emphasize that an item pool is a planned library and not an amorphous collection. One cannot assemble an item pool simply by contributing old test questions or writing new ones. Such an unstructured procedure would produce only a hodgepodge of items, many unrelated to the objectives of the program for which the system is being evolved.

Therefore, the first step in the creation of an item pool is the development by the teachers of a blueprint which outlines the specifications of the pool. Of course, once these specifications have been determined, teachers will find that many of their old test items and techniques do in fact fit various specifications and can be incorporated into the pool. These specifications are nothing more or less than a clear delineation of the objectives of the course or program for which the item pool is being developed. It can take the form of a two-dimensional table, one axis containing subject matter, the other, behaviors (see Chapters 2 and 4); or in the case of formative evaluation it can assume the hierarchical structure of a unit or chapter in a textbook (see Chapter 6). For a desired balance of items in the pool, each cell in the table of specifications should be given a value weighting (see Chapter 4).

Contributions
Once the table of specifications has been decided upon, each teacher in the group contributes a number of items designed to evaluate a particular aspect of the table.

Instead of having to build a separate and complete exam for a given unit, each teacher need only contribute items for a fraction of the total table of specifications. Since a person is often more adept at writing certain types of items than other kinds, this division of labor also utilizes the item-writing strengths and competencies of each member of the group to maximum advantage. For example, persons more at home with a particular content area may take responsibility for items in that area; certain teachers may be more facile in developing items to test the higher mental processes (Chapters 9 and 10), while others may work more effectively on knowledge items (Chapter 8); some teachers may be more creative in developing affective than cognitive techniques (Chapter 11).

Screening of contributions
The contributed items, generally written on 3-by-5-inch file cards, must be screened against the general and specific writing suggestions described in this chapter. One screening method that eliminates long group discussions is to have members of the group read the items independently and privately. The group can then meet to discuss those items judged by two or more teachers to be in need of revision. All individual suggestions for improvement can be passed on to the item writer for consideration. Such individual and group screening can go a long way toward eliminating ambiguities, wrongly keyed answers, and other technical weaknesses. Further, these procedures help ensure that an item adequately measures the behavior and content in question.

Coding of items
Once the item has passed the screening process, it is ready to be coded for filing purposes. Like a library, an item pool must incorporate a coding system that permits the user to locate items easily. Since the purpose of the pool is to allow the teacher or department to assemble an instrument designed to measure particular objectives, the coding system must relate readily to the objectives. While coding

systems will necessarily differ from one locality to another, depending on specific needs, a code might include the following fields:

Field I: A number denoting the subject area. For example:
1.0 Algebra I
2.0 Geometry
3.0 Algebra II
4.0 General mathematics

Field II: A letter denoting the intended taxonomic level of items. For example:
A.0 Knowledge
B.0 Comprehension
C.0 Application
D.0 Analysis
E.0 Synthesis
F.0 Evaluation

Field III: A number denoting a content topic in the given subject the question deals with.

Field IV: A number denoting the textbook or curriculum guide for which the question is designed.

Field V: A number denoting the chapter within the textbook or curriculum guide for which the item is designed.

Field II could be further coded by specific behaviors under each major taxonomic category. For example, under Knowledge, A.1 might represent recall of specific facts, A.2 recognition of terminology, and so forth. Field III could likewise be subdivided as desired.

The following is an example of an item coded for the five fields just described. (The codes for fields III, IV, and V would have been previously specified.) The asterisk indicates the correct answer.

	I	A.2	2.9	2	7				.79	.43
Fields:	I	II	III	IV	V	VI	VII	VIII	IX	X

Which of the following is an example of alternation?
  a. $3/5 = 6/10$ and $-2/5 = -4/10$
  b. $x/y = 2/3$ and $x/3 = 2/7$
*c. $x/y = 2/3$ and $3/7 = 2/x$
  d. $5/3 = 10/6$ and $3/5 = 6/10$

The empty fields can be used for additional code meanings as the necessity arises. For example, where the practice of departmental examinations is followed, it may be desirable to code an item to indicate that it is to be used only for quarterly and final examinations. Further, as each item is used, item analysis data can be computed (described in Chapter 4) and entered in a reserved field on the item file card; for example, the difficulty and discrimination indices for the above items have been entered in fields IX and X, respectively; poorly constructed items not caught in the initial screening process can thus be detected and either corrected or dropped. When item statistics are entered on an item card, the user must remember that these statistics are situationally dependent (Baker, 1977). That is, the same item could behave quite differently when used with a different population of examinees, or a larger number of examinees, or in a test with a different configuration of items. Statistics appearing on an item card in a pool should therefore be used with caution and only as rough indicators of how the item might function when used again. Each time an item is used, separate item statistics should be entered along with information about the number of students and their characteristics (grade level, sex, etc.).

Using the pool

The pool should be constantly restocked and kept up to date as objectives are added, modified, or dropped. After a period of time, the pool will place at the disposal of teachers a large number of tried and proven items for each objective in the table of specifications. When a teacher wishes to build a formative or summative instrument to evaluate a unit of instruction, he or she can, by using the predetermined codes, choose items that fit the specifications for the test. The teacher can arrange the items according to behavior, content, difficulty level, or type of test. The items are then refiled for further use.

For a more in-depth treatment of the development of item pools, the reader should consult Childs (1978), Choppin (1978), Lippey (1974), and Wood and Skurnik (1969).

A SUMMARY CHECKLIST FOR ITEM WRITING

Table 7-3 (pages 208–209) shows an excellent and very practical summary of item-writing principles developed by Hambleton and Eignor (1978). This checklist can be used by a teacher in the final screening of items for inclusion in a test. The appropriate answer for each question is indicated by (√). The same set of criteria can also be applied when choosing items from an item pool; if these or similar screens are used before the item is included in the pool, then the principal criteria in selecting items are content and validity.

EXERCISES

1. Review the instructional objectives you wrote after reading Chapter 2.
   a. Divide a piece of paper into two columns. In one column list the behavioral verbs used in your objectives. In the second column list the item types which are appropriate to a demonstration of each behavior.
   b. Look back over the lists. What types of behaviors are best suited to supply items? To selection items? To either supply or selection items?
2. Take out the table of specifications you constructed as an exercise for Chapter 2.
   a. Using this table along with your list of objectives and the list of appropriate item types from exercise 1 above, write two or three test items for each objective. Whenever possible, write items of different types for the same objective. When appropriate, construct a supply item and a selection item for the same objective.
   b. Review the items you have just written. For each objective decide which item type is most appropriate. What criteria govern your decisions?
   c. Look very carefully at the objectives for which you have written both supply- and selection-type items. Are the items equivalent? Do they both tap the behavior indicated in the objective? How might the examinee's thought process differ with different item types?
3. Put your items aside for a day or two. Then screen your items on the following bases:
   (1) Content validity.
   (2) Construct validity. How would you go about empirically examining construct validity?
   (3) The mechanics of good item writing. Use Hambleton and Eignor's summary checklist (pages 208–209). Make a list of flaws you find. Revise flawed items.
4. Exchange your list of test items with a colleague. Again using Hambleton and Eignor's checklist, screen and edit each other's items. What kinds of flaws does one tend to overlook in one's own items?
5. Assume for the moment that you are the assistant superintendent for evaluation in a public school system. You have set a task to develop item pools for certain of your middle school curricula.
   a. Write up a plan to follow in building the item pools. Include in your plan such things as personnel requirements, time requirements, and procedures to be followed.
   b. Write a set of guidelines to be provided to users of the item pools.

TABLE 7-3   A SUMMARY CHECKLIST FOR ITEM WRITING

	Yes	No
1. Have I used items measuring important parts of the curriculum?	√	
2. Have I avoided using items that are presented in an ambiguous fashion?	√	
3. Have I followed standard rules of punctuation and grammar in constructing items?	√	
4. Have I constructed only items that have a right or a clearly best answer?	√	
5. Have I kept the level of reading difficulty appropriate to the group being tested?	√	
6. Have I constructed test items from statements taken verbatim from instructional materials (for example, textbooks)?		√
7. If any items are based on an opinion or authority, have I stated whose opinion or what authority?	√	
8. Do items offer clues for answering other items in the text?		√
9. Do students learn things from items that help them answer other items in the test?		√
10. Do any of the items contain irrelevant cues?		√
11. Have I made any items overly difficult by requiring unnecessarily exact or difficult operations?		√
12. Do any of my items have words such as "always," "never," "none," or "all" in them?		√
13. Have I included any "trick" items in the test?		√
14. Have I checked the items with other teachers or item writers to try and eliminate ambiguity, technical errors, and other errors in item writing?	√	
15. Do any of the items try to test more than a single idea?		√
16. Have I restricted the number of item formats in the test?	√	
17. Were the most "valid" item formats used in the test?	√	
18. Have I grouped items presented in the same format together?	√	
19. Do the correct answers follow essentially a random pattern?	√	

Multiple-choice items

	Yes	No
1. Is each item designed to measure an important objective?	√	
2. Does the item stem clearly define the problem?	√	
3. Have I included as much of the item in the stem as possible?	√	
4. Have I put any irrelevant material in the item stem?		√
5. Have I included any grammatical cues in the item stem?		√
6. Have I kept to a minimum the number of negatively stated item stems?	√	
7. If the negative is used in an item stem, have I clearly emphasized it?	√	
8. Is there one correct or clearly best answer?	√	
9. Have I avoided the use of answers such as "all of the above" and "none of the above"?	√	
10. Have I made sure that all answers are grammatically consistent with the item stem and parallel in form?	√	
11. Have I avoided stating the correct answer in more detail?	√	
12. Have I made sure that all distractors represent plausible alternatives to examinees who do <u>not</u> possess the skill measured by the test item?	√	
13. Have I avoided including two answers that mean the same, such that both can be rejected?	√	
14. Have I avoided the use of modifiers like "sometimes" and "usually" in the alternatives?	√	
15. Have I made sure to use important-sounding words in the distractors as well as the correct answer?	√	
16. Are all answers of the same length and complexity?	√	
17. Have I made the answers as homogeneous as possible?	√	
18. Have I varied the length of the correct answer, thereby eliminating length as a potential clue?	√	
19. Have I listed answers on separate lines, beneath each other?	√	
20. Have I used letters in front of the answers?	√	
21. Have I used new material for the students in formulating problems to measure understanding or ability to apply principles?	√	

Matching items

	Yes	No
1. Are the entries in the two sets homogeneous in content?	√	
2. Are there more answers than premises?	√	
3. Is each answer a plausible alternative for each premise?	√	

Source: Adapted from Hambleton and Eignor, 1978, pp. 61–66.

TABLE 7-3 (CONTINUED)

	Yes	No
4. Is the set too long (greater than 8-10 premises)?		✓
5. Are the entries in the sets arranged in some logical order?	✓	
6. Have I indicated whether an answer can be used more than once?	✓	
7. Do my directions specify the basis on which the match is to be made?	✓	
8. Have I made sure that the matching exercise is on one page?	✓	
9. Have I used headings for the premise and answer choices?	✓	
10. Have I made sure that the information couldn't be better obtained using another format, such as multiple-choice?	✓	

True-false items

	Yes	No
1. Would another item format be more appropriate?		✓
2. Is the item definitely true or false?	✓	
3. Does each item contain a single important idea?	✓	
4. Is the item short?	✓	
5. Is simple language used?	✓	
6. Have I made sure that one part of the item isn't true while another part of the item is false?	✓	
7. Does an insignificant word or phrase influence the truth or falsity of an item?		✓
8. Have I avoided using negative statements?	✓	
9. Have I avoided using vague words such as "seldom" and "frequently"?	✓	
10. Have I avoided use of words that give clues to the correct answer, for example, "always," "never," "usually," and "may"?	✓	
11. Have I made sure my true statements are no longer than my false statements?	✓	
12. Are there approximately an equal number of true and false statements in the test?	✓	

Completion items

	Yes	No
1. Would another item format be more appropriate?		✓
2. Is the item written so that a single brief answer is possible?	✓	
3. Have I omitted unimportant words?	✓	
4. Have I left too many blanks?		✓
5. Are the blanks near the end of the item?	✓	
6. Have I avoided the use of specific determiners, such as "a" and "an," and singular and plural verbs?	✓	
7. Have I made sure the length of my answer blank is equal from question to question?	✓	
8. If the problem requires a numerical answer, have I indicated the units I want the answer stated in?	✓	
9. If the problem requires a written answer, do students know how spelling errors will be scored?	✓	
10. Is each problem written so clearly that there is a single correct answer?	✓	

Essay items

	Yes	No
1. Are essay questions only being used to measure higher-order objectives?	✓	
2. Are the questions closely matched to the objectives they were written to measure?	✓	
3. Does each question present a clear task to the student?	✓	
4. Is there sufficient time for answering questions?	✓	
5. Are students aware of the time limits?	✓	
6. Do students know the points for each question in the test?	✓	
7. Have I used new or interesting material in my essay questions?	✓	
8. Have I tried to start the questions with words or phrases such as "Compare," "Contrast," "Give the reason for," "Give original examples of," "Explain how," "Predict what would happen if," "Criticize"?	✓	
9. Have I written a set of directions for the essays?	✓	
10. If several essays are used, have I used a range of complexity and difficulty in the questions?	✓	
11. Have I prepared an "ideal" answer to each essay question before administering the test?	✓	
12. Have I allowed the students a choice of questions only in those instances when students aren't going to be compared?	✓	

REFERENCES

Association of American Geographers (High School Geography Project). *The Geography of Culture Change Test.* Washington, D.C.: Author, 1967.

Baker, F. B. Advances in item analysis. *Review of Educational Research,* 1977, 47(1), 141–178.

Carroll, J. B., Davies, P., & Richman, B. *The American Heritage word frequency book.* New York: American Heritage; Boston: Houghton Mifflin, 1971.

Cherry, C. *On human communication* (2nd ed.). Cambridge: Massachusetts Institute of Technology Press, 1966.

Childs, R. *Item banking* (Basic Testing Series). Slough: National Foundation for Educational Research in England and Wales, 1978.

Choppin, B. *Item banking and the monitoring of achievement: An introductory paper.* Slough: National Foundation for Educational Research in England and Wales, 1978.

Coffman, W. E. Essay examination. In R. L. Thorndike (Ed.), *Educational measurement* (2nd ed.). Washington, D.C.: American Council on Education, 1971.

College Entrance Examination Board, Commission on English. *Freedom and discipline in English.* New York: Author, 1963.

Davis, D. An exercise to test perception of unifying formal elements in painting. Unpublished test. Iowa City: University of Iowa, 1968.

Ebel, R. L. How to write true-false test items. *Educational and Psychological Measurement,* 1971, *31,* 417–426.

Educational Testing Service. *Making your own test.* Princeton, N.J.: Sound Filmstrip Cooperative Test Division, Educational Testing Service, n.d.

Eduational Testing Service. *Making the classroom test: A guide for teachers.* Princeton, N.J.: Educational Testing Service, 1961.

Educational Testing Service. *Cooperative science tests, chemistry, form B.* Princeton, N.J.: Educational Testing Service, 1963. (a)

Educational Testing Service. *Cooperative science tests, physics, form B.* Princeton, N.J.: Educational Testing Service, 1963. (b)

Hambleton, R. K., & Eignor, D. R. A practitioner's guide to criterion-referenced test development, validation, and test score usage (Laboratory of Psychometric and Evaluative Research Report No. 70). Amherst, Mass.: School of Education, University of Massachusetts, 1978.

Hoffman, B. *The tyranny of testing.* New York: Crowell-Collier, 1962.

Houts, P. L. (Ed.). *The myth of measurability.* New York: Hart, 1977.

Jackson, P. *Life in classrooms.* New York: Holt, 1968.

Jones, M. H. *The unintentional memory load in tests for young children* (CSE Report No. 57). Los Angeles: University of California, 1970.

Kennedy, G. *The language of tests for young children* (CSE Working Paper No. 7). Los Angeles: University of California, 1970.

Klein, S. P. The uses and limitations of standardized tests in meeting the demands of accountability. *UCLA Evaluation Comment* (Center for the Study of Evaluation), 1971, 2(4), 1–7.

Klopfer, L. E. Evaluation of learning in science. In B. S. Bloom, J. T. Hastings, & G. F. Madaus (Eds.), *Handbook on formative and summative evaluation of student learning.* New York: McGraw-Hill, 1971.

Lippey, G. (Ed.). *Computer-assisted test construction.* Englewood Cliffs, N.J.: Educational Technology Publications, 1974.

Madaus, G. F., Airasian, P. W., & Kellaghan, T. *School effectiveness: A reassessment of the evidence.* New York: McGraw-Hill, 1980.

Madaus, G. F. & Macnamara, J. *Public examinations: A study of the Irish Leaving Certificate.* Dublin, Ireland: Educational Research Centre, St. Patrick's College, 1970.

Millman, J., & Pauk, W. *How to take tests.* New York: McGraw-Hill, 1969.

Moore, W. J., & Kennedy, L. D. Evaluation of learning in the language arts. In B. S. Bloom, J. T. Hastings, & G. F. Madaus (Eds.),

Handbook on formative and summative evaluation of student learning. New York: McGraw-Hill, 1971.

Orasanu, J. Constraints of text and setting of measurement of mental ability (Working Paper 3). New York: Rockefeller University Laboratory of Comparative Human Cognition and Institute for Comparative Human Development, 1977.

Orlandi, L. R. Evaluation of learning in secondary school social studies. In B. S. Bloom, J. T. Hastings, & G. F. Madaus (Eds.), *Handbook on formative and summative evaluation of student learning.* New York: McGraw-Hill, 1971.

Payne, S. L. *The art of asking questions.* Princeton, N.J.: Princeton University Press, 1951.

Purves, A. C. Evaluation of learning in literature. In B. S. Bloom, J. T. Hastings, & G. F. Madaus (Eds.), *Handbook on formative and summative evaluation of student learning.* New York: McGraw-Hill, 1971.

Rice, M. The futility of the spelling grind. *The Forum,* 1897, 23, 163–172.

Rutherford, F. J. et al. *Harvard Project Physics Unit Tests.* Cambridge, Mass.: Harvard Project Physics, 1966.

Schmeiser, C. B., & Whitney, D. R. *The effect of selected poor item-writing practices on test difficulty, reliability and validity: A replication* (Research report #66). Iowa City: University of Iowa, University Evaluation and Examination Service, 1973.

Schultz, M. *Tests for comparative political systems: An inquiry approach.* New York: Holt, 1967.

Stalnaker, J. M. The essay type of examination. In E. F. Lindquist (Ed.), *Educational measurement.* Washington, D.C.: American Council on Education, 1951.

Storey, A. G. *The measurement of classroom learning.* Chicago: Science Research Associates, 1970.

Thorndike, E. G. & Lorge, I. *The teacher's word book of 30,000 words.* New York:

Teachers College, Columbia University, 1944.

Trismen, D. A. *Evaluation of the Education through Vision curriculum, phase I* (Project 7–0049). Princeton, N.J.: U. S. Office of Education, Bureau of Research, 1968.

University of Chicago, College. *Diagnostic reports in comprehensive examinations.* Chicago: Author, 1948.

University of Chicago, Examiners Office. *University of Chicago General Examination.* Chicago: Author, n.d.

University of London. *General Certificate of Education Examination: Chemistry 2.* London: University of London, University Entrance and School Examinations Council, June 1974.

Valette, R. M. Evaluation of learning in a second language. In B. S. Bloom, J. T. Hastings, & G. F. Madaus (Eds.), *Handbook on formative and summative evaluation of student learning.* New York: McGraw-Hill, 1971.

Wesman, A. G. Writing the test item. In R. L. Thorndike (Ed.), *Educational Measurement* (2nd ed.), Washington, D.C.: American Council on Education, 1971.

Wilson, B. G. Evaluation of learning in art education. In B. S. Bloom, J. T. Hastings, & G. F. Madaus (Eds.), *Handbook on formative and summative evaluation of student learning.* New York: McGraw-Hill, 1971.

Wilson, J. W. Evaluation of learning in secondary school mathematics. In B. S. Bloom, J. T. Hastings, & G. F. Madaus (Eds.), *Handbook on formative and summative evaluation of student learning.* New York: McGraw-Hill, 1971.

Wood, R. Multiple choice: A state of the art report. *Evaluation in Educational International Progress,* 1977, I(3), 191–280.

Wood, R., & Skurnik, L. S. *Item banking.* Slough, England: National Foundation for Educational Research in England and Wales, 1969.

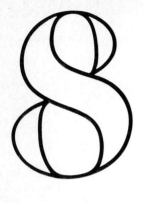

Evaluation Techniques for Knowledge and Comprehension Objectives

Chapter Highlights

INTRODUCTION: THE PLACE OF KNOWLEDGE AND COMPREHENSION OBJECTIVES

The goals or objectives defined as "knowledge" have held a precarious position in American education for 40 years. Not so "comprehension"! The difference is this: "knowledge" gets put down (to use a current phrase) every decade or so on the ground that it implies recall or recognition of a myriad inconsequential details with no understanding or systematization of those details; "comprehension," on the other hand, suggests that the learner "understands"—or internalizes and systematizes—the knowledge. However, if one looks at almost any of the various tables of specifications of content-behavior outcomes in this book (see Chapters 4 and 6), one finds that knowledge of such things as terminology, principles, and rules appears as part of the behavior-content objectives. This situation is not peculiar to this book; statewide and local courses of study include knowledge as a basic part of the curriculum.

KNOWLEDGE OBJECTIVES

The Importance of Knowledge Objectives

The phrase "knowledge objectives," as used in this book, implies recall or recognition of specific elements in a subject area. Perhaps the widest range of types of things which are taught for the purpose of immediate recall appears in the *Taxonomy of Educational Objectives*. Handbook 1, *Cognitive Domain* (Bloom, 1956, pp. 62–77). In that treatise there are examples of knowledge objectives as disparate in content as "the recall of major facts about particular cultures" (p. 66) and "knowledge of a relatively complete formulation of the theory of evolution" (p. 77). Terminology, conventions, and criteria can each be the substance of knowledge.

The objective of the ability to recall does not in itself suggest either the existence or the nonexistence of the capability of using or applying that knowledge. Certainly any self-respecting educator—or educational system—would expect acquired knowledge to be useful in some fashion, whether for the solution of problems (knowledge of the relationship between temperature and pressure) or for personal enjoyment (recall of lines from a poem by E. A. Robinson). It is true that much of what we term knowledge is forgotten after a period of disuse, but this does not deny that such knowledge was a worthy outcome at the time it was learned. For example, most readers of this book had a course in algebra at one time which required recall of the general quadratic equation, $ax_2 + bx + c = 0$. Unless you have been engaged in work (or games) which use it or unless you are a mathematics buff, the chances are that you could not have recalled it exactly at this point. However, when you took algebra, it was important to *know* it both for the solving of exercises and for the more general purpose of acquiring usable concepts about relationships between first-order and second-order equations.

Although many of the specifics which we learn to recall or recognize during our formal instruction are forgotten within a few months or years, knowledge of them at the time of learning is *extremely important* for the development of ideas which do stay with us for interpretative and associational uses. Therefore, during the instruction period it is important for the teacher to test such knowledge as one facet of the evaluation of students' learning. In many cases assessment of recall of specific facts is more a function of formative evaluation (Chapter 6) than of summative evaluation (Chapter 4). We need to have evidence of whether the student can recall certain terms, facts, or methods in order to make inference about difficulties or their treatments.

If we turn to Gagné's method of defining educational objectives, discussed in Chapter 2 (see pages 34–36 and Figure 2-1), we will find time after time that knowledge of a particular term, relationship, or operation is an essential part of the pyramid of prerequisite capabilities for the desired terminal behavior. In some cases, perhaps in many, the underlying knowledge may be important only during the learning process, but at that point it is *essential*. Thus testing for it is highly desirable if one is to understand what is happening to the students.

Statements of Knowledge Objectives

As noted before, knowledge objectives abound in curriculum guides at all levels, in books on the pedagogy of particular subjects, and in books on the measurement of educational outcomes. The following statements are typical of the manner in which such objectives are worded:

1. "Knowledge of reliable sources of information for wise purchasing" (Bloom, 1956, p. 67)
2. "Knowledge of the standard representational devices and symbols in maps and charts" (Bloom, 1956, p. 70)

3. "To define technical terms by giving their attributes, properties, or relations" (Bloom, 1956, p. 64)
4. "Recall the specific definition of negative camber" (Bloom, Hastings, & Madaus, 1971, p. 872)
5. "To recognize a Shakespearean sonnet" in "a group of sonnets" (Bloom et al., 1971, p. 707)
6. "Know biographical information" (Bloom et al., 1971, p. 724)
7. "To identify letters of the alphabet" (Cleveland Heights School District. 1964, p. 18)
8. "The differentiation and discrimination among patterns and elements" (Bloom et al., 1971, p. 823)
9. "The ability to recognize the meanings or the definitions of words and of those terms which are necessary for study in the language arts" (Bloom et al., 1971, p. 412)

Any reader who is at all familiar with education can list many more statements of knowledge objectives. The reason for the selection of the few preceding ones is to present the common forms in which they appear. Those just stated differ from each other in two obvious ways—first, in the objects of the behaviors, and second, in the verbs or implied verbs (for example, "knowledge" meaning "to know"). There are other differences which are not quite so obvious but which are very important when it comes to evaluating students' learning. These are the differences in specificity and type of content and observability and type of behavior.

In terms of specificity of content, perhaps statements 4 and 7 are the most explicit. Statement 4 deals with one definition of one term. It is easy to see several clear ways of testing for this objective; for example, the teacher need only ask the student to state orally or in writing the definition wanted. For the statement dealing with letters of the alphabet, there would be more items, certainly, since there are twenty-six letters, but the area of content is clear and finite.

Statements 1 and 9 indeed present limited content, but for either there would be some question of the limits. Some procedure would have to be used to determine which are the "*reliable* sources of information for *wise* purchasing," but even then the number of specific ones might be so large that the evaluator would find it desirable to sample only a few of them in order to estimate the extent of the student's knowledge. Much the same thing can be said about statement 9, but with the additional note that it includes as content "the meanings or the definitions." The act of implementing this statement in testing situations would have to take into account the possible differences between "meanings" and "definitions." One way to obviate this latter concern is to cut one or the other of the two words out of the statement. We would argue against doing so on the ground that intended outcomes would be altered *in order to make it easier to test for them*. This should never be the criterion. On the other hand, one simply must not overlook the difference in meaning between the two words.

In terms of content, statement 5 deals with sonnets by Shakespeare and sonnets by others. This may suggest a field which is functionally infinite, since one could presumably write sonnets for this purpose. However, the necessary decision here, different from those in 1 and 9, concerns the dimensions along which one wants the student to differentiate and the closeness of the differentiation. One could say that the comparisons should treat subject matter or word choice or word orders—or all these and others. None of this is meant to suggest that this particular statement of a knowledge objective is poorly stated or is less than useful; it does imply that the teacher who is attempting to evaluate learning outcomes in the light of such an objective must keep these possible concerns in mind.

The final observation about the content end of statements of knowledge objectives is directed at statement 3. At first glance this statement may seem to deal with much the same order of things as 4 (the definition of negative camber) and 9 (definitions of words in the language arts). On second reading it is clear that the real content is not subject matter in any restrictive sense; rather it is a method or technique. The knowledge re-

quired is how to define technical terms by citing attributes, properties, or relations of the things to which the terms refer. There are other ways in which to show knowledge of a term—for example, by using it in a sentence, identifying an incorrect use of it, and giving an example of the class to which it refers. We must assume that the objective in statement 3 is not intended to entail any single subject matter or group of subject areas. The intent is to develop in students a particular way of defining technical terms. Therefore, if one wishes to assess the extent to which learners have developed this ability, sampling across technical terms in various areas (at their level of learning) would seem to be demanded.

Several paragraphs earlier it was stated that the list of statements of knowledge objectives also illustrates differences in observability and type of behavior. Chapter 2 has discussed differences in the behavioral aspect of behavior-content objectives as formulated by various people, among them Tyler and Gagné. The nine statements of knowledge objectives illustrate certain concerns for the teacher who is assessing students' learning. For instance, statement 4 (to recall a specific definition) and statement 8 (to differentiate and discriminate) suggest or imply different behaviors. As an example, if we ask you to differentiate and discriminate between the terms "square" and "parallelogram" and you simply list the characteristics of each, you are scarcely delivering the behavior we requested. This doesn't mean that you are naughty—or that you can't distinguish between the two. It means that you didn't give evidence of the sort of behavior which was solicited.

Statement 1 in the list implies that the students know the reliable sources. When we wish to convert this statement into a test item, we must decide what acts or behavior on the students' part satisfies our meaning of "knowing." It could be that if they *list* the sources either orally or in writing when requested, we will be satisfied that they know them. If they do not do this, we may question whether they do not know the sources or whether they do not—for whatever reason—

wish to comply with our request. This is why in Chapter 3, Learning for Mastery, and Chapter 6, Formative Evaluation, it was suggested that the emphasis on grading students be dropped in many circumstances and that learning be assessed for the sole purpose of improving the instruction and learning. Under such circumstances, if the students can be taught to believe in these ground rules, they will be much more willing to respond to our requests to "list the sources." Then the fact that one student lists fewer or less acceptable sources than another means that the one so doing needs more help to arrive at mastery.

Statement 1 might mean that the students are given a list of possible sources of information on which they check those which are reliable for wise purchasing and leave blank those which do not fit this category. Such behavior is observable. One can see whether or not the students check a certain alternative; one cannot see whether or not they *know*. Similarly, with a literal meaning attached to statement 4, one cannot observe whether students "recall" but can observe whether they write, state, or choose a given definition.

There are those (Mager, 1962; Popham, 1969) who demand that any statement of an objective be put in terms of "observable behavior." The authors of this book feel that in general it is useful to express objectives in terms of such categories as "recall," "recognize," and "remember," with the expectation that each teacher or other evaluator of students' learning will look for several possible ways of observing the behavior. We feel that different students may express their knowledge in different ways; we also believe that our collective knowledge of the contingencies among different acts (explicit behaviors) is not yet strong enough to allow for a prescription of the *best* way of expressing knowledge.

Both statement 5 and statement 9 use the word "recognize." Ordinarily this means something different from "recall." In the former case one expects to deal with a choice item, defined in Chapter 7 as one in which the students are asked to select from among alternatives which are given. The word "re-

call," on the other hand, more frequently carries the meaning of having the students respond to a supply item, that is, one in which they are asked to provide a response instead of select among several responses. (In this chapter, examples are given of both supply and choice items.) It is true, however, that if the students choose a response from among several which are given—whether they select the correct one or not—they are *recalling* something. One could say also that when the students supply an answer ("List the five most reliable sources") instead of choosing among sources given ("From the following ten sources select the five most reliable"), they are *recognizing* the appropriate responses among the several or many which come to mind.

In other words, the terms "recognize" and "recall" do not in themselves explicate the observable behavior which is intended any more than does the expression "to know." Persons who are developing tests for these objectives must think of the various observable behaviors which could be used to demonstrate "recognizing," "recalling," and "knowing." They may be satisfied with using one such behavior for all students for a given knowledge objective. On the other hand, they may wish to use several different types of behavior and require that the student demonstrate competence with each. Finally, they may wish to use several different ones but require that the student be competent only with any one of them.

Illustrative Test Items for Knowledge Objectives

The intent of this section is to give the reader examples of a few of the main item formats and indicate the knowledge behaviors for which they are appropriate. Items designed to test knowledge have been more prevalent in tests—teacher-made or published—in almost all fields of study than have items directed at application, analysis, and other uses of knowledge. Examples of types of items which can be used to test knowledge abound both in such tests and in books whose purpose is to present item types and functions. Perhaps one of the most complete sets of illustrations of various item types is in the book by J. Raymond Gerberich, *Specimen Objective Test Items* (1956). Another excellent source of item types, ordered according to subcategories of knowledge (for example, knowledge of conventions, knowledge of trends and sequences, and knowledge of methodology), is the *Taxonomy of Educational Objectives* (Bloom, 1956). Some of the illustrations in this section have been chosen from other works. For each such item, the source is indicated.

There are two very important characteristics of good knowledge items. First, a good item is at a level of exactness and discrimination which is very similar to the level used in the original learning. If one is teaching at a beginning level for knowledge of conventions in language usage or knowledge of methodology in history, test items on the material should never call for finer discrimination or more exact usage than that for which the teaching might account. If they do, some behavior beyond knowledge is being tested; the student must in some way use other principles, generalizations, or criteria to respond correctly. This is not to say that such testing is not useful; it simply suggests that it does not fall in the knowledge category.

The second characteristic is that items should not be couched in terms or settings which are new to the student. This is just the opposite of the rule for testing application or analysis (see Chapter 9). If one has taught a child that the materials deep inside the earth are hot, then one should not test for this knowledge with an item using terms like "interior" and "igneous fusion" unless it is known that these are familiar to the child. If unfamiliar terms are used, then the teacher is testing not for knowledge taught but rather for unfamiliar vocabulary.

As stated earlier, the two main classes of knowledge items are *supply* and *choice*.

Perhaps the simplest form of the supply type is the completion item.

1. The name of the third president of the United States is
——————————.

2. The Crimean War took place in the years
———— to ————.

3. If 6 is multipled by 8, the answer is
————.

4. Two triangles are congruent if they have
———— and ———— of
one equal respectively to
———— and ———— of
the other.

Items such as these are usually best for testing knowledge of specific names, technical terms, and definitions. In building them one must be sure to leave enough space for the word or words to be placed in the blanks. Also, it should be obvious that care must be taken to phrase the statement so that it is unambiguous. For example, as we pointed out in Chapter 7, if the second item were worded "The Crimean War took place in——————————," an appropriate answer might be any of the following: "1853 to 1856," "the Crimea," "the nineteenth century," "southern Russia."

There are those who contend that this type of item leads more directly to rote learning or verbalization without meaning than other types do. Because of the two characteristics cited a few paragraphs earlier, knowledge items in general can motivate students toward rote learning and verbalization if the instruction sets the stage for this and if there is no testing for other capabilities, such as translation, application, and synthesis. One must remember that knowledge test items are intended to discover whether the student recalls certain important things—in much the same form as they were learned. If these things are taught in a meaningless fashion, if there is no attempt to measure understanding in addition to knowledge, the result may well be mere verbalization. This is scarcely the fault of the type of item.

Another kind of supply item which is familiar to most teachers is the direct request for a definition, the statement of a principle or convention, or the steps of a method.

5. State the law relating temperature, pressure, and volume of a gas.

6. List in order the steps which should be taken in adjusting the timer on a six-cylinder engine.

7. Write the definition for similar triangles.

One of the main difficulties with this type of item is that the decisions on scoring them may be very complex. How many different wordings of the response to item 5 should be accepted as satisfactory? What differential scoring should be used on the responses to item 6 if the ordering of the steps differs from that desired? Should the student's response be counted as all wrong if one of the steps is not described adequately? Does a slight misstatement in a student's reply to item 7 mean that the student does not know the definition, or simply that the student's ability to express the idea is not good? There can be answers to such questions, but the process of determining them is time-consuming for both the examinees and the teacher. When the rules are set up for scoring, it would be well to check them out with someone else in the subject area. It is also important that every attempt be made in the directions to convey the ground rules—the exact limits of responses—to the students.

The type of completion item for which the response consists of one to three words obviates some of the difficulties with scoring. The choice item (see below) is usually more efficient in amount of information gained in a set period of time and in scoring time. However, it must be recognized that the examiner is not demanding the same behavior in the supply items just illustrated as in completion or choice types. The one who is evaluating the student's learning must decide which sort of behavior satisfies the knowledge objective.

There is one other type of supply item which bears mentioning. This is one in which the stimulus for recall is visual or auditory.

8. For each of the following figures, write the name below the figure.

9. I will play parts of each of six musical selections on the record player. At the end of each selection I will pause while you write the name of the composer on the line for that selection.

a. _____
b. _____
c. _____
d. _____
e. _____
f. _____

Obvious variations on this item would be to ask for the name of the composition or the type of musical selection.

Item 10 is another example of this type of supply item:

10. As I show you certain pieces of laboratory equipment one at a time, write down the name of the equipment on the lines provided.

a. _____
b. _____
c. _____
d. _____

One could ask instead for the function of the equipment or for an example of use.

Such items as these elicit a type of behavior which is valued in many kinds of learning. The form itself can be adapted to many different subject areas, but it is probably best suited to use in the fine arts classroom, the laboratory, and the shop. It should be noted that the choice of a written answer as opposed to an oral one is not required by the intent of the item. The written response and the prescribed places for responses allow for group use and for standardization of procedure. One should recognize that in this item, as in the preceding set, scoring requires decisions about limits of acceptability of responses. For example, in item 8 should one accept for the second figure both "parallelogram" and "quadrilateral"? In item 9 should one allow an approximate phonic spelling of names—as long as they are recognizable—or demand something more exact? It seems to us that the answers to these sorts of questions rest upon a careful determination of the behavior and content meaning of the knowledge objective.

Choice items for knowledge objectives take many different forms to fit special needs. We will present several of the most common ones, again with comments on some benefits and some dangers involved in using them for testing knowledge objectives. Perhaps the readers can best satisfy their requirements by practicing with a few of these forms. Then, if they want more detailed information on particular rules and on statistical techniques for improving tests, they can refer to some of the books designed especially for test construction, such as those by Ahmann and Glock (1971), Ebel (1965), and Gronlund (1976).

One of the most commonly used forms is that in which the examinee is asked a question and then presented with several alternatives from which one correct answer must be selected. Here is one which parallels item 1 above.

11. Who was the third president of the United States? (Circle the letter of the correct name.)
    a. Adams
    b. Clay
    c. Jackson
    d. Jefferson
    e. Madison

The advantages that this type of item has over the completion form are that there can be no room for ambiguity and in general more items can be sampled in a given time period. Studies have indicated that when the same students are given a large sample of each type testing the same material, the results for the students, in terms of their standing on the tests, is very nearly the same. There may be reasons in a given situation for wanting to sample the supply behavior instead of the choice type, but if the two place students in about the same order, it is usually more efficient to use the choice type.

This multiple-choice form is quite well suited to testing for knowledge of terminology or specific facts, as is illustrated in the following:

12. A synapse can best be described as
    a. a mass or layer of protoplasm having many nuclei but lacking distinct cell boundaries.
    b. a lapse of memory caused by inadequate circulation of blood to the brain.
    c. the pairing of maternal with paternal chromosomes during maturation of the germ cell.
    d. the long cylindrical portion of an axon.
    e. the point at which the nervous impulse passes from one neuron to another.

(Bloom, 1956, p. 79, item 1)

13. Negative camber is the
    a. inward tilt of the kingpin at the top.
    b. outward tilt of the kingpin at the top.
    c. forward tilt of the kingpin.
    d. backward tilt of the kingpin.

(Bloom, Hastings, & Madaus, 1971, p. 872)

In most multiple-choice items, the distracters (nonpreferred alternatives) provided can make discrimination between them and the "correct" choice more or less difficult. If in item 11 we make the alternatives to "Jefferson" such names as "Kalderwehki" and "Kawakami," the student is apt to choose on other grounds than knowledge of the third president's name. It should also be recognized that one can ask for a "best choice" from among those given, as opposed to "the correct choice." This possibility is frequently needed in the social sciences and humanities, but it is certainly applicable to other areas. Take this example:

14. An important difference between a trapezoid and parallelogram is that the latter has.
    a. angles which sum to 360 degrees.
    b. sides of equal length.
    c. opposite angles which are equal.
    d. two angles which are obtuse.

Alternative c is not necessarily the only correct difference or the best of all possible answers, but it is the best alternative given.

Another design of choice item which is useful for the rapid sampling of many knowledge objectives is the true-false format. Following is an example:

15. For each of the following statements, put a T or an F on the blank in front of the statement according to whether you believe it is true (T) or false (F).
    a. _____The opposite sides of a parallelogram are equal.
    b. _____A quadrilateral has four equal angles.
    c. _____An isosceles triangle has three equal sides.

The list may continue with many such statements.

This type of item demands that the students match their memory of a fact, a convention, a definition, or some other statement with the one presented to them. It should be recognized that this is exactly what many multiple-choice items do except that they test one piece of knowledge with several statements and ask the student to identify only the one which is "true." A great difficulty with this type is that in many subject areas it is very difficult to make true or false statements without the use of such conditioners as "usually," "in general," "always," and "never." In statements such as "Elm trees are usually found in temperate climates" and "Cacti never grow outside of subtropical or tropical climates," the student, particularly the clever student, is quite apt to react to the words "usually" and "never," marking the former "true" and the latter "false." The chances of being correct are increased, but you are not testing for the knowledge behavior you intended. This does not mean that the true-false item type is necessarily poor; it merely means that great care must be taken in writing such items.

The third type of choice item is called a "matching" item. Items 16 and 17 are illustrative of this type.

16. On the line to the left of each phrase in *Column A,* write the letter of the word in *Column B* that best matches the phrase. Each word in *Column B* may be used once, more than once, or not at all.

Column A	Column B
_____1. Name of the *answer* in addition problems	a. Difference
_____2. Name of the *answer* in subtraction problems.	b. Dividend
	c. Multiplicand
_____3. Name of the *answer* in multiplication problems	d. Product
	e. Quotient
_____4. Name of the *answer* in division problems	f. Subtrahend
	g. Sum

(Gronlund, 1971, p. 165)

17. Identify the author of each title in the left-hand column by putting the letter which appears before the name in the right-hand column in the blank before the title. One author may have written several of the works named or none of them.

_____1. *The Taming of the Shrew*	a. Benét
	b. Byron
_____2. *Ode on a Grecian Urn*	c. Longfellow
_____3. *Talifer*	d. Melville
_____4. *Moby Dick*	e. Robinson
_____5. *John Brown's Body*	f. Shakespeare
_____6. *Tristram*	g. Keats

Items in this category, like true-false items, provide efficiency in terms of coverage per unit of time. They are, however, very difficult to construct. For example, the terminology of the title should not suggest the period or school of the author. In general there should be more choices in the right-hand column than things to be identified in the left-hand column. Otherwise, the student responding may select one or two on some principle of elimination, not on the basis of knowledge.

In summary, when testing for knowledge objectives, one resorts to either the supply item, in which the students offer the answer *out of their memory,* or choice items, in which they select from some set of *given alternatives.* There are several ways in which to ask for either. If units of information per period of time are important, some of the item formats are likely to be more useful than others. Supply items are likely to be more difficult to score than are the choice type. On the other hand, they are easier to invent. The final question which a teacher should ask, however, is, "What observable behavior will satisfy my objective of knowledge of . . . ?"

See Chapter 7 for a more complete treatment of writing test items.

COMPREHENSION OBJECTIVES

The foregoing section on knowledge objectives dealt with behavior that could be (educators forbid!) mere rote learning or verbalization. In 1946 the National Society for the Study of Education issued a yearbook devoted to the measurement of understanding as opposed to rote memory and verbalization

(Henry, 1946). The idea of the publication was to emphasize that knowledge alone is not enough; use of the knowledge is more important. The authors of the chapters treated understanding operationally as any behavior from stating a proposition in words different from those of the original statement through giving examples of a referent in a definition to applying a principle in a situation new to the learner. Ten years after that publication, the *Taxonomy of Educational Objectives*, Handbook 1, *Cognitive Domain* (Bloom, 1956), treated many of the same operations and some additional ones, but classified them into levels of cognition. In the scheme presented in the *Taxonomy*, the category called "comprehension" is the first level beyond the category of "knowledge."

Comprehension is described in terms of three different operations. The lowest order is that of *translation*, in which the known concept or message is put in different words or changed from one kind of symbolic system to another. Evidence of translation is present when a person puts into words the parts of a graph which shows trends over time in the cost of living—that is, expresses points of the graph in words. Obviously, if one changes a statement in French to its equivalent in English, one is engaging in translation. The ability to translate is frequently very important in such tasks as applying principles of physics to a mechanical problem, analyzing a document, or creating a work of art.

The second level of comprehension is *interpretation*. Evidence of this behavior is present when students can go beyond recognizing the separate parts of a communication—translating the graph mentioned in the preceding paragraph—and see the interrelations among the parts. They can relate the various parts of the graph to actual events. Also, they must be able to differentiate the essentials of the message from aspects unimportant to the message, such as the color of the graph or the size of the time-scale units.

The third level of comprehension is *extrapolation*. In this category the receiver of a communication is expected to go beyond the literal communication itself and make inferences about consequences or perceptibly extend the time dimensions, the sample, or the topic. In the example of the graph showing cost-of-living trends, extrapolation would demand such behaviors as inferring what the next time unit—beyond the graph—might show, suggesting the possible meaning of the graph for different sorts of commodities, or presenting the effects which the situation described by the message might have on wages or taxes. In this sense extrapolation is much akin to interpretation, but it exceeds the literal limits of the message.

Although it is very useful for both instructional and evaluative purposes for the teacher to be concerned with each of the three subcategories independently, they are highly interrelated. In certain tasks and behaviors, one may draw a line too fine by attempting to say, "This is translation and not interpretation" or "That is interpretation but not extrapolation." There are cases, however, in which the distinctions are clear. Therefore, in the remainder of this chapter we will present objectives, test items, and discussions of the items under the more general heading of "comprehension," although the subcategories are indicated where appropriate.

Statements of Comprehension Objectives

Objectives in this area appear in courses of study and in methods books in various subject areas almost as frequently as statements of knowledge objectives. Some rather typically worded statements are these:

1. "The ability to translate an abstraction, such as some general principle, by giving an illustration or sample" (Bloom, 1956, p. 92).
2. "The ability to read musical scores" (Bloom, 1956, p. 92).
3. "The ability to comprehend the connotative value in words" in a literary work (Bloom, Hastings, & Madaus, 1971, p. 737).
4. "Give a literal translation [of a sentence from French into English] and a meaningful English equivalent" (Bloom et al., 1971, p. 832).
5. "A major aspect of reading in the social sciences is geared to the interpretation of

maps, globes, graphs, tables, and charts, and cartoons" (Bloom et al., 1971, p. 476).

6. "To write a one- or two-paragraph summary based on reading material, observation, or listening" (Cleveland Heights School District, 1964, p. 37).

7. "The ability to comprehend the significance of particular words in a poem in the light of the context of the poem" (Bloom et al., 1971, p. 412).

8. "The ability to recognize puns or verbal ambiguities" (Bloom et al., 1971, p. 736).

9. The ability "to extrapolate from data presented in a table" (Bloom et al., 1971, p. 476).

10. "The ability to estimate or predict consequences of courses of action described in a communication" (Bloom, 1956, p. 96).

11. "Skill in predicting continuation of trends" (Bloom, 1956, p. 96).

12. "The ability to be sensitive to factors which may render predictions inaccurate" (Bloom, 1956, p. 96).

The readers would do well to spend some time looking through methods books and courses of study or curriculum guidelines in their own fields in order to find statements like the foregoing. If you are a teacher and have not developed statements like these for your own class, you should try your hand at some right now. Note that statements 1 and 2 concern translation. Statements 3 and 4 certainly involve translation as a main ingredient, but each may entail some interpretation in that an assessment of the relationship among elements of the message *may* be demanded. Interpretation is clearly the level of statements 5 to 8, whereas extrapolation is the focus of 9 to 12.

Even a cursory study of the list above will show that comprehension, as defined in this setting, is not the sole property of one or two fields of study. For example, statements 5 and 2 represent geography and music respectively; language arts, literature, and foreign language are the subject areas of statements 3, 4, and 6 to 8; and science, social studies, and mathematics can be the contents of statements 1, 9, and 12 in that order.

In the preceding section, it was pointed out that items built for the purpose of evaluating knowledge outcomes should stick as nearly as possible to the form and the level of precision used in instruction. In comprehension items—ranging from translation to extrapolation—the opposite is true. If the students are asked to translate in *exactly* the same situation as the one in which they were taught to translate, they may be working much more at the knowledge level than in the comprehension category. For example, if we teach for statement 1 by using certain principles accompanied by particular illustrations and then assess learning by items which use those same principles and allow the identical illustrations, the student's correct response is more likely to be direct recall than it is a generalized translation ability.

On the other hand, items which call for interpretation in a totally different setting from the one in which instruction was given probably come much nearer to testing application and analysis than to measuring interpretation in the meaning which is used here. For instance, if we have instructed students along the lines suggested by statement 8 above, and then we test them on their ability to comprehend objects in a cartoon in the light of the total cartoon, we are probably asking them to use higher-order abilities than we had intended.

In many ways statements of comprehension objectives provide more direction in their very wording for writing questions and examination items than do statements of knowledge objectives. Note statement 2, which deals with music. The obvious way of testing for this is by giving students musical scores and asking them to translate the symbols into actual notes. However, it would still be translation if the students were required to write in words the notes, phrasing, and other characteristics. Or again, statement 5 suggests that one give the examinees a map and then ask them questions about how to get from here to there, or ask them to describe the terrain. However, if the objective is statement 11, there may be several routes to the evaluation of the outcomes. One could set up a situation in which the "continuation" has occurred— inflation in the 1880s—and judge the students' response against the fact. Unfortunately, this might be a knowledge item for some students. An alternative would be to use current data and expert judgments on the probability of the choice of trends.

The main consideration with comprehension objectives is to see whether students can go beyond the *knowledge* objectives—which are highly specific—to *understanding* (Henry, 1946). If the students can translate, interpret, and extrapolate from messages which are used as input, they have gone beyond verbalization of knowledge. They have to some extent a "command of substantive knowledge" (Ebel, 1965, p. 38).

Illustrative Test Items for Comprehension Objectives

The characteristics of comprehension items are fairly clear. The material for translation, interpretation, or extrapolation must not be the same as was used in instruction, but it should have similar characteristics in terms of language or symbols, complexity, and content. Translation should involve elements instead of the relationships between elements in the message to be translated. Interpretation items will involve the translation of elements with the additional requirement that the student see interrelationships among elements of the total message. Extrapolation items will call for going beyond the limits of the literal message and will involve both translation and interpretation.

18. The following sentence is stated as a definition, but the italicized words are fictitious. Your task is to read the definition and choose the formula below the statement which states the same thing. "The *calong* (C) is equal to the sum over the entire set of the squared differences between the *lorang* (L,) and the beland (B) divided by twice the number of *graks* (G)."

   a. ___ $C = \dfrac{\Sigma(B^2 - L)}{G^2}$ c. ___ $C = \dfrac{\Sigma L^2 - \Sigma B^2}{2G}$

   b. ___ $C = \dfrac{\Sigma(L - B)^2}{2G}$ d. ___ $C = \dfrac{\Sigma(L - B)}{G^2}$

An item like 18 could be built around a real law or definition and still require the student

to translate from words to symbols. The difficulty with using a real definition is that the students may have memorized the formula, in which case this is likely to become a knowledge item.

19. A group of examiners is engaged in the production of a taxonomy of educational objectives. In ordinary English, what are these persons doing?
   a. Evaluating the progress of education
   b. Classifying teaching goals
   c. Preparing a curriculum
   d. Constructing learning exercises

   (Bloom, 1956, p. 99, item 1)

Item 19 requires a simple translation of the word "taxonomy" into "classification" and of "educational objectives" into "teaching goals." This item illustrates that translation can be at a very simple level. It should be noted, however, that if the student has been instructed that "classification" can substitute for "taxonomy," the item will represent the knowledge category

20. When a current is induced by the relative motion of a conductor and a magnetic field, the direction of the induced current is such as to establish a magnetic field that opposes the motion. This principle is illustrated by
   a. a magnet attracting a nail.
   b. an electric generator or dynamo.
   c. the motion of a compass needle.
   d. an electric doorbell.

   (Bloom, 1956, p. 99, item 3)

Item 20 requires a student to translate from a formal and fairly abstract definition into a specific example. If the example had been used in the instructional setting, then one might be testing straight recall of a verbal tie.

21. While listening to lectures in physical science you have heard the following terms frequently used: "hypotheses," "theories," "scientific laws," "scientific method," and "scientific attitude." In a series of paragraphs, indicate in your own words and in terms of everyday experience what these terms mean to you.

   (Bloom, 1956, p. 99, item 4)

Item 21 illustrates that supply (as opposed to choice) situations can be very useful for evaluating translation. It should be recognized that item 18, above, could have been put in supply form. As a matter of fact, giving an item such as that in supply form to a small group of learners is one way to generate alternatives for the choice item.

22. A comparatively easy achievement test was given to a group of good learners. Which of the following graphs—in which f represents the frequency of a score among the examinees and s represents the score scale from low to high—shows the distribution you would expect?

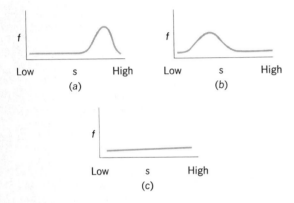

Translation of an idea into graphic form, as in item 22, is an important behavior in many subject areas. One could turn the direction of translation around by giving a graph and then requesting the student to choose among several verbal descriptions.

Items 23 to 30 are examples of a complex item.

Directions: Use the following numbers to indicate your answer [to each of the questions concerning Figure 8-1].
  1. The statement is supported by the evidence given in the chart.

  2. Whether the statement is correct or incorrect cannot be determined by the evidence in the chart.

  3. The statement is contradicted by the evidence given in the chart.

Questions on [Figure 8-1]
23. The total farm economy of the United States depends upon exports.

24. Less than 50 percent of exports of agricultural products are government-sponsored.

25. The American farmer would suffer great loss of income if government-sponsored programs were to be dropped.

26. Rice was the largest item in government-sponsored programs.

27. The United States consumes about two-thirds of the tobacco produced.

28. The United States keeps for its own use over half of the rice and wheat grown.

29. The graph demonstrates that economic health in the United States depends upon economic health of the countries that import our products.

30. Cotton exports would suffer least from the withdrawal of government-sponsored programs.

(Morse & McCune, 1964, pp. 62–63, items 33–40,
quoted in Bloom, Hastings, & Madaus, 1971,
pp. 476–477, items 36–43)

This kind of complex item can be very useful for evaluating comprehension. Most of these statements appear to involve all three levels of comprehension, although some focus more upon one level than another. Statements 27 and 28 call mostly for translation from graphics into words—if we assume that what is not exported is used within the country. Statements 24 and 30 emphasize interpretation, since the student must interrelate various elements in the graph. Extrapolation is demanded in 25 and 29, which ask the examinee to go beyond the limits of the message.

The following group of items (31–39) is an excellent example of testing for both translation and interpretation. Although the group appears in the *Taxonomy* with examples of interpretation items, it is obvious that parts of it (for example, items 31 to 33) are almost completely translation from one set of terms to another. One could increase or decrease the translation behavior by making the statements to be judged either less or more similar in language to the descriptions of the experiments. Again, as in items 23 and 30, one

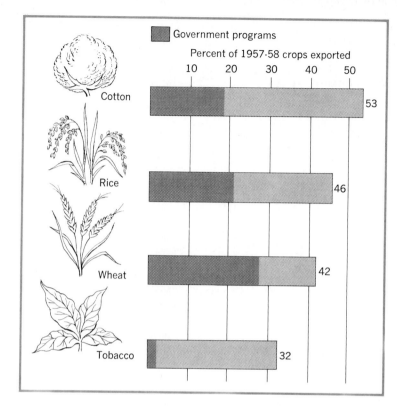

Figure 8-1 American agriculture depends on exports. (U.S. Department of State, U.S. Department of Defense, & International Cooperation Administration. *Mutual security program, fiscal year 1960: A summary presentation.* Washington, D.C.: USDS, USDD, and ICA, March 1959. Reprinted in Morse & McCune, 1964, p. 62; reproduced in Bloom, Hastings, & Madaus, 1971, p. 476.)

could test for extrapolation using this item form by simply going outside the exact boundaries of the message (the descriptions) and asking for predictions or estimates of related events.

A scientist cultivated a large colony of disease-producing bacteria. From them, he extracted a bacteria-free material referred to as substance X. A large dose of substance X was then injected into each of a group of animals (group A). These animals promptly developed some of the symptoms normally produced in infection by the bacteria in question. Then, into each of a number of other animals (group B), the scientist made a series of injections of small doses of substance X. Three weeks after this series of injections, and continuing for two years thereafter, this group of animals (group B) could be made to develop the disease by injecting them with several thousand times the number of bacteria which was fatal to untreated animals.

After the item number on the answer sheet, blacken space A—if the data given above definitely show that the item correctly completes the introductory statement.

B—if the data given above do not definitely show that the item correctly completes the introductory statement.
(Be careful to make your judgments in terms of the data given in the description of the experiment.)

Substance X acted upon the animals of group A as if it were a

31. poison.

32. destroyer of poisons.

33. stimulator causing animals of group A to produce destroyers of the bacterial poison.

With reference to its effect upon the animals of group B, substance X appeared to act as

34. a means of counteracting the effects of the disease-producing bacteria.

35. a destroyer of the bacteria or of their poisonous products.

36. a poisonous product of the bacteria.

225

Ten months after the series of injections described above, the scientist prepared serum from the blood of the animals of group B. He injected this serum into each of a large group (group C) of animals infected with the disease. A control group, also infected with the disease, was given no serum. There was a higher percentage of prompt recoveries in group C than in the control group.

Serum from the animals of group B acted in the animals of group C to

37. stimulate the animals of group C to produce a destroyer of the disease-producing bacteria or their poisonous products.

38. destroy the disease-producing bacteria or their poisonous products.

39. hasten the deleterious effects of the disease-producing bacteria upon animals of group C.

(Bloom, 1956, pp. 111–112, items 40–48.)

The following sort of items set (40–41) is intended basically for translation, but it does have some characteristics of interpretation, since the successful student must be aware of relationships between elements of the message. The selections can be made more difficult by increasing the number of relationships to be noted.

Each of the following selections concerns a mathematical situation. The activities described and the numbers used are correct, but in some cases the wrong term (mathematical word) is used. You are to read the selection and underline the terms which you believe have been used incorrectly.

40. In a problem which John was working, it was necessary to add 618, 431, and 215. He added them and found their product to be 1,264. He checked by readding in the other direction.

41. In making arrangements to redecorate his home, Mr. Gray found that he needed to use some mathematics. The ratio between the height, 12 feet, and the width, 10 feet, of a certain room was 2 feet. It was also necessary to find the area of the air in the room for purposes of heating. To solve the problem of lighting the room, Mr. Gray had to determine certain angles formed by lines drawn from various points in the room to the center of each window.

In the next two item groups (42–56 and 57–71), interpretation of a message is important.

In this problem you are to follow the directions in the box below to judge the statements about the accompanying table.

Public Debt of the United States

Year	Total national debt, dollars	Per capita debt, dollars
1900	1,263,416,913	16.60
1905	1,132,357,095	13.51
1910	1,146,939,969	12.41
1915	1,191,264,068	11.85
1920	24,299,321,467	228.23
1925	20,516,193,888	167.12
1930	16,185,309,831	131.51
1935	28,700,892,625	225.55
1940	42,967,531,038	325.59
1945	258,682,187,410	1,853.21

The figures in the table were compiled and published by the United States Treasury Department. The column headed "Per capita debt" shows the amount of money each person living in the United States that year would have owed if the national debt had been divided equally.

Make a decision about each of the numbered statements on the basis of the above information and the graphs, and indicate your decisions on the answer sheet as follows:
1. It is *true*.
2. It is *probably true*.
3. The facts alone are *not sufficient* to indicate whether there is any degree of truth or falsity in the statement.
4. It is *probably false*.
5. It is *false*.

42. In 1940 the per capita debt in the United States was approximately two times as great as in 1925.
43. This table shows that the United States needs a better system of taxation.
44. The total national debt was greater in 1916 than in 1911.
45. In 1948 the people of the United States had lowered the per capita debt to about the 1935 level.
46. The reason for the decrease in the total debt between 1920 and 1930 was that during those years the United States had presidents who were excellent administrators of the national wealth.

47. For those years shown in the period from 1905 to 1915 inclusive, the size of the total national debt decreased.

48. The dollar amount of the debt resulting from the programs of national defense and relief was greater in 1940 than in 1935. (About 65 percent of the debt was due to these programs.)

49. There was a sharp drop in the per capita debt in 1942.

50. The decrease in the per capita debt from 1910 to 1915 was much greater than the decrease from 1900 to 1905.

51. From 1920 to 1945 there was a steady and continuous increase in the total national debt.

52. In 1947 the per capita debt was less than it was in 1940.

53. The United States Treasury Department published these facts to show people how greatly wars increase the national debt. (A large part of the debt in 1945 was caused by military expenditures.)

54. The total debt of the United States was somewhat greater in 1900 then in 1915.

55. Poor administration of government funds caused the heavily increased per capita debt in 1935.

56. In 1890 the per capita debt was less than it was in 1920.

In this problem [items 57–71] you are to follow the directions in the box [below] in judging the statements which are made about the graphs [in Figure 8-2].

The graphs were published by the Safety Council of Middleburg, West Virginia. The information plotted for each given hour is the total number of accidents in the year 1949 in the 3-hour span from 1½ hours before to 1½ hours after the hour stated. For example, a point at "3 A.M." represents the total number of accidents that occurred during the year in that part of the day from 1:30 A.M. to 4:30 A.M. Of the registered drivers in Middleburg, 70 percent were men and 30 percent were women.

> Make a decision about each of the numbered statements on the basis of the above information and the graph, and indicate your decisions on the answer sheet as follows:
> 1. It is *true*.
> 2. It is *probably true*.
> 3. The facts alone are *not sufficient* to indicate whether there is any degree of truth or falsity in the statement.
> 4. It is *probably false*.
> 5. It is *false*.

57. The total number of accidents showed a sharp drop between midnight and 3 A.M.

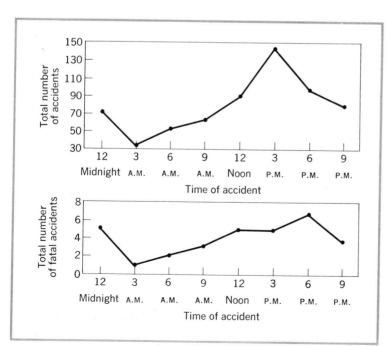

Figure 8-2 Number of traffic accidents at given hours in Middleburg, West Virginia, 1949.

58. Most fatal accidents occurring between midnight and 3 A.M. were a result of drunken driving.
59. The accident rate at 10 A.M. was less than the rate at 11 A.M.
60. The greatest number of fatal accidents occurred at midnight.
61. Over half of the drivers involved in the accidents between noon and midnight were men.
62. In the downtown area, the accident rate was slightly lower in the afternoon than in the morning. (A recent traffic count revealed that a large majority of the car owners drive in the downtown area each day.)
63. There were fewer fatal accidents between midnight and 6 A.M. than there were between 3 P.M. and 9 P.M.
64. This chart was published to show that people ought to drive more carefully. (Ten percent of the drivers in Middleburg were involved in a traffic accident in 1949.)
65. In many other cities of this size in the United States, there are more fatal traffic accidents in the late afternoon hours than in the early morning.
66. Between midnight and noon the total number of accidents showed a steady increase.
67. The total number of accidents per hour was greater at 5 A.M. than at 1 A.M.
68. More women then men were involved in the accidents which occurred during the late afternoon period.
69. The police department of Middleburg ought to increase their traffic force.
70. The total number of accidents at 12:30 A.M. was greater than the number which occurred at 2:30 A.M.
71. Any person who causes and survives an accident fatal to someone else should have his driver's license suspended.

Although the approach used in both sets of item complexes, 42 to 56 and 57 to 71, is especially useful for testing comprehension in the social and natural sciences, the idea can be adapted to industrial arts, business education, and even certain areas of the humanities. The item groups obviously call for interpretation of a message. Translation from one set of symbols to another is especially prominent in items 57 to 71 because most of the message is given in graph form. It should be noted that such items as 52 and 56 call for extrapolation in time. Item 70 requires the learner to be sensitive to how far one can estimate beyond the data.

These last two sets of items, 42 to 56 and

57 to 71, also afford some interesting and useful scoring possibilities. Each statement about the data is keyed as true (T), probably true (PT), not sufficiently indicated by the data (NS), probably false (PF), or false (F). Thus, item 42 would be keyed as T, 43 as NS, 44 (representing a variety of the extrapolation-level item) as PT, 45 as PF, and 47 as F. Obviously a student's responses could be scored, as on most tests, by a mark of either correct (like the key) or incorrect (unlike the key) on each response. However, the evaluation staff of the Eight-Year Study of secondary education (Smith & Tyler, 1942, pp. 48–56) worked out a scoring scheme which gives more detailed information. The chart in Table 8-1 is basic to the system.

The letter "A" in the body of the chart represents an *accurate* response; that is, the student's response matches the key. "C" stands for a *cautious* answer. If the statement is in fact true but the student responds with "PT" or "NS," the student is not using or interpreting all the data available—he or she is being cautious. "CE" represents a *crude error*; the student who says that a statement keyed "T" is either probably false or false is really missing the translation, interpretation, or extrapolation.

A student who indicates that he or she believes a statement keyed "PT" or "NS" is in fact true, "T," is going *beyond the data*, "BD." Also, the student can go beyond the

TABLE 8-1   CHART SHOWING HOW SCORES ARE DERIVED

		Student's response to statement				
		T	PT	NS	PF	F
	T	A	C	C	CE	CE
	PT	BD	A	C	CE	CE
Key	NS	BD	BD	A	BD	BD
	PF	CE	CE	C	A	BD
	F	CE	CE	C	C	A

Source: Adapted from Smith & Tyler, 1942, p. 54.

data in interpretation at the "false" end of the scale.

Any response a student makes can be put into one of these four categories: accurate answer, cautious answer, crude error, or answer beyond the data. For example, if a student responded to most statements with "NS" when all five types of statements appeared in the problem, he or she would be classified as cautious in ability to comprehend the data. On the other hand, were the student always—or almost always—to say "true" or "false" to statements many of which were only probably true or probably false and for some of which there were not sufficient data to say either way, we would certainly have evidence that the student's tendency was to go beyond the data, that is, to overinterpret.

This type of scoring could be very useful in either summative evaluation (Chapter 4) or formative evaluation (Chapter 6). It is also possible with this type of item to score in terms of the three levels of comprehension—translation, interpretation, and extrapolation—if the test maker sees to it that all three types of statements are present. For example, item 57 calls mainly for translation, since the elements to be related are so close together and the descending line translates to "drop." Item 63, however, puts most of the weight on the interrelations between several elements and is therefore interpretation. Any item, such as 70, which asks for information not explicitly plotted on the graph is dealing with extrapolation.

EXERCISES

Objective: Construct test items appropriate to the evaluation of knowledge and comprehension objectives.

Preparation: The objectives and test items developed for Chapters 2 and 7 may be useful in doing the exercises for this chapter and Chapters 9 and 10.

1. *Preparing objectives.* Prepare two sets of objectives—one set of knowledge and one set of comprehension objectives. The following guidelines may be useful.

   a. Select some objectives from ones you have written previously, from curriculum guides, from books on teaching, or from books on educational measurement.

   b. Write some new objectives as well.

   c. It is not necessary to limit yourself to one instructional unit. Better that you get the experience of writing objectives for the same cognitive levels for different units, even different subjects. It may be interesting to try your hand at writing objectives for subjects you do not ordinarily teach.

   d. Make an attempt to write comprehension objectives for each of the three subcategories: translation, interpretation, and extrapolation.

2. *Operationalizing behaviors.*

   a. Make a list of all the behavioral verbs used in your objectives. Note that some may represent actions that are more directly observable than others.

   b. For each of the verbs, list several specific actions or behaviors which would demonstrate existence of the behavior in the original objective.

3. *Item writing.*

   a. Write one or more test items for each of your objectives, making use of the demonstrable behaviors you specified above. Try to use a variety of item types, ensuring that the type you use is appropriate to the behavior.

   b. Time permitting, screen your items, following the procedure for exercise 3 in Chapter 7. For content validity ask a teacher of the subject to relate the items to your statements of objectives.

REFERENCES

Ahmann, J. S., & Glock, M. D. *Evaluating pupil growth.* Boston: Allyn & Bacon, 1971.

Bloom, B. S. (Ed.). *Taxonomy of educational objectives: The classification of edu-*

cational goals. Handbook 1. *Cognitive domain.* New York: McKay, 1956.

Bloom, B. S., Hastings, J. T., & Madaus, G. F. *Handbook on formative and summative evaluation of student learning.* New York: McGraw-Hill, 1971.

Cleveland Heights School District. *A sequential program in composition.* Cleveland: Author, 1964.

Ebel, R. L. *Measuring educational achievement,* Englewood Cliffs, N.J.: Prentice-Hall, 1965.

Gerberich, J. R. *Specimen objective test items: A guide to achievement test construction.* New York: Longmans, Green, 1956.

Gronlund, N. E. *Measurement and evaluation in teaching.* New York: Macmillan, 1976.

Henry, N. B. (Ed.). *The measurement of understanding: The forty-fifth yearbook of the National Society for the Study of Education.* Chicago: University of Chicago Press, 1946.

Mager, R. F. *Preparing objectives for programmed instruction.* San Francisco: Fearon, 1962.

Morse, H. T., & McCune, G. H. *Selected items for the testing of study skills and critical thinking* (Bulletin No. 15, 4th ed.). Washington, D.C.: National Council for the Social Sciences, 1964.

Popham, W. J. Objectives and instruction. *AERA Monograph Series on Curriculum Evaluation,* 1969, No. 3, pp. 32–52.

Smith, E. R., & Tyler, R. W. *Appraising and recording student progress. Adventures in American Education Series.* Vol 3. New York: McGraw-Hill, 1942.

Evaluation Techniques for Application and Analysis Objectives

Chapter Highlights

APPLICATION OF PRINCIPLES AND GENERALIZATIONS

Application is "the use of abstractions in particular and concrete situations. The abstractions may be in the form of general ideas, rules of procedures, or generalized methods. The abstractions may also be technical principles, and theories which must be remembered and applied" (Bloom, 1956, p. 205).

The ability to apply principles and generalizations to new problems and situations is a type of educational objective which is found in most courses of instruction beginning with the elementary school and is increasingly stressed at the high school, college, graduate, and professional school levels.

Teachers and curriculum makers have long recognized that students don't really "understand" an idea or principle unless they can use it in new problem situations. Thus, application is frequently regarded as an indication that a subject has been adequately mastered. More commonly, teachers and curriculum makers have stressed this objective in its own right. They have regarded the ability to apply principles and generalizations to new problems and situations as one of the more complex and difficult objectives of education. They may see it as important because it makes the learning constantly useful in problem solving, it enables students to gain some degree of control over various aspects of their environment and the problems it poses, or it represents one of the outcomes of learning which enable a student to cope with conditions and problems in a complex and rapidly changing society. Then too, students who have demonstrated a high level of ability in this type of objective have acquired an intellectual independence which in part frees them from continual dependence on teachers, experts, and other adult authorities. Finally, there is some evidence that once the ability to make application is developed, it is likely to be one of the more permanent acquisitions in learning. If the ability is retained well, in part because it is so serviceable, then it becomes an especially important objective for education, wherever it is appropriate.

Whatever the reasons for stressing this objective, its importance for evaluation can be demonstrated by the frequency with which it is stated in various courses and programs at the elementary, secondary, and higher education levels. In Figure 9-1 we have listed objectives which may be classified under the general category of *Application* established in the *Taxonomy of Educational Objectives* (See Appendix, page 331).

It will be seen from this list that the application objectives generally include or imply three phrases which are in need of further refinement and definition. These are "ability to apply," "principles and generalizations," and "new problems and situations." In the following discussion we will attempt to clarify each of these three phrases. However, we will do this in reverse order.

New Problems and Situations

By "new problems and situations" we mean problems and situations which are *likely* to be new to the student. These are similar to those which were included in the instruction but have some elements of newness or unfamiliarity for the student. Students should not be able to solve the new problems and situations merely by remembering the solution to or the precise method of solving a similar problem in class. It is not a new problem or situation if it is exactly like others solved in class except that new quantities or symbols are used (as in mathematics or physics). It is not a new problem or situation if it is the same as one solved in class with only some new names or other slight changes altering the original form.

It is a new problem or situation if the student has not been given instruction or help on a given problem and must do some of the following with the statement of the problem before solving it:

1. The statement of the problem must be modified in some way before it can be attacked.
   a. The student must search through the statement to find exactly what is given and what is needed before it can be attacked or solved.
   b. The student must recognize that there are extraneous or irrelevant elements in the statement which he or she must delete or ignore.
   c. The student must recast the problem by putting its parts in a different order from that found in the statement.
   d. The student may have to restate or redefine the problem before it becomes clear exactly what he or she is to do to solve it.
2. The statement of the problem must be put in the form of some paradigm or model before the student can bring the principles or generalizations previously learned to bear on it. This is especially true of mathematics and science problems where the student has previously been given problem types and models and some practice in using them. It may be more difficult to find such forms and structures in the social sciences and humanities.
3. The statement of the problem requires the student to search through memory for relevant principles and generalizations. Further, it is a new problem if the student must use the principles and generalizations somewhat differently from the way he or she used them previously.

The posing of new problems and situations is a difficult art in evaluation. It requires the evaluator to find or make new problems and situations within the grasp of particular students. It is especially useful if the problems are real ones rather than contrived ones with artificial or fictitious elements. Students find real problems more satisfying to attack than patently contrived problems, which can seem rather like puzzles and tricks to be solved. Problems occurring in

The ability to present ideas [orally or in writing] in accordance with the principles of grammar (1, p. 18).

The ability to present ideas [in written form] in accordance with the principles of rhetoric [e.g., principles relating to coherence, transition, unity, and emphasis] (1, p. 19).

To consistently apply scientific knowledge and understandings in the solution of personal and social problems (1, p. 42).

To apply the generalizations [facts, and theories established by the investigations] to explain phenomena (1, p. 54).

To apply a scientific generalization [or method] to interpret the natural phenomena related to the social or personal problem (1, p. 54).

To judge the probable applicability of the generalization or method by evaluating its warranted assertability as an explanation of natural phenomena (1, p. 54).

Application to the phenomena discussed by a paper, of the scientific terms and concepts used in other papers (2, p. 124).

The ability to apply social science generalizations and conclusions to actual social problems (2, p. 124).

The ability to predict the probable effect of a change in a factor on a biological situation previously at equilibrium (2, p. 124).

The ability to apply science principles, postulates, theorems, or other abstractions to new situations (2, p. 124).

Apply principles of psychology in identifying the characteristics of a new social situation (2, p. 124).

The ability to relate principles of civil liberties and civil rights to current events (2, p. 124).

Skill in applying principles of democratic group action to participation in group and social situations (2, p. 124).

The ability to apply the laws of trigonometry to practical situations (2, p. 124).

To develop some skill in applying Mendel's laws of inheritance to experimental findings on plant genetic problems (2, p. 124).

To apply the major principles, concepts and ideas of Civics to specific new situations (3, p. 25).

To apply the principles of Social Studies to the solution of social problems....(3, p. 25).

To relate geographic principles and knowledge to problems involving the development of material resources (3, p. 77).

Explains events in daily life in terms of scientific principles, concepts and theories (3, p. 105).

Recognises the limits within which a scientific principle is applicable (3, p. 105).

Applies the principles of science to determine appropriate courses of action in gardening and other home activities (3, p. 105).

The ability to apply principles of Physics to new situations (3, p. 133).

The student will develop the ability to apply economic knowledge to problems of economic policy (4, p. 59).

(continued)

---

[1] Tyler, 1954.

[2] Bloom, 1956.

[3] All India Council, 1958.

[4] University Grants Commission, 1961.

[5] French, 1957.

Figure 9-1 Statements of objectives for *Application.*

The student will develop the ability to apply knowledge of political science to solve current problems in politics and administration (4, p. 95).

The student should develop the ability to apply the facts, concepts and theories to actual life situations (4, p. 123).

The student should know the limitation of the applications of psychology (4, p. 123).

The students are able to apply chemistry to daily life (4, p. 185).

The student will develop the ability to apply the physical laws to explain various natural phenomena (4, p. 207).

The student will develop the ability to apply basic principles in solving physical problems (4, p. 207).

The student should be able to apply the principles of botany to new problems (4, p. 229).

The student should become aware of the limitations in the applicability of botany (4, p. 229).

The student will develop the ability to solve problems on the basis of the theories and methods learned (4, p. 247).

Ability to apply scientific fact and principle (5, p. 107).

---

[1] Tyler, 1954.

[2] Bloom, 1956.

[3] All India Council, 1958.

[4] University Grants Commission, 1961.

[5] French, 1957.

Figure 9-1 Continued.

real life, problems found in the specialized literature of a given subject, and problems encountered by specialists in the field are more likely to be interesting and useful to solve than problems dreamed up by a teacher or evaluator just for the purposes of testing the students. Then too, the relations between the principles and the problem are more likely to be the real or natural relations rather than those imposed by the evaluator.

In one case in which the students were given examinations with obviously contrived and artificial problem situations requiring the application of principles, the students expressed some resentment and were of the opinion that they were supposed to outwit the examiners. They indicated that solving such problems depended mainly on their ability to figure out just what the tester was up to. When the problems were more real, they had a sense of working on worthwhile questions and even when they had difficulty, they expressed some satisfaction with the meaningfulness of attempting to solve such problems.

Principles and Generalizations

In each subject field there are some basic ideas which summarize much of what scholars have learned over the long history of the field. These ideas give meaning to much that has been learned, and they provide the basic ideas for dealing with many new problems as they are encountered by people who have learned what the field has to offer. We believe that it is a primary obligation of the scholars as well as teachers of the subject to search constantly for these abstractions, to find ways of helping students learn them, and especially to help students learn how to use them in a great variety of problem situations. To learn such principles and generalizations adequately is to become a very different human being. Through them one comes to appreciate the beauty and orderliness of the universe. Through them one learns to appreciate the great power of the human mind. To learn to use such principles is to possess a powerful way of dealing with the world.

For example, the student who has learned the law of gravity has possession of an abstraction which applies to phenomena throughout the universe. It is as applicable to the movement of a baseball as it is to the movement of a planet. With it one can understand the special problems of sending a rocket into space or of throwing a discus in an athletic contest. One also becomes aware of the enormous feat of conceptualizing and using such a powerful law of nature.

We distinguish several levels of abstractions which can be applied to new problems.

Principles

By "principle" we mean a statement about a process or relation which describes a fundamental truth or a law accepted and used by the scholars in a field. Some examples are:

The pressure of a given quantity of gas increases with an increase of temperature.
A learned act is not repeated unless it is reinforced.
The capacity of air to hold water increases with an increase in temperature.
A body remains at rest or in a state of uniform motion in a straight line unless a force acts on it.

These principles are statements which hold under a great range of conditions. They represent relatively precise inferences from a large body of observations and experiments or are deductions from a body of theory or accepted assumptions.

Generalizations

By "generalizations" we mean general statements or inferences which summarize a body of information or other particulars and which can be applied in new situations. Examples:

Frustration increases anxiety.
Crime is greatest among individuals who are alienated from society.
The educational aspirations of students are related to their parents' socioeconomic status.
Institutional patterns exercise strong control over conduct.
Japanese children are disciplined by being made fun of.

Hybrids are more vigorous than closely inbred individuals.
In undisturbed sedimentary rocks, the youngest layer is on top.

A generalization holds under limited conditions, and the special problem it poses to the student is to recognize its tentativeness, the particular circumstances under which it may hold true, and its value in quickly ordering new phenomena. One hopes that the student will be able to understand the basis for the generalization, the underlying phenomena at work, and the restricted truth which the generalization summarizes.

We recognize that the distinctions between principles and generalizations are not always clear, and we must leave it to experts in the different subjects to determine the types of abstractions they may have which are basic to their own fields. It is clear that the sciences have some of the most powerful principles, whereas the social sciences and the humanities have great difficulty formulating generalizations which are more than commonsense statements. When such generalizations are stated, they seem so obvious that few would disagree with them—but it is difficult to determine just how they help summarize our present knowledge. Or there are so many exceptions to the generalization that we do not find them very helpful in dealing with new problems.

Principles and generalizations are developed in a number of different ways. Some are developed by definition and convention. Workers in the field agree on a rule, definition, or relationship.

The circumference of a circle equals $2\pi r$.
Force = mass $\times$ acceleration
Friction exists between any two bodies in contact with each other.

Such abstractions are conventions which are very effective in classifying and organizing a great many specific phenomena in their respective fields. There is an arbitrary quality about these generalizations since they are true only by definition. The student must learn what they include and what they do not include and must also learn what specific phenomena, concrete objects, and events illustrate the rule and which ones do not. The student may also be expected to know various relations among the abstractions—whether the relations are chronological, superordinate and subordinate, concomitant variation, or cause and effect. The student may also be expected to know whether the abstractions are parts of a theory, taxonomy, or classification scheme.

Since these abstractions are true by definition, it is not possible for the student to discover them on his or her own. The student may come to see the specific *phenomena* on his or her own, but must find the *terms* and *definitions* by reference to the history of the subject. One might speculate that among other approaches, an effective way for the student to learn about such abstractions would be to begin with situations in which he or she must recognize specific, clear instances of the abstraction. Then the student can be given opportunities to learn the use of the abstraction to name, classify, or organize such phenomena. Finally, the student should be helped to explore the range of phenomena included in the abstraction.

Another set of abstractions are the result of empirical research and scholarship. Boyle's law, the effects of combinations of genes, and the relationship between intelligence and academic achievement are examples of principles and generalizations discovered through investigations of existing phenomena. These generalizations are true—within certain limits—and they can be used to organize many specific events, actions, facts, and so forth. Abstractions of this type may be "discovered" afresh by each student if the phenomena and the necessary measuring and observational techniques are available. The student who has "discovered" the abstraction is likely to find the exact statement of the generalization useful as a more precise and parsimonious formulation of the relationship among the phenomena. In any case, learning experiences must somehow help the student relate specific and concrete phenomena to the statement of the abstraction. One without the other is unlikely to be very useful or meaningful to the student.

A third type is a more limited set of generalizations derived from the observation. The following are illustrations of this type:

Hemingway's heroes usually overcome conflicts between man and nature.
Frustrated children tend to show regressive behavior.
Smoking cigarettes may cause cancer.
Too rigid toilet training may produce personality disorders.
High interest rates reduce capital investment.

These generalizations may be statements of trends, tendencies, and regularities which are far from universal laws and principles; that is, they may occur frequently but there are many exceptions. They may be examples of an effect which may also be produced by quite different causes, or illustrations of phenomena which have multiple causation. For example, although smoking may cause cancer, there are many other causes of the disease, and smoking does not always cause it. Many of these generalizations concern phenomena and events for which there is not a full understanding of the reasons that they occur or the process which relates one part of the statement to the other. Such generalizations have so many exceptions to them that the student must learn to be cautious in using them. Here also, the student may discover some of these generalizations independently, but must be alerted to their limited nature. Again, the student must be given opportunities to relate the abstract statement to specific and concrete examples.

A final set represents generalizations which are deductions from a larger theory, model, or point of view. Such generalizations may rarely describe existing phenomena but are statements of what would occur under special circumstances or ideal conditions. Examples are:

If children are given sufficient love and attention, they will not develop anxiety.
Children's ego identity gains real strength only from consistent recognition of real accomplishment.

Dialectic methods attempt to remove or transcend some contradictions.

Equal volumes of gases at the same temperature and pressure contain about the same number of molecules.

Population tends to multiply faster than its means of subsistence.

Such generalizations represent a particular (and somewhat restricted) view of the world, and they are true if a particular set of assumptions are accepted. In learning such generalizations the student must clearly recognize the point of view which they represent and should be helped to understand that they represent one alternative when others may also exist.

Gagné (1965) has emphasized that there is a hierarchical process in the learning of principles, generalizations, and concepts. He believes that these are best learned as a result of a movement from concrete phenomena to higher-order abstractions. In his model, the student is expected to move from specific facts and terms to relationships among them to the eventual development of the larger abstraction. Gagné believes that a student who has failed to understand and master some of the lower-order phenomena will have difficulty in understanding the generalization or abstraction. In Chapter 6 we have indicated the way in which formative tests may be developed to determine where the student has difficulty in Gagné's model of learning and what learning problems are posed by specific difficulties at different levels of the model.

The Ability to Apply

"Ability to apply" implies that with appropriate training, practice, and other kinds of help students become able to apply principles and generalizations to new problems and situations. That is, they can use principles and generalizations appropriately in solving problems that are new to them. The implication is that there is a generalized ability which grows out of the students' learning experiences such that, when faced with new problems and situations, they can make use of the ability to apply principles and generalizations.

In terms of students' behaviors, the ability to apply might include some of the following:

The student can determine which principles or generalizations are appropriate or relevant in dealing with a new problem situation (A).

The student can restate a problem so as to determine which principles or generalizations are necessary for its solution (B).

The student can specify the limits within which a particular principle or generalization is true or relevant (C).

The student can recognize the exceptions to a particular generalization and the reasons for them (D).

The student can explain new phenomena in terms of known principles or generalizations (E).

The student can predict what will happen in a new situation by the use of appropriate principles or generalizations (F).

The student can determine or justify a particular course of action or decision in a new situation by the use of appropriate principles and generalizations (G).

The student can state the reasoning he or she employs to support the use of one or more principles or generalizations in a given problem situation (H).

These behaviors will be discussed in the next section as we attempt to define them further and illustrate testing techniques appropriate to them.

TESTING FOR APPLICATION

It is possible to determine the requirements or rules for making test items for the application of principles and generalizations from the foregoing analysis of the three phases "ability to apply," "principles and generalizations," and "new problems and situations."

Some of the requirements are these:

1. The problem situation must be new, unfamiliar, or in some way different from those

used in the instruction. The difficulty of the problem will be determined in part by how different it is from problems encountered in the instruction.

2. The problem should be solvable in part by the use of the appropriate principles or generalizations.

3. One or more of the behaviors listed above under the subsection "The Ability to Apply" should be sampled by the test problem.

Since the behaviors discussed under "The Ability to Apply" give useful clues to how questions might be formed, our test illustrations will follow that listing. Most of the test illustrations have been drawn from the files of the University Examiner's Office of the University of Chicago. We have used these because they illustrate a variety of test forms in a number of different subject areas. When the source of the illustration is not the Examiner's Office, we have accompanied the item with indications of the specific source.

Test Problems for Application Behaviors A and B

The student can determine which principles or generalizations are appropriate or relevant in dealing with a new problem situation (A).

The student can restate a problem so as to determine which principles or generalizations are necessary for its solution (B).

In this type of problem, the students do not actually have to solve the problem completely; all they need to do is determine the principles or generalizations which are appropriate. In the following examples, it will be noted that examinees must do little more than exhibit a grasp of what the problem is about and what principles or generalizations are relevant, useful, or pertinent. One cannot be sure from such problems that the students could actually solve the problem in a detailed way, but one can be sure that they have some grasp of what is required. The great value of this type of problem is the efficiency with which one can sample a great variety of problems and principles of generalizations.

In the following set of questions, the principles are stated and the students have only to determine which ones are relevant to each governmental practice. They may have to reformulate some of the practices in order to determine which of the given principles is relevant. It would be a more difficult task if the students were not given a list of principles but had to state the political principles underlying each statement.

1. The following are some of the basic principles upon which our [Canadian] federal government has been built:
   A. majority rule
   B. the federal government having primary responsibility only in certain areas
   C. responsible government
   D. other principles not listed above

For each of the following practices . . . indicate the principle involved. Mark D if none of the above principles are involved.
   (1) Mr. Pearson as leader of the Liberal Party is Prime Minister.
   (2) The federal government provides unemployment insurance.
   (3) The federal government collects excise taxes.
   (4) The governor-general may request the leader of the opposition to form a government.

(Ayers, 1966.)

In the set of questions below, two of the principles are named rather than stated in a more complete form. (1) and (3) require the student to restate the problem before the appropriate principle can be determined, whereas (2) is likely to be stated in the form in which the student originally learned it and to require little more than remembering what it was supposed to illustrate. The set of questions would probably be more difficult (and realistic) if some of the problems required more than a single explanatory principle.

2. *Directions:* For each statement of fact below, blacken the answer space corresponding to the one explanatory principle, from the list preceding the statements, which is most directly useful in explaining the fact. If none of the principles listed is applicable, blacken answer space E. NOTE THAT EACH ITEM REQUIRES ONE ANSWER ONLY.

Explanatory principles [A–E]
   A. Force is equal to mass times acceleration.

B. Friction exists between any two bodies in contact with each other.
C. Conservation of momentum.
D. Conservation of energy.
E. None of the foregoing.

(1) To be opened slowly a given door requires a small force; to be opened quickly it requires a much greater force.
(2) The velocity of a body moving along a curve cannot be constant.
(3) A brick can be pulled along a fairly smooth surface by means of a string; the string would break, however, if jerked sharply.

The next set of questions is very similar to the preceding set. However, the problems are more likely to be different from the illustrations used in the instruction given to explain the principles. It would be slightly more difficult if the student were asked to supply new illustrations for the principles or to state the principles relevant to each fact or observation.

3. *Directions: Blacken* the answer space corresponding to the one principle which is most useful in explaining each statement of fact.

Explanatory principles
A. Force is equal to mass times acceleration.
B. The momentum of a body tends to remain constant.
C. The moment or turning effect of a force is proportional to its distance from the axis of rotation.
D. Friction exists between bodies in contact and moving with respect to one another.
E. The sum of kinetic and potential energies in an isolated system is a constant.

(1) Shears used to cut sheet metal have long handles.
(2) The force exerted on a brake by the driver's foot is much less than that exerted on the brake drums.
(3) A rocket can propel itself in a vacuum.
(4) If a rapidly rotating grindstone bursts, the fragments fly outward in straight lines.
(5) Streamlining an automobile reduces the amount of power necessary to maintain a speed of 60 miles per hour.

In the following type of question, the student must determine the validity of the generalization, its relevance, and whether it supports or questions the trend. Note that it is possible to have several generalizations which are applicable to the trend. The trend could have been presented in more detail in the form of observations about governmental practices at different levels and at different times. This would have made the problem less familiar to the student and somewhat more realistic.

4. The trend in the United States is toward greater concentration of power in the national government as compared to state and local governments. It is sometimes argued that this is both *inevitable* and *desirable*.
Directions: The following statements represent various points of view concerning this issue. *Blacken* answer space
A—if the statement presents a *valid* argument *supporting* the inevitability or desirability of this trend
B—if the statement presents a *valid* argument questioning either the inevitability or desirability of this trend
C—if the statement is *invalid* or *irrelevant* to the issue

(1) Increasing industrial and economic centralization makes local regulation of economic affairs largely ineffective.
(2) Decentralization of authority permits more adequate experimentation in various forms of political control.
(3) The policies of decentralized governmental units coincide more closely with public opinion then do the policies of centralized government.
(4) If local areas were redefined to correspond to industrial or social units, decentralized authority could be made more effective.

In the following item, the use of "good comment" (which had to be further defined in a note) makes this an academic exercise. It might be more effective if the students were merely asked which generalizations are relevant or had to determine which generalizations are relevant to some predictions or particular events or practices in Russia. In the original test problem, there were many more generalizations than those included here.

5. *Directions: Consider the following statement:*
"A writer on Russia asserted that Communism cannot suppress the Russian peasant's instinct of religion. He later pointed to the recognition of the Greek Catholic Church by the Soviet Union as evidence to support his opinion that there was such an instinct, which could not be suppressed."

Following are some comments on this statement. For each item, *blacken* answer space

A—if you think it is a *good* comment

B—if you think it is a *bad* comment

Note: A good comment is one which shows informed understanding of the subject under discussion.

(1) Strongly entrenched habits are often mistaken for instincts.

(2) Institutional patterns exercise strong control over conduct.

In the next set of questions, each of the three conceptions of evolution includes several principles which are not differentiated. The questions might have been more searching if the directions had stated the specific principles instead of merely naming the theory. The list of alternatives requires the student to make very clear distinctions. Perhaps this set would have been less searching if the student had only to determine consistency with each of the conceptions. It is evident that a great range of phenomena might be sampled in this type of problem.

6. *Directions:* For each of the following statements, *blacken* answer space

A—if the statement is consistent with the *Darwinian* conception of evolution, but not with the *Lamarckian* conception of evolution or the hypothesis of *special creation*

B—if the statement is consistent with both the *Darwinian* and *Lamarckian* evolutionary conceptions, but *not* with the hypothesis of *special creation*

C—if the statement is consistent with the *Darwinian* conception and *special creation* hypothesis, but *not* with the *Lamarckian*

D—if the statement is consistent with *all three* conceptions

E—if the statement is inconsistent with the *Darwinian* conception

(1) The wolf and the fox have a common ancestor.

(2) Trees growing along the Pacific coast often bend inland away from the wind, whether grown there from seed or planted there as small trees.

(3) The descendants of the trees in item [2], which have been grown for many generations in this windy place, if reared in a calm site grow as erect as trees native to that calm site.

(4) A breeding experiment is conducted with many generations of rats. Short-haired animals are selectively mated to each other, and only that half of

each generation with shorter hair is retained in the experiment. The laboratory, however, is kept at a temperature well below that of the natural habitat of these rats. At the end of the experiment, the average length of hair based on all the individuals in the last generation is very much less than the average hair length based on all individuals in the first generation.

(5) While the Carlsbad caverns are inhabited primarily by blind animals, successive generations of mice reared there in a small laboratory in total darkness have eyesight as good as that of their normal forebears.

(6) In both plant and animal kingdoms, offspring tend to resemble their parents.

(7) The serum of a rabbit which has been inoculated with the serum of a pig is agglutinated less strongly by chicken serum than horse serum, still less strongly by shark serum, imperceptibly by earthworm serum. Other similar experiments reveal that, in each case, the serum of a rabbit which has been sensitized to that of a particular animal is more strongly agglutinated by the sera of animals thought to be closely related phylogenetically to the sensitizing animal than by the sera of animals thought to be more distantly related.

(8) It is impossible to improve the commercial value of domestic plants and animals by breeding.

(9) The birth rate among residents of upper- and middle-class urban areas is much lower than among slum residents.

Test Problems for Application Behaviors C and D

The student can specify the limits within which a particular principle or generalization is true or relevant (C).

The student can recognize the exceptions to a particular generalization and the reasons for them (D).

When these behaviors are being tested, the problems should include applications which go beyond the limits of the generalization or principle as well as applications where the generalization or principle is applicable. It should be remembered that these problems have the purpose of determining whether or not the student is aware of the boundary conditions under which the principles or generalizations are operative. For the most part, the evaluation procedures for these behaviors can be relatively simple, and the student may be asked to do little more than recognize or supply illustrations which are within or outside the limits and in some cases to indicate the reasons the application or illustration is outside the limits within which the principle or generalization is true, useful, or relevant.

If the conclusions are generalizations, this type of question can be used to determine whether the student can recognize situations which question or support the generalization. The use of "C—if neither A nor B clearly applies" is a further check on the relevance of the generalization to the situation. Item 7 is an example.

7. *Directions:* In each of the following items, you are given a fact followed by a conclusion. *Blacken* answer space

A—if the fact is good evidence to *support* the conclusion

B—if the fact is good evidence to *disprove* the conclusion

C—if neither A nor B clearly applies

(1) FACT: The native tribes of Australia have a very complex social organization and a very simple technology.
CONCLUSION: The complexity of nonmaterial culture is not dependent upon high technological development.

(2) FACT: The number of shareholders in most large corporations has increased considerably during the last 30 years.
CONCLUSION: Control of corporations has become more democratic in the last 30 years.

(3) FACT: The machine has stimulated a progressively greater division of labor with an emphasis upon more and more minutely detailed operations.
CONCLUSION: The individual worker in modern society is typically without insight into the workings of the total social mechanism.

In each of the following questions (items 8–12), the student is to recognize the limits, special conditions, or assumptions under which the generalization or principle may be true or useful. This type of behavior is especially useful in subjects where principles or generalizations have limited applicability. The forms suggested here are the simple forms for testing this behavior.

8. The statement is made that the altitude of the celestial pole is equal to the geographic latitude of the observer. This is correct
A. if the diameter of the earth is considered negligible compared to the distances to the stars
B. only if the earth is considered spherical
C. only if the altitude is measured from the plane of the ecliptic
D. if the observation is made at 12:00 noon
E. only if the altitude of the celestial pole is equal to its zenith distance

9. In using the equation $s = \frac{1}{2}gt^2$ to calculate the time it takes a given body to fall from a height h to the ground, which of the two factors [below] would introduce the greater error?
A. Factor 1 (Variation in gravity).
B. Factor 2 (Variation in air resistance).
C. Factor 1 for heights above a certain value; Factor 2 for lesser heights
D. Factor 2 for heights above a certain value; Factor 1 for lesser heights.

10. Lobachevsky based his geometry on the assumption that through a given external point any number of straight lines can be drawn parallel to a given straight line. This assumption
A. has been found true under certain circumstances and is now considered a basic law of nature
B. is obviously incorrect but is useful in checking the accuracy of other geometries
C. can be shown to be incorrect by drawing lines through the point and demonstrating that all but one line intersects the given line
D. cannot be established or disproved experimentally
E. is entirely arbitrary, having no relation to the other assumptions and theorems of Lobachevsky's geometry

11. A defect of Rousseau's generalization that those laws are compatible with liberty which are in accordance with the "general will" is that
A. it makes no provision for the liberty of minority groups
B. it offers no criterion by which we can decide when the commands of government are an expression of the "general will"
C. it does not recognize that a government must have the sanction of force behind its commands
D. it fails to recognize that to consent willingly to a government, knowing it necessarily to have imperfections, is to consent to the imperfections

12. "The best economic system is that one which allows individuals the most freedom to pursue their own interests. In so doing, they will compete one with another, the end result being to the benefit of society."
   (1) A necessary condition if the theory stated in the quotation is to be true is that
      A. government regulate the prices of a few basic commodities and let individuals make their decisions accordingly
      B. individuals have access to the necessary information
      C. individuals be morally sound
      D. government be made up of experts
   (2) If true, which of the following is best evidence *against* the application of the theory stated in the quotation?
      A. Individuals, when left free to pursue their own interests, have unequal incomes.
      B. Ever increasing concentration of capital is accompanied by continuous reduction in prices.
      C. Individuals have other motivations in addition to the desire for profit.
      D. Governments with unlimited power tend toward corruption.

Test Problems for Application Behavior E

The student can explain new phenomena in terms of known principles or generalizations (E).

The problems testing for this behavior should include new phenomena, new illustrations, or new situations which must be explained by the use of principles or generalizations. The explanations most frequently take the form "A occurs because of Y," where Y is a principle or generalization. The explanation may use the principle or generalization to show *why* something happens, *how* it happens, or under *what conditions* it occurs.

The following questions require a relatively precise recognition of the principles or generalizations which can explain the given phenomena. These simple test forms are useful for a wide range of application problems.

13. If one frequently raises the cover of a vessel in which a liquid is being heated, the liquid takes longer to boil because
   A. boiling occurs at a higher temperature if the pressure is increased

   B. escaping vapor carries heat away from the liquid
   C. permitting the vapor to escape decreases the volume of the liquid
   D. the temperature of a vapor is proportional to its volume at constant temperature
   E. permitting more air to enter results in increased pressure on the liquid

14. Dilute sulfuric acid reacts readily with iron strips and yet concentrated sulfuric acid can be safely stored in iron vessels. This is because
   A. concentrated sulfuric acid is less ionized than dilute sulfuric acid
   B. iron is above hydrogen in the activity series
   C. the iron vessel, being more massive, conducts away the heat of reaction
   D. iron contains carbon which is not affected by sulfuric acid
   E. the sulfur in the sulfuric acid coats the iron and protects it.

15. The steps leading to a swimming pool appear bent where they enter the water. Which *one* of the following gives the best explanation of this phenomenon?
   A. Diffraction of light by the surface of the water
   B. Dispersion of light on entering water
   C. Refraction of light due to difference in speed of light in air and water
   D. Light does not travel in straight lines in water
   E. Suspended particles in the water

The following questions require the student to relate a principle or generalization to the problem situation and to indicate the particular way in which the principle or generalization relates to the situation.

16. *Principle:* A metal owes its magnetism to an orderly arrangement of relatively large units (called "domains") each composed of thousands of atoms. In a magnetized material these domains may be compared to tiny magnets all pointing in the same direction.
   Directions: For each statement below, *blacken* answer space
   A—if it is supported by the principle
   B—if it is contradicted by the principle
   C—if it is neither supported nor contradicted by the principle
   (1) A current of electricity flowing in a nearby wire *cannot* cause a bar of metal to become magnetic.
   (2) A hot bar of iron is harder to magnetize than a cold bar.
   (3) The best conductors are also capable of the strongest magnetization.

17. *Directions:* In these questions, select the one best *numbered* response and then select the one best *lettered* response.

The radial velocities of a star can be detected by
(1) photographing the stars at two different times
(2) comparing their spectra with spectra obtained in the laboratory
(3) measuring variations in the angle of parallax
This method depends upon the principle that: (A- Radial motion is very minute. B- The apparent motions of such distant objects is small. C- Relative motion of source of waves and observer alters the frequency. D- Parallax measurements yield the distance of stars. E- The radius of a star varies with temperature and therefore with spectral type.)

While question 18 is a relatively complex test form, it lends itself to the examination of a great variety of relations between generalizations and phenomena, including the use of generalizations to explain given phenomena.

18. *Directions:* Below you are given a group of statements about the culture of the Japanese. These statements are followed by comments which describe certain personality or behavior traits of the Japanese and questions about each comment. Read the statements as if they were a paragraph description of the Japanese. Then answer the questions following each of the comments.

Statements:
A. Japanese children are teased a great deal by their parents. In fact, the child is disciplined by being made fun of.
B. There is a marked discontinuity in the upbringing of Japanese boys. As infants, all satisfactions are possible to them and they are treated like little gods. But at the age of six or seven increasingly heavy responsibility is placed on them and this responsibility is upheld by the most drastic sanctions.
C. There is very little in Japanese life that permits the harmless diffusion of emotion. There is everything that locks it in, represses it, frustrates it, chokes it.
D. If a boy is disrespectful to his teachers, his family may cast him out. He is made to realize that he is his family's representative before the world.
E. Japanese children are taught that they owe a great debt to their parents.
Consider the above statements in the light of what you have learned regarding the analysis of culture. Unless

otherwise directed, *blacken* the answer space corresponding to the letter of the above statement which supplies the *one best answer* to the question following the comments.

Comment: In Japan the individual is sure of support from his own group only as long as approval is given by other groups.
(1) Which statement above furnishes data for this comment?

Comment: The great moral decisions of the Japanese have hinged not on the battle of good and evil of the individual's inner consciousness, but on the opposition between the individual's personal inclinations and his social duty.
(2) Which *two* statements above describe a fact of Japanese life which would be likely to produce the phenomenon described in the comment?

Comment: In Japan, the approval of the "outside world" takes on an importance probably unparalleled in any other society.
(3) Which statement most strikingly exemplifies this comment?

Comment: Japanese behavior is full of contradictions and gives evidence of a deeply implanted dualism.
(4) Which statement describes a condition which would be likely to produce the behavior described in the comment?

Comment: Fear of ridicule is one of the strongest social restraints.
(5) Which statement describes a fact which would be likely to produce the attitude described in the comment?

Test Problems for Application Behavior F

The student can predict what will happen in a new situation by the use of appropriate principles or generalizations (F).

In tests for this behavior, the new situation may be a common observation, or it may be a situation in which something has happened or will happen and for which the student is to predict the outcome. The predictions may involve qualitative or quantitative changes likely to occur. With respect to the quantitative changes, the predictions may be very precise or only according to rough orders of magnitude. The difficulty of the problem may be determined by the precision with which the change must be estimated or calculated. In many of the problems, the student must use a principle or generalization to predict but may not be asked to state or cite the basis for the prediction. In other problems, the student must not only predict but also indicate the basis for the prediction.

19. Suppose an elevator is descending with a constant acceleration of gravity "g." If a passenger attempts to throw a rubber ball upward, what will be the motion of the ball with respect to the elevator? The ball will
   A. remain fixed at a point the passenger releases it
   B. rise to the top of the elevator and remain there
   C. not rise at all, but will fall to the floor
   D. rise, bounce, then move toward the floor at a constant speed
   E. rise, bounce, then move toward the floor at an increasing speed

20. If the temperature of the sun were suddenly to change from 6,000° to 12,000°, while the mass, radius, and position in relation to the earth remained the same, the following effects would be noted:
   (1) The color of the sun would be (A- more blue; B- more red; C- essentially unchanged).
   (2) The sun would appear (A- brighter; B- about as bright; C- appreciably less bright).
   (3) More molecular bands (A- would; B- would not) appear in the solar spectrum.

21. *Directions:* Following are some predictions. For each item, *blacken* answer space
   A—if it is highly probable;
   B—if it is highly improbable;
   C—if neither of these judgments can be made.
   (1) State governments will take over most of the functions now exercised by the federal government within the next 50 years.
   (2) Productivity of labor will increase in the United States within the next 30 years.
   (3) The influence of the small stockholder on the management of corporations will increase after the war.
   (4) During the next decade net reproduction rates in large American cities will be sufficiently high to replace their present population.

22. For each hypothetical experimental modification of the normal functioning of an animal described below, a series of statements of possible consequences is given.
   Directions: For each numbered statement, *blacken* answer space
   A—if the consequence described would be expected *to follow*

B—if the consequence described would be expected *not to follow*

The thyroid gland is removed from a rabbit. Examination of the animal is made five weeks after recovery from the operation.
   (1) In a cold room body temperature will be lower than in normal rabbits in the same room.
   (2) Vasoconstriction of skin vessels when the animal is in an environment of 40°F will be greater than before the operation.
   (3) Average amount of carbon dioxide exhaled is found to be lower than before the operation.
   (4) Urine production is found to be lower than before the operation.
   (5) Body weight of the animal is found to be lower than before the operation.

A dog is placed in a chamber, the air of which is maintained at the normal concentration of oxygen but with a concentration of carbon dioxide 100 times the normal concentration in the atmosphere.
   (6) Rate of division of red cells in the circulating blood will increase.
   (7) Rate of division of cells in the red bone marrow will increase.
   (8) Rate of respiration will rise above the average rate before the experiment.

23. *Directions:* In the following items you are to judge the effects of a particular policy on the distribution of income. In each case assume that there are no other changes in policy which would counteract the effects of the policy described in the item. For each item, *blacken* answer space
   A—if the policy described would tend to *reduce* the existing degree of inequality in the distribution of income
   B—if the policy described would tend to *increase* the existing degree of inequality in the distribution of income
   C—if the policy described would have no effect, or would have an indeterminate effect, on the distribution of income

   (1) Increasingly progressive income taxes
   (2) Introduction of a national sales tax
   (3) Provision of educational and medical services, and low-cost public housing
   (4) Reduction in the degree of business monopoly
   (5) Increasing taxes in periods of prosperity and decreasing them in periods when depressions threaten

24. *Directions:* In each of the following items a certain social or economic condition or policy is described and a certain group or groups are mentioned. You are to judge the effect of this condition or policy on consensus *within* the group, if only one group is mentioned; or on consensus *between* the two groups, if two groups are mentioned. *Blacken* answer space

A—if the policy or condition is likely to result in *increased* consensus.

B—if the policy or condition is likely to result in *decreased* consensus.

C—if the policy or condition is likely to have no effect or an indeterminate effect on the level of consensus.

Condition or policy	Group or groups involved
(1) Decentralization of urban centers	Farmers and urban dwellers
(2) Teaching of morality based on individual self-interest	Student body of a university
(3) Voluntary sharing of responsibility for factory administration	Shop foremen and shop stewards
(4) More stringent divorce laws	Newly married couples
(5) Administration of local school system by combined boards of educational specialists and representatives from various civic and labor groups	School teachers and parents of community

In all the preceding items (19–24), the student must use an unstated principle or generalization in order to make the prediction.

These would be more searching questions if the student also had to indicate the principle which was being used to make the prediction.

The following items (items 25–28) illustrate the latter point. In these questions, the student has to make a prediction as well as indicate the principle or generalization which is applicable.

25. Would the air in a closed room be heated or cooled by the operation of an electric refrigerator in the room with the refrigerator door open?

A. heated, because the heat given off by the motor and the compressed gas would exceed the heat absorbed

B. cooled, because the refrigerator is a cooling device

C. cooled, because compressed gases expand in the refrigerator

D. cooled, because liquids absorb heat when they evaporate

E. neither heated nor cooled   (Ayers, 1965.)

26. A car having a mass of 2,000 pounds is given the maximum acceleration which the motor can produce. If a load of 2,000 pounds is now placed in the car, the maximum acceleration that can be given to the car is

(1) twice as great

(2) the same

(3) one-half as great

In solving this problem, which of the following was used directly? (A- Newton's first law of motion; B- Newton's second law of motion; C- Newton's law of gravitation; D- law of falling bodies; E- definition.)

27. Regions lying 10 degrees to the north or south of the equator and near to the coast are normally

(1) subject to heavy rains (in excess of 60 inches per year)

(2) desert

(3) subject to only moderate rains (30 to 40 inches per year)

because (A- air currents are dominantly descending; B- the rate of evaporation in the tropics is low; C- cyclonic storms occur every few weeks; D- air currents are dominantly ascending; E- dry winds blow in from the deserts to the north and south).

28. A body of air with temperature of 60°F has a relative humidity of 40 percent. If the temperature of this body is raised to 80° without addition of any water, the relative humidity will be:

(1) increased   (3) unaffected

(2) decreased

because (A- the capacity of air to hold water decreases with increase in temperature; B- the capacity of air to hold water is independent of the temperature of the air; C- the capacity of air to hold water increases with the increase of temperature; D- the rate of evaporation will be increased; E- the ratio of the weight of water vapor to the weight of the air remains the same).

Test Problems for Application Behavior G

The student can determine or justify a particular course of action or decision in a new situation by the use of appropriate principles and generalizations (G).

This behavior involves decision making of some type—on policy, practical courses of action, ways of correcting a particular situation, and so forth—and the use of principles or generalizations to support or justify the action or decision. Behavior *G* is especially relevant to policy decisions in the social sciences. The illustrations given below all deal with social policy problems. In these questions the course of action is stated, and the student has only to indicate the principles or generalizations which support or oppose it.

29. Which *two* of the following state possible weaknesses in the application of banking and monetary policy as the sole means of stabilizing the economy? (TWO ANSWERS)
    A. Monetary policies do not affect the real rate of return on investment.
    B. "Cheap money" policies may not be sufficient to encourage pessimistic enterprisers and householders to take credit.
    C. Inflationary tendencies may start long before a satisfactory level of employment and prosperity is reached.
    D. In the causation of cumulative changes in total effective demand, quantity of money is unimportant compared with the velocity of its circulation.
    E. Creditors will apply political pressures to promote inflationary policies and debtors will try to promote deflationary tendencies.

30. Which of the following constitutes the most important objection against relying primarily upon changes in tax rates as a means to counteract a downswing?
    A. Increases in income and corporation tax rates tend to discourage the investment of "venture capital."
    B. Reductions in tax rates leave too much purchasing power in the hands of business or consumers and will tend to cause an inflation.
    C. While reductions in tax rates leave more purchasing power in the hands of the public, there is no assurance that these funds would be spent.
    D. Increases in income and corporation tax rates are sure to raise costs and therefore prices.
    E. There is no need to decrease tax rates in a downswing, for tax revenue will fall anyway.

In the problem below (item 31), the students have only to indicate the course of action which would bring about a particular result. This item would be a more searching set of questions if the students had also to cite the principle or the generalization which they were using as a basis for the policy decisions.

31. *Directions:* Many people predict that there will be an extreme inflationary period following the war. If you were a financial adviser to the Treasury Department, under the conditions described above, what would be your advice about the following policies? For each numbered item, *blacken* answer space

    A—if you would *advocate* it, if you wished to retard the trend described above
    B—if you would *not advocate* it, if you wished to retard the trend described above

    (1) Raising the rediscount rate
    (2) Increasing facilities by which more firms could borrow money at fair terms
    (3) Get people to cash their bonds immediately
    (4) Forced savings
    (5) Expansion of a public works program
    (6) Decrease taxes drastically

Test Problems for Application Behavior H

The student can state the reasoning he or she employs to support the use of one or more principles or generalizations in a given problem situation (H).

Behavior *H* is the most complex behavior under *Application*, since it requires the examinee to explain the reasoning used as well as to determine the principles and generalizations which are relevant to a given situation.

It is likely that items of the essay form could well be used in testing for this type of behavior, although the following illustrations (items 32 and 33) are of the recognition type.

Notice the complexity of these two items, and the degree of detail in the directions to the student.

32. Assume that the principle of national self-determination can be stated as follows: "Every nation has a right to choose freely the political, social, and economical arrangements under which it will live."

   Directions: Before each of the following items write

   A—if it is a logical consequence of the principle of self-determination

   B—if it is a logical consequence of the principle but if carried into effect by only one country, would tend to destroy or weaken the conditions under which other countries could apply the principle

   C—if it is a logical contradiction of the principle

   D—if it is neither a logical consequence nor a logical contradiction of the principle but an empirical condition that would facilitate the universal application of the principle

   E—if it is neither a logical consequence nor a contradiction of the principle but an empirical condition that would tend to obstruct the universal application of the principle

   (1) The world should be dominated by those national or racial groups best fitted to rule.

   (2) A substantial inequality in the distribution of military and economic power as between large states and small states.

   (3) The right to depreciate the national currency.

   (4) The unlimited right of a representative government to declare war.

   (5) Establishment of a separate political unit for every linguistic or ethnic group.

33. The water supply for a certain big city is obtained from a large lake, and sewage is disposed of in a river flowing from the lake. This river at one time flowed into the lake, but during the glacial period its direction of flow was reversed. Occasionally, during heavy rains in the spring, water from the river backs up into the lake. What should be done to safeguard effectively and economically the health of the people living in this city?

   Directions: Choose the conclusion which you believe is most consistent with the facts given above and most reasonable in the light of whatever knowledge you might have, and mark the appropriate space on the Answer Sheet. . . .

   Conclusions:

   A. During the spring season, the amount of chemicals used in purifying the water should be increased.

   B. A permanent system of treating the sewage before it is dumped into the river should be provided.

   C. During the spring season, water should be taken from the lake at a point some distance from the origin of the river.

   Directions: Choose the reasons you would use to explain or support your conclusion and fill in the appropriate spaces on your Answer Sheet. Be sure that your marks are in one column only—the same column in which you marked the conclusion. . . .

   Reasons:

   (1) In light of the fact that bacteria cannot survive in salted meat, we may say that they cannot survive in chlorinated water.

   (2) Many bacteria in sewage are not harmful to man.

   (3) Chlorination of water is one of the least expensive methods of eliminating harmful bacteria from a water supply.

   (4) An enlightened individual would know that the best way to kill bacteria is to use chlorine.

   (5) A sewage treatment system is cheaper than the use of chlorine.

   (6) Bacteriologists say that bacteria can be best controlled with chlorine.

   (7) As the number of micro-organisms increases in a given amount of water, the quantity of chlorine necessary to kill the organisms must be increased.

   (8) A sewage treatment system is the only means known by which water can be made absolutely safe.

   (9) By increasing the amount of chlorine in the water supply, the health of the people in this city will be protected.

   (10) Harmful bacteria in water are killed when a small amount of chlorine is placed in the water.

   (11) When bacteria come in contact with chlorine they move out of the chlorinated area in order to survive.

   (12) Untreated sewage contains vast numbers of bacteria, many of which may cause disease in man.

   (13) In most cities it is customary to use chlorine to control harmful bacteria in the water supply.

   (14) Sewage deposited in a lake tends to remain in an area close to the point of entry.

   (Progressive Education Association, 1939, p. 8, problem VII.)

This type of problem is very complex in form and requires very specific directions. However, it lends itself to a detailed analysis of the quality of the reasoning used by the student in support of particular decisions or courses of action chosen. The errors made by the students may include the use of inappropriate generalizations and principles; or the examinees may show weakness by using irrelevant arguments. Such problems require a good deal of testing time, and their use may be justified best when a detailed diagnosis of the students' thinking and reasoning is to be made for formative testing purposes.

ANALYSIS

Analysis is "the breakdown of a communication into its constituent elements or parts such that the relative hierarchy of ideas is made clear and/or the relations between the ideas expressed are made explicit. Such analyses are intended to clarify the communication, to indicate how the communication is organized, and the way in which it manages to convey its effects, as well as its basis and arrangement" (Bloom, 1956, p. 205).

The ability to analyze a problem, communication, or approach to attacking a problem is a complex ability which makes use of knowledge, comprehension, and application but goes beyond them. Such an ability may be regarded as a further step in the "comprehension" of an idea, problem, or document, as a prelude to a complex evaluation of the idea or document, or as a preliminary step to a creative synthesis for a problem of some complexity.

Analysis is not frequently found in elementary school objectives; it is more common at the secondary school and higher education levels. Some justification of this may be found in Piaget's work, which questions how far preadolescents can pursue the kind of reasoning and the analytic processes which are so central in what we have termed "analysis." Analysis presupposes that one not only can comprehend what has been stated in a document (literally as well as figuratively) but also can separate oneself from the message to view it in terms of how it does what it does.

In a real sense, analysis requires the student to "see" the underlying machinery, devices, and ideas employed in a document, which can only be inferred from what the author of the communication has done. Frequently not even the author will be fully aware of what he or she did, and the reader is expected to detect the underlying framework with little explicit help from the author.

There is little doubt that the analysis objectives are very difficult to teach and to learn. Instructors and curriculum makers may stress such objectives because of the greater understanding they give the student about a problem, approach to a problem, or

document. In a society where changes in ideas, problems, and methods are so rapid, analytic abilities are necessary in order to go below surface manifestations to explore the basis for these changes and distinguish those which are real and fundamental from those which are not. While analysis is a slower and more difficult process than comprehension, it is very important to use where a deeper understanding is required before decisions are reached, problems are attacked, or significant evaluations are made. Especially in a society where complex problems and issues must be faced and attacked in a deeper way, analytic abilities must be developed if the problems and issues are to be dealt with in more than a superficial way.

It is likely that once analytic abilities are developed in a number of fields of knowledge, they can be applied to new problems in a creative way. It is also likely that once such abilities are developed to a reasonable degree, they will be retained and will be available to the individual long after much of the detailed knowledge has been forgotten. What the student must learn is both how to make analyses and under what conditions the analytic abilities can and should be employed.

In Figures 9-2 to 9-4 we have listed objectives which may be classified under the general taxonomy category of *Analysis*. We have distinguished among these objectives using the analysis subcategories of the *Taxonomy of Educational Objectives* (Bloom, 1956; see the Appendix of the present book).

Figure 9-2 presents some objectives which emphasize the taxonomic classification *Analysis of elements*. These are primarily concerned with the identification of the underlying elements in a communication, such as the assumptions, values, and views being used by the author of the communication. Analysis of elements may also be used to determine the nature and function of particular statements in the communication.

In Figure 9-3 the objectives emphasize the taxonomic subcategory *Analysis of relationships*. These are primarily concerned with the interrelationships of elements and parts of a communication, such as the relationship of hypotheses to evidence, assump-

[The ability to recognize] basic terms and their interrelationships; supporting evidence; the difference between subjective and objective statements, etc. (1, p. 39).

The ability to distinguish factual from normative statements (2, p. 146).

Ability to distinguish a conclusion from statements which support it (2, p. 146).

The ability to recognize unstated assumptions (2, p. 146).

Skill in identifying motives and in discriminating between mechanisms of behavior with reference to individuals and groups (3, p. 35).

Recognize both defensible and indefensible techniques used in attempts to influence thought and behavior: propaganda, rumors, stereotypes, emotional appeals, etc. (4, p. 101).

---

[1] Tyler, 1954.

[2] Bloom, 1956.

[3] American Council on Education Studies, 1944.

[4] French, 1957.

Figure 9-2 Statements of objectives for *Analysis of elements.*

[The ability to recognize] basic terms and their interrelationship; the problem or question; the author's argument and his conclusions; supporting evidence; the purpose, assumptions, and pre-suppositions of the author (1, p. 29).

Ability to check the consistency of hypotheses with given information and assumptions (2, p. 147).

Ability to recognize which facts or assumptions are essential to a main thesis or to the argument in support of that thesis (2, p. 147).

...To identify unstated assumptions which are necessary to a line of argument (3, p. 101).

Ability to recognize what particulars are relevant to the validation of a judgment (2, p. 147).

Ability to recognize the causal relations and the important and unimportant details in an historical account (2, p. 147).

[The habit of thinking] critically (i.e. to recognize untoward emotional appeal, detect false inferences or unsubstantiated generalizations) (1, p. 20).

[Development of skill in recognizing] the assumptions underlying [theoretical economic] models (4, p. 81).

The ability to establish cause and effect relationships in economic phenomena (4, p. 59).

[The ability to distinguish] cause and effect relationships from other sequential relationships (5).

---

[1] Tyler, 1954.

[2] Bloom, 1956.

[3] French, 1957.

[4] University Grants Commission, 1961.

[5] Ayers, 1966.

Figure 9-3 Statements of objectives for *Analysis of relationships.*

250

The ability to infer the author's purpose, point of view, or traits of thought and feeling as exhibited in his work (1, p. 148).

The ability to recognize the tone, mood, and purpose of the author (2, p. 17).

[The ability to detect] the purpose, point of view, attitude, or general conception of the author (3).

Ability to analyze, in a particular work of art, the relation of materials and means of production to the "elements" and to the organization (1, p. 148).

The ability to recognize form and pattern in literary works as a means of understanding their meaning (4, p. 44).

Ability to recognize the point of view or bias of a writer in an historical account (1, p. 148).

[The ability to recognize] such different methods of scientific inquiry as classification, relational or analogical, inquiry, causal inquiry, etc. (2, p. 52).

[1] Bloom, 1956.

[2] Tyler, 1954.

[3] Ayers, 1965.

[4] American Council on Education Studies, 1944.

Figure 9-4 Statements of objectives for *Analysis of organizational principles.*

tions to arguments, casual relationships, and sequential relationships. They also include the logical or necessary relationships among the elements or parts.

A third group of objectives, like those shown in Figure 9-4, primarily emphasize *Analysis of organizational principles.* These objectives involve the ability to deal with the organization, systematic arrangement, and structure which hold an entire work together. The taxonomic subcategory includes analyses of the way in which the entire work is predicated on a particular form, point of view, purpose, or conception of the author's.

It will be seen by scanning the lists of analysis objectives in the figures that all involve some *ability* to recognize, identify, classify, distinguish, discriminate, or relate particular qualities or characteristics of a work. It can be inferred from these statements that the ability or skill is to be used on *new problems, materials, or situations*, and that the adequacy of the student's analysis is to be judged against the ability of some expert or experts to make a similar analysis with the same givens. We will attempt to clarify the terms "new problems, materials, or situations" and "ability to analyze."

New Problems, Materials, or Situations

One learns to make analysis of the kinds suggested in these objectives by actually engaging in the process with selected materials and problems. Thus, "the ability to recognize unstated assumptions" or "to distinguish factual from normative statements" is likely to be developed by practice in *doing* what is suggested by the objective with real material in a learning situation. The teacher would undoubtedly begin with relatively easy materials, in which the unstated assumptions or factual as against normative statements are relatively evident to many students, and gradually move to more complex materials, in which more effort and skill are required to discern, distinguish, or recognize the assumptions or types of statements.

Obviously the evaluation of analysis abilities and skills require that the students demonstrate the appropriate behaviors in a *new problem or situation.* Otherwise they would be doing no more than revealing their memory or knowledge of an analysis carried out by themselves or the teacher in the learning situation. By "new" we mean material that is new to the students, or at least material that is unlikely to have been analyzed in this way by or for them previously.

The selection of new materials and situations on which the student is to be evaluated entails fine judgment on the part of the teacher or other evaluator. One can imagine a range of materials from examples so simple that almost all students could make the appropriate discriminations to others so complex that only the most skilled analyst could discern the relationships and qualities sought. No simple rule can be given for this selection other than that the analysis required should be at the level of complexity and difficulty expected of the students at the appropriate level in their learning of this set of skills—whether the evaluation is formative or summative. At least the new task should be as complex as the material used at this stage in the student's learning experiences for analysis purposes.

Ideally the new problem, material, or situation should be real; that is, it should be selected from work or documents that already exist rather than prepared expressly for the evaluation exercise. As we said earlier, real materials are more likely to be of interest to the students, who in our experience prefer to exercise their analytic skills on genuine problems rather than on puzzle solving, in which the task is to figure out where or how the evaluator "hid" the required assumptions, types of statements, and so forth.

The Ability to Analyze

The ability to analyze is a complex set of skills and behaviors which the student can learn through practice with a variety of materials. It is assumed that this practice requires help from the teacher in order for the student to focus on the particular qualities desired; to develop and recognize systematic ways of proceeding to make the analysis; to learn the symptoms or cues that are helpful in distinguishing assumptions, relations, and other elements of a problem; and to learn the criteria by which one can judge the adequacy of the analysis. Practice without guidance, help, and corrections is not likely to be very

effective. Practice on materials which vary in difficulty, complexity, form, and other aspects is likely to be more effective for learning these skills than is repeated practice on the same kinds of materials.

In terms of students' behaviors, the ability to analyze might include the following:

The student can classify words, phrases, and statements in a document using given analytic criteria; this is the taxonomic subcategory *Analysis of elements* (A).

The student can infer particular qualities or characteristics not directly stated from clues available in the document; this is also *Analysis of elements* (B).

The student can infer from the criteria and relations of material in a document what underlying qualities, assumptions, or conditions must be implicit, required, or necessary; the taxonomic subcategory is *Analysis of relationships* (C).

The student can use criteria (such as relevance, causation, and sequence) to discern a pattern, order, or arrangement of material in a document: *Analysis of organizational principles* is involved here (D).

The student can recognize the organizational principles or patterns on which an entire document or work is based—again, an instance of *Analysis of organizational principles* (E).

The student can infer the particular framework, purpose, and point of view on which the document is based; this is another form of *Analysis of organizational principles* (F).

TESTING FOR ANALYSIS

It is possible to determine the requirements for making analysis test items from the foregoing exposition of behaviors and new situations. Some of the requirements are these:

1. The problem situation, document, or material to be analyzed must be new, unfamiliar, or in some way different from that used in instruction.

2. The new situation, document, or material should be available to the students as they make the analysis, and they should be able to refer to it as they attempt to answer the questions or solve the problems posed by the evaluator.

3. One or more of the behaviors listed in the subsection "The Ability to Analyze" should be sampled by the test problem.

4. The adequacy of a particular analysis should be determined by a comparison with that made by competent persons in the field or by a judgment of the adequacy with which evidence is used to infer particular unstated qualities or characteristics.

In the following subsections, we will attempt to illustrate some of the testing procedures which have been used to evaluate analytic abilities. We will organize these illustrations under the six types of behavior listed above because these appear to provide a useful way of making clear what the test problem is attempting to evaluate and because the behaviors provide a rough scale of complexity of the analytic tasks. Most of the illustrations are in objective test form because such forms make it very clear what skills are being tested. However, there is no doubt that essay or completion forms could be used to evaluate the same skills. As was true of the *Application* illustrations, most of the examples are drawn from the extensive files of the Examiner's Office of the University of Chicago, which provides the richest and most varied collection of illustrations for our purpose. Where examples are drawn from other sources, this is indicated in the note accompanying the illustration.

Test Problems for Analysis Behavior A

The student can classify words, phrases, and statements in a document using given analytic criteria (A).

This is the simplest type of analysis, in which the student, given analytic criteria or suggestions, can distinguish, classify, code, recognize, or otherwise discern particular elements of the material, document, or state-

ment which are appropriate. Such elements are explicitly stated or contained in the communication, and the student's only task is to recognize and classify them appropriately. It is believed that this type of analysis is a first step in an overall analysis because it is necessary to sort or classify those elements explicit in the document before one can move to the more difficult task of inferring what is implicit in or underlying the material contained in the document.

It should be pointed out that this type of analytic problem need not directly test the student's comprehension or evaluation of the statement. Rather, the questions attempt to determine whether or not the student recognizes the *function, purpose,* or *use* made of the particular elements in the document.

In the items below the students are expected to know what is meant by the terms "experiment," "theory," and "definition" and to be able to recognize or classify statements in relation to these terms. They are also expected to know enough about the phenomena described by each of the statements to determine the type of evidence or support on which it is based as well as its truth or falsity. This problem does test the students' knowledge as well as their ability to use the criteria.

34. *Directions:* Each statement below is to be marked on the answer sheet as
    A—if it is *factual* and has been found *true* by experiment or observation
    B—if it is *factual* and has been found *false* by experiment or observation
    C—if it is a *part* of an accepted theory
    D—if it is in *contradiction* to an accepted theory
    E—if it is true merely by *definition* of a word or words used

    (1) Water freezes at 0° Centigrade.
    (2) The interior of an atom is mostly empty space.
    (3) Pressure exerted by a gas is due to the weight of molecules.
    (4) Iron rusts by combining with oxygen.
    (5) Equal volumes of gases at the same temperature and pressure have the same weight.
    (6) The resistance of two conductors in series is greater than their resistance in parallel.

In the next items the student must determine the way in which the statements are related to the phenomena described, only one of which has been included here. It is clear that the student must have a good deal of knowledge about each phenomenon in order to make the relatively simple type of analysis required here.

35. A biological situation is listed below. In each situation, a *specific phenomenon* is *underlined [italicized]*. After each situation is a numbered list of statements, each of which may or may not be directly related to the specific phenomenon.
    Directions: For each numbered statement *blacken* the answer space, in accordance with the series of choices given below, which best characterizes the statement.
    Blacken answer space
    A—if the statement helps to *explain* the cause of the phenomenon
    B—if it *merely describes* the phenomenon
    C—if it describes a *consequence* of the phenomenon
    D—if the statement does not directly relate to the phenomenon
    A flower box is kept near a south window. All the plants in the box *bend toward the window.*
    (1) The plants were exposed to unequal illumination on opposite sides.
    (2) Growth rates differ on the exposed and shaded portions of the stems.
    (3) Cell division proceeds at a greater rate on the shaded side.
    (4) The rate of photosynthesis is greater on the exposed side.
    (5) The plants receive an increased illumination due to the bending.
    (6) The plants exhibit positive phototropism.
    (7) Within certain limits, cell elongation is directly proportional to the quantity of active auxin present.

In the following problem the student is expected to have information about the historical events in order to proceed to the type of analysis required. A student may fail it if he or she lacks the information, can't use the criteria, or both.

36. *Directions:* For items 1–6, mark the answer spaces to indicate whether each of the statements about the Benedictine monastic movement refers to
    A—its fundamental purpose
    B—achievements that were incidental to its fundamental purpose
    C—evidence of regard for the movement on the part of the laity
    D—evidence of corruption within the movement
    E—none of the above
    (1) The scholarly interests of monks assured the preservation of arts and letters.
    (2) The monasteries came into possession of great landed estates stocked with serf labor.
    (3) The monks did much to bring about the improvement of agriculture.
    (4) The monks' day and night were organized about periods of prayer and worship.
    (5) By forbidding the monks to hold personal property, the Benedictine rule demonstrated the idea of communal ownership of property.
    (6) Travellers seeking shelter at monasteries kept the monks informed on current news.

The next question is a more difficult problem of analysis, in which the student must distinguish among hypothesis, assumption, and findings and must determine which of these are being referred to in a relatively complex report of a social sciences investigation. While this type of test approaches that of the next type of behavior (B), the relatively straightforward distinctions below require only a few clues to the underlying structure of the document. (Students were given a selection from a social science study in advance of the test.)

37. *Directions:* You may refer to the reading material and to your own notes as frequently as you wish in answering these questions. For each of the statements below which refer to the study, *blacken* answer space
    A—if the statement is an hypothesis whose validity the author seeks to investigate . . .
    B—if the statement is an assumption on which this study is based *but not an hypothesis* which the study was designed to test
    C—if the statement is a finding of the study *but was not an hypothesis which the study was designed to test*
    D—if none of the above clearly applies.
    (1) An individual's social and economic attitudes are closely related to his class identification and both are related to his role in the economic system.
    (2) Some middle-class persons are more radical in

terms of the author's definition than some working-class persons.

(3) A majority of Americans believe themselves to be members of the working class.

(4) An individual's social class position can be determined with reasonable accuracy by knowing the amount and steadiness of his income.

(5) The reactions of members of different social classes to questionnaires are sufficiently comparable so that different responses can be taken to represent different opinions.

(6) A social class is characterized by common attitudes and beliefs.

(7) It is possible to state the issues involved in a liberal or conservative socioeconomic attitude in terms having substantially the same meaning for all Americans.

(8) Results obtained from a sample of 1,100 persons are valid when generalized to the American people as a whole.

Test Problems for Analysis Behavior B

The student can infer particular qualities or characteristics not directly stated from clues available in the document (B).

In general this type of behavior requires the students to recognize a variety of clues in the documents and to use these as the basis for their inferences. Here they must do more than classify explicit statements; they must infer the qualities rather than merely recognize them. However, the emphasis in this behavior is primarily on *specific* qualities, characteristics, or elements.

It is clear that for an evaluation of this behavior, it is necessary for the students to have the document or material available to refer to as frequently as they wish. While it may in some instances be possible for the students to remember the document well enough to refer to it in memory, it is likely that analytic problems based on this condition will be very rare.

In the following example, the student must recognize the underlying assumption which the writer was making. Note that the assumption must be derived from several clues in the document. In the actual test in which this passage was used, there were a number of questions to evaluate the student's

comprehension of the document. In general, questions on a lengthy passage will rarely be restricted to analysis. Analytic questions are likely to be part of a set of items dealing with comprehension, application, evaluation, and so forth.

Passage A (written in 1789)

"A plural Legislature is as necessary to good Government as a single Executive. It is not enough that your Legislature should be numerous; it should also be divided. Numbers alone are not a sufficient Barrier against the Impulses of Passion, the Combinations of Interest, the intrigues of Faction, the Haste of Folly, or Spirit of Encroachment . . .

"Hence it is that the two Branches should be elected by Persons differently qualified; and in short, that, as far as possible, they should be made to represent different interests. Under this Reasoning I would establish a Legislature of two Houses. The Upper should represent the Property; the Lower the Population of the State. The Upper should be chosen by Freemen possessing in Lands and Houses one thousand Pounds; the Lower by all such as had resided four years in the Country, and paid Taxes. The first should be chosen for four, the last for two years. They should in Authority be coequal."

—An anonymous author writing on the Pennsylvania Constitution

38. *Directions:* The following questions refer to Passage A. For each question *blacken* the answer space corresponding to the *one best* answer or completion.

(1) Of the assumptions which the writer of the passage makes, one is that

A. decisions made by a government in which there is a heavy representation of property will always be wise decisions.

B. the principle basic to politics is that various groups strive to achieve their own economic ends.

C. under a good form of government, "factions" will be eliminated.

D. under a good form of government the drives which people have of using government to promote their own economic ends will be eliminated.

In the next example it is to be noted that the student is to determine the effect of the assumptions made by the writer. While these questions relate to the entire document or investigation, they deal primarily with the more immediate effect of particular elements in the paper.

[The student has the paper available for reference during the examination.]

39. (1) In Leibnitz' discussion of "quantity of motion," his first assumption establishes
    A. a definition of the term "force" acquired by a body in falling from height A.
    B. a relationship between falling bodies and bodies projected upward against gravity.
    C. that the momentum acquired by a body falling from height h is sufficient to carry it back to height h.
    D. the equivalence of weight and motive force.

(2) His second assumption establishes
    A. a definition of the term "force."
    B. a relationship between height of fall and velocity acquired.
    C. a relationship between height of fall and weight of body.
    D. the special case arising in consideration of machines.

(3) In discussing the separation of particles, Lavoisier does *not* assert or assume that
    A. any body expanded by heating can be contracted by cooling.
    B. there is a range of attainable temperature below the point at which bodies remain constant in size despite further cooling.
    C. the size of the individual particles is unaffected by heat.
    D. there is a point on the temperature scale below which further markings are meaningless.

In the following example the students are probably helped by their general knowledge of Jefferson's political position. However, they must answer these analytic questions primarily from a careful reading of the letter from Jefferson to Madison. These two questions illustrate the rather close relation between comprehension and analysis. In one sense both deal with conclusions that may be inferred from Jefferson's arguments. In another sense both deal with propositions or assumptions underlying these arguments.

40. [The students are presented with a letter from Thomas Jefferson to James Madison. They can refer to it repeatedly as they attempt to answer a series of questions related to it.]
    (1) A fundamental political tenet underlying Jefferson's argument is that
        A. a little liberty is a dangerous thing; men must choose between complete freedom and unlimited authority.
        B. anarchy is a better state than tyranny, and possibly the best state for man; but it is not a real alternative for American society.
        C. rebellions are a wholesome, if rather bitter, medicine for government, since they generally lead men a little closer to the ideal of society without government.
        D. government is a necessary evil, but it should be stripped of power, since all power tends to corrupt.
        E. all of the above.

    (2) A futher underlying proposition is that
        A. the perils of extensive liberty in the hands of the people, however great, are less serious than the perils of arbitrary power in the hands of officials, whether royal or republican.
        B. men in general have the capacity for self-government.
        C. rebellions in general are a sign of public health, showing that men care enough about their rights to defend them at great risk.
        D. rebellions in general are a sign of public degeneracy, in that they testify to governmental encroachments on popular liberties.
        E. all the above.

In the following three questions, the students are called upon to analyze specific words and phrases in the poem. They are expected to use clues throughout the poem in answering these relatively simple analytic questions. It is evident that this type of analysis can be made only if the material (the poem, in this case) is available at the time of the evaluation.

41. *Directions:* Read the following poem carefully; then consider items 1 to 3, which refer to it, blackening the answer space corresponding to the *one* best completion.

POEM II

Go, go, quaint follies, sugared sin,	
Shadow no more my door;	2
I will no longer cobwebs spin,	
I'm too much on the score.	4
For since amidst my youth and night	
My great preserver smiles.	6
We'll make a match, my only light,	
And join against their wiles;	8

Blind, desp'rate fits, that study how
To dress and trim our shame.   10
That gild rank poison, and allow
Vice in a fairer name;   12

The purls of youthful blood and bowels,
Lust in the robes of love,   14
The idle talk of fev'rish souls,
Sick with a scarf or glove;   16

Let it suffice my warmer days
Simpered and shined on you.   18
Twist not my cypress with your bays,
Or roses with my yew;   20

Go, go, seek out some greener thing,
It snows and freezeth here;   22
Let nightingales attend the spring,
Winter is all my year.   24

(1) In addressing "quaint follies" and "sugared sin" [stanza 1], the speaker expresses his specific purpose of
  A. reconciling himself to the physical limitations of old age.
  B. rejecting his earlier practice of amorous versifying.
  C. rejecting his earlier indolent habits in favor of industrious and constructive activity.
  D. abandoning his former attitude of toleration toward the sinful, and adopting a policy of positive denunciation.

(2) The smiling of the "great preserver" (line 6) symbolizes
  A. God's grateful recognition and acceptance of a life spent serving Him and hating His enemies.
  B. the nearness of death (i.e., heavenly bliss) for the speaker.
  C. the love of God for man, and God's consequent willingness to redeem man from eternal damnation.
  D. the benevolent attitude toward the author of the poem of an unidentified patron.

(3) Among the meanings for "match" (line 7) which were in use at the time of the composition of Poem II . . . the poet has drawn especially upon two, namely:
  A. "a compact or agreement" and "an article furnishing illumination."
  B. "a contest or competition" and "an article furnishing illumination."
  C. "a compact or agreement" and "a similarity or sameness."
  D. "a contest or competition" and "a similarity or sameness."

Test Problems for Analysis Behavior C

The student can infer from the criteria and relations of material in a document what underlying qualities, assumptions, or conditions must be implicit, required, or necessary (C).

In behaviors A and B the student is expected to use analytic criteria on parts or elements of the document, passage, poem, or other material. For the most part, behaviors A and B could be evidenced in the handling of excerpts from the larger document, since the necessary clues are usually available within the excerpt itself. In behavior C the emphasis is on the entire document or idea, although the analysis still deals with particulars which have a bearing on the document as a whole.

A relatively simple type of analysis is evidenced below in the use of logical relations. Although the document or idea as a whole is relatively restricted, we see these illustrations as examples of behavior C. There are many forms in which syllogistic reasoning can be demonstrated; these are only a few of the possible variations.

42. *Directions:* In each of the following items, blacken answer space
  A—if the conclusion logically follows;
  B—if the conclusion does *not* logically follow.
  (1) *Statements:* if X exists, then Y exists. X exists.
  Conclusion: Y exists.
  (2) *Statements:* if X exists, then Y exists. X does not exist.
  Conclusion: Y does not exist.

Directions: In each of the following items, select the best lettered response.

43. *Statements:* No lover of sophistry respects the truth. All skeptics love sophistry.
  Conclusions:
  A. All skeptics respect the truth.
  B. Some skeptics respect the truth.
  C. None who respect the truth are non-skeptics
  D. Some skeptics do not respect the truth.
  E. None of the foregoing.

44. *Statements:* It is true that, if perfect competition exists, the cost of production inevitably equals selling price. But perfect competition never did exist, does not exist, and never will exist.

Conclusion: Cost of production cannot equal selling price.

Comments:

A. The conclusion follows logically.

B. It is impossible to be sure that competition never did and never will exist.

C. It is not stated that perfect competition is the only condition that permits cost of production to equal selling price.

D. An argument that begins with "if" cannot lead to any certain conclusion.

E. The argument sounds plausible but contains an important fallacy.

45. *Statements:* Let me explain how you can establish whether one thing or event is the cause of another. We will speak of two things or events, x and y. If you begin at any time, and observe when x happens, and after that you notice that y always follows x, and y never happens except after x, then you can say with certainty that x is the cause of y.

I began once to make such observations and noticed that whenever the sun set, it was followed later by the rising of the sun, and the sun never rose without being preceded by the setting of the sun.

Conclusion: The setting of the sun is the cause of the rising of the sun.

Comments:

A. The conclusion follows logically.

B. The second part of the "statement" is an unfair use of the first part; this is an exceptional case.

C. An important assumption has been omitted from the statements.

D. The conclusion is absurd, so it cannot be logical.

E. The statement about "cause" is somewhat fallacious.

In the following examples the student is to determine which type of evidence supports a particular theoretical statement. The problem of relating evidence to theory could be put in different forms. The simplest form is that of selecting the best evidence for a statement. The most complex is probably that of determining the criteria which must be met for evidence or experimental findings to support or refute a particular theoretical position. In the problems below, the student must have a good deal of prior knowledge about the theoretical statements in order to make the type of analysis required. It is to be noted that the student is not asked to determine the truth or falsity of the different choices—only their relevance to the theoretical statement. In some items all the choices are true, but they differ in the criteria specified in the test question.

46. Light has wave characteristics. Which one of the following offers the best experimental support for this statement?

A. Light can be reflected by a mirror.

B. A beam of light spreads out on passing through a small opening.

C. A beam of light can be broken into colors by a prism.

D. Light causes a current to flow in a photoelectric cell circuit.

E. Light carries energy.

47. Geologists subscribe to the hypothesis that the earth has been shrinking. Which of the following is the best evidence for this hypothesis?

A. The earth is not a perfect sphere.

B. The density of the interior of the earth is considerably higher than that of the surface layers.

C. The force of gravity varies in different parts of the earth.

D. The earth came originally from the sun as heterogeneous material and has been readjusting to the force of gravity.

E. Mountain ranges consist of series of folds.

48. In the past, glaciers covered the Great Lakes region. Which of the following offers the most direct experimental support for this statement?

A. The region is relatively cool in the summer.

B. Unsorted deposits are found in the region.

C. Igneous rocks are found in the region.

D. Ice sheets are still present in Greenland.

E. Tropical vegetation is absent in the region.

49. Two theories are advanced to explain the burning of material in air. Both theories assume that no substance can have negative mass or weight.

Theory A. During combustion, the burning material unites with a certain component of the air.

Theory B. During combustion, a substance escapes from the burning material into the surrounding air. The capacity of air to take up this escaping substance is limited.

Directions: Consider each fact below and decide

whether the fact *taken by itself* constitutes better evidence for one theory than for the other, is nearly equally good evidence for either theory, or furnishes no evidence for either theory. For each of the facts given below, *blacken* answer space

A—if the fact lends more direct support to Theory A than to Theory B;

B—if the fact lends more direct support to Theory B than to Theory A;

C—if the fact supports the two theories about equally well;

D—if the fact could not be used to support either theory.

Facts

(1) A candle in a closed jar containing air stops burning before the candle is used up.

(2) The product formed by burning iron in air weighs more than the original iron.

(3) Some products of combustion, when heated in air which no longer supports combustion, restore the original properties of the air.

(4) A candle burns more brightly in a breeze than in still air.

(5) Illuminating gas burns more brightly in chlorine than in air.

In the next items the student must determine the necessary relations, definitions, and conditions for the logical and theoretical developments in Galileo's writing.

50. (1) Assume that the definition of mass developed in the excerpt [based on a writing by Galileo] is the only definition of mass utilized by the author. In order then to have his theory of mechanics cover the common experience of the varying *weights* of bodies, he must establish a relationship between.

A. weight and force.

B. weight and inertia.

C. weight and acceleration.

(2) One postulate necessary to the logical development of the excerpt is contained in the statement (do *not* assume that *postulate* necessarily means *unreal*)

A. bodies differ in weight.

B. two bodies mutually affect the acceleration of each other.

C. mass is a ratio of two accelerations.

D. acceleration is inversely proportional to inertia.

(3) In the excerpt, the use of the acceleration of a particle due solely to the mutual action of it and

one other particle in determining masses is justifiable

A. only if no other particles affect the two particles considered.

B. only if the initial acceleration of each particle is used, since the acceleration of each particle will depend on the distance between the particles.

C. only if the total acceleration of a particle is analyzable into component accelerations each of which can be considered as affecting the particle independently.

D. since acceleration is itself a directly measurable quantity.

Additional examples of behavior C are afforded by the following examples from literature, the social sciences, and music. These are isolated questions from a series of questions based on a work in each subject. In each case students must base their answers on a comprehension of the entire work, although the specific clues are for the most part to be found in a particular excerpt.

51. Which one of the following statements best explains the diction of lines 7–11 [from *King Lear*]?

A. Only the language used in these lines is really appropriate to a king.

B. The language reveals Lear's innate tendency to exaggeration in circumstances that excite his anger.

C. The language, chosen by the playwright primarily with a view to the effect on the spectator or reader, achieves a skillful contrast by the creation of emotional stress after the emotional relaxation in lines 1–6.

D. The imaginative quality of the language vividly shows Lear's awareness, as a result of his own painful experience, of the sufferings of the poor in general.

52. (1) The author [of a social science paper] is assuming as *basic* to his argument the idea that

A. the main problem of government is to get common action even though people are divided on their basic interests.

B. public discussion is important in that it allows an opportunity for the "experts" to inform the public of its true interests.

C. government is good to the degree that it achieves the welfare of the people.

D. true democracy consists of rule by majority.

259

(2) A belief basic to the author's argument is that
   A. under the correct conditions, what the public wants is the best clue to what will be for the public good.
   B. the importance of intelligence has been over-emphasized in discussion of how public policy should be made.
   C. the democratic movement was essentially transitional and . . . another means for determining public policy must be discovered.
   D. experts are specialists and have nothing to do with how public policy is formed.

53. *The Theme and Variation 1 will each be played ONCE.* The livelier effect of Variation 1 as compared with the Theme is due to
   A. the faster tempo of Variation 1.
   B. the more rapid succession of notes of Variation 1.
   C. both faster tempo and more rapid succession of notes.
   D. neither faster tempo nor more rapid succession of notes.

Test Problems for Analysis Behaviors D, E, and F

The student can use criteria (such as relevance, causation, and sequence) to discern a pattern, order, or arrangement of material in a document (D).

The student can recognize the organizational principles or patterns on which an entire document or work is based (E).

The student can infer the particular framework, purpose, and point of view on which the document is based (F).

All three types of behavior require students to make particular kinds of analysis in which they are able to discern the pattern, organizational principle, framework, or point of view on which an entire work is based. Appropriate test problems for these types of analysis behaviors require students to relate the entire work to a given analytic question or problem.

In the items below, the student must relate parts of a poem to the entire work. The second and third questions attempt to determine whether the student can discern pattern in the relation between several of the stanzas (behavior D). The fourth question attempts to determine whether the student can analyze the progression of thought or pattern in the entire work (E). The first question attempts to determine the poet's point of view in the entire work (F). Typically questions of this type would come toward the end of a set of questions on a particular work since they depend in part on knowledge, comprehension, and application as well as on more specific kinds of analysis of details of the work. They thus form the more complex behaviors or questions in a hierarchy of cognitive abilities and skills as applied to a new work.

54. (1) The poet shows [in the poem given to the students with the examination] that his frustrated desire to aid the sufferers on the ship is due to
   A. his inexperience and lack of wisdom.
   B. his inability to get himself accepted as one of them.
   C. his inability to move the oppressors to pity.
   D. a combination of A and C.
   E. a combination of B and C.
   (2) Stanza B serves chiefly
   A. to relieve the emotional strain aroused by stanza 7.
   B. to intensify the distress of the men before the mast who were "reckless" or "aghast."
   C. to sharpen by contrast the reader's picture of the situation in the noisome hold.
   D. to give a more definite idea of injustice in the situation on the ship.
   (3) Stanza 9 serves the purpose chiefly of
   A. giving the reader a realistic picture of the return of the fishing fleet.
   B. returning the reader to the scene established in stanza 1.
   C. providing material for extending the simile of the ship to a final point.
   D. delaying the end to make the poem symmetrical.
   (4) Which of the following [choices A, B, C, and D] describes the progression of thought in the poem most accurately and most completely?
   A. The beauty of a particular spot suggests the harmony of the motion of the Earth in the universe; pleasure in this idea is marred by the

sins of men against each other and the inequities in their lots. Reflection on these evils causes fear for the ultimate destiny of Earth.

B. The sight of boats at sea suggests that Earth is like a ship carrying all sorts of men. The poet reflects that unless men unite in brotherhood, the ship will be wrecked and he implores us to right the ship before it is too late.

C. The poet feels that Earth, like ships at sea, is in constant danger both from tyrants (captains) and from labor agitators (slavers in the hold). There are some passengers but these are thwarted by the selfish men.

D. The poem contemplates the beauty of Earth and prays to God that this beauty may be kept intact among men as it is in nature.

The next questions are all related to a new work of sculpture presented to the students at the time of the examination. The first two questions attempt to evaluate the student's ability to discern particular aspects of the arrangement of material and form (behavior D). The next four test the student's recognition of some of the organizational principles underlying the work (E), while the last question focuses on the overall framework or quality of the sculpture (F).

55. (1) The feeling of mass in the work [a sculpture] results from
    A. the material.
    B. the color.
    C. the form.
    D. the treatment of surfaces.
(2) The sculpture is unified chiefly by
    A. repetition of parallel planes.
    B. color, texture, and repetition of lines and volumes.
    C. bilateral symmetry.
    D. repetition of identical shapes.
(3) One principle movement in the sculpture is created by
    A. the parallel turning of front and back planes of the figure.
    B. a single cylindrical volume running from top to base.
    C. an unbroken curve encircling the figure.
    D. a vertical core-line extending from top to base.

(4) Linear movements felt in this work are
    A. vertical
    B. diagonal.
    C. horizontal.
    D. all of these.
(5) The principal linear movements in the sculpture are
    A. repeated by the volumes, and repeated by the grain of the wood.
    B. repeated by the volumes, but opposed by the grain of the wood.
    C. opposed by the volumes, but repeated by the grain of the wood.
    D. opposed by the volumes, and opposed by the grain of the wood.
(6) The medium affects the work chiefly
    A. by limiting the nature of the design.
    B. by its color and grain.
    C. by its structure and hardness.
    D. by the difficulty of carving it.
(7) This work is best described as
    A. close representation of the natural object.
    B. selective representation of the natural object.
    C. abstraction based upon geometrical principles.
    D. nearly nonobjective.

In the set of questions below, the students are expected to analyze a statement about *Hamlet* on the basis of their knowledge of the play. Item 3 gets at the students' ability to analyze the overall pattern of the play (D). Item 2 attempts to have them discern the organizing principle to be inferred from the quoted passage (E), while item 1 concerns the point of view adopted by the writer of the passage (F).

56. Consider the following statement [relating to an excerpt shown on the test]:
    "1) Hamlet is given a command by the ghost of his murdered father to take vengeance upon the murderer, Claudius. 2) He is not able to do so immediately because he does not have sufficient proof that Claudius has murdered his father. 3) In the process of finding this proof, Hamlet unwittingly allows the king to discover his suspicions. 4) As the action proceeds, Hamlet cannot take vengeance because he never has a real opportunity to do so. 5) As the action ends, Hamlet becomes involved in a duel arranged by Claudius which has as its consequences the death of the

hero and his adversary as well as the more important of the subordinate characters."

(1) This statement may best be described as
  A. an *interpretation* of the play (as the word "interpretation" is used in the syllabus for the course).
  B. an analysis of *character* (as the word "character" is used in the syllabus for the course).
  C. a summary of the *thought* of the play (as the word "thought" is used in the syllabus for the course).
  D. an analysis of the *mode of dramatic representation* (as that phrase is used in the syllabus for the course).
  E. an account of the events in *Hamlet* which are presented *on stage*.

(2) An inference could be made from this statement as to the *element* which the writer of the statement takes to be the *organizing principle* of the play (as these concepts are defined in the syllabus for the course). Judging by this statement, we may say that for its writer, the play seems to be organized by
  A. action.
  B. character.
  C. thought.
  D. diction.
  E. manner of presentation.

(3) A consideration of the problems raised throughout this play leads to
  A. the view that Hamlet is not "essentially a speculative person" but, on the contrary, essentially a man of *action*.
  B. the view that Hamlet delays in carrying out the ghost's command because he has *moral scruples* against the act of murder.
  C. a serious doubt of the validity of *characterizing* Hamlet as "the kind of man who is always substituting thinking for action."
  D. a serious doubt of the validity of the final "except-clause" of the statement ("except when he is forced by external circumstances to act on the instant").

EXERCISES

Objective: Construct test items appropriate to the evaluation of application and analysis objectives.

Preparation: The objectives and test items developed for Chapters 2 and 7 may be useful in doing the exercises for this chapter and Chapter 10.

1. *Preparing objectives.* Prepare two sets of objectives—one for application behaviors and one for analysis behaviors.
   a. Select some objectives from ones you have written previously, from curriculum guides, from books on teaching, or from books on educational measurement.
   b. In addition, try your hand at writing some objectives.
   c. Given the difficulty of writing objectives and test items at the levels of application and analysis, limit yourself throughout to a unit or subject with which you are particularly comfortable. It is most useful if you stick with the unit you chose for the Chapter 2 and 7 exercises. One goal of the *Taxonomy* is to sequence instruction within a subject or unit area.
   d. Try to write objectives for the subcategories within the application and analysis levels.
2. *Operationalizing behaviors.*
   a. List the behavioral verbs used in your objectives.
   b. For each verb identify a specific action or task which can form the basis for a test item.
3. *Item writing.*
   a. Write a test item for each of your objectives. Use the examples in the chapter as models or suggestions.
   b. Review your items to ensure that they tap the intended behavior from whatever subcategory the objective is derived.
   c. Screen the items for technical adequacy.
   d. Have a teacher or independent judge determine content validity of your test items using the behavioral statements as the criteria.

REFERENCES

American Council on Education Studies. *A design for general education.* Washington, D.C.; Author, 1944.

Ayers, J. D., et al. *Summary description of grade nine science objectives and test items.* Edmonton, Alberta, Can.: Department of Education, High School Entrance Examinations Board, 1965.

Ayers, J. D., et al. *Summary description of grade nine social studies objectives and test items.* Edmonton, Alberta, Can.: Department of Education, Examinations Board, 1966.

Bloom, B. S. (Ed.). *Taxonomy of educational objectives; The classification of educational goals.* Handbook 1. *Cognitive domain*, New York: McKay, 1956.

Bloom, B. S. (Ed.). *Evaluation in secondary schools.* New Delhi: All India Council for Secondary Education, 1958.

Bloom, B. S. (Ed.) *Evaluation in higher education.* New Delhi: University Grants Commission, 1961.

French, W., & Associates. *Behavioral goals of general education in high school.* New York: Russell Sage Foundation, 1957.

Gagné, R. M. *The conditions of learning.* New York: Holt, Author, 1965.

Progressive Education Association. Test 1.3a; *Application of principles in science: Evaluation in the Eight-Year Study.* Chicago: Author, 1939.

Tyler, R. W. The fact-finding study of the testing program of the United States Armed Forces Institute, 1952–1954 (Report to the USAFI). University of Chicago, Author, 1954.

10 Evaluation Techniques for Synthesis and Evaluation Objectives

---

Chapter Highlights

Synthesis
    Definition: "The Putting Together of Elements and Parts So
        as to Form a Whole . . . a Pattern or Structure Not Clearly
        There Before."
    Divergent Thinking
    A Culminating Outcome of Education
    Subcategories
        Production of a Unique Communication
        Production of a Plan or Proposed Set of Operations
        Derivation of a Set of Abstract Relations
    Development of a Master-Apprentice Relationship between
        Teacher and Student
    Quality of Product as More Important Than Specific Behaviors
Testing for Synthesis
    New Problem; Student Has a Part in Defining It
    References and Other Materials Are Available as Needed
    Types of Products Vary
    Adequacy of Product Is Judged in Various Ways
    Essay or Production of Something Takes Place during
        the Testing Situation
Evaluation
    Definition: "The Making of Judgments about the Value,
        for Some Purpose, of Ideas, Works, Solutions, Methods,
        Materials, etc., . . . Involves the Use of Criteria as Well
        as Standards."
    Complex Cognitive Behaviors
    Informed Judgment
    Explicit Criteria

SYNTHESIS

Synthesis is "the putting together of elements and parts so as to form a whole. This involves the process of working with pieces, parts, elements, etc., and arranging and combining them in such a way as to constitute a pattern or structure not clearly there before" (Bloom, 1956, p. 206).

There has been much discussion and research on creativity during the past decades (see summaries in Taylor & Barron, 1963). Creativity has been regarded as one of the more important types of educational outcome, especially for the academically gifted. It has also been viewed as a kind of self-expression in which a student is urged and helped to produce something novel or different, bearing the stamp of personal uniqueness and individuality. Much of the emphasis on creativity has undoubtedly come as a reaction against authoritarian modes of teaching and highly structured educational programs. It is also a reaction against the relatively extreme type of rote learning frequently emphasized in such teaching or educational programs.

Creativity has also been deemed to emphasize divergent thinking in contrast with convergent thinking. In divergent thinking the answer to a problem cannot be fixed in advance (as in multiple-choice questions), and each person may be expected or desired to produce a unique answer. In convergent thinking the correct answer to a problem or question can be known in advance since it is fixed by the requirements of the subject matter or the problem or both. For the most part, the categories of the *Taxonomy of Educational Objectives* (Bloom, 1956) up to the level of *Synthesis—Knowledge, Comprehension, Application*, and *Analysis*—can be regarded as convergent thinking, and the test illustrations for the majority of these behaviors can be of a form in which the correct or best answer can be determined in advance.

Synthesis, however, appears to be a type of divergent thinking in that it is unlikely that the right solution to a problem can be set in advance. In synthesis each student may provide a unique response to the questions or problems posed, and it is the task of the teacher or evaluator to determine the merits of the responses in terms of the process exhibited, the quality of the product, or the quality of evidence and arguments supporting the synthetic work.

Whether or not we identify creativity with synthesis, we can justify the development of objectives involving synthesis. As a form of divergent thinking, synthesis represents one of the terminal outcomes of education. No longer are the students displaying to the teacher the particular types of knowledge or skills and abilities they have developed; they are now producing ideas, plans, and products which they perceive as their own. Thus synthesis is one of the culminating objectives of education in that individuals become scholars or artists in their own right.

Synthesis can also be regarded as educationally important because of the pride of authorship, sense of creativity, and sense of communication and relevance which accompany the creation of something unique—especially when the students feel that they have done an adequate job with the materials and ideas at their command.

In a world of rapidly changing problems and answers, the schools are largely organized around fixed problems and set answers. Education emphasizing synthetic problems that can be approached in highly individual ways represents a clear departure from the catechisms under the control of curriculum makers and teachers. Eventually individuals will be placed in positions where they are expected to make unique contributions in the industrial world, in the professions, in the arts, or in scholarship. Synthesis is what is frequently expected of the mature worker, and the sooner the students are given opportunities to make syntheses on their own, the sooner they will feel that the world of the

school has something to contribute to them and to the life they will live in the wider society.

In Figures 10-1 to 10-3 we list a series of objectives which are included in the large category of *Synthesis*. We differentiate these objectives using the subcategories developed in the *Taxonomy of Educational Objectives* (Bloom, 1956; see also Appendix, page 331).

In Figure 10-1 are some synthesis objectives which emphasize the *Production of a unique communication*. These are primarily concerned with the development of a communication in which the author—writer, speaker, artist—attempts to convey ideas, feelings, relationships, or experiences to others. The communication may be in the form of a verbal statement (written or oral), a poem, a painting, a musical composition, or a mathematical statement, among others.

Figure 10-2 contains some synthesis objectives which emphasize the *Production of a plan or proposed set of operations*. These are primarily concerned with the development of a plan of work or the proposal of a plan of operations. The plan should satisfy the re-

---

Skill in writing, using an excellent organization of ideas and statements (1, p. 169).

Ability to write creatively a story, essay, or verse . . . (1, p. 169).

To develop effective written expression—the ability to adapt . . . material to a level of language and form suitable to the purpose and situation (2, p. 19).

Expresses his ideas in speech, writing, or in some artistic form with increasing clarity and correctness (3, p. 97).

Ability to write simple musical compositions, as in setting a short poem to music (1, p. 169).

The ability to participate [effectively] . . . in at least one of the arts or crafts or in some form of musical expression (4, p. 45).

The ability to participate effectively in group discussions of social problems . . . coordinating different suggestions, suggesting solutions, and orienting these solutions to the goals of the group (2, p. 28).

Skill in constructing . . . graphic materials (2, p. 49).

---

[1] Bloom, 1956.

[2] Tyler, 1954.

[3] French, 1957.

[4] American Council on Education Studies, 1944.

Figure 10-1 Statements of objectives for *Production of a unique Communication.*

Ability to propose ways of testing hypotheses (1, p. 170).

Devising . . . suitable experiments for testing hypotheses; providing controls for experimental variables; recognizing and allowing for uncontrolled variables; setting up . . . laboratory equipment needed (2, p. 39).

Ability to plan a unit of instruction for a particular teaching situation (1, p. 171).

Ability to design a building according to given specifications (1, p. 171).

[1] Bloom, 1956.

[2] Tyler, 1954.

Figure 10-2 Statements of objectives for *Production of a plan or proposed set of operations.*

quirements of a task which may be given to the students or which they may select or develop for themselves.

In Figure 10-3 the synthesis objectives listed emphasize the *Derivation of a set of abstract relations.* These are concerned with the development of a set of abstract relations to classify or explain particular data or phenomena. They may also include deduction of propositions and relations from a set of basic propositions or symbolic representations.

The reader will see by scanning the lists of synthesis objectives in these figures that they all involve the student's developing some new organization of material and ideas to meet the requirements of a problem or task or to express some feelings or ideas.

It is evident that the problem or task must be a new one for the student; otherwise the outcome might be a remembered synthesis rather than a new one produced by the student. It also seems likely that students must have a great deal of latitude in defining the problem or task if they are to relate their own ideas, feelings, or experiences to it. While a common task or problem may be given to a group, the redefinition of the problem and the approach of each student may be quite unique. It is also possible for a student to set his or her own synthesis task or problem.

It is not necessary that the problem be new and original in the field involved—only that it be new to the student. Nor must the synthetic solution be a new development,

Development of a tentative hypothesis based on the data at hand (1, p. 39).

Ability to formulate appropriate hypotheses based upon an analysis of factors involved, and to modify such hypotheses in the light of new factors and considerations (2, p. 172).

Ability to make mathematical discoveries and generalizations (2, p. 172).

Makes logical experiments; i.e. assumes the truth of a proposition which he suspects is false, and then makes logical deductions from this proposition (as in certain proofs in demonstrative geometry) (3, p. 98).

Ability to perceive possible ways in which experience may be organized to form a conceptual structure (2, p. 172).

[1] Tyler, 1954.

[2] Bloom, 1956.

[3] French, 1957.

Figure 10-3 Statements of objectives for *Derivation of a set of abstract relations.*

creation, or discovery for the field involved— only a unique development as far as the student is concerned.

Synthesis objectives like those in Figures 10-1 to 10-3 require new views and roles from both teachers and students. The students are expected to produce something which is unique and different. They are expected to produce this when provided with a task or problem, a set of specifications, or a collection of materials. In doing this they must have a goal in view, a prospective audience in mind, and some criteria of what constitutes an adequate job. In contrast, teachers for synthesis objectives are no longer pedagogues. They are more like coaches, guides, or master craftsmen working with apprentices. The teacher may also form the audience or critic for whom the unique production is intended. Ideally, the judgments of such a teacher about the products are not the "pass-fail" or a series of letter grades. Rather, like most formative judgments, they are directed to helping the students find aspects of their work which are adequate as well as aspects which could be improved or strengthened. The point is that no synthesis is ever really perfect but that each one opens up vistas of future products and syntheses. This requires that teacher and student move from the pedagogue-pupil to the master-apprentice relationship—a most difficult new relationship which demands much from both teacher and student.

For the other categories of the *Taxonomy*, we have been able to state relatively specific student behaviors. For *Synthesis*, the emphasis is on the quality of the products created rather than on the specific processes or behaviors involved in their creation. However, since it does seem that somewhat different products are involved in the three subcategories, we will present test illustrations under these subcategories:

Production of a unique communication (A)
Production of a plan or proposed set of operations (B)
Derivation of a set of abstract relations (C)

TESTING FOR SYNTHESIS

Some of the requirements for developing synthesis problems and tests may be summarized briefly.

1. The problem, task, or situation involving synthesis should be new or in some way different from those used in the instruction. The student may set the task or problem for himself or herself, or at least may have considerable freedom in redefining it.

2. The student may attack the problem with a variety of references or other available materials as these are needed. Thus, synthesis problems may be open-book examinations, in which the student may use notes, references, the library, and other resources as appropriate. Ideally synthesis problems should be as close as possible to the situation in which a scholar (or artist, or engineer, and so forth) attacks a problem he or she is interested in. The time allowed, conditions of work, and other stipulations should be as far from the typical, controlled examination situation as possible.

3. The type of product developed may be one of the types listed under the general category of *Synthesis* or any other which is appropriate to the particular educational objective being evaluated.

4. The adequacy of the final product may be judged in terms of the effect it has on the reader, observer, or audience; the adequacy with which it has accomplished the task; or evidence on the adequacy of the process by which it was developed.

Most of the examples to be presented in the following sections are drawn from the files of the Examiner's Office of the University of Chicago. With a few exceptions these illustrations are of the essay type or involve the production of a new set of materials, work, or other product. It is unlikely that recognition test forms would be of great value in testing for this category of objective.

Test Problems for Synthesis A: Production of a Unique Communication

In the type of synthesis classified as *Production of a unique communication*, the student is attempting to convey an idea, feeling, or experience to others. In doing this the student must have in mind the effects to be achieved, the nature of the audience to be influenced or affected, the particular medium or form to be used (written or spoken, painted, expressed in scientific symbols, and so forth), and the ideas, feelings, or experiences to be communicated.

It is obvious that the student must have considerable freedom in defining the task for himself or herself, or in redefining the problem or task that has been set.

In this example of the typical English essay problem, the students are given a relatively general task which they must further define for themselves. They are offered a number of suggestions to help them get started. However, they are provided with little in the way of criteria or standards they must meet in their papers.

Session III (3 hours)

1. *Directions:* On many campuses a favorite target for student criticism is the university newspaper. At Harvard or Chicago, for example, the charge is sometimes made that the *Crimson* or the *Maroon* is unfair or inaccurate, that it is too radical or too conservative, that the staff is limited to a clique, that the style is bad and the articles dull, that too much or too little space is given to sports or music or to this or that group of campus politicians, and so on. To such complaints the editor of the college paper often rejoins that student criticism is merely unconstructive griping and that students don't know what they want of their paper anyway.

This afternoon you are to explain and describe what you want a college or university paper to be. You may center your discussion on a particular newspaper on a particular campus—say the *Chicago Maroon*—or you may, if you prefer, discuss college papers in general. In any case, present your ideas about the characteristics that you believe a college paper ought to possess and develop these ideas out of a clearly expressed and coherently formulated conception of the proper role of college and university newspapers and of

the interests and conditions which they should reflect. What should be the purpose or purposes of the paper? What needs should it serve? By what standards should it be judged? For instance, should a college newspaper limit itself to articles and editorials dealing only with campus events, issues, and personalities, or should it also deal with national and international news? Or, again, are certain responsibilities and duties rightly to be expected of a college paper because on most campuses it has no competitor?

Do not write merely a series of answers to these questions. They are intended to help you think about the problem. After you have done your thinking and planning, write an essay that will have a beginning, a middle, and an end, in which the parts will be linked by some principle of progression. Reserve time toward the close of the examination for proofreading what you have written. Write on every other line of the essay booklet so you can make corrections and insertions neatly and legibly.

In preparation for the following essay, the student is given a series of brief articles which deal with various aspects of the subject. Here the student is given relatively detailed specifications for the paper, with some suggestions of the criteria to be used in judging it. Note in point 7 the provisions for objectivity and the attempt to encourage the student to use wide latitude in expressing opinions.

2. *Directions:* Write a unified paper on some restricted aspect of the question of the future of private property in America. The paper may be either an argument in support of some form of ownership which you favor, or an attack upon some form which you oppose, or both. It must, however, observe the following stipulations [1–7 below]:

   (1) It must include a discussion of the *moral bases* and *social effects* of the kind of ownership which you favor or wish to attack. For example, what ultimate right has anyone to claim anything as his own? What should he be allowed to do with what he owns? How should such rights be achieved, or protected, or limited? What will be the effects on society of the policies which you discuss?

   (2) It must relate to your thesis the arguments pro and con . . . the *passages* distributed before the examination which are relevant to your position. It must not merely report what these passages said in

the order in which they were printed. In the course of developing your own position you must make use of the arguments which support it and refute the arguments which oppose it.

(3) It must show some *application* of your theoretical position to one or more examples of property rights drawn from your own experience, observation, or reading. The following examples may suggest possibilities: private property in the family, or in the dormitory; rented, owned, and cooperative housing; public and private schools; independent, chain, and cooperative stores; making the university bookstore a cooperative; municipal ownership of utilities and transportation; nationalization of banks, coal mines, railroads, and communications; national developments such as TVA; the rights of capital, management, labor, and consumers in the control of large corporations, etc.

(4) In form, the paper must be an *argument*. It must not be a mere assertion of your opinions supported by a description of the practices which you favor. It must give reasons for the position which you favor and against the positions which you oppose. The reasoning must be logical, but it need not make explicit reference to logical forms.

(5) The argument should be clear, interesting, and acceptable to the *audience* to which it is addressed. In a preliminary paragraph, separate from the rest of the paper, describe briefly the traits of your audience which you intend to keep in mind while writing your paper.

(6) The paper must be effectively organized and well written. It must not follow the points given above as a writing outline. It must not ignore them, however. Students are expected to deal with the assignment.

(7) The nature of the opinions expressed in this paper will have no effect on grades, and will never be revealed. Papers will be read only by members of the English 3 staff, and only after the names of the writers have been removed.

In preparation for the following social science problem, the students are provided with several readings relevant to the problem. The "comment" is intended to help them get started as well as to state the problem.

Essay (Suggested time: 2-2½ hours)

3. *Directions:* Read the following comment on Selections I and II of the Reading Materials and answer the question based on them.

Comment: "Each of the three statements—of a leading American policy planner, of Britain's (1951) Foreign Secretary, and of one of the Soviet Union's official newspapers—claims to prescribe indispensable conditions for the achievement of peace. But no one of the statements really deals with the crucial factors which underlie the conflict between East and West. No one of them indicates the fundamental policies, both domestic and foreign, which are necessary to achieve peace."

Question: Do you agree or disagree with this Comment? In defending your answer, make clear your own view of the indispensable conditions, both within and between nations, of lasting peace, and describe and defend a major line of policy which the United States might now employ.

[Your essay will be judged *not* in terms of the particular view which you accept but in terms of the thoughtfulness and consistency of your essay as a whole, and the adequacy of the information which you bring to bear upon the issues with which you deal. Refer, when appropriate, to authors read in the Social Sciences 3 Course, but do not use such references as a substitute for presenting your own consistent, coherent point of view.]

The next example is an interesting problem in that the student is provided with both the words and the music during the examination and must now relate them. However, this is a relatively restricted synthesis problem with very little freedom for the student to develop a unique communication.

Essay (40 minutes)

4. Write an essay in which you consider the relationship between words and music in the song "Orpheus with His Lute" by Sir Arthur Sullivan. The text and the vocal line of the song are printed on Music Plate XIX. The text is taken from Act III, Scene I, of *King Henry the Eighth.* The song will be played once as you begin work on this essay, and twice more thereafter, at ten-minute intervals.

It is recommended that you first spend about ten minutes of the time alloted to this essay in planning your remarks.

Although the text is printed on the music plate, it may be useful for you to see how it appears when printed as verse.

Orpheus with his lute made trees.
And the mountain tops that freeze
   Bow themselves when he did sing.

To his music plants and flowers
Ever sprung, as sun and showers
   There had made a lasting spring.
Every thing that heard him play,
Even the billows of the sea,
   Hung their heads, and then lay by,
In sweet music is such art,
Killing care and grief of heart
   Fall asleep, or hearing die.

Art products are especially good examples of unique communications. In the following three examples, explicit criteria are set for the task (Wilson, 1971, p.551):

5. *Directions:* Using a full size of 14-inch by 20-inch paper plan a composition to be rendered in watercolor, tempera, or a combination of some other media. Select one of the following titles for your composition:
   a. "Ocean Bathers"
   b. "Metamorphosis"
   c. "Building Site"
   Write the name of the title you have selected in the upper right-hand corner of your composition. Your work will be judged for:
   1. creation of a mood
   2. the quality and originality of the composition
   3. expressive handling of media.

6. *Directions:* Artists have often rearranged elements from the way they appeared in nature to suit the purpose of the particular work of art they were producing. The photograph of a landscape before you is just as it appears in nature. Your task is to rearrange the landscape so that the composition forms a concentric pattern. (Medium: pencil on paper; time: one hour.)

7. *Directions:* Make a tempera painting of a single figure. The painting is to have a mood or feeling of turbulence. The feeling should result from the attitude of the figure, from the use of colors, textures, lines, and shapes, and from the composition of the painting. (One hour.)

Test Problems for Synthesis B: Production of a Plan or Proposed Set of Operations

In this type of synthesis, the student is to develop a plan or propose some procedures for dealing with a task or problem. The plan or proposed set of operations should, in the view of the student, meet the requirements of the task, provide for the specifications or data to be taken into account, and satisfy the standards and criteria generally accepted in the subject field. It is important to remember that the student is not actually executing the plan, but only making the plan or proposing the operations necessary.

In the next three illustrations the student is not required to make his or her own synthesis—only to judge particular details of a proposed set of operations. The value of this test form is that it can sample a variety of details in a brief amount of time. However, these would be clearer illustrations of synthesis if the student were asked to propose the hypotheses and state how he or she would test them.

8. *Facts:* Gases X and Y react readily when mixed in a glass flask. If, however, just before the gases are introduced, the flask is heated strongly and cooled, no reaction takes place. If a copper container is used, no reaction occurs.
   Directions: Consider each hypothesis below in the light of the facts above. If the hypothesis is untenable or is not stated in a way that could be tested experimentally, blacken answer space A. Otherwise choose the experiment which will best test the hypothesis and blacken the corresponding answer space.
   (1) Water is a *necessary* participant in the reaction.
      A. Hypothesis is not tenable or cannot be tested experimentally.
      B. Dry the flask without heating it before introducing the gases.
      C. Leave the flask open after mixing the gases.
      D. Moisten the walls of the copper container before introducing the gases.
      E. Heat the glass flask strongly, allow it to cool, and leave it open for several days before introducing the gases.
   (2) When glass is present, molecules are absorbed in the glass in such a way that their active portions project inward.
      A. Hypothesis is not tenable or cannot be tested experimentally.
      B. Fill the container with broken glass and note any change in the rate of reaction.
      C. Dry the flask without heating it before introducing the gases.
      D. Cover the interior of the flask with paraffin.
      E. Examine the inside walls of the container with a microscope during the reaction.

(3) Copper forms a stable compound with the gas X and prevents reaction with the other gas.
   A. Hypothesis is not tenable or cannot be tested experimentally.
   B. Analyze the interior surface of the copper container.
   C. Increase the gas concentration of gas X in a glass flask and note whether the rate finally reaches a constant limiting value.
   D. Moisten the walls of the copper container before introducing the gases.
(4) The reaction takes place by a simple collision of X and Y in the body of the gas.
   A. Hypothesis is not tenable or cannot be tested experimentally.
   B. Fill the container with broken glass and note any change in the rate of reaction.
   C. Carry out the reaction with gases X and Y dissolved in water.
   D. Cover the interior of the flask with paraffin.
   E. Increase the gas concentrations of gas X in a glass flask and note whether the rate finally reaches a constant limiting value.

9. A measurement is to be made of the heat evolved in the complete combustion of a certain type of coal. The sample of coal is placed in a thin metal capsule; oxygen is admitted; and the capsule is sealed. The capsule is immersed in water contained in an insulated vessel and the contents are ignited by means of an electric spark. The amount of heat evolved in the capsule is determined from the rise of the temperature of the surrounding water.
Directions: Keeping in mind the purpose of the determination described above, choose the *one* best alternative for each of the following items and *blacken* the corresponding answer space.
(1) The weight of the coal sample
   A. must be known accurately
   B. need only be known approximately, i.e. to about 50%
   C. need not be known, but must at least equal the weight of water
   D. is entirely immaterial
(2) The amount of the water in the vessel
   A. must be known accurately
   B. must be known only well enough to permit addition of water to balance evaporation
   C. is immaterial as long as it covers the capsule completely
   D. is immaterial but should not cover the capsule completely

10. An experiment is being planned to determine the amount of radiation emitted through a 25-square-foot opening in a furnace during a one-minute period. A paper-thin flat sheet of metal one foot square is held in the path of the radiation at a distance of five feet from the opening. Its rise in temperature is measured by means of a thermocouple.
Directions: You are to decide which of the following factors are important in this experiment. For each factor below, *blacken* answer space
A—if the factor must be taken into account before even a rough estimate of the amount of radiation emitted can be made
B—if the factor need be taken into account only if a fairly accurate estimate is to be made
C—if the factor is not likely to affect the estimate to any measurable degree
(1) The shape of the metal sheet
(2) The angle at which it is held relative to the opening
(3) Whether the surface of the metal is blackened or shiny
(4) The temperature of the room

Item 11 is another illustration of use of the objective test form to get at the student's ability to propose a plan to solve a problem. In this case it might have been simpler to have the student state his or her own hypotheses and propose experiments for testing them.

11. A hitherto unknown ray has been discovered in the Arctic regions but in spite of diligent investigation no trace has been found elsewhere. On exposure to this ray, salt acquires a considerable charge; the odor of chlorine can be detected in the vicinity. Water, on like treatment, also assumes a powerful charge and becomes quite sour in taste; no other changes are observed.
Directions: In the *first* blank at the left of each of the items below, classify the following hypotheses concerning the nature of the ray as:
A. possibly correct and capable of experimental verification
B. possibly correct but expressed in terms which are not specific enough to lend themselves to experimental verification
C. untenable in the light of the facts given above
Next, for each statement which you have marked "A," select from [the following list] that *one* experiment which is the most direct test of that statement. Place its number in the remaining blank to the right of "A." If no appropriate experiment is listed, write a zero sign (0) in the blank.

List of experiments [for item 11]
(1) Determine whether chlorine can be detected in water after the water has been irradiated.
(2) Pass the ray between charged condenser plates.
(3) Examine the ray with a spectroscope.
(4) Determine the intensity of the ray at different altitudes.
(5) Analyze irradiated salt for traces of hydrogen.
(6) Determine whether the ray will pass through an evacuated space.
(7) Carry out experiments on the ray in the tropics.
(8) Determine whether the ray is attracted toward one of the poles of a magnet.
(9) Determine the direction of the path of the ray.
(10) Determine whether the ray can be focused by means of a lens.
(11) Determine the penetrating power of the ray.
(12) Determine whether interference patterns can be produced on a screen covered with salt crystals.

Hypotheses
___ ___ The ray originates in outer space.
___ ___ The ray is a stream of high velocity sodium ions.
___ ___ The ray contains a transverse wave motion of frequency beyond the ultraviolet.
___ ___ The ray contains a longitudinal (compression) wave motion.
___ ___ The ray is a stream of high velocity protons.
___ ___ The ray is a stream of particles having no mass and no charge.

In the example below the student is provided with relevant readings and is asked to propose a set of foreign policy objectives and principles and to defend them by reference to particular characteristics of the contemporary situation. It is possible that this would be better tested in a term paper or essay written over a more extended period of time. In some ways this synthesis task is as appropriate to subcategory A (unique communication) as it is to subcategory B (production of a plan).

Directions for Essay (Suggested time: 2-2 ½ hours)
12. *Comment:* "It is true that nowadays any program for American domestic policy must take account of the limitations imposed by the present international situation and proper goals with respect to it. But similarly, any proposals with respect to American foreign policy must reckon with their implications for domestic policies, including the limits imposed by current domestic conditions and by the values we seek in our domestic life. Regarded either individually or collec-

tively, the proposals of Lippmann, Stevenson, and Eisenhower do not take adequate account of the second half of this circle."

In terms of the above comment write an essay on American foreign policy. In the course of your essay, describe the principles which, in your view, should guide current policy; describe and defend the objectives which current policy should seek and the particular policies which should be followed (in case of doubt, intensive treatment of a limited policy problem, the broader ramifications of which have been made clear, is preferable to a broader, but superficial coverage of policies); and make it clear which characteristics of the contemporary domestic and international situation you regard as important to the justification of your policy proposals.

Your essay will be judged not on the basis of the particular view you adopt but on the basis of its thoughtfulness and consistency as a whole, the adequacy of the information and analytical skill which you bring to bear upon the issues with which you deal, and the appropriateness with which you organize what you have to say. When appropriate, refer to authors read in the Social Sciences 3 Course, but do not use such references as a substitute for presenting clearly your own point of view.

Test Problems for Synthesis C: Derivation of a Set of Abstract Relations

The student is to produce a set of hypotheses or explanations to account for given phenomena; to create a classification scheme, explanatory model, conceptual scheme, or theory to account for a range of phenomena, data, and observations; or to determine the logical statements and hypotheses which can be deduced from a theory, set of propositions, or set of abstract relations. The student's work must meet the requirements of the phenomena and the logical possibilities inherent in the relationships among the phenomena or propositions.

In items 13 and 14 the student is to develop a set of hypotheses to account for phenomena and findings in a series of experiments.

13. A physiologist found that:
(1) Even with all nerves to the pancreas cut, pancreatic enzymes were secreted when food entered the intestine.
(2) When a wash from a piece of small intestine from

an unfed dog was injected into the blood of normal animals no pancreatic enzyme secretion occurred. When intestinal tissue was first treated with hydrochloric acid, and a wash then made and injected into normal animals, pancreatic enzyme secretion occurred.

(3) Intestinal tissue was first treated with pure starch, fat, and protein. A wash from the treated intestine, when injected into the blood of a normal unfed animal, resulted in no pancreatic stimulation.

(4) Injection of hydrochloric acid alone into the blood of normal animals did not stimulate pancreatic secretion.

(5) The stomach of normal animals secretes hydrochloric acid.

From these facts, the physiologist formed the tentative hypothesis that pancreatic secretion is stimulated by a hormone produced by the small intestine; the presence of hydrochloric acid is the necessary and sufficient condition under which the small intestine will secrete its pancreas-stimulating hormone.

He then performed another experiment, as follows:

The stomach was removed from a number of animals and the esophagus connected directly to the small intestine. From such animals he discovered four additional facts.

(6) When the animal was fed a meal consisting of starch, pure fat, and pure protein, pancreatic enzyme secretion, though delayed, nevertheless occurred.

(7) Blood taken from such animals 1 hour after they were fed a diet of pure starch, pure fat, and pure protein, would, when injected into normal animals, stimulate a flow of pancreatic juice.

(8) Blood taken from such animals after 24 hours without food did not stimulate secretion of pancreatic juice when injected into normal animals.

(9) In such stomach-less animals, the duct from pancreas to small intestine was tied off. After recovery, the animals were given a meal of pure protein, pure fat, and pure starch. One hour later the contents of the small intestine were removed and found to contain not only the pure foods previously ingested, but also small amounts of the digestion-products of protein, fat, and starch.

In the light of these new data carefully devise and state a refined and expanded hypothesis concerning stimulation of pancreatic enzyme secretion. Be sure that your answer (1) corrects any statements in the tentative hypothesis which the new data indicate to have been false or overstated; (2) accounts for stimulation of pancreatic secretion in *normal* animals; (3) accounts for all cases of pancreatic stimulation in the experimental animals above.

14. A physiologist found that:
    (1) bile salts break up fats into fine droplets:
    (2) the lymph leaving the small intestine contains fine droplets of fats:
    (3) the absorbing cells of the intestine contain small fat droplets.

From these facts, the physiologist formed the tentative hypothesis that: fats are emulsified by the bile salts and are absorbed and carried away from the intestine in this form.

He then found in addition that:
    (4) in the absence of pancreatic juice, no fat is absorbed from the intestine (even when the fat has been emulsified by bile);
    (5) pancreatic juice transforms fats into glycerol and fatty acids;
    (6) careful examination of the absorbing cells of the intestine showed that there were no fat droplets in that part of each absorbing cell that projects into the intestine, but that the fat droplets were confined to that portion of each absorbing cell farthest from the cavity of the intestine.

Carefully devise and state a refined and expanded hypothesis concerning the digestion and absorption of fat. Explain clearly the successive steps necessary to account for all the facts presented above.

In the next example the student is expected to take more and more data and observations into consideration as the experiments proceed. The student's hypotheses and explanations are to account for an increasingly complex set of results.

15. The experiments described below have actually been performed, with the results which are given. They are basic to the theories which have been proposed to account for the manner in which cells accomplish chemical transformations which either do not occur spontaneously or occur spontaneously at extremely slow rates.

In answering the questions following these experiments, you are to use the evidence given by the experiments themselves, interpreting these as nearly as possible in the terms considered appropriate by cell physiologists such as Potter and Dixon.

To understand the methods employed in these experiments, you will need the following preliminary information.

Information: Methylene blue is a synthetic dye whose blue color disappears when its solution is treated with a mild reducing agent. Hydrogen gas itself does not decolorize methylene blue solution. When reduced methylene blue solution is shaken with air or oxygen gas, the solution absorbs oxygen and becomes blue again. The absorbed oxygen has combined with hydrogen from the reduced methylene blue to form water. Thus, methylene blue can act as a hydrogen acceptor in some cases, and, after having received the hydrogen, can yield it to oxygen to form water.

Note: Many of the necessary technical details in these experiments have been omitted from the descriptions. One such detail is that the mixtures for the experiments are made up with neutral buffer substances which keep the mixtures neutral even though an acid or a base is added in reasonable amounts.

Experiment A: Methylene blue solution was placed in a closed flask filled with helium, an inert gas. *Lactic acid* solution was added to the mixture without opening the flask. No color change was observed. Analysis of a sample showed that the lactic acid was still present.

Experiment B: A living frog was decapitated. One of its larger leg muscles was finely chopped, washed in several changes of physiological salt solution. The washed muscle was mixed with a methylene blue solution in helium gas as in *A*. No color change was observed.

Experiment C: The mixture from *A* was added to the flask in *B*. The blue color disappeared and analysis showed much less lactic acid than had been used in *A*.

Experiment D: When a similar muscle was heated to the boiling temperature before chopping, no change occurred and no lactic acid disappeared, in a test situation such as in *C*.

(1) What kind of atoms were probably added to or removed from the lactic acid?

(2) Use your knowledge of living tissues to invent an explanation for the difference between the results in *A, B, C,* and *D*.

Experiment E: Minced fresh frog muscle was washed in physiological salt solution *much longer* than in Experiment *B*. Then, Experiment *C* was repeated, using the more thoroughly washed muscle tissue. On this occasion the muscle produced almost no change in the color of methylene blue or in the quantity of lactic acid.

Experiment F: Juice from cooked minced frog muscle was added to the mixture from *E*. The methylene blue color now disappeared and the quantity of lactic acid was greatly lessened.

(3) In the light of your knowledge of cell chemistry, what hypothesis or modification of your earlier hypothesis would best explain the results in *E* and *F*?

Experiment G: Experiments *A* through *D* were repeated, using *succinic acid* instead of lactic acid. The results obtained were similar.

Experiment H: A solution of succinic acid and methylene blue was placed in a closed flask, the space above the solution being filled with *oxygen* gas. The flask was attached to an apparatus arranged to measure changes in gas volume. During a period of an hour, no oxygen was used, no succinic acid had disappeared, and the color remained blue.

Experiment I: Fresh, chopped frog muscle was prepared *as in B*, except that no methylene blue solution was used. The mixture was placed in a flask such as was used in *H*, the space above the mixture being filled with oxygen. During a period of an hour, very little oxygen was used.

Experiment J: Succinic acid solution (with no methylene blue) was added to the mixture in *I*. At once, oxygen began to disappear relatively rapidly and continued until practically all the succinic acid had been used.

(4) What hypothesis or hypotheses would satisfactorily explain these results?

In the example below, the student is given more freedom to develop and illustrate a simple theory about the social changes that might take place.

Social Sciences Essay

16. Imagine that you are able to travel into the future and study the culture of the United States two thousand years from now. You find that at that time the majority of positions of influence and honor are filled by women. When you question people, they tell you that intelligence, kindness, and a respect for creative work are the ideal human attributes and that women, by nature, excel men in these matters. Write an essay in which you describe what other significant social changes might accompany the change described above.

EVALUATION

"Evaluation is defined as the making of judgments about the value, for some purpose, of ideas, works, solutions, methods, material, etc. It involves the use of criteria as well as standards for appraising the extent to which particulars are accurate, effective, economical, or satisfying. The judgments may be either quantitative or qualitative, and the criteria may be either those determined by the student or those which are given to him" (Bloom, 1956, p. 185).

Judgments such as "good-bad," "like-dislike," and "desirable-undesirable" are constantly being made by all of us. We have difficulty refraining from making a judgment about anything that comes within our view, whether it is a person, a thing, an idea, or a situation.

Many of these judgments are expressions of taste, whim, convention, or habit—"I like this," "I don't like that," "I have always liked this type of music," and so on. While such expressions of personal taste and feeling are real and important to the one making them, they are not illustrations of the types of evaluation found in educational objectives. Judgments which are primarily dictated by taste and habit are relatively simple; they are rarely examined; they are private; and they are rarely based on criteria and standards which can be made explicit.

In contrast, the types of evaluation found in educational objectives appear to us to be among the most complex cognitive behaviors. In the *Taxonomy of Educational Objectives* (Bloom, 1956), *Evaluation* is placed as the last category of objectives. Implicit in this placement of evaluation in the cognitive domain is the assumption that objectives in this category require some competence in all the previous categories—*Knowledge, Comprehension, Application, Analysis*, and *Synthesis*. Evaluation, however, goes beyond these in that the student is presumably required to make judgments about something he or she knows, analyzes, synthesizes, and so forth, on the basis of criteria which can be made explicit.

Educational objectives involving evaluation, as defined in the *Taxonomy,* are found mainly at the secondary school and higher education levels. This type of informed judgment is likely to be so complex that teachers and curriculum makers include it relatively late in the education process. Perhaps it is so difficult to teach because it requires a temporary suspension of one's own quick judgment about something (for example, a work of art or a social policy) while one systematically appraises it by means of explicit and relatively complex criteria.

In spite of its complexity, evaluation appears to be one of the most important categories of educational objectives in our society. Increasingly, the citizen in a democracy is called upon to participate in making evaluations of social policies, political decisions, and governmental actions. Problems of pollution, war and peace, and urban conditions are so complex that the citizen must be exceedingly well informed in order to participate meaningfully in the appraisal and evaluation of past as well as future decisions and actions. Given the increasingly complex and difficult set of problems posed in modern society, it seems evident that evaluation as it has been defined here is most relevant for the education of citizens throughout the world.

So too the nature of music, art, literature, and even the substantive disciplines of the sciences and social sciences places more and more emphasis on evaluation. Rapid changes in the arts, new approaches to the sciences and the social sciences, and rapid communication about these developments require that a person be able to suspend judgment about the new while making appropriate analyses and evaluations of it. To reject the new and different because it is new and different is to reject the opportunity of participating in the modern world. On the other hand, to accept the new and different because it is the current fad and fashion is not adaptive either. Thus, we are expressing the view that the development of adequate evaluative behavior is especially required for a person's well-being in a rapidly changing society where

Judging by internal standards, the ability to assess general probability of accuracy in reporting facts from the care given to exactness of statement, documentation, proof, etc. (1, p. 189).

The ability to apply given criteria (based on internal standards) to the judgment of the work (1, p. 189).

The ability to recognize the accuracy, completeness and relevance of data (2, p. 17).

The ability to distinguish between valid and invalid inferences, generalizations, arguments, judgments, and implications (2, p. 17).

The ability to verify the accuracy of the computations and check the validity of the inferences by examining the logic of the inductive or deductive proof [mathematics] (2, p. 48).

[The ability] to determine if the data, method of inquiry, and argument support the conclusions (2, p. 53).

[The ability] to evaluate a proposition about natural phenomena; to recognize the accuracy and reliability of the observations warranted by the nature of the problem, the chosen procedure, and the instruments used (2, p. 53).

[The ability to] recognize bias and emotional factors in a presentation and in his own thinking (3, p. 101).

The ability to distinguish between valid and invalid arguments and conclusions; recognizing adequacy, completeness and relevance of data; recognizing misrepresentation of data, partial truths, and incompleteness in over-all treatment of an issue (2, p. 29).

The student will be able to recognize gaps, contradictions, and redundance in a given set of postulates and to detect fallacies in mathematical arguments (4, p. 254).

---

[1] Bloom, 1956.

[2] Tyler, 1954.

[3] French, 1957.

[4] University Grants Commission, 1961.

Figure 10-4 Statements of objectives for *Judgments in terms of internal evidence.*

new choices, decisions, and consequences are ever present. Effective participation in a rapidly changing society continually requires evaluative behaviors of a very high order.

In Figures 10-4 and 10-5 we list objectives which may be classified under the general taxonomy category of *Evaluation*. We again distinguish among these objectives according to the evaluation subcategories of the *Taxonomy of Educational Objectives* (Bloom, 1956).

In Figure 10-4 are some evaluation objectives which emphasize *Judgments in terms of internal evidence*. These are primarily concerned with judgments of the accuracy of a communication from such evidence as logical accuracy and consistency.

Figure 10-5 (see page 278) presents some evaluation objectives which emphasize *Judgments in terms of external criteria*. They primarily entail evaluation of materials, objects, and policies by reference to selected criteria. These may be criteria developed by the student, criteria in the form of other related works, or standards and criteria formulated by specialists in the relevant fields.

It will be seen from the two lists of objectives in these figures that they all involve some *ability to evaluate* works, policies, or situations, among other things. It can be inferred from these statements that the ability or skill is to be used on *new problems, materials, or situations* and that the adequacy of the student's evaluation is to be judged

The ability to apply self-developed [aesthetic] standards to the choice and use of the ordinary objects of the everyday environment (1, p. 192).

The ability to recognize artistic quality in contemporary works of music and art (2, p. 45).

[The ability to] distinguish between art objects which represent good design, line, color, and texture and those which do not (3, p. 111).

The ability to judge the overall literary quality of the work (4, p. 17).

Judging by external standards, the ability to compare a work with the highest known standards in the field—especially with other works of recognized excellence (1, p. 192).

Skill in recognizing and weighing values involved in alternative courses of action (1, p. 192).

The ability to identify and appraise judgments and values that are involved in the choice of a course of action (1, p. 192).

[The ability] to recognize those instances in which a scientific finding supports or is in conflict with doctrines explaining the constitution and processes of the physical world (4, p. 55).

[The ability] to evaluate a proposition about natural phenomena (4, p. 53).

The comparison of major theories, generalizations, and facts about particular cultures (1, p. 192).

The ability to evaluate the adequacy of the solution reached for the settlement of the original problematic situation [mathematics] (4, p. 48).

The student will develop the ability to critically assess traditional beliefs, institutions, and behavior patterns in relation to the functions of the state (5, p. 95).

The student will develop the ability . . . to formulate judgments [about controversial political problems] (5, p. 95).

The student will develop the ability to . . . evaluate current developments in politics at the national and international level (5, p. 95).

[Develops the ability to] evaluate his community government in terms of its contribution to the quality of living for families who reside there: protection, cultural stimulation, educational and recreational opportunities (3, p. 179).

---

1 Bloom, 1956.

2 American Council on Education Studies, 1944.

3 French, 1957.

4 Tyler, 1954.

5 University Grants Commission, 1961.

Figure 10-5 Statements of objectives for *Judgments in terms of external criteria.*

against the ability of some expert or experts to make a similar evaluation with the same material or against an expert judgment about the adequacy of the criteria used and the process by which the evaluation has been made. The phrases "new problems, materials, or situations" and "ability to evaluate" are further developed in the following discussion.

New Problems, Materials, or Situations

It is obvious that evaluations made by the students should be related to new works not treated this way in the classroom. Otherwise the evaluations would represent little more than memory or knowledge of evaluations already made by the students or the teacher in the learning situation. By "new" we mean material which is new to the student or which is unlikely to have been evaluated in the same way by or for the student previously.

No simple rule can be given for the selection of new material for evaluation. One might expect that the new material, problems, and so forth might be similar to those evaluated in the learning situation in terms of difficulty or complexity.

Ideally the new material should be real in that it is selected from works, documents, situations, or other sources that already exist rather than be expressly developed for the evaluation problems. As we have pointed out previously, students are likely to find real evaluation problems more interesting than obviously contrived ones. The type of material to be evaluated is in large part dictated by the statement of the objective (see Figures 10-4 and 10-5) and by the particular behaviors deemed relevant.

Ability to Evaluate

The ability to evaluate or judge works or other givens is a complex set of skills and behaviors which the student is expected to learn through practice with a variety of works and problems. While the ability is dependent on the student's acquisition of prior types of learning—knowledge, comprehension, application, analysis, and synthesis—it includes in addition specific behaviors involving judgments and evaluation.

In terms of students' behaviors, evaluation includes the following:

The student can make judgments of a document or work in terms of the accuracy, precision, and care with which it has been made (internal accuracy; A).

The student can make judgments of a document or work in terms of the consistency of the arguments; the relations among assumptions, evidence, and conclusions; and the internal consistency of the logic and organization (internal consistency; B).

The student can recognize the values and points of view used in a particular judgment of a work (internal criteria; C).

The student can make judgments of a work by comparing it with other relevant works (external criteria; D).

The student can make judgments of a work by using a given set of criteria or standards (external criteria; E).

The student can make judgments of a work by using his or her own explicit set of criteria or standards (external criteria; F).

TESTING FOR EVALUATION

It is possible to determine the requirements for making evaluation test problems from the foregoing analyses of behaviors and situations.

Some of the requirements are:

1. The problem situation, document, work, or material to be evaluated must be new, unfamiliar, or in some way different from those used in instruction.
2. The new problem situation, work, or other matter should be available to the students as they make the evaluation, and they should be able to refer to it as they attempt to answer the evaluative questions or problems posed by the evaluator (or themselves).
3. One or more of the behaviors listed in the foregoing subsection, "Ability to Evaluate," should be sampled in the test situation.
4. The adequacy of a particular evaluation should be determined by a comparison of it with that made by competent experts in the field or by a judgment on the adequacy with which a particular evaluation is explained, argued, or defended.

In the following sections we will attempt to illustrate some of the testing procedures which have been used to appraise evaluative abilities. The illustrations will be grouped under the six types of behavior listed above, since these behaviors provide a useful way of making clear what the test problem is attempting to do and furnish a rough scale of complexity of the evaluative tasks. The test illustrations will be of both the objective and the essay form. In some ways it does seem that the essay form is superior to the recognition forms for testing evaluation. However, for purposes of illustrating the behaviors being tested, the objective form is simpler and somewhat clearer because it provides both the questions and the possible answers. It would take too much space to indicate the possible answers or scoring procedures for the essay problems.

The examples are drawn from the files of the Examiner's Office of the University of Chicago because of the care with which these test materials were constructed and because of the great variety of illustrations available in these files.

Test Problems for Evaluation Behavior A

The student can make judgments of a document or work in terms of the accuracy, precision, and care with which it has been made (internal accuracy; A).

This is the simplest type of evaluation, calling on the student to recognize the extent to which particular details of a document or work are accurate, precise, or carefully done. While this behavior does resemble some aspects of knowledge, comprehension, and analysis, these illustrations should emphasize not only the recognition of accuracy (or inaccuracy) in details but also a judgment on the adequacy of the work in terms of its internal accuracy. (We have provided only a single illustration of this behavior because we believe that there should be little difficulty in constructing tests for this type of evaluation.)

17. Two investigators, Smith and Jones, after studying the foregoing data, tested their conclusions in the laboratory.

Investigator Smith collected eggs from lake H and performed the following experiment: He distributed the eggs equally into each of 10 tanks which were known to be identical in all respects except temperature. Each tank was held at a *different, constant* temperature in a range of 5°C to 30°C. He recorded the number of fin-rays of the fish which developed in each tank.

Investigator Jones performed a series of six experiments. Each experiment was just like that one experiment performed by investigator Smith, but in this case the eggs for
experiment 1 were taken from lake L,
experiment 2 were taken from lake I,
experiment 3 were taken from lake G,
experiment 4 were taken from lake H,
experiment 5 were taken from lake B,
experiment 6 were taken from lake A.
Now state explicitly what biological factor is uncontrolled in Smith's experiment, but well-sampled by those of Jones.

In this illustration the student is to determine the features of the experiments which make one investigation more accurate and valid than the other.

Test Problems for Evaluation Behavior B

The student can make judgments of a document or work in terms of the consistency of the arguments; the relations among assumptions, evidence, and conclusions; and the internal consistency of the logic and organization (internal consistency; B).

This type of behavior requires the student to recognize the ways in which the details and parts of a work fit together in terms of consistency, order, and organization. The student must recognize the internal consistency of a work, the parts and details which are not consistent, and the ways in which the parts relate to each other. While the emphasis in this behavior is primarily on specific details and their internal logic, it is also expected that the student will make some final judgment about the work in terms of consistency among these details.

It is clear that in the tests for this behavior, the students will need to have the document or work available to them as they make the necessary distinctions and judgments. Only rarely can the student be expected to make such judgments on the basis of memory of the work.

In the next illustrations the student is judging the relations between parts of an argument or between a conclusion and evidence. While the problem may be new to the student, it is likely that some aspects of it have been previously learned. These would be clearer illustrations of evaluation if the detailed judgments were followed by some overall judgment about the theory or situation. These illustrations overlap considerably with some that we have considered under the category of analysis. However, the emphasis here is on the validity and consistency of the details and parts.

18. *Directions:* A dissolved substance lowers the freezing point of the solvent because of a mechanical hindrance offered by solute molecules to the process of the assumption of regular lattice arrangement by the solvent molecules during crystal formation. The lowering of the freezing point is a linear function of the hindrance, that is, of the concentration of solute molecules only. Mark each of the following factors as

A—if the factor is *not* likely to interfere with accurate applicability of the theory

B—if the factor is such that the theory is applicable if great accuracy is unimportant

C—if the factor makes the theory not applicable

D—if the information given is not sufficient to decide between A, B, and C

(1) The dissolved substance has a very small vapor pressure.

(2) The dissolved substance consists of charged particles.

(3) The substance has a great tendency to unite chemically with the solvent.

(4) The crystal lattice formed upon freezing contains alternating solute and solvent molecules.

(5) The solution is concentrated.

(6) The atmospheric pressure varies from one determination to the next.

19. The existence of complexly folded rock strata can be used as evidence for a shrinking earth

A. provided this fact is supplemented by evidence that compensating tensions have not existed in other regions.

B. provided the rock folds are in a general north-south direction.

C. provided similarly folded rock strata can be found at great depth, i.e., over 100 miles.

D. provided one assumes that the earth is undergoing a cooling process

E. without reservations; folding must always result in a surface shortening.

In item 20 the student is to judge consistency or lack of consistency between pairs of statements and the basis on which the two statements may be related to each other.

20. *Directions:* Following is a series of pairs of propositions dealing with a single topic. In the case of each pair of propositions, you are to locate the source of their 'opposition,' real or apparent, by *blackening* the letter of the completion which best accounts for it. You will need, of course, to consider the context of each quotation as it appeared in your readings.

(1) (a) "Scientific discovery must ever depend upon some happy thought, of which we cannot trace the origin; in some fortunate cast of intellect, rising above all rules."

(b) "For my way of discovering the sciences goes far to level men's wits, and leaves but little to individual excellence."

The 'opposition' between these two statements is

A. merely verbal.

B. ascribable to the fact that while (a) refers to 'scientific discovery,' (b) refers to 'discovering sciences.'

C. ascribable to the fact that (a) has to do with induction, whereas (b) is concerned with deduction.

D. ascribable to different underlying notions of the relation between data and ideas.

E. ascribable to different underlying notions of the relation between observation and experiment.

(2) (a) "In any other case, it is no evidence of the truth of the hypothesis that we are able to deduce the phenomena from it."

(b) "The doctrine which is the *hypothesis* of the deductive reasoning, is the *inference* of the inductive process. . . . And in this manner the deduction establishes the induction. The principle which we gather from the facts is true, because the facts can be derived from it by rigorous demonstration."

The 'opposition' between these two statements is

A. merely verbal.

B. ascribable to the distinction implied in (a) between 'phenomena' and 'causes.'

C. ascribable to different underlying conceptions of the relation between sense and intellect.

D. ascribable to different underlying conceptions of the relation between deductive truths and prediction of unobserved cases.

E. ascribable to different underlying conceptions of the nature and role of proof in 'the science of discovery.'

281

(3) (a) "Human beings in society have no properties but those which are derived from, and may be resolved into, the laws of the nature of individual men."

(b) "Thus the great movements of enthusiasm, indignation, and pity in a crowd do not originate in any one of the individual consciousnesses."

The 'opposition' between these two statements

A. is merely verbal.

B. implies opposing conceptions of the psychology of individual men.

C. is ascribable to the inclusion of the 'social phenomena' cited in (b) within the scope of the 'laws of the nature of individual men' cited in (a).

D. is ascribable to the difference between the 'nature' of (a) and the 'consciousnesses' of (b).

E. expresses opposing attitudes toward Mill's conception of the 'Chemical' method in the social sciences.

The primary task in the next illustration is to determine the consistency between arguments and selected policies. Again, it would be a clearer evaluation problem if there were a final question on the soundness of the two policies in terms of the arguments presented.

21. Early in 1951, the public became aware that the Federal Reserve authorities and the Treasury had for some time been in conflict regarding the proper open market policy of the Federal Reserve Banks and regarding the proper related "debt management" policy to be pursued by the U. S. Treasury. The Federal Reserve authorities have insisted that the Treasury's "pressure" on them to buy government securities has interfered with their aims of counteracting credit expansion. Treasury officials, supported by other high government officials, in turn have charged the Federal Reserve system with attempting to sabotage the Treasury's debt-management policy; i.e., the policy of keeping the market price for government bonds stable and the interest rate on the public debt relatively constant at the low level of about 2½%. The Treasury stresses this point in view of the imminent need to refund a large amount of maturing bond issues.

Directions: For each of the following items, you are asked to decide whether

A. the argument tends to support the Treasury's policy;

B. the argument tends to support the Federal Reserve authorities' policy;

C. the argument is likely to be accepted by both participants in the struggle and does not support either side in the issue at stake more than the other;

D. the argument is likely to be rejected by both groups in the struggle.

Note: Give only the *one best* answer.

(1) Holding down the yields and supporting the prices of government bonds keeps down interest payments on the federal debt; this is particularly important in a period in which tax revenue is urgently needed for armaments.

(2) If we fight inflation largely by price controls, we will curtail freedom and efficiency. If we rely primarily on sharp tax increases, we will find that they are politically unobtainable, or if attained, would produce undesirable economic effects. We must not confine ourselves to these strategies.

(3) The maintenance of government security prices at a constant level is desirable because it protects investors, including commercial banks, against depreciation of their investments.

(4) If the policy of maintaining stable prices of government bonds contributes significantly to the continuation of an inflationary process, such a policy will not be in the interest of actual or prospective bondholders. They will tend to consider the decrease in the *real* purchasing power of their principal and interest earnings more important than the maintenance of the dollar bond price.

(5) An increase in the level of interest rates, though fairly ineffective as a direct anti-inflationary measure, might have a negative effect on productive investment, especially in durable capital goods.

Test Problems for Evaluation Behavior C

The student can recognize the values and points of view used in a particular judgment of a work (internal criteria; C).

Here the student is not expected to make a judgment but rather is to identify the values, points of view, and assumptions on which the judgments given are based. Again, the behavior must be regarded as only one aspect of a more complex behavior—the final process of judgment. We place it here primarily because it appears to be one step toward the more complex behaviors D, E, and F. It is likely that students who can demonstrate this behavior can also recognize the values they use to make an evaluative judgment.

In the following example, the student is provided with brief evaluative statements and is to determine the point of view or assumptions on which they could be based. It is clear that this type of test item could be used in many subject fields besides science.

22. (1) The statement is often made, "Physics and chemistry are basic sciences; astronomy and geology are derived sciences." Which of the following is the best interpretation of the statement?

A. Physics and chemistry rest on a sound foundation of proven laws; much of astronomy and geology is pure speculation.

B. The development of astronomy and geology necessitates the use of physics and chemistry; the converse is not true.

C. The entire subject matter of astronomy and geology could have been derived by using the laws and methods of physics and chemistry.

D. Physics and chemistry are of more basic importance to human activity than are astronomy and geology.

E. It is possible to carry out laboratory experiments in physics and chemistry but not in astronomy or geology.

(2) Which of the following best interprets and clarifies the statement: "Geology for the most part is an observational science rather than an experimental science?"

A. The phenomena of geology are usually too vast in time and scale for investigation under controlled conditions.

B. It is impossible to investigate geological phenomena in the laboratory.

C. An open mind can better be retained by observing nature as it is than as it performs under artificial conditions.

D. As long as geological processes are easily visible, it is unnecessary to carry out experiments.

E. The statement is based on the erroneous distinction between direct evidence such as that obtained through our senses and inference obtained by reasoning from facts; the statement is self-contradictory.

The poem "The Revenge" is available to the students as they answer these next questions. The questions are intended to determine whether the student recognizes the point of view or type of detail on which the critical remarks are based.

23. The following questions are based on Tennyson's narrative poem "The Revenge," which was printed in full in the original examination.

Directions: The following sentences are characteristic of the kinds of critical remarks people make about literary works. Read each statement carefully and mark in the space at the LEFT:

(1) if the statement concerns the relation of the author to his work;

(2) if the statement concerns the organization of the poem as a relationship of parts to the whole;

(3) if the statement concerns the relationship between historical events and events treated in the poem;

(4) if the statement is an evaluation made by the reader in terms of his own ideas;

(5) if the statement is concerned with the classification of poems or with their metrical form.

____ The history of the ship, Revenge, unifies the poem.

____ Grenville's reputation as a naval commander makes him an appropriate hero for the poem.

____ The poem is written in imitation of the traditional ballad form.

____ The poem is bad because it does not arouse sympathy for the Spanish.

____ The poem was written from the English point of view because Tennyson was an Englishman.

____ Grenville's decision to fight the superior Spanish fleet initiates the actions which follow.

____ The action is improbable because no man with only one ship would fight a fleet of fifty-three.

____ The poem is written in trochaic metre.

____ The Revenge had been commanded by Drake in the fight against the Armada in 1588.

____ Grenville's devotion to "Queen and Faith" explains his actions throughout the poem.

In the next item (item 24) the student, who has studied Hemingway's novel *A Farewell to Arms,* is provided with statements taken from book reviews written by four critics (only two are illustrated here). What the student must do is to recognize the values, points of views, and assumptions made by each of the critics.

The last two questions of item 24—that is, questions (8) and (9)—determine whether the student can extend the critic's points of view to other sets of details about the book.

This is a relatively complex test situation which can be used to get at relatively subtle aspects of evaluation.

24. Two Critics on *A Farewell to Arms*

Directions: The following statements are taken from
. . . book reviews written at the time of the first
publication of *A Farewell to Arms*. . . .

Critic I

In its depiction of war, the novel bears comparison
with its best predecessors. But it is in the hero's
perhaps unethical quitting of the battle line to be with
the woman he has gotten with child that it achieves its
greatest significance. Love is more maligned in literature than any other emotion, by romantic distortion on
the one hand, by carnal diminution on the other. But
Author Hemingway knows it at its best to be a blend of
desire, serenity, and wordless sympathy. His man and
woman stand incoherently together against a shat-
tered, dissolving world. They express their feelings by
such superficially trivial things as a joke, a gesture in
the night, an endearment as trite as "darling." And as
they make their escape from Italy in a rowboat, survey
the Alps from their hillside lodgings, move on to
Lausanne where there are hospitals, gaze at each
other in torment by the deathbed of Catherine, their
tiny shapes on the vast landscape are expressive of the
pity, beauty, and doom of mankind.

Critic II

It is not the plot that counts, it is the circumstance and
the complete realization of the characters. In this book
you get your own times in typical essence to wonder
about and interpret. Yet I do not believe that
Hemingway's strength lies in character creation. His
Catherine and his Henry have nothing strange or novel
in their personalities. Catherine is a fine girl who needs
a lover. Henry is an individualist who acts by instinct
rationalized, not by principle, and makes his friends
love him. Hemingway's art is to make such not
unfamiliar characters articulate when he finds them.
. . . It isn't *what* they are, it is *how* they are that seems
important, and of course that is a true principle in art.
Anyone can outline a psychology, but how many can
give you, whole and self-interpreting, just a darky
crossing the road, or a man nursing his first wound!
Hemingway works almost entirely through a simple
record of incident and dialogue which he stretches to
include mediation in the rhythm of thought. . . . He is
after voice rhythms and voice contrasts. It is the way
these people talk, not what they say, that lifts the
scene into reality.

Directions: [Questions (1) through (9)] are based on
the passages [above]. . . . For [these items] blacken
the answer space corresponding to the *one* best
completion.

(1) Critic I finds the "significance" of the novel to lie
especially in
  A. its account of the psychology of a deserter
  B. its evocation of pity and fear
  C. its representation of the true nature of love
  D. its combination of realistic fatalism and sym-
    bolic beauty

(2) In support of this view, Critic I directs attention to
certain details in the novel. When he describes the
characters' methods of expressing their feelings as
"superficially trivial," one understands that he
must mean that
  A. these "things" are trivial only on the surface
  B. the characters are mediocre and lacking in
    depth
  C. the novelist has been deficient in invention
  D. there is a clear, but unimportant, weakness in
    the direction of the novel

(3) The last sentence of the passage implies that
  A. the human figures are distorted by the roman-
    tic setting of the action
  B. the emotions of the characters, being the
    common experience of all men, are shared by
    the reader
  C. the particulars of the novel stand for universal
    propositions about life
  D. the inevitable consequence of errors in conduct
    is symbolized in the outcome of this action

(4) Consequently, it is apparent that Critic I is judging
the novel primarily as
  A. an imitation of life
  B. an interpretation of life
  C. a means to the end of good conduct
  D. an extension of the reader's experience

(5) Critic II, on the other hand, is judging the novel
primarily as
  A. an imitation of life
  B. an interpretation of life
  C. a source of aesthetic pleasure
  D. an extension of the reader's experience

(6) From what he says about plot, character, and
dialogue, it may be inferred that this critic is
concerned, before judging a novel, with
  A. determining the organizing principle of the
    whole
  B. determining what aspect of reality the writer is
    trying to imitate
  C. analyzing the personalities of the characters
  D. analyzing his own subjective reactions to it

(7) His criteria for judgment, so far as this excerpt
indicates them, are primarily concerned with
  A. the truth and novelty of the subject matter
  B. the complete realism of the diction
  C. the adequacy of execution to conception
  D. the complete convincingness of the imitation

If these two critics analyzed the function of the narrator in *A Farewell to Arms*, each would emphasize, it is assumed in the next two [questions], different points. You are warned to consider in these items, not only whether the completion is *appropriate* to the critic, but also whether it is *accurate* for the novel.

(8) Critic I would emphasize the fact that

A. the apparent incompleteness of emotional expression is accounted for by the character of the narrator and his involvement in the action

B. the apparent incompleteness of emotional expression is accounted for by the limited knowledge available to a narrator-observer

C. the symbolic significance of the action is heightened by the narrator's use of elaborate descriptive details, as in allegory

D. the symbolic significance of the action is brought to the attention of the reader by the narrator's comments on the symbols

(9) Critic II would emphasize the fact that

A. unity is achieved by the use of a single, limited point of view

B. the selection of a central character as narrator almost automatically gives one a "self-interpreting" action

C. the narrator's habit of directly addressing the reader makes the whole action seem more immediate

D. the first-person point of view, if well handled, gives one the most natural view of an action— as it really seems to a particular individual

Test Problems for Evaluation Behaviors D and E

The student can make judgments of a work by comparing it with other relevant works (external criteria; D).

The student can make judgments of a work by using a given set of criteria or standards (external criteria; E).

In both of these behaviors, the student is making judgments about a work by the use of some external criteria—another work, a set of criteria, or a known standard. In most of the illustrations that follow, the student is expected to analyze and judge a specific *new* subject—a work, document, proposal, policy—by relating it to some other works, books, positions, standards, and so forth which he or she has *previously studied* in connection with a relevant course.

In the example below, the students have read and discussed Kennan's book and are to use it in evaluating the position stated in the quotation. The directions are rather general and the student is given little guidance on what to do.

ESSAY II—Time: 30 minutes

25. "If we will grant that what we want is *peace*, and that *justice* is the only way to peace, then we may begin dimly to perceive both the outlines of a policy for the present and the *constitutional* foundations of a future world order. We are required to abandon a policy of power and purchase and pursue a policy of justice at home and abroad."

Directions: Analyze and evaluate this position, using the principles and ideas in Kennan's *American Diplomacy*.

In the next example the students are to relate the President's Economic Report to Simons's book. The judgments concern the effects of particular economic policies. The test form and directions are relatively complex.

26. *Directions:* The United States is confronted with international tensions which, as policy is now being carried out, require a large outlay for goods and services that will not find their way into consumers' markets.

Various techniques have been proposed for financing this outlay and for determining the items to be produced. These techniques may serve or conflict with various values. For example, some techniques may (I) place serious restrictions on at least some economic freedoms which Simons (*Positive Program for Laissez-faire*) regards as essential to the maintenance of a free enterprise system. These same or other techniques may (II) conflict with goals of economic policy (other than freedom) in that they (i) would have "adverse effects" on the distribution of income (i.e., making it more unequal). (ii) would hamper the defense effort itself by intensifying the dangers of inflation, or (iii) would hamper the defense effort by failing to bring about production of the type and quantity of goods needed for the defense effort. For items (1) to (6) you are to judge the consequences of various policies for (I) freedom on the one hand vs. their effects on (II) these other goals of economic policy. A policy is to be considered as "conflicting with other goals of economic policy" if it appears to conflict significantly with *any*

285

one of the goals listed in (II) above. For each item blacken answer space

A—if the policy would be *compatible with* the maintenance of the *economic freedoms* which Simons regards as essential to the maintenance of a free enterprise system and *would not conflict* with other goals of economic policy

B—if the policy would be *compatible with* the maintenance of the *economic freedoms* which Simons regards as essential to the maintenance of a free enterprise system but *would conflict* with other goals of economic policy

C—if the policy would involve at least *some restriction on the economic freedoms* which Simons regards as essential to the maintenance of a free enterprise system but *would not conflict* with other goals of economic policy

D—if the policy would involve at least *some restriction on the economic freedoms* which Simons regards as essential to the maintenance of a free enterprise system and *would also conflict* with other goals of economic policy

E—if none of the above clearly applies

Note: In answering these items, judge the effects of the policy in terms of the current situation as described in the *President's Economic Report.* In answering each item assume that the policy stated is not counteracted by other policies or devices employed at the same time.

(1) A moderate increase in income taxes (the increase to be of a type which does not change the progressiveness of the present tax structure).

(2) Legislation to prohibit automobile manufacturers from mass producing new models during the crisis.

(3) A policy of permitting wages to rise in defense industries to the extent necessary to attract a sufficient number of workers to such jobs.

(4) An increase of social security deductions so that less purchasing power finds its way into consumers' hands, and higher pension payments may be made when the crisis is over.

(5) Imposition on all finished consumer goods of a uniform general sales tax sufficient to balance the budget.

(6) A policy of government subsidization of all families earning an income of less than $2,500 for four people, where such an amount is clearly necessary for the maintenance of minimum living standards.

The next example is a simpler test form. The students are to judge a particular regulation using the views of selected philosophers and documents studied in the course.

27. *Directions:* Let us suppose that in 1952 the school board of Centerville, an American city of 50,000, prescribes for all teachers and students of all its elementary and secondary public schools a compulsory oath which is to be recited at regular intervals at such occasions as assemblies and class meetings. The oath is to include the conventional pledge of allegiance and also to affirm that the speaker "does not subscribe, will never subscribe, and has never in the past subscribed to any principles of any organization advocating a form of government alien to that of the United States or advocating violence as a means of changing the government."

We may conceive at least four different views of such a regulation:

A. The regulation is thoroughly improper.

B. The regulation is proper as regards students but not as regards teachers.

C. The regulation is proper as regards teachers but not as regards students.

D. The regulation is thoroughly proper.

The statements which follow were made by various speakers at a town meeting to discuss the regulation. For items (1) to (8) blacken the answer space corresponding to the letter of the above view which is most similar to that expressed by the speaker. *Blacken answer space E if no one of the above clearly applies*

(1) Hobbes is the only accurate philosopher of loyalty.

(2) In his essay on *Civil Government Locke*, in contrast with Hobbes, advised citizens properly in regard to what they should do about arbitrary government.

(3) Plato's standards for education are essentially sound.

(4) Education is, as Mill said, a process in which free men help others to become free.

(5) Mill was right in arguing that political conclusions require deliberations upon experience.

(6) The clue to all loyalty oath questions is to be found in Mill's doctrine on the difference between thoughts and actions as proper objects of social control.

(7) The requirement of an oath would violate the First Amendment by not making exceptions on religious grounds.

(8) The principles underlying the Supreme Court's decisions in the second of the flag salute cases before it in 1940–43 are the correct ones.

In the following illustration a new set of criteria for scientific theories is given, and the student is to use it in making particular judgments about scientific theories studied.

Note the relatively simple test form used to get at very complex judgments.

28. Questions [1 to 4] deal with the following passage, concerning the general nature of science.

At bottom, science admits only one test of the validity of its theories, namely *concordance;* consequences drawn by purely deductive reasoning from observations together with the theories of science must not contradict one another.

The purpose of science is to discover order in the world, that is, to find relations connecting the various observed phenomena. For this purpose it is necessary to construct theories. These theories always postulate the existence of entities (such as atoms, fields of force, or the mass of the sun) which cannot be directly perceived in any observations, but which serve to unify our picture of the world behind our observations. The unification consists in the circumstance that by means of the nonobservable entities and the relations which are postulated to hold among them, we can draw conclusions from one set of observations concerning another such set.

In particular, scientific theories are often quantitative in form, the postulated entities are characterized by numbers, and the relations which hold among them are mathematical. In this case, the "theoretical" quantities must be capable of being computed on the basis of observations, and the observations themselves must, therefore, be quantitative—i.e., they must be measurements. Furthermore, each "theoretical" quantity must, at least in some situations, be computable independently from *more than one* set of measurements. The agreement among the results of independent measurements is the concordance which tests the theory; if such independent determinations are impossible, there can be no test of the theoretic results; the theoretic quantity involved serves no useful function and is therefore redundant.

(1) Which of the following observations, taken by itself, provides a test of the "concordance" achieved by Newton's particle theory of light?
   A. observation of the path of a particle, under the conditions described in Newton's first theorem concerning "very small bodies"
   B. measurement of the angle of incidence and the angle of refraction for a single ray of light passing from one medium to another
   C. measurement of the angle of incidence and the angle of reflection for a single ray of light reflected from a surface separating two media
   D. measurement of the angle at which total reflection occurs for a single ray of light passing from water into air

(2) Which of the following is the most probable judgment of the author of the above passage, concerning the relative merits of a treatment of light which takes such generalizations as the laws of reflection and refraction as its basic premises, and a treatment like that of Newton's "On Very Small Bodies" or Huygens' *Treatise?*
   A. A theory of light like Newton's or Huygens' is to be desired, because it is concerned not merely to describe but to *explain* the properties of light.
   B. A theory of light like Newton's or Huygens' is relatively valueless if it postulates entities (like light rays) whose properties cannot be tested by any observations; since all the optical phenomena can be comprehended by laws like those of reflection and refraction, the "concordance" of optical phenomena can be fully achieved by a treatment based on such laws.
   C. A treatment of light based upon the laws of reflection and refraction is not sufficiently mathematical to serve the purposes of science as well as a theory like Huygens' or Newton's.
   D. A theory of light like Huygens' or Newton's is superior, because it relates optical phenomena to a wider class of phenomena (mechanical phenomena), and because it provides general principles in terms of which it should be possible to investigate the behavior of light in situations not covered by the known generalizations.
   E. A treatment of light based on generalizations like the law of refraction is preferable, because it is more directly concerned with expressing the order found in observed phenomena, which is the true purpose of science.

(3) Which of the following would the author of the above passage be most likely to regard as a decisive reason for rejecting a scientific theory?
   A. The theory is not quantitative.
   B. The theory is not concordant with certain phenomena.
   C. The theory contains redundant elements.
   D. The theory contains postulates which assign to certain entities properties which differ from any that have ever been found in visible objects or processes.
   E. Each of the above would probably constitute a decisive reason for rejecting the theory.

(4) Which of the following [choices A–E] is *not* a reason for regarding Young's work as a scientific advance, from the point of view of the above passage?
   A. Young discovered a new optical phenomenon,

287

previously unknown, namely the "internal fringes" in a shadow; this is an advance because a new phenomenon involves new relations of this phenomenon to others.
  B. Young discovered a quantitative relation previously undiscerned in phenomena which Newton had observed.
  C. Young applied to light a theoretical conception—that of wave-length—in terms of which a much wider concordance of optical phenomena was achieved than had been previously.
  D. Young devised a way of determining the ratio of the velocities of light in two media independently of the law of refraction.
  E. Each of the above states a reason regarding Young's work as an advance.

The following material is part of a much larger test in which the student is given a new poem and then asked a series of questions to elicit particular elements of knowledge, comprehension, and analysis. In the questions the student is asked to judge specific aspects of the poem, using three critical points of view. The students study the three critics Aristotle, Plato, and Olson in the course and are now using them as bases for their judgments.

29. Now we will attempt to apply to this poem the doctrines of three of the critics you have studied this year.
  I. *Aristotle's Poetics:*
    (1) If a critic were to apply the principles of the *Poetics* to a study of this poem, he would be most likely to regard the *object* of imitation as
      A. the "subject." . . .
      B. the poet's universal idea about this "subject."
      C. the speaker going through an emotional response to this "subject."
      D. the nature of mankind.
      E. the poet's moral character.
    (2) And he would regard the *manner* of imitation as
      A. lyric.
      B. dramatic.
      C. narrative.
      D. mixed.
      E. sonnet.

    (3) Viewing the poem as a whole, he would be most likely to *praise* it *primarily* for
      A. its clear and convincing demonstration of a universal truth of human nature.
      B. its forceful warning to its readers to avoid a very great danger—a danger to which man, because of his basic nature, is especially susceptible.
      C. its unified plot.
      D. its vivid and moving rendition of a recognizably human action.
      E. its evocation and purgation of the audience's pity and fear.
  II. Elder Olson's *Prolegomena to a Poetics of the Lyric:*
    (4) A critic applying the principles of Olson to a study of this poem would come to a different conclusion. One important reason for this difference can be found in Olson's general conception of poetry, for Olson, unlike Aristotle, believes that
      A. poetry must be judged without regard to the character of the poet.
      B. poetry has no reference to the real world.
      C. a poem is a whole composed of mutually related parts.
      D. the purpose of poetry is to state universal truths.
      E. the purpose of poetry is not to state universal truths.
    (5) Because of this belief, a critic using Olson's principles would be most likely to regard the poem before us as
      A. a complex structure of related terms.
      B. the imitation of a human action.
      C. a warning to the readers.
      D. the expression of the poet's feelings.
      E. the expression of a universal truth about the "subject." . . .
    (6) Because of this view, he might very well *censure* the last two lines of this poem because
      A. they inculcate an attitude of resignation toward a great evil.
      B. "the world" did not appear in the situation the poet originally set up.
      C. it is in fact false that no one "knows well to shun the heaven that leads men to this hell."
      D. they are not "in character" for the speaker of the poem.
      E. they violate the rules of the particular poetic "form" within which the poet is working.

III. Plato's *Phaedrus*:

(7) A critic using the principles of the *Phaedrus* would emerge with still a third view of this poem. One important reason for his difference from the two preceding critics can be found in Plato's general conception of poetry, for Plato, *unlike either* Aristotle or Olson, believes that

A. a poem is a whole composed of mutually related parts.

B. poetry is related to real life.

C. poetry must not be judged by cold, logical criteria.

D. poetry must be judged without regard to the character of the poet.

E. poetry is a form of moral activity.

(8) Because of this belief, a critic using Plato's principles would most likely *censure* the last two lines of this poem because they

A. are not "in character" for the speaker of the poem.

B. are written rather than spoken aloud.

C. fail to state a general conclusion about the "subject." . . .

D. inculcate an attitude of resignation toward a great evil.

E. violate the rules of the particular poetic "form" within which the poet is working.

(9) The deficiency of these last two lines (indicated in the correct response to the preceding item), this critic might say, really results from the poet's improper handling of his subject in the rest of the poem. We can see, from the way Plato handles a similar subject in the *Phaedrus*, that a "Platonic" critic would claim this poet has erred because he

A. has never risen above the lowest level of his subject, the level of "excess."

B. has risen from the level of "excess" to that of "temperance," but has failed to go on to the highest level on which his subject can be viewed.

C. has begun on the highest level of his subject and worked down, instead of moving in the opposite and more correct direction.

D. has tried to grapple with a high level of his subject without going through the necessary preliminary investigation of the lower levels.

E. is treating his subject on a level that is not befitting the conversation of a moral dialectician.

In the following set of questions, the students have the Senate hearings available to them. The first set of questions involve relating particular judgments to specific positions taken by representatives of different groups during the hearings. The second set of questions require the use of particular criteria and standards in making judgments about selected methods of dealing with the problem.

FULL AND STABLE EMPLOYMENT POLICIES

30. The following two sets of items deal with (I) some of the basic *objectives* and underlying values stressed by different participants in the Senate discussion of the Murray Bill leading to the Employment Act of 1946; and (II) *methods* of policy appropriate for different stabilization objectives under specified conditions. . . .

I. Basic goals stressed by different groups in the 1945 Senate hearings on S. 380 (Murray, Full Employment Bill).

Directions: For each item, blacken the answer space corresponding to the letter of the *one* group which would accept the formulation of basic values or goals stated in the item. Note: Give only the *one best answer.*

(1) "Full and stable employment means security and security is such an outstanding value that we should be prepared to pay any price for it." This statement would be accepted by

A. proponents of the Full Employment Bill.

B. at least some of the businessmen testifying.

C. all representatives of organized labor.

D. all of the above.

E. none of the above.

(2) "Freedom and security are largely mutually compatible and even supporting goals. But they can conflict if either is pursued too exclusively. Full and stable employment should be pursued only to the degree and by such methods as are compatible with the maintenance of basic economic and political freedoms." This statement would be accepted by

A. sponsors of the Full Employment Bill.

B. at least some of the businessmen testifying.

C. all representatives of organized labor.

D. all of the above.

E. none of the above.

(3) "Freedom, in the traditional American sense of the free enterprise system including economic and political freedoms, is the best, and in principle, sufficient condition for the achievement and maintenance of a reasonable level of employment and degree of stability. Government should normally confine itself to the removal of obstacles and the protection of traditional freedoms." This statement would be accepted by

A. sponsors of the Full Employment Bill.

B. at least some spokesmen for business or farmers.

C. other spokesmen for business and farmers, *and* representatives of organized labor.

D. all of the above.

II. Methods appropriate to different stabilization objectives.

Assuming general agreement about the desirability both of stabilizing employment at a high level and of the preservation of the freedoms accepted by all participants in the hearings on S. 380 as basic to a "free enterprise economy," we may distinguish several more specific policy objectives and methods appropriate to these specific objectives. Specific policy objectives may be classified as

A. *Structural Reform:* Those policies which aim at long-range structural reforms (including institutions and rules of the game) which would (i) decrease the economy's disposition toward cumulative processes of contraction and unemployment or of overexpansion and inflation, and (ii) strengthen its capacity to sustain a high and stable rate of progressive expansion.

B. *Anti-depression* or *Recovery:* Those policies which aim at counteracting an incipient or already developed depression and stimulating a process of recovery in the direction of "full employment."

C. *Anti-inflation:* Those policies which aim at preventing or counteracting an incipient or already developed inflationary boom.

Directions: The following items describe methods which may be appropriate to one or another of the above objectives. For each item, blacken the answer space corresponding to the letter of the above objective to which it is most appropriate. In answering the items assume that the method described is not counteracted by simultaneous methods which would have opposite effects and that freedoms basic to a "free enterprise economy" are to be preserved. Since almost all

methods may be said to curtail at least some freedoms of some individual or groups, the condition of "preservation of essential freedoms" means that the method should be such that its probable *net* results for the economy as a whole would not involve serious curtailment of the basic freedoms designated above. Blacken answer space

D. if none of the above apply (i.e., the method would not contribute to any of the objectives, or would violate the freedom condition).

(4) Increase in expenditures for public works financed by government borrowing from banks or by the use of public funds accumulated in previous years.

(5) Policies aiming at a reduction of monopoly power which is likely to be used for restriction of output.

(6) Increase in the reserve requirements for member banks of the Federal Reserve System towards legal maxima.

(7) Initiation of a "cheap money" policy by reduction in interest rates.

(8) Comprehensive planning and permanent direct controls on all prices, wages, production, and jobs.

(9) Replacement of the fractional reserve system by a 100% reserve requirement for commercial banks.

In these next three questions (item 31), the students are to evaluate the three paragraphs on particular criteria. In the fourth question, the students may choose the criteria they wish to use to evaluate a poem they have been given (Purves, 1971, pp. 744–745):

31. I. "Hello, my girlie. Let's sit down here and hearken to those fellows playing music. It's quiet enough. Then we'll both go home. What say to that, my girl?"

II. "The moon presents a nice picture as its rich glorious rays come down on this wonderful big bank. Let us rest down here and listen to the precious music, which sounds most sweet in the peaceful quiet of the soft, stilly night. Is not this scene nearly perfect, Jessica? Come here, gentle musicians, and let your sweetest divine music charm us. The angelic moon shines in most precious glory. Let us stay and listen to the heavenly melodies, most sweet, most immortal of harmonies."

III. "How sweet the moonlight sits upon this bank. Here will we sit and let the sound of music creep in our ears. Soft stillness and the night become the touches of sweet harmony. Sit, Jessica. Such harmony is in immortal souls. Come ho! and wake Diana with a hymn. With sweetest touches pierce your mistress' ear, and draw her home with music."

(1) In the . . . three paragraphs
a. paragraph II shows the best choice of words
b. paragraph I shows the best choice of words
c. paragraph III shows the best choice of words

(2) In the . . . three paragraphs
a. paragraph III is most convincing
b. paragraph II is most convincing
c. paragraph I is most convincing

(3) In the . . . three paragraphs
a. paragraph II is spoiled by too much exaggeration
b. paragraph III is spoiled by too much exaggeration
c. paragraph I is spoiled by too much exaggeration

(Speer & Smith, 1937, p. 3, items 1,2,3)

(4) Which of the following come closest to what you think about this poem? Make one, two, or three choices, but no more than three. [Circle the letter of your choice or choices.]
a. It is a good poem because it makes me see the world differently.
b. It is a good poem because it makes me feel good.
c. It is a good poem because it is about one thing and doesn't use any extra words.
d. It is a good poem because it asks an important question.
e. It is a good poem because the words are right for what it is talking about.
f. It is poor because it does not rhyme.
g. It is a poor poem because it does not teach a lesson.
h. It is a poor poem because it does not make sense.
i. It is a poor poem because it does not hang together.
j. It is a poor poem because it uses simple words.
k. It is a poor poem because it deals with an unimportant subject.
l. It is a poor poem because it does not make me feel anything.

Each of the following four questions in item 32 (Wilson, 1971, p. 545) requires the use of a different basis for esthetic evaluation. It is of interest to note that even elementary-grade students can learn to apply different bases for criticism and evaluation. By varying the selection of works of art and the level of language used in the questions, this general form can be used at almost any grade level.

32. (1) Some people who have studied this painting by Paul Cézanne ["Still Life"] have said it is very successful because of the way the various parts fit together to form a complete painting. In the space below write about the parts in the painting and how well you think they fit together. (15 minutes)

(2) Some people who have studied this painting ["My Gems," by Harnett] have said it is successful because of the pleasure one receives from looking at it. Write why you think one *could* or *could not* get pleasure from looking at the painting. (15 minutes)

(3) Some people who have studied this painting ["Girl with a Plant," by Diebenkorn] have said it is successful because of the vivid and intense quality experienced while looking at it. Write about whether you agree or don't agree that the work is capable of creating a vivid and intense experience. (15 minutes)

(4) Some people who have studied this painting ["Temprano," by Albers] have said it is successful because it represents and tells something important about the twentieth century. Write about whether you think it is successful in representing our time. (15 minutes)

The next illustration (item 33) is an interesting example of evaluation in that the student is to evaluate his or her own writing by using the specific criteria indicated. It is thus possible for the instructor to do the same and compare the two evaluations for formative and summative purposes. It is also of interest to note that this type of evaluation can be used from about the fourth grade up. Evaluation types of objectives and testing procedures for them can be used at almost every school grade level.

33. *Directions:* Before you hand your composition in, go through the checklist. Answer the questions completely. The checklist should serve to guide you in the evaluation of your paper.
    (1) Do I try to write creatively?
    (2) Does the story have a good beginning?
    (3) Is the story interesting?
    (4) Are the details organized?
    (5) Are the words and phrases colorful?
    (6) Have I taken care of periods, commas, etc.?

(Moore & Kennedy, 1971, p. 429; adapted from Lamb, 1967, p. 350)

Test Problems for Evaluation Behavior F

The student can make judgments of a work by using his or her own explicit set of criteria or standards (external criteria; F).

The final type of behavior for evaluation is the student's use of his or her own standards or criteria. In this type of behavior, the students are to make their criteria or standards explicit and to demonstrate how they are relevant to judgments evolved about a particular work, document, policy, or situation. Since each student may have his or her own criteria or standards, it is not likely that objective or recognition types of question forms could be used in testing for this behavior. Thus the major problem of the evaluator is to judge the adequacy of the students' use of their own criteria in evaluating a particular work or other material. The evaluator may in passing also judge the adequacy of the students' critical criteria or standards.

This essay requires the student to make his or her own criteria explicit and to apply them in judging a poem which was assigned for reading but not discussed in the course. The directions given to the student make it clear what is to be done and on what basis the essay will be judged.

Essay Question (one hour, 40 points)

34. Write an essay of 400 to 600 words on one of the four poems assigned for outside reading during the third quarter:
    Bridges, *Nightingales;*
    Frost, *The Death of the Hired Man;*
    Housman, *To an Athlete Dying Young;*
    Tate, *Ode to the Confederate Dead.*

Your essay should meet the following three conditions:
(1) It should offer one or more judgments about the poem (e.g., the value of its intention, the success of its means to that end, its truth, its beauty, etc.).
(2) It should make explicit the nature of each criterion employed, and explain what assumptions concerning the nature or ends of poetry make this criterion a significant basis for judgment.
(3) It should discuss in considerable detail (the major part of your essay) whatever parts or aspects of the poem are pertinent to the judgment made—as proof that your conclusions are justified.

The following test requires the student to relate a critic's position to his or her own with respect to a particular characteristic of the novel *Madam Bovary.* Again, the directions make it clear what the student is expected to do.

Essay in Criticism: Madame Bovary (Time: 2 hours)

35. A critic has said of *Madam Bovary:*
    "Whatever virtues *Madame Bovary* may have, it certainly does not possess that of unity. This is supposed to be the story of Emma Bovary, yet it begins, not with her early life (which we learn of later only from a few brief comments), but with a detailed description of Charles' history from childhood on. Nor does the novel end where it should, but goes on after Emma's death to recount the subsequent fortunes of Charles and M. Homais. And why, even before Emma's death, is so much attention devoted to Homais? Or, for that matter, to Hippolyte, the club foot, or to the hideous blind beggar? Clearly, none of these characters plays a very significant part in Emma's catastrophe."

    Do you agree or disagree with the above judgment of the unity of *Madame Bovary*? In a well-organized, coherent essay of from 300 to 600 words, expound and defend your position, supporting your argument with specific references to the novel wherever possible. Your discussion *must* take into account all the episodes and characters mentioned by the above critic, although you should feel free to deal with them in any order you wish, and to bring in any others that you consider relevant. While your treatment of this problem will consider all these particulars, it should be directed to a judgment of the novel as a whole of some sort. Your essay should reveal your general critical position; but your understanding of this position should be demonstrated by your intelligent and sensitive *application* of it to the critical problem here presented, rather than by any elaborate excursion into esthetic theory.

You are to assume that you are writing for a literature reader, who has read *Madame Bovary* and the critical texts of Humanities 3, but who must be *convinced* of your judgment of the novel.

Remember that you will be judged, not only on what you say, but on how effectively you say it. It is suggested that you give at least 20 minutes to the careful planning of your essay before beginning to write, 80 minutes to the actual writing, and 20 minutes at the end to proofreading and revision, so that the essay in its final form represents your best intention.

This next essay question (item 36) is somewhat more general than the preceding illustrations. Here the students may select what they wish in presenting their evaluation of the picture. The picture is available to the students during this part of the examination.

Essay in Critical Evaluation (Time: 2 hours)
36. Write an essay on *The Bewitched Mill* (1913), an oil painting by the 20th century German artist Franz Marc (1880–1916), in which you express your own critical evaluation of the picture, supporting your evaluation by specific discussion of the work.

During the course of your essay indicate the criteria you have used in your judgments, and reveal the assumptions about art on which your views are based. You may, if you wish, refer to various authors whose works have been studied in the course; this should be undertaken only as a natural and connected part of your essay and should not appear as a parade of knowledge or authority. These references should not be a substitute for the exposition of your own views, since your essay must stand by itself.

In item 37 the student is to judge the song from the position of two critics as well as from his or her own position. Note that the student is not asked to write about his or her own standards and criteria but instead to be judged on the basis of the application of those critical principles to the music. The student has the score of the *Serenade* available while preparing the essay.

Critical Essay (Time: 2 hours)
37. Write a well-organized, coherent essay of from 300 to 600 words on the song entitled "Nocturne" from Benjamin Britten's *Serenade* for tenor solo, horn, and strings. Your essay should consist of three parts: the "Nocturne" (1) as viewed from the critical position of James Beattie, (2) as viewed from the critical position of Ernest Newman, and (3) your own critical evaluation and conclusion.

In writing the first two parts of your essay, bear in mind in each case the problems that it would be appropriate to pose. Do not rehearse the critical principles of Beattie and Newman; rather, write freely in what you consider to be their vein. Throughout your essay you should concentrate upon the most significant and compelling points that can be made, and should support your argument with explicit references to the song wherever possible. The principles upon which your judgment is based should be demonstrated rather by your intelligent and sensitive *application* of them to the song than by any elaborate excursion into esthetic theory.

In item 38 the student is asked to compare two poems as well as to make explicit the criteria used in judging them.

Essay on the Comparison of Two Lyric Poems (Time: 2 hours)
38. Below are printed two complete poems with certain similarities of subject. Write a well-organized, coherent essay of from 300 to 600 words, comparing the two poems, indicating which one you consider to be superior, and justifying your choice with as forceful an argument as you can produce. Although many things can be said about the two poems, you should concentrate upon the most significant and compelling points which can be made, and should support your argument with explicit references to the texts wherever possible. You should recognize, too, that appropriate treatment of this problem, while it will consider all significant details, will be directed to a judgment of the two poems as poetic wholes. Your essay should reveal the principles upon which your judgment is based, but your understanding of these principles should be demonstrated by your intelligent and sensitive *application* of them to the critical problem here presented, rather than by any elaborate excursion into esthetic theory.

Remember that you will be judged, not only on what you say, but on how effectively you say it. It is suggested that you give at least 20 minutes to the careful planning of your essay before beginning to write, 80 minutes to the actual writing, and 20 minutes at the end to proofreading and revision, so that the essay in its final form represents your best work. *Write legibly in ink, skipping every other line.*

POEM A

I taste a liquor never brewed,
From tankards scooped in pearl;
Not all the vats upon the Rhine
Yield such an alcohol!

Inebriate of air am I,
And debauchee of dew,
Reeling, through endless summer days,
From inns of molten blue.

When landlords turn the drunken bee
Out of the foxglove's door,
When butterflies renounce their drams,
I shall but drink the more!

Till seraphs swing their snowy hats,
And saints to windows run,
To see the little tippler
Leaning against the sun!

POEM B

Away, where leaves scarce grown are strown,
O'er the hills by the dewdrops known,
Across the dales by the dewdrops known,
Away from the city I'll flee.

I'll seek me a hilly throne of stone,
Where summer flowers by the winds are blown.
Where woodland smells by the winds are blown,
And free as the winds I'll be.

There on my hilly throne alone,
Where skies of blue to me are shown,
Where wonderful shrubs to me are shown,
Laurel tree and buzzing bee.

EXERCISES

Objective: Construct test items appropriate to the evaluation of synthesis and evaluation objectives.
Preparation: The objectives and test items developed for Chapters 2 and 7 may be useful in doing these exercises.
1. *Preparing objectives.* Prepare two sets of objectives—one for synthesis and one for evaluation.

a. Select some objectives from ones you have written previously, from curriculum guides, from books on teaching, or from books on educational measurement.
b. In addition, write some new objectives. Given the complexity of the behaviors involved, ensure that the difficulty level is appropriate to the level of student for which the objective is intended.
c. It would be useful to stay within the subject or unit used for the Chapter 9 exercises.
d. If it is appropriate to your subject, write objectives requiring different types of products at the synthesis level.
e. Write objectives for different types of evaluation behaviors.
2. *Operationalizing behaviors.*
a. It is likely that the synthesis objectives make clear what the intended behavior and product are. Ensure that this is the case.
b. For your evaluation objectives, identify a specific action or task which would demonstrate the desired behavior.
3. *Item writing.*
a. Write a test item for each of your objectives. Make clear what materials, documents, works, etc., would be available during testing.
b. Prepare a scoring plan for your items. Make clear what criteria would be used to judge the adequacy of the synthesis and evaluation test results.

REFERENCES

American Council on Education Studies. *A design for general education*, Washington, D.C.: Author 1944.

Bloom, B. S. (Ed.). *Taxonomy of educational objectives: The classification of educational goals.* Handbook 1. *Cognitive domain.* New York: McKay, 1956.

Bloom, B. S. (Ed.) *Evaluation in higher education.* New Delhi: University Grants Commission, 1961.

Bloom, B. S., Hastings, J. T., & Madaus, G. F. *Handbook on formative and summative evaluation of student learning.* New York: McGraw-Hill, 1971.

French, W., & Associates. *Behavioral goals of general education in high school.* New York: Russell Sage Foundation, 1957.

Lamb, P. *Guiding children's language learning.* Dubuque, Iowa: Brown, 1967.

Moore, W. J., & Kennedy, L. D. Evaluation of learning in the language arts. In B. S. Bloom, J. T. Hastings, & G. F. Madaus, *Handbook on formative and summative evaluation of student learning.* New York: McGraw-Hill, 1971.

Purves, A. C. Evaluation of learning in literature. In B. S. Bloom, J. T. Hastings, & G. F. Madaus, *Handbook on formative and summative evaluation of student learning.* New York: McGraw-Hill, 1971.

Taylor, C. W., & Barron, F. *Scientific creativity: Its recognition and development.* New York: Wiley, 1963.

Tyler, R. W. The fact-finding study of the testing program of the United States Armed Forces Insititute, 1952–1954 (Report to the USAFI). University of Chicago, 1954.

Wilson, B. G., Evaluation of learning in art education. In B. S. Bloom, J. T. Hastings, & G. F. Madaus, *Handbook on formative and summative evaluation of student learning.* New York: McGraw-Hill, 1971.

11 Evaluation Techniques for Affective Objectives

Chapter Contents

... We must ask whether in immersing our-selves so exclusively in this cognitive function of education—in education for verbal-conceptual abilities—we have not severely neglected other important and sometimes simpler facets of personality and life—the esthetic pleasures, for instance, that accrue from sharpening the instruments of sensory perception, or the intrinsic values in the appreciation of poetry and art which are available to those whose education has cultivated their intuitive powers and refined their capacities for sympathy and feeling. (McMurrin, 1967, p. 42. Reprinted from the *Saturday Review*, January 14, 1967, a special issue produced in cooperation with the Committee for Economic Development, by permission of the publisher.)

INTRODUCTION:
AFFECT IN THE CURRICULUM

American education continues to maintain that among its most important ideals is the development of such attributes as interests, desires, attitudes, appreciation, values, commitment, and willpower. The quotation from McMurrin, however, documents the reality that the types of outcomes which in fact receive the highest priorities in our schools, to the detriment of these affective goals, are cognitive in nature.

The reasons for this emphasis on the cognitive in preference to the affective are several and interactive. Our system of education is geared to producing people who can deal with the words, concepts, and mathematical or scientific symbols necessary for success in our technological society. These skills can be achieved through the communi-cation of both specific and generalized knowledge and through the development of deductive and inductive habits of thought.

Such outcomes lend themselves to the well-defined verbal-conceptual methods of lectures, conversations, demonstrations, discussions, and the printed word, all so widely used in our schools. In contrast, not nearly so well-defined are the techniques a teacher might use to help students change their attitude toward a minority group, develop an esthetic sensibility, or learn to enjoy studying mathematics.

Further, there tends to be more concern about the attainment of cognitive outcomes, and less controversy associated with them, than there is for affective goals. Clearly, schools are more frequently criticized over students' shortcomings in such cognitive areas as reading and mathematics than any shortcomings related to affective objectives. When a school district *does* seek to develop affect concerning a contemporary social issue, it can find itself embroiled in controversy.

This is not to imply that realizations of cognitive outcomes are not accompanied by changes in affect—quite the contrary: these separate outcomes may be very closely related. As B. O. Smith points out (1966, p. 53), "to teach any concept, principle, or theory is to teach not only for its comprehension, but also for an attitude toward it—the acceptance or rejection of it as useful, dependable, and so forth." Indeed, certain established pedagogic techniques for producing acceptable cognitive outcomes—for example, extensive and intensive drill in arithmetic—can destroy the positive feeling students might have toward the subject area. Suffice it to say it is possible for a learner to understand and be quite proficient in a subject matter area and still have a deep aversion or other negative affect toward the discipline. This would be an example of the unintentional and unanticipated negative outcomes discussed in Chapter 2.

While cognitive learning can change affect, affect can also influence cognitive learning. Up to one-fourth of the variance on achievement tests can be accounted for by individuals' affective entry characteristics (Bloom, 1976). During instruction negative affect can result from being made fun of, ignored, frequently scolded, or punished by an unfeeling or unthinking teacher; these negative feelings in turn can adversely influence the student's progress in cognitive areas.

This chapter deals with the problems of writing or selecting affective objectives and of developing or selecting evaluation techniques to measure them. Before proceeding, let us first examine in more detail some of the reasons why American education has failed to emphasize affective goals.

REASONS FOR THE NEGLECT OF AFFECTIVE GOALS

Fear of Indoctrination

One of the reasons for the failure to give instructional emphasis to affective outcomes is related to the Orwellian overtones which attitudinal and value-oriented instruction often conjures up in the minds of teachers and the public. Can we teach attitudes and values without espousing a particular political or sectarian position and without employing the techniques of preachment, indoctrination, and brainwashing which are so foreign to our democratic system? Scriven deals specifically with this problem in his excellent paper "Student Values as Educational Objectives" (1966). He makes a distinction between values acquired in conjunction with cognitive learning—such as the valuing

of objectivity and the scientific methods—and moral values—such as empathy and sympathy—which cannot be taught exclusively with cognitive techniques.

In regard to cognitive-related values, Scriven (1966) points out that not teaching these is "not just cowardice but incompetence, professional incompetence." On the subject of moral behavior and conclusions, he points out that there is a moral imperative to instruct in these areas so that students will not be "ignorant of the empirical punch behind the morality behind the law and the institutions which incorporate this country's virtues and permit its vices" (p. 42).

The teaching of both cognitive and moral values can, however, avoid the charge of brainwashing if three notions are held in mind:

1. We teach as facts only those assertions which can really be objectively established . . .; others we teach as hypotheses. Hence, we do not violate the rights of others to make their own choices where choice is rationally possible, nor their right to know the truth where it is known.
2. Good teaching does not consist primarily in requiring the memorization of conclusions the teacher thinks are true, but in developing the skills needed to arrive at and test conclusions. . . .
3. That certain conclusions should now be treated as established does not mean they cannot ever turn out to be wrong. . . .

(Scriven, 1966, pp. 44–45)

Contrary, then, to fears of brainwashing or indoctrination, if the dangers of a totalitarian society are to be avoided, schools have an obligation to work toward the realization of affective objectives.

Prevalent Beliefs about the Role of the School and the Nature of Affect

Tyler (1973) describes two widely held beliefs about affective objectives that have inhibited their pursuit. First it is the belief of many that the development of feelings, values, and commitments is the proper task of home and religion rather than school. However, while the roles of the family and religion remain important in the development of affect, there are many legitimate areas within the affective domain where the school plays an essential role.

We alluded to a second common belief in the introduction to this chapter, namely, that appropriate affect develops automatically from knowledge and experience with content and does not need special instruction. However, we now realize that positive affect does not automatically follow from knowledge or understanding of material. In fact, as noted above, unanticipated negative affect can also follow such experiences. Many attitudes, interests, and values can in fact be specifically taught for, using techniques that may not be appropriate in the cognitive area (Khan & Weiss, 1973).

Fear of Invasion of Privacy

A third reason for neglect in stressing affective objectives is that, unlike cognitive achievement, affect is considered a private rather than a public matter. A person's attitudes on social issues, religious beliefs or lack of them, and political preferences are private concerns—and their privacy is protected by our Constitution. How one spends leisure time, what one likes in literature, art, music, or cinema are considered questions of personal preference in our society. Because of this private quality of the affective life, teachers are hesitant to enter into these areas in their instruction and evaluations. However as we shall see, if certain conditions are met, it is possible to address affective outcomes without intruding on a person's privacy.

Failure to Evaluate Affective Outcomes

Teacher-made tests used to assess students' performance are geared almost exclusively to cognitive outcomes. Standardized tests used by the schools compare their students' performance with that of some national norm group or against some criterion or standard of performance. Both norm- and criterion-referenced standardized tests lay stress on intellectual tasks involving recognition or recall of previously learned knowledge and the reordering or application of this knowledge to solve problems posed.

There are cogent explanations given for the exclusive focus on cognitive outcomes and the failure to evaluate affective objectives. First, it is often assumed that, unlike most cognitive objectives, affective objectives cannot be attained in the relatively short instructional period of a week, month, semester, or year; therefore they cannot be evaluated in the school setting. This belief is implied in the statements of teachers who claim their goals are intangible or so long-range that the attitudes, values, interests, and appreciations they have tried to develop in their students may not reveal themselves until much later in life—long after formal education has been completed. If this assumption were always correct, then it would indeed be difficult to evaluate affective objectives. While the time it takes to bring about an affective behavioral change is undoubtedly a function of the complexity of the behavior being sought, this is also true for desired changes in cognitive behavior. There is evidence however that, like certain cognitive objectives, many affective objectives *can* be attained relatively quickly and *are* amenable to evaluation.

A second reason for the hesitancy to evaluate affective objectives is that, as mentioned above, some people feel that to try to assess a person's feelings, interests, and attitudes is to infringe on that person's right to privacy. Closely related to this proper reluctance to impinge on a person's privacy is the fact that most educators do not consider it appropriate to record a grade for a student's attitudes, values, interests, or appreciations. Thus, though affective characteristics may impinge, favorably or unfavorably, in an unofficial way on the grade a student receives, for most teachers an attempt to grade affect itself would be unthinkable. For these reasons teachers have avoided evaluating affective goals. However it is possible to attain affective outcomes and to evaluate them without "grading" students and without violating an individual's right to privacy. The point is that when teachers disregard affective outcomes in the evaluation process, they are apt to disregard them unintentionally in the instructional process.

IMPORTANCE OF EVALUATING AFFECTIVE OBJECTIVES

"A spirit of inquiry," "compliance with the law and school regulations," "ability to appreciate the structure of the real number system," "listening with pleasure to good music," and "increased appetite and taste for what is good in literature"—if the aims of the school include such affective outcomes as these in addition to cognitive objectives, it then has the obligation to evaluate the effectiveness of the curriculum in forming those behaviors. If it does not evaluate them, it has no evidence on which to base modifications of its curriculum and pedagogic methods for purposes of affective instruction. Further, a failure to evaluate leads, as we have previously stated, to the eventual disregard of the affective aspect of education and to exclusive emphasis on cognition. This failure is due in part to a narrow view of the concept of evaluation and to a disregard of the distinction between the formative and summative evaluation of both the student and the curriculum. Evaluation should not be equated with assigning a grade or giving an examination, for it is a much broader practice that employs a multitude of evidence-gathering techniques to help in decisions about the quality of performance by an individual or group, or about the success of a curriculum in relation to stated objectives. Let us consider briefly how the evaluation of affect can help improve both individual learning and a curriculum.

Although it is bad practice to assign a summative grade for affective behavior, it is often desirable to evaluate a student's affective behavior for proper diagnosis and placement (see Chapter 5). As mentioned above, each student brings to instruction an affective history that can influence the way he or she approaches school in general or learning in a particular course (Bloom, 1976; Khan & Weiss, 1973). A student who begins a course with a positive affect (other entry behaviors being equal) should learn more easily and rapidly than the classmate who begins without enthusiasm, enjoyment, or interest, or the classmate who is anxious or fearful about the material to be studied (Bloom, 1976). Of course students vary greatly in the manner in which entering affect influences learning. For example, one student with negative affect toward chemistry can block completely and fail while another disregards the same negative affect, knowing that college admission requires good grades. Despite such individual differences, it is important for a teacher at the beginning of a course to know as much as possible about each student's affective entry level. Such knowledge can help the teacher plan remedial procedures to deal with the diagnosed affect.

Once instruction is underway, a student may experience difficulty. Formative evaluation of affect toward the subject may reveal that the cause is a developing fear of the subject or a lack of self-confidence. The student may be caught in the vicious circle of a self-fulfilling prophecy—"I'm not doing well in arithmetic. It makes me nervous. I like arithmetic less each day"—and this attitude leads to failure, which in turn strengthens the negative affect. Such knowledge alerts the teacher to the need for positive reinforcement and encouragement to pull the student from the vicious circle.

Finally, on the broader level of curriculum, information on how a *group* reacts to certain techniques or materials designed to achieve an affective objective is important formative information. Further, if a large proportion of a *class* does not attain the affective objective the course was designed in part to achieve, this information is valuable in the summative evaluation. In both cases, techniques that assure anonymity and privacy can be used to gather *group* information.

Thus it is possible to evaluate a curriculum's affective objectives both formatively and summatively without grading an individual's private and personal affective behavior.

STATING AFFECTIVE OBJECTIVES

The role of clear, unambiguous statements of educational objectives as the first step in instructional planning and evaluation was emphasized in Chapter 2. Such statements are no less important for affective than for cognitive objectives. However, because of the numerous interpretations people can place on affective concepts, the specification of students' actions or products that are acceptable as indicators of the construct is often neglected. This is not to imply that affective objectives cannot be stated in terms of an action or product; teachers, however, often neglect to give careful thought to specifying those actions which will lead them to infer the presence or absence of some affective construct.

Many teachers find it more difficult to describe affective objectives behaviorally than they do cognitive ones. Furthermore, the large number of affective objectives found in the literature use concepts such as "attitudes," "values," "appreciation," and "interest" in a wide variety of ways. For example, objectives dealing with interest can encompass behaviors ranging from mere awareness that a given phenomenon exists to avid pursuit of experience of the phenomenon. "Appreciation" can also refer to a simple behavior such as mere perception of a phenomenon or to such a complex, emotionally toned behavior as active enjoyment when experiencing the phenomenon.

As we saw in Chapter 2, the essential step in defining an objective in an unambiguous way, be it cognitive, affective, or psychomotor, is to start with the general construct and then write statements of observable actions or products that will serve as indicators of the construct. A list of action verbs helpful in describing affective objectives is shown in Figure 11-1 (see page 302): as can be seen, all the verbs deal with observable actions.

The experience of the Evaluation Committee of the Eight-Year Study (Smith & Tyler, 1942) with the objective "appreciation of literature" illustrates how the constructs were described in terms of observable actions or products. The committee members selected seven general constructs they felt were central to appreciation; they specified these further by listing examples of overt acts and verbal responses which they would accept as evidence of the presence or absence of each of the seven.

The results were as follows (Smith & Tyler, 1942, pp. 251–252):

1. SATISFACTION IN THE THING APPRECIATED
   1.1. He reads aloud to others, or simply to himself, passages which he finds unusually interesting.
   1.2. He reads straight through without stopping, or with a minimum of interruption.
   1.3. He reads for considerable periods of time.
2. DESIRE FOR MORE OF THE THING APPRECIATED
   2.1. He asks other people to recommend reading which is more or less similar to the thing appreciated.
   2.2. He commences this reading of similar things as soon after reading the first as possible.
   2.3. He reads subsequently several books, plays, or poems by the same author.
3. DESIRE TO KNOW MORE ABOUT THE THING APPRECIATED
   3.1. He asks other people for information or sources of information about what he has read.
   3.2. He reads supplementary materials, such as biographies, history, criticism, etc.
   3.3. He attends literary meetings devoted to reviews, criticisms, discussions, etc.
4. DESIRE TO EXPRESS ONE'S SELF CREATIVELY
   4.1. He produces, or at least undertakes to produce, a creative period more or less after the manner of the thing appreciated.

Accepts	Enrolls	Questions
Acts	Evaluates	Reacts
Adopts	Explores	Recommends
Advocates	Expresses (views)	Rejects
Aids	Gathers (information)	Requests
Annotates	Goes out of his way	Responds
Answers	Helps	Salvages
Argues (a position)	Imitates	Searches
Asks	Initiates	Seeks
Attempts	Investigates	Selects
Attends	Joins	Shares
Brings	Judges	Sleeps
Builds	Keeps (preserves)	Specifies
Buys	Leads	Spends (money, time)
Challenges	Listens	Stimulates
Chooses	Meets	Studies
Collects	Obeys	Submits
Completes	Objects (to an idea)	subscribes
Consults	Offers	Suggests
Contributes	Organizes	Supports
Convinces	Participates	Talks (about)
Cooperates	Perseveres	Tells
Corrects	Persists	Tests
Creates	Plays	Tries
Criticizes	Points (out)	Visits
Defends	Praises	Volunteers
Delays (response)	Presents	Votes (for)
Demonstrates	Promotes	Waits
Designs	Proposes	Wears
Develops (a hobby)	Purchases	Weighs (judges)
Disputes	Qualifies	Writes
Emulates	Queries	Yearns

Figure 11-1 Action verbs helpful in writing or selecting affective objectives. (Lieberman, Brown, Neidlinger, & Swanson, 1970, p. 16; and Eiss & Harbeck, 1972.)

4.2. He writes critical appreciations.

4.3. He illustrates what he has read in some one of the graphic, spatial, musical or dramatic arts.

5. IDENTIFICATION OF ONE'S SELF WITH THE THING APPRECIATED

5.1. He accepts, at least while he is reading, the persons, places, situations, events, etc., as real.

5.2. He dramatizes, formally or informally, various passages.

5.3. He imitates, consciously and unconsciously, the speech and actions of various characters in the story.

6. DESIRE TO CLARIFY ONE'S OWN THINKING WITH REGARD TO THE LIFE PROBLEMS RAISED BY THE THING APPRECIATED

6.1. He attempts to state, either orally or in writing, his own ideas, feelings, or information concerning the life problems with which his reading deals.

6.2. He examines other sources for more information about these problems.

6.3. He reads other works dealing with similar problems.

7. DESIRE TO EVALUATE THE THING APPRECIATED

7.1. He points out, both orally and in writing, the elements which in his opinion make it good literature.

7.2. He explains how certain unacceptable elements (if any) could be improved.

7.3. He consults published criticisms.

Additional clarification of an objective such as "appreciation of literature" occurs when items are developed for inclusion in an inventory. Items taken from the *Literature Questionnaire: The Novel, Test 3.22,* of the Eight-Year Study (Progressive Education Association, 1940) illustrate for each of the seven appreciation constructs described above how the process of description is carried through to the item-development stage.

The student was instructed to mark each question in the following manner:

A. means that you answer the question *Yes*

U. means that you are unable to answer *Yes* or *No* to the question

D. means that your answer to the question is *No*

[Derives satisfaction from reading]

____ 1. After you had started this novel, were you more interested in finishing it than in doing almost anything else?

[Wants to read more]

____ 2. Do you have any desire to read this novel or any parts of it again?

[Becomes curious about reading]

____ 3. Would you like to know more about the life of the author?

[Expresses himself creatively]

____ 4. If you were an artist would you like to illustrate this novel?

[Identifies himself with reading]

____ 5. Were you able to picture in your mind how some of the characters in the novel must have looked?

[Relates his reading to life]

____ 6. Do you feel that reading this novel has helped you to understand more clearly why people act as they do in various circumstances?

[Evaluates his reading]

____ 7. Did you read this novel without giving much thought to the merits or defects of the plot?

(Progressive Education Association, 1940, items 55, 27, 11, 16, 6, 63, 21.)

Thus in the process of stating affective objectives a teacher might emulate the steps followed in the Eight-Year Study by:

1. Identifying the affective objective in terms of a broad general construct such as appreciation, interest, etc.
2. Narrowing the broad construct to component constructs.
3. Describing each component construct in terms of an action verb like those shown in Figure 11-1.
4. Developing specific situations or items to elicit evidence of the presence or absence of construct.

By following these four steps the teacher will develop the kind of clear, unambiguous statements of an affective objective that can then be used to plan instruction and evaluation.

As pointed out in Chapter 2, the process of stating objectives needs to be viewed as cyclical. That is, the experience of teaching leads to the identification of new or unanticipated objectives and to the refinement of previously stated objectives.

TAXONOMY OF EDUCATIONAL OBJECTIVES: AFFECTIVE DOMAIN

In working in the area of affective education a key resource in stating affective objectives (as discussed in the preceding section) and in selecting affective objectives from available sources (as discussed in the next section) is the *Taxonomy of Educational Objectives,* Handbook 2, *Affective Domain* (Krathwohl, Bloom, & Masia, 1964).

As we saw in Chapter 2, it provides the teacher with a useful guide for describing and classifying educational objectives which emphasize positive or negative feelings, an emotion, or a degree of acceptance or rejection. Further, it provides the reader with a rich source both of objectives and of methods of evaluating. The affective *Taxonomy* is summarized in the Appendix of this book along with Handbook 1, *Cognitive Domain*. Let us now consider in more detail this important resource.

Relationship between the Cognitive and Affective Domains

As noted earlier in this chapter, there is an intimate relationship between cognitive and affective behavioral changes. This relationship is operative at the instructional as well as the evaluation level. As the authors of the affective *Taxonomy* point out,

> Each affective behavior has a cognitive behavior counterpart of some kind and vice versa. An objective in one domain has a counterpart in the opposite domain, though often we do not take cognizance of it. . . . Each domain is sometimes used as a means to the other, though the more common route is from the cognitive to the affective. Theory statements exist which permit us to express one in terms of the other and vice versa. (Krathwohl, Bloom, & Masia, 1964, p. 62; copyright © 1964 by Longman, Inc., and reprinted by permission of Longman.)

The interaction between the two domains has implications for evaluation. Krathwohl, Bloom, and Masia point out that teachers more often reward a student on the basis of whether or not he or she *can do* a task—a cognitive consideration—than on the affective consideration of whether the student *does do* it after learning it. A teacher concerned only with cognition will be satisfied with a "can do" evaluation: can the student recite, read, write, etc.? However, as Cazden (1971) aptly points out,

> . . . a teacher with both cognitive and affective objectives in mind would look for evidence that the child actually uses these abilities in the part of his life not directed by the teacher. Transfer to new situations can rightfully be

considered simply a more stringent criterion of successful cognitive learning, but the criterion of frequent appropriate performance goes beyond that, into the affective domain. Here abilities must be linked to attitudes and values. Spontaneous questions depend not only on ability to ask questions but also on the desire to find out; using language for planning, by oneself or with others, depending not only on the ability to construct sentences but also on the belief that one can affect the environment with words. (p. 353)

As part of the evaluation process the teacher should be constantly on the lookout for student-initiated actions in the cognitive areas like reading, writing, speaking, etc., for these often are compelling indications of progress toward affective outcomes.

Categories of the Affective Taxonomy

The *Taxonomy* arranges objectives along a hierarchical continuum. At the lowest point on this continuum, the students are merely aware of a phenomenon, simply able to perceive it. At the next level they are willing to attend to the phenomenon. The next step finds the students responding to the phenomenon with feeling. At the next point they go out of their way to respond to the phenomenon. Next they conceptualize behavior and feelings and organize these into a structure. The highest point in the hierarchy is reached when the structure becomes an outlook on life.

The authors of the *Taxonomy* describe this continuum as one of internalization, in which the affective component passes from a level of bare awareness to a position of some power and then to control of a person's behavior.

Thus the *Taxonomy* comprises five major categories of internalization: *Receiving, Responding, Valuing, Organization*, and *Characterization*. These five categories are in turn further subdivided into levels.

Figure 11-2 shows how each level of the *Taxonomy* translates into statements of affective objectives. Each of the five major categories is briefly described; then, drawing

	Examples of infinitives	Examples of direct objects
1.0 Receiving (attending) The first category is defined as sensitivity to the existence of certain phenomena and stimuli, that is, the willingness to receive or attend to them. A typical objective at this level would be: "The student develops a tolerance for a variety of types of music."		
1.1 Awareness	To differentiate, to separate, to set apart, to share	Sights, sounds, events, designs, arrangements
1.2 Willingness to receive	To accumulate, to select, to combine, to accept	Models, examples, shapes, sizes, meters, cadences
1.3 Controlled or selected attention	To select, to posturally respond to, to listen (for), to control	Alternatives, answers, rhythms, nuances
2.0 Responding "Responding" refers to a behavior which goes beyond merely attending to the phenomena; it implies active attending, doing something with or about the phenomena, and not merely perceiving them. Here a typical objective would be: "The student voluntarily reads magazines and newspapers designed for young children."		
2.1 Acquiescence in responding	To comply (with), to follow, to command, to approve	Directions, instructions, laws, policies, demonstrations
2.2 Willingness to respond	To volunteer, to discuss to practice, to play	Instruments, games, dramatic works, charades, burlesques
2.3 Satisfaction in response	To applaud, to acclaim, to spend leisure time in, to augment	Speeches, plays, presentations, writings
3.0 Valuing Behavior which belongs to this level of the taxonomy goes beyond merely doing something with or about certain phenomena. It implies perceiving them as having worth and consequently revealing consistency in behavior related to these phenomena. A typical objective at this level would be: "Writes letters to the press on issues he feels strongly about."		[Continued on page 306]

Figure 11-2 Translating the levels of the affective taxonomy into statements of objectives. (Adapted from Metfessel, Michael, & Kirsner, 1969, pp. 227–231.)

	Examples of infinitives	Examples of direct object
3.1 Acceptance of a value	To increase measured proficiency in, to increase numbers of, to relinquish, to specify	Group membership(s), artistic production(s), musical productions, personal friendships
3.2 Preference for a value	To assist, to subsidize, to help, to support	Artists, projects, viewpoints, arguments
3.3 Commitment	To deny, to protest, to debate, to argue	Deceptions, irrelevancies, abdications, irrationalities

4.0 Organization Organization is defined as the conceptualization of values and the employment of these concepts for determining the interrelationship among values. Here a typical objective might be: "Begins to form judgments as to the major directions in which American society should move."

4.1 Conceptualization of a value	To discuss, to theorize (on), to abstract, to compare	Parameters, codes, standards, goals
4.2 Organization of a value system	To balance, to organize, to define, to formulate	Systems, approaches, criteria, limits

5.0 Characterization The organization of values, beliefs, ideas, and attitudes into an internally consistent system is called "characterization." This goes beyond merely determining interrelationships among various values: it implies their organization into a total philosophy or world view. Here a typical objective would include: "Develops a consistent philosophy of life" (Krathwohl et al., 1964, pp. 176–185).

5.1 Generalized set	To revise, to change, to complete, to require	Plans, behavior, methods, effort(s)
5.2 Characterization	To be rated high by peers in, to be rated high by superiors in, to be rated high by subordinates in	Humanitarianism, ethics, integrity, maturity
	and	
	To avoid, to manage, to resolve, to resist	Extravagance(s), excesses, conflicts, exorbitancy/exorbitancies

Figure 11-2 Continued.

on the work of Metfessel, Michael, and Kirsner (1969), subdivisions of the category are listed in the first column, together with infinitives or action verbs in the second column, and direct objects in the third column. The infinitives in the second column are action verbs similar to those listed in Figure 11-1 which can be used by a teacher to state in terms of a student's behavior or actions an objective corresponding to the category in question. The infinitives listed of course are not exhaustive but are intended to illustrate the type of verb necessary for a clear statement of an objective. The "direct objects" column lists in very general terms examples of subject matter that can be matched with one or more of the verbs to complete the statement of the object.

Using Figure 11-2 a statement of an affective objective dealing with interest in music might be found in the following way. Under the category *Responding*, "willingness to respond" might be translated into an actual statement of an objective by choosing from column 2 the infinitive "to practice" and from column 3 the direct object "instruments." The final statement might then read, "The student practices chords on the guitar."

As noted earlier, commonly used terms such as "interest," "appreciation," "attitude," "value," and "adjustment" take on a variety of meanings in relation to the taxonomic categories. By way of example consider the broad objective "appreciation of literature" from the Eight-Year Study which was described earlier. "Appreciation of literature" is a common objective among English teachers. As further clarified in the Eight-Year Study, the construct "appreciation" involves behaviors that cut across at least three of the taxonomic categories of internalization shown in Figure 11-2: *Responding, Valuing,* and *Organization*. "Reading for considerable periods of time" or "reading straight through without stopping" are subsumed under the category *Responding*. "He (she) imitates, consciously and unconsciously, the speech and actions of various characters in the story" could be classified under *Valuing*. "He

(she) points out, both orally and in writing, the elements which in his (her) opinion make it good literature" would fall under the category *Organization*. The reader should notice that this last behavior classified under *Organization* is closely related to *Evaluation* in the cognitive *Taxonomy*.

To further illustrate how the categories of the affective *Taxonomy* might be used in developing statements of objectives and evaluation techniques, let us consider each of the first four categories separately in terms of *possible* items that can be used to evaluate the category. (The fifth category, *Characterization*, is a longer-term objective, usually beyond the scope of a single teacher; Krathwohl, Bloom, & Masia, 1964.)

The items used to illustrate each of the four categories are drawn from reading, music, and mathematics. They were selected for the purpose of clarifying further the essential behavioral component of the category.

1.0 Receiving

At the first level of internalization—*Receiving*—one is trying to determine if the student will be willing to attend to, to be receptive to, to consider, or to be aware of a stimulus such as a book, concert, or design. Is the student open to reading, listening to music, or mathematics?

The key element in the following questions is the attempt to establish the student's willingness to *be open to* an object or an experience:

Do you wish you had more time to devote to reading?

[Yes or no]

Do you have in mind one or two books which you would like to read sometime soon? [Yes or no]

(Lewy, 1966, p. 168)

I have never had the wish to improve my understanding of music. [True or not true]

I would like to devote some time to listening to good music. [True or not true]

(pp. 160–161)

Do you feel that the designs (shown) are just a lot of uninteresting lines and shapes?   [Yes or no]

Do you think that (either) of these designs (is) attractive?
                                                   [Yes or no]
                                            (pp. 150–151)

2.0 Responding

At the second level of internalization—*Responding*—the student's action goes beyond a willingness to *consider* an activity or object to some voluntary *action*. There is the element of preference, enjoyment, pleasure— a lack of boredom in responding. There is a lack of difficulty, an element of ease. Notice that the following questions all seek to determine whether the student follows through and reads a book, listens to music, or solves mathematics problems of his or her *own accord*.

Once you have begun a book, do you usually finish it within a few days' time?   [Yes or no]

Is it unusual for you to spend a whole afternoon or evening reading a book?   [Yes or no]
                                    (Lewy, 1966, pp. 168–170)

Being with friends or in a party, I usually welcome suggestions to listen to records of classical music.
                                              [True or not true]

It is unusual for me to listen to music continuously for a period of two hours.   [True or not true]
                                            (pp. 160–166)

You probably had to prove geometric problems like the following:

Prove that if a pentagon inscribed in a circle has equal angles then its sides are equal.

Did you often wish you should not have to bother with problems like this?   [Yes or no]

Would it be unusual for you to try to solve problems like this on your own accord?   [Yes or no]

Would you enjoy helping students to solve problems like this?   [Yes or no]
                                            (pp. 150–158)

3.0 Valuing

The third level of internalization—*Valuing*— includes voluntary actions but goes beyond and includes elements of involvement, consistency, enthusiasm, and frequency. The student perceives the activity or object as satisfying or worthwhile or useful in itself. The following questions try to determine whether the student becomes involved or absorbed in, or will go out of the way to pursue, an activity, whether he or she recommends it to friends or tries to persuade them to engage in or value the activity.

Is it very unusual for you to become so enthusiastic about a book that you urge several of your friends to read it?
                                                   [Yes or no]

Do you have a collection of your own books, not counting school textbooks?   [Yes or no]

If some book is not available in your school library, would it be unusual for you to try to borrow it from some other library?   [Yes or no]
                                    (Lewy, 1966, pp. 168–170)

If I like a certain musical piece, I often recommend it to my friends for the purpose of listening to it. [True or not true]

In several instances I tried to convince my friends that they should devote some time for listening to music.

[True or not true]

(pp. 160–166)

Mathematics (Algebra, Geometry, etc.) is not useful for problems of everyday life. [True or not true]

Would you spend some time intensively studying the meaning of a complex design? [Yes or no]

(pp. 150–158)

4.0 Organization

At the fourth level of internalization— *Organization*—one attempts to determine if a student has conceptualized certain values to the extent that he or she uses them as a basis for making judgments about concepts, activities, events, etc. The following questions try to determine if the student has been influenced by an action, the extent to which events or concepts are discussed, how opinions are formed, and whether such opinions are voiced.

Have any of the books which you read markedly influenced your views about social problems like unemployment?

[Yes or no]

Have any of the books you read markedly influenced your views about marriage or family life? [Yes or no]

(Lewy, 1966, pp. 168–170)

The key element in the following questions is the attempt to establish whether the student's reactions to events, activities, concepts, etc., are controlled by underlying values.

I like to exchange views on the quality of performance with others who have heard the same program.

[True or not true]

Have you ever had to explain or discuss the [question] What makes a musical composition immortal? [Yes or no]

In your writing or speeches, have you ever tried expressing your opinion on the importance of mathematics in our life?

[Yes or no]

Have you ever thought about what is the meaning of "beauty in mathematics?" [Yes or no]

(Lewy, 1966, pp. 150–158)

The preceding examples, drawn from Lewy's work, illustrate the type of question that can be used to evaluate learning at each level of the *Taxonomy*. Further, they show how statements of affective objectives derived from the *Taxonomy* can be clarified in terms of questions designed to evaluate them. The illustrations used above are all forced-choice questionnaire items; however there are numerous additional techniques available to those interested in evaluating affective outcomes. A variety of techniques will be surveyed in a subsequent section, followed by a description of sources a teacher might use to select evaluation techniques in the affective domain. Let us now consider in more detail the problems associated with evaluating affective objectives and steps that might be taken to alleviate them.

PROBLEMS OF EVALUATION IN THE AFFECTIVE DOMAIN

We saw earlier that one of the reasons affective outcomes are often neglected is because they are not evaluated, and we alluded to the fact that this was partly because evaluation of affect is beset with more problems than evaluation of cognition. In this section we shall discuss general problems associated with the measurement of affective objectives. In the next section we shall treat specific problems related to particular techniques that may be used to assess affect.

"Credibility Gap"

Perhaps the single most troublesome problem is that students' actions or products specified as indicators of such affective constructs as interest, attitudes, and values might in fact be reflecting no more than a desire to please or to give the socially acceptable response. In other words, a teacher cannot always take at face value students' responses to affective questions. This "credibility gap" is less of a problem in the cognitive domain and least troublesome in the psychomotor domain, where the behavior itself is the objective sought (Eiss & Harbeck, 1972).

The "credibility gap" associated with behavioral indicators in the affective domain can develop in several ways. Younger children are often anxious to simply please adults and thus tend to say or do what they think the teacher wants them to say or do (Ball, 1971). Older students may try to please the teacher, play on perceived biases of the teacher (Orlandi, 1971), or try to give what they feel is the socially acceptable answer, simply to stay on the right side of the teacher in hopes of good grades. Credibility is a particularly thorny problem when self-report items are used. For example, consider the following question:

What is the most time you have ever spent working on an interesting mathematics problem?
    a. about 30 minutes or less
    b. about 1 hour
    c. up to 4 hours
    d. off and on for several days

A student could select choices b or c or d because he or she actually spent that much time or because of a wish to impress the mathematics teacher.

The tendency among some students to try to please the teacher or try to give only what they perceive to be socially acceptable responses can be counteracted by the use of group data. Group data on affective behavior are all that is required for curriculum evaluation. The use of group results for the evaluation of curriculum outcomes makes it possible for the teacher to guarantee the students' anonymity by allowing them to omit their names from any affective instruments.

Sometimes, however, it is desirable to identify individuals so that the affective information can be used for formative self-evaluation and guidance. When this is the case, the students have to be assured that their responses will not be criticized, let alone graded. This assurance can serve the same purpose as a guarantee of anonymity, once the students are convinced that the results

are treated scrupulously in a confidential, unthreatening manner. Such trust is the basis of any good guidance program, and there is no reason teachers cannot treat affective information the way it is handled in a counselor-counselee relationship. If this trust exists, then the validity of self-report techniques is enhanced.

Another way to lessen the credibility problem associated with self-reporting is to use direct observations of students' actions. Thus a music teacher might accept as an indicator of valuing music the fact that the student voluntarily signs up for the glee club. Another teacher might feel that an indicator of interest, or lack thereof, would be the number of class cuts. Even these direct observable actions can result in incorrect inferences, however. In the first instance a student's real motive for joining the glee club might simply be that it looks good on a college admission form. In the second instance a student could cut a number of classes that fell during the first two periods of the day because of early-morning bouts of asthma. That a child is quiet and does not volunteer may indicate a lack of interest in a subject or instead may indicate shyness. A number of different types of observations over an extended period of time can lessen the likelihood of incorrect inferences about an affective outcome.

Superficial Changes in Attitudes

A different dimension to the problem of measuring affect involves the fact that many attitudes are resistant to change but can appear changed because of some exhilarating experience, such as a motion picture (Orlandi, 1971). If a scale were administered before and after a film on a sensitive topic, it might appear that an attitude change had come about. However, such a "change" might be superficial and vanish after a brief time period. Further, Orlandi points out that even when students answer attitude questions honestly, the change can easily be simply verbal in nature and personal behavior has remained unaltered.

Instability of Young Children's Attitudes

There is a special set of problems associated with measuring affect in young children. Ball (1971) notes that there is little stability in the attitudes of children 4 to 7. Young children can be easily influenced by momentary considerations. Thus patterns of behavior over extended periods of time should be used as the basis for inferences about affective objectives in young children (Kamii, 1971). While they are more honest about their feelings, Aiken (1970) questions the degree of self-insight and conscientiousness with which primary students respond to affective inventories. Because children of this age group have difficulty reading, writing, and following directions, affective evaluations should be individually administered in preschool and to very small groups in the early primary grades (Ball, 1971).

A teacher who wishes to evaluate affective outcomes needs to proceed with caution. The teacher must be satisfied that any instrument used is valid and take various precautions to close the "credibility gap" as far as possible.

Teachers are safer in making inferences about groups than about individuals. When anonymity can be ensured, behavioral decisions can be made because the student trusts the teacher not to abuse, reveal, or grade the response.

METHODS OF EVALUATING AFFECTIVE OUTCOMES

This section is a brief review of the range of possible techniques a teacher might use to evaluate affective outcomes. It is beyond the scope of this chapter to explore the details of each technique. Instead, the techniques will be briefly described, examples given of their uses in evaluating affect, and—where appropriate—problems with the techniques noted. Sources a teacher can consult to investigate each technique in more detail are provided.

Observation

Teachers directly observe their students every day in a variety of settings, under all types of conditions. What better opportunity to make inferences about intended and unintended affective outcomes or for that matter cognitive or psychomotor outcomes? Observation permits immediate, on-the-spot assessment of affective behavior. Further, as mentioned above, daily observation over an extended period permits more direct, safer inferences about patterns of affective behavior than data from a single administration of a paper-and-pencil instrument. By listening to what students say to others and about themselves and by observing them in their daily routine, patterns of affective behavior can be identified. Cazden (1971), for example, calls the teacher's attention to the following:

> . . . When they first come to school in the morning, do they initiate conversation with other children? With adults? Do they often voluntarily participate in a small discussion group or listen to a story or talk over yesterday's visitor? On trips, do they ask more questions about what they see and hear? (p. 381)

A teacher should be alert to such signals as thoroughness in checking arithmetic answers, joining extracurricular clubs, helping a classmate with homework, continually being late for class, frequently "forgetting" the arithmetic book, working alone with minimal supervision, being prompt in beginning assignments. These kinds of observations of course are an essential part of teaching. The blank, bored, anxious, or guilty look, the eagerly raised hand, the knowing smile, the giggle, etc., provide the on-the-spot cues the teacher needs to adjust instruction. However, a teacher who wishes to use observations to make systematic inferences about affective outcomes might systematically record the observations to be employed. If observations are not recorded soon after the event, important aspects of the event may be forgotten. One technique of recording observations is to keep a daily log. In such a log the teacher should record what the student actually did, said, or produced and the situation in which these actions took place. Subjective impressions and interpretations of these actions should be clearly distinguished from the record of events. Recording daily, specific instances of overt behavior indicative of affect can be particularly helpful with students experiencing difficulty in the class. The log can reveal patterns of actions which might otherwise go undetected.

One problem not unique to this technique is that the observer's own biases, expectations, and preferences can distort inferences made from the data. While this problem can never be completely overcome, it can be minimized by concentrating attention on recording observable behavior of students and specific circumstances.

A rating form is another device that a teacher might use to record observed behavior as it happens, at the end of the day or at least on a weekly basis. For example Kamii (1971, pp. 305–306) suggests that the socioemotional objectives of preschool can be described in behavorial terms and then every few days a teacher can rate children on each behavior. The objective the student develops, "Achievement motivation and pride of mastery," can be further specified in terms of the following component behaviors:

Completes assignments
Is hesitant to try, or gives up easily
Takes time to reflect in making decisions
Can stay with one activity for some time
Has a short attention span
Brings treasures to school

(Adapted from Kamii, p. 306)

The teacher can periodically rate each student on the frequency of each specified behavior. The following familiar five-point scale might be employed: VF for "very frequently," F for "frequently," S for "sometimes," I for "infrequently," and VI for "very infrequently." These letter symbols could of course be converted into a numerical scale of 1 to 5, where 5 always indicates the *most desirable* response. Thus a VF for "completes assignments" would get a value of 5, while a similar VF for "short attention span" would

receive a 1. This numerical coding permits the teacher to do two things with the data. First, the teacher can compute the average score for the class for each behavior. Second, the teacher can sum across all behaviors associated with a single objective.

There are two problems in using rating scales. First, there is a tendency to use one or two positions on the scale to the exclusion of others. Such a tendency is related to the more general response bias of being either overcautious or overgenerous (Green, 1977). Second, Green points out that ratings on specific traits are often influenced by global impressions the teacher has of the student. Teachers who rate a student high or low on one trait often rate the student high or low across all the traits on the rating scale. Teachers who use a rating scale to record their daily observations should attempt as far as possible to use the full range of rating categories and should be aware of the "halo affect" when rating a particular student.

An alternative to the rating scale is the simpler checklist. The teacher uses a check ($\sqrt{}$) when the behavior is observed. Some checklists call for a plus or minus sign to indicate the presence of a desirable or undesirable action.

The partial checklist shown in Table 11-1 along with directions for its use illustrates how a science teacher might record observed affective behavior.

The reader is referred to Whisler and Harper (1962) for a more detailed treatment of the development and use of rating scales and checklists.

Unobtrusive Techniques

An unobtrusive measure of an affective outcome is a related observational technique. An unobtrusive measure does not require the cooperation of the student in responding. Further, it is nonreactive in that it does not contaminate the response by influencing through its very use the behavior in question (Webb, Campbell, Schwartz, & Sechrest, 1966).

TABLE 11-1 PARTIAL CHECKLIST

How to use the checklist:

Write the students' names or numbers at the top of the checklist and the desired behaviors down the left-hand margin; check the appropriate behaviors beneath the students' names or numbers whenever they are observed exhibiting them. Also, you may wish to use minus signs to indicate "negative behaviors" that are observed, that is, when the student exhibits a behavior that is the opposite of what is desired. Additional behaviors may be added in the blanks at the bottom of the page.

Desired behaviors	Mary	Kathy	Joe	George	Eileen	Sarah	Martha	Chris	Matt	Etc.
Verbal behaviors										
Argues:										
Advocates desirable actions										
Defends desirable actions										
Criticizes plans and suggestions	✓		✓					✓		
Asks:										
Inquires for further information										
Examines others' ideas by further questioning	✓	✓				✓		✓		
Reads:										
Science magazines				✓			✓			
Science books				✓						
Science articles in the daily or weekly press				✓						
Nonverbal behaviors										
Participates:										
Joins science clubs				✓	✓		✓		✓	
Participates actively in science clubs										
Contributes:										
Time to science projects	✓			✓						
Money to science projects				✓			✓			
Time and money to agencies attempting to improve the environment				✓						
Visits:										
Science centers, etc.				✓					✓	
Assists in laboratory preparations and operations, etc.	✓									
Repairs:										
Adjusts science equipment, etc.				✓						
Purchases:										
Science equipment, etc.				✓						
(Other items should be added as needed.)										

Students' names (or numbers)

Source: Adapted from Eiss & Harbeck, 1972, pp. 37–38.

Examples of unobtrusive affective measures include school records (e.g., attendance, tardiness, library checkouts), students' products (papers, notebooks, etc.), and physical evidence (voluntary seating arrangements, the library books or class materials that are most worn from use, etc.). Foley (1971) sums up the use of nonreactive measure to assess affect connected with writing as follows:

> The evaluation depends most often upon the ingenuity of the teacher in structuring situations for the unobtrusive gathering of evaluative data. Simple observation can transform journals, workbooks and notebooks into eloquent witnesses—if the evaluator is sensitive and cautious about ways in which the act of observing affects what is observed. (p. 800)

The use of unobtrusive measures does involve ingenuity and creativity on the part of a teacher, but the results can often be well worth the effort. The reader is referred to Webb et al. (1966) for a more detailed treatment of the topic of unobtrusive measures.

The Interview

The interview technique involves a face-to-face encounter in which the interviewer asks carefully developed questions of the student. The interview can be structured or unstructured in format.

In the structured interview, the wording and sequence of the questions are fixed. The interviewer is given little or no freedom to deviate from the fixed schedule except to clarify misunderstanding or ambiguities and to branch into other sections of the schedule when certain criteria are met. The principal job of the interviewer is to present the question to the student and record the answer.

The following questions are samples of structural interview items developed for a summative evaluation of affect toward an experimental course in Russian.* The respondents were culturally disadvantaged high school students who had long records of scholastic failure. The interviewer asked each question and then marked the alternative which most closely corresponded to the student's free answer.

*This illustration is borrowed from items 1, 5, and 7 of an unpublished instrument developed by Peter W. Airasian, presently at Boston College, for the late Wayne Fisher of the University of Chicago Laboratory School.

How much do you like your Russian course?
- a) a lot
- b) indifferent
- c) not much
- d) don't know

Why?
- a) teacher
- b) subject matter
- c) fact that it's a special class
- d) friends are not in it
- e) get credit without work
- f) hardness or easiness
- g) _____

What is the most important thing you've learned in your Russian course so far?
- a) all teachers are not bad
- b) a good teacher can make a subject interesting
- c) content response
- d) I can do something well
- e) a new respect for school
- f) a new understanding of other school topics
- g) a better understanding of current events
- h) the relation between what goes on in school and out of school
- i) _____

What do other students in the course think of it?
- a) like
- b) dislike
- c) indifferent
- d) don't talk about it
- e) afraid to say

What do students not in the class think of it?
- a) a good idea
- b) wish they had a course like it
- c) don't ever say
- d) dislike it
- e) _____

The similarities between the structured interview questions and items on a self-report questionnaire are obvious. The principal difference involves the face-to-face encounter which gives greater assurance that the student understands the intent of the questions.

In the unstructured interview, a limited number of key questions are raised. In the unstructured interview, the interviewer listens and probes. Here the approach is much more nondirective, and the interviewer has almost unlimited freedom to explore subtle nuances, thereby clarifying a respondent's answer. The unstructured interview broadens and deepens the evaluative information by encouraging a more spontaneous and more immediately personal expression of attitudes on the part of the student. It enables the student to indicate the whys and wherefores of the values and attitudes expressed.

Obviously the unstructured interview is more time-consuming both to conduct and to process than the structured interview. Despite this drawback, the unstructured interview can give a teacher information impossible to gather in any other way. Further, the unstructured interview can serve to suggest ideas for writing structured items; when used with a small sample in addition to a structured-interview technique, it allows the investigator to check on the validity of the structured data; finally, it can fill out the skeletal findings of the structured approach.

There are problems with both kinds of interviews. Because an interpersonal encounter is involved, several factors can influence the student's responses to the interview situation. First, if the student is reticent, he or she may need extra encouragement to answer; and the interviewer needs to be sensitive to this possibility.

Second, students of different backgrounds might interpret questions differently. Pretesting with carefully chosen samples can help identify questions that are interpreted differently because of differences in social or linguistic backgrounds.

Third, students' responses might be governed by their perceptions of the power relationship in the interview (Labov, 1972). For example, if the classroom teacher is the interviewer and a student has had negative experiences in the class, the student may view the situation not as an interview but as an investigation and accordingly may say what he or she thinks the teacher wants to hear. In such cases a "neutral" interviewer should be used. Another reactive situation might occur when the race, ethnicity, or sex of the interviewer differs from that of the interviewee.

Fourth, young children may misunderstand a question which may be clear to older children and perfectly reasonable to the adult who framed it. As Blank (1975, p. 245) points out, adults "reinterpret the question so that it better represents what they believe the experimenter must be driving at." Younger children seldom have this ability, and therefore their answers can appear to be off the point. Because of his or her frame of reference, the adult may continue even after pretesting to be unaware of the fact that the child has misunderstood the intent of the question.

Finally, in employing the unstructured interview to gather information about affective objectives, the teacher must be careful not to lead the respondents or influence them so that they give what they consider to be the expected answer. The reader is referred to Sidney and Brown (1961); Richardson, Dohrenwend, and Klein (1965); and Dyer (1976) for a more detailed treatment of interview techniques. Another excellent source is Payne's (1951) book *The Art of Asking Questions*.

The Open-Ended Question

The open-ended question calls for a written statement which may vary in length. Raths, Harmin, and Simon list some open-ended questions which have been effective in getting at attitudes, beliefs, activities, and values.

With a gift of $100, I would . . .
  If this next weekend *were* a three-day weekend, I would want to . . .
My best friends can be counted on to . . .
My bluest days are . . .
I can hardly wait to be able to . . .
My children won't have to . . . Because . . .
People can hurt my feelings the most by . . .
If I had a car of my own . . .
I've made up my mind to finally learn how to . . .
If I could get a free subscription to two magazines, I would select . . . Because . . .
Some people seem to want only to . . .
The night I stayed up later than ever before I . . .
If I could have seven wishes . . .
I believe . . .
Secretly I wish . . .
My advice to the world would be . . .

(Raths, Harmin, & Simon, 1966, pp. 137–138, items 1–16.)

315

The open-ended questionnaire has been widely used to measure attitude structure and socialization. Getzels and Walsh (1958) report on an interesting technique that can be used not only to measure socialization but also to reduce the tendency of respondents to indicate attitudes more favorable than their true beliefs. Their approach to the open-ended questionnaire involves the use of two instruments: the paired "direct" and "projective" questionnaires. In the direct questionnaire each item includes a first-person pronoun; in the projective questionnaire the same items are phrased in the third person.

In responding to the direct instrument, the subject is fully aware of the self-revelatory and possibly evaluative nature of his responses. Because of this the response represents "the level of behavior at which the individual permits society to look at him" (Getzels & Walsh, 1958, p. 3). The projective questionnaire, in contrast, is devoid of personal reference and thus affords a truer measure of respondents' beliefs. Several illustrative items from Getzels and Walsh's monograph follow:

When I break a window while playing I . . .	When Alice breaks a window while playing, she . . .
Whenever they ask me to be in charge, I . . .	Whenever they ask Freda to be in charge, she . . .
If the teacher caught me cheating on the test, I . . .	If the teacher caught Bea cheating on the test, Bea . . .

(Getzels & Walsh, 1958, pp. 29–33, items 5, 23, 36; pp. 32–36, items 23, 13, 36.)

When used in the formative or summative evaluation of a curriculum that purports to change attitudes, the "projective" version will reduce the conscious and unconscious tendencies students have to give what they consider to be the socially acceptable response. The proportion of negative responses on the projective version to positive responses on the direct instrument gives a discrepancy score between personal hypotheses and expressed reactions. This technique, coupled with assurances of confidentiality to the respondent, could help construct a truer picture of the curriculum's impact on attitudes.

The open-ended technique has two principal advantages from an evaluation point of view. First, it is an excellent device for making a formative evaluation of either the curriculum or the student. The responses of the class to open-ended questions can show the teacher areas of common concern and points of misunderstanding and negative affect, which can then receive additional instruction emphasis while the curriculum is still fluid.

Second, when the student realizes that he or she is free to answer such questions or not and knows that the responses will not be graded, the experience of answering the open-ended questions can provide valuable insights. Insights about affect can be further enhanced when the teacher, either in writing or in discussion, asks the student to clarify his or her response further, points out inconsistencies or assumptions that have been made, underlines extreme statements, and asks the student such questions as "Have you done anything about this?" All these actions give the student formative evaluative information about the present status, growth, or development of his or her interests, attitudes, and values (Raths, Harmin, & Simon, 1966). However, if responses to open-ended questions are used to help the students gain insights about themselves, Cronbach's (1977, p. 748) warning needs to be heeded:

> Only a qualified therapist can safely undertake to make the student highly conscious of his beliefs and feelings about personal matters. Making a student self-conscious can be damaging. . . . There is a place for the adolescent or the advanced student to examine closely his philosophy of life; such a systematic review is not undertaken in the spirit of short-term feed-backs.

Like the unstructured interview, the open-ended question technique can be a rich source for possible alternative answers in a closed format. A problem with the open-ended technique is that the answers are time-consuming and sometimes difficult to read and interpret. Concerning interpretation, it is important that the teacher have explicit guidelines in order to recognize reliable indications of the affective constructs under consideration.

The Closed-Item Questionnaire

The questionnaire with fixed alternatives is similar to the structured interview described earlier except that the respondent completes it without the aid of an interviewer. The closed-item instrument takes several forms.

Ranking or forced choice

These questionnaires require the student to rank or choose statements in terms of their appeal. This item type could ask for a simple ranking from high to low. Alternatively the students are required to choose among three or more statements that one that is most appealing and the one that is least appealing. An example of this forced-choice type is the following item taken from the field of vocational education:

Responding to alternative automotive repair jobs
Listed below are three tasks which a mechanic is expected to perform. In the blank space next to the tasks, write an "M" to indicate the one you would like to do *most,* and an "L" for the one you would like to do *least.*
_____Perform a valve and ring job
_____Trace a short in the electrical system
_____Repair a hydraulic brake system
(Baldwin, 1971, p. 890)

Another type of forced-choice item asks the student simply to check off from a longer list of statements describing an activity, job, etc., a limited number that are most interesting, appealing, important, etc.

A more complicated form of ranking asks the student to read through an extensive list of statements and pick a fixed number that are most important (or appealing), then go back and rank the statements chosen in order of importance (or appeal). For example, the

following questions were used in evaluating a literature course:

Below are twenty questions which people have asked about _____. Some of them you may think are more important than others. Read through the questions and put an X in front of the nine questions that you think are important to your understanding of _____. When you have done that, look at the nine questions you have chosen and put a 1 next to the one that you think is most important, a 2 next to the one you think is next most important, and so on until you have rated five of the nine questions.
  a. Is this a proper subject for a story?
  b. How does_____make me feel?
  c. Are any of the characters in _____ like people I know?
  d. Has the writer used words differently from the way people usually use them?
  e. What tricks that authors use are in this story?
  f. What happens in_____?
  g. Does the way it is told fit what _____ is about?
  h. How does the story develop?
  i. What does the author think about the people he is writing about in_____?
  j. What type of story is_____? Is it like any other story I know?
  k. When was_____written? What is the background of the story?
  l. Is there one part of_____that explains the whole story?
  m. Is there anything in_____that has a hidden meaning?
  n. How can we explain the way people behave in_____?
  o. What does_____tell me about the way people are?
  p. What does_____tell us about people in general?
  q. Does_____teach us a lesson?
  r. Is_____effective in making me feel the way I am supposed to?
  s. Is_____well-written?
  t. Does_____have something important to say?
(Purves, 1971, pp. 748–749)

Two difficulties associated with ranking or forced-choice techniques are, first, that the list to be ranked can become unwieldy for the student. The number of statements to be ranked should stay within the ability of the age group to hold the statements in mind while considering the ranking. Second, by its very nature the technique forces students to choose between alternatives. If the choices to be ranked or chosen are very similar in appeal, then the resulting ranks or choices could lead to an overinterpretation of the students' preferences.

Scales

A common item type asks students to choose from a point on a scale that corresponds to his or her answer to a question. The scales, which can take many forms, consist of two or more points. For example, as we saw above, a student might be asked to answer yes or no to a question—a two-point scale—or to indicate whether he or she strongly agrees with, agrees with, is uncertain about, disagrees with, or strongly disagrees with a particular statement—a five-point scale. These types of rating scales differ from those described previously in that the students are rating themselves rather than having their actions or products rated by the teacher or some observer.

Often it is desirable to secure a measure of the intensity of a student's affect toward a phenomenon. Several response modes make this possible; they are illustrated by the following items in mathematics:

I would like to be a mathematician.
    a. strongly disagree
    b. disagree
    c. don't know
    d. agree
    e. strongly agree
I would like to study mathematics
    a. no more
    b. one more year
    c. two more years
    d. three more years
Outside of school, I would like to use mathematics
    a. every chance I get
    b. often
    c. sometimes
    d. hardly ever
    e. never

I use mathematics outside of school in my games, reading, hobbies, or when watching TV
    a. very often
    b. quite often
    c. sometimes
    d. hardly ever
    e. never

(Wilson et al., 1968, p. 217)

As we saw with the rating scale, the verbal categories in the scale can be assigned number values. A conversion with the highest numbers going to the most-favored category should be followed. Thus in the example above, "strongly disagree" would be coded 1; "disagree," 2; "don't know," 3; "agree," 4; and "strongly agree," 5. As mentioned earlier, these numeric values can be summed across items to yield a total score on a construct. Further, they can be used to compute group averages for summative evaluation.

In using scales such as the one described above, a teacher needs to be aware that elementary students may not be able to make distinctions between adjacent scale values. Reducing the number of categories can help alleviate this problem. For example in the first item above, three categories—"agree," "no opinion," and "disagree"—could be used instead of five. The following is a simple two-point scale that is often used for students in the middle grades:

Directions: The purpose of this questionnaire is to determine how you feel about the things we do in class. There are no right answers. Check the blank for "yes" if you agree with the statement. Check the blank for "no" if you disagree with the statement.

Yes No
___ ___ 87. I like to read orally.
___ ___ 88. I like to work on committees to discuss reading.
___ ___ 89. I like to answer questions about my reading.
___ ___ 90. I enjoy making reports of books.
___ ___ 91. I enjoy reading certain parts of books orally.

(Moore & Kennedy, 1971, p. 434)

A pictorial response mode is often preferable to verbal categories when assessing affect of children in the primary grades. For example, the following is a pictorial scale item from the primary version (scales 1–23) of the *Survey of School Attitudes* (Hogan, 1975a):

The teacher reads the following aloud:

Now go down to the next row. In the box you see a plant that has grown. Fill in the face to show whether or not you like to study about how plants grow. (p. 15)

The student then fills in one of the three faces described as follows:

One of the faces is smiling—it's a happy face.

Another face has a frown on it—it looks very sad.

And the face in the middle looks neither happy nor sad.

(Hogan, 1975b, item 3)

O'Hara (1958) describes a simple and speedy but highly valid format for measuring students' vocational self-concept in the areas of interests, general values, work values, and aptitudes. This method involves taking definitions of a particular trait or construct of interest to the investigator from either the test manual or the test itself, and asking students to rate themselves regarding the trait or construct on a nine-point scale. The following is an example of the self-concept scale corresponding with the artistic interest scale of the Kuder Preference Record. Notice that in this scale the student is asked to make a norm-referenced comparison; the scale positions (shown in Table 11-2) are stated in terms of the student's interests in relation to a group. The student checks the space that describes the amount of his or her interest.

ARTISTIC INTEREST—Artistic interest means liking to do creative work with your hands—usually work that has "eye appeal," involving attractive design, colors and materials.

(O'Hara, 1958)

This form of item can encompass any concept so that by changing the description from "artistic interest" to, say, "ability to think for oneself," a teacher can obtain an indication of the student's self-rating on many constructs. Using these scales as pre- and posttests can give a teacher an indication of how the instruction is affecting the students' rating of themselves on the pertinent trait. This scale could be shortened by eliminating categories 1, 3, 7, and 9.

A variation of the rating scale technique asks the student to use the scale points to fill in a blank between two separate activities. For example, consider the following item (remember that although the item is broken across pages in this book, that would not be done on a test):

Directions: Each sentence below has a blank space in the middle. Following each sentence are *five* ways you can fill

TABLE 11-2 SELF-CONCEPT SCALE FOR "ARTISTIC INTEREST"

1	2	3	4	5	6	7	8	9
My interest ranks with the lowest group in this field	I have very much less interest than most people	I have much less interest than most people	I have less interest than most people	I have the same amount of interest as most people	I have a little more interest than most people	I have much more interest than most people	I have very much more interest than most people	My interest ranks with the highest group in this field

Source: O'Hara, 1958.

the blank. After you read the sentence carefully, choose the one answer which is MOST like the way you really feel. Choose ONLY ONE answer for each sentence. Remember, there are no right or wrong answers to any of these sentences. When you have decided which answer is most like the way you feel, CIRCLE the letter *in front of* your choice.

(1) I like reading about a great writer

_____ reading about scientific discoveries

a. a lot more than   d. a little less than

b. a little more than   e. a lot less than

c. just as much as

(2) I like talking about problems in science

_____talking about problems in social studies. [Same alternatives as in question (1).]

(3) I like writing answers to social studies questions

_____ writing answers to science questions. [Same alternatives as in question (1).]

(Shoresman, 1965, items 1, 6, 7)

The format allows a comparison between two stated activities by forcing a simultaneous consideration of both.

Sometimes it is desirable to combine the advantages of the open-ended question and the closed-item format. This technique provides the evaluator with both quantitative and qualitative information while also giving data that allow for validity checks. The following example from the Independent Activities Questionnaire of the Educational Testing Service (1965) illustrates this combination.

	NO	YES
During the last year have you read an entire book of either fiction or nonfiction other than for a classroom assignment?	☐	☐
If "no" place an X in the "NO" box and [skip the next two questions]. If "yes" place an X in the "YES" box and go to [the two questions] below.		
Do you frequently discuss with family or friends ideas or impressions you have gained from books you have read?	☐	☐
Describe most recent example: _____		
Have you, on your own initiative, written out quotations, notes, or critiques of books that you have read?	☐	☐
Describe most recent example: _____		

(Educational Testing Service, 1965, items 23, 23a, 23b.)

A modification of the paired direct and projective technique of Getzels and Walsh discussed above also lends itself to the closed-item format, as is illustrated in the following item. The directions instruct the respondent to guess how the person described, an average person, would act in a difficult situation and then how the respondent would act under the same circumstances.

A man is walking down a deserted street at 2:00 A.M. As he turns the corner he sees a hoodlum striking a woman about the head and trying to take her purse. She holds on to the purse tenaciously. The man knows that he should go to her aid. There is no one else to call for help in the area. The man could turn back around the corner and no one would know.

If a man goes to her aid the attacker might become frightened and run. The attacker does not seem armed.

Would the man try to help the woman?	Would you try to help the woman?
___a. Definitely	___a. Definitely
___b. Probably	___b. Probably
___c. Probably not	___c. Probably not
___d. Definitely not	___d. Definitely not

(Klausner, 1963)

The reader should recall that the most difficult problem associated with using scales such as those described above involves the "credibility gap" of self-report data discussed earlier. The reader interested in pursuing self-report and scaling techniques in more detail is referred to Shaw and Wright (1967) and Oppenheim (1966).

The semantic differential (SD) technique of Charles Osgood (Osgood, Suci, & Tannenbaum, 1967) is a valuable and comprehensive tool for measuring generalized attitudes. The form of the instrument involves a list of bipolar adjective pairs; the student checks the scale value along the adjective continuum corresponding with his or her attitude toward the concept in question.

For example:

Concept
Polar term X . . . : ___: ___: ___: ___: ___: ___: Polar term Y
                1 2 3 4 5 6 7

These scaled positions, generally 5 or 7 between the two polar terms, are then defined.

Definitions might, for instance, be written as follows:

(1) extremely X
(2) quite X
(3) slightly X
(4) neither X nor Y; equally X and Y
(5) slightly Y
(6) quite Y
(7) extremely Y

To measure generalized attitudes, Osgood recommends the use of adjectives he has labeled "evaluative" to form the polar terms. Examples of such evaluative adjective pairs that form the polar terms X and Y illustrated in the general form above are "good-bad," "beautiful-ugly," "clean-dirty," "valuable-worthless," "beneficial-harmful," and "pleasant-unpleasant." A lengthy list of evaluative adjectives can be found in Osgood, Suci, and Tannenbaum's book *The Measurement of Meaning* (1967).

Almost any concept of interest could be used to form polar terms. For example, an English teacher might want to explore generalized attitudes toward drama, poetry, essay writing, or a Shakespearean play. Each concept is repeated separately with the same set of adjectives that form the polar opposites. *The Social Studies Evaluation Program* of the Education Development Center (1969) uses this technique to evaluate attitudes toward concepts contained in their social studies materials on Netsilik Eskimos. For example, attitudes toward the concept "Arctic" are assessed by the following semantic differential scales. Notice the use of opposing adjectives to form the ends of the scale:

Arctic
(The Arctic is the area near the North Pole.)

changing : ___:___:___:___:___ : changeless
windy   : ___:___:___:___:___ : calm
strange   : ___:___:___:___:___ : familiar
explored : ___:___:___:___:___ : unexplored
tame   : ___:___:___:___:___ : wild
good   : ___:___:___:___:___ : bad
deserted : ___:___:___:___:___ : inhabited
fierce   : ___:___:___:___:___ : gentle
livable   : ___:___:___:___:___ : not livable

(The Social Studies Evaluation Program, 1969, items 15–24)

An excellent sample of the instructions to students sitting for the semantic differential is provided by Rutherford et al. (1966).

Directions: In this study, we want to find out how you describe different things. There are no "right" or "wrong" answers. On each page in this booklet you will find a heading printed like this:

CHEMISTRY

The rest of the page contains pairs of words that you will use to describe your image of the heading at the top of the page. Each pair of words will be on a scale which looks like this:

Quick □ □ □ □ □ Slow

You are to make a check in the box which best represents how you feel that word pair describes the heading at the top of the page. For example, you might check the "QUICK-SLOW" scale this way for "CHEMISTRY"

If you feel that "CHEMISTRY" is very closely connected with "QUICK," check the scale like this:

Quick ☑ □ □ □ □ Slow

If you feel that "CHEMISTRY" is only somewhat connected with "QUICK," check the scale like this:

Quick □ ☑ □ □ □Slow

If you feel that "CHEMISTRY" is equally connected with "QUICK" and "SLOW," or *not connected with either,* check the scale like this:

Quick □ □ ☑ □ □ Slow

If you feel that "CHEMISTRY" is somewhat connected with "SLOW" or very closely connected with "SLOW," you would check one of the two boxes next to "SLOW" just as above.

Look at the heading at the top of the page; get an impression of it in your mind, and then work down the page checking the scales as *quickly* as you can. We are interested in your first impressions, so work rapidly and, do not go back and change any marks. *Be sure to check every scale* and only make one check on each scale.

PHYSICS

Safe □	□	□	□	□ Dangerous
Uninvolved □	□	□	□	□ Involved
Enjoyable □	□	□	□	□ Unenjoyable
Threatening □	□	□	□	□ Comforting
Refreshing □	□	□	□	□ Weary
Solemn □	□	□	□	□ Cheerful
Organized □	□	□	□	□ Messy
Unproductive □	□	□	□	□ Productive
Complex □	□	□	□	□ Simple
Important □	□	□	□	□ Unimportant
Interesting □	□	□	□	□ Dull
Gloomy □	□	□	□	□ Joyful
Worthless □	□	□	□	□ Worthwhile
Risky □	□	□	□	□ Sure
Boring □	□	□	□	□ Exciting

(Rutherford et al., 1966)

Using this technique the teacher-evaluator can determine differences between concepts or between individuals or groups on a concept. For a more technical treatment of the analysis of SD data, the reader is referred to Osgood, Suci, and Tannenbaum's text.

SOURCES OF AFFECTIVE OBJECTIVES AND EVALUATIVE TECHNIQUES

We shall now consider sources a teacher might use to select affective objectives and affective evaluation techniques. In doing so we will make a distinction between sources for affective objectives and evaluation techniques that are subject-specific and those that cover more general constructs related to school. The examples from the Eight-Year Study and from Lewy described above are examples of the former, while more general constructs like academic self-concept, attitude toward school, need achievement, level of educational aspiration, test anxiety, etc., are examples of the latter.

Sources of Subject-Related Affective Objectives and Evaluation Techniques

We have already discussed two excellent sources of subject-related affective objectives and techniques for their evaluation, *The Eight-Year Study* (Smith & Tyler, 1942) and *The Taxonomy of Educational Objectives*, Handbook 2, *Affective Domain* (Krathwohl, Bloom, & Masia, 1964).

Part II of the *Handbook of Formative and Summative Evaluation of Student Learning* (Bloom, Hastings, & Madaus, 1971), described in Chapter 2, is another source from which it is possible to select both subject-specific affective objective and evaluation techniques. The authors of ten of the eleven different subject matter chapters use language identical or similar to the affective *Taxonomy* in discussing affective outcomes in their disciplines and provide illustrations of techniques that can be used to evaluate such outcomes. The single exception is the chapter by Constance Kamii (1971), who discusses and de-

scribes "socioeducational objectives" and evaluation techniques in terms of the following more general constructs: dependence on the teacher; inner controls; interaction with other children; ability to get along with other children; comfort in school; achievement, motivation, and pride of mastery; curiosity; and creativity.

The National Assessment of Education Progress has described affective objectives for each of the ten subject matter areas described in Chapter 2. For example, in the area of writing there are three affective objectives:

a. Recognize the value of writing for social, business, and scholastic needs.
b. Write to fulfill these needs.
c. Get satisfaction from having written something well.

Those who teach in the subject areas covered by NAEP would do well to consider the affective goals for each age group that have been specified by the various NAEP committees. Accompanying each affective objective are descriptions of individual actions that are indicative of the objectives.

Teachers should be aware of the work of *professional associations* in specifying subject-related affective objectives and techniques for their evaluation. For example, the National Science Supervisors Association (NSSA) has a booklet, *Behavioral Objectives in the Affective Domain* (Eiss & Harbeck, 1972), which is an excellent source for science teachers to consult. The following are three affective objectives in science at the level of *Valuing* (p. 30):

15. patience
    a. is willing to wait for something worthwhile, i.e., data.
    b. undertakes long-term projects where no immediate results are possible.
    c. is willing to perform time-consuming procedures without attempting questionable shortcuts.

National curriculum development groups also provide interested teachers with a pool of affective objectives and related techniques. For example, the School Mathematics Study Group (SMSG) (B. G. Wilson, 1971) has developed a series of instruments to measure affect in mathematics. The following are two such items designed to measure interest in mathematics. The first is an example of *Receiving* (attending); the second, an example of *Responding*.

I would like to learn to program a computer
a. not at all   c. quite well
b. just a little   d. expertly

I use mathematics outside of school in my games, reading, hobbies, or when watching TV
a. very often   d. hardly ever
b. quite often   e. never
c. sometimes

(Wilson et al., 1968, p. 217)

Another source of subject-specific affective objectives is the *Report on the Evaluation Workshop in the Affective Domain of the Downers Grove Public School District Evaluation for Individualized Instruction Project* (Lieberman, Brown, Needlinger, & Swanson, 1970). (This source also contains more general school-related affective objectives). The report contains the following sections: samples of published tests in the area of affective objectives; school and institutional objectives; and samples of self-concept objectives. The final three sections are devoted to instruments to measure affective objectives specific to a given area of the curriculum, school and institutional affective objectives, and self-concept. The following is an example of an affective objective for German from the Downers Grove report.

The student will demonstrate his appreciation of the German people and language by:
1. voluntarily attempting to speak German
2. talking to other people about Germany and the German language
3. listening to other people talk about Germany and the German language
4. voluntarily reading books and materials about Germany
5. corresponding in German with a person in Germany

It would be impossible to mention all the possible sources from which a teacher may select affective objectives for school subjects. One should consult the latest *Mental Measurement Yearbooks* (Buros, 1972, 1978) for reviews of commercially available instruments. These yearbooks also review research instruments designed to measure affective objectives. Teachers should periodically check the professional literature in their discipline for critical reviews dealing with affective evaluation. For example, Aiken (1969, 1970, 1976) provides a periodic review of the available literature concerning attitudes toward mathematics.

The teacher needs to keep abreast of the rapid development of sources and materials that are being developed in the affective area. However, the sources mentioned above are good places to begin the search for sources from which one can select or adapt affective subject-related objectives.

In *selecting* affective objectives the reader needs to recall the cautions outlined in Chapter 2 governing the screens that need to be employed before an objective is adopted by a teacher. Figure 11-3 shows a summary worksheet developed by Walker (1977) which teachers might use to help them systematically screen affective instruments. The worksheet presents the information that should be examined when reviewing an affective instrument for possible adoption.

Sources of School-Related Affective Objectives and Evaluation Techniques

Two sources of subject-related affective material—the affective *Taxonomy* and the Downers Grove project—also contain excellent school-related affective material. There are several other avenues to be explored by a teacher or a group of teachers interested in selecting techniques to measure more general affective objectives, such as academic self-concept and attitude toward school.

First, commercial publishers market instruments that are designed to measure these general affective outcomes. Teachers should consult the *Mental Measurement Yearbooks*

Name of instrument _____

Author/developer _____

Address where measure is obtained _____

_____

DIRECTIONS

Answer the following with respect to the instrument listed above. Check all responses that apply or follow other directions. (Note: NA means no information was available to judge.)

UTILITY OF RESULTS

1. What type of evaluation and use of results from the affective measures is planned?

___Summative   ___Formative   ___Diagnostic

2. Is the desired affective variable assessed by the measure?

___Totally   ___Partially   ___Uncertain   ___Not at all

3. List intended audiences for the evaluation results (circle those who would be satisfied with the type of information produced by the measure).

_____

_____

APPROPRIATENESS FOR TARGET POPULATION

1. Is the instrument's content appropriate with respect to the following variables?

    a. Child's developmental level   _Yes   _No   _Uncertain   _NA

    b. Child's reading level   _Yes   _No   _Uncertain   _NA

    c. Child's oral comprehension   _Yes   _No   _Uncertain   _NA

    d. Child's vocabulary   _Yes   _No   _Uncertain   _NA

    e. Child's attention span   _Yes   _No   _Uncertain   _NA

2. Is the instrument's content biased with respect to the following:

    a. Race   _Yes   _No   _Uncertain   _NA

    b. Culture   _Yes   _No   _Uncertain   _NA

    c. Sex   _Yes   _No   _Uncertain   _NA

    d. Other (specify)   _Yes   _No   _Uncertain   _NA

3. Is the test format both appropriate and appealing?

_Yes   _Somewhat   _No   _Uncertain   _NA

4. Are the instructions for the administration of the measure clear and standardized?

_Yes   _No   _Uncertain   _NA

If applicable, are the instructions appropriate for the target population?

_Yes   _No   _Uncertain   _NA

5. Is the procedure for recording the child's responses appropriate and adequate?

_Yes   _No   _Uncertain   _NA

Figure 11-3 Summary worksheet for information considered in the selection of an affective measure. (Walker, 1977, pp. 75–79.)

(Buros) for reviews of such instruments and satisfy themselves that the instruments are valid measures of the constructs they purport to measure. Another source of reviews of published affective instruments is the *CSE-RBS Test Evaluations: Tests of Higher Or-der Cognitive, Affective and Interpersonal Skills* (Hoepfner et al., 1972).

Second, the *Head Start Test Collection Report* (Collier & Guthrie, 1971) is an annotated bibliography of a variety of self-concept measures appropriate for use with children

ADMINISTRATIVE USABILITY

1. Is the instrument easy and convenient to administer?
   _Yes   _No   _Uncertain   _NA
2. How long does the assignment procedure take each time it is used?

   _____

   How many times will the assessments be made during the evaluation?

   _____

   When? _____
3. Who should administer the procedure? _____

   How much formal training is needed to adequately administer the procedure?
   _None   _Minimal   _Some   _A lot   _NA
4. What is the approximate average cost per student for each time the assessment procedure is used? ___
   Overall, the costs associated with using the measure in the evaluations are
   _Extremely high   _High   _Moderate   _Low   _NA

TECHNICAL QUALITY (E—excellent; G—good; F—fair; P—poor)

1. Is the assessment procedure reliable? (Circle the most appropriate rating).

a. Internal consistency estimates	E	G	F	P	NA
b. Stability estimates	E	G	F	P	NA
c. Intertester-interjudge estimates	E	G	F	P	NA

   List eligible reliability coefficients: _____

   _____

2. Is the assessment procedure valid? (Circle the most appropriate rating.)

a. Content validity estimates	E	G	F	P	NA
b. Criterion-related validity					
Concurrent validity	E	G	F	P	NA
Predictive validity	E	G	F	P	NA
c. Construct validity estimates	E	G	F	P	NA

   List available validity data: _____

   _____

3. Are norms for the measure available?   _Yes   _No   _NA
   If so, for what age range? _____
   If so, are the norma adequate?   _Yes   _No   _Uncertain   _NA
4. Is there a ceiling or floor effect for some items in the measure?
   _Yes   _No   _Uncertain   _NA

ADEQUACY OF SCORING PROCEDURES

1. Is the scoring procedure understandable?
   _Yes   _No   _Uncertain   _NA
2. Who does the scoring? _____
   Is training necessary?   _Yes   _No   _Uncertain   _NA
3. Are interpretations from the scores clear and reasonable?
   _Yes   _No   _Uncertain   _NA

Figure 11-3 Continued.

from the preschool level through the third grade. The bibliography is meant to be an initial screening device to draw the reader's attention to measures which might otherwise be overlooked. The user should obtain copies of the instruments along with validity data before deciding to adopt any instrument described in the bibliography. The last is good advice and should be followed in selecting any instrument purporting to measure affective objectives, be it school- or subject-related. The following is an example of an entry from the bibliography (Collier & Guthrie, 1971, p. 6):

> 13. Gordon, I. J., *How I See Myself Scale*
>   *From:* Ira J. Gordon, Director, Institute for Development of Natural Resources, College of Education, University of Florida, Gainesville, Florida 32601. Manual available from the Florida Educational Research and Development Council, College of Education, University of Florida, Gainesville, Florida 32601, for $1.00.
>
> Designed to measure self-concept with regard to body, peers, teachers, school, and emotional control in children from the third through the sixth grade (elementary form). The test is self-administered and untimed. The test assumes that self-concept is not a unitary trait, but has a factor structure. Test items require the child to respond to bipolar statements on a scale from 1 to 5. No training is necessary to administer the test. Test-retest reliability for 34 third graders was .78 for the total score. Norms are provided for grades 3–12 by sex, race, and social class.

The *How I See Myself Scale* is an example of an instrument developed initially for research purposes. Anyone who is interested in exploring an instrument such as this should also consult the *Mental Measurement Yearbook* for possible reviews. On the basis of this review one might then order an examination copy and manual for a closer look.

Along lines similar to the Collier and Guthrie (1971) work, Knapp (1972) has completed *An Omnibus of Measures Related to School Based Attitudes*. Educational Testing Service (ETS) through its ERIC Clearinghouse has published test collections on attitudes toward school and school adjustment for grades 4–6 (1973a) and 7–12 (1973b).

Another source of more general school-related affective objectives and evaluation techniques for grades K–12 is the *Instructional Objectives Exchange* (IOX), described in Chapter 2. This source contains attitude measures in some commonly taught *subjects* as well.

IOX has drawn heavily on Title III programs (ESEA, 1965) from a number of states that were concerned with the development of affective objectives and measures of these objectives. The affective instruments in the IOX collection are meant for group, not individual, assessment. Therefore the validity of any of the attitudinal measures for an individual was not considered. Since these devices were not intended to be used to make decisions about an individual, some error in responses could be tolerated (IOX, nd). A user needs to keep this restriction in mind when considering the measures contained in the IOX pools.

Another source to consult in selecting affective objectives and evaluation techniques is state departments of education. Many of them have included general affective questions as part of their state needs-assessment programs. Teachers should routinely check with their state education department if they are in the process of selecting affective objectives or evaluation techniques.

As was the case with sources of subject-related affective materials, the teacher needs to keep abreast of professional journals for critical reviews of literature dealing with more general affective topics. For example, Shavelson, Hubner, and Stanton (1976) provide an excellent review entitled *Self-Concept: Validation of Construct Interpretation*.

In closing this description of sources from which a teacher might select affective objectives or instruments, we would remind the reader once again of the cautions needed in selecting objectives in general and affective objectives in particular (see pages 42–43). Further, we again remind the teacher of the need to keep abreast of developments in the field. Tools like ERIC—Educational Resources Information Center—can assist in this process with, for example, works such as *Measuring Attitudes toward Reading: An Annotated ERIC Bibliography* by Hahn (1977).

Finally, we would reiterate that before

selecting an instrument to measure affective outcomes, be they subject-related or school-related, teachers must satisfy themselves that the test is valid. It is not enough that the items look as if they measure interest or attitudes, etc., or that the items deal with a specific curricular area. Content validity is not sufficient for affective instruments (Hogan, 1975a). As mentioned, an instrument may simply be measuring the student's desire to please the teacher or give the socially acceptable response. Evidence of validity should be scrutinized carefully. Correlations between scales measuring affect in different subject areas or between more general affective constructs like academic self-concepts and attitudes toward school should be examined to see if they are in the predicted direction.

SUMMARY

Affective objectives can and should become integral goals of American education. The effectiveness of the schools in developing desired affective outcomes can and should be assessed. The real and imagined dangers associated with evaluating such instructional outcomes are reduced when the distinction between formative and summative evaluation is observed. Assuring students of anonymity or assuring them that they will not be penalized for their response can lead to valid evidence about affective outcomes.

Thus the abuses often associated with affective evaluation can be overcome. Models of well-defined affective objectives and a variety of techniques to evaluate them are available to the teacher or school system willing to accept the obligation to assess previously neglected but important affective curriculum components.

EXERCISES

Objective: Develop a set of objectives in the affective domain and an appropriate evaluative instrument.

Preparation:

A. Select a unit outline from your lesson plans or a curriculum or teacher's guide. It may be useful to use the outline and objectives developed at the end of Chapter 2. Writing affective objectives for the same unit will help stress the relationship between the cognitive and affective domains. If you prefer, use an outline for a longer term with a view toward writing long-term affective objectives.

B. Review the list of source materials discussed in the last part of the chapter. Given the difficulty of writing affective objectives and evaluative items, you may want to use some of these sources for the exercises below. At the very least, you should consult the Taxonomy of Krathwohl et al. (1964).

1. *Identifying constructs.* Review your outline or list of cognitive objectives, looking for clues to implicit affective objectives.
    a. What broad, general constructs in the affective domain do you consider important for the unit?
    b. Select one or two of these general constructs as the basis for writing affective objectives. Justify your choice in terms of importance to the unit and appropriateness for classroom instruction.
    c. For each of the general constructs list more specific component constructs. (The example from the Eight-year Study is useful here. Note how the broad construct "appreciation of literature" was broken down into seven component constructs.

2. *Writing affective objectives.*
    a. Write several statements for each component construct taking care to use an appropriate action verb. (See Figure 11-1 for suggested action verbs.)
    b. Categorize these statements of objectives according to the taxonomy of Krathwohl et al. (1964). Use the descriptions in Figure 11-2 as the basis for the categorization. You may find that statements for one component construct fall into different categories.
    c. Revise the statements of objectives

using the examples of infinitives and direct objects from Figure 11-2.

3. *Evaluating affective objectives.*

   a. Select a method or methods to use in evaluating your affective objectives. Why did you choose the method or methods?

   b. Prepare an evaluative instrument for your affective objectives. The form of the instrument is dictated by choice of method made above.

   c. What difficulties do you anticipate in your use of this evaluative instrument? How will you counteract these?

   d. Administer your affective evaluation. Interpret the results.

REFERENCES

Aiken, L. R. Attitudes toward mathematics. In J. W. Wilson & L. R. Carry (Eds.), *Reviews of recent research in mathematics education* (SMSG Studies in Mathematics, Vol. 19). Stanford, Calif.: School of Mathematics Study Group, 1969.

Aiken, L. R. Attitudes toward mathematics. *Review of Educational Research, 40* (4), 1970, 551–596.

Aiken, L. R. Attitudes toward mathematics. *Review of Educational Research, 46* (2), 1976, 293–311.

Airasian, P. W. *Formative evaluation instruments: A construction and validation of tests to evaluate learning over short time periods.* Unpublished doctoral dissertaion, University of Chicago, 1968.

Baldwin, T. S. Evaluation of learning in industrial education. In B. S. Bloom, J. T. Hastings, & G. F. Madaus, *Handbook on formative and summative evaluation of student learning.* New York: McGraw-Hill, 1971.

Ball, S. *Assessing the attitudes of young children toward school* (Head Start Test Collection). Princeton, N.J.: Educational Testing Service, 1971.

Blank, M. Eliciting verbalization from young children in experimental tasks: A methodological note. *Child Development, 46* (1), 1975. 244–251.

Bloom, B. S. *Human characteristics and school learning.* New York: McGraw-Hill, 1976.

Bloom, B. S., Hastings, J. T., & Madaus, G. F. (Eds.). *Handbook on formative and summative evaluation of student learning.* New York: McGraw-Hill, 1971.

Buros, O. K. (Ed.). *The seventh mental measurement yearbook.* Highland Park, N.J.: Gryphon Press, 1972.

Buros, O. K. (Ed.). *The eighth mental measurements yearbook.* Highland Park, N.J.: Gryphon Press, 1978.

Cazden, C. B. Evaluation of learning in preschool education: Early language development. In B. S. Bloom, J. T. Hastings, & G. F. Madaus (Eds.), *Handbook on formative and summative evaluation of student learning.* New York: McGraw-Hill, 1971.

Collier, A. R., & Guthrie, P. D. *Self-concept measures: An annotated bibliography.* (Head Start Test Collection). ERIC Clearing House on Tests, Measurements and Evaluation. Princeton, N.J.: Educational Testing Service, 1971.

Columbia University, Bureau of Applied Social Research, Inc. *Action in difficult situations.* New York: Author, 1963.

Cronbach, L. J. *Educational psychology* (4th ed.). New York: Harcourt Brace Jovanovich, 1977.

Dyer, H. S. The interview as a measuring device (TM Report 56) *Evaluation.* ERIC Clearinghouse on Tests, Measurement and Evaluation. Princeton, N.J.: Educational Testing Service, 1976.

Educational Testing Service. *Independent activities questionnaire.* Princeton, N.J.: Author, 1965.

Educational Development Center. *The social studies evaluation program* (Netsilik Unit Test). Cambridge, Mass.: Author, 1969.

Educational Testing Service. *Test Collection: Attitudes toward school and school adjustment, grades 4–6.* Princeton, N.J.: Author, 1973. (a)

Educational Testing Service. *Test Collection: Attitudes toward school and school adjustment, grades 7–12.* Princeton, N.J.: Author, 1973. (b)

Eiss, A. F., & Harbeck, M. B. *Behavioral*

objectives in the affective domain. Washington, D.C.: National Science Teachers Association, 1972.

Foley, J. T. Evaluation of learning in writing. In B. S. Bloom, J. T. Hastings, & G. F. Madaus (Eds.), *Handbook on formative and summative evaluation of student learning.* New York: McGraw-Hill, 1971.

Getzels, J. W., & Walsh, J. J. The method of paired direct and projective questionnaires in the study of attitude structure and socialization. *Psychological Monographs*, 1958, 73 (1), Whole 454.

Green, D. H. Attitudes. In S. Ball (Ed.), *Motivation in education.* New York: Academic Press 1977.

Hahn, C. T. *Measuring attitudes toward reading: An annotated ERIC bibliography.* ERIC Clearinghouse on Tests, Measurement and Evaluation. Princeton, N.J.: Educational Testing Service, 1977.

Hoepfner, R., Hemenway, J., DeMuth, J., Tenopyr, M. L., Granville, A. C., Petrosko, J. M., Krakower, J., Silberstein, R., & Nadeau, M. A. *CSE-RBS evaluations: Tests of higher order cognitive, affective and interpersonal skills.* Los Angeles UCLA Graduate School of Education, Center for Study of Evaluations, 1972.

Hogan, T. P. *Survey of school attitudes: Manual for administering and interpreting.* New York: Harcourt Brace Jovanovich, 1975. (a)

Hogan, T. P. *Survey of school attitudes: Primary form A.* New York: Harcourt Brace Jovanovich, 1975. (b)

Instructional Objectives Exchange (IOX). *Attitude toward school, K–12.* Los Angeles: Author, 1970.

Kamii, C. K. Evaluation in learning in preschool education: Socio-emotional, perceptual-motor, cognitive development. In B. S. Bloom, J. T. Hastings, & G. F. Madaus (Eds.), *Handbook on Formative and summative evaluation of student learning.* New York: McGraw-Hill, 1971.

Khan, S. B., & Weiss, J. The teaching of affective responses. In R. M. W. Travers (Ed.), *Second handbook of research in teaching.* Chicago: Rand McNally, 1973.

Klausner, S. Z. *Action in difficult situa-tions.* Washington, D.C.: Bureau of Social Research, Inc., 1963.

Knapp, J. *An omnibus of measures related to school based attitudes.* Princeton, N.J.: Center for Statewide Educational Assessment, Educational Testing Service, 1972.

Krathwohl, D. R., Bloom, B. S., & Masia, B. B. *Taxonomy of educational objectives: The classification of educational goals. Handbook 2. Affective domain.* New York: McKay, 1964.

Labov, W. The logic of non-standard English, Part II. In W. Labov, *Language in the inner city: Studies in the Black English vernacular.* Philadelphia: University of Pennsylvania Press, 1972.

Lewy, A. *The empirical validity of major properties of a taxonomy of affective educational objectives.* Unpublished doctoral dissertation. University of Chicago, 1966.

Lieberman, M., Brown, L., Needlinger, W., & Swanson, L. *Report on the evaluation workshop in the affective classroom.* Downers Grove, Ill.: Downers Grove Public School District 99, 1970.

McMurrin, S. M. What tasks for the schools? *Saturday Review, 50* (2), 1967, 40–43.

Metfessel, N. S., Michael, W. O., & Kirsner, D. A. Instrumentation of Bloom's and Krathwohl's taxonomies for the writing of educational objectives. *Psychology in the Schools*, 1969, 6 (3), 227–331.

Moore, W. J., & Kennedy, L. D. Evaluation of learning in the language arts. In B. S. Bloom, J. T. Hastings, & G. F. Madaus (Eds.), *Handbook on formative and summative evaluation of student learning.* New York: McGraw-Hill, 1971.

National Assessment of Education Progress. *Writing objectives.* Ann Arbor, Mich.: Committee on Assessing the Progress of Education, 1969.

O'Hara, R. P. *A cross-sectional study of growth in the relationship of self-ratings and test scores.* Unpublished doctoral dissertation, Harvard University, 1958.

Oppenheim, A. N. *Questionnaire design and attitude measurement.* New York: Basic Books, 1966.

Orasanu, J. Constraints of test and setting of measurement of mental ability. (Working Paper 3). New York: Rockefeller University Laboratory of Comparative Human Cognition and Institute for Comparative Human Development, 1976.

Orlandi, L. R. Evaluation of learning in secondary school social studies. In B. S. Bloom, J. T. Hastings, & G. F. Madaus (Eds.), *Handbook on formative and summative evaluation of student learning.* New York: McGraw-Hill, 1971.

Osgood, C., Suci, G., & Tannenbaum, P. *The measurement of meaning.* Urbana: University of Illinois Press, 1967.

Payne, S. *The art of asking questions.* Princeton, N.J.: Princeton University Press, 1951.

Progressive Education Association. *Literature Questionnaire: The Novel, Test 3.22.* Chicago, Author, 1940.

Purves, A. C. Evaluation of learning in literature. In B. S. Bloom, J. T. Hastings, & G. F. Madaus (Eds.), *Handbook on formative and summative evaluation of student learning.* New York: McGraw-Hill, 1971.

Raths, L. Harmin, M., & Simon, S. *Values and teaching: Working with values in the classroom.* Columbus: Merrill, 1966.

Richardson, S., Dohrenwend, B., & Klein, D. *Interviewing: Its forms and functions.* New York: Basic Books, 1965.

Rutherford, F. J. et al. *Semantic differential test.* Cambridge, Mass.: Harvard Project Physics, 1966.

Scriven, M. Student values as educational objectives. *Proceedings of the 1965 Invitational Conference on Testing Problems.* Princeton, N.J.: Educational Testing Service, 1966.

Shavelson, R. J., Hubner, J. J., & Stanton, G. D. Self-concept: Validation of construct interpretations. *Review of Educational Research,* 1976, 46(3), 407–441.

Shaw, M., & Wright, J. *Scales for the measurement of attitudes.* New York: McGraw-Hill, 1967.

Shoresman, P. B. *Interests and ideas. Form AV.* Urbana: University of Illinois, Elementary School Science Project, 1965.

Sidney, E., & Brown, M. *The skills of interviewing.* Whitstable, England: Tavistock Publications, 1961.

Smith, B. O. Teaching and testing values. *Proceedings of the 1965 Invitational Conference on Testing Problems.* Princeton, N.J.: Educational Testing Service, 1966.

Smith, E. R., & Tyler, R. W. *Appraising and recording student progress* (Adventures in American Education Series, Vol. 3). New York: Harper, 1942.

Tyler, R. W. Assessing educational achievement in the affective domain. *Measurement in Education,* 1973, 4(3), 1–8.

Walker, D. K. *A guide to assessing program impact on children's affective development.* Washington, D.C.: U. S. Office of Education, Office of Planning Budget and Evaluation, 1977.

Webb, E. J., Campbell, D. T., Schwartz, R. D., & Sechrest, L. *Unobtrusive measures: Nonreactive research in the social sciences.* Chicago: Rand McNally, 1966.

Whisler, T., & Harper, S. *Performance appraisal: Research and practice.* New York: Holt, 1962.

Wilson, J. W., Cohen, L. S., & Begle, E. G. (Eds.). *Z-population test batteries* (NLSMA Report No. 2). Stanford, Calif.: School Mathematics Study Group, 1968.

Wilson, B. G. Evaluation of learning in art education. In B. S. Bloom, J. T. Hastings, & G. F. Madaus (Eds.), *Handbook on formative and summative evaluation of student learning.* New York: McGraw-Hill, 1971.

Appendix

Condensed Version of the Taxonomy of Educational Objectives*

COGNITIVE DOMAIN

Knowledge

1.00 Knowledge

Knowledge, as defined here, involves the recall of specifics and universals, the recall of methods and processes, or the recall of a pattern, structure, or setting. For measurement purposes, the recall situation involves little more than bringing to mind the appropriate material. Although some alteration of the material may be required, this is a relatively minor part of the task. The knowledge objectives emphasize most the psychological processes of remembering. . . .

1.10 *Knowledge of specifics* The recall of specific and isolable bits of information. The emphasis is on symbols with concrete refer-

*Sources: B. S. Bloom (Ed.). *Taxonomy of educational objectives: The classification of educational goals*. Handbook 1. *Cognitive domain*. New York: McKay, 1956. Pp. 201–207; D. R. Krathwohl, B. S. Bloom, & B. B. Masia. *Taxonomy of educational objectives: The classification of educational goals*. Handbook 2. *Affective domain*. New York: McKay, 1964. Pp. 176–185.

ents. This material, which is at a very low level of abstraction, may be thought of as the elements from which more complex and abstract forms of knowledge are built. . . .

1.20 *Knowledge of ways and means of dealing with specifics* Knowledge of the ways of organizing, studying, judging, and criticizing. This includes the methods of inquiry, the chronological sequences, and the standards of judgment within a field as well as the patterns of organization through which the areas of the fields themselves are determined and internally organized. . . .

1.30 *Knowledge of the universals and abstractions in a field* Knowledge of the major schemes and patterns by which phenomena and ideas are organized. These are the large structures, theories, and generalizations which dominate a subject field or which are quite generally used in studying phenomena or solving problems. These are at the highest levels of abstraction and complexity. . . .

Intellectual Abilities and Skills

Abilities and skills refer to organized modes of operation and generalized techniques for dealing with materials and problems. The materials and problems may be of such a nature that little or no specialized and technical information is required. Such information as is required can be assumed to be part of the individual's general fund of knowledge. Other problems may require specialized and technical information at a rather high level such that specific knowledge and skill in dealing with the problem and the materials are required. The abilities and skills objectives emphasize the mental processes of organizing and reorganizing material to achieve a particular purpose. The materials may be given or remembered.

2.00 Comprehension

This represents the lowest level of understanding. It refers to a type of understanding or apprehension such that the individual knows what is being communicated and can make use of the material or idea being communicated without necessarily relating it to other material or seeing its fullest implications.

2.10 Translation Comprehension as evidenced by the care and accuracy with which the communication is paraphrased or rendered from one language or form of communication to another. Translation is judged on the basis of faithfulness and accuracy, that is, on the extent to which the material in the original communication is preserved although the form of the communication has been altered. . . .

2.20 Interpretation The explanation or summarization of a communication. Whereas translation involves an objective, part-for-part rendering of a communication, interpretation involves a reordering, rearrangement, or a new view of the material. . . .

2.30 Extrapolation The extension of trends or tendencies beyond the given data to determine implications, consequences, corollaries, effects, etc., which are in accordance with the conditions described in the original communication. . . .

3.00 Application

The use of abstractions in particular and concrete situations. The abstractions may be in the form of general ideas, rules of procedures, or generalized methods. The abstractions may also be technical principles, ideas, and theories which must be remembered and applied. . . .

4.00 Analysis

The breakdown of a communication into its constituent elements or parts such that the relative hierarchy of ideas is made clear and the relations between the ideas expressed are made explicit. Such analyses are intended to clarify the communication, to indicate how the communication is organized, and [to show] the way in which it manages to convey its effects, as well as its basis and arrangement.

4.10 Analysis of elements Identification of the elements included in a communication. . . .

4.20 Analyses of relationships The connections and interactions between elements and parts of a communication. . . .

4.30 Analysis of organizational principles The organization, systematic arrangement, and structure which hold the communication together. This includes the "explicit" as well as "implicit" structure. It includes the bases, necessary arrangement, and the mechanics which make the communication a unit. . . .

5.00 Synthesis

The putting together of elements and parts so as to form a whole. This involves the process of working with pieces, parts, elements, etc., and arranging and combining them in such a way as to constitute a pattern or structure not clearly there before.

5.10 Production of a unique communication The development of a communication in which the writer or speaker attempts to convey ideas, feelings, and/or experiences to others. . . .

5.20 *Production of a plan or proposed set of operations* The development of a plan of work or the proposal of a plan of operations. The plan should satisfy requirements of the task which may be given to the student or which he may develop for himself. . . .

5.30 *Derivation of a set of abstract relations* The development of a set of abstract relations either to classify or [to] explain particular data or phenomena, or the deduction of propositions and relations from a set of basic propositions or symbolic representations. . . .

6.00   Evaluation

Judgments about the value of material and methods for given purposes. Quantitative and qualitative judgments about the extent to which material and methods satisfy criteria. Use of a standard of appraisal. The criteria may be those determined by the student or those which are given to him.

6.10 *Judgments in terms of internal evidence* Evaluation of the accuracy of a communication from such evidence as logical accuracy, consistency, and other internal criteria. . . .

6.20 *Judgments in terms of external criteria* Evaluation of material with reference to selected or remembered criteria. . . .

AFFECTIVE DOMAIN

1.0   Receiving (attending)

At this level we are concerned that the learner be sensitized to the existence of certain phenomena and stimuli; that is, that he be willing to receive or to attend to them. This is clearly the first and crucial step if the learner is to be properly oriented to learn what the teacher intends that he will. . . .

The category of *Receiving* has been divided into three subcategories to indicate three different levels of attending to phenomena. While the division points between the subcategories are arbitrary, the subcategories do represent a continuum. From an extremely passive position or role on the part of the learner, where the sole responsibility for the evocation of the behavior rests with the teacher—that is, the responsibility rests with him for "capturing" the student's attention—the continuum extends to a point at which the learner directs his attention, at least at a semiconscious level, toward the preferred stimuli.

1.1 *Awareness* *Awareness* is almost a cognitive behavior. But unlike *Knowledge*, the lowest level of the cognitive domain, we are not so much concerned with a memory of, or ability to recall, an item or fact as we are that, given appropriate opportunity, the learner will merely be conscious of something—that he take into account a situation, phenomenon, object, or state of affairs. Like *Knowledge* it does not imply an assessment of the qualities or nature of the stimulus, but unlike *Knowledge* it does not necessarily imply attention. There can be simple awareness without specific discrimination or recognition of the objective characteristics of the object, even though these characteristics must be deemed to have an effect. The individual may not be able to verbalize the aspects of the stimulus which cause the awareness.

1.2 *Willingness to receive* In this category we have come a step up the ladder but are still dealing with what appears to be cognitive behavior. At a minimum level, we are here describing the behavior of being willing to tolerate a given stimulus, not to avoid it. Like *Awareness*, it involves a neutrality or suspended judgment toward the stimulus. At this level of the continuum, the teacher is not concerned that the student seek it out, nor even, perhaps, that in an environment crowded with many other stimuli the learner will necessarily attend to the stimulus. Rather, at worst, given the opportunity to attend in a field with relatively few competing stimuli, the learner is not actively seeking to avoid it. At best he is willing to take notice of the phenomenon and give it his attention.

1.3 Controlled or selected attention

At a somewhat higher level we are concerned with a new phenomenon, the differentiation of a given stimulus into figure and ground at a conscious or perhaps semiconscious level—the differentiation of aspects of a stimulus which is 'perceived as clearly marked off from adjacent impressions. The perception is still without tension or assessment, and the student may not know the technical terms or symbols with which to describe it correctly or precisely to others. In some instances it may refer not so much to the selectivity of attention as to the control of attention, so that when certain stimuli are present they will be attended to. There is an element of the learner's controlling the attention here, so that the favored stimulus is selected and attended to despite competing and distracting stimuli.

2.0 Responding

At this level we are concerned with responses which go beyond merely attending to the phenomenon. The student is sufficiently motivated that he is not just 1.2 *Willing to attend* [receive]; perhaps it is correct to say that he is actively attending. As a first stage in a "learning by doing" process the student is committing himself in some small measure to the phenomena involved. This is a very low level of commitment, and we would not say at this level that this was "a value of his" or that he had "such and such an attitude." These terms belong to the next higher level that we describe. But we could say that he is doing something with or about the phenomenon besides merely perceiving it, as would be true at the next level below this of 1.3 *Controlled or selected attention*.

This is the category that many teachers will find best describes their "interest" objectives. Most commonly we use the term to indicate the desire that a child become sufficiently involved in or committed to a subject, phenomenon, or activity that he will seek it out and gain satisfaction from working with it or engaging in it.

2.1 Acquiescence in responding

We might use the word "obedience" or "compliance" to describe this behavior. As both of these terms indicate, there is a passiveness so far as the initiation of the behavior is concerned, and the stimulus calling for this behavior is not subtle. Compliance is perhaps a better term than obedience, since there is more of the element of reaction to a suggestion and less of the implication of resistance or yielding unwillingly. The student makes the response, but he has not fully accepted the necessity for doing so.

2.2 Willingness to respond

The key to this level is in the term "willingness," with its implication of capacity for voluntary activity. There is the implication that the learner is sufficiently committed to exhibiting the behavior that he does so not just because of a fear of punishment, but "on his own" or voluntarily. It may help to note that the element of resistance or of yielding unwillingly, which is possibly present at the previous level, is here replaced with consent or proceeding from one's own choice.

2.3 Satisfaction in response

The additional element in the step beyond the *Willingness to respond* level, the consent, the assent to responding, or the voluntary response, is that the behavior is accompanied by a feeling of satisfaction, an emotional response, generally of pleasure, zest, or enjoyment. The location of this category in the hierarchy has given us a great deal of difficulty. Just where in the process of internalization the attachment of an emotional response, kick, or thrill to a behavior occurs has been hard to determine. For that matter there is some uncertainty as to whether the level of internalization at which it occurs may not depend on the particular behavior. We have even questioned whether it should be a category. If our structure is to be a hierarchy, then each category should include the behavior in the next level below it. The emotional component appears gradually through the range of internalization categories. The attempt to specify a given position in the hierarchy as *the* one at which the emotional component is added is doomed to failure.

The category is arbitrarily placed at this point in the hierarchy where it seems to appear most frequently and where it is cited as or appears to be an important component of the objectives at this level on the continuum. The category's inclusion at this point serves the pragmatic purpose of reminding us of the presence of the emotional component and its value in the building of affective behaviors. But it should not be thought of as appearing and occurring at this one point in the continuum and thus destroying the hierarchy which we are attempting to build.

3.0 Valuing

This is the only category headed by a term which is in common use in the expression of objectives by teachers. Further, it is employed in its usual sense: that a thing, phenomenon, or behavior has worth. This abstract concept of worth is in part a result of the individual's own valuing or assessment, but it is much more a social product that has been slowly internalized or accepted and has come to be used by the student as his own criterion of worth.

Behavior categorized at this level is sufficiently consistent and stable to have taken on the characteristics of a belief or an attitude. The learner displays this behavior with sufficient consistency in appropriate situations that he comes to be perceived as holding a value. At this level, we are not concerned with the relationships among values but rather with the internalization of a set of specified, ideal values. Viewed from another standpoint, the objectives classified here are the prime stuff from which the conscience of the individual is developed into active control of behavior.

This category will be found appropriate for many objectives that use the term "attitude" (as well as, of course, "value").

An important element of behavior characterized by *Valuing* is that it is motivated, not by the desire to comply or obey, but by the individual's commitment to the underlying value guiding the behavior.

3.1 Acceptance of a value At this level we are concerned with the ascribing of worth to a phenomenon, behavior, object, etc. The term "belief," which is defined as "the emotional acceptance of a proposition or doctrine upon what one implicitly considers adequate ground" . . . describes quite well what may be thought of as the dominant characteristic here. Beliefs have varying degrees of certitude. At the lowest level of *Valuing* we are concerned with the lowest levels of certainty; that is, there is more of a readiness to reevaluate one's position than at the higher levels. It is a position that is somewhat tentative.

One of the distinguishing characteristics of this behavior is consistency of response to the class of objects, phenomena, etc., with which the belief or attitude is identified. It is consistent enough so that the person is perceived by others as holding the belief or value. At the level we are describing here, he is both sufficiently consistent that others can identify the value, and sufficiently committed that he is willing to be so identified.

3.2 Preference for a value The provision for this subdivision arose out of a feeling that there were objectives that expressed a level of internalization between the mere acceptance of a value and commitment or conviction in the usual connotation of deep involvement in an area. Behavior at this level implies not just the acceptance of a value to the point of being willing to be identified with it, but the individual is sufficiently committed to the value to pursue it, to seek it out, to want it.

3.3 Commitment Belief at this level involves a high degree of certainty. The ideas of "conviction" and "certainty beyond a shadow of a doubt" help to convey further the level of behavior intended. In some instances this may border on faith, in the sense of its being a firm emotional acceptance of a belief upon admittedly nonrational grounds. Loyalty to a position, group, or cause would also be classified here.

The person who displays behavior at this level is clearly perceived as holding the value. He acts to further the thing valued in some way, to extend the possibility of his developing it, to deepen involvement with it and with the things representing it. He tries to convince others and seek converts to his cause. There is a tension here which needs to be satisfied; action is the result of an aroused need or drive. There is a real motivation to act out the behavior.

4.0 Organization

As the learner successively internalizes values, he encounters situations for which more than one value is relevant. Thus necessity arises for (a) the organization of the values into a system, (b) the determination of the interrelationships among them, and (c) the establishment of the dominant and pervasive ones. Such a system is built gradually, subject to change as new values are incorporated. This category is intended as the proper classification for objectives which describe the beginnings of the building of a value system. . . .

4.1 Conceptualization of a value   In the previous category, 3.0 *Valuing,* we noted that consistency and stability are integral characteristics of the particular value or belief. At this level (4.1) the quality of abstraction or conceptualization is added. This permits the individual to see how the value relates to those that he already holds or to new ones that he is coming to hold.

Conceptualization will be abstract, and in this sense it will be symbolic. But the symbols need not be verbal symbols. Whether conceptualization first appears at this point on the affective continuum is a moot point. . . .

4.2 Organization of a value system   Objectives properly classified here are those which require the learner to bring together a complex of values, possibly disparate values, and to bring these into an ordered relationship with one another. Ideally, the ordered relationship will be one which is harmonious and internally consistent. This is, of course, the goal of such objectives, which seek to have the student formulate a philosophy of life. In actuality, the integration may be something less than entirely harmonious. More likely the relationship is better described as a kind of dynamic equilibrium which is, in part, dependent upon those portions of the environment which are salient at any point in time. In many instances the organization of values may result in their synthesis into a new value or value complex of a higher order.

5.0 Characterization by a value or value complex

At this level of internalization the values already have a place in the individual's value hierarchy, are organized into some kind of internally consistent system, have controlled the behavior of the individual for a sufficient time that he has adapted to behaving this way; and an evocation of the behavior no longer arouses emotion or affect except when the individual is threatened or challenged.

The individual acts consistently in accordance with the values he has internalized at this level, and our concern is to indicate two things: (a) the generalization of this control to so much of the individual's behavior that he is described and characterized as a person by these pervasive controlling tendencies and (b) the integration of these beliefs, ideas, and attitudes into a total philosophy or world view. These two aspects constitute the subcategories.

5.1 Generalized set   The generalized set is that which gives an internal consistency to the system of attitudes and values at any particular moment. It is selective responding at a very high level. It is sometimes spoken of as a determining tendency, an orientation toward phenomena, or a predisposition to act in a certain way. The generalized set is a response to highly generalized phenomena. It is a persistent and consistent response to a

family of related situations or objects. It may often be an unconscious set which guides action without conscious forethought. The generalized set may be thought of as closely related to the idea of an attitude cluster, where the commonality is based on behavioral characteristics rather than the subject or object of the attitude. A generalized set is a basic orientation which enables the individual, to reduce and order the complex world about him and to act consistently and effectively in it.

5.2 Characterization This, the peak of the internalization process, includes those objectives which are broadest with respect both to the phenomena covered and to the range of behavior which they comprise. Thus, here are found those objectives which concern one's

view of the universe, one's philosophy of life, one's *Weltanschauung*—a value system having as its object the whole of what is known or knowable.

Objectives categorized here are more than generalized sets in the sense that they involve a greater inclusiveness and, within the group of attitudes, behaviors, beliefs, or ideas, an emphasis on internal consistency. Though this internal consistency may not always be exhibited behaviorally by the students toward whom the objective is directed, since we are categorizing teachers' objectives, this consistency feature will always be a component of *Characterization* objectives.

As the title of the category implies, these objectives are so encompassing that they tend to characterize the individual almost completely.

Name Index

Page references in **boldface** refer to tables or illustrations.

Subject Index

Page references in **boldface** refer to tables or illustrations.

2463